Lecture Notes in Computer Science   **9615**

Commenced Publication in 1973
Founding and Former Series Editors:
Gerhard Goos, Juris Hartmanis, and Jan van Leeuwen

More information about this series at http://www.springer.com/series/7410

Chen-Mou Cheng · Kai-Min Chung
Giuseppe Persiano · Bo-Yin Yang (Eds.)

Public-Key Cryptography – PKC 2016

19th IACR International Conference
on Practice and Theory in Public-Key Cryptography
Taipei, Taiwan, March 6–9, 2016
Proceedings, Part II

 Springer

Editors
Chen-Mou Cheng
National Taiwan University
Taipei
Taiwan

Kai-Min Chung
Academia Sinica
Taipei
Taiwan

Giuseppe Persiano
Università di Salerno
Fisciano
Italy

Bo-Yin Yang
Academia Sinica
Taipei
Taiwan

ISSN 0302-9743   ISSN 1611-3349   (electronic)
Lecture Notes in Computer Science
ISBN 978-3-662-49386-1   ISBN 978-3-662-49387-8   (eBook)
DOI 10.1007/978-3-662-49387-8

Library of Congress Control Number: 2016930549

LNCS Sublibrary: SL4 – Security and Cryptology

Printed on acid-free paper

This Springer imprint is published by SpringerNature
The registered company is Springer-Verlag GmbH Berlin Heidelberg

Preface

The 19th IACR International Conference on Practice and Theory of Public-Key Cryptography (PKC 2016) was held March 6–9, 2016 in Taipei (Taiwan). The conference, sponsored by the International Association for Cryptologic Research (IACR), focuses on all technical aspects of public-key cryptography. These proceedings contain 34 papers selected by the Program Committee from 143 submissions. The many high-quality submissions made it easy to build a strong program but also required rejecting good papers. Each submission was judged by at least three reviewers, or four in the case of submissions by Program Committee members. The selection process included one whole month of independent review (each Program Committee member was assigned about 14 papers) followed by five more weeks of discussions. We tried to make the review and discussion system more interactive and used a new feature of the review system that allows Program Committee members to send specific questions to the authors.

We would like to thank the many authors from all over the world for submitting their papers—without them there would not be a conference. We are deeply grateful to the Program Committee for their hard work to ensure that each paper received a thorough and fair review. We gratefully acknowledge the external reviewers listed on the following pages. Our thanks go to Shai Halevi: the committee's work was tremendously simplified by his submission/review software.

January 2016

Giuseppe Persiano
Bo-Yin Yang

PKC 2016

The 19th International Conference on the Theory and Practice of Public-Key Cryptography

Taipei, Taiwan

March 6–9, 2016

Sponsored by the *International Association of Cryptologic Research*

General Chairs

Chen-Mou Cheng	National Taiwan University, Taiwan
Kai-Min Chung	Academia Sinica, Taiwan

Program Chairs

Giuseppe Persiano	Università di Salerno, Italy
Bo-Yin Yang	Academia Sinica, Taiwan

Program Committee

Joel Alwen	IST, Austria
Paulo Barreto	University of Sao Paulo, Brazil and University of Washington Tacoma, USA
Carlo Blundo	University of Salerno, Italy
Dario Catalano	University of Catania, Italy
Melissa Chase	Microsoft Research, USA
Tung Chou	TU Eindhoven, The Netherlands
Dana Dachman-Soled	University of Maryland, USA
Emiliano De Cristofaro	UCL, UK
Yvo Desmedt	UT at Dallas, USA and UCL, UK
Leo Ducas	CWI, The Netherlands
Dario Fiore	IMDEA Software Institute, Spain
Pierre-Alain Fouque	University of Rennes 1, France
Sanjam Garg	University of California, Berkeley, USA
Tim Gneysu	University of Bremen, Germany
Yuval Ishai	The Technion, Israel and UCLA, USA
Tanja Lange	TU Eindhoven, The Netherlands
Benot Libert	ENS Lyon, France
Feng-Hao Liu	Florida Atlantic University, USA
Hemanta Maji	Purdue University, USA
Alexander May	RU Bochum, Germany

Phong Q. Nguyen	Inria, France and University of Tokyo, Japan
Jesper Buus Nielsen	Aarhus University, Denmark
Tatsuaki Okamoto	NTT, Japan
Rafail Ostrovsky	UCLA, USA
Omkant Pandey	University of California, Berkeley, USA
Christophe Petit	UCL, UK
David Pointcheval	ENS Paris, France
Ahmad-Reza Sadeghi	TU Darmstadt, Germany
Dominique Schrder	Saarland University, CISPA, Germany
Peter Schwabe	Radboud University, The Netherlands
Daniel Smith-Tone	NIST, USA
Damien Stehl	ENS Lyon, France
Mehdi Tibouchi	NTT, Japan
Weng-Guey Tzeng	National Chiao Tung University, Taiwan
Daniele Venturi	Sapienza University of Rome, Italy
Moti Yung	Google and Columbia University, USA

External Reviewers

Shweta Agrawal
Shashank Agrawal
Jacob Alperin-Sheriff
Daniel Apon
Saikrishna
 Badrinarayanan
Shi Bai
Lejla Batina
Fabrice Ben Hamouda
Daniel J. Bernstein
Sanjay Bhattacherjee
Nina Bindel
Olivier Blazy
Jonathan Bootle
Florian Bourse
Andrea Cerulli
Jie Chen
Ming-Shing Chen
Cline Chevalier
Chitchanok
 Chuengsatiansup
Kai-Min Chung
Michele Ciampi
Sandro Coretti
Ana Costache
Geoffroy Couteau

Cas Cremer
Bernardo David
Gareth Davies
Angelo De Caro
Jean-Christophe
 Deneuville
Jérémie Detrey
Julien Devigne
Nico Doettling
Xiong Fan
Antonio Faonio
Houda Ferradi
Nils Fleischhacker
Eiichiro Fujisaki
Steven Galbraith
Luke Garratt
Essam Gheddafi
Satrajit Ghosh
Esha Gosh
Divya Gupta
Florian Göpfert
Brett Hemenway
Jens Hermans
Gottfried Herold
Felix Heuer
Yun-Ju Huang

Vincenzo Iovino
Malika Izabachene
Zahra Jafargholi
Aayush Jain
Chen Jie
Ali El Kaafarani
Dakshita Khurana
Eike Kiltz
Chong-Hee Kim
Taechan Kim
Paul Kirchner
Katriel Kohn-Gordon
Venkata Koppula
Luke Kowalczyk
Mukul Kulkarni
Po-Chun Kuo
Fabien Laguillaumie
Tancrède Lepoint
Bernardo Magri
Giulio Malavolta
Ingo von Maurich
Peihan Miao
Ameer Mohammed
Amir Moradi
Fabrice Mouhartem
Pratyay Mukherjee

Soheil Nematihaji
Gregory Neven
Khoa Nguyen
Ruben Niederhagen
Luca Nizzardo
Tobias Oder
Cristina Onete
Ilya Ozerov
Geovandro Pereira
Thomas Peters
Duong Hieu Phan
Krzysztof Pietrzak
Antigoni Polychroniadou
Angel Perez del Pozo
Benjamin Pring

Bartosz Przydatek
Thomas Pöppelmann
Max Rabkin
Carla Rafols
Somindu Ramanna
Carla Ràfols
Akshayaram Srinivasan
Carla Rafols Salvador
Pascal Sasdrich
Sven Schäge
Vipin Singh Sehrawat
Mark Simkin
Luisa Siniscalchi
Daniel Slamanig
Pierre-Jean Spaenlehauer

Bjrn Tackmann
Katsuyuki Takashima
Susan Thomson
Mehdi Tibouchi
Junichi Tomida
Hoang Viet Tung
Niels de Vreede
Tianhao Wang
Hoeteck Wee
Mor Weiss
Daniel Wichs
Jenny Yuan-Chun Yeh
Thomas Zacharias

Contents – Part II

Primitives

Contents – Part I

Signatures

Cryptanalysis

Algebraic Approaches for the Elliptic Curve Discrete Logarithm Problem over Prime Fields

Christophe Petit[1](✉), Michiel Kosters[2], and Ange Messeng[3]

[1] Mathematical Institute, University of Oxford,
Andrew Wiles Building, Radcliffe Observatory Quarter, Woodstock Road,
Oxford OX2 6GG, UK
christophe.f.petit@gmail.com
[2] University of California, Irvine, 340 Rowland Hall, Irvine, CA 95697-3875, USA
kosters@gmail.com
[3] Faculty of Mathematics, University of Passau, InnStrasse 33, IM207,
94032 Passau, Germany
messeng.ange2@gmail.com

Abstract. The elliptic curve discrete logarithm problem is one of the most important problems in cryptography. In recent years, several index calculus algorithms have been introduced for elliptic curves defined over extension fields, but the most important curves in practice, defined over prime fields, have so far appeared immune to these attacks.

In this paper we formally generalize previous attacks from binary curves to prime curves. We study the efficiency of our algorithms with computer experiments and we discuss their current and potential impact on elliptic curve standards.

Our algorithms are only practical for small parameters at the moment and their asymptotic analysis is limited by our understanding of Gröbner basis algorithms. Nevertheless, they highlight a potential vulnerability on prime curves which our community needs to explore further.

1 Introduction

The elliptic curve discrete logarithm problem (ECDLP) is widely believed to be one of the hardest computational number theory problem used in cryptography. While integer factorization and discrete logarithms over finite fields suffer from index calculus attacks of subexponential or even quasipolynomial complexity, recommended key sizes for elliptic curve cryptography correspond to the birthday paradox bound complexity of generic discrete logarithm algorithms.

In the last ten years starting from the seminal work of Semaev [19], index calculus algorithms have progressively been adapted to elliptic curve discrete logarithm problems. However, the most efficient attacks target parameters that are not used in standards; attacks against binary curves rely on poorly understood Gröbner basis assumptions; and almost no attacks at all have been proposed against the most important family of curves, namely elliptic curves defined over prime fields.

C.-M. Cheng et al. (Eds.): PKC 2016, Part II, LNCS 9615, pp. 3–18, 2016.
DOI: 10.1007/978-3-662-49387-8_1

Contributions. In this paper, we provide new index calculus algorithms to solve elliptic curve discrete logarithm problems over prime fields of cardinality p.

The factor bases in our algorithms are of the form $\mathcal{F} := \{(x, y) \in E(K) | L(x) = 0\}$, where L is a large-degree rational map. We additionally require that L is a composition of small-degree rational maps L_j, $j = 1, \ldots, n'$, such that the large-degree constraint $L(x) = 0$ can be replaced by a system of low degree constraints $x_2 = L_1(x)$, $x_3 = L_2(x_2)$, $x_4 = L_3(x_3)$, $\ldots$, $x_{n'} = L_{n'-1}(x_{n'-1})$, $L_{n'}(x_{n'}) = 0$. Relations are computed by solving a polynomial system constructed from Semaev's summation polynomials and the above decomposition of the map L.

Our factor bases generalize the factor bases used in previous works: Diem and Gaudry's attacks [6,10] implicitly use $L(x) = x^q - x$ where q is the size of a subfield; small characteristic, prime degree extension attacks [7–9,12,17,21] implicitly use the linearized polynomial corresponding to a vector space; and Semaev's original factor basis [19] implicitly uses $L(x) = \prod_{\alpha < B}(x - \alpha)$ for some B of appropriate size. The potential advantage of our polynomials L compared to the one implicitly used by Semaev is that they can be re-written in the form of a system of low degree polynomial equations, similar to systems occurring in the characteristic 2 case, which we then solve using Gröbner basis algorithms.

We specify two concrete instances of the above algorithm. In the first instance, we assume that $p - 1$ has a large divisor which is smooth, and we define L such that its roots form precisely a coset of a subgroup of smooth order. In the second instance, we assume the knowledge of an auxiliary curve over the same field with a large enough smooth subgroup, and we define L using the isogeny corresponding to that subgroup. We complete the second instance with two different algorithms to compute an auxiliary curve over a finite field, and we compare both methods.

Interestingly, the standardized curve NIST P-224 falls into the framework of our first algorithm. We also show that computing a finite field and an auxiliary curve for this field is as far as we know much easier than computing an auxiliary curve for a given finite field.

The complexity of our algorithms remains an open problem. We implemented both of them in Magma, and compared their performances to previous attacks on binary curves of comparable sizes. The experimental results suggest that in spite of a common structure, the systems are a bit more efficient to solve in binary cases than in prime cases. They also suggest that all the systems we studied are easier to solve than generic systems of "comparable parameters". This may look encouraging from a cryptanalytic point of view, but we stress that the set of experiments is too limited to draw any conclusion at this stage (see also [11] for a criticism of the analysis of [17]). At the moment all attacks are outperformed by generic discrete logarithm algorithms for practically relevant parameters.

Perspectives. Our paper introduces a new algorithmic framework to solve ECDLP over prime fields. We hope that these ideas revive research in this area and lead to a better understanding of the elliptic curve discrete logarithm problem.

Proving meaningful complexity bounds for our algorithms appears very challenging today as they use Gröbner basis algorithms on non-understood families of polynomial systems with a special structure. At the time of writing it is not clear yet whether the special structure introduced in this paper leads to asymptotic improvements with respect to generic discrete logarithm algorithms. Of course, Gröbner basis algorithms may also not be the best tools to solve these systems. At the end of the paper we suggest that better, dedicated algorithms to solve these systems, inspired from existing root-finding algorithms, could perhaps lead to substantial efficiency and analysis improvements of our algorithms.

Related work. In recent years many index calculus algorithms have been proposed for elliptic curves [6–10,12,17,19,21]. All these papers except Semaev's paper [19] focus on elliptic curves defined over extension fields, and Semaev did not provide an algorithm to compute relations. Moreover, our work offers a natural large prime counterpart to recent characteristic 2 approaches, and an avenue to generalize any future result on these approaches to the even more interesting large prime case.

We are aware of two other types of attacks that first exploited smoothness properties of $p - 1$ and were later generalized using elliptic curves. The first one is Pollard's $p - 1$ factorization method generalized to the celebrated elliptic curve factorization method [13]. The second one is den Boer's reduction of the computational Diffie-Helman problem to the discrete logarithm problem, which was generalized by Maurer [5,14]. We point out that the smoothness requirements on the auxiliary curve order are much weaker in our attacks than in these contexts.

Because of these attacks, there may also be a folklore suspicion in the community that using primes with special properties could lead to improved attacks on elliptic curves, but to the best of our knowledge this was not supported by any concrete attack so far, and in fact all NIST curves use generalized Mersenne primes.

Outline. The remaining of the paper is organized as follows. In Sect. 2 we describe related work, particularly on binary curves. In Sect. 3 we describe our main results. We first sketch our main idea and provide a partial analysis of our general algorithm, leaving aside precomputation details and the complexity of the Gröbner basis step. We then describe the $p - 1$ smooth and isogeny versions of our algorithms, and we analyze the complexity of computing an auxiliary curve in the second case. In Sect. 4 we describe our experimental evaluation of the attack. Finally, Sect. 5 summarizes our results and provides routes towards improvements.

2 Previous Work on (binary) Curves

Let K be a finite field; let E be an elliptic curve defined over K; and let $P, Q \in E(K)$ such that Q is in the subgroup $G \subset E(K)$ generated by P. The discrete logarithm problem is the problem of finding an integer k such that $Q = kP$.

In the following we assume that the order r of G is prime, as it is usually the case in cryptographic applications.

2.1 Index Calculus for Elliptic Curves

Index calculus algorithms use a subset $\mathcal{F} \subset G$ often called a *factor basis*. The simplest algorithms run in two stages. The first stage consists in collecting *relations* of the form

$$a_i P + b_i Q + \sum_{P_j \in \mathcal{F}} e_{ij} P_j = 0.$$

The second stage consists in performing linear algebra on these relations to deduce a relation of the form

$$aP + bQ = 0,$$

from which the discrete logarithm $k = -a/b \mod r$ is easily deduced.

Since the seminal work of Semaev [19], index calculus algorithms for elliptic curves have used a basis of the form

$$\mathcal{F} := \{(x, y) \in E(K) | x \in V\}$$

where V is some subset of K. Relations are obtained by computing $R = (X, Y) = aP + bQ$ for random a and b, then solving a polynomial equation

$$S_{m+1}(x_1, \ldots, x_m, X) = 0$$

with the additional constraints that $x_i \in V$ for all i. Here S_ℓ is such that for $X_1, \ldots, X_\ell \in \overline{K}$ one has $S_\ell(X_1, \ldots, X_\ell) = 0$ if and only if there exist $P_i = (X_i, Y_i) \in E(\overline{K})$ with $P_1 + \ldots + P_\ell = 0$. The polynomials S_ℓ are called *summation polynomials*.

When $K = \mathbb{F}_p$, Semaev originally proposed to use $V = \{x \in \mathbb{Z}_{\geq 0} | x < p^{1/m}\}$. This was inspired by the factor bases used for discrete logarithms over finite fields. However, Semaev did not suggest any algorithm to compute relations with this factor basis.

2.2 Weil Restriction on Vector Spaces

In the case of an extension field $K = \mathbb{F}_{q^n}$, developments of Semaev's ideas by Gaudry, Diem and Faugère-Perret-Petit-Renault [6–8,10] led to choosing V as a linear subspace of $\mathbb{F}_{q^n}/\mathbb{F}_q$ with dimension $n' \approx \lceil n/m \rceil$. In order to compute relations, we then proceed to a *Weil descent* or *Weil restriction* of the summation polynomial onto the vector space.

Concretely we fix a basis $\{v_1, \ldots, v_{n'}\}$ for V, we define mn' variables x_{ij} over $\mathbb{F}_q$, we substitute x_i by $\sum_j x_{ij} v_j$ in S_{m+1}, and by fixing a basis $\{\theta_1, \ldots, \theta_n\}$ of $\mathbb{F}_{q^n}/\mathbb{F}_q$ we see the resulting equation over $\mathbb{F}_{q^n}$ as a system of n polynomial equations over $\mathbb{F}_q$. Namely, we write

$$S_{m+1}\left(\sum_j x_{1j} v_j, \ldots, \sum_j x_{mj} v_j, X\right) = 0$$

in the form

$$\sum_k \theta_k f_k(x_{ij}) = 0$$

which implies that for all k we have

$$f_k(x_{ij}) = 0.$$

This polynomial system is then solved using generic methods such as resultants or Gröbner basis algorithms.

A particular case of this approach consists in taking $V := \mathbb{F}_q$. The resulting index calculus algorithm is more efficient than generic algorithms for fixed $n > 3$ and large enough q, and has subexponential time when q and n increase simultaneously in an appropriate manner [6, 10].

Another particular case occurs when q is a very small constant (typically $q = 2$). In this case the efficiency of Gröbner basis algorithms is increased by adding the so-called *field equations* $x_{ij}^q - x_{ij} = 0$ to the system. Experimental results and a heuristic analysis led Petit and Quisquater to conjecture that the algorithm could also have subexponential time in that case [17].

2.3 Limits of Previous Works

From a practical point of view, the subexponential result in [6] is of little interest as elliptic curves that appear in leading cryptographic standards are defined either over prime fields or binary fields with a prime extension degree. Semaev's seminal paper [19] proposes one factor basis for the prime case, but as mentioned above, it does not provide any corresponding algorithm to compute relations.

Binary curves may be vulnerable to index calculus algorithms for large enough parameters, according to Petit and Quisquater's analysis and following works [9, 12, 17, 21]. However, generic algorithms currently outperform these algorithms for the parameters used in practice, and the complexity estimates for larger parameters depend on the so-called *first fall degree assumption*. This assumption on Gröbner basis algorithms holds in some cases including for HFE systems [11, 15], but it is also known to be false in general. The systems occurring in binary ECDLP attacks are related to HFE systems, but at the time of writing it is not clear whether or not, or to which extent the assumption holds in their case. On the other hand, as the systems in play are clearly not generic, one should a priori be able to replace Gröbner basis by other, more dedicated tools.

2.4 Alternative Systems

One idea in that direction is to completely avoid the Weil descent methodology. The vector space constraints $x_i \in V$ are equivalent to the constraints $L(x_i) = 0$ where

$$L(x) := \prod_{v \in V} (x - v).$$

It is easy to prove (see [2, Chap. 11]) that L is a linearized polynomial, in other words L can be written as

$$L(x) = \sum_{j=0}^{n'} c_j x^{q^j}$$

where $c_j \in \mathbb{F}_{q^n}$. Moreover (see also [16]) L can be written as a composition of degree q maps

$$L(x) = (x^q - \alpha_{n'}x) \circ \ldots \circ (x^q - \alpha_1 x) \tag{1}$$

for well-chosen $\alpha_i \in \mathbb{F}_{q^n}$. Abusing the notations x_{ij}, the problem of finding $x_i \in V$ with $S_{m+1}(x_1, \ldots, x_m, X) = 0$ can now be reduced to solving either

$$\begin{cases} S_{m+1}(x_{11}, \ldots, x_{m1}, X) = 0 & \\ x_{ij} = x_{i,j-1}^q & i = 1, \ldots, m; j = 2, \ldots, n' \\ \sum_{j=0}^{n'} c_i x_{ij} = 0 & i = 1, \ldots, m \end{cases} \tag{2}$$

or

$$\begin{cases} S_{m+1}(x_{11}, \ldots, x_{m1}, X) = 0 & \\ x_{ij} = x_{i,j-1}^q - \alpha_{j-1}x_{i,j-1} & i = 1, \ldots, m; j = 2, \ldots, n' \\ 0 = x_{i,n'}^q - \alpha_{n'}x_{i,n'} & i = 1, \ldots, m. \end{cases} \tag{3}$$

The two systems have been suggested in [11,15,16]. Compared to polynomial systems arising from a Weil descent, both systems have the disadvantage to be defined over the field $\mathbb{F}_{q^n}$ but on the other hand they are much sparser and a priori easier to study. In fact, these systems are equivalent to polynomial systems arising from a Weil descent under linear changes of equations and variables, and in the univariate case ($m = 1$) their study has allowed to derive bounds on the corresponding Weil descent systems [11,15].

While Systems (2) and (3) can be solved with generic Gröbner basis algorithms, their simple structures might lead to better algorithms in the future. Most importantly for this article, they open the way to a generalization of previous algorithms to elliptic curves over prime fields.

3   Algebraic Attacks on Prime Curves

3.1   Main Idea

We replace the map L in Eq. (1) by another algebraic or rational map over $\mathbb{F}_p$ which for a given m similarly satisfies the following two conditions

1. $|\{x \in \mathbb{F}_p | L(x) = 0\}| \approx |\{x \in \overline{\mathbb{F}_p} | L(x) = 0\}| \approx p^{1/m}$,
2. L can be written as a composition of low degree maps L_j.

The resulting index calculus algorithm is summarized as Algorithm 1. For an optimal efficiency, the parameter m will have to be fixed depending on the cost of the relation search. At the moment, we have not investigated the existence of any algorithm better than Gröbner basis algorithms to solve System (4).

Algorithm 1. Index calculus algorithm for prime curves

Require: p, E, P, Q defining a discrete logarithm problem
Ensure: discrete logarithm k such that $Q = kP$
1: Fix m
2: Find a suitable map L and its decomposition $L = \circ_{j=1}^{n'} L_j$
3: Define a factor base $\mathcal{F} = \{(x, y) \in E(K) | L(x) = 0\}$
4: Compute $\deg L + \Delta$ relations as follows

    a. Pick $a, b \in \mathbb{F}_p$ randomly and compute $(X, Y) = aP + bQ$.
    b. Construct and solve the system

$$\begin{cases} S_{m+1}(x_{11}, \ldots, x_{m1}, X) = 0 \\ x_{i,j+1} = L_j(x_{i,j}) & i = 1, \ldots, m; j = 1, \ldots, n' - 1 \\ 0 = L_{n'}(x_{i,n'}) & i = 1, \ldots, m. \end{cases} \quad (4)$$

    (If the L_j are rational maps, their denominators are put on the left-hand sides
    to obtain a polynomial system.)
    c. For any solution found (modulo symmetries, namely permutations of the x_{i1}),
    if there are $P_i = (x_i, y_i) \in \mathcal{F}$ such that $\sum_i P_i = 0$, then store this relation.

5: Use linear algebra to solve the discrete logarithm

The parameter Δ can be a priori fixed to 10; its aim is to account for linear depencies that may occur with a low probability between the relations.

    The above conditions on L are such that: (1) most solutions of the system are defined over $\mathbb{F}_p$; (2) heuristically, we expect that the system has a constant probability to have a solution; (3) all the equations in the system have low degree. Note that System (4) is very similar to System (2) and System (3). We now show how these conditions can be satisfied, first for primes p such that $p - 1$ has a large smooth factor, and then for arbitrary primes.

3.2 Partial Analysis

We consider a computation model where both arithmetic operations in $\mathbb{F}_p$ and elliptic curve scalar multiplications have unitary cost. This is of course a very rough approximation as scalar multiplications require a polynomial number of field operations, but the approximation will be sufficient for our purposes.

    Let $T(E, m, L)$ be the time needed to solve System (4) for X chosen as in the algorithm. Let $P(p, m)$ be the *precomputation* time required to perform Step 2. The expected number of different solutions of the system in Steps 4b and 4c is about

$$\frac{(\deg L)^m}{m! \cdot p}.$$

Indeed, $|\mathcal{F}|$ is about $\deg(L)$ and $|E(K)|$ is about p. A given point (X, Y) is in the image of $\mathcal{F}^n \to E(K)$, $(P_r)_{r=1}^n \to \sum_{r=1}^n P_r$ about $\frac{(\deg L)^m}{m! \cdot p}$ times on average. The cost of Step 5 is

$$(\deg L)^\omega$$

where $2 < \omega \le 3$ depends on the algorithm used for linear algebra. The total cost of the attack is therefore

$$P(p, m) + \frac{m! \cdot p}{(\deg L)^{m-1}} T(E, m, L) + (\deg L)^{\omega}.$$

Our algorithm will outperform generic discrete logarithm algorithms when this complexity is smaller than $p^{1/2}$. When $(\deg L)^m \approx m! \cdot p$, this will happen when one can solve $T(E, m, L)$ more efficiently than $p^{1/2 - 1/m}$.

3.3   Attack When $p - 1$ Has a Large Smooth Factor

Let us first assume that $p - 1 = r \prod_{i=1}^{n'} p_i$ where the p_i are not necessarily distinct primes, all smaller than B, and $\prod_{i=1}^{n'} p_i \approx p^{1/m}$. We do not impose any particular condition on r. We define V as the subgroup G of order $\prod_{i=1}^{n'} p_i$ in $\mathbb{F}_p^*$. We then set $L_j(x) = x^{p_j}$ for $j = 1, \ldots, n' - 1$, and $L_{n'}(x) = 1 - x^{p_{n'}}$. The function $L := \circ_{j=1}^{n'} L_j$ satisfies all the properties required.

Alternatively, we could also choose V as a coset aG of G, and adapt the maps accordingly.

Due to Pohlig-Hellman's attack [18], finite fields with smooth order, or an order with some large smooth factor, have long been discarded for the discrete logarithm problem over finite fields, but to the best of our knowledge there has been no similar result nor even warning with respect to elliptic curves. In fact, NIST curves use pseudo-Mersenne numbers and are therefore potentially more vulnerable to our approach than other curves. In particular, the prime number used to define NIST P-224 curve is such that

$$p - 1 = 2^{96} \cdot 3 \cdot 5 \cdot 17 \cdot 257 \cdot 641 \cdot 65537 \cdot 274177 \cdot 6700417 \cdot 67280421310721$$

hence it satisfies the prerequisites of our attack already for $m \ge 3$ and $B = 2$.

3.4   Generalization to Arbitrary p

Let now p be an arbitrary prime number, in particular not necessarily of the previous form. Our second attack assumes the knowledge of an auxiliary elliptic curve $E'/\mathbb{F}_p$ with an order $N = r \prod_{i=1}^{n'} p_i$ where the p_i are not necessarily distinct primes, all smaller than B, and $\prod_{i=1}^{n'} p_i \approx p^{1/m}$. Note that the auxiliary curve is a priori unrelated to the curve specified by the elliptic curve discrete logarithm problem, except that it is defined over the same field. Let H be a subgroup of $E'(\mathbb{F}_p)$ of cardinality $\prod_{i=1}^{n'} p_i$. The set V will consist of the x-coordinates of all points $(x, y) \in E'(\mathbb{F}_p)$ in a coset of H. Let $\varphi : E' \to E'$ be the isogeny with kernel H. This isogeny can be efficiently written as a composition

$$\varphi = \varphi_{n'} \circ \ldots \circ \varphi_1$$

where $\deg \varphi_i = p_i$ and moreover all these isogenies can be efficiently computed using Vélu's formulae [23]. There exist polynomials ξ_j, ω_j, ψ_j such that

$$\varphi_j = \left(\frac{\xi_j(x)}{\psi_j^2(x)}, y \frac{\omega_j(x)}{\psi_j^3(x)} \right).$$

We then choose $L_j = \frac{\xi_j(x)}{\psi_j^2(x)}$ for $j = 1, \ldots, n'-1$ and $L_{n'} = \frac{\xi_{n'}(x)}{\psi_{n'}^2(x)} - \chi$, where χ is the x-coordinate of a point in the image of φ which is not 2-torsion. It is easy to check that the map $L = \circ_{j=1}^{n'} L_j$ then satisfies all properties required:

Lemma 1. *In the above construction, $\{x \in \mathbb{F}_p | L(x) = 0\}$ has size $\prod_{i=1}^{n'} p_i$.*

Proof. By construction, the isogeny φ has a kernel of size N/s, and so does any kernel coset. We claim that all the points in a coset have distinct x-coordinate if χ is not the x-coordinate of a point of order 2. Indeed, let $P_1 \neq P_2$ with $\varphi(P_1) = \varphi(P_2)$. If P_1 and P_2 have the same x-coordinate, then we have $P_2 = -P_1$ hence $\varphi(P_2) = \varphi(-P_1) = -\varphi(P_1)$. Therefore $\varphi(P_1) = -\varphi(P_1)$ has order 2. $\square$

In Sect. 3.5 we discuss how the auxiliary curve E' can be found, first assuming that p has been fixed and cannot be changed, second assuming that we have some flexibility in choosing p as well.

3.5 Finding an Auxiliary Curve

We now consider the cost of Step 2 of our algorithm for general prime numbers. We propose two algorithms to perform this task: the first one just picks curves at random until one that has the good properties is found, the second one uses the theory of complex multiplication. As many applications will be using standardized curves such as NIST curves, these costs can be considered as precomputation costs in many applications. Finally, we show that they can be greatly reduced for an attacker who can choose the prime p.

Random Curve Selection. The simplest method to perform the precomputation is to pick curves over $\mathbb{F}_p$ at random until one is found with a smooth enough order. To simplify the analysis, let us first consider a smoothness bound $B = 2$. The probability that the order of a random curve over $\mathbb{F}_p$ can be written as $N = 2^s \cdot r$ with $2^s \approx p^{1/m}$ is approximately $1/2^s \approx p^{-1/m}$, hence we expect to try about $p^{1/m}$ curves before finding a good one. Note that $p^{1/m}$ is essentially the size of the factor basis, hence the precomputation costs will always be dominated by at least the linear algebra costs in the whole index calculus algorithm. In practice we might be able to choose B bigger than 2, and this will make the precomputation cost even smaller, as shown by Table 1.

Table 1. Expected number of trials before finding a good curve, such that a factor at least $p^{1/m}$ is B-smooth. A number k in the table means that 2^k trials are needed on average. The numbers provided are for $|p| = 160$ and $|p| = 256$.

B/m	2	3	4	5
2	80.0	54.0	40.0	32.0
3	75.3	49.2	36.3	28.6
5	71.5	45.9	33.3	25.9
7	68.3	43.3	31.0	23.9
11	65.7	41.2	29.3	22.3
13	63.4	39.4	27.8	21.1
17	61.5	37.8	26.5	20.0

B/m	2	3	4	5
2	128.0	86.0	64.0	52.0
3	122.7	80.6	59.6	47.2
5	118.2	76.6	56.1	43.9
7	114.4	73.4	53.2	41.3
11	111.2	70.7	50.9	39.2
13	108.3	68.4	48.9	37.5
17	105.8	66.3	47.2	36.0

Complex Multiplication. The existence of a curve with N points over $\mathbb{F}_p$ within the Hasse-Weil bound is equivalent to the existence of an integer solution to the equation

$$(N + 1 - p)^2 - Df^2 = 4N$$

with $D < 0$ (see [3, Eq. 4.3]). Once this solution is known, the curve can be constructed using the complex multiplication algorithm [3, p.30], provided however that the *reduced discriminant* D is not too large to compute the Hilbert class polynomial H_D mod p. To the best of our knowledge, the best algorithm for this task is due to Sutherland [22] and runs in quasi-linear time in $|D|$. Sutherland reports computations up to $|D| \approx 10^{13}$.

We can rewrite the above equation as $(p + 1 - N)^2 - Df^2 = 4p$ and try to solve it for some small D using Cornacchia's algorithm [4]. More precisely, we can solve the equation $x^2 - Dy^2 = 4p$ and check if the solution produces a number N which is divisible by a large enough smooth factor. This approach is relatively slow since the number of such N is relatively small. With $B = 2$, one needs to try about $p^{1/m}$ different values of D.

Faster Precomputation for Chosen p. We now consider a different attack scenario, where p is not fixed but can be chosen by the attacker. In this setting, we first construct a number N in such a way that we know its factorization, and that N has a large enough smooth factor. We then solve $x^2 - Dy^2 = 4N$ for some small $|D|$ (using the factorization of N). We check if the appropriate value for p is indeed prime, and if not we try a different small $|D|$. The probability of p being prime is about $1/\log(p) \approx 1/\log(N)$. This method allows to use much smaller $|D|$ and it will outperform previous methods in general.

We remark that this approach can potentially be applied to produce a sort of "back door" when choosing primes for elliptic curve cryptography standards. However, this seems unlikely for the following two reasons. First, as soon as a user is aware of the potential existence of such a back door, it can easily detect it by solving the above equation for the given p and all small values of D. Second, other equally useful auxiliary curves can be constructed in a time dominated by other steps of the index calculus algorithm.

4   Gröbner Basis Experiments

In this section we describe preliminary computer experiments to evaluate the complexity of relation search in our approach, and compare it to the binary case.

4.1   Experimental Set-Up

In the binary case, we selected random curves over $\mathbb{F}_{2^{2n_1}}$ and a fixed vector space $V = \langle 1, x, x^2, \ldots, x^{n_1} \rangle$, for $1 \leq n_1 \leq 11$.

For the attack of Sect. 3.3 we chose the smallest prime p such that 2^{n_1} divides $p - 1$ with $p \geq 2^{2n_1}$, and V equal to the subgroup of order 2^{n_1} in $\mathbb{F}_p^*$.

For the attack of Sect. 3.4 we fixed $D = 7$. We selected parameters N and p such that there exists a curve of order N over $\mathbb{F}_p$, 2^{n_1} divides N, $N \in [2^{2n_1} - 2^{2n_1-2}; 2^{2n_1} + 2^{2n_1-1}]$ and N is the closest to 2^{2n_1} among those parameters. Using complex multiplication, we generated an elliptic curve E' over $\mathbb{F}_p$ with N rational points, and we computed a reduced Weierstrass model for this curve. We finally chose V as the projection on the x-coordinate of a coset of a subgroup of order 2^{n_1} of E', such that V had cardinality 2^{n_1}.

In all cases we selected a random (reduced Weierstrass model) curve over the field of consideration and a random point P on the curve. We then attempted to write $P = P_1 + P_2$ with P_i in the factor basis by reduction to polynomial systems and resolution of these systems with the Gröbner Basis routine of Magma. In the binary case we experimented on systems of the forms (2) and (3). In the other two cases we generated the systems as described in Sect. 3. We repeated all sets of experiments 100 times.

All experiments were performed on a CPU with 16-cores Intel Xeon Processor 5550, running at 2.67 GHz with a L3 cache of 18MB. The Operating System was Linux Ubuntu 12.04.5 LTS with kernel version GNU/Linux 3.5.0-17-generic x86_64 and 24GB memory. The programming platform was Magma V2.18-5 in its 64-bit version.

4.2   Experimental Results

In the tables below (Tables 2, 3, 4 and 5) *nbsols* is the average number of solutions of the system, *Av. time* is the average time in seconds and *Max. mem* is the maximum amount of memory used. The values D_{av} and D_{av}^{corr} are the average values of two measures of the degree of regularity from Magma's verbose output. For D_{av} we take the largest "step degree" occurring during a Gröbner Basis computation. This corresponds to the degrees reported in [17]. For D_{av}^{corr} we correct that by removing any step in which no pair was reduced, as these steps should arguably not significantly impact the overall complexity of the algorithm. This corresponds to the degrees reported in [20] and [11].

Based on this (limited) set of experiments we make the following observations:

1. The corrected version of the degree of regularity is a very stable measure: except for very small parameters, no variation was observed within any set of 100 experiments.

Table 2. Binary case, SRA system

n_1	n	D_{av}	D_{av}^{corr}	nbsols	Av. time (s)	Max. mem (MB)
1	2	2.76	2.76	0.59	0.00	14
2	4	3.93	3.93	0.73	0.00	14
3	6	3.99	3.99	0.72	0.00	14
4	8	3.99	3.98	1.03	0.00	15
5	10	4.36	4.00	1.19	0.02	41
6	12	4.50	4.00	1.30	0.09	80
7	14	4.64	4.00	1.04	0.43	213
8	16	4.62	4.00	1.03	2.21	622
9	18	4.56	4.00	0.78	9.27	1555
10	20	5.14	4.00	1.26	38.83	4170
11	22	4.93	4.00	0.94	207.72	53173

Table 3. Binary case, System (2)

n_1	n	D_{av}	D_{av}^{corr}	nbsols	Av. time (s)	Max. mem (MB)
1	2	2.60	2.60	0.95	0.00	14
2	4	3.93	3.93	0.54	0.00	14
3	6	4.00	4.00	0.96	0.00	14
4	8	4.38	4.00	1.14	0.00	15
5	10	4.35	3.99	1.06	0.01	25
6	12	4.39	4.00	0.98	0.05	18
7	14	4.32	4.00	0.91	0.20	19
8	16	4.66	4.00	1.18	2.04	24
9	18	4.74	4.00	1.18	4.90	34
10	20	4.62	4.00	0.98	39.00	65
11	22	4.70	4.00	1.00	4989.96	256

2. In our experiments, systems in the form (2) require much less memory than the corresponding SRA systems.
3. Timing comparison is less clear: while systems in the form (2) are more efficient up to $n_1 = 10$, SRA systems are much better at $n_2 = 11$.
4. The degrees of regularity, time and memory requirements are similar in the subgroup and isogeny versions of our attack.
5. The degrees of regularity, time and memory requirements seem to increase a bit faster in the prime case than in the binary case in general.

According to Bardet [1, Prop 4.1.2], homogeneous semi-generic systems with n equations of degree 2 and 1 equation of degree 4 in n variables have a degree of regularity equal to $(3+n)/2$. In all our experiments we observed a much smaller

Table 4. Prime case, $p - 1$ subgroups

n_1	p	D_{av}	D_{av}^{corr}	nbsols	Av. time (s)	Max. mem (MB)
1	5	4.00	4.00	0.59	0.00	9
2	17	4.00	4.00	0.79	0.00	9
3	73	4.00	4.00	0.84	0.00	9
4	257	4.01	4.00	1.14	0.00	9
5	1153	4.48	4.00	1.34	0.02	10
6	4289	5.00	5.00	1.08	0.13	13
7	17921	5.36	5.00	0.99	1.14	17
8	65537	5.36	5.00	0.96	9.09	35
9	262657	5.78	5.00	1.06	59.87	98
10	1051649	6.36	6.00	0.96	454.79	501
11	4206593	6.29	6.00	0.76	4975.07	2266

Table 5. Prime case, isogeny kernel

N	p	D_{av}	D_{av}^{corr}	nbsols	Av. time (s)	Max. mem (MB)
$2^1 \cdot 4$	11	4.00	4.00	0.25	0.00	11
$2^2 \cdot 7$	29	5.00	5.00	0.44	0.00	11
$2^3 \cdot 7$	71	5.00	5.00	0.91	0.01	11
$2^4 \cdot 22$	359	5.00	5.00	0.52	0.01	11
$2^5 \cdot 29$	967	5.00	5.00	0.97	0.03	11
$2^6 \cdot 53$	3467	5.42	5.00	1.23	0.15	12
$2^7 \cdot 106$	13619	5.47	5.00	1.17	1.16	18
$2^8 \cdot 203$	52291	5.42	5.00	1.13	9.08	34
$2^9 \cdot 414$	212587	5.92	5.00	1.19	51.87	95
$2^{10} \cdot 791$	811763	6.44	6.00	1.04	438.57	367
$2^{11} \cdot 1548$	3173683	6.45	6.00	1.06	5163.46	1945

dependency in n of the degree of regularity, suggesting that the systems occurring in our attacks are easier to solve than semi-generic systems with comparable parameters.

5 Conclusion, Further Work and Perspectives

Our algorithms generalize previous index calculus attacks from binary curves to prime curves, and therefore considerably increase their potential impact. All attacks including ours (implicitly) reduce the relation search in index calculus algorithms to an instance of the following problem:

Problem 1 (Generalized Root-Finding Problem). *Given a finite field K, given $f \in K[X_1, \ldots, X_m]$, and given $L \in K(X)$, find $X_i \in K$ such that $f(X_1, \ldots, X_m) = 0$ and $L(X_i) = 0$ for all i.*

We have suggested to focus on special polynomials L, which can be written as compositions of low degree maps, so that the generalized root-finding problem can be reduced to a polynomial system similar to "SRA systems" [16, Sect. 6], and then solved using Gröbner basis algorithms. Our computer experiments suggest that the resulting systems are a bit harder to solve than the corresponding systems in binary cases, but easier to solve than generic systems of comparable parameters.

The attacks are not practical at the moment and we do not know their asymptotic complexity. Still, we believe that they do unveil potential vulnerabilities that cryptanalysts need to study further. In particular, we showed that the standardized curve NIST P-224 satisfies the requirements of our first attack.

Following a suggestion by the PKC 2016 committee, we have also compared our approach with a variant of Semaev's original attack using Groebner basis algorithms to solve the system $S(x_1, x_2, X) = 0$, $L(x_1) = 0$, $L(x_2) = 0$ with $L(x) = \prod_{\alpha < B}(x - \alpha)$. Intriguingly, our preliminary results show that these systems are easier to solve than ours using Groebner basis algorithms on similar parameters. This can perhaps be explained by the much smaller number of variables, and may either suggest that our approach is unlikely to be efficient asymptotically, or that Semaev's original attack should be revisited from an algebraic perspective.

Important open problems include providing a satisfactory theoretical explanation for our experiments, and predicting the complexity of all algorithms for large parameters.

An even more important problem is to design a dedicated algorithm for the generalized root-finding problem, which would not rely on Gröbner basis algorithms at all. It is worth noticing that the Weil descent and Gröbner basis approach, when applied to classical root-finding problems (where f is univariate and $L(x) = x^{|K|} - x$), provides an algorithm with complexity exponential in $O(\log n \cdot \deg f)$ under a somewhat controversial heuristic assumption, whereas the best algorithms for this problem have a provable complexity exponential in $O(\log n + \deg f)$. A similar improvement for the above generalized version of the root-finding problem will greatly impact elliptic curve cryptography.

Acknowledgement. We thank Steven Galbraith, Sze Ling Yeo and Andreas Enge for discussions and suggestions related to this work. We also thank the program committee for their numerous and helpful suggestions. The research leading to these results has received funding from the European Research Council under the European Union's Seventh Framework Programme (FP/2007-2013) / ERC Grant Agreement no. 307937, the Engineering and Physical Sciences Research Council grant EP/J009520/1, and GCHQ through a research grant. The second author was initially funded by TL@NTU, but is currently affiliated to UCI.

References

1. Bardet, M.: Etude des systèmes algébriques surdéterminés. Applications aux codes correcteurs et à la cryptographie. Ph.D. thesis, Université Paris 6 (2004)
2. Berlekamp, E.R.: Algebraic Coding Theory. Aegean Park Press, Laguna Hills (1984)
3. Bröker, R.: Constructing elliptic curves of prescribed order. PhD thesis, University of Leiden (2006)
4. Cornacchia, G.: Su di un metodo per la risoluzione in numeri interi dell' equazione $\sum_{h=0}^{n} c_h x^{n-h} y^h = p$. Giorn. Mat. Battaglini **46**, 33–90 (1903)
5. den Boer, B.: Diffie-Hellman is as strong as discrete log for certain primes. In: Goldwasser, S. (ed.) CRYPTO 1988. LNCS, vol. 403, pp. 530–539. Springer, Heidelberg (1990)
6. Diem, C.: On the discrete logarithm problem in elliptic curves. Compos. Math. **147**, 75–104 (2011)
7. Diem, C.: On the discrete logarithm problem in elliptic curves II. Algebra Number Theory **7**, 1281–1323 (2013)
8. Faugère, J.-C., Perret, L., Petit, C., Renault, G.: Improving the complexity of index calculus algorithms in elliptic curves over binary fields. In: Pointcheval, D., Johansson, T. (eds.) EUROCRYPT 2012. LNCS, vol. 7237, pp. 27–44. Springer, Heidelberg (2012)
9. Galbraith, S.D., Gebregiyorgis, S.W.: Summation polynomial algorithms for elliptic curves in characteristic two. In: Meier, W., Mukhopadhyay, D. (eds.) INDOCRYPT 2014. LNCS, vol. 8885, pp. 409–427. Springer, Heidelberg (2014)
10. Gaudry, P.: Index calculus for abelian varieties of small dimension and the elliptic curve discrete logarithm problem. J. Symb. Comput. **44**(12), 1690–1702 (2009)
11. Huang, M.A., Kosters, M., Yeo, S.L.: Last fall degree, HFE, and Weil descent attacks on ECDLP. In: Gennaro, R., Robshaw, M. (eds.) CRYPTO 2015, Part I. LNCS, vol. 9215, pp. 581–600. Springer, Heidelberg (2015)
12. Huang, Y.-J., Petit, C., Shinohara, N., Takagi, T.: Improvement of faugère *et al.*'s method to solve ecdlp. In: Sakiyama, K., Terada, M. (eds.) IWSEC 2013. LNCS, vol. 8231, pp. 115–132. Springer, Heidelberg (2013)
13. Lenstra, H.W.: Factoring integers with elliptic curves. Ann. of Math. **126**, 649–673 (1987)
14. Maurer, U.M.: Towards the equivalence of breaking the diffie-hellman protocol and computing discrete logarithms. In: Desmedt, Y.G. (ed.) CRYPTO 1994. LNCS, vol. 839, pp. 271–281. Springer, Heidelberg (1994)
15. Petit, C.: Bounding HFE with SRA (2014). http://perso.uclouvain.be/christophe.petit/files/SRA_GB.pdf
16. Petit, C.: Finding roots in $GF(p^n)$ with the successive resultant algorithm. LMS J. Comput. Math. **17A**, 203–217 (2014)
17. Petit, C., Quisquater, J.-J.: On polynomial systems arising from a weil descent. In: Wang, X., Sako, K. (eds.) ASIACRYPT 2012. LNCS, vol. 7658, pp. 451–466. Springer, Heidelberg (2012)
18. Pohlig, S.C., Hellman, M.E.: An improved algorithm for computing logarithms over $GF(p)$ and its cryptographic significance (corresp.). IEEE Trans. Inf. Theory **24**(1), 106–110 (1978)
19. Semaev, I.: Summation polynomials and the discrete logarithm problem on elliptic curves. Cryptology ePrint Archive, Report /031 (2004). http://eprint.iacr.org/

20. Semaev, I.: New algorithm for the discrete logarithm problem on elliptic curves. Cryptology ePrint Archive, Report /310 (2015). http://eprint.iacr.org/
21. Shantz, M., Teske, E.: Solving the elliptic curve discrete logarithm problem using semaev polynomials, weil descent and gröbner basis methods – an experimental study. In: Fischlin, M., Katzenbeisser, S. (eds.) Buchmann Festschrift. LNCS, vol. 8260, pp. 94–107. Springer, Heidelberg (2013)
22. Sutherland, A.V.: Computing Hilbert class polynomials with the Chinese remainder theorem. Math. Comput. **80**(273), 501–538 (2011)
23. Vélu, J.: Isogénies entre courbes elliptiques. Communications de l'Académie royale des Sciences de Paris **273**, 238–241 (1971)

Degenerate Curve Attacks
Extending Invalid Curve Attacks to Edwards Curves and Other Models

Samuel Neves[1]($\boxtimes$) and Mehdi Tibouchi[2]

[1] CISUC, Department of Informatics Engineering,
University of Coimbra, Coimbra, Portugal
sneves@dei.uc.pt
[2] Okamoto Research Laboratory, NTT Secure Platform Laboratories,
Musashino-shi, Japan
tibouchi.mehdi@lab.ntt.co.jp

Abstract. Invalid curve attacks are a well-known class of attacks against implementations of elliptic curve cryptosystems, in which an adversary tricks the cryptographic device into carrying out scalar multiplication not on the expected secure curve, but on some other, weaker elliptic curve of his choosing. In their original form, however, these attacks only affect elliptic curve implementations using addition and doubling formulas that are independent of at least one of the curve parameters. This property is typically satisfied for elliptic curves in Weierstrass form but not for newer models that have gained increasing popularity in recent years, like Edwards and twisted Edwards curves. It has therefore been suggested (e.g. in the original paper on invalid curve attacks) that such alternate models could protect against those attacks.

In this paper, we dispel that belief and present the first attack of this nature against (twisted) Edwards curves, Jacobi quartics, Jacobi intersections and more. Our attack differs from invalid curve attacks proper in that the cryptographic device is tricked into carrying out a computation not on another elliptic curve, but on a group isomorphic to the multiplicative group of the underlying base field. This often makes it easy to recover the secret scalar with a single invalid computation.

We also show how our result can be used constructively, especially on curves over random base fields, as a fault attack countermeasure similar to Shamir's trick.

Keywords: Elliptic curve cryptography · Edwards curves · Implementation issues · Fault attacks · Countermeasures

1 Introduction

Elliptic curve cryptography (ECC) was introduced in the 1980s by Miller [44] and Koblitz [38], following the successful application of elliptic curves to integer factorization [39]. Compared to its finite field alternatives, ECC offers shorter

© International Association for Cryptologic Research 2016
C.-M. Cheng et al. (Eds.): PKC 2016, Part II, LNCS 9615, pp. 19–35, 2016.
DOI: 10.1007/978-3-662-49387-8_2

keys, higher speeds, and additional structure that enables constructions such as bilinear pairings. ECC rests on the hardness of the elliptic curve discrete logarithm problem (ECDLP), which has remained intractable so far—for well-chosen curves.

Regardless of the theoretical security of elliptic curve cryptosystems, attacks targeting their *implementations* are numerous. One particularly powerful attack class is the *fault attack* [12,13], which consists in injecting faults before or during a cryptographic operation, and inspecting the resulting output to recover key information. Fault attacks directed at elliptic curve scalar multiplication implementations were first published in [9] and further developed in many other works, including [11,15,20,36].

A conceptually simpler attack pointed out by Antipa et al. [1] and extended in several further works [35,37], the *invalid curve attack*, exploits implementations that fail to verify that input points to a scalar multiplication belong to the correct elliptic curve, and where point addition and doubling formulas are independent of at least one curve parameter. In such cases, the attacker can query its target with a specially-crafted point outside of the correct elliptic curve. Then, because the formulas used in the scalar multiplication do not depend on all curve parameters, the implementation really computes a normal scalar multiplication by the same scalar, but on a *different* curve depending on the invalid input point. Choosing invalid points in such a way that the corresponding curves are weak, the attacker can then quickly recover secret keys from observing the outputs (or the hashed outputs) of the scalar multiplications. Although the attack and recommended countermeasures are well-known to cryptographers, recent research has found that a number of widely-used cryptographic libraries in the wild are vulnerable [29].

The attack of Antipa et al. was originally introduced in the context of elliptic curves in Weierstrass form $y^2 = x^3 + ax + b$, where the usual formulas for point addition and doubling are independent of the curve parameter b. Nowadays, however, alternate elliptic curve models and addition laws are gaining prominence: models such as Montgomery [4,45] and Edwards [7,18] curves are being proposed for wide Internet usage[1], and several others are known to have desirable properties for cryptographic applications [10,33,34,40,53].

Invalid curve attacks generalize directly to those alternate models *provided that* the crucial property of independence of the arithmetic on at least one curve parameter is satisfied. But many of the newer models for elliptic curves, including Edwards curves, use all parameters in their most common addition formulas. It is thus reasonable to expect, then, that invalid curve attacks would not apply to those curves. In fact, the use of addition formulas depending on all curve parameters was specifically mentioned by Antipa et al. [1] as a possible countermeasure to thwart their attack.

Our Contribution. In this paper, we re-examine the feasibility of invalid curve attacks against newer elliptic curve models like Edwards curves, and find that

---

[1] See https://tools.ietf.org/html/draft-irtf-cfrg-curves.

a new variant of the attack of Antipa et al. *will* indeed break the security of implementations that do not carry out proper point validation. The new attack works by reducing the problem of finding the secret scalar to solving discrete logarithms not on a weaker elliptic curve, but in the multiplicative group of the base field, which is easy for typical curve sizes.

The idea behind the attack is roughly to let one of the parameters in the curve family vary, and consider the degenerate curves (those of genus 0) among them. On those special curves, the group law degenerates to the multiplicative group (or in rare cases, the additive group), and while in principle the group formulas should still involve the curve parameter that was made to vary, it often ends up being multiplied by the constant zero for all points on the degenerate curve. As a result, the same formulas as for scalar multiplication on the correct curve yield an exponentiation in the degenerate group.

When only a hash value of the result of the scalar multiplication is provided (as in hashed Diffie–Hellman), our new attack is somewhat less flexible than invalid curve attacks, since it is no longer possible to vary the weak curve as done by Antipa et al. However, using a baby-step-giant-step-like time-memory tradeoff, we show that we can still easily break curves over some of the largest fields commonly used for elliptic curve cryptography, such as $\mathbb{F}_{2^{521}-1}$.

This new attack underscores the importance of point validation even over newer elliptic curve models.

Finally, the properties we exploit in the attack can also be used constructively, to thwart fault attacks. We present a concrete countermeasure, similar to Shamir's trick [50], that detects faults injected during scalar multiplication particularly efficiently. This is done by lifting the computation on the elliptic curve over $\mathbb{F}_p$ to the composite order ring $\mathbb{Z}/pr\mathbb{Z}$ for some small constant r, and making sure that the component modulo r of the lifted curve is degenerate in the sense mentioned above. Then, verifying that the computation modulo r was correct becomes a simple field exponentiation, which is much faster than the usual scalar multiplication. This technique applies to Weierstrass curves as well as newer models.

Organization of the Paper. In Sect. 2, we provide a rundown of some of the most common curve models and addition laws used in elliptic curve cryptography. In Sect. 3, we first recall the traditional invalid curve attack, and then present our extension of it to newer models of elliptic curves using the degenerate curve technique. In Sect. 4, we explain how the new attack can be applied when only a hash of the result of the scalar multiplication is available. And finally, in Sect. 5, we present our concrete fault attack countermeasure using degenerate curves.

2   Elliptic Curve Models

We begin by presenting the elliptic curve forms and respective group laws studied in this paper. This is not an exhaustive list; there are many other addition laws in the literature, and the interested reader can see an overview of many of them in [8]. Every base field $\mathbb{F}_p$ throughout this paper is assumed to have characteristic ≥ 5.

2.1 Weierstrass Model

The canonical short Weierstrass form of an elliptic curve is given by the equation $y^2 = x^3 + ax + b$, with a point at infinity $\mathcal{O} = (0 : 1 : 0)$. Addition on Weierstrass curves is derived directly from the chord and tangent method [52, Chapter III.2]:

$$
\begin{aligned}
x_3 &= \lambda^2 - x_1 - x_2 \\
y_3 &= \lambda(x_1 - x_3) - y_1
\end{aligned}
\quad \text{where } \lambda =
\begin{cases}
\frac{y_1 - y_2}{x_1 - x_2} & \text{if } (x_1, y_1) \neq (x_2, \pm y_2), \\
\frac{3x_1^2 + a}{2y_1} & \text{if } (x_1, y_1) = (x_2, y_2).
\end{cases}
\tag{1}
$$

2.2 Twisted Edwards Model

Edwards curves were introduced in 2007 [7,18]. Here we look at their generalization, *twisted* Edwards curves [5], which cover more curves. A twisted Edwards curve is defined by the equation $ax^2 + y^2 = 1 + dx^2y^2$, with neutral affine point $\mathcal{O} = (0,1)$. The general complete group law for twisted Edwards curves is

$$
(x_3, y_3) = \left(\frac{x_1 y_2 + y_1 x_2}{1 + dx_1 x_2 y_1 y_2}, \frac{y_1 y_2 - a x_1 x_2}{1 - dx_1 x_2 y_1 y_2} \right).
\tag{2}
$$

An addition formula, no longer complete, which does not require the d parameter, was found by Hisil, Wong, Carter, and Dawson [25]:

$$
(x_3, y_3) =
\begin{cases}
\left(\frac{x_1 y_1 + x_2 y_2}{y_1 y_2 + a x_1 x_2}, \frac{x_1 y_1 - x_2 y_2}{x_1 y_2 - y_1 x_2} \right) & \text{if } (x_1, y_1) \neq (x_2, y_2), (-x_1, -y_1) \\
\left(\frac{2 x_1 y_1}{y_1^2 + a x_1^2}, \frac{y_1^2 - a x_1^2}{2 - y_1^2 - a x_1^2} \right) & \text{if } (x_1, y_1) = (x_2, y_2)
\end{cases}.
\tag{3}
$$

2.3 Huff's Model

Huff curves are a recently rediscovered elliptic curve model [34] previously used in the study of a certain Diophantine equation [27]. They are defined by the equation $ax(y^2 - 1) = by(x^2 - 1)$, and have the affine neutral point $\mathcal{O} = (0,0)$. Huff's addition formula, complete for points of odd order, is independent of the curve's parameters:

$$
(x_3, y_3) = \left(\frac{(x_1 + x_2)(1 + y_1 y_2)}{(1 + x_1 x_2)(1 - y_1 y_2)}, \frac{(y_1 + y_2)(1 + x_1 x_2)}{(1 - x_1 x_2)(1 + y_1 y_2)} \right).
\tag{4}
$$

2.4 Hessian Model

The Hessian form of an elliptic curve, introduced in [14] (also in [17,24,33,46, 53]), is defined by the equation $x^3 + y^3 + 1 = 3dxy$, with a point at infinity $\mathcal{O} = (1, -1, 0)$ as neutral element. The group law is given by

$$
(x_3, y_3) =
\begin{cases}
\left(\frac{y_1^2 x_2 - y_2^2 x_1}{x_2 y_2 - x_1 y_1}, \frac{x_1^2 y_2 - x_2^2 y_1}{x_2 y_2 - x_1 y_1} \right) & \text{if } (x_1, y_1) \neq (x_2, y_2) \\
\left(\frac{y_1(1 - x_1^3)}{x_1^3 - y_1^3}, \frac{x_1(y_1^3 - 1)}{x_1^3 - y_1^3} \right) & \text{if } (x_1, y_1) = (x_2, y_2).
\end{cases}
\tag{5}
$$

2.5   Twisted Hessian Model

The twisted Hessian form [6,8] is defined by equation $ax^3 + y^3 + 1 = dxy$, with neutral element $\mathcal{O} = (0, -1)$. Unlike the original Hessian form, twisted Hessian curves have an affine neutral point and complete addition formula

$$(x_3, y_3) = \left(\frac{x_1 - y_1^2 x_2 y_2}{ax_1 y_1 x_2^2 - y_2}, \frac{y_1 y_2^2 - ax_1^2 x_2}{ax_1 y_1 x_2^2 - y_2} \right). \tag{6}$$

2.6   Twisted Jacobi Intersections

Jacobi intersections were suggested by Chudnovsky and Chudnovsky [14], and were among the first competitive candidates for fast single-coordinate arithmetic[2]. Here we present Hisil et al.'s generalization [26], defined by the intersection of $bs^2 + c^2 = 1$ and $as^2 + d^2 = 1$, with neutral affine point $\mathcal{O} = (0, 1, 1)$ and complete addition formula

$$(s_3, c_3, d_3) = \left(\frac{s_1 c_2 d_2 + c_1 d_1 s_2}{1 - abs_1^2 s_2^2}, \frac{c_1 c_2 - bs_1 d_1 s_2 d_2}{1 - abs_1^2 s_2^2}, \frac{d_1 d_2 - as_1 c_1 s_2 c_2}{1 - abs_1^2 s_2^2} \right). \tag{7}$$

2.7   Extended Jacobi Quartics

Extended Jacobi quartics [14,26] are defined by the equation $y^2 = dx^4 + 2ax^2 + 1$, with $\mathcal{O} = (0, 1)$ and group law

$$(x_3, y_3) = \left(\frac{x_1 y_2 + y_1 x_2}{1 - dx_1^2 x_2^2}, \frac{(1 + dx_1^2 x_2^2)(y_1 y_2 + 2ax_1 x_2) + 2dx_1 x_2(x_1^2 + x_2^2)}{(1 - dx_1^2 x_2^2)^2} \right).$$
$$\tag{8}$$

3   Invalid Curve Attacks

3.1   Review of the Weierstrass Curve Case

We begin by describing the classic invalid curve attack against short Weierstrass curves $E_{a,b}$: $y^2 = x^3 + ax + b$ over the finite field $\mathbb{F}_p$. The key insight is that formulas defining the arithmetic on that curve, given by Eq. (1), do not depend on the parameter b of the curve equation. All the curves $E_{a,b'}$ for all b' actually share the same addition and doubling formulas.

Now consider a cryptographic device that performs scalar multiplications in $E_{a,b}(\mathbb{F}_p)$ by a constant secret scalar k, and that, furthermore, does not check that input points actually belong to that curve. An attacker trying to recover k can then query the device on an invalid point $\widetilde{P} = (\widetilde{x}, \widetilde{y}) \notin E_{a,b}(\mathbb{F}_p)$. That point belongs to a well-defined curve of the form $E_{a,b'}$, namely $E_{a,\tilde{b}}(\mathbb{F}_p)$ with $\tilde{b} =$

---

[2] Miller [44] also suggested x-only arithmetic for Diffie–Hellman. However he suggested using division polynomials for scalar multiplication, which is far more computationally expensive.

$\tilde{y}^2 - \tilde{x}^3 - a\tilde{x}$. As a result, on input $\widetilde{P}$, the device actually computes the scalar multiplication $k \cdot \widetilde{P}$ in the group $E_{a,\tilde{b}}(\mathbb{F}_p)$ and returns that value.

The discrete logarithm problem in the subgroup $\langle \widetilde{P} \rangle$ generated by $\widetilde{P}$ in $E_{a,\tilde{b}}(\mathbb{F}_p)$ will typically be much easier than in the original group $E_{a,b}(\mathbb{F}_p)$, and the attacker can even choose the invalid point and curve to make the problem particularly easy. This allows him to efficiently recover k modulo the order of $\langle \widetilde{P} \rangle$, and then all of k by repeating the process a few times with different invalid curves.

The whole attack can thus be summarized as follows:

1. Find a curve $E_{a,\tilde{b}}(\mathbb{F}_p)$ and a point $\widetilde{P}$ on it such that discrete logarithms in $\langle \widetilde{P} \rangle$ are easy;
2. Query the cryptographic device on $\widetilde{P}$ to get $k \cdot \widetilde{P}$;
3. Solve the discrete logarithm in the easy group, revealing $k \, mod \, \mathrm{ord}(\widetilde{P})$;
4. Repeat until k is recovered in its entirety.

Finding a curve and point such that discrete logarithms are easy can be done in several different ways. The original approach, inspired by [41], was to use invalid curves containing subgroups of very small orders and an input point in those subgroups; such curves are easy to find, but quite a few queries are needed to recover all of k.

Another approach is to use a curve of smooth order [43]: this is somewhat harder to construct, but may allow a full recovery of k in a single query. Alternatively, using a singular curve [35] yields a discrete logarithm problem in a form of the multiplicative group over $\mathbb{F}_p$ (or the additive group when $a = 0$), which is typically easy to solve and again makes the single-query recovery of k possible [28, Sect. 3.7].

The attack also extends to the situation when the cryptographic device only returns a hash of the resulting point of the scalar multiplication (the hashed Diffie–Hellman setting): in that case, the small subgroup approach is typically the most efficient. That is the approach taken by Jager, Schwenk and Somorovsky in their paper attacking ECDH key exchange in actually deployed TLS libraries [29].

3.2   Parameter-Independent Formulas

The invalid curve attack translates easily to the case of alternate curve models for which the addition and doubling formulas are independent of at least one of the curve parameters: when querying the cryptographic device on a point $\widetilde{P}$ outside of the valid curve E, the computations still amount to a scalar multiplication on a different curve $\widetilde{E}$ in the same family, obtained by adjusting the independent parameter appropriately.

This is the case for (twisted) Hessian and Huff curves. Additionally, efficient d-less formulas exist for Edwards curves (cf. Eq. (3)), Jacobian quartics and Jacobian intersections [26].

On the other hand, in the case of addition laws depending on all curve parameters, the result of sending an arbitrary invalid input point to the device can no longer be interpreted as a scalar multiplication on a well-defined invalid curve: the attack of Antipa et al. does not generalize directly to that setting.

3.3 Our New Approach: The Degenerate Curve Attack Against Edwards Curves

As is easily observed in Eq. (2), the typical Edwards addition formulas depend on all curve parameters and are therefore not vulnerable to the original invalid curve attack as described above. However, there is one interesting property of this addition law that helps us transfer elliptic curve discrete logarithms to the curve's underlying field, rendering them solvable by sieve methods [16, 21].

Theorem 1. *Let $E_{a,d}$ be a twisted Edwards curve over $\mathbb{F}_p$. The subset $\widetilde{G} \subset \mathbb{F}_p^2$ of the affine plane consisting of points of the form $(0, y)$, $y \neq 0$, endowed with the addition law defined by the same formula as $E_{a,d}$, given by Eq. (2), forms a group isomorphic to $\mathbb{F}_p^*$ under the isomorphism $y \mapsto (0, y)$.*

Proof. The map $\varphi \colon \mathbb{F}_p^* \to \widetilde{G}$, $y \mapsto (0, y)$ is by definition a bijection. It suffices to check that it is a homomorphism to conclude. But this is indeed the case since adding the points $(0, y_1)$ and $(0, y_2)$ yields, according to Eq. (2):

$$\varphi(y_1) + \varphi(y_2) = \left(\frac{0 \cdot y_2 + y_1 \cdot 0}{1 + d \cdot 0 \cdot 0 \cdot y_1 y_2}, \frac{y_1 y_2 - a \cdot 0 \cdot 0}{1 - d \cdot 0 \cdot 0 \cdot y_1 y_2} \right) = (0, y_1 y_2) = \varphi(y_1 y_2)$$

as required. ☐

As a result, given a cryptographic device performing scalar multiplications in the group $E_{a,d}(\mathbb{F}_p)$ without input point validation, as in the original attack of Sect. 3.1, an attacker can send as input an invalid point $\widetilde{P}$ of the form $(0, \tilde{y})$, and receive as result the scalar multiplication of $\widetilde{P}$ by the secret k in the group $\widetilde{G}$, namely $(0, \tilde{y}^k)$. Therefore, recovering k is reduced to solving the discrete logarithm problem in the multiplicative group $\mathbb{F}_p^*$, which as we have mentioned above is much easier than in $E_{a,d}(\mathbb{F}_p)$ owing to well-known subexponential attacks.

For elliptic curve sizes used in practice (up to 500 or so bits), the finite field discrete log is easy! By choosing y as a generator of $\mathbb{F}_p^*$ (which is always a cyclic group), the attacker can thus recover all of k in a single query. This yields our generalization of invalid curve attacks to the case of Edwards curves: we call this attack a *degenerate curve attack* for reasons that will become apparent shortly.

Remark 1. An obvious but important observation is that, while we have described our attack in affine coordinates, it also works in the (likely) case when the device performs its computation in projective coordinates, using the projective versions of the same group operations. It is straightforward to check, for example, that $(0 : Y_1 : 1) + (0 : Y_2 : 1) = (0 : Y_1 Y_2 : 1)$ (and generalizations with other values of the Z-coordinates go through similarly).

One can wonder why, despite the dependence of the group law Eq. (2) on all curve parameters, we can still find an invalid curve in the affine plane where the same formulas induce a group structure. A rough explanation is as follows. First, the y-axis $Y: x = 0$ in the plane is actually a limit (in the usual sense of one-parameter families) of the twisted Edwards curves $E_{a,d}$ for fixed d: it is the fiber above $a = \infty$. This is easily seen by rewriting the equation of $E_{a,d}$ in terms of $a' = 1/a$, as $x^2 + a'y^2 = a'(1 + dx^2y^2)$, and setting $a' = 0$. Since Y is of genus 0, the Edwards group law should degenerate on Y (minus a finite number of points) as the additive or the multiplicative group. The expression of the group law need not a priori be the same as on the original curve $E_{a,d}$ itself, but it does turn out to be the case, because the only term depending on the parameter a cancels out along $Y: x = 0$.

Now the line Y is not itself singular (although it should perhaps really be seen as the non-reduced double line $x^2 = 0$), but it is where the family degenerates, hence the name of our attack.

3.4   Degenerate Curve Attacks Against Other Models

The idea of the previous attack generalizes easily to other models of elliptic curves, including all of those mentioned in Sect. 2. We now describe those generalizations in affine coordinates below; they of course also work in projective coordinates.

Extended Jacobi Quartics. Let $E_{a,b}: y^2 = dx^4 + 2ax^2 + 1$ be an extended Jacobi quartic curve over $\mathbb{F}_p$, and consider the set $\widetilde{G}$ of points in $\mathbb{F}_p^2$ of the form $(0, y)$, $y \neq 0$. Endow this set with the same addition law as $E_{a,d}$, defined by Eq. (8). It then forms a group isomorphic to $\mathbb{F}_p^*$ under the isomorphism $\varphi: y \mapsto (0, y)$. Indeed, this map is a bijection and we have:

$$\varphi(y_1) + \varphi(y_2) = \left(\frac{0 \cdot y_2 + y_1 \cdot 0}{1 - d \cdot 0 \cdot 0}, \frac{(1 + d \cdot 0 \cdot 0)(y_1 y_2 + 2a \cdot 0 \cdot 0) + 2d \cdot 0 \cdot 0 \cdot 0}{(1 - d \cdot 0 \cdot 0)^2} \right)$$
$$= (0, y_1 y_2) = \varphi(y_1 y_2),$$

so φ is an isomorphism as required.

Therefore, we can carry out our attack as before, by sending to a device performing scalar multiplications on $E_{a,d}$ the invalid input point $(0, y)$ for some generator y of $\mathbb{F}_p^*$.

In this case, the y-axis appears as the degenerate limit of the family $E_{a,d}$ for fixed a and varying d, taken for $d = \infty$.

Twisted Jacobi Intersections. Let $E_{a,b}: as^2 + c^2 = bs^2 + d^2 = 1$ be a twisted Jacobi intersection over $\mathbb{F}_p$, and consider the sets $\widetilde{G}_1$ and $\widetilde{G}_2$ of points in $\mathbb{F}_p^3$ of the form $(0, c, 0)$, $c \neq 0$, and $(0, 0, d)$, $d \neq 0$, respectively. Endow both of these sets with the same addition law as $E_{a,b}$, defined by Eq. (7). Then they form groups isomorphic to $\mathbb{F}_p^*$ under the isomorphisms $\varphi_1: c \mapsto (0, c, 0)$ and $\varphi_2: d \mapsto (0, 0, d)$ respectively. Indeed, those maps are both bijections and we have:

$$\varphi_1(c_1) + \varphi_1(c_2) = \left(\frac{0 \cdot c_2 \cdot 0 + c_1 \cdot 0 \cdot 0}{1 - ab \cdot 0 \cdot 0}, \frac{c_1 c_2 - b \cdot 0 \cdot 0 \cdot 0}{1 - ab \cdot 0 \cdot 0}, \frac{0 \cdot 0 - b \cdot 0 \cdot c_1 \cdot 0 \cdot c_2}{1 - ab \cdot 0 \cdot 0} \right)$$

$$= (0, c_1 c_2, 0) = \varphi_1(c_1 c_2)$$

and similarly for φ_2 by symmetry.

This provides two families of invalid points using which we can carry out our attack exactly as before.

Twisted Hessian Curves. The case of twisted Hessian curves is somewhat less interesting, since this model has a group law independent of the curve parameter d, and hence the original invalid curve attack applies to it. Nevertheless, we can mention for completeness that our approach generalizes rather directly to those curves as well.

Indeed, if $E_{a,d} : ax^3 + y^3 + 1 = dxy$ is a twisted Hessian curve, the map $\varphi : y \mapsto (0, -y)$ defines an isomorphism between $\mathbb{F}_p^*$ and the set of elements of the form $(0, y)$, $y \neq 0$ in $\mathbb{F}_p^2$ endowed with the same addition law as $E_{a,d}$, defined by Eq. (6). Indeed:

$$\varphi(y_1) + \varphi(y_2) = \left(\frac{0 + y_1^2 \cdot 0 \cdot y_2}{-a \cdot 0 \cdot y_1 \cdot 0 + y_2}, \frac{-y_1 y_2^2 - a \cdot 0 \cdot 0}{-a \cdot 0 \cdot y_1 \cdot 0 + y_2} \right)$$

$$= (0, -y_1 y_2) = \varphi(y_1 y_2).$$

Huff Curves. As with Hessian curves, Huff curves have a parameter-independent group law and hence are not the most relevant setting for us, but we can again extend our attack to them.

For the Huff curve $E_{a,b} : ax(y^2 - 1) = by(x^2 - 1)$ with the group law of Eq. (4), we can consider the set $\widetilde{G}$ of points in $\mathbb{F}_p^2$ of the form $(0, y)$. The sum of two such points under the addition law given by the same formula is given by:

$$(0, y_1) + (0, y_2) = \left(\frac{0 \cdot (1 + y_1 y_2)}{1 \cdot (1 - y_1 y_2)}, \frac{(y_1 + y_2) \cdot 1}{1 \cdot (1 + y_1 y_2)} \right) = \left(0, \frac{y_1 + y_2}{1 + y_1 y_2} \right).$$

Thus, if we consider the map $\varphi : \mathbb{F}_p^* \to \widetilde{G}$ defined outside -1 by $\varphi(t) = \left(0, (1 - t)/(1 + t) \right)$, it is easy to check that $\varphi(t_1) + \varphi(t_2) = \varphi(t_1 t_2)$, and therefore we again have a group isomorphic to $\mathbb{F}_p^*$ to carry out our attack.

Remark 2. It may be worth noting that for some curve models, we are also able to find degenerate curves on which the addition law induces a group structure isomorphic to the twisted form of the multiplicative group (i.e. the subgroup of order $p + 1$ of elements of norm 1 in $\mathbb{F}_{p^2}^*$). Huff curves offer a simple concrete example: consider the set of points of the form $(x, x) \in \mathbb{F}_p^2$ with the Huff addition law of Eq. (4). The sum of two such points is given by $(x_1, x_1) + (x_2, x_2) = (x_3, x_3)$ where

$$x_3 = \frac{x_1 + x_2}{1 - x_1 x_2}.$$

When -1 is a quadratic nonresidue in $\mathbb{F}_p$, this is well-known to be the so-called "compressed form" of the twisted multiplicative group [49].

4　The Hashed Case

The previous section considered attacks on a cryptographic device that performs elliptic curve scalar multiplications without validation of input points, and returns the actual result of the scalar multiplication. This is a somewhat idealized attack model, however.

One real-world protocol where a similar situation arises is (static) Diffie–Hellman key exchange over elliptic curves, one variant of which is presented in Fig. 1. In an invalid curve attack on that protocol, Bob would send Alice his invalid point B, and Alice would use it to compute the product $k_A \cdot B$ where k_A is her static secret key. The resulting point $k_A \cdot B$ is not directly sent back to Bob, however, but used to derive a key $K = \text{KDF}(k_A \cdot B)$ used in subsequent communication. In effect, what Bob receives is the image of $k_A \cdot B$ under a fixed, public one-way function, usually with low collision probability (in Fig. 1, it would be the authentication message M).

We model that situation by considering an oracle which, on input of a point P (still unvalidated), computes the scalar multiplication $k \cdot P$ by a fixed secret k, and returns the image $H(k \cdot P)$ of the result under a public hash function H. In that more restrictive setting, degenerate curve attacks are not as devastating as previously described, but we will see that it is often still possible to recover k quite quickly in practice, depending on the smoothness of the order $p - 1$ of $\mathbb{F}_p^*$ (or of $p + 1$ in the case of degenerate groups isomorphic to the twisted multiplicative group; we will describe the attack in the $\mathbb{F}_p^*$ case to fix ideas).

The idea is simply to apply the Pohlig–Hellman algorithm [47]. Using the naive variant of the algorithm, the attacker can, for each prime divisor ℓ of $p - 1$, choose a point $\widetilde{P}$ of order ℓ in the degenerate group, obtain $H(k \cdot \widetilde{P})$ from the oracle, and perform an exhaustive search in the subgroup $\langle \widetilde{P} \rangle$ to find the point $\widetilde{Q}$ such that $H(k \cdot \widetilde{P}) = H(\widetilde{Q})$, revealing $k \bmod \ell$. Prime powers are dealt with similarly, and in the end the attacker recovers all of k with only a few oracle queries, in time quasilinear in the largest prime factor $P_1(p - 1)$ of $p - 1$. Furthermore, if a higher query complexity is acceptable, we can use Shanks'

Fig. 1. Basic unauthenticated elliptic curve Diffie–Hellman protocol, under which invalid curve attacks may be mounted. The protocol works over a curve $E_{a,b}(\mathbb{F}_p)$, with a generator point P of prime order n. KDF$(\cdot)$ is an arbitrary key-derivation function taking points of $E_{a,b}(\mathbb{F}_p)$ as input; $E(K, M)$ is taken to be some authenticated encryption primitive, e.g., AES–GCM.

baby-step giant-step time-memory tradeoff [51] to recover k in time quasilinear in $\sqrt{P_1(p-1)}$, also using a number of queries and a space complexity quasilinear in $\sqrt{P_1(p-1)}$.

In general, even $\sqrt{P_1(p-1)}$ need not be much smaller than the complexity of the discrete logarithm problem in the original curve. However, newer models like Edwards curves are often used over special base fields $\mathbb{F}_p$ with particularly efficient arithmetic. Table 1 lists those efficient primes for usual curve sizes together with the bit size of $P_1(p-1)$, and we can see that for many of them, the degenerate curve attack is quite efficient: for example, for curves over the Mersenne prime field $\mathbb{F}_{2^{521}-1}$ (used to construct the highest security elliptic curves, including E-521 [2]), the complexity of an $\mathbb{F}_p^*$ degenerate curve attack would be around $O(2^{44})$, which is very practical. And it would be $O(2^{57.5})$, also quite fast, over $\mathbb{F}_{2^{448}-2^{224}-1}$, the field of definition of Ed448-Goldilocks [22].

5   A Fault Attack Countermeasure

Soon after the announcement of the Bellcore attack on RSA, Shamir proposed a countermeasure [50] that relies on the Chinese remainder theorem to detect faults during modular exponentiation. The basic idea of Shamir is to replace computations modulo a prime p by computations in the ring modulo the composite pr, where r is a small randomly-selected integer, and then compare the result modulo r against an independent equivalent computation modulo r.

While Shamir's trick[3] works well on RSA, due to its simple structure, it is trickier to apply this countermeasure to the elliptic curve case. Nevertheless, countermeasures based on Shamir's trick have been devised. The first one was invented by Blömer, Otto, and Seifert [11] (BOS), and consisted of two elliptic curve scalar multiplications—one over $\mathbb{Z}/pr\mathbb{Z}$, the other over $\mathbb{Z}/r\mathbb{Z}$. Baek and Vasyltov [3] suggested the use of the curve $Y^2Z + pYZ^3 = X^3 + aXZ^4 + BZ^6 \in \mathbb{Z}/pr\mathbb{Z}$, where $B = y^2 + py - x^3 - ax$, which clearly is equivalent to the original when reduced modulo p. This method is limited to projective coordinates, since not every intermediate result may have an inverse in the extended ring. Their method also has some potential weaknesses owing to its reliance on random integers r instead of adequately selected primes [31]. It has been recently pointed out that the original BOS countermeasure is not correct when coupled with group laws containing exceptions [48], and thus group laws used in BOS-like countermeasures must be *test-free*.

More recently, Joye [30,32] proposed a variant of the BOS countermeasure, where one works instead over $\mathbb{Z}/pr^2\mathbb{Z}$ (resp. $\mathbb{Z}/r^2\mathbb{Z}$). To accelerate the second scalar multiplication, Joye takes advantage of the isomorphism between the set of points of $E(\mathbb{Z}/r^2\mathbb{Z})$ that reduce to the neutral point modulo r, and the additive group $\mathbb{F}_r^+$. For example, the set of affine points $(\alpha r, 1) \in E(\mathbb{Z}/r^2\mathbb{Z})$, coupled with the Edwards group law, yields the useful identity $k \cdot (\alpha r, 1) = (k \cdot \alpha r, 1) \pmod{r^2}$,

---

[3] Not to be confused with Shamir's double-exponentiation trick, pointed out by ElGamal [19, p. 471] and originally discovered by Straus [54].

Table 1. For primes p suitable for fast elliptic curve cryptography [23], size in bits of the largest prime factor of $p-1$ and $p+1$, and complexity of our BSGS-style hashed Diffie–Hellman attack in $\mathbb{F}_p^*$ ($(p-1)$ attack) and in the twisted multiplicative group ($(p+1)$ attack).

p	$\log_2 P_1(p-1)$	$(p-1)$ attack	$\log_2 P_1(p+1)$	$(p+1)$ attack
$2^{191}-19$	90	$O(2^{45})$	93	$O(2^{46.5})$
$2^{196}-15$	64	$O(2^{32})$	165	$O(2^{82.5})$
$2^{216}-2^{108}-1$	107	$O(2^{53.5})$	19	$O(2^{9.5})$
$2^{221}-3$	73	$O(2^{36.5})$	42	$O(2^{21})$
$2^{224}-2^{96}+1$	46	$O(2^{23})$	157	$O(2^{78.5})$
$2^{226}-5$	127	$O(2^{63.5})$	49	$O(2^{24.5})$
$2^{230}-27$	101	$O(2^{50.5})$	136	$O(2^{68})$
$2^{251}-9$	235	$O(2^{117.5})$	70	$O(2^{35})$
$2^{255}-19$	236	$O(2^{118})$	95	$O(2^{47.5})$
$2^{266}-3$	37	$O(2^{17.5})$	125	$O(2^{62.5})$
$2^{285}-9$	237	$O(2^{118.5})$	60	$O(2^{30})$
$2^{291}-19$	259	$O(2^{129.5})$	114	$O(2^{57})$
$2^{322}-2^{161}-1$	133	$O(2^{66.5})$	64	$O(2^{32})$
$2^{336}-3$	166	$O(2^{83})$	214	$O(2^{107})$
$2^{338}-15$	166	$O(2^{83})$	204	$O(2^{102})$
$2^{369}-25$	192	$O(2^{96})$	252	$O(2^{126})$
$2^{383}-31$	88	$O(2^{44})$	97	$O(2^{48.5})$
$2^{389}-21$	247	$O(2^{123.5})$	311	$O(2^{155.5})$
$2^{401}-31$	48	$O(2^{24})$	209	$O(2^{104.5})$
$2^{416}-2^{208}-1$	60	$O(2^{30})$	96	$O(2^{48})$
$2^{448}-2^{224}-1$	115	$O(2^{57.5})$	49	$O(2^{24.5})$
$2^{450}-2^{225}-1$	88	$O(2^{44})$	54	$O(2^{27})$
$2^{452}-3$	88	$O(2^{44})$	266	$O(2^{133})$
$2^{468}-17$	209	$O(2^{104.5})$	164	$O(2^{82})$
$2^{480}-2^{240}-1$	163	$O(2^{81.5})$	36	$O(2^{18})$
$2^{489}-21$	263	$O(2^{131.5})$	260	$O(2^{130})$
$2^{495}-31$	158	$O(2^{79})$	319	$O(2^{159.5})$
$2^{521}-1$	88	$O(2^{44})$	1	$O(2^{0.5})$

which can be used to detect a fault very efficiently. Our proposed countermeasure is conceptually similar, but takes advantage of the multiplicative and additive identities of degenerate curves described in Sect. 3 instead. The countermeasure is described, in its most general form, in Algorithm 1.

Algorithm 1: Fault attack countermeasure for elliptic curves with degenerate points allowing "shortcut" scalar multiplications.

Input:

A curve $E(\mathbb{F}_p)$;

A point $P = (x, y) \in E(\mathbb{F}_p)$;

A scalar exponent $k \in \mathbb{Z}$;

A security parameter b;

An efficiently-computable "shortcut" map $f(k, P) : E(\mathbb{F}_r) \to E(\mathbb{F}_r)$ implementing scalar multiplication by k.

Output: $k \cdot P$

begin

   $r \leftarrow$ random b-bit prime

   $E_r \leftarrow$ DegenerateCurve(r) // **Pick degenerate curve, model-dependent**

   $P_r \leftarrow (x_r, y_r) \in E_r(\mathbb{F}_r)$ // **Pick appropriate degenerate point on** E_r

   $E' \leftarrow E \times E_r \ / \ \mathbb{Z}/pr\mathbb{Z}$

   $P' \leftarrow \Big(\mathrm{CRT}_{p,r}(x(P), x_r), \mathrm{CRT}_{p,r}(y(P), y_r)\Big) \in E'(\mathbb{Z}/pr\mathbb{Z})$

   $Q' \leftarrow k \cdot P'$

   if $Q' \bmod r \neq f(k, P' \bmod r)$ **then**   // **Check for fault**

      | **return** *"error"*

   else

      | **return** $\Big(x(Q') \bmod p, y(Q') \bmod p\Big)$

   end

end

One can view our proposed countermeasure as the BOS [11] countermeasure coupled with a "shortcut" $f(k, P)$ to compute the second scalar multiplication—$k \cdot P$ in $E(\mathbb{F}_r)$—much faster than by using the standard formulas. This shortcut takes different forms depending on which curve shape we are working over. Generically, we begin by picking a curve E_r over $\mathbb{F}_r$ for which there is at least one point for which scalar multiplication is easy to compute. Then, the extended curve E' is the direct product $E'(\mathbb{Z}/pr\mathbb{Z}) = E(\mathbb{F}_p) \times E_r(\mathbb{F}_r)$, and the countermeasure consists of checking whether $k \cdot P' \in E'$, reduced modulo r, equals the same multiplication performed independently in E_r. The correctness of this method follows from the correctness of BOS [11]; our concrete contribution is the shortcuts taken to reduce the computation overhead of the scalar multiplication in E_r. The following considers two popular shapes—Weierstrass and Edwards curves—but others are similarly easy to derive.

5.1   Weierstrass Curves

In Weierstrass curves, we may take advantage of the unique singular curve $y^2 = x^3$. This curve is notable for degenerating into the *additive* group $\mathbb{F}_r^+$ via the map $(x, y) \mapsto x/y$ and $\infty \mapsto 0$, with inverse $t \mapsto (t^{-2}, t^{-3})$ and $0 \mapsto \infty$ [28, Sect. 3.7]. This immediately suggests a very efficient shortcut map for E_r:

$$f(k, P) = \left((kt)^{-2}, (kt)^{-3}\right),$$

where $t = x/y$ or $t = 0$ if $P = \infty$.

The resulting correctness test only requires a few multiplications modulo r, which is more efficient than both BOS [11] and Baek–Vasyltsov [3], and is comparable with Joye's approach [30]. Note that the inversions are avoidable by using projective coordinates.

5.2   Edwards Curves

Unlike Weierstrass curves, Edwards curves do not have any additive degeneration. However, we can use the results of Sect. 3.3 to devise a similar countermeasure using a multiplicative degeneration. The shortcut map for E_r is

$$f(k, P) = \left(0, y^k\right),$$

where $P = (0, y)$ for any $y \notin \{0, 1\}$ that generates the group $\mathbb{F}_r^*$. In this case the computational overhead is larger than in the Weierstrass case—a modular exponentiation modulo r—but is still far cheaper than a scalar multiplication.

5.3   Comparison with Previous Countermeasures

The above methods offer some advantages relatively to previous Shamir-inspired fault attack countermeasures:

Only one full-fledged scalar multiplication is required. This is in contrast with Blömer–Otto–Seifert [11, Sect. 8] which requires 2 scalar multiplications—one modulo pr, another modulo r. In the case of Weierstrass curves, our countermeasure is faster than any other targeting the same curve shape.

Works both in affine and projective coordinates. This is in contrast with Baek–Vasyltsov [3], which due to working on Weierstrass curves, breaks down when faced with the corner cases in the addition and doubling formulas of those curves.

Although our method may not suit every use case, it is another useful tool for hardened implementations of elliptic curves. It is particularly suitable for implementations of curves over random primes, which hardware implementers tend to favor [42], since multiplication modulo pr is straightforward to implement, and the overhead remains small. On the other hand, highly structured primes, usually very close to a power of 2, would likely suffer a higher performance impact, since modular reduction would no longer be a linear-time operation.

References

1. Antipa, A., Brown, D.R.L., Menezes, A., Struik, R., Vanstone, S.A.: Validation of elliptic curve public keys. In: Desmedt, Y.G. (ed.) PKC 2003. LNCS, vol. 2567, pp. 211–223. Springer, Heidelberg (2002)

2. Aranha, D.F., Barreto, P., Pereira, G., Ricardini, J.E.: A note on high-security general-purpose elliptic curves. Cryptology ePrint Archive, Report 2013/647 (2013). http://eprint.iacr.org/

3. Baek, Y.-J., Vasyltsov, I.: How to prevent DPA and fault attack in a unified way for ECC scalar multiplication – ring extension method. In: Dawson, E., Wong, D.S. (eds.) ISPEC 2007. LNCS, vol. 4464, pp. 225–237. Springer, Heidelberg (2007). http://dx.doi.org/10.1007/978-3-540-72163-5_18

4. Bernstein, D.J.: Curve25519: new Diffie-Hellman speed records. In: Yung, M., Dodis, Y., Kiayias, A., Malkin, T. (eds.) PKC 2006. LNCS, vol. 3958, pp. 207–228. Springer, Heidelberg (2006)

5. Bernstein, D.J., Birkner, P., Joye, M., Lange, T., Peters, C.: Twisted Edwards curves. In: Vaudenay, S. (ed.) AFRICACRYPT 2008. LNCS, vol. 5023, pp. 389–405. Springer, Heidelberg (2008)

6. Bernstein, D.J., Chuengsatiansup, C., Kohel, D., Lange, T.: Twisted Hessian curves. In: Lauter, K., Rodríguez-Henríquez, F. (eds.) LatinCrypt 2015. LNCS, vol. 9230, pp. 269–294. Springer, Heidelberg (2015)

7. Bernstein, D.J., Lange, T.: Faster addition and doubling on elliptic curves. In: Kurosawa, K. (ed.) ASIACRYPT 2007. LNCS, vol. 4833, pp. 29–50. Springer, Heidelberg (2007)

8. Bernstein, D.J., Lange, T.: Explicit-formulas database (2015). https://hyperellip tic.org/EFD/. Accessed 1 May 2015

9. Biehl, I., Meyer, B., Müller, V.: Differential fault attacks on elliptic curve cryptosystems. In: Bellare, M. (ed.) CRYPTO 2000. LNCS, vol. 1880, pp. 131–146. Springer, Heidelberg (2000)

10. Billet, O., Joye, M.: The Jacobi model of an elliptic curve and side-channel analysis. In: Fossorier, M.P.C., Høholdt, T., Poli, A. (eds.) AAECC 2003. LNCS, vol. 2643, pp. 34–42. Springer, Heidelberg (2003). https://eprint.iacr.org/2002/125

11. Blömer, J., Otto, M., Seifert, J.-P.: Sign change fault attacks on elliptic curve cryptosystems. In: Breveglieri, L., Koren, I., Naccache, D., Seifert, J.-P. (eds.) FDTC 2006. LNCS, vol. 4236, pp. 36–52. Springer, Heidelberg (2006). http://dx.doi.org/10.1007/11889700_4

12. Boneh, D., DeMillo, R.A., Lipton, R.J.: On the importance of checking cryptographic protocols for faults. In: Fumy, W. (ed.) EUROCRYPT 1997. LNCS, vol. 1233, pp. 37–51. Springer, Heidelberg (1997)

13. Boneh, D., DeMillo, R.A., Lipton, R.J.: On the importance of eliminating errors in cryptographic computations. J. Cryptol. **14**(2), 101–119 (2001)

14. Chudnovsky, D.V., Chudnovsky, G.V.: Sequences of numbers generated by addition in formal groups and new primality and factorization tests. Adv. Appl. Math. **7**(4), 385–434 (1986). http://dx.org/10.1016/0196-8858(86)90023-0

15. Ciet, M., Joye, M.: Elliptic curve cryptosystems in the presence of permanent and transient faults. Des. Codes Crypt. **36**(1), 33–43 (2005). http://dx.org/10.1007/s10623-003-1160-8

16. Coppersmith, D., Odlyzko, A.M., Schroeppel, R.: Discrete logarithms in $GF(p)$. Algorithmica **1**(1), 1–15 (1986). http://dx.org/10.1007/BF01840433

17. Desboves, A.: Résolution, en nombres entiers et sous la forme la plus générale, de l'équation cubique, homogène, à trois inconnues. Nouvelles annales de mathématiques, journal des candidats aux écoles polytechnique et normale **5**(3), 545–579 (1886). http://www.numdam.org/item?id=NAM_1886_3_5_545_0

18. Edwards, H.M.: A normal form for elliptic curves. Bull. Am. Math. Soc. **44**(3), 393–422 (2007). http://dx.org/10.1090/S0273-0979-07-01153-6

19. ElGamal, T.: A public key cryptosystem and a signature scheme based on discrete logarithms. IEEE Trans. Inf. Theory **31**, 469–472 (1985)
20. Fouque, P., Lercier, R., Réal, D., Valette, F.: Fault attack on elliptic curve Montgomery ladder implementation. In: Breveglieri, L., Gueron, S., Koren, I., Naccache, D., Seifert, J. (eds.) 2008 Fifth International Workshop on Fault Diagnosis and Tolerance in Cryptography, FDTC 2008, Washington, DC, USA, 10 August 2008, pp. 92–98. IEEE Computer Society (2008). http://dx.org/10.1109/FDTC.2008.15
21. Gordon, D.M.: Discrete logarithms in $GF(p)$ using the number field sieve. SIAM J. Discret. Math. **6**(1), 124–138 (1993). http://dx.org/10.1137/0406010
22. Hamburg, M.: Ed448-Goldilocks. In: Workshop on Elliptic Curve Cryptography Standards (2015)
23. Harris, B., et al.: The Pareto frontiers of sleeveless primes. The Curves mailing list, October 2014. https://moderncrypto.org/mail-archive/curves/2014/000324.html
24. Hesse, O.: Über die Elimination der Variabeln aus drei algebraischen Gleichungen vom zweiten Grade mit zwei Variabeln. Journal für die reine und angewandte Mathematik **28**, 68–96 (1844). http://resolver.sub.uni-goettingen.de/purl?GDZPPN002144069
25. Hisil, H., Wong, K.K.-H., Carter, G., Dawson, E.: Twisted Edwards curves revisited. In: Pieprzyk, J. (ed.) ASIACRYPT 2008. LNCS, vol. 5350, pp. 326–343. Springer, Heidelberg (2008)
26. Hisil, H., Wong, K.K., Carter, G., Dawson, E.: An exploration of affine group laws for elliptic curves. J. Math. Cryptol. **5**(1), 1–50 (2011). http://dx.org/10.1515/jmc.2011.005
27. Huff, G.B.: Diophantine problems in geometry and elliptic ternary forms. Duke Math. J. **15**(2), 443–453 (1948)
28. Husemöller, D.: Elliptic Curves, Graduate Texts in Mathematics, vol. 111, 2nd edn. Springer, New York (2004)
29. Jager, T., Schwenk, J., Somorovsky, J.: Practical invalid curve attacks on TLS-ECDH. In: Pernul, G., Y A Ryan, P., Weippl, E. (eds.) ESORICS. LNCS, vol. 9326, pp. 407–425. Springer, Heidelberg (2015). doi:10.1007/978-3-319-24174-6_21
30. Joye, M.: Fault-resistant calculcations on elliptic curves, June 2013. http://www.google.com/patents/US8457303, US Patent 8,457,303
31. Joye, M.: On the security of a unified countermeasure. In: Breveglieri, L., Gueron, S., Koren, I., Naccache, D., Seifert, J. (eds.) 2008 Fifth International Workshop on Fault Diagnosis and Tolerance in Cryptography, FDTC 2008, Washington, DC, USA, 10 August 2008, pp. 87–91. IEEE Computer Society (2008). http://dx.org/10.1109/FDTC.2008.8
32. Joye, M.: Elliptic curve cryptosystems in the presence of faults. In: Fischer, W., Schmidt, J. (eds.) 2013 Workshop on Fault Diagnosis and Tolerance in Cryptography, Los Alamitos, CA, USA, 20 August 2013, p. 73. IEEE Computer Society (2013). http://conferenze.dei.polimi.it/FDTC13/shared/FDTC-2013-keynote-2.pdf
33. Joye, M., Quisquater, J.-J.: Hessian elliptic curves and side-channel attacks. In: Koç, Ç.K., Naccache, D., Paar, C. (eds.) CHES 2001. LNCS, vol. 2162, pp. 402–410. Springer, Heidelberg (2001)
34. Joye, M., Tibouchi, M., Vergnaud, D.: Huff's model for elliptic curves. In: Hanrot, G., Morain, F., Thomé, E. (eds.) ANTS-IX. LNCS, vol. 6197, pp. 234–250. Springer, Heidelberg (2010). http://dx.doi.org/10.1007/978-3-642-14518-6_20

35. Karabina, K., Ustaoğlu, B.: Invalid-curve attacks on (hyper)elliptic curve cryptosystems. Adv. Math. Commun. **4**(3), 307–321 (2010). http://cryptolounge.net/pdf/KarUst10.pdf
36. Kim, T., Tibouchi, M.: Bit-flip faults on elliptic curve base fields, revisited. In: Boureanu, I., Owesarski, P., Vaudenay, S. (eds.) ACNS 2014. LNCS, vol. 8479, pp. 163–180. Springer, Heidelberg (2014)
37. Kim, T., Tibouchi, M.: Invalid curve attacks in a GLS setting. In: Tanaka, K., Suga, Y. (eds.) IWSEC 2015. LNCS, vol. 9241, pp. 41–55. Springer, Heidelberg (2015)
38. Koblitz, N.: Elliptic curve cryptosystems. Math. Comput. **48**, 203–209 (1987). http://dx.org/10.1090/S0025-5718-1987-0866109-5
39. Lenstra Jr., H.W.: Factoring integers with elliptic curves. Ann. Math. **126**(3), 649–673 (1987). http://www.jstor.org/stable/1971363
40. Liardet, P., Smart, N.P.: Preventing SPA/DPA in ECC systems using the Jacobi form. In: Koç, Ç.K., Naccache, D., Paar, C. (eds.) CHES 2001. LNCS, vol. 2162, pp. 391–401. Springer, Heidelberg (2001)
41. Lim, C.H., Lee, P.J.: A key recovery attack on discrete log-based schemes using a prime order subgroup. In: Kaliski Jr., B.S. (ed.) CRYPTO 1997. LNCS, vol. 1294, pp. 249–263. Springer, Heidelberg (1997)
42. Lochter, M., Merkle, J., Schmidt, J.M., Schütze, T.: Requirements for standard elliptic curves. Cryptology ePrint Archive, Report 2014/832 (2014). http://eprint.iacr.org/2014/832
43. Menezes, A.: Another look at HMQV. J. Math. Cryptol. **1**, 47–64 (2007). http://dx.org/10.1515/JMC.2007.004
44. Miller, V.S.: Use of elliptic curves in cryptography. In: Williams, H.C. (ed.) CRYPTO 1985. LNCS, vol. 218, pp. 417–426. Springer, Heidelberg (1986)
45. Montgomery, P.L.: Speeding the Pollard and elliptic curve methods of factorization. Math. Comput. **48**(177), 243–264 (1987). http://www.ams.org/journals/mcom/1987-48-177/S0025-5718-1987-0866113-7/
46. Mumford, D.: On the equations defining Abelian varieties. I. Inventiones Math. **1**(4), 287–354 (1966). http://dash.harvard.edu/handle/1/3597241
47. Pohlig, S.C., Hellman, M.E.: An improved algorithm for computing logarithms over GF(p) and its crytographic significance. IEEE Trans. Inf. Theory **24**, 106–110 (1978)
48. Rauzy, P., Moreau, M., Guilley, S., Najm, Z.: Using modular extension to provably protect ECC against fault attacks. Cryptology ePrint Archive, Report 2015/882 (2015). http://eprint.iacr.org/2015/882
49. Rubin, K., Silverberg, A.: Compression in finite fields and torus-based cryptography. SIAM J. Comput. **37**(5), 1401–1428 (2008)
50. Shamir, A.: How to check modular exponentiation, May 1997. (presented at the rump session of EUROCRYPT 1997)
51. Shanks, D.: Class number, a theory of factorization, and genera. In: Lewis, D.J. (ed.) 1969 Number Theory Institute. Proceedings of Symposia in Pure Mathematics, vol. 20, pp. 415–440. American Mathematical Society, Providence, Rhode Island (1971)
52. Silverman, J.H.: The Arithmetic of Elliptic Curves, Graduate Texts in Mathematics, vol. 106, 2nd edn. Springer, New York (2009). http://www.math.brown.edu/jhs/AECHome.html
53. Smart, N.P.: The Hessian form of an elliptic curve. In: Koç, Ç.K., Naccache, D., Paar, C. (eds.) CHES 2001. LNCS, vol. 2162, pp. 118–125. Springer, Heidelberg (2001)
54. Straus, E.G.: Addition chains of vectors (problem 5125). Am. Math. Monthly **71**(7), 806–808 (1964). http://www.jstor.org/stable/2310929

Easing Coppersmith Methods Using Analytic Combinatorics: Applications to Public-Key Cryptography with Weak Pseudorandomness

Fabrice Benhamouda[1]([⊠]), Céline Chevalier[2]([⊠]), Adrian Thillard[1,3]([⊠]),
and Damien Vergnaud[1]([⊠])

[1] ENS, CNRS, INRIA, and PSL, Paris, France
{fabrice.ben.hamouda,damien.vergnaud}@ens.fr, adrianthillard@gmail.com
[2] CRED, Université Panthéon-Assas, Paris, France
celine.chevalier@ens.fr
[3] ANSSI, Paris, France

Abstract. The *Coppersmith methods* is a family of lattice-based techniques to find small integer roots of polynomial equations. They have found numerous applications in cryptanalysis and, in recent developments, we have seen applications where the number of unknowns and the number of equations are non-constant. In these cases, the combinatorial analysis required to settle the complexity and the success condition of the method becomes very intricate.

We provide a toolbox based on *analytic combinatorics* for these studies. It uses the structure of the considered polynomials to derive their generating functions and applies complex analysis techniques to get asymptotics. The toolbox is versatile and can be used for many different applications, including multivariate polynomial systems with arbitrarily many unknowns (of possibly different sizes) and simultaneous modular equations over different moduli. To demonstrate the power of this approach, we apply it to recent cryptanalytic results on number-theoretic pseudorandom generators for which we easily derive precise and formal analysis. We also present new theoretical applications to two problems on RSA key generation and randomness generation used in padding functions for encryption.

Keywords: Coppersmith methods · Analytic combinatorics · Cryptanalysis · Pseudorandom generators · RSA key Generation · Encryption padding

1 Introduction

Many important problems in (public-key) cryptanalysis amount to solving polynomial equations with partial information about the solutions. In 1996, Coppersmith introduced two celebrated lattice-based techniques [11–13] for finding small roots of polynomial equations. They have notably found many important

© International Association for Cryptologic Research 2016
C.-M. Cheng et al. (Eds.): PKC 2016, Part II, LNCS 9615, pp. 36–66, 2016.
DOI: 10.1007/978-3-662-49387-8_3

applications in the cryptanalysis of the RSA cryptosystem (see [27] and references therein). The first technique works for a univariate modular polynomial whereas the second one deals with a bivariate polynomial over the integers. In these methods, a family of polynomials is first derived from the polynomial whose roots are wanted; this family naturally gives a lattice basis and short vectors of this lattice possibly provide the wanted roots. Since 1996 many generalizations of the methods have been proposed to deal with more variables (e.g., [8,20,22]) or multiple moduli (e.g., [28–30]).

Most of the applications of the Coppersmith methods in cryptanalysis involve a constant number of multivariate polynomial equations in a constant number of variables. However, in recent developments, we have seen applications of the methods where the number of unknowns is non-constant (e.g., [2,18,29]). These applications typically involve a number-theoretic pseudorandom number generator that works by iterating an algebraic map on a secret random initial seed value and outputting the state value at each iteration. It has been shown that in many cases Coppersmith's methods can be applied to recover some secret value. The difficulty comes from the fact that the polynomial system to solve involves all iterates of the pseudorandom generator. It is very tedious to analyze the attack complexity (i.e., the dimension of the lattice derived from the polynomial system whose roots are wanted) and its success condition (i.e., the total degrees of the polynomials and monomials families used in the lattice construction). For instance in [2,18], this analysis is a bit loose; it uses a nice simplifying trick in order to analyze the condition of success but does not permit to estimate the attack complexity. The main intent of this paper is to promote the use of *analytic combinatorics* in order to perform these computations. In order to demonstrate the power of this approach, we apply it to known cryptanalytic results [2] for which we easily derive precise and formal analysis. We also present new theoretical applications to two problems that were left open in [16] on RSA key generation and randomness generation used in padding functions for encryption.

Prior Work. As illustrations of our toolbox, we apply it to the following problems from the literature:

- *Number-theoretic pseudorandom generators.* A *pseudorandom generator* is a deterministic algorithm that maps a random seed to a longer string that cannot be distinguished from uniformly random bits by a computationally bounded algorithm. As mentioned above, a *number-theoretic* pseudorandom generator iterates an algebraic map F over a residue ring $\mathbb{Z}_N$ on a secret random seed $v_0 \in \mathbb{Z}_N$ and computes the intermediate states $v_{i+1} = F(v_i)$ mod N for $i \in \mathbb{N}$. It outputs (some consecutive bits of) the state value v_i at each iteration. The well-known *linear congruential generator* corresponds to the case where F is an affine function. It is efficient and has good statistical properties but Boyar [10] proved that one can recover the seed in time polynomial in the bit-size of M and this is also the case even if one outputs only the most significant bit of each v_i (see [9,23,31]). In [2], Bauer, Vergnaud, and Zapalowicz studied the security of number-theoretic generators for rational map F and proposed attacks based on Coppersmith's techniques showing that for low degree F the generators are polynomial time predictable if sufficiently many consecutive bits of the v_i's are revealed (see also [5,6]). Their lattice constructions are intricate and the analysis of their attacks is complex.

- *Key generation and Paddings from weak pseudorandom generator.* The former attacks assume that the adversary has direct access to sufficiently many consecutive bits of a certain number of outputs. However, it may be possible that using such a generator in a cryptographic protocol does not make the resulting protocol insecure. For instance, in [25], Koshiba proved that the linear congruential generator can be used to generate randomness in the ElGamal encryption scheme (based on some plausible assumption). This security results holds because the adversary against ElGamal encryption scheme does not have access to the actual outputs of the generator. *A contrario*, in 1997, Bellare et al. [4] broke the Digital Signature Algorithm (DSA) when the random nonces used in signature generation are computed using a linear congruential generator. Recently, Fouque et al. [16] analyzed the security of public-key schemes when the secret keys are constructed by concatenating the outputs of a linear congruential generator. They obtained a time/memory tradeoff on the search for the seed when such generators are used to generate the prime factors of an RSA modulus (using multipoint polynomial evaluation). They left open the problem to extend it to different scenarios, such as the generation of randomness used in padding functions for encryption and signatures.

Technical Tools. In *Coppersmith methods*, one usually considers an irreducible multivariate polynomial f defined over $\mathbb{Z}$, having a small root $\boldsymbol{x}$ modulo a known integer N and one generates a collection of polynomials having $\boldsymbol{x}$ as a modular root (usually, multiples and powers of f are chosen). The problem of finding $\boldsymbol{x}$ can be reformulated by constructing a matrix using the collection of polynomials (see Sect. 2). The methods succeed (heuristically) if some conditions on the matrix hold and these conditions can be checked by enumerating the polynomials involved in the collection and the total degree of the monomials appearing in the collection. The success condition is usually stated as a bound $\boldsymbol{x} < N^\delta$ where δ is an asymptotic explicit constant derived from the combinatorial analysis. However, in order to actually reach this bound in practice, the constructed matrix is of huge dimension and the computation which is theoretically polynomial-time becomes in practice prohibitive[1]. These attacks based on this method are obviously strong evidence of a weakness in the underlying cryptographic scheme and there exist method that makes it possible to use matrices of reasonable dimension

---

[1] Following Lipton's terminology we can often qualify as *galactic* the resulting polynomial-time algorithm for the asymptotic value of δ [26].

(e.g., by performing an exhaustive to retrieve a small part of x and Coppersmith technique with a smaller matrix to retrieve the other (bigger) part).

The combinatorial analysis in Coppersmith methods is usually easy to perform but as mentioned above it can be very intricate if one considers multivariate polynomial equations in a non-constant number of variables. *Analytic combinatorics* is a celebrated technique — which was mostly developed by Flajolet and Sedgewick [15] — of counting combinatorial objects. It uses the structure of the objects considered to derive their generating functions and applies complex analysis techniques to get asymptotics.

Contributions. The main contribution of the paper is to provide a toolbox based on analytic combinatorics for the study of the complexity and the success condition of Coppersmith methods. The toolbox is versatile and can be used for many different applications, including multivariate polynomial systems with arbitrarily many unknowns (of possibly different sizes) and simultaneous modular equations over different moduli.

In order to illustrate the usefulness of this toolbox, we then revisit the analysis of previous cryptanalytic results from the literature on number-theoretic pseudo-random generators [2]. In particular, we precise the complexity analysis of the attacks described in [2] by giving generating functions and asymptotics for the dimension of the matrix involved in the attack. We provide a complete analysis of the success condition of the attacks described in [2,29]. The technique uses simple formal manipulation on the generating functions and are readily done using any computer algebra system. In particular, this shows that the toolbox is very generic and can be applied in many settings (and does not require any clever tricks).

Eventually, we provide new applications of the toolbox to RSA key generation and encryption paddings from weak pseudorandom generator. We improve Fouque *et al.* time/memory tradeoff attack and we propose a (heuristic) polynomial-time factorization attack when the RSA prime factors are constructed by concatenating the outputs of a linear congruential generator. Our attack applies when the primes factors are concatenation of three (or more) consecutive outputs of the generator, i.e., when the seed is at most $N^{1/6}$ (for which the time/memory tradeoff attack has the prohibitive complexity $O(N^{1/12})$). The attack is theoretical since it makes use of a matrix of large dimension. Following their suggestion, we also apply our toolbox to the setting of the randomness generation used in padding functions for encryption. To illustrate our technique, we consider RSA Encryption with padding as described in PKCS#1 v1.5; it has been known to be insecure since Bleichenbachers chosen ciphertext attack [7] but, unfortunately, this padding is still in used about everywhere (e.g., TLS, XML encryption standard, hardware token, ...). We consider several scenario, namely linear congruential generator (LCG), truncated LCG, and LCG used in n consecutive ciphertext. We apply our toolbox to all of them and for an RSA modulus N with a public exponent e and a LCG with modulus M, our attacks are polynomial-time in $\log(N)$ for the following (asymptotic) M's:

Key generation	PKCS#1 v1.5		
with LCG	LCG	Truncated LCG	LCG and multiple ciphertexts
$M \leqslant N^{1/6}$	$M < N^{1/e}$	$M < N^{1/e}$	$M < N^{n/e}$

2   Coppersmith Methods

In this section, we give a short description of Coppersmith method for solving a multivariate modular polynomial system of equations over multiple moduli. We refer the reader to [22,30] for details and proofs.

Problem Definition. Let $f_1(y_1, \ldots, y_n), \ldots, f_s(y_1, \ldots, y_n)$ be irreducible multivariate polynomials defined over $\mathbb{Z}$, having a root $(x_1, \ldots, x_n)$ modulo respective known integers $N_1, \ldots, N_n$, that is $f_i(x_1, \ldots, x_n) \equiv 0 \mod N_i$. This root is *small* in the sense that each of its components is bounded by a known value, namely $|x_1| < X_1, \ldots, |x_n| < X_n$. We need to bound the sizes of X_i (for $i \in \{1, \ldots, n\}$) allowing to recover the desired root in polynomial time.

Polynomials Collection. In a first step, for each modulus N_i, one generates a collection of polynomials $\{\tilde{f}_{i,1}, \ldots, \tilde{f}_{i,r(i)}\}$ having $(x_1, \ldots, x_n)$ as a root modulo N_i. Usually, multiples and powers of the original polynomial f_i are chosen, namely $\tilde{f}_{i,j} = y_1^{k_{i,j,1}} \cdots y_n^{k_{i,j,n}} f_i^{k_{i,j,\ell}}$ for some integers $k_{i,j,1}, \ldots, k_{i,j,n}, k_{i,j,\ell}$. By construction, such polynomials satisfy the relation $\tilde{f}_{i,j}(x_1, \ldots, x_n) \equiv 0 \mod N_i^{k_{i,j,\ell}}$, i.e., there exists an integer $c_{i,j,k}$ such that $\tilde{f}_{i,j,k}(x_1, \ldots, x_n) = c_{i,j,k} N_i^{k_{i,j,\ell}}$. If some moduli N_i are equals, one can also consider multiples and powers of products of the corresponding original polynomials f_i.

From now, we denote for each $i \in \{1, \ldots, s\}$, the polynomials $\{\tilde{f}_{i,1}, \ldots, \tilde{f}_{i,r(i)}\}$ constructed as above. Considering the union of such sets if some moduli N_i are equals, we can assume without loss of generality that the moduli N_i are *pairwise distinct* and even *pairwise coprime*. Let us denote as $\mathscr{P}$ the set of all the polynomials and $\mathscr{M}$ the set of monomials appearing in the collection $\mathscr{P}$. In the paper, we use the following essential condition for the method to work: for each $i \in \{1, \ldots, s\}$, the polynomials $\{\tilde{f}_{i,1}, \ldots, \tilde{f}_{i,r(i)}\}$ are *linearly independent*.

Matrix Construction. The problem of finding small modular roots of these polynomials can now be reformulated in a vectorial way. Indeed, each polynomial from our chosen collection can be expressed as a vector over $\mathbb{Z}^t$ by extracting its coefficients and putting them into a vector with respect to a chosen order on $\mathcal{M}$. We hence construct a matrix $\mathfrak{M}$ as follows and we define as $\mathcal{L}$ the lattice generated by its rows:

$$
\mathfrak{M} = \left(
\begin{array}{ccc|ccc}
 & & & & & \\
\multicolumn{3}{c|}{\begin{matrix} 1 & & \\ & X_1^{-1} & \\ & & \ddots \\ & & X_1^{-a_1}\ldots X_n^{-a_n} \end{matrix}} & \multicolumn{3}{c}{\bigstar} \\
\hline
\multicolumn{3}{c|}{\mathbf{0}} & \multicolumn{3}{c}{\begin{matrix} N_1^{k_{1,1,\ell}} & & \\ & \ddots & \\ & & N_s^{k_{s,r(s),\ell}} \end{matrix}}
\end{array}
\right)
\begin{array}{c}
1 \\ y_1 \\ \vdots \\ y_1^{a_1}\ldots y_n^{a_n} \\ \\ \\ \\
\end{array}
$$

$$\tilde{f}_{1,1} \cdots \tilde{f}_{s,r(s)}$$
$$\downarrow \quad \cdots \quad \downarrow$$

On that figure, every row of the upper part is related to one monomial of $\mathcal{M}$ (we assume in the figure that $\mathcal{M}$ contains 1, y_1, and $y_1^{a_1}\ldots y_n^{a_n}$ among other monomials). The left-hand side contains the bounds on these monomials (e.g., the coefficient $X_1^{-1}X_2^{-2}$ is put in the row related to the monomial $y_1 y_2^2$). The right-hand side is formed by all vectors coming from the union of the collections $\{\tilde{f}_{i,1}, \ldots, \tilde{f}_{i,r(i)}\}$.

A Short Vector in a Sublattice. Let us now consider the row vector

$$r_0 = (1, x_1, \ldots, x_1^{a_1}\ldots x_n^{a_n}, -c_1, \ldots, -c_r).$$

By multiplying this vector by the matrix $\mathfrak{M}$, one obtains:

$$s_0 = \left(1, \left(\frac{x_1}{X_1}\right), \ldots, \left(\frac{x_1}{X_1}\right)^{a_1} \cdots \left(\frac{x_n}{X_n}\right)^{a_n}, 0, \ldots, 0\right).$$

By construction, this vector which, *in some sense*, contains the root we are searching for, belongs to $\mathcal{L}$ and its norm is very small. Thus, the recovery of a small vector in $\mathcal{L}$, will likely lead to the recovery of the desired root $(x_1, \ldots, x_n)$. To this end, we first restrict ourselves in a more appropriated subspace. Indeed, noticing that the last coefficients of s_0 are all null, we know that this vector belongs to a sublattice $\mathcal{L}'$ whose last coordinates are composed by zero coefficients. By doing elementary operations on the rows of $\mathfrak{M}$, one can easily construct that sublattice and prove that its determinant is the same as the one of $\mathcal{L}$.

Method Conclusion. From that point, one computes an LLL-reduction on the lattice $\mathcal{L}'$ and computes the Gram-Schmidt's orthogonalized basis $(b_1^\star, \ldots, b_t^\star)$ of the LLL output basis $(b_1, \ldots, b_t)$. Since s_0 belongs to $\mathcal{L}'$, this vector can be expressed as a linear combination of the $b_i^\star$'s. Consequently, if its norm is smaller than those of $b_t^\star$, then s_0 is orthogonal to $b_t^\star$. Extracting the coefficients appearing in $b_t^\star$, one can construct a polynomial p_1 defined over $\mathbb{Z}$ such that $p_1(x_1, \ldots, x_n) = 0$. Repeating the same process with the vectors $b_{t-1}^\star, \ldots, b_{t-n+1}^\star$ leads to the system $\{p_1(x_1, \ldots, x_n) = 0, \ldots, p_n(x_1, \ldots, x_n) = 0\}$. Under the (heuristic) assumption that all created polynomials define an algebraic variety of dimension 0, the previous system can be solved (e.g., using elimination techniques such as Groebner basis) and the desired root recovered in polynomial time.

The conditions on the bounds X_i that make this method work are given by the following (simplified) inequation (see [30] for details):

$$\prod_{y_1^{k_1} \ldots y_n^{k_n} \in \mathcal{M}} X_1^{k_1} \cdots X_n^{k_n} < \prod_i N_i^{\sum_{i=1}^{n} \sum_{j=1}^{r(i)} k_{i,j,\ell}} . \tag{1}$$

For such techniques, the most complicated part is the choice of the collection of polynomials, what could be a really intricate task when working with multiple polynomials.

3 Analytic Combinatorics

We now recall the analytic combinatorics results that we need in the remaining of this paper. We deliberately omit some of the formalism in order to simplify the techniques used. See [15] for more details. In the following, we denote by $|\mathcal{A}|$ the cardinal of a set $\mathcal{A}$.

3.1 Introduction

As explained in the former section, Coppersmith's method requires polynomials which are usually constructed as $f_{\mathbf{k}} = y_1^{k_1} \ldots y_n^{k_n} f^{k_\ell}$ (with f being a polynomial of degree e in the variables $y_1, \ldots, y_n$). In the following, we thus consider a set of polynomials looking like[2]

$$\mathcal{P} = \{f_{\mathbf{k}} = y_1^{k_1} \ldots y_n^{k_n} f^{k_\ell} \mod N^{k_\ell} \mid 1 \leqslant k_\ell < t$$
$$\text{and } \deg(f_{\mathbf{k}}) = k_1 + \ldots + k_n + k_\ell e < te\},$$

where the notation $\mod N^{k_\ell}$ is only here to recall that the considered solution verifies $f_{\mathbf{k}} \equiv 0 \mod N^{k_\ell}$ (to make things clearer). We suppose that f is not just a monomial (i.e., is the sum of at least two distinct monomials) and therefore each $\mathbf{k}$ corresponds to a distinct polynomial $f_{\mathbf{k}}$.

The set of monomials appearing in the collection $\mathcal{P}$ will usually look like

$$\mathcal{M} = \{y_{\mathbf{k}} = y_1^{k_1} \ldots y_n^{k_n} \mid 0 \leqslant \deg(y_{\mathbf{k}}) = k_1 + \ldots + k_n < te\}.$$

---

[2] We only use one polynomial f and one modulus N for the sake of simplicity. Furthermore, this exact set $\mathcal{P}$ could actually not appear in the Coppersmith methods, as the polynomials are not linearly independent. However, it is easier to explain analytic combinatorics tools on this set $\mathcal{P}$. We show later, in Sect. 4 and throughout this paper, how to adapt these tools to useful variants of this set.

By construction, since $(x_1, \ldots, x_n)$ is a modular root of the polynomials $f_{\mathbf{k}}$, there exists an integer $c_{\mathbf{k}}$ such that $f_{\mathbf{k}}(x_1, \ldots, x_n) = c_{\mathbf{k}} N^{k\ell}$ (see Sect. 2). Furthermore, this root is *small* in the sense that each of its components is bounded by a known value, namely $|x_1| < X_1, \ldots, |x_n| < X_n$. These considerations imply that for the final condition in Coppersmith's method (see Eq. (1)), one needs to compute the values

$$\psi = \sum_{f_{\mathbf{k}} \in \mathscr{P}} k_\ell \quad \text{and} \quad \forall i \in \{1, \ldots, n\}, \quad \alpha_i = \sum_{y_{\mathbf{k}} \in \mathscr{M}} k_i.$$

These values correspond to the exponent of N and X_i (for $i \in \{1, \ldots, n\}$) in Eq. (1) respectively.

For the sake of readability for the reader unfamiliar with analytic combinatorics, we first show how to compute the number of polynomials in $\mathscr{P}$ or $\mathscr{M}$ of a certain degree and then how to compute these sums ψ and α_i but only for polynomials in $\mathscr{P}$ or $\mathscr{M}$ of a certain degree. These computations are of no direct use for Coppersmith's method but are a warm-up for the really interesting computation, namely these sums ψ and a_i for polynomials in $\mathscr{P}$ or $\mathscr{M}$ up to a certain degree.

3.2 Combinatorial Classes, Sizes, and Parameters

A combinatorial class is a finite or countable set on which a size function is defined, satisfying the following conditions: (i) the size of an element is a non-negative integer and (ii) the number of elements of any given size is finite. Polynomials of a "certain" form and up to a "certain" degree can be considered as a combinatorial class, using a size function usually related to the degree of the polynomial.

In the following, we can consider the set $\mathscr{P}$ as a combinatorial class, with the size function $S_{\mathscr{P}}$ defined as $S_{\mathscr{P}}(f_{\mathbf{k}}) = \deg(f_{\mathbf{k}}) = k_1 + \ldots + k_n + k_\ell e$. In order to compute the sum of the k_ℓ as explained in Sect. 3.1, we define another function $\chi_{\mathscr{P}}$, called a *parameter* function, such that $\chi_{\mathscr{P}}(f_{\mathbf{k}}) = k_\ell$. This function will enable us, instead of counting "1" for each polynomial, to count "k_ℓ" for each polynomial, which is exactly what we need (see Sect. 3.4 for the details).

As for the monomials, we will also consider the set $\mathscr{M}$ as a combinatorial class, with the size function $S_{\mathscr{M}}$ defined as $S_{\mathscr{M}}(y_{\mathbf{k}}) = k_1 + \ldots + k_n$. In the case the bounds on the variables are equal ($X_1 = \ldots = X_n = X$), the parameter function corresponding to the exponent α_1 of X_1 in the final condition in Coppersmith's method will be set as $\chi_{\mathscr{M}}(y_{\mathbf{k}}) = k_1 + \ldots + k_n$. Otherwise, one will be able to define other parameter functions in case the bounds are not equal (see again Sect. 3.4).

3.3 Counting the Elements: Generating Functions

The counting sequence of a combinatorial class $\mathcal{A}$ with size function S is the sequence of integers $(A_p)_{p \geqslant 0}$ where $A_p = |\{a \in \mathcal{A}_p \mid S(a) = p\}|$ is the number

44   F. Benhamouda et al.

of objects in class $\mathcal{A}$ that have size p. For instance, if we consider the set $\mathcal{M}$ defined in Sect. 3.1, we have the equality $M_1 = n$ since there are n monomials in n variables of degree 1.

Definition 1. *The ordinary generating function (OGF) of a combinatorial class $\mathcal{A}$ is the generating function of the numbers A_p, for $p \geqslant 0$, i.e., the formal[3] power series $A(z) = \sum_{p=0}^{+\infty} A_p z^p$.*

For instance, if we consider the set $\mathcal{M}^{(1)} = \{y_1^{k_1} \mid 1 \leqslant k_1 < t\}$ of the monomials with one variable, then one gets $M_p^{(1)} = 1$ for all $p \in \mathbb{N}$, implying that $M^{(1)}(z) = \sum_{p=0}^{+\infty} z^p = \frac{1}{1-z}$.

In the former example, we constructed the OGF $A(z)$ from the sequence of numbers A_p of objects that have size p. Of course, what we are really interested in is to do it the other way around. We now describe an easy way to construct the OGF, and we will deduce from this function and classical analytic tools the value of A_p for every integer p. We assume the existence of an "atomic" class, comprising a single element of size 1, here a variable, usually denoted as $\mathcal{Z}$. We also need a "neutral" class, comprising a single element of size 0, here 1, usually denoted as ε. Their OGF are $Z(z) = z$ and $E(z) = 1$. We show in Table 1 the possible admissible constructions that we will need here, as well as the corresponding generating functions.

One then recovers the formula $M^{(1)}(z) = \frac{1}{1-z}$ from $Z(z) = z$ and the construction $\mathrm{SEQ}(\mathcal{Z})$ to describe $\mathcal{M}^{(1)}$. Similarly, if we now consider the set $\mathcal{M}^{(2)} = \{y_{\mathbf{k}} = y_1^{k_1} y_2^{k_2} \mid 0 \leqslant k_1 + k_2 < t\}$ of the monomials with two variables, with the size function $S(y_{\mathbf{k}}) = k_1 + k_2$, then one gets $M^{(2)}(z) = M^{(1)}(z) \cdot M^{(1)}(z) = \frac{1}{(1-z)^2}$ from $\mathcal{M}^{(2)} = \mathcal{M}^{(1)} \times \mathcal{M}^{(1)}$. Finally, since $\frac{1}{(1-z)^2} = \sum_{p=1}^{+\infty} p z^{p-1}$, one gets, for all $p \geqslant 1$, $(M_2)_p = p + 1$, which is exactly the number of monomials with two variables of size p.

When the class contains elements of different sizes (such as variables of degree 1 and polynomials of degree e), the variables are represented by the atomic

Table 1. Combinatorics constructions and their OGF

	Construction	OGF
Atomic class	$\mathcal{Z}$	$Z(z) = z$
Neutral class	ε	$E(z) = 1$
Disjoint union	$\mathcal{A} = \mathcal{B} + \mathcal{C}$ (when $\mathcal{B} \cap \mathcal{C} = \emptyset$)	$A(z) = B(z) + C(z)$
Complement	$\mathcal{A} = \mathcal{B} \setminus \mathcal{C}$ (when $\mathcal{C} \subseteq \mathcal{B}$)	$A(z) = B(z) - C(z)$
Cartesian product	$\mathcal{A} = \mathcal{B} \times \mathcal{C}$	$A(z) = B(z) \cdot C(z)$
Cartesian exponentiation	$\mathcal{A} = \mathcal{B}^k = \mathcal{B} \times \cdots \times \mathcal{B}$	$A(z) = B(z)^k$
Sequence	$\mathcal{A} = \mathrm{SEQ}(\mathcal{B}) = \varepsilon + \mathcal{B} + \mathcal{B}^2 + \dots$	$A(z) = \frac{1}{1 - B(z)}$

---

[3] We stress that it is a "formal" series, i.e., with no need to worry about the convergence.

element $\mathcal{Z}$ and the polynomials by the element $\mathcal{Z}^e$, in order to take into account the degree of the polynomial f. If we consider for instance the set $\mathscr{P}^{(1,2)} = \{f_{\mathbf{k}} = y_1^{k_1} f^{k_\ell} \mid 1 \leqslant k_\ell < t \text{ and } \deg(f_{\mathbf{k}}) = k_1 + 2k_\ell < 2t\}$, with f a polynomial of degree 2, this set is isomorphic to $\mathrm{SEQ}(\mathcal{Z}) \times \mathcal{Z}^2 \mathrm{SEQ}(\mathcal{Z}^2)$, since $\deg(f) = 2$. This leads to an OGF equals to

$$\frac{1}{1-z}\frac{z^2}{1-z^2} = \sum_{q=0}^{+\infty} q z^q \sum_{r=1}^{+\infty} r z^{2r} = \sum_{p=0}^{+\infty} \sum_{r=1}^{\lfloor p/2 \rfloor} (p - 2r) r z^p,$$

which gives $P_p^{(1,2)} = \sum_{r=1}^{\lfloor p/2 \rfloor} (p-2r)r$, which is exactly the number of polynomials of degree p contained in the class.

3.4 Counting the Parameters of the Elements: Bivariate Generating Functions

As seen in the former section, when one considers a combinatorial class $\mathcal{A}$ of polynomials and computes the corresponding OGF $A(z)$, classical analytic tools enable to recover A_p as the coefficient of z^p in the OGF. As explained in the introduction of this section, however, Coppersmith's method requires a computation a bit more tricky, which involves an additional parameter. For the sake of simplicity, we describe this technique on an example.

For instance, consider our monomial set example $\mathcal{M}^{(2)}$, but now assume that $X_1 \neq X_2$. Our goal is to compute $\sum k_1$, where the sum is taken over all the monomials in $\mathcal{M}^{(2)}$ of size p. We set a parameter function[4] $\chi(y_{\mathbf{k}}) = k_1$ and we do not compute $M_p^{(2)}$ (for $p \geqslant 1$) anymore, but rather

$$\chi_p(\mathcal{M}^{(2)}) = \sum_{y_{\mathbf{k}} \in \mathcal{M}^{(2)} \mid S(y_{\mathbf{k}})=p} \chi(y_{\mathbf{k}}) = \sum_{y_{\mathbf{k}} \in \mathcal{M}^{(2)} \mid S(y_{\mathbf{k}})=p} k_1$$

where, informally speaking, instead of counting for 1, every monomial counts for the value of its parameter (here the degree k_1 in y_1).

The value $\chi_p(\mathcal{M}^{(2)})$ cannot be obtained by the construction of $\mathcal{M}^{(2)}$ as $\mathrm{SEQ}(\mathcal{Z}) \times \mathrm{SEQ}(\mathcal{Z})$ that we used in the former section, since the two atomic elements $\mathcal{Z}$ do not play the same role (the first one is linked with the parameter, whereas the second one is not). The classical solution is simply to "mark" the atomic element useful for the parameter, with a new variable u: With this new parameter function, $\mathcal{M}^{(2)}$ is seen as $\mathrm{SEQ}(u\mathcal{Z}) \times \mathrm{SEQ}(\mathcal{Z})$, defining the bivariate ordinary generating function (BGF)[5] $M_2(z, u) = \frac{1}{1-uz}\frac{1}{1-z}$. We remark that when we set $u = 1$, we get the original non-parameterized OGF. Informally speaking, the BGF of a combinatorial class $\mathcal{A}$ with respect to a size function S

---

[4] Note that it is possible to count the exponents of both X_1 and X_2 at once using two parameters, but it is usually easier to count them separately, which often boils down to the same computation. See concrete examples in Sect. 4.

[5] In complex cases, the marker u can be put to some exponent k, for instance if the parameter considered has a value equal to k for the atomic element.

and a parameter function χ is obtained from the corresponding OGF by replacing each z by $u^k z$ where k is the value of the parameter taken on the atomic element $\mathcal{Z}$. We then obtain $\chi_p(\mathcal{A})$ via the following result:

Theorem 2. *Assume $\mathcal{A}$ is a combinatorial class with size function S and parameter function χ, and assume $A(z,u)$ is the bivariate ordinary generating funtion for $\mathcal{A}$ corresponding to this parameter (constructed as explained above). Then, if we define*

$$\chi_p(\mathcal{A}) = \sum_{a \in \mathcal{A} \mid S(a) = p} \chi(a)$$

the ordinary generating function of the sequence $(\chi_p(\mathcal{A}))_{p \geqslant 0}$ is equal to the value $(\partial A(z,u)/\partial u)_{u=1}$, meaning that we have the equality

$$\left. \frac{\partial A(z,u)}{\partial u} \right|_{u=1} = \sum_{p=0}^{+\infty} \chi_p(\mathcal{A}) z^p \overset{def}{=} \chi(\mathcal{A})(z).$$

Coming back to our example, one then gets

$$\chi(\mathscr{M}^{(2)})(z) = \sum_{p=0}^{+\infty} \chi_p(\mathscr{M}^{(2)}) z^p = \left. \frac{\partial M^{(2)}(z,u)}{\partial u} \right|_{u=1} = \frac{z}{(1-z)^3} = \sum_{p=1}^{+\infty} \frac{p(p-1)}{2} z^{p-1}.$$

meaning that $\chi_p(\mathscr{M}^{(2)}) = p(p+1)/2$ (remind that it is an equality on formal series). Finally, the sum of the degrees k_1 of the elements of size p is $p(p+1)/2$, which can be checked by enumerating them: $y_2^p, y_1 y_2^{p-1}, y_1^2 y_2^{p-2}, \ldots, y_1^{p-1} y_2, y_1^p$. It is easy to see that the result is exactly the same for X_2, without any additional computation, by symmetry.

3.5 Counting the Parameters of the Elements up to a Certain Size

We described in the former section a technique to compute the sum of the (partial) degrees of elements of size p, but how about computing the same sum for elements of size *up to p*? Using the notations of the former section, we want to compute

$$\chi_{\leqslant p}(\mathcal{A}) = \sum_{a \in \mathcal{A} \mid S(a) \leqslant p} \chi_p(a).$$

The naive way is to sum up the values $\chi_i(\mathcal{A})$ for all i between 0 and p:

$$\chi_{\leqslant p}(\mathcal{A}) = \sum_{i=0}^{p} \sum_{a \in \mathcal{A} \mid S(a) = i} \chi_i(a),$$

but an easier way to do so is to artificially force all elements a of size less than or equal to p to be of size exactly p by adding enough times a dummy element y_0 such that $\chi(y_0) = 0$.

In our context of polynomials, the aim of the dummy variable y_0 is to homogenize the polynomial. If we consider again the set $\mathscr{M}^{(2)}$ of monomials of two variables y_1 and y_2, with size function equal to $S(y_{\mathbf{k}}) = k_1 + k_2$ and parameter function equal to $\chi(y_{\mathbf{k}}) = k_1$, and if we are interested in the sum of the degrees k_1 of the elements in this set of size *up to* p, we now describe this set as $\mathrm{SEQ}(u\mathcal{Z}) \times \mathrm{SEQ}(\mathcal{Z}) \times \mathrm{SEQ}(\mathcal{Z})$, the last part being the class of monomials in the unique variable y_0. This variable is not marked, since its degree is not counted. One obtains the new bivariate generating function $M^{(2)}(z, u) = \frac{1}{1-uz}\frac{1}{(1-z)^2}$ and

$$
\chi_{\leqslant}(M^{(2)})(z) = \sum_{p=0}^{+\infty} \chi_{\leqslant p}(\mathscr{M}^{(2)})z^p = \left.\frac{\partial M^{(2)}(z, u)}{\partial u}\right|_{u=1} = \frac{z}{(1-z)^4}
$$

$$
= \sum_{p=2}^{+\infty} \frac{p(p-1)(p-2)}{6} z^{p-2},
$$

meaning that $\chi_{\leqslant p}(\mathscr{M}^{(2)}) = p(p+1)(p+2)/6$ (remind that it is an equality on formal series). Finally, the sum of the degrees k_1 of the elements of size up to p (i.e., the exponent of X_1 in Coppersmith's method) is $p(p+1)(p+2)/2$, which can be checked by the computation

$$
\sum_{i=0}^{p} \frac{i(i+1)}{2} = \frac{p(p+1)(p+2)}{6}.
$$

Again, it is easy to see that the result is exactly the same for X_2, without any additional computation.

3.6   Asymptotic Values: Transfer Theorem

Finding the OGF or BGF of the combinatorial classes is usually an easy task, but finding the exact value of the coefficients can be quite painful. Coppersmith's method is usually used in an asymptotic way. Singularity analysis enables us to find the asymptotic value of the coefficients in an simple way, using the technique described in [15, Corollary VI.1(sim-transfer), p. 392]. Adapted to our context, their transfer theorem can be stated as follows:

Theorem 3 (Transfer Theorem). *Assume $\mathcal{A}$ is a combinatorial class with an ordinary generating function F regular enough such that there exists a value c verifying*

$$
F(z) \underset{z \to 1}{\sim} \frac{c}{(1-z)^\alpha}
$$

for a non-negative integer α. Then the asymptotic value of the coefficient F_n is

$$
F_n \underset{n \to \infty}{\sim} \frac{cn^{\alpha-1}}{(\alpha-1)!}.
$$

4   A Toolbox for the Cryptanalyst

We now describe how to use the generic tools recalled in the former section to count the exponents of the bounds $X_1, \ldots, X_n$ and of the modulo N (as in the previous section, we consider the simplified case with only one modulus N) on the monomials and polynomials appearing in Coppersmith's method (see Sect. 2). For the sake of simplicity, we describe the technique on several examples, supposedly complex enough to be easily combined and adapted to most of the useful cases encountered in practice.

4.1   Counting the Bounds for the Monomials (Useful Examples)

First Example. In this example, we consider

$$\mathscr{M} = \{ y_1{}^{i_1} \cdots y_m{}^m \cdot y_{m+1}{}^{m+1} \cdots y_n{}^{i_n} \mid 1 \leqslant i_1 + \ldots + i_n < t \}$$

with the bounds $|y_i| < X$ for $1 \leqslant i \leqslant m$ et $|y_i| < Y$ for $m < i \leqslant n$. In order to obtain the exponent for the bound X, we consider the size function $S(y_1{}^{i_1} \ldots y_n{}^{i_n}) = i_1 + \ldots + i_n$ and the parameter function $\chi_X(y_1{}^{i_1} \ldots y_n{}^{i_n}) = i_1 + \ldots + i_m$.

We describe $\mathscr{M}$ as $\prod_{i=1}^{m} \mathrm{SEQ}(u\mathcal{Z}) \times \prod_{i=m+1}^{n} \mathrm{SEQ}(\mathcal{Z}) \times \mathrm{SEQ}(\mathcal{Z}) \setminus \varepsilon$ (the last $\mathrm{SEQ}(\mathcal{Z})$ being for the dummy value y_0), which leads to the OGF

$$F(z, u) = \left(\frac{1}{1 - uz} \right)^m \left(\frac{1}{1 - z} \right)^{n-m+1} - 1.$$

The next step is to compute the partial derivative in u at $u = 1$:

$$\left. \frac{\partial F(z, u)}{\partial u} \right|_{u=1} = \frac{mz}{(1 - uz)^{m+1}} \left(\frac{1}{1 - z} \right)^{n-m+1} \Bigg|_{u=1} = \frac{mz}{(1 - z)^{n+2}}$$

and take the equivalent value when $z \to 1$:

$$\left. \frac{\partial F(z, u)}{\partial u} \right|_{u=1} \underset{z \to 1}{\sim} \frac{m}{(1 - z)^{n+2}},$$

which finally leads, using Theorem 3, to $\chi_{X, <t}(\mathscr{M}) \sim \frac{m(t-1)^{n+1}}{(n+1)!} \sim \frac{mt^{n+1}}{(n+1)!}$.

Finally, it is easy to see that if one denotes $\chi_Y(y_1{}^{i_1} \ldots y_n{}^{i_n}) = i_{m+1} + \ldots + i_n$, one gets $\chi_{Y, <t}(\mathscr{M}) \sim \frac{(n-m)t^{n+1}}{(n+1)!}$. This set of monomials used in Coppersmith's method thus leads to the bound $X^{\frac{mt^{n+1}}{(n+1)!}} Y^{\frac{(n-m)t^{n+1}}{(n+1)!}}$. In the particularly useful case where $X = Y$, the bound becomes $X^{\frac{nt^{n+1}}{(n+1)!}}$ for all the monomials in n variables of degree up to t.

Second Example. In this example, we consider

$$\mathscr{M} = \{y_1{}^{i_1} \ldots y_n{}^{i_n} \mid (i_1 = 0 \text{ or } i_2 = 0)$$
$$\text{and } 1 \leqslant i_3 \leqslant e \text{ and } 1 \leqslant i_1 + \ldots + i_n < t\}$$

with the bounds $|y_i| < X$ for $1 \leqslant i \leqslant n$. We use the size function $S(y_1{}^{i_1} \ldots y_n{}^{i_n}) = i_1 + \ldots + i_n$ and the parameter function $\chi(y_1{}^{i_1} \ldots y_n{}^{i_n}) = i_1 + \ldots + i_n$ (since the bound X is the same for all variables).

The first step is to split $\mathscr{M}$ into disjoint subsets. In our case, the three disjoint subsets correspond to $i_1 = i_2 = 0$, ($i_1 = 0$ and $i_2 \neq 0$) and ($i_1 \neq 0$ and $i_2 = 0$). Taking into account the dummy value y_0, we describe them as

$$(\mathcal{Z} + \ldots + \mathcal{Z}^e) \times \prod_{i=1}^{n-3} \text{SEQ}(u\mathcal{Z}) \times \text{SEQ}(\mathcal{Z})$$

for the first one and

$$(u\mathcal{Z}) \times \text{SEQ}(u\mathcal{Z}) \times (\mathcal{Z} + \ldots + \mathcal{Z}^e) \times \prod_{i=1}^{n-3} \text{SEQ}(u\mathcal{Z}) \times \text{SEQ}(\mathcal{Z})$$

for the two others (since the presence of y_1 or y_2 is mandatory). This leads to the OGF

$$F(z, u) = \left(1 + \frac{uz}{1 - uz} + \frac{uz}{1 - uz}\right)(z + \ldots + z^e)\left(\frac{1}{1 - uz}\right)^{n-3}\frac{1}{1 - z}$$
$$= \frac{1 + uz}{(1 - uz)^{n-2}}\frac{z + \ldots + z^e}{1 - z},$$

which gives, after computations,

$$\left.\frac{\partial F(z, u)}{\partial u}\right|_{u=1} = \frac{z((n-3)uz + n - 1)}{(1 - uz)^{n-1}}\left.\frac{z + \ldots + z^e}{1 - z}\right|_{u=1} \underset{z \to 1}{\sim} \frac{(2n-4)e}{(1 - z)^n},$$

which finally leads to $\chi_{<t}(\mathscr{M}) \sim \frac{(2n-4)e(t-1)^{n-1}}{(n-1)!} \sim \frac{(2n-4)et^{n-1}}{(n-1)!}$, using Theorem 3.

4.2 Counting the Bounds for the Polynomials (Example)

We now consider the set

$$\mathscr{P} = \{f_{\mathbf{k}} = y_1^{k_1} \ldots y_n^{k_n} f^{k_\ell} \mod N^{k_\ell} \mid 1 \leqslant k_\ell < t$$
$$\text{and } \deg(f_{\mathbf{k}}) = k_1 + \ldots + k_n + k_\ell e < te\}$$

with the bounds $X_1 = \ldots = X_n = X$ for the variables. In order to obtain the exponent for the modulus N, we consider the size function $S(y_1^{k_1} \ldots y_n^{k_n} f^{k_\ell}) = k_1 + \ldots + k_n + k_\ell$ and the parameter function $\chi_N(y_1^{k_1} \ldots y_n^{k_n} f^{k_\ell}) = k_\ell$.

For the sake of simplicity, we can consider $0 \leqslant k_\ell < t$ since the parameter function is equal to 0 on the elements $f_{\mathbf{k}}$ such that $k_\ell = 0$. We describe $\mathscr{P}$ as

$\prod_{i=1}^{n} \text{SEQ}(\mathcal{Z}) \times \text{SEQ}(u\mathcal{Z}^e) \times \text{SEQ}(\mathcal{Z})$ (the last one being for the dummy value y_0), since only f needs a marker and its degree is e. This leads to the OGF

$$F(z, u) = \left(\frac{1}{1-z}\right)^{n+1} \frac{1}{1 - uz^e}.$$

The next step is to compute the partial derivative in u at $u = 1$:

$$\frac{\partial F(z, u)}{\partial u}\bigg|_{u=1} = \frac{z^e}{(1 - uz^e)^2}\left(\frac{1}{1-z}\right)^{n+1}\bigg|_{u=1} = \frac{z^e}{(1 - z^e)^2}\left(\frac{1}{1-z}\right)^{n+1}$$

and take the equivalent value when $z \to 1$, using the formula $1 - z^e \sim e(1 - z)$:

$$\frac{\partial F(z, u)}{\partial u}\bigg|_{u=1} \underset{z \to 1}{\sim} \frac{1}{e^2 (1 - z)^{n+3}},$$

which finally leads, using Theorem 3, to $\chi_{N, < te}(\mathscr{P}) \sim \frac{(te)^{n+2}}{e^2 (n+2)!}$.

5 Number-Theoretic Pseudorandom Generators (Following [2])

As mentioned in the introduction, number-theoretic pseudorandom generators work by iterating an algebraic map F over a residue ring $\mathbb{Z}_N$ on a secret random initial seed value $v_0 \in \mathbb{Z}_N$ to compute the intermediate state values $v_{i+1} = F(v_i)$ mod N for $i \in \mathbb{N}$ and outputting (some consecutive bits of) the state value v_i at each iteration. In [2], Bauer et al. showed that such a pseudorandom generator defined by a known iteration polynomial function F can be broken under the condition that sufficiently many bits are output by the generator at each iteration (with respect to the degree of F).

Let $F(X)$ be a polynomial of degree d in $\mathbb{Z}_N[X]$ and let v_0 be a secret seed. As in [2], we assume that the generator outputs the k most significant bits of v_i at each iteration (with $k \in \{1, \ldots, n\}$ where n is the bit-length of N). More precisely, if $v_i = 2^{n-k} w_i + x_i$, with $0 \leqslant x_i < 2^{n-k} = M = N^\delta$ which is unknown to the adversary and w_i is output by the generator. The adversary wants to recover x_i for some $i \in \mathbb{N}$ from consecutive values of the pseudorandom sequence (with M as large as possible). We have $v_{i+1} = F(v_i)$ mod N (for $i \in \mathbb{N}$) for a known polynomial F and $2^{m-k} w_{i+1} + x_{i+1} = F(2^{m-k} w_i + x_i)$ mod N. We can therefore define explicitly a family of bivariate polynomials of degree d, $f_i(y_i, y_{i+1}) \in \mathbb{Z}_N[y_i, y_{i+1}]$, such that $f_i(x_i, x_{i+1}) = 0 \mod N$, for $i \in \{0, \ldots, n\}$ whose coefficients publicly depend on the approximations w_i, w_{i+1} and F's coefficients. The goal is to compute the (small) modular root $(x_0, x_1, \ldots, x_n)$ of the polynomial system $\{f_0(y_0, y_1) = 0, \ldots, f_n(y_n, y_{n+1}) = 0\}$ in polynomial time.

Description of the attack. In order to solve this system, Bauer *et al.* [2] applied Coppersmith method for multivariate modular polynomial system to the following collection of polynomials:

$$\mathscr{P} = \{y_0^j f_0^{i_0} \ldots f_n^{i_n} \mid d(i_0 + d i_1 + \ldots + d^n i_n) + j \leqslant dm \wedge (i_0 + \ldots + i_n > 0)\}$$

where $m \geq 1$ is a fixed integer. They showed that the set of monomials occurring in the collection is:

$$\{y_0^j y_1^{i_0} \ldots y_{n+1}^{i_n} \mid d(i_0 + d i_1 + \ldots + d^n i_n) + j \leqslant dm\}.$$

To analyze their algorithm, Bauer *et al.* used a trick from [18] and only computes the quotient of the two quantities involved in Coppersmith success condition (1) (thanks to a fortunate simplification). In the following, we will use our toolbox to recompute (more) easily the bounds on these two quantities. We also obtain more precise estimates since our toolbox also permits to obtain the dimensions of the matrix used in Coppersmith method (and therefore the actual complexity of the attack).

Bound for the Polynomials. We consider the set $\mathscr{P}$ defined as

$$\{y_0^j f_0^{i_0} \ldots f_n^{i_n} \bmod N^{i_n} \mid d(i_0 + d i_1 + \ldots + d^n i_n) + j \leqslant dm \wedge i_0 + \ldots + i_n > 0)\}$$

as a combinatorial class, with the size function $S_f(y_0^j f_0^{i_0} \ldots f_n^{i_n}) = d(i_0 + d i_1 + \ldots + d^n i_n) + j$ and the parameter function $\chi_f(y_0^j f_0^{i_0} \ldots f_n^{i_n}) = i_0 + \ldots + i_n$. For the sake of simplicity, we can consider $i_0 + \ldots + i_n \geqslant 0$ since the parameter function is equal to 0 on the elements such that $i_0 + \ldots + i_n = 0$. We split the parameter functions into $(n+1)$ parts $\chi_{f,j}(y_0^j f_0^{i_0} \ldots f_n^{i_n}) = i_j$ (for $j \in \{0, \ldots, n\}$), do the computation for each of them and sum the obtained asymptotic equivalents (and this can be done legitimately by computing the corresponding limits).

Let $j \in \{0, \ldots, n\}$. Since the degree of each f_k is d^{k+1}, we consider $\mathscr{P}$ as

$$\underbrace{\mathrm{SEQ}(\mathcal{Z})}_{y_0} \times \underbrace{\prod_{\substack{k=0 \\ k \neq j}}^{n} \mathrm{SEQ}(\mathcal{Z}^{d^{k+1}})}_{f_k} \times \underbrace{\mathrm{SEQ}(u \mathcal{Z}^{d^{j+1}})}_{f_j} \times \underbrace{\mathrm{SEQ}(\mathcal{Z})}_{\text{dummy var.}} \setminus \underbrace{\mathrm{SEQ}(\mathcal{Z})}_{y_0} \times \underbrace{\mathrm{SEQ}(\mathcal{Z})}_{\text{dummy var.}}$$

which leads to the following generating function

$$F_j(u, z) = \frac{1}{1-z} \left(\prod_{\substack{k=0 \\ k \neq j}}^{n} \frac{1}{1 - z^{d^{k+1}}} \right) \frac{1}{1 - u z^{d^{j+1}}} \frac{1}{1-z} - \frac{1}{1-z} \frac{1}{1-z}.$$

We take the partial derivative in u and then let $u = 1$:

$$\left. \frac{\partial F_j}{\partial u}(u, z) \right|_{u=1} = \left(\frac{1}{1-z} \right)^2 \times \left(\prod_{\substack{k=0 \\ k \neq j}}^{n} \frac{1}{1 - z^{d^{k+1}}} \right) \times \frac{z^{d^{j+1}}}{(1 - z^{d^{j+1}})^2}.$$

We take the equivalent when $z \to 1$, using the formula $1 - z^n \sim n(1-z)$:

$$\frac{\partial F_j}{\partial u}(u,z)\bigg|_{u=1} \underset{z \to 1}{\sim} \left(\frac{1}{1-z}\right)^2 \times \left(\prod_{\substack{k=0 \\ k \neq j}}^{n} \frac{1}{d^{k+1}(1-z)}\right) \times \frac{1}{(d^{j+1})^2(1-z)^2} .$$

$$\underset{z \to 1}{\sim} \frac{1}{(1-z)^{n+4}} \frac{1}{d^{(n+1)(n+2)/2}d^{j+1}}$$

Applying Theorem 3, one finally gets

$$\chi_{f,j,\leqslant dm}(\mathscr{P}) \sim \frac{1}{(n+3)!}(dm)^{n+3}\frac{1}{d^{(n+1)(n+2)/2}d^{j+1}} ,$$

which leads to

$$\chi_{f,\leqslant dm}(\mathscr{P}) \sim \left(\sum_{j=0}^{n}\frac{1}{d^{j+1}}\right)\frac{1}{(n+3)!}(dm)^{n+3}\frac{1}{d^{(n+1)(n+2)/2}} .$$

Bound for the Monomials. We consider the set $\mathscr{M}$ defined as

$$\{y_0{}^j y_1{}^{i_0} \ldots y_{n+1}{}^{i_n} \mod M^{i_0 + \ldots + i_n} \mid d(i_0 + di_1 + \ldots + d^n i_n) + j \leqslant dm\}$$

as a combinatorial class, with the size function $S_y(y_0{}^j y_1{}^{i_0} \ldots y_{n+1}{}^{i_n}) = d(i_0 + di_1 + \ldots + d^n i_n) + j$ and the parameter function $\chi_y(y_0{}^j f_0{}^{i_0} \ldots f_n{}^{i_n}) = i_0 + \ldots + i_n$. As before, we split the parameter functions into $(n+1)$ parts $\chi_{y,j}(y_0{}^j y_1{}^{i_0} \ldots y_{n+1}{}^{i_n}) = i_j$ (for $j \in \{0,\ldots,n\}$) and do the computation for each of them. As each y_k "counts for" d^k in the condition of the set, we consider $\mathscr{M}$ as

$$\underbrace{\text{SEQ}(\mathcal{Z})}_{y_0} \times \underbrace{\prod_{\substack{k=1 \\ k \neq j}}^{n+1}\text{SEQ}(\mathcal{Z}^{d^k})}_{y_k} \times \underbrace{\text{SEQ}(u\mathcal{Z}^{d^j})}_{y_j} \times \underbrace{\text{SEQ}(\mathcal{Z})}_{\text{dummy var.}} ,$$

which leads to the following generating function

$$G_j(u,z) = \frac{1}{1-z}\left(\prod_{\substack{k=1 \\ k \neq j}}^{n+1}\frac{1}{1-z^{d^k}}\right)\frac{1}{1-uz^{d^j}}\frac{1}{1-z} .$$

We take the partial derivative in u and then let $u = 1$:

$$\frac{\partial G_j}{\partial u}(u,z)\bigg|_{u=1} = \left(\prod_{\substack{k=0 \\ k \neq j}}^{n+1}\frac{1}{1-z^{d^k}}\right) \times \left(\frac{1}{1-z}\right) \times \frac{z^{d^j}}{(1-z^{d^j})^2} .$$

We take the equivalent when $z \to 1$, using the formula $1 - z^n \sim n(1-z)$:

$$\frac{\partial G_j}{\partial u}(u,z)\bigg|_{u=1} \underset{z \to 1}{\sim} \left(\prod_{\substack{k=0 \\ k \neq j}}^{n+1}\frac{1}{d^k(1-z)}\right) \times \left(\frac{1}{1-z}\right) \times \frac{1}{(d^j)^2(1-z)^2}$$

$$\underset{z \to 1}{\sim} \frac{1}{(1-z)^{n+4}}\frac{1}{d^{(n+1)(n+2)/2}d^j} .$$

Applying Theorem 3, one finally gets

$$\chi_{y,j,\leqslant dm}(\mathcal{M}) \sim \frac{1}{(n+3)!}(dm)^{n+3}\frac{1}{d^{(n+1)(n+2)/2}d^j},$$

which leads to

$$\chi_{y,\leqslant dm}(\mathcal{M}) \sim \left(\sum_{j=0}^{n+1}\frac{1}{d^j}\right)\frac{1}{(n+3)!}(dm)^{n+3}\frac{1}{d^{(n+1)(n+2)/2}}.$$

Condition. If we denote by $\mu = \chi_{f,\leqslant dm}(\mathcal{P})$ and $\xi = \chi_{y,\leqslant dm}(\mathcal{M})$, the condition for Coppersmith's method is $N^\mu > M^\xi$, i.e., $N^{\mu/\xi} > M$, where

$$\frac{\mu}{\xi} = \frac{\chi_{f,\leqslant dm}(\mathcal{P})}{\chi_{y,\leqslant dm}(\mathcal{M})} \sim \frac{\sum_{j=0}^{n}\frac{1}{d^{j+1}}}{\sum_{j=0}^{n+1}\frac{1}{d^j}} = \frac{\frac{1}{d}\frac{1-1/d^{n+1}}{1-1/d}}{\frac{1-1/d^{n+2}}{1-1/d}} \sim \frac{1}{d},$$

which leads to the expected bound $M < N^{1/d}$ that was given in [2], for which the algorithm (heuristically) outputs the the (small) modular root $(x_0, x_1, \ldots, x_n)$ of the polynomial system $\{f_0(y_0, y_1) = 0, \ldots, f_n(y_n, y_{n+1}) = 0\}$ in polynomial time.

Complexity. In order to compute the dimensions of the matrix used in Coppersmith methods, we have to compute the cardinality of the sets $\mathcal{P}$ and $\mathcal{M}$ (i.e., with the constant parameter functions $\chi_f = 1$ and $\chi_{y,j} = 1$). We obtain the generating functions

$$\frac{1}{1-z}\left(\prod_{k=0}^{n}\frac{1}{1-z^{d^{k+1}}}\right)\frac{1}{1-z} - \frac{1}{1-z}\frac{1}{1-z} \underset{z\to 1}{\sim} \frac{1}{(1-z)^{n+3}}\frac{1}{d^{(n+1)(n+2)/2}}$$

and

$$\frac{1}{1-z}\left(\prod_{k=1}^{n+1}\frac{1}{1-z^{d^k}}\right)\frac{1}{1-z} \underset{z\to 1}{\sim} \frac{1}{(1-z)^{n+3}}\frac{1}{d^{(n+1)(n+2)/2}}$$

for $\mathcal{P}$ and $\mathcal{M}$ (respectively). We thus obtain as above for the cardinality of both sets $\mathcal{P}$ and $\mathcal{M}$ (and therefore essentially for the dimensions of the matrix), the asymptotics

$$\frac{(dm)^{n+2}}{(n+2)!}\frac{1}{d^{(n+1)(n+2)/2}}.$$

Remark 4. A computer algebra program can compute the first coefficients of the formal series for μ and ξ and for the cardinality of the sets $\mathcal{P}$ and $\mathcal{M}$, for any given d and n. Therefore, given d, n, and $\log M/\log N$, it enables to compute the minimum value m such that the attack works (i.e., such that $\mu/\xi > \log M/\log N$, using the simplified condition, assuming the heuristic assumption holds) and then to compute the corresponding number of polynomials in $\mathcal{P}$ and of monomials in $\mathcal{M}$, which then yield the size of the matrix. For an example of such an analysis see end of Sect. 6.1.

6   New Applications

6.1   Key Generation from Weak Pseudorandomness

In [16], Fouque, Tibouchi and Zapalowicz analyzed the security of key generation algorithms when the prime factors of an RSA modulus are constructed by
concatenating the outputs of a linear congruential generator. They proposed an
(exponential-time) attack based on multipoint polynomial evaluation to recover
the seed when such generators are used to generate one prime factor of an RSA
modulus. In this section, we propose a new heuristic (polynomial-time) algorithm based on Coppersmith methods that allows to factor an RSA modulus
when both its primes factors are constructed by concatenating the outputs of a
linear congruential generator (with possible different seeds).

Let $M = 2^k$ be a power of 2 (for $k \in \mathbb{N} \setminus \{0\}$). For the ease of exposition, we
consider a straightforward method to generate a prime number in which the key
generation algorithm starts from a random seed modulo M, iterates the linear
congruential generator and performs a primality test on the concatenation of
the outputs (and in case of an invalid answer, repeat the process with another
random seed until a prime is found). Let v_0 and w_0 be two random seeds for a
linear congruential generator with public parameters a and b in $\mathbb{Z}_M$ that defines
the pseudorandom sequences:

$$v_{i+1} = av_i + b \mod M \quad \text{and} \quad w_{i+1} = aw_i + b$$

for $i \in \mathbb{N}$. We assume that the adversary is given as input a (balanced) RSA
modulus $N = p \cdot q$ where p and q are (kn)-bit primes where $p = v_0 + Mv_1 +
\ldots + M^n v_n$ and $q = w_0 + Mw_1 + \ldots + M^n w_n$.

Description of the attack. The adversary is given as inputs the RSA modulus N
and the generator parameters a and b and its goal is to factor N (or equivalently
to recover one of the secret seed v_0 or w_0 used in the key generation algorithm).
This can be done by solving the following multivariate system of polynomial
equations over the moduli N and M with unknowns $v_0,\ldots,v_n,w_0,\ldots,w_n$:

$$\begin{cases} f = (v_0 + Mv_1 + \ldots + M^n v_n)(w_0 + Mw_1 + \ldots + M^n w_n) \equiv 0 \mod N \\ g_0 = v_1 - (av_0 + b) \equiv 0 \mod M \\ \quad \vdots \\ g_{n-1} = v_n - (av_{n-1} + b) \equiv 0 \mod M \\ h_0 = w_1 - (aw_0 + b) \equiv 0 \mod M \\ \quad \vdots \\ h_{n-1} = w_n - (aw_{n-1} + b) \equiv 0 \mod M. \end{cases}$$

In order to apply Coppersmith technique, the most complicated part is the
choice of the collection of polynomials constructed from the polynomials that

occur in this system. After several attempts, we choose to use the following polynomial family (parameterized by some integer $t \in \mathbb{N}$):

$$\tilde{f}_{i_0,\ldots,i_n,j_0,\ldots,j_n,k} = v_0^{i_0} \ldots v_n^{i_n} \cdot w_0^{j_0} \ldots w_n^{j_n} \cdot f^k \quad \bmod N^k$$
$$\text{with } 1 \leq k < t, \ (i_0 = 0 \text{ or } j_0 = 0)$$
$$\text{and } \deg(\tilde{f}_{\ldots}) = i_0 + \ldots + i_n + j_0 + \ldots + j_n + 2k < 2t$$

$$\tilde{g}_{i_0,\ldots,i_n,j_0,\ldots,j_n} = g_0^{i_0} \ldots g_{n-1}^{i_{n-1}} \cdot v_n^{i_n} \cdot h_0^{j_0} \ldots h_{n-1}^{j_{n-1}} \cdot w_n^{j_n} \quad \bmod M^\ell$$
$$\text{with } 1 \leq \ell = i_0 + \ldots + i_{n-1} + j_0 + \ldots + j_{n-1}$$
$$\text{and } \deg(\tilde{g}_{\ldots}) = i_0 + \ldots + i_n + j_0 + \ldots + j_n < 2t.$$

The moduli N and M are *coprime* (since N is an RSA modulus and M is a power of 2) and it is easy to see that the polynomials $\tilde{f}_{i_0,\ldots,i_n,j_0,\ldots,j_n,k}$ on one hand and the polynomials $\tilde{g}_{i_0,\ldots,i_n,j_0,\ldots,j_n}$ on the other hand are linearly independent.

We have a system of modular polynomial equations in $2n + 2$ unknowns and the Coppersmith method does not necessarily imply that we can solve the system of equations. As often in this setting, we have to assume that if the method succeeds, we will be able to recover the prime factors p and q from the set of polynomials we will obtain:

Heuristic 1. *Let $\mathcal{F}$ denote the polynomial set*

$$\mathcal{P} = \left\{ \tilde{f}_{i_0,\ldots,i_n,j_0,\ldots,j_n,k} \ \middle| \ \begin{array}{c} 1 \leq k < t, \ (i_0 = 0 \text{ or } j_0 = 0) \\ i_0 + \ldots + i_n + j_0 + \ldots + j_n + 2k < 2t \end{array} \right\}$$
$$\bigcup \left\{ \tilde{g}_{i_0,\ldots,i_n,j_0,\ldots,j_n} \ \middle| \ \begin{array}{c} 1 \leq \ell = i_0 + \ldots + i_{n-1} + j_0 + \ldots + j_{n-1} \\ \deg(\tilde{g}_{\ldots}) = i_0 + \ldots + i_n + j_0 + \ldots + j_n < 2t \end{array} \right\}.$$

We assume that the set of polynomials we get by applying Coppersmiths method with the polynomial set $\mathcal{P}$ define an algebraic variety of dimension 0.

Theorem 5. *Under Heuristic 1, given as inputs an RSA modulus $N = p \cdot q$ and the linear congruential generator parameters a and b such that $p = v_0 + Mv_1 + \ldots + M^n v_n$ and $q = w_0 + Mw_1 + \ldots + M^n w_n$. (where v_0 and w_0 are two random seeds and $v_{i+1} = av_i + b \ \bmod M$ and $w_{i+1} = aw_i + b$ for $i \in \mathbb{N}$), we can recover the prime factors p and q in polynomial time in $\log(N)$ for any $n \geqslant 2$.*

Bounds for the Polynomials Modulo N. We consider the set

$$\mathcal{P}_f = \{ \tilde{f}_{i_0,\ldots,i_n,j_0,\ldots,j_n,k} = v_0^{i_0} \ldots v_n^{i_n} \cdot w_0^{j_0} \ldots w_n^{j_n} \cdot f^k \quad \bmod N^k$$
$$| \ 1 \leq k < t, \ (i_0 = 0 \text{ or } j_0 = 0)$$
$$\text{and } \deg(\tilde{f}_{i_0,\ldots,i_n,j_0,\ldots,j_n,k}) = i_0 + \ldots + i_n + j_0 + \ldots + j_n + 2k < 2t\}$$

as a combinatorial class, with the size function $S_f(\tilde{f}_{i_0,\ldots,i_n,j_0,\ldots,j_n,k}) = i_0 + \ldots + i_n + j_0 + \ldots + j_n + 2k$ and the parameter function $\chi_f(\tilde{f}_{i_0,\ldots,i_n,j_0,\ldots,j_n,k}) = k$.

The degree of each variable $v_0, \ldots, v_n, w_0, \ldots, w_n$ is 1, whereas the degree of f is 1. For the sake of simplicity, we can consider $0 \leqslant k < t$ since the parameter function is equal to 0 on the elements $f_{\mathbf{k}}$ such that $k = 0$. We use the technique described in the second example of Sect. 4.2 to write $\mathscr{P}_f$ as a disjoint union of three sets (depending on the values i_0 and j_0) and consider it as

$$\underbrace{(\varepsilon + \mathcal{Z}\mathrm{SEQ}(\mathcal{Z}) + \mathcal{Z}\mathrm{SEQ}(\mathcal{Z}))}_{v_0, w_0} \times \prod_{k=1}^{n} \underbrace{\mathrm{SEQ}(Z)}_{v_k} \times \prod_{k=1}^{n} \underbrace{\mathrm{SEQ}(Z)}_{w_k} \times \underbrace{\mathrm{SEQ}(uZ^2)}_{f} \times \underbrace{\mathrm{SEQ}(Z)}_{\text{dummy var,}}$$

which leads to the following generating function:

$$F(u, z) = \left(1 + \frac{z}{1-z} + \frac{z}{1-z}\right) \frac{1}{(1-z)^{2n}} \frac{1}{1-uz^2} \frac{1}{1-z} = \frac{1+z}{(1-z)^{2n+2}} \frac{1}{1-uz^2}.$$

We take the partial derivative in u, then let $u = 1$, and finally take the equivalent when $z \to 1$:

$$\left.\frac{\partial F}{\partial u}(u, z)\right|_{u=1} = \frac{z^2}{(1-z)^{2n+4}(1+z)} \underset{z \to 1}{\sim} \frac{1}{2(1-z)^{2n+4}}.$$

Applying Theorem 3, since $2t \sim 2t - 1$, one finally gets

$$\chi_{f, <2t}(\mathscr{P}_f) \sim \frac{1}{2(2n+3)!}(2t)^{2n+3}.$$

Bounds for the Polynomials Modulo M. We consider the set

$$\mathscr{P}_g = \{\tilde{g}_{i_0, \ldots, i_n, j_0, \ldots, j_n} = g_0^{i_0} \cdots g_{n-1}^{i_{n-1}} \cdot v_n^{i_n} \cdot h_0^{j_0} \cdots h_{n-1}^{j_{n-1}} \cdot w_n^{j_n} \mod M^\ell$$
$$| \ 1 \leq \ell = i_0 + \ldots + i_{n-1} + j_0 + \ldots + j_{n-1}$$
$$\text{and } \deg(\tilde{g}_{i_0, \ldots, i_n, j_0, \ldots, j_n}) = i_0 + \ldots + i_n + j_0 + \ldots + j_n < 2t\}$$

as a combinatorial class, with the size function $S_g(\tilde{g}_{i_0, \ldots, i_n, j_0, \ldots, j_n}) = i_0 + \ldots + i_n + j_0 + \ldots + j_n$ and the parameter function $\chi_g(\tilde{g}_{i_1, \ldots, i_n, j_0, \ldots, j_n}) = i_0 + \ldots + i_{n-1} + j_0 + \ldots + j_{n-1}$. The degree of each polynomial g_k is 1, as well as the degrees of v_n and w_n. For the sake of simplicity, we can consider $0 \leqslant \ell$ since the parameter function is equal to 0 on the elements such that $\ell = 0$. We thus consider $\mathscr{P}_g$ as

$$\prod_{k=0}^{n-1} \underbrace{\mathrm{SEQ}(uZ)}_{g_k} \times \underbrace{\mathrm{SEQ}(Z)}_{v_n} \times \prod_{k=0}^{n-1} \underbrace{\mathrm{SEQ}(uZ)}_{h_k} \times \underbrace{\mathrm{SEQ}(Z)}_{w_n} \times \underbrace{\mathrm{SEQ}(Z)}_{\text{dummy var.}}$$

which leads to the following generating function:

$$G(u, z) = \frac{1}{(1-uz)^{2n}} \frac{1}{(1-z)^2} \frac{1}{1-z}.$$

We take the partial derivative in u, then let $u = 1$, and finally take the equivalent when $z \to 1$:

$$\frac{\partial G}{\partial u}(u,z)\bigg|_{u=1} = \frac{2nz}{(1-z)^{2n+4}} \underset{z \to 1}{\sim} \frac{2n}{(1-z)^{2n+4}}.$$

Applying Theorem 3, since $2t \sim 2t - 1$, one finally gets

$$\chi_{g,<2t}(\mathscr{P}_g) \sim \frac{2n}{(2n+3)!}(2t)^{2n+3}.$$

Bounds for the Monomials Modulo M. We consider the set

$$\mathscr{M} = \{v_0{}^{i_0} \dots v_n{}^{i_n} \cdot w_0{}^{j_0} \dots w_n{}^{j_n} \quad \mathrm{mod} \ M^\ell \mid 0 \leqslant \ell = i_0 + \dots + i_n + j_0 + \dots + j_n < 2t\}$$

as a combinatorial class, with the size function $S_x(v_0{}^{i_0} \dots v_n{}^{i_n} \cdot w_0{}^{j_0} \dots w_n{}^{j_n}) = i_0 + \dots + i_n + j_0 + \dots + j_n$ and the parameter one $\chi_x(v_0{}^{i_0} \dots v_n{}^{i_n} \cdot w_0{}^{j_0} \dots w_n{}^{j_n}) = i_0 + \dots + i_n + j_0 + \dots + j_n$. The degree of each variable x_k is 1. We thus consider $\mathscr{M}$ as

$$\prod_{k=0}^{n} \underbrace{\mathrm{SEQ}(uZ)}_{v_k} \times \prod_{k=0}^{n} \underbrace{\mathrm{SEQ}(uZ)}_{w_k} \times \underbrace{\mathrm{SEQ}(Z)}_{\text{dummy var,}}$$

which leads to the following generating function:

$$H(u,z) = \frac{1}{(1-uz)^{2n+2}} \frac{1}{1-z}.$$

We take the partial derivative in u, then let $u = 1$, and finally take the equivalent when $z \to 1$:

$$\frac{\partial H}{\partial u}(u,z)\bigg|_{u=1} = \frac{(2n+2)z}{(1-z)^{2n+4}} \underset{z \to 1}{\sim} \frac{2n+2}{(1-z)^{2n+4}}.$$

Applying Theorem 3, since $2t \sim 2t - 1$, one finally gets

$$\chi_{x,<2t}(\mathscr{M}) \sim \frac{2n+2}{(2n+3)!}(2t)^{2n+3}.$$

Condition. If we denote by $\nu = \chi_{f,<te}(\mathscr{P}_f)$, $\mu = \chi_{g,<te}(\mathscr{P}_g)$ and $\xi = \chi_{x,<te}(\mathscr{M})$, the condition for Coppersmith's method is $N^\nu \cdot M^\mu > M^\xi$, where

$$\frac{\nu}{\xi - \mu} = \frac{\chi_{f,<te}(\mathscr{P}_f)}{\chi_{x,<te}(\mathscr{M}) - \chi_{g,<te}(\mathscr{P}_g)} \underset{z \to 1}{\sim} \frac{\frac{1}{2(2n+3)!}(2t)^{2n+3}}{\frac{2n+2}{(2n+3)!}(2t)^{2n+3} - \frac{2n}{(2n+3)!}(2t)^{2n+3}} \underset{z \to 1}{\sim} \frac{1}{4}$$

which leads to the bound $M < N^{1/4}$ (and since N is an even power of M we obtain $M \leqslant N^{1/6}$ and thus $n \geqslant 2$).

Table 2. Bounds in Coppersmith (simplified) success condition (1)

n	t	1	2	3	4	5	6	7	8
2	Polynomial bound	4	38	186	654	1866	4602	10182	**20706**
	Monomial bound	6	48	216	720	1980	4752	10296	**20592**
3	Polynomial bound	6	68	402	1688	5682	**16340**		
	Monomial bound	8	80	440	1760	5720	**16016**		
4	Polynomial bound	10	152	1206	6704	**29416**			
	Monomial Bound	12	168	1260	6720	**28560**			
5	Polynomial bound	12	206	1842	**11486**				
	Monomial bound	14	224	1904	**11424**				

Remark 6. In the previous attack, we actually considered a very naive prime number generation algorithm. However, a prime number generation algorithm based on this (bad) design principle would probably use instead an incremental algorithm and output prime numbers $p = (v_0 + Mv_1 + \ldots + M^n v_n) + \alpha$ and $q = (w_0 + Mw_1 + \ldots + M^n w_n) + \beta$ for some α and β in $\mathbb{N}$. Thanks to the prime number theorem, these values are likely to be small and the previous algorithm can be run[6] after an exhaustive search of α and β.

Concrete bounds. The previous analysis leads to the bound $M < N^{1/4}$ when t goes to ∞. Actually to reach the (simplified) success condition (1) in Coppersmith method for $n \geqslant 2$, we need only small values of t as shown in Table 2.

Unfortunately, even if t is small, the constructed matrix is of huge dimension (since the number of monomials is quite large) and the computation which is theoretically polynomial-time becomes in practice prohibitive (for instance, for $n = 3$ and $t = 6$, the matrix is of dimension 6473). These attacks are netherthe-less good evidence of a weakness in this key generation scheme. For $n = 1$ (i.e., $M = N^{1/4}$), the polynomial time attack does not apply, but one may combine it with an exhaustive search to retrieve a small part of v_0, v_1, w_0 and w_1 to retrieve the other (bigger) part of the seeds.

6.2 PKCS#1 V1.5 Padding Encryption with Weak Pseudorandomness

PKCS#1 v1.5 describes a particular encoding padding for RSA encryption. Let N be RSA an modulus of byte-length k (i.e., $2^{8(k-1)} < N < 2^{8k}$, e be a public exponent coprime to the Euler totient $\varphi(N)$ and m be a message of ℓ-byte with $\ell < k - 11$. The PKCS#1 v1.5 padding of m is defined as follows:

1. A randomizer r consisting in $k - 3 - \ell \geqslant 8$ nonzero bytes is generated uniformly at random;

---

[6] Alternatively, one can also adapt the algorithm by adding unknowns for α and β to the multivariate modular polynomial system.

2. $\mu(m, r)$ is the integer converted from the octet-string:

$$\mu(m, r) = 0002_{16}||r||00_{16}||m. \tag{2}$$

The encryption of m is then defined as $c = \mu(m, r)^e \mod N$. To decrypt $c \in \mathbb{Z}_N^*$, compute $c^d \mod N$ (where $ed \equiv 1 \mod \varphi(N)$), convert the result to a k-byte octet-string and parse it according to Eq. (2). If the string cannot be parsed unambiguously or if r is shorter than eight octets, the decryption algorithm $\mathcal{D}$ outputs $\bot$; otherwise, $\mathcal{D}$ outputs the plaintext m.

The PKCS#1 v1.5 padding has been known to be insecure for encryption since Bleichenbachers famous chosen ciphertext attack [7]. Several additionnal attacks were published since 1998 (e.g., [1, 14, 21]).

Fouque *et al.* [16] suggested to consider the setting of the randomness generation used in padding functions for encryption. In PKCS#1 v1.5 padding, the randomizer shall be pseudorandomly generated (according to the RFC which defines it [24]) and since it is still widely used in practice (e.g., TLS, XML Encryption standard, Hardware token...)n it seems interesting to investigate its security when the randomizer is constructed by concatenating the outputs of a linear congruential generator. We consider several scenarios (linear congruential generator, truncated linear congruential generators, multiple ciphertexts ...) and we apply our toolbox to all of them.

Scenario 1: Linear Congruential Generator. The first attack scenario can be seen as a *chosen distribution attack*. These attacks were introduced by Bellare et al. [3] to model attacks where an adversary can control the distribution of both messages and random coins used in an encryption scheme. We assume that the adversary can control the message (as in the classical notion of semantic security for public-key encryption schemes [17]) and that the randomizer used in the PKCS#1 v1.5 padding is constructed by concatenating the outputs of a linear congruential generator (with a seed picked uniformly at random). The adversary will choose two messages m_0 and m_1 of the same byte-length $\ell < k - 11$ (where k is the byte length of the RSA modulus N) and the challenger will pick at random a seed x_1 of byte-length ρ. It will compute

$$x_{i+1} = ax_i + b \mod M$$

for $i \in \{2, \ldots, n-1\}$ where $n = (k-3-\ell)/\rho$ and $M = 2^{8\rho}$. The challenge ciphertext will be $c = \mu(m_b, r)^e \mod N$ where b is a bit picked uniformly at random by the challenger and the randomizer r is the concatenation of $x_1, \ldots, x_n$. We have

$$\mu(m_b, r) = 0002_{16}||r||00_{16}||m_b$$
$$= 0002_{16}||x_1||x_2||\ldots||x_n||00_{16}||m_b$$
$$= (\tilde{\alpha}_1 x_1 + \tilde{\alpha}_2 x_2 + \ldots + \tilde{\alpha}_n x_n + \tilde{\beta})$$

where this last expression is the integer converted from the octet-string with the $\tilde{\alpha}_i$'s are known public constant and $\tilde{\beta}$ is the integer converted from the string

m_b. If we divide c by $\tilde{\alpha_1}^e$, we obtain

$$c = (x_1 + \alpha_2 x_2 + \ldots + \alpha_n x_n + \beta)^e \mod N$$

where $\alpha_i = \tilde{\alpha_i}/\tilde{\alpha_1}$ for $i \in \{2, \ldots, n\}$ and $\beta = \tilde{\beta}/\tilde{\alpha_1}$.

Description of the attack. The adversary is therefore looking for the solutions of the following modular multivariate polynomial system: of *monic* polynomial equations:

$$\begin{cases} f = (x_1 + \alpha_2 x_2 + \ldots + \alpha_n x_n + \beta)^e \mod N \\ g_1 = x_1 - ax_2 + b \mod M \\ \quad \vdots \\ g_{n-1} = x_{n-1} - ax_n + b \mod M \end{cases}$$

where β can be derived easily from the value m_b. The attack consists in applying Coppersmith Method for multivariate polynomials with two moduli (see Sect. 2) to the two systems derived from the two possible values for m_b.

As above, the most complicated part is the choice of the collection of polynomials constructed from the polynomials that occur in this system. Our analysis brought out the following polynomial family (parameterized by some integer $t \in \mathbb{N}$):

$$\tilde{f}_{i_1,\ldots,i_n,j} = x_1^{i_1} \ldots x_n^{i_n} \cdot f^j \mod N^j$$

with $1 \le j < t$, $0 \le i_1 < e$ and $\deg(\tilde{f}_{\ldots}) = i_1 + \ldots + i_n + je < te$

$$\tilde{g}_{i_1,\ldots,i_n} = g_1^{i_1} \ldots g_{n-1}^{i_{n-1}} \cdot x_n^{i_n} \mod M^k$$

with $1 \le k = i_1 + \ldots + i_{n-1}$ and $\deg(\tilde{g}_{\ldots}) = i_1 + \ldots + i_n < te$.

As in the previous section, the moduli N and M are *coprime* (since N is an RSA modulus and M is a power of 2). Moreover, it is easy to see that the polynomials $\tilde{f}_{i_1,\ldots,i_n,j}$ on one hand and the polynomials $\tilde{g}_{i_0,\ldots,i_n}$ on the other hand are linearly independent. Indeed, these polynomials have distinct leading monomials and are monic.

We have a system of modular polynomial equations in n unknowns and the Coppersmith method does not necessarily imply that we can solve the system of equations. Thus, we also have to assume that if the method succeeds, we will be able to recover the seed x_1 from the set of polynomials we will obtain:

Heuristic 2. *Let $\mathscr{P}$ denote the polynomial set*

$$\mathscr{P} = \left\{ \tilde{f}_{i_1,\ldots,i_n,j} \;\middle|\; \begin{matrix} 1 \le j < t,\ 0 \le i_1 < e \\ i_1 + \ldots + i_n + je < te \end{matrix} \right\}$$

$$\bigcup \left\{ \tilde{g}_{i_1,\ldots,i_n} \;\middle|\; \begin{matrix} 1 \le k = i_1 + \ldots + i_{n-1} \\ i_1 + \ldots + i_n < te \end{matrix} \right\}.$$

We assume that the set of polynomials we get by applying Coppersmiths method with the polynomial set $\mathscr{P}$ define an algebraic variety of dimension 0.

Theorem 7. *Under Heuristic 2, given as inputs an RSA modulus N, the linear congruential generator parameters a and b, two messages m_0 and m_1 and a* PKCS#1 *v1.5 ciphertext $c = \mu(m_b, r)$ for some bit $b \in \{0, 1\}$ such that the randomizer r is the concatenation of $x_1, \ldots, x_n$ (where x_1 is a random seed of size M and $x_{i+1} = ax_i + b \mod M$ for $i \in \mathbb{N}$), we can recover the seed x_1 (and thus the bit b) in polynomial time in $\log(N)$ as soon as $M < N^{1/e}$.*

Bounds for the Polynomials Modulo N. We consider the set

$$\mathscr{P}_f = \{\tilde{f}_{i_1,\ldots,i_n,j} = x_1^{i_1} \cdots x_n^{i_n} \cdot f^j \mod N^j \mid 1 \leq j < t, 0 \leq i_1 < e$$
$$\text{and } \deg(\tilde{f}_{i_1,\ldots,i_n,j}) - i_1 \mid \ldots + i_n + je < te\}$$

as a combinatorial class, with the size function $S_f(\tilde{f}_{i_1,\ldots,i_n,j}) = i_1 + \ldots + i_n + je$ and the parameter function $\chi_f(\tilde{f}_{i_1,\ldots,i_n,j}) = j$. The degree of each variable x_k is 1, whereas the degree of f is e. For the sake of simplicity, we can consider $0 \leqslant j < t$ since the parameter function is equal to 0 on the elements such that $j = 0$. We thus consider $\mathscr{P}_f$ as

$$\underbrace{(\varepsilon + \mathcal{Z} + \ldots + \mathcal{Z}^{e-1})}_{x_1} \times \prod_{k=2}^{n} \underbrace{\text{SEQ}(\mathcal{Z})}_{x_k} \times \underbrace{\text{SEQ}(u\mathcal{Z}^e)}_{f} \times \underbrace{\text{SEQ}(\mathcal{Z})}_{\text{dummy var.}}$$

which leads to the following generating function:

$$F(u, z) = (1 + z + \ldots + z^{e-1})\frac{1}{(1-z)^{n-1}}\frac{1}{1 - uz^e}\frac{1}{1 - z}.$$

We take the partial derivative in u and then let $u = 1$:

$$\left.\frac{\partial F}{\partial u}(u, z)\right|_{u=1} = (1 + z + \ldots + z^{e-1})\frac{1}{(1-z)^n}\frac{z^e}{(1 - z^e)^2}.$$

We take the equivalent when $z \to 1$, using the formula $1 - z^e \sim e(1 - z)$:

$$\left.\frac{\partial F}{\partial u}(u, z)\right|_{u=1} \underset{z \to 1}{\sim} \frac{1}{e(1 - z)^{n+2}}.$$

Applying Theorem 3, since $te \sim te - 1$, one finally gets

$$\chi_{f,<te}(\mathscr{P}_f) \sim \frac{1}{e(n + 1)!}(te)^{n+1}.$$

Bounds for the Polynomials Modulo M. We consider the set

$$\mathscr{P}_g = \{\tilde{g}_{i_1,\ldots,i_n} = g_1^{i_1} \cdots g_{n-1}^{i_{n-1}} \cdot x_n^{i_n} \mod M^{i_1+\cdots+i_{n-1}} \mid 1 \leq k = i_1 + \cdots + i_{n-1}$$
$$\text{and } \deg(\tilde{g}_{i_1,\ldots,i_n}) = i_1 + \ldots + i_n < te\}$$

as a combinatorial class, with the size function $S_g(\tilde{g}_{i_1,\ldots,i_n}) = i_1 + \ldots + i_n$ and the parameter function $\chi_g(\tilde{g}_{i_1,\ldots,i_n}) = i_1 + \ldots + i_{n-1}$. The degree of each polynomial g_k is 1, as well as the degree of x_n. For the sake of simplicity, we can consider $0 \leqslant k$ since the parameter function is equal to 0 on the elements such that $k = 0$. We thus consider $\mathscr{P}_g$ as

$$\prod_{k=1}^{n-1} \underbrace{\text{SEQ}(uZ)}_{g_k} \times \underbrace{\text{SEQ}(Z)}_{x_n} \times \underbrace{\text{SEQ}(Z)}_{\text{dummy var,}}$$

which leads to the following generating function:

$$G(u,z) = \frac{1}{(1-uz)^{n-1}} \frac{1}{1-z} \frac{1}{1-z}.$$

We take the partial derivative in u, then let $u = 1$, and finally take the equivalent when $z \to 1$:

$$\frac{\partial G}{\partial u}(u,z)\bigg|_{u=1} = \frac{(n-1)z}{(1-z)^{n+2}} \underset{z \to 1}{\sim} \frac{n-1}{(1-z)^{n+2}}.$$

Applying Theorem 3, since $te \sim te - 1$, one finally gets

$$\chi_{g,<te}(\mathscr{P}_g) \sim \frac{n-1}{(n+1)!}(te)^{n+1}.$$

Bounds for the Monomials Modulo M. We consider the set

$$\mathscr{M} = \{x_1^{i_1} \ldots x_n^{i_n} \mod M^{i_1+\ldots+i_n} \mid 0 \leqslant i_1 + \ldots + i_n < te\}.$$

as a combinatorial class, with the size function $S_x(x_1^{i_1} \ldots x_n^{i_n}) = i_1 + \ldots + i_n$ and the parameter function $\chi_x(x_1^{i_1} \ldots x_n^{i_n}) = i_1 + \ldots + i_n$. The degree of each variable x_k is 1. We thus consider $\mathscr{M}$ as

$$\prod_{k=1}^{n} \underbrace{\text{SEQ}(uZ)}_{x_k} \times \underbrace{\text{SEQ}(Z)}_{\text{dummy var,}}$$

which leads to the following generating function:

$$H(u,z) = \frac{1}{(1-uz)^n} \frac{1}{1-z}.$$

We first take the partial derivative in u, then let $u = 1$, and finally take the equivalent when $z \to 1$:

$$\frac{\partial H}{\partial u}(u,z)\bigg|_{u=1} = \frac{nz}{(1-z)^{n+2}} \underset{z \to 1}{\sim} \frac{n}{(1-z)^{n+2}}.$$

Applying Theorem 3, since $te \sim te - 1$, one finally gets

$$\chi_{x,<te}(\mathscr{M}) \sim \frac{n}{(n+1)!}(te)^{n+1}.$$

Condition. If we denote by $\nu = \chi_{f,<te}(\mathscr{P}_f)$, $\mu = \chi_{g,<te}(\mathscr{P}_g)$ and $\xi = \chi_{x,<te}(\mathscr{M})$, the condition for Coppersmith's method is $N^\nu \cdot M^\mu > M^\xi$, where

$$\frac{\nu}{\xi - \mu} = \frac{\chi_{f,<te}(\mathscr{P}_f)}{\chi_{x,<te}(\mathscr{M}) - \chi_{g,<te}(\mathscr{P}_g)} \underset{z\to 1}{\sim} \frac{\frac{1}{e(n+1)!}(te)^{n+1}}{\frac{n}{(n+1)!}(te)^{n+1} - \frac{n-1}{(n+1)!}(te)^{n+1}} \underset{z\to 1}{\sim} \frac{1}{e}$$

which leads to the expected bound $M < N^{1/e}$.

Scenario 2: Truncated Linear Congruential Generator. In 1997, Bellare et al. [4] broke the Digital Signature Algorithm (DSA) when the random nonces used in signature generation are computed using a linear congruential generator. They also broke the DSA signature scheme if the nonces are computed by a *truncated* linear congruential generator. In order to pursue the parallel with their work, in the second attack scenario, we the previous analysis to the case where the randomize in PKCS#1 v1.5 padding is constructed by concatenating any consecutive bits of the outputs of a linear congruential generator (with a seed picked uniformly at random).

More precisely, the seed of the linear congruential generator is now denoted $v_1 = y_1 + x_1 \cdot 2^{\gamma_y \log M} + z_1 \cdot 2^{\gamma_x \log M + \gamma_y \log M}$, where y_1 has $\gamma_y \log M$ bits, x_1 has $\gamma_x \log M$ bits, z_1 has $\gamma_z \log M$ bits and $\gamma_x + \gamma_y + \gamma_z = 1$. We define the (weak)pseudorandom sequence by $v_{i+1} = av_i + b \mod M$ for $i \in \mathbb{N}$ (with public a, b and M). We denote $v_i = y_i + x_i \cdot 2^{\gamma_y \log M} + z_i \cdot 2^{\gamma_x \log M + \gamma_y \log M}$, where y_i has $\gamma_y \log M$ bits, x_i has $\gamma_x \log M$ bits and z_i has $\gamma_z \log M$ bits.

As above, the challenge ciphertext will be $c = \mu(m_b, r)^e \mod N$ where b is a bit picked uniformly at random by the challenger and the randomizer r is the concatenation of $x_1, \ldots, x_n$ for $n = (k - 3 - \ell)/(8\gamma_x \log M)$. We have

$$\mu(m_b, r) = 0002_{16}||r||00_{16}||m_b$$
$$= (\tilde{\alpha}_1 x_1 + \tilde{\alpha}_2 x_2 + \ldots + \tilde{\alpha}_n x_n + \tilde{\beta}).$$

Description of the attack. The adversary is looking for the solutions of the following multivariate modular polynomial system: of *monic* polynomial equations:

$$\begin{cases} f = (x_1 + \alpha_2 x_2 + \ldots + \alpha_n x_n + \beta)^e \mod N \\ g_1 = x_1 + a'y_1 + a''z_1 + bx_2 + b'y_2 + b''z_2 + c \mod M \\ \quad \vdots \\ g_{n-1} = x_{n-1} + a'y_{n-1} + a''y_{n-1} + bx_n + b'y_n + b''z_n + c \mod M \end{cases}$$

where β can be derived easily from the value m_b and the constants $\alpha_2, \ldots, \alpha_N$, a', a'', b, b' and b'' are public. As in the previous scenario, the attack consists in applying Coppersmith Method for multivariate polynomials with two moduli (see Sect. 2) to the two systems derived from the two possible values for m_b.

For the choice of the polynomials collection, we choose in this scenario the following polynomial family (parameterized by some integer $t \in \mathbb{N}$):

$$\tilde{f}_{i,i',i'',j} = x_1^{i_1} \ldots x_n^{i_n} \cdot y_1^{i'_1} \ldots y_n^{i'_n} \cdot z_1^{i''_1} \ldots z_n^{i''_n} \cdot f^j \quad \bmod N^j$$

$$\text{with } 1 \leq j < t, \, 0 \leq i_1 < e \text{ and } \deg(\tilde{f}_{\ldots}) < te$$

$$\tilde{g}_{i,i',i''} = g_1^{i_1} \ldots g_{n-1}^{i_{n-1}} \cdot x_n^{i_n} \cdot y_1^{i'_1} \ldots y_n^{i'_n} \cdot z_1^{i''_1} \ldots z_n^{i''_n} \quad \bmod M^k$$

$$\text{with } 1 \leq k = i_1 + \ldots + i_{n-1} \text{ and } \deg(\tilde{g}_{\ldots}) < te.$$

As above, the moduli N and M are *coprime* and the polynomials $\tilde{f}_{i_1,\ldots,i_n,j}$ on one hand and the polynomials $\tilde{g}_{i_0,\ldots,i_n}$ on the other hand are linearly independent.

Again the Coppersmith method does not necessarily imply that we can solve the system of equations and we have to make the following heuristic:

Heuristic 3. *Let $\mathscr{P}$ denote the polynomial set*

$$\mathscr{P} = \left\{ \tilde{f}_{i,i',i'',j} \mid \begin{array}{c} 1 \leq j < t, \, 0 \leq i_1 < e \\ i_1 + \ldots + i_n + +i'_1 + \ldots + i'_{n-1} + i''_1 + \ldots + i''_{n-1} + je < te \end{array} \right\}$$

$$\bigcup \left\{ \tilde{g}_{i,i',i''} \mid \begin{array}{c} 1 \leq k = i_1 + \ldots + i_{n-1} \\ i_1 + \ldots + i_n + +i'_1 + \ldots + i'_{n-1} + i''_1 + \ldots + i'_{n-1} < te \end{array} \right\}.$$

We assume that the set of polynomials we get by applying Coppersmiths method with the polynomial set $\mathscr{P}$ define an algebraic variety of dimension 0.

Theorem 8. *Under Heuristic 3, given as inputs an RSA modulus N, the truncated linear congruential generator parameters a and b, two messages m_0 and m_1 and a PKCS#1 v1.5 ciphertext $c = \mu(m_b, r)$ for some bit $b \in \{0, 1\}$ such that the randomizer r is the concatenation of truncations of $v_1, \ldots, v_n$ (where v_1 is a random seed of size M and $v_{i+1} = av_i + b \bmod M$ for $i \in \mathbb{N}$), we can recover the seed v_1 (and thus the bit b) in polynomial time in $\log(N)$ as soon as $M < N^{1/e}$.*

Due to lack of space, the details of the computation are provided in the full version.

Scenario 3: Truncated Linear Congruential Generator and Multiple Ciphertexts.

We can also extend the first *chosen distribution attack* by letting the adversary control m pair of messages (as in the semantic security for multiple ciphertexts, see e.g. [19]) and that the randomizer used in all the PKCS#1 v1.5 paddings are constructed by concatenating the successive outputs of a linear congruential generator (with a unique seed picked uniformly at random). We also apply our toolbox to this scenario and for an RSA modulus N with a public exponent e and a linear congruential generator with modulus M, our heuristic attacks are polynomial-time in $\log(N)$ for the $M < N^{m/e}$ (see details in the full version).

Acknowledgments. The authors are supported in part by the French ANR JCJC ROMAnTIC project (ANR-12-JS02-0004). The authors thank Aurélie Bauer for her participation and contributions in the early stage of this work.

References

1. Bauer, A., Coron, J.-S., Naccache, D., Tibouchi, M., Vergnaud, D.: On the broadcast and validity-checking security of PKCS#1 v1.5 encryption. In: Zhou, J., Yung, M. (eds.) ACNS 2010. LNCS, vol. 6123, pp. 1–18. Springer, Heidelberg (2010)
2. Bauer, A., Vergnaud, D., Zapalowicz, J.-C.: Inferring sequences produced by nonlinear pseudorandom number generators using Coppersmith's methods. In: Fischlin, M., Buchmann, J., Manulis, M. (eds.) PKC 2012. LNCS, vol. 7293, pp. 609–626. Springer, Heidelberg (2012)
3. Bellare, M., Brakerski, Z., Naor, M., Ristenpart, T., Segev, G., Shacham, H., Yilek, S.: Hedged public-key encryption: how to protect against bad randomness. In: Matsui, M. (ed.) ASIACRYPT 2009. LNCS, vol. 5912, pp. 232–249. Springer, Heidelberg (2009)
4. Bellare, M., Goldwasser, S., Micciancio, D.: "Pseudo-random" number generation within cryptographic algorithms: the DSS case. In: Kaliski Jr., B.S. (ed.) CRYPTO 1997. LNCS, vol. 1294, pp. 277–291. Springer, Heidelberg (1997)
5. Blackburn, S.R., Gómez-Pérez, D., Gutierrez, J., Shparlinski, I.: Predicting nonlinear pseudorandom number generators. Math. Comput. **74**(251), 1471–1494 (2005)
6. Blackburn, S.R., Gómez-Pérez, D., Gutierrez, J., Shparlinski, I.: Reconstructing noisy polynomial evaluation in residue rings. J. Algorithms **61**(2), 47–59 (2006)
7. Bleichenbacher, D.: Chosen ciphertext attacks against protocols based on the RSA encryption standard PKCS #1. In: Krawczyk, H. (ed.) CRYPTO 1998. LNCS, vol. 1462, pp. 1–12. Springer, Heidelberg (1998)
8. Blömer, J., May, A.: A tool kit for finding small roots of bivariate polynomials over the integers. In: Cramer, R. (ed.) EUROCRYPT 2005. LNCS, vol. 3494, pp. 251–267. Springer, Heidelberg (2005)
9. Boyar, J.: Inferring sequences produced by a linear congruential generator missing low-order bits. J. Cryptology **1**(3), 177–184 (1989)
10. Boyar, J.: Inferring sequences produced by pseudo-random number generators. J. ACM **36**(1), 129–141 (1989)
11. Coppersmith, D.: Finding a small root of a bivariate integer equation; factoring with high bits known. In: Maurer, U.M. (ed.) EUROCRYPT 1996. LNCS, vol. 1070, pp. 178–189. Springer, Heidelberg (1996)
12. Coppersmith, D.: Finding a small root of a univariate modular equation. In: Maurer, U.M. (ed.) EUROCRYPT 1996. LNCS, vol. 1070, pp. 155–165. Springer, Heidelberg (1996)
13. Coppersmith, D.: Small solutions to polynomial equations, and low exponent RSA vulnerabilities. J. Cryptology **10**(4), 233–260 (1997)
14. Coron, J.-S., Joye, M., Naccache, D., Paillier, P.: New attacks on PKCS#1 v1.5 encryption. In: Preneel, B. (ed.) EUROCRYPT 2000. LNCS, vol. 1807, pp. 369–381. Springer, Heidelberg (2000)
15. Flajolet, P., Sedgewick, R.: Analytic Combinatorics. Cambridge University Press, Cambridge (2009)
16. Fouque, P.-A., Tibouchi, M., Zapalowicz, J.-C.: Recovering private keys generated with weak PRNGs. In: Stam, M. (ed.) IMACC 2013. LNCS, vol. 8308, pp. 158–172. Springer, Heidelberg (2013)
17. Goldwasser, S., Micali, S.: Probabilistic encryption. J. Comput. Syst. Sci. **28**(2), 270–299 (1984)
18. Herrmann, M., May, A.: Attacking power generators using unravelled linearization: when do we output too much? In: Matsui, M. (ed.) ASIACRYPT 2009. LNCS, vol. 5912, pp. 487–504. Springer, Heidelberg (2009)

19. Hofheinz, D., Jager, T.: Tightly secure signatures and public-key encryption. In: Safavi-Naini, R., Canetti, R. (eds.) CRYPTO 2012. LNCS, vol. 7417, pp. 590–607. Springer, Heidelberg (2012)

20. Howgrave-Graham, N.: Finding small roots of univariate modular equations revisited. In: Darnell, M. (ed.) Cryptography and Coding 1997. LNCS, vol. 1355, pp. 131–142. Springer, Heidelberg (1997)

21. Jager, T., Schinzel, S., Somorovsky, J.: Bleichenbacher's attack strikes again: breaking PKCS#1 v1.5 in XML encryption. In: Foresti, S., Yung, M., Martinelli, F. (eds.) ESORICS 2012. LNCS, vol. 7459, pp. 752–769. Springer, Heidelberg (2012)

22. Jochemsz, E., May, A.: A strategy for finding roots of multivariate polynomials with new applications in attacking RSA variants. In: Lai, X., Chen, K. (eds.) ASIACRYPT 2006. LNCS, vol. 4284, pp. 267–282. Springer, Heidelberg (2006)

23. Joux, A., Stern, J.: Lattice reduction: a toolbox for the cryptanalyst. J. Cryptology 11(3), 161–185 (1998)

24. Kaliski, B.: PKCS #1: RSA Encryption Version 1.5. RFC 2313, Internet Engineering Task Force, March 1998. http://www.rfc-editor.org/rfc/rfc2313.txt

25. Koshiba, T.: On sufficient randomness for secure public-key cryptosystems. In: Naccache, D., Paillier, P. (eds.) PKC 2002. LNCS, vol. 2274, pp. 34–47. Springer, Heidelberg (2002)

26. Lipton, R.J., Regan, K.W.: People, Problems, and Proofs - Essays from Gödel's Lost Letter: 2010. Springer, Berlin (2013)

27. May, A.: Using lll-reduction for solving RSA and factorization problems. In: Nguyen, P.Q., Vallée, B. (eds.) The LLL Algorithm - Survey and Applications. Information Security and Cryptography, pp. 315–348, Springer, Heidelberg (2010). http://dx.org/10.1007/978-3-642-02295-1

28. May, A., Ritzenhofen, M.: Solving systems of modular equations in one variable: how many RSA-encrypted messages does eve need to know? In: Cramer, R. (ed.) PKC 2008. LNCS, vol. 4939, pp. 37–46. Springer, Heidelberg (2008)

29. May, A., Ritzenhofen, M.: Implicit factoring: on polynomial time factoring given only an implicit hint. In: Jarecki, S., Tsudik, G. (eds.) PKC 2009. LNCS, vol. 5443, pp. 1–14. Springer, Heidelberg (2009)

30. Ritzenhofen, M.: On efficiently calculating small solutions of systems of polynomial equations: lattice-based methods and applications to cryptography. Ph.D. thesis, Ruhr University Bochum (2010). http://www-brs.ub.ruhr-uni-bochum.de/netahtml/HSS/Diss/RitzenhofenMaike/

31. Stern, J.: Secret linear congruential generators are not cryptographically secure. In: 28th FOCS, pp. 421–426. IEEE Computer Society Press, October 1987

How to Generalize RSA Cryptanalyses

Atsushi Takayasu[1,2](✉) and Noboru Kunihiro[1]

[1] The University of Tokyo, Chiba, Japan
a-takayasu@it.k.u-tokyo.ac.jp, kunihiro@k.u-tokyo.ac.jp
[2] AIST, Tokyo, Japan

Abstract. Recently, the security of RSA variants with moduli $N = p^r q$, e.g., the Takagi RSA and the prime power RSA, have been actively studied in several papers. Due to the unusual composite moduli and rather complex key generations, the analyses are more involved than the standard RSA. Furthermore, the method used in some of these works are specialized to the form of composite integers $N = p^r q$.

In this paper, we generalize the techniques used in the current best attacks on the standard RSA to the RSA variants. We show that the lattices used to attack the standard RSA can be transformed into lattices to attack the variants where the dimensions are larger by a factor of $(r+1)$ of the original lattices. We believe the steps we took present to be more natural than previous researches, and to illustrate this point we obtained the following results:

- Simpler proof for small secret exponent attacks on the Takagi RSA proposed by Itoh et al. (CT-RSA 2008). Our proof generalizes the work of Herrmann and May (PKC 2010).
- Partial key exposure attacks on the Takagi RSA; generalizations of the works of Ernst et al. (Eurocrypt 2005) and Takayasu and Kunihiro (SAC 2014). Our attacks improve the result of Huang et al. (ACNS 2014).
- Small secret exponent attacks on the prime power RSA; generalizations of the work of Boneh and Durfee (Eurocrypt 1999). Our attacks improve the results of Sarkar (DCC 2014, ePrint 2015) and Lu et al. (Asiacrypt 2015).
- Partial key exposure attacks on the prime power RSA; generalizations of the works of Ernst et al. and Takayasu and Kunihiro. Our attacks improve the results of Sarkar and Lu et al.

The construction techniques and the strategies we used are conceptually easier to understand than previous works, owing to the fact that we exploit the exact connections with those of the standard RSA.

Keywords: RSA · Takagi RSA · Prime power RSA · Cryptanalysis · Small secret exponent · Partial key exposure · Lattices · Coppersmith's method

© International Association for Cryptologic Research 2016
C.-M. Cheng et al. (Eds.): PKC 2016, Part II, LNCS 9615, pp. 67–97, 2016.
DOI: 10.1007/978-3-662-49387-8_4

1   Introduction

Background. RSA [RSA78] is one of the most well-known cryptosystems. Let N be the public RSA modulus, a product of two distinct primes p and q with the same bit sizes. The public and secret exponents are positive integers such that $ed = 1 \mod (p-1)(q-1)$. The RSA cryptosystem has been extensively studied in numerous papers including lattice based cryptanalysis. In this paper, we introduce two well-analyzed attacks; *small secret exponent attacks* and *partial key exposure attacks*. Boneh and Durfee [BD00] showed that a public RSA modulus N can be factorized when a secret exponent d is small, e.g., they proposed a weaker result $d < N^{0.284}$ and a stronger result $d < N^{0.292}$. Several papers [BM03, EJMW05, SGM10, TK14] have studied the security of RSA when some portions of the most significant bits (MSBs) or the least significant bits (LSBs) of d are exposed to attackers. The attack of Ernst et al. [EJMW05] are the best results for general cases, e.g., the MSBs or the LSBs are exposed for general sizes of e and d. Although Blömer and May [BM03] and Sarkar et al. [SGM10] achieved the same result, they are only special cases of Ernst et al., e.g., Blömer and May's attack works only with the LSBs and the attack of Sarkar et al. works only with the MSBs and large e. Takayasu and Kunihiro [TK14] proposed an improved attack of Ernst et al. for specific parameters, e.g., small d.

There are some variants of RSA. In this paper, we study two of them that we call the *Takagi RSA* [Tak98] and the *prime power RSA*. Both have a public RSA modulus $N = p^r q$ for $r \geq 2$ with distinct primes p and q with the same bit sizes. A public and a secret exponent $e \approx N^{\alpha}$ and $d \approx N^{\beta}$ satisfy

$$ed = 1 \mod (p-1)(q-1)$$

for the Takagi RSA and

$$ed = 1 \mod p^{r-1}(p-1)(q-1)$$

for the prime power RSA, respectively. The security of the variants have been analyzed; May [May04] proposed small secret exponent attacks and partial key exposure attacks on the prime power RSA, and Itoh et al. [IKK08] proposed small secret exponent attacks on the Takagi RSA. Recently, the research area becomes a hot topic and several papers have been published. Huang et al. [HHX+14] proposed partial key exposure attacks on the Takagi RSA. Sarkar [Sar14] proposed small secret exponent attacks on the prime power RSA, and further improved the result in [Sar15] with a result for partial key exposure attacks. The result is better than May for small r. Lu et al. [LZPL15] proposed small secret exponent attacks and partial key exposure attacks on the prime power RSA that fully improve May's attack and are better than Sarkar's attack for $r \geq 5$.

Attacks of May [May04], and Lu et al. [LZPL15] make use of the special structure of a public modulus $N = p^r q$ and a key generation equality of the prime power RSA. Then, their attacks do not work for the standard RSA. However, a naive approach for the analysis of RSA variants should be generalizations of the attacks on the standard RSA. By definition, the Takagi RSA and the prime power RSA become the same as the standard RSA for $r = 1$. Hence, the attacks on the variants for $r = 1$ should completely cover the currently known best attacks on the standard RSA; the stronger Boneh-Durfee small secret exponent attack, partial key exposure attacks of Ernst et al., and Takayasu and Kunihiro. Since a public modulus N and key generations for the variants are more involved than the standard RSA, the analyses also become involved. Indeed, almost all the algorithm constructions and their strategies are too complicated to understand since the connections with those for the standard RSA are unclear. Moreover, existing attacks on the variants for $r = 1$ do not fully cover the currently known best attacks on the standard RSA.

Our Results. In this paper, we study the security of the Takagi RSA and the prime power RSA. The main focus of this paper is to generalize the currently known best attacks on the standard RSA, e.g., small secret exponent attacks and partial key exposure attacks, to the variants and to exploit the connections between their algorithm constructions. We show that the lattices used to attack the standard RSA can be transformed into lattices to attack the variants with simple operations. More concretely, the lattices used to attack the standard RSA can be transformed into lattices to attack the Takagi RSA (resp. the prime power RSA) by multiplying $\{1, q, pq, p^2q, \ldots, p^{r-1}q\}$ (resp. $\{q^a, pq^a, p^2q^a, \ldots, p^{r-1}q^a, p^{r-1}q^{a+1}\}$ with some integer a) to all the polynomials in the bases. Hence, dimensions of the lattices that we use to attack the variants are larger by a factor of $(r + 1)$ of the original lattices to attack the standard RSA. We believe that the connections offer better understanding for our algorithm constructions and enable us to easily generalize other attacks for their variants. As applications of our generalizations, we obtain the following results:

– In Sect. 3, we propose a partial key exposure attack on the Takagi RSA that fully generalizes the attack of Ernst et al. [EJMW05]. Our attack becomes the same as Huang et al. [HHX+14] with the exposed LSBs and better than the attack with the exposed MSBs for all α, β, and r.
– In Sect. 4, we give a simpler proof for the Itoh et al. small secret exponent attack on the Takagi RSA that fully generalizes the stronger Boneh-Durfee attack [BD00]. Our alternative proof fully generalizes that of Herrmann and May [HM10] for the stronger Boneh-Durfee attack and enables us to understand the Itoh et al. attack in detail. Based on the understanding, we propose a partial key exposure attack on the Takagi RSA with the exposed LSBs that fully generalizes Takayasu and Kunihiro's attack [TK14]. The attack is better than our attack in Sect. 3 and that of Huang et al. [HHX+14] for all α and r when β is small.
– In Sect. 5, we propose a small secret exponent attack on the prime power RSA that fully generalizes the weaker Boneh-Durfee attack [BD00]. To obtain the attack is technically easy since it is an extension of Sarkar's attack [Sar15] for arbitrary α. However, the extension reveals an important fact. Although Sarkar's attack, which captures only for $\alpha = 1$, is weaker than Lu et al. [LZPL15] for $r \geq 5$, our attack is better than Lu et al. for all r when α is small.

In addition, we propose a partial key exposure attack that fully generalizes the Ernst et al. [EJMW05]. Our attack is better than Sarkar's result for small α and β, and is better than Lu et al. [LZPL15] for small r.

- In Sect. 6, we propose a small secret exponent attack on the prime power RSA that (almost) fully generalizes the stronger Boneh-Durfee [BD00]. The attack is better than our attack in Sect. 5. In addition, we propose a partial key exposure attack that (almost) fully generalizes Takayasu and Kunihiro [TK14]. The attack is better than all known attacks for small r and β.

Since the elliptic curve method factorization [Len87] becomes efficient for large r and Boneh et al. [BDH99] revealed that only a $1/(r+1)$ fraction of the most significant bits of p suffices to factorize the modulus, they are the more important for small r. Then, we mainly compare our results and previous works for $r = 2$ and 3 throughout the paper, although we analyze the security for arbitrary r.

Technical Overview. In 1996, Coppersmith introduced lattice based methods to solve univariate modular equations [Cop96a] and bivariate integer equations [Cop96b], and they can be extended to more variables with a reasonable assumption (that we discuss later). The method is useful to evaluate the security of RSA. See [Cop97, Cop01, NS01, May03, May10]. Indeed, small secret exponent attack was firstly mentioned by Wiener [Wie90]. The attack is based on a continued fraction approach and works when $d < N^{0.25}$. Later, Boneh and Durfee revisited the attack and improved the bound to $d < N^{0.292}$ using the Coppersmith method. Although the original Coppersmith method is conceptually involved, simpler reformulations have been proposed; for modular equations by Howgrave-Graham [How97] and for integer equations by Coron [Cor04, Cor07]. In short, the methods construct a lattice whose bases consist of coefficients of polynomials that have the same roots as the original equations. By finding short lattice vectors using the LLL reduction, the original equations can be solved. The methods can solve modular (resp. integer) equations when sizes of roots are to some extent smaller than the modulus (resp. the norm of polynomial).

To maximize solvable root bounds, appropriate selections of lattice bases are essential. Jochemsz and May [JM06] proposed a conceptually simple strategy for the lattice constructions. Although the strategy does not always offer the best results, usually offers the best or similar bounds. For example, the Boneh-Durfee weaker result $d < N^{0.284}$ can be obtained based on the strategy. Especially, the strategy is the more compatible with integer equations based analysis. To the best of our knowledge, there are no algorithms solving integer equations outperforming the Jochemsz-May strategy; currently known best algorithms solving any integer equations can be captured by the Jochemsz-May strategy. Furthermore, most algorithms by solving modular equations based on the Jochemsz-May strategy can also be obtained by solving integer equations based on the strategy although reverse does not always hold. For example, in the context of partial key exposure attacks on the standard RSA, Ernst et al. [EJMW05] solved integer equations, whereas Blömer and May [BM03], and Sarkar et al. [SGM10] solved modular equations, and all these results are captured by the Jochemsz-May strategy. As we noted, attacks of Blömer and May, and Sarkar et al. are only the special cases of Ernst et al. However, in the context of security analyses of the Takagi RSA and the prime power RSA, there are no results known that solved integer equations. Therefore, we solve integer equations for the Takagi RSA (Sect. 3) and the prime power RSA (Sect. 5), and fully generalize the weaker Boneh-Durfee and Ernst et al.

Although the differences are small, there are some results beyond the Jochemsz-May strategy that solve modular equations, e.g., the stronger Boneh-Durfee attack $d < N^{0.292}$ [BD00]. In general, analyses to obtain attacks outperforming the Jochemsz-May strategy are difficult. Indeed, there are no results known that attack the Takagi RSA or the prime power RSA outperforming the Jochemsz-May strategy except the Itoh et al. small secret exponent attack on the Takagi RSA [IKK08]. In the context of the stronger Boneh-Durfee attack, the proof is involved since determinants of lattices, whose basis matrices are non-triangular, should be calculated. For the purpose, Boneh and Durfee introduced geometrically progressive matrix although the notion is unfamiliar. Since Itoh et al. followed the proof, the analysis is also involved. The fact makes it difficult to obtain partial key exposure attacks on the Takagi RSA outperforming the Jochemsz-May strategy. As the hope of such situations, Herrmann and May [HM10] gave a simpler proof for the stronger Boneh-Durfee attack. They used unravelled linearization [HM09] and transformed Boneh and Durfee's non-triangular basis matrices to triangular. The simpler proof offers better understanding of the attack. Based on the understanding, Takayasu and Kunihiro extended the stronger Boneh-Durfee attack to partial key exposure attacks outperforming the Jochemsz-May strategy. As the same way, we give a simpler proof of the Itoh et al. and propose a partial key exposure attack on the Takagi RSA outperforming the Jochemsz-May strategy (Sect. 4). Moreover, we analyze better lattice constructions and propose small secret exponent attacks and partial key exposure attacks on the prime power RSA outperforming the Jochemsz-May strategy (Sect. 6).

2   Preliminaries

In the beginning of this section, we formulate the exposed bits that will be used to analyze partial key exposure attacks. In the remaining of this section, we introduce tools to solve modular equations and integer equations; lattices and the LLL algorithm, the overview of the Coppersmith method, and the Jochemsz-May strategy. The experts of the research area can skip this part.

Exposed Bits. In this paper, we analyze partial key exposure attacks when some portions of the MSBs or the LSBs are exposed. In this section, we formulated the exposed bits. When the MSBs (resp. LSBs) are exposed, let $d_0 > N^{\beta-\delta}$ denote the exposed MSBs (resp. LSBs) and $d_1 < N^\delta$ denote the unknown LSBs (resp. MSBs). The secret exponent can be written as $d = d_0 M + d_1$ (resp. $d = d_1 M + d_0$) with an integer $M = 2^{\lfloor \delta \log N \rfloor}$ (resp. $M = 2^{\lfloor (\beta-\delta) \log N \rfloor}$). We also use $\tilde{d}$ to denote $d_0 M$ (resp. d_0).

Lattices and the LLL Algorithm. Let $b_1, \ldots, b_n \in \mathbb{Z}^{n'}$ be linearly independent n'-dimensional vectors. All vectors are row representations. The lattice $L(b_1, \ldots, b_n)$ spanned by the basis vectors $b_1, \ldots, b_n$ is defined as $L(b_1, \ldots, b_n) = \{\sum_{j=1}^{n} c_j b_j : c_j \in \mathbb{Z}\}$. We also use matrix representations $B \in \mathbb{Z}^{n \times n'}$ for the bases where each row corresponds to a basis vector $b_1, \ldots, b_n$. Then, a lattice spanned by the basis matrix B is defined as $L(B) = \{cB : c \in \mathbb{Z}^n\}$. We call n a rank of the lattice, and n' a dimension of the lattice. We call the lattice full-rank when $n = n'$. We define a determinant of a lattice $\det(L(B))$ as $\det(L(B)) = \sqrt{\det(BB^t)}$ where B^t is a trasprose of B. By definition, a determinant of a full-rank lattice can be computed as $\det(L(B)) = |\det(B)|$.

For a cryptanalysis, to find short lattice vectors is a very important problem. In 1982, Lenstra et al. [LLL82] proposed a polynomial time algorithm to find short lattice vectors, called the LLL algorithm.

Proposition 1 (LLL algorithm [LLL82, May03]) *Given a matrix $B \in \mathbb{Z}^{n \times n'}$, the LLL algorithm finds vectors b_1' and b_2' in a lattice $L(B)$. Euclidean norms of the vectors are bounded by*

$$\|b_1'\| \le 2^{(n-1)/4}(\det(L(B)))^{1/n} \text{ and } \|b_2'\| \le 2^{n/2}(\det(L(B)))^{1/(n-1)}.$$

The running time is polynomial time in n, n', and input length.

Although the outputs of the LLL algorithm are not the shortest lattice vectors in general, the fact is not the matter when we use the Coppersmith method.

The Coppersmith Methods. Instead of the original Coppersmith method, we introduce Howgrave-Graham's reformulation to solve modular equations [How97] and Coron's reformulation to solve integer equations [Cor04]. Although Coron's method [Cor04] is less efficient than the original Coppersmith method [Cop96b] and Coron's method [Cor07], it is simpler to analyze than the other methods.

For a k-variate polynomial $h(x_1, \ldots, x_k) = \sum h_{i_1, \ldots, i_k} x_1^{i_1} \cdots x_k^{i_k}$, we define a norm of a polynomial $\|h(x_1, \ldots, x_k)\| = \sqrt{\sum h_{i_1, \ldots, i_k}^2}$ and $\|h(x_1, \ldots, x_k)\|_\infty = \max_{i_1, \ldots, i_k} |h_{i_1, \ldots, i_k}|$. At first, we show a modular method since an integer method makes use of the modular method. The Coppersmith method can find solutions $(\tilde{x}_1, \tilde{x}_2)$ of a bivariate modular equation $h(x_1, x_2) = 0 \mod e$ when $|\tilde{x}_1| < X_1, |\tilde{x}_2| < X_2$, and $X_1 X_2$ is reasonably smaller than e. Let m be a positive integer. We construct n polynomials $h_1(x_1, x_2), \ldots, h_n(x_1, x_2)$ that have the roots $(\tilde{x}_1, \tilde{x}_2)$ modulo e^m. Then, we construct a matrix B whose rows consist of coefficients of $h_1(x_1 X_1, x_2 X_2), \ldots, h_n(x_1 X_1, x_2 X_2)$. Applying the LLL algorithm to B and we obtain two short vectors b_1' and b_2', and their corresponding polynomials $h'(x_1, x_2)$ and $h_2'(x_1, x_2)$. If norms of these polynomials are small, they have roots $(\tilde{x}_1, \tilde{x}_2)$ over the integers. The fact comes from the following lemma.

Lemma 1 [How97]. *Let $h(x_1, \ldots, x_k) \in \mathbb{Z}[x_1, \ldots, x_k]$ be a polynomial over the integers that consists of at most n monomials. Let $X_1, \ldots, X_k$, and R be positive*

integers. If the polynomial $h(x_1, \ldots, x_k)$ *satisfies the following two conditions:*
1. $h(\tilde{x}_1, \ldots, \tilde{x}_k) = 0 \pmod{R}$, *where* $|\tilde{x}_1| < X_1, \ldots, |\tilde{x}_k| < X_k$,
2. $\|h(x_1 X_1, \ldots, x_k X_k)\| < R/\sqrt{n}$.
Then, $h(\tilde{x}_1, \ldots, \tilde{x}_k) = 0$ *holds over the integers.*

Therefore, if $h'(x_1, x_2)$ and $h_2'(x_1, x_2)$ satisfy Lemma 1, we can compute Gröbner bases or a resultant of them and easily recover $(\tilde{x}_1, \tilde{x}_2)$.

Next, we show an integer case. The Coppersmith method can find solutions $(\tilde{x}_1, \tilde{x}_2, \tilde{x}_3)$ of a trivariate equation $h(x_1, x_2, x_3) = 0$ over the integers when $|\tilde{x}_1| < X_1, |\tilde{x}_2| < X_2, |\tilde{x}_3| < X_3$, and $X_1 X_2 X_3$ is reasonably smaller than $\|h(x_1 X_1, x_2 X_2, x_3 X_3)\|_\infty$. Although we omit details of the method, we set a reasonable integer R and remaining procedures are almost the same as modular case by solving a modular equation $h(x_1, x_2, x_3) = 0 \mod R$. New polynomials $h'(x_1, x_2, x_3)$ and $h_2'(x_1, x_2, x_3)$ obtained by outputs of the LLL algorithm are provably algebraically independent of $h(x_1, x_2, x_3)$. See [Cor04] for the detail.

We should note that the methods need heuristic argument. There are no assurance if new polynomials obtained by outputs of the LLL algorithm are algebraically independent. In this paper, we assume that these polynomials are always algebraically independent and resultants of polynomials will not vanish since there have been few negative reports that contradict the assumption. Moreover, most our attacks use sublattices of lattices that are used in previous works. Hence, validities of previous attacks justify validities of our results.

The Jochemsz-May Strategy. We summarize lattice constructions to solve integer equations based on the Jochemsz-May strategy [JM06]. Let l_j denote the largest exponent of x_j in the polynomial $h(x_1, \ldots, x_k) = \sum h_{i_1, \ldots, i_k} x_1^{i_1} \cdots x_k^{i_k}$. We set an (possibly large) integer W such that $W \leq \|h(x_1, \ldots, x_k)\|_\infty$. Next, we set an integer $R := W X_1^{l_1(m-1)+t} \prod_{u=2}^{k} X_j^{l_u(m-1)}$ with some positive integers m and $t = O(m)$ such that $\gcd(R, h_{0, \ldots, 0}) = 1$. We compute $c = h_{0, \ldots, 0}^{-1} \mod R$ and $h'(x_1, \ldots, x_k) := c \cdot h(x_1, \ldots, x_k) \mod R$. We define shift-polynomials g and g' as

$$g : x_1^{i_1} \cdots x_k^{i_k} \cdot h(x_1, \ldots, x_k) \cdot X_1^{l_1(m-1)+t-i_1} \prod_{u=2}^{k} X_j^{l_u(m-1)-i_j} \quad \text{for } x_1^{i_1} \cdots x_k^{i_k} \in S,$$

$$g' : x_1^{i_1} \cdots x_k^{i_k} \cdot R \quad \text{for } x_1^{i_1} \cdots x_k^{i_k} \in M \backslash S,$$

for sets of monomials

$$S := \bigcup_{0 \leq j \leq t} \{ x_1^{i_1+j} \cdots x_k^{i_k} \mid x_1^{i_1} \cdots x_k^{i_k} \text{ is a monomial of } h(x_1, \ldots, x_k)^{m-1} \},$$

$$M := \{ \text{monomials of } x_1^{i_1} \cdots x_k^{i_k} \cdot h(x_1, \ldots, x_k) \text{ for } x_1^{i_1} \cdots x_k^{i_k} \in S \}.$$

All these shift-polynomials g and g' modulo R have the roots $(\tilde{x}_1, \ldots, \tilde{x}_k)$ that are the same as $h(x_1, \ldots, x_k)$. We construct a lattice with coefficients of $g(x_1 X_1, \ldots, x_k X_k)$ and $g'(x_1 X_1, \ldots, x_k X_k)$ as the bases. The shift-polynomials generate a triangular basis matrix. Ignoring low order terms of m, LLL outputs short vectors that satisfy Lemma 1 when

$$\prod_{j=1}^{k} X_j^{s_j} < W^{|S|} \text{ for } s_j = \sum_{x_1^{i_1} \cdots x_k^{i_k} \in M \setminus S} i_j.$$

When the condition holds, we can find all small roots. See [JM06] for the detail.

3 Attacks on the Takagi RSA by Solving Integer Equations

In this section, we analyze the security of the Takagi RSA by solving integer equations. In Sect. 3.1, we give an alternative proof of the Itoh et al. small secret exponent attack [IKK08] that was proposed by solving modular equations. In Sect. 3.2, we propose a partial key exposure attack that fully generalizes the attack of Ernst et al. [EJMW05].

3.1 Small Secret Exponent Attack

In this section, we revisit the Itoh et al. small secret exponent attacks [IKK08]. The result fully generalizes the weaker Boneh-Durfee [BD00] in the sense that it completely covers their attack, i.e., $\beta < (7 - 2\sqrt{7})/6$ for $r = 1$ and $\alpha = 1$.

Theorem 1 [IKK08]. *Let $N = p^r q$ be a public modulus and let $e \approx N^\alpha$ and $d \approx N^\beta$ be public exponent and secret exponent of the Takagi RSA, respectively. If*

$$\beta < \frac{7 - 2\sqrt{1 + 3(r+1)\alpha}}{3(r+1)} \text{ for } \alpha \leq \frac{1}{r+1}$$

holds, then the Takagi RSA modulus N can be factorized in polynomial time.

Although the original paper [IKK08] solved modular equations for the attack, we solve integer equations and give an alternative proof. The proof is convenient to analyze partial key exposure attacks in Sect. 3.2. Moreover, we exploit the exact connection between the algorithm constructions of Itoh et al. and the weaker Boneh-Durfee.

Alternative Proof of Theorem 1. Looking at a key generation for the Takagi RSA; $ed = 1 + \ell(p-1)(q-1)$ with some integer $|\ell| \approx N^{\alpha+\beta-2/(r+1)}$. To recover the secret exponent d, we use the following polynomial

$$f_{T.SSE.i}(x, y, z_1, z_2) = 1 + ex + y(z_1 + 1)(z_2 + 1)$$

whose roots over the integers are $(x, y, z_1, z_2) = (-d, \ell, -p, -q)$. The absolute values are bounded by $X := N^\beta, Y := N^{\alpha+\beta-2/(r+1)}, Z_1 :=$

$2N^{1/(r+1)}, Z_2 := 2N^{1/(r+1)}$. We also use a notation $Z = Z_1 = Z_2$ for simplicity. We set an (possibly large) integer W such that $W < N^{\alpha+\beta}$ since $\|f_{T.SSE.i}(xX, yY, z_1Z_1, z_2Z_2)\|_\infty \geq |eX| \approx N^{\alpha+\beta}$. Next, we set an integer $R := W(XY)^{m-1}Z^{m+r-1+t}$ with some integers $m = \omega(r)$ and $t = \tau m$ where $\tau \geq 0$. We define shift-polynomials $g_{T.SSE.i}$ and $g'_{T.SSE.i}$ as

$$g_{T.SSE.i} : x^{i_X} y^{i_Y} z_1^{i_{Z_1}} z_2^{i_{Z_2}} \cdot f_{T.SSE.i} \cdot X^{m-1-i_X} Y^{m-1-i_Y} Z^{m+r-1+t-i_{Z_1}-i_{Z_2}}$$

$$\text{for } x^{i_X} y^{i_Y} z_1^{i_{Z_1}} z_2^{i_{Z_2}} \in S_1 \cup S_2,$$

$$g'_{T.SSE.i} : x^{i_X} y^{i_Y} z_1^{i_{Z_1}} z_2^{i_{Z_2}} \cdot R \quad \text{for } x^{i_X} y^{i_Y} z_1^{i_{Z_1}} z_2^{i_{Z_2}} \in (M_1 \cup M_2)\backslash(S_1 \cup S_2),$$

for sets of monomials

$$S_1 := \bigcup_{0 \leq j \leq t} \left\{ x^{i_X} y^{i_Y} z_1^{i_{Z_1}+j} \, \middle| \, \begin{array}{l} x^{i_X} y^{i_Y} z_1^{i_{Z_1}} \text{ is a monomial of} \\ f_{T.SSE.i}(x, y, z_1, z_2)^{m-1} \end{array} \right\},$$

$$S_2 := \bigcup_{0 \leq j \leq t} \left\{ x^{i_X} y^{i_Y} z_1^{i_{Z_1}} z_2^{i_{Z_2}+j} \, \middle| \, \begin{array}{l} x^{i_X} y^{i_Y} z_1^{i_{Z_1}} z_2^{i_{Z_2}} \text{ is a monomial of} \\ \tilde{s} \cdot f_{T.SSE.i}(x, y, z_1, z_2)^{m-1} \text{ for } i_{Z_2} \geq 1 \\ \text{where } \tilde{s} = \{z_1^{r-1} z_2, z_1^{r-2} z_2, \ldots, z_1 z_2\} \end{array} \right\},$$

$$M_1 := \left\{ x^{i_X} y^{i_Y} z_1^{i_{Z_1}} \, \middle| \, \begin{array}{l} \text{monomials of } x^{i'_X} y^{i'_Y} z_1^{i'_{Z_1}} \cdot f_{T.SSE.i}(x, y, z_1, z_2) \\ \text{for } x^{i'_X} y^{i'_Y} z_1^{i'_{Z_1}} \in S_1 \end{array} \right\},$$

$$M_2 := \left\{ x^{i_X} y^{i_Y} z_1^{i_{Z_1}} z_2^{i_{Z_2}} \, \middle| \, \begin{array}{l} \text{monomials of } x^{i'_X} y^{i'_Y} z_1^{i'_{Z_1}} z_2^{i'_{Z_2}} \cdot f_{T.SSE.i}(x, y, z_1, z_2) \\ \text{for } i_{Z_2} \geq 1 \text{ where } x^{i'_X} y^{i'_Y} z_1^{i'_{Z_1}} z_2^{i'_{Z_2}} \in S_2 \end{array} \right\}.$$

By definition of sets of monomial S_1, S_2, M_1, and M_2, it follows that

$$x^{i_X} y^{i_y} z_1^{i_{Z_1}} \in S_1 \Leftrightarrow i_X = 0, 1, \ldots, m-1; i_Y = 0, 1, \ldots, m-1-i_X;$$
$$i_{Z_1} = 0, 1, \ldots, i_Y + t,$$

$$x^{i_X} y^{i_y} z_1^{i_{Z_1}} z_2^{i_{Z_2}} \in S_2 \Leftrightarrow i_X = 0, 1, \ldots, m-1; i_Y = 0, 1, \ldots, m-1-i_X;$$
$$i_{Z_1} = 0, 1, \ldots, r-1; i_{Z_2} = 1, 2, \ldots, i_Y + t + 1,$$

$$x^{i_X} y^{i_y} z_1^{i_{Z_1}} \in M_1 \Leftrightarrow i_X = 0, 1, \ldots, m; i_Y = 0, 1, \ldots, m-i_X;$$
$$i_{Z_1} = 0, 1, \ldots, i_Y + t,$$

$$x^{i_X} y^{i_y} z_1^{i_{Z_1}} z_2^{i_{Z_2}} \in M_2 \Leftrightarrow i_X = 0, 1, \ldots, m; i_Y = 0, 1, \ldots, m-i_X;$$
$$i_{Z_1} = 0, 1, \ldots, r-1; i_{Z_2} = 1, 2, \ldots, i_Y + t + 1.$$

All these shift-polynomials $g_{T.SSE.i}$ and $g'_{T.SSE.i}$ modulo R have the roots $(x, y, z_1, z_2) = (-d, \ell, -p, -q)$ that are the same as $f_{T.SSE.i}(x, y, z_1, z_2)$. We replace each occurrence of $z_1^r z_2$ by N and construct a lattice with coefficients of $g_{T.SSE.i}(xX, yY, z_1Z_1, z_2Z_2)$ and $g'_{T.SSE.i}(xX, yY, z_1Z_1, z_2Z_2)$ as the bases. The shift-polynomials generate a triangular basis matrix. Ignoring low order terms of m, based on the Jochemsz-May strategy [JM06], LLL outputs short vectors that satisfy Lemma 1 when

$$X^{(r+1)(\frac{1}{6}+\frac{\tau}{2})m^3} Y^{(r+1)(\frac{1}{3}+\frac{\tau}{2})m^3} Z^{(r+1)(\frac{1}{6}+\frac{\tau}{2}+\frac{\tau^2}{2})m^3} < W^{(r+1)(\frac{1}{6}+\frac{\tau}{2})m^3} \quad (1)$$

that leads to

$$0 < -(r+1)\alpha - (r+1)(2+3\tau)\beta + 3 + 3\tau - 3\tau^2.$$

To maximize the right hand side of the inequality, we set the parameter $\tau = (1-(r+1)\beta)/2$ and the condition becomes

$$\beta < \frac{7 - 2\sqrt{1+3(r+1)\alpha}}{3(r+1)}$$

as required. To satisfy the restriction $\tau \geq 0$, the condition $\beta \leq \frac{1}{r+1}$ should hold. The condition results in $\alpha \geq \frac{1}{r+1}$.   □

The algorithm construction fully generalizes that of Ernst et al. that is a partial key exposure extension of the weaker Boneh-Durfee by solving integer equations, although the connection is hard to follow from the original proof in [IKK08]. In [EJMW05], Ernst et al. used a similar polynomial as $f_{T.SSE.i}$ and the condition becomes $X^{\left(\frac{1}{6}+\frac{\tau}{2}\right)m^3} Y^{\left(\frac{1}{3}+\frac{\tau}{2}\right)m^3} Z^{\left(\frac{1}{6}+\frac{\tau}{2}+\frac{\tau^2}{2}\right)m^3} < W^{\left(\frac{1}{6}+\frac{\tau}{2}\right)m^3}$. Clearly, the condition relates to that of Eq. (1). The connection comes from our definition of sets of monomials S_1, S_2, M_1, and M_2 that are generalizations of those of Ernst et al. by a factor of $(r+1)$. More concretely, each of our S_1 and S_2 for $i_{Z_1} = 0, 1, \ldots, r-1$ play the same role as that for Ernst et al. and so do M_1 and M_2 for $i_{Z_1} = 0, 1, \ldots, r-1$. Hence, our n, s_X, s_Y, and s_Z are larger by a factor of $(r+1)$ of Ernst et al. As a result, we successfully proposed a generalization the weaker Boneh-Durfee. In Sect. 3.2, we use the same sets of monomials S_1, S_2, M_1, and M_2 and construct a generalization of the partial key exposure attack of Ernst et al.

3.2 Partial Key Exposure Attack

In this section, we propose partial key exposure attacks on the Takagi RSA that satisfy the following property.

Theorem 2. *Let* $N = p^r q$ *be a public modulus and let* $e \approx N^\alpha$ *and* $d \approx N^\beta$ *be public exponent and secret exponent of the Takagi RSA, respectively. When* $(\beta - \delta) \log N$ *bits of the most significant bits or the least significant bits are exposed, if*

$$\delta < \frac{5 - 2\sqrt{-5 + 3(r+1)(\alpha+\beta)}}{3(r+1)} \ for \ \frac{2}{r+1} \leq \alpha + \beta$$

holds, then the Takagi RSA modulus N *can be factorized in polynomial time.*

The result fully generalizes Ernst et al. [EJMW05] in the sense that it completely covers their attack, i.e., $\beta < \left(5 - 2\sqrt{-5 + 6(\alpha + \beta)}\right)/6$ for $r = 1$. When the LSBs are exposed, our attack becomes the same as Huang et al. [HHX+14]. Although the attack of Huang et al. with the MSBs is weaker than that with the

LSBs, our attacks work in the same conditions. We can obtain the advantage by solving integer equations.

Proof of Theorem 2. Looking at a key generation for the Takagi RSA with the exposed bits (regardless of the MSBs or the LSBs); $e\left(\tilde{d} + (d - \tilde{d})\right) = 1 + \ell(p - 1)$ $(q - 1)$ with some integer $|\ell| \approx N^{\alpha+\beta-2/(r+1)}$. To recover unknown parts $d - \tilde{d}$, we use the following polynomial

$$f_{T.PKE.i}(x, y, z_1, z_2) = 1 - e\tilde{d} + eMx + y(z_1 + 1)(z_2 + 1)$$

where $M = 1$ (resp. $M = 2^{\lfloor(\beta-\delta)\log N\rfloor}$) with the exposed MSBs (resp. LSBs) whose roots over the integers are $(x, y, z_1, z_2) = (-(d - \tilde{d}), \ell, -p, -q)$. The absolute values are bounded by $X := N^\delta, Y := N^{\alpha+\beta-2/(r+1)}, Z_1 :=$ $2N^{1/(r+1)}, Z_2 := 2N^{1/(r+1)}$. We also use a notation $Z = Z_1 = Z_2$ for simplicity.

These formulations and those for small secret exponent attacks in Sect. 3.1 are essentially the same when we use the Jochemsz-May strategy. That means the Newton polygons of polynomials $f_{T.SSE.i}(x, y, z_1, z_2)$ and $f_{T.PKE.i}(x, y, z_1, z_2)$ are the same, e.g., there are six monomials for variables $1, x, y, yz_1, yz_2$, and yz_1z_2. Hence, we use almost the same algorithm construction. We set an (possibly large) integer W such that $W < N^{\alpha+\beta}$ since $\|f_{T.SSE.i}(xX, yY, z_1Z_1, z_2Z_2)\|_\infty \geq$ $\max\{|1 - e\tilde{d}|, |eMX|\} \approx N^{\alpha+\beta}$. Next, we set an integer $R := W(XY)^{m-1} \cdot$ $Z^{m+r-1+t}$ with some integers $m = \omega(r)$ and $t = \tau m$ where $\tau \geq 0$ such that $\gcd(R, 1 - e\tilde{d}) = 1$. We compute $c = (1 - e\tilde{d})^{-1} \mod R$ and $f'_{T.PKE.i}(x, y, z_1, z_2)$ $:= c \cdot f_{T.PKE.i}(x, y, z_1, z_2) \mod R$. We define shift-polynomials $g_{T.PKE.i}$ and $g'_{T.PKE.i}$ as

$$g_{T.PKE.i} : x^{i_x} y^{i_Y} z_1^{i_{Z_1}} z_2^{i_{Z_2}} \cdot f'_{T.PKE.i} \cdot X^{m-1-i_x} Y^{m-1-i_Y} Z^{m+r-1+t-i_{Z_1}-i_{Z_2}}$$

$$\text{for } x^{i_x} y^{i_Y} z_1^{i_{Z_1}} z_2^{i_{Z_2}} \in S_1 \cup S_2,$$

$$g'_{T.PKE.i} : x^{i_x} y^{i_Y} z_1^{i_{Z_1}} z_2^{i_{Z_2}} \cdot R \quad \text{for } x^{i_x} y^{i_Y} z_1^{i_{Z_1}} z_2^{i_{Z_2}} \in (M_1 \cup M_2)\backslash(S_1 \cup S_2),$$

for sets of monomials S_1, S_2, M_1, and M_2 that are the same as in Sect. 3.1 where $f_{T.SSE.i}$ is replaced by $f'_{T.PKE.i}$. All these shift-polynomials $g_{T.PKE.i}$ and $g'_{T.PKE.i}$ modulo R have the roots $(x, y, z_1, z_2) = (-(d - \tilde{d}), \ell, -p, -q)$ that are the same as $f_{T.PKE.i}(x, y, z_1, z_2)$. We replace each occurrence of $z_1^r z_2$ by N and construct a lattice with coefficients of $g_{T.PKE.i}(xX, yY, z_1Z_1, z_2Z_2)$ and $g'_{T.PKE.i}(xX, yY, z_1Z_1, z_2Z_2)$ as the bases. Hence, ignoring low order terms of m, based on the Jochemsz-May strategy [JM06], LLL outputs short lattice vectors that satisfy Lemma 1 when the inequality Eq. (1) holds. For partial key exposure attacks (regardless of the MSBs or the LSBs are exposed), the inequality becomes

$$0 < -(r + 1)(\alpha + \beta) - (r + 1)\delta(1 + 3\tau) + 3 + 3\tau - 3\tau^2.$$

To maximize the right hand side of the inequality, we set the parameter $\tau = (1 - (r + 1)\delta)/2$ and the condition becomes

$$\delta < \frac{5 - 2\sqrt{-5 + 3(r + 1)(\alpha + \beta)}}{3(r + 1)}$$

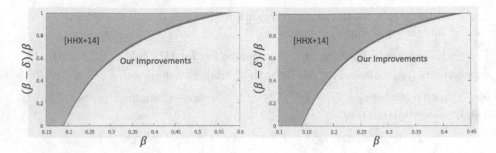

Fig. 1. Comparisons of partial key exposure attacks on the Takagi RSA when the MSBs are exposed for $\alpha = 1/(r+1)$. We compare how much portions of d should be exposed for β between the attack of Huang et al. [HHX+14] and our Theorem 2. The left figure is for $r = 2$ and the right figure is for $r = 3$.

as required. To satisfy the restriction $\eta \geq 0$, the condition $\delta \leq \frac{1}{r+1}$ should hold. The condition results in $\frac{2}{r+1} \leq \alpha + \beta$.   □

As we claimed in Sect. 3.1, the algorithm construction fully generalizes Ernst et al.

When the MSBs are exposed, our attack is always better than Huang et al. [HHX+14] that works when $\delta < \frac{7 - \sqrt{-39 + 24(r+1)(\alpha+\beta)}}{4(r+1)}$. Figure 1 compare Theorem 2 and Huang et al. for $r = 2$ and 3. Our attack is the better for all β, e.g., our attack works with less partial information.

In Sect. 4.2, we propose an improved attack when the LSBs are exposed. It seems that our Theorem 2 with the exposed MSBs is hard to be improved. Although there exist attacks that are better than Ernst et al. (the other attack of Ernst et al. [EJMW05] and Takayasu and Kunihiro's attack [TK14]), by definition, it seems difficult to generalize the attacks for the Takagi RSA since both attacks make use of the MSBs of ℓ. To compute the MSBs of ℓ, we have to know the MSBs of $(p-1)(q-1)$. It is possible for the standard RSA since $pq = N$. However, it seems difficult for the Takagi RSA. Hence, to improve Theorem 2, we have to exploit the special structure of the Takagi RSA or improve the attacks on the standard RSA without the knowledge of the MSBs of ℓ.

4   Attacks on the Takagi RSA by Solving Modular Equations

In this section, we analyze the security of the Takagi RSA by solving modular equations. In Sect. 4.1, we give an alternative proof of the Itoh et al. small secret exponent attack [IKK08] that is analogous to Herrmann and May [HM10]. In Sect. 4.2, we propose a partial key exposure attack that fully generalizes Takayasu and Kunihiro's result [TK14].

4.1 Small Secret Exponent Attack

In this section, we prove the following Itoh et al. small secret exponent attack. The result fully generalizes the stronger Boneh-Durfee [BD00] in the sense that it completely covers their attack, i.e., $\beta < 1 - 1/\sqrt{2}$ for $r = 1$ and $\alpha = 1$.

Theorem 3 [IKK08]. *Let $N = p^r q$ be a public modulus and let $e \approx N^\alpha$ and $d \approx N^\beta$ be public exponent and secret exponent of the Takagi RSA, respectively. If*

$$\beta < \frac{2 - \sqrt{(r+1)\alpha}}{r+1} \; for \; \frac{1}{r+1} \le \alpha$$

holds, then the Takagi RSA modulus N can be factorized in polynomial time.

The original proof in [IKK08] is involved since they used geometrically progressive matrix. We use unravelled linearization [HM09] and offer simpler proof. Moreover, we exploit the exact connection between the algorithm constructions of Itoh et al. and the stronger Boneh-Durfee.

Alternative Proof of Theorem 3. Looking at a key generation for the Takagi RSA modulo $N = p^r q$, $ed = 1 + \ell(p-1)(q-1)$ with some integer $|\ell| \approx N^{\alpha+\beta-2/(r+1)}$. Itoh et al. [IKK08] considered a polynomial

$$f_{T.SSE.m}(x, y_1, y_2) = 1 + x(y_1 + 1)(y_2 + 1).$$

The polynomial modulo e has roots $(x, y_1, y_2) = (\ell, -p, -q)$. The absolute values are bounded by $X := N^{\alpha+\beta-2/(r+1)}, Y_1 = Y_2 := 2N^{1/(r+1)}$. Let $m = \omega(r)$ be an integer and $\tau \ge 0$. To solve a modular equation $f_{T.SSE.m}(x, y_1, y_2) = 0 \mod e$, we use shift-polynomials

$$g_{T.SSE.m}(x, y_1, y_2) = x^{i_X} y_1^{i_{Y_1}} y_2^{i_{Y_2}} f_{T.SSE.m}^u(x, y_1, y_2) e^{m-u}$$

with indices in

$$\mathcal{I}_{x1} \Leftrightarrow u = 0, 1, \ldots, m; i_X = 0, 1, \ldots, m - u; i_{Y_1} = 0; i_{Y_2} = 0, \text{or}$$
$$\mathcal{I}_{x2} \Leftrightarrow u = 0, 1, \ldots, m; i_X = 0, 1, \ldots, m - u; i_{Y_1} = 0, 1, \ldots, r - 1; i_{Y_2} = 1,$$
$$\mathcal{I}_{y1} \Leftrightarrow u = 0, 1, \ldots, m; i_X = 0; i_{Y_1} = 1, 2, \ldots, \lceil \tau u \rceil; i_{Y_2} = 0, \text{or}$$
$$\mathcal{I}_{y2} \Leftrightarrow u = 0, 1, \ldots, m; i_X = 0; i_{Y_1} = 0, 1, \ldots, r - 1; i_{Y_2} = 2, 3, \ldots, \lceil \tau u \rceil.$$

All these shift-polynomials $g_{T.SSE.m}$ modulo e^m have the roots $(x, y_1, y_2) = (\ell, -p, -q)$ that are the same as $f_{T.SSE.m}$. We replace each occurrence of $y_1^r y_2$ by N and construct a lattice with coefficients of $g_{T.SSE.m}(xX, y_1 Y_1, y_2 Y_2)$ as the bases.

Here, we observe why the construction offers a bound outperforming the Jochemsz-May strategy. In the above $\mathcal{I}_{y1}$ and $\mathcal{I}_{y2}$, i_{Y_1} and i_{Y_2} are upper bounded by $\lceil \tau u \rceil$ that depend on u. In the Jochemsz-May strategy, the corresponding indices ($i_{Z_1} - i_Y$ and $i_{Z_2} - i_Y$ in S_1, S_2, M_1, and M_2 in Sect. 3.1) are bounded by $t = \tau m$ that only depends m. Since the former covers the latter, we can analyze broader classes of lattice constructions. The restriction of the Jochemsz-May strategy offers simpler analysis with a triangular basis matrix although that does not always offer the best bound. Moreover, the parameter is eventually set to $\tau = 1 - (r+1)\beta$. The optimization follows from the fact that shift-polynomials $g_{T.SSE.m}$ with indices in $\mathcal{I}_{y1}$ and $\mathcal{I}_{y2}$ reduce the norm of outputs of the LLL algorithm, e.g., the diagonals for the shift-polynomials are smaller than the modulus e^m. This observation enables readers to understand our improvements in Sect. 6 easily.

However, the former selection requires involved analysis since the shift-polynomials generate non-triangular basis matrices. The dependence of the Jochemsz-May strategy always generates triangular basis matrices and the analysis is easy. To construct partial key exposure attacks outperforming the Jochemsz-May strategy, we require better understanding for small secret exponent attacks. For the purpose, we show an analogous elementary proof to Herrmann and May [HM10]. Although the above shift-polynomials generate non-triangular basis matrices, we can transform it to be triangular by using unravelled linearization.

Lemma 2. *Using a linearization $z_1 = 1 + xy_1$ and $z_2 = 1 + xy_2$, the above shift-polynomials generate a triangular basis matrix. The diagonals of the basis matrix for $g_{T.SSE.m}$ are*

$$- X^{u+i_X} Y_1^u e^{m-u} \qquad \text{for indices in } \mathcal{I}_{x1},$$
$$- X^{u+i_X} Y_1^{i_{Y_1}} Y_2^{u+1} e^{m-u} \quad \text{for indices in } \mathcal{I}_{x2},$$
$$- Y_1^{i_{Y_1}} Z_1^u e^{m-u} \qquad \text{for indices in } \mathcal{I}_{y1},$$
$$- Y_1^{i_{Y_1}} Y_2 Z_2^u e^{m-u} \qquad \text{for indices in } \mathcal{I}_{y2}.$$

Indeed, the transformation is analogous to Herrmann and May [HM10], and show the exact connection with the stronger Boneh-Durfee and the Itoh et al. attack although the connection is hard to follow from the original proof [IKK08]. The shift-polynomials for indices in $\mathcal{I}_{x1}$ and $\mathcal{I}_{x2}$ for $i_{Y_1} = 0, 1, \ldots, r-1$ (resp. $\mathcal{I}_{y1}$ and $\mathcal{I}_{y2}$ for $i_{Y_1} = 0, 1, \ldots, r-1$) play the same role as x-shifts (resp. y-shifts) of the stronger Boneh-Durfee. Ignoring low order terms of m, the dimension of the lattice is $(r+1)\left(\frac{1}{2} + \frac{\tau}{2}\right)m^2$, and the determinant of the basis matrix is $X^{(r+1)\left(\frac{1}{3} + \frac{\tau}{3}\right)m^3} Y^{(r+1)\left(\frac{1}{6} + \frac{\tau}{3} + \frac{\tau^2}{6}\right)m^3} e^{(r+1)\left(\frac{1}{3} + \frac{\tau}{6}\right)m^3}$. Notice that $Z_1 = Z_2 \approx XY$. Again, we stress the connection with the stronger Boneh-Durfee. In the proof, a dimension of a lattice is $\left(\frac{1}{2} + \frac{\tau}{2}\right)m^2$ and its determinant is $X^{\left(\frac{1}{3} + \frac{\tau}{3}\right)m^3} Y^{\left(\frac{1}{6} + \frac{\tau}{3} + \frac{\tau^2}{6}\right)m^3} e^{\left(\frac{1}{3} + \frac{\tau}{6}\right)m^3}$. Hence, it is clear that the algorithm construction of Itoh et al. is a generalization of that for the stronger Boneh-Durfee. We set the parameter $\tau = 1 - (r+1)\beta$, and obtain Theorem 3. Here, we omit overall calculations since they are completely the same as those in [IKK08]. $\square$

4.2   Partial Key Exposure Attack

In this section, we propose a partial key exposure attack on the Takagi RSA that satisfies the following property.

Theorem 4. *Let $N = p^r q$ be a public modulus and let $e \approx N^\alpha$ and $d \approx N^\beta$ be public exponent and secret exponent of the Takagi RSA, respectively. When $(\beta - \delta) \log N$ bits of the least significant bits are exposed, if*

$$\delta < \frac{2 + (r+1)\beta - \sqrt{-12 + 4(r+1)\alpha + 12(r+1)\beta - 3(r+1)^2\beta^2}}{2(r+1)} \quad and$$

$$\beta \leq \frac{9 - \sqrt{-3 + 12(r+1)\alpha}}{6(r+1)}$$

hold, then the Takagi RSA modulus N can be factorized in polynomial time.

The result fully generalizes Takayasu and Kunihiro's result [TK14] in the sense that it completely covers their attack, i.e., $\delta < \left(1 + \beta - \sqrt{-1 + 6\beta - 3\beta^2}\right)/2$ and $\beta < (9 - \sqrt{21})/12$ for $r = 1$ and $\alpha = 1$.

Proof of Theorem 4. Looking at a key generation for the Takagi RSA with the exposed LSBs; $e(d_1 M + d_0) = 1 + \ell(p-1)(q-1)$ with some integer $|\ell| \approx N^{\alpha+\beta-2/(r+1)}$. To recover the unknown MSBs of the secret exponent d_1, we use the following polynomials

$$f_{T.PKE.m1}(x, y_1, y_2) = 1 - ed_0 + x(y_1 + 1)(y_2 + 1) \text{ and}$$

$$f_{T.PKE.m2}(x, y_1, y_2) = 1 + x(y_1 + 1)(y_2 + 1)$$

whose roots with appropriate moduli are $(x, y_1, y_2) = (\ell, -p, -q)$, e.g., $f_{T.PKE.m1}(\ell, -p, -q) = 0 \mod eM$ and $f_{T.PKE.m2}(\ell, -p, -q) = 0 \mod e$. The absolute values are bounded by $X := N^{\alpha+\beta-2/(r+1)}, Y_1 = Y_2 := 2N^{1/(r+1)}$. Let $m = \omega(r)$ be an integer and define a function

$$l_r(k) = \max\left\{0, \frac{k - (r+1)(\beta - \delta)m}{1 + (r+1)(\delta - 2\beta)}\right\}.$$

To solve modular equations $f_{T.PKE.m1}(x, y_1, y_2) = 0 \mod eM$ and $f_{T.PKE.m2}(x, y_1, y_2) = 0 \mod e$ simultaneously, we use following shift-polynomials

$$g_{T.PKE.m1}(x, y_1, y_2) = x^{i_X} y_1^{i_{Y_1}} y_2^{i_{Y_2}} f_{T.PKE.m1}^u(x, y_1, y_2)(eM)^{m-u},$$

$$g_{T.PKE.m2}(x, y_1, y_2) = y_1^{i_{Y_1}+k_1} y_2^{i_{Y_2}+k_2} f_{T.PKE.m1}^{u-\lceil l_r(k_1+k_2)\rceil}(x, y_1, y_2)\cdot$$
$$f_{T.PKE.m2}^{\lceil l_r(k_1+k_2)\rceil}(x, y_1, y_2)e^{m-u} M^{m-(u-\lceil l_r(k_1+k_2)\rceil)}.$$

To construct a lattice we use $g_{T.PKE.m1}$ with indices in $\mathcal{I}_{x1}, \mathcal{I}_{x2}$ and $g_{T.PKE.m2}$ with indices in $\mathcal{I}_{y1}, \mathcal{I}_{y2}$ where

$$\mathcal{I}_{x1} \Leftrightarrow u = 0, 1, \ldots, m; i_X = 0, 1, \ldots, m-u; i_{Y_1} = 0; i_{Y_2} = 0,$$
$$\mathcal{I}_{x2} \Leftrightarrow u = 0, 1, \ldots, m; i_X = 0, 1, \ldots, m-u; i_{Y_1} = 0, 1, \ldots, r-1; i_{Y_2} = 1,$$
$$\mathcal{I}_{y1} \Leftrightarrow u = 0, 1, \ldots, m; i_{Y_1} = 0; i_{Y_2} = 0;$$

$$k_1 = 1, 2, \ldots, \lfloor (r+1)(\beta - \delta)m + (1 + (r+1)(\delta - 2\beta))u \rfloor; k_2 = 0,$$
$$\mathcal{I}_{y2} \Leftrightarrow u = 0, 1, \ldots, m; i_{Y_1} = 0, 1, \ldots, r-1; i_{Y_2} = 1; k_1 = 0;$$
$$k_2 = 1, 2, \ldots, \lfloor (r+1)(\beta - \delta)m + (1 + (r+1)(\delta - 2\beta))u \rfloor.$$

All these shift-polynomials $g_{T.PKE.m1}$ and $g_{T.PKE.m2}$ modulo $(eM)^m$ have the roots $(x, y_1, y_2) = (\ell, -p, -q)$ that are the same as $f_{T.PKE.m}$. We replace each occurrence of $y_1^r y_2$ by N and construct a lattice with coefficients of $g_{T.PKE.m1}(xX, y_1Y_1, y_2Y_2)$ and $g_{T.PKE.m2}(xX, y_1Y_1, y_2Y_2)$ as the bases.

As in the proof of Theorem 3, the shift-polynomials $g_{T.PKE.m1}$ with indices in $\mathcal{I}_{x1}$ and $\mathcal{I}_{x2}$ for $i_{Y_1} = 0, 1, \ldots, r-1$ (resp. $g_{T.PKE.m2}$ with indices in $\mathcal{I}_{y1}$ and $\mathcal{I}_{y2}$ for $i_{Y_1} = 0, 1, \ldots, r-1$) play the same role as x-shifts (resp. y-shifts) of Takayasu and Kunihiro. The shift-polynomials generate a triangular basis matrix using a linearization $z_1 = 1 + xy_1$ and $z_2 = 1 + xy_2$. Assume $1 + (r+1)(\delta - 2\beta) \geq 0$ and the diagonals of the basis matrix are

- $X^{u+i_X} Y_1^u e^{m-u}$ for $g_{T.PKE.m1}$ with indices in $\mathcal{I}_{x1}$,
- $X^{u+i_X} Y_1^{i_{Y_1}} Y_2^{u+1} e^{m-u}$ for $g_{T.PKE.m1}$ with indices in $\mathcal{I}_{x2}$,
- $X^{u-\lceil l_r(k_1) \rceil} Y_1^{u-\lceil l_r(k_1) \rceil + k_1} Z_1^{\lceil l_r(k_1) \rceil} e^{m-u} M^{m-(u-\lceil l_r(k_1) \rceil)}$
  for $g_{T.PKE.m2}$ with indices in $\mathcal{I}_{y1}$,
- $X^{u-\lceil l_r(k_2) \rceil} Y_1^{i_{Y_1}} Y_2^{u-\lceil l_r(k_2) \rceil + k_2 + 1} Z_2^{\lceil l_r(k_2) \rceil} e^{m-u} M^{m-(u-\lceil l_r(k_2) \rceil)}$
  for $g_{T.PKE.m2}$ with indices in $\mathcal{I}_{y2}$.

In $\mathcal{I}_{y1}$ and $\mathcal{I}_{y2}$, k_1 and k_2 are upper bounded by $\lfloor (r+1)(\beta-\delta)m+(1+(r+1)(\delta-2\beta))u \rfloor$. As Takayasu and Kunihiro, the definition follows from the fact that the shift-polynomials reduce norms of output vectors by the LLL algorithm.

As the proof of Theorem 3, all these values are larger by a factor of $(r+1)$ of Takayasu and Kunihiro's. Ignoring low order term of m, the LLL algorithm outputs short vectors that satisfy Lemma 1 when

$$(r+1)^2\delta^2 - (r+1)(2 + (r+1)\beta)\delta + 4 - (r+1)\alpha - 2(r+1)\beta + (r+1)^2\beta^2 > 0.$$

Hence, we obtain the bound of Theorem 4

$$\delta < \frac{2 + (r+1)\beta - \sqrt{-12 + 4(r+1)\alpha + 12(r+1)\beta - 3(r+1)^2\beta^2}}{2(r+1)}$$

as required. To satisfy the restriction $1 + (r+1)(\delta - 2\beta) \geq 0$, the condition $\beta \leq \frac{9-\sqrt{-3+12(r+1)\alpha}}{6(r+1)}$ should hold. $\square$

When the LSBs are exposed and $\beta \leq \frac{9-\sqrt{-3+12(r+1)\alpha}}{6(r+1)}$, our attack is better than Huang et al. [HHX+14] that works when $\delta < \frac{5-2\sqrt{-5+3(r+1)(\alpha+\beta)}}{3(r+1)}$. Figure 2 compare our results and Huang et al. for $r = 2$ and 3. Our attack is the better for small β, e.g., our attack works with less partial information.

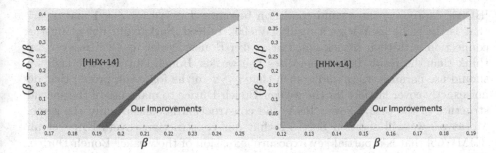

Fig. 2. Comparisons of partial key exposure attacks on the Takagi RSA when the LSBs are exposed and $\alpha = 1/(r+1)$. We compare how much portions of d should be exposed for β between the attack of Huang et al. [HHX+14] and our Theorem 4. The left figure is for $r = 2$ and the right figure is for $r = 3$.

5   Attacks on the Prime Power RSA by Solving Integer Equations

In this section, we analyze the security of the prime power RSA by solving integer equations. In Sect. 5.1, we propose a small secret exponent attack that fully generalizes the weaker Boneh-Durfee result [BD00]. In Sect. 5.2, we propose a partial key exposure attack that fully generalizes Ernst et al. [EJMW05].

5.1   Small Secret Exponent Attack

In this section, we propose small secret exponent attacks on the prime power RSA that satisfy the following property.

Theorem 5. *Let $N = p^r q$ be a public modulus for $r \geq 2$ and let $e \approx N^\alpha$ and $d \approx N^\beta$ be public exponent and secret exponent of the prime power RSA, respectively. If*

$$0 < -r(r+1)^2\alpha + r(r+1)(1 - \beta)(2(r+1) + 3r\tau) - 1 - 3r\eta(1 + r\eta)$$
$$- r^3(1 - \eta + \tau)^3 + r^2(\eta - \tau)^3 \ where$$
$$\eta = \frac{r(r+1)(1 - \beta) - 1}{2r} \ and \ \tau = \eta - \frac{r - \sqrt{-r + (r+1)^2(1 - \beta)}}{r+1}$$
$$for \ \frac{3r^3 + r^2 + r - 1}{4(r+1)} \leq \alpha, \ or$$
$$\beta < \frac{r + (\sqrt{r} - 1)^2}{2r(r+1)} - \frac{\alpha}{2} \ for \ \frac{r + (\sqrt{r} - 1)^2}{r(r+1)} < \alpha \leq \frac{3r^3 + r^2 + r - 1}{4(r+1)}$$

holds, then prime power RSA modulus N can be factorized in polynomial time.

The result extends Sarkar's attack [Sar15] for arbitrary α although they solved modular equations. The result for $r = 1$ does not cover the weaker Boneh-Durfee

[BD00]. Moreover, the second condition becomes $\beta < 1/4$ for $r = 1$ and $\alpha = 1$ that is the same as Wiener's result [Wie90]. Indeed, Sarkar did not claim the connection with their attack and the weaker Boneh-Durfee at all. However, we think that the result fully generalizes the weaker Boneh-Durfee. Although we should use parameters (η and τ such that $\eta \geq \tau$ in the following proof) that do not exactly cover lattices for the weaker Boneh-Durfee to make use of the special structure of the prime power RSA, the construction is conceptually the same. Moreover, we will show in Sect. 5.2 that our construction covers Ernst et al. [EJMW05] that is a partial key exposure extension of the weaker Boneh-Durfee. The proof is convenient to analyze partial key exposure attacks in Sect. 3.2.

Proof of Theorem 5. Looking at a key generation for the prime power RSA; $ed = 1 + \ell p^{r-1}(p-1)(q-1)$ with some integer $|\ell| \approx N^{\alpha+\beta-1}$. To recover the secret exponent d, we use the following polynomial

$$f_{PP.SSE.i}(x, y, z_1, z_2) = 1 + ex + yz_1^{r-1}(z_1 - 1)(z_2 - 1)$$

whose roots over the integers are $(x, y, z_1, z_2) = (-d, \ell, p, q)$. The absolute values are bounded by $X := N^\beta, Y := N^{\alpha+\beta-1}, Z_1 := 2N^{1/(r+1)}, Z_2 := 2N^{1/(r+1)}$. We also use a notation $Z = Z_1 = Z_2$ for simplicity. We set an (possibly large) integer W such that $W < N^{\alpha+\beta}$ since $\|f_{PP.SSE}(xX, yY, z_1Z_1, z_2Z_2)\|_\infty \geq |eX| \approx N^{\alpha+\beta}$. Next, we set an integer $R := W(XY)^{m-1}Z^{r(m-1-a+t)}$ with some integers $m = \omega(r), t = \tau m$, and $a = \eta m$ where $\tau \geq 0$ and $\eta \geq \tau$. We define shift-polynomials $g_{PP.SSE.i}$ and $g'_{PP.SSE.i}$ as

$$g_{PP.SSE.i} : x^{i_X} y^{i_Y} z_1^{i_{Z_1}} z_2^{i_{Z_2}} \cdot f_{PP.SSE.i} \cdot X^{m-1-i_X} Y^{m-1-i_Y} Z^{r(m-1-a+t)-i_{Z_1}-i_{Z_2}}$$

$$\text{for } x^{i_X} y^{i_Y} z_1^{i_{Z_1}} z_2^{i_{Z_2}} \in S,$$

$$g'_{PP.SSE.i} : x^{i_X} y^{i_Y} z_1^{i_{Z_1}} z_2^{i_{Z_2}} \cdot R \quad \text{for } x^{i_X} y^{i_Y} z_1^{i_{Z_1}} z_2^{i_{Z_2}} \in M \backslash S,$$

for sets of monomials

$$S := \bigcup_{0 \leq j \leq rt} \left\{ x^{i_X} y^{i_Y} z_1^{i_{Z_1}+j} z_2^{i_{Z_2}} \,\middle|\, \begin{array}{l} x^{i_X} y^{i_Y} z_1^{i_{Z_1}} z_2^{i_{Z_2}} \text{ is a monomial of} \\ \tilde{s} \cdot f_{PP.SSE.i}(x, y, z_1, z_2)^{m-1} \text{ where} \\ \tilde{s} = \{z_2^a, z_1 z_2^a, z_1^2 z_2^a, \ldots, z_1^r z_2^a, z_1^{r-1} z_2^{a+1}\} \end{array} \right\},$$

$$M := \left\{ x^{i_X} y^{i_Y} z_1^{i_{Z_1}} z_2^{i_{Z_2}} \,\middle|\, \begin{array}{l} \text{monomials of } x^{i'_X} y^{i'_Y} z_1^{i'_{Z_1}} z_2^{i'_{Z_2}} \cdot f_{PP.SSE.i}(x, y, z_1, z_2) \\ \text{where } x^{i'_X} y^{i'_Y} z_1^{i'_{Z_1}} z_2^{i'_{Z_2}} \in S \end{array} \right\},$$

with an integer $a = \eta m$ for $\eta \geq \tau$. By definition, it follows that

$$x^{i_X} y^{i_y} z_1^{i_{Z_1}} z_2^{i_{Z_2}} \in S \Leftrightarrow i_X = 0, 1, \ldots, m - a + t - 1;$$

$$i_Y = a - t, a - t + 1, \ldots, m - 1 - i_X;$$

$$i_{Z_1} = 0, 1, \ldots, r(i_Y - a + t); i_{Z_2} = 0, \text{ and}$$

$$i_X = 0, 1, \ldots, m - 1; i_Y = 0, 1, \ldots, m - 1 - i_X;$$

$$i_{Z_1} = \max\{0, r - i_Y + r(i_{Z_2} - 1 - a)\}, \ldots, r - 1;$$

$$i_{Z_2} = a+1, a+2, \ldots, a + \lceil (i_Y+1)/r \rceil, \quad \text{and}$$
$$i_X = 0, 1, \ldots, m-1; i_Y = 0, 1, \ldots, m-1-i_X;$$
$$i_{Z_1} = 0, 1, \ldots, r-1;$$
$$i_{Z_2} = \max\{0, -i_Y + a - t\}, \ldots, a,$$
$$x^{i_X} y^{i_v} z_1^{i_{Z_1}} z_2^{i_{Z_2}} \in M \Leftrightarrow i_X = 0, 1, \ldots, m-a+t;$$
$$i_Y = a-t, a-t+1, \ldots, m-i_X;$$
$$i_{Z_1} = 0, 1, \ldots, r(i_Y - a + t); i_{Z_2} = 0, \quad \text{and}$$
$$i_X = 0, 1, \ldots, m; i_Y = 0, 1, \ldots, m-i_X;$$
$$i_{Z_1} = \max\{0, r - i_Y + r(i_{Z_2} - 1 - a)\}, \ldots, r-1;$$
$$i_{Z_2} = a+1, a+2, \ldots, a + \lceil (i_Y+1)/r \rceil, \quad \text{and}$$
$$i_X = 0, 1, \ldots, m; i_Y = 0, 1, \ldots, m-i_X;$$
$$i_{Z_1} = 0, 1, \ldots, r-1;$$
$$i_{Z_2} = \max\{0, -i_Y + a - t\}, \ldots, a.$$

All these shift-polynomials $g_{PP.SSE.i}$ and $g'_{PP.SSE.i}$ modulo R have the roots $(x, y, z_1, z_2) = (-d, \ell, -p, -q)$ that are the same as $f_{PP.SSE.i}(x, y, z_1, z_2)$. We replace each occurrence of $z_1^r z_2$ by N and construct a lattice with coefficients of $g_{PP.SSE.i}(xX, yY, z_1 Z_1, z_2 Z_2)$ and $g'_{PP.SSE.i}(xX, yY, z_1 Z_1, z_2 Z_2)$ as the bases. The shift-polynomials generate a triangular basis matrix.

Ignoring low order terms of m, based on the Jochemsz-May strategy [JM06], LLL outputs short vectors that satisfy Lemma 1 when

$$X^{\left(\frac{r+1}{6} + \frac{r}{2}\tau\right)m^3} Y^{\left(\frac{r+1}{3} + \frac{r}{2}\tau\right)m^3} Z_1^{\left(\frac{r^2(1-\eta+\tau)^3}{6}\right)m^3} Z_2^{\left(\frac{1}{6r} + \frac{1}{2}\eta + \frac{r}{2}\eta^2 - \frac{r}{6}(\eta-\tau)^3\right)m^3}$$
$$< W^{\left(\frac{r+1}{6} + \frac{r}{2}\tau\right)m^3} \qquad (2)$$

that leads to

$$0 < - r(r+1)^2 \alpha + r(r+1)(1-\beta)(2(r+1)+3r\tau)$$
$$- 1 - 3r\eta(1+r\eta) - r^3(1-\eta+\tau)^3 + r^2(\eta-\tau)^3. \qquad (3)$$

To maximize the right hand side of the inequality, we set parameters $\eta = \frac{r(r+1)(1-\beta)-1}{2r}$ and $\tau = \eta - \frac{r - \sqrt{-r+(r+1)^2(1-\beta)}}{r+1}$ that results in the first condition of Theorem 5.

To satisfy the restriction $\tau \geq 0$, the condition $\beta \leq \frac{r^2-r-1+2\sqrt{r}}{r(r+1)}$ should hold. The condition results in $\alpha \geq \frac{3r^3+r^2+r-1}{4(r+1)}$. Other restrictions $\eta \geq \tau$ and $\eta \geq 0$ always hold.

In the other cases, e.g. $\alpha \leq \frac{3r^3+r^2+r-1}{4(r+1)}$, we fix the parameter $\tau = 0$. To maximize the right hand side of the inequality Eq. (3), we set the other parameter $\eta = 1 - 1/\sqrt{r}$ and the condition becomes

$$\beta < \frac{r + (\sqrt{r}-1)^2}{2r(r+1)} - \frac{\alpha}{2}$$

as required. Since the prime power RSA satisfies $\alpha + \beta > 1$ by definition, $\alpha > \frac{r+(\sqrt{r}-1)^2}{r(r+1)}$ should hold. □

This attack is an extension of Sarkar's attack [Sar15] for arbitrary α. However, the extension offers an advantage of the approach although Sarkar did not claim. Lu et al. [LZPL15] claimed that their attack, which works when $\beta < \frac{r(r-1)}{(r+1)^2}$, is better than Sarkar's attack for $r \geq 5$. Indeed, the attack of Lu et al. is better than Theorem 5 for $\alpha = 1$ (that is equivalent to Sarkar's attack). However, our attack becomes better than the attack of Lu et al. for small α. Considering the restriction $\alpha + \beta > 1$, although the attack of Lu et al. works when $\alpha > \frac{3r+1}{(r+1)^2}$, our attack works when $\alpha > \frac{r+(\sqrt{r}-1)^2}{r(r+1)}$. Hence, our attack works for smaller α than Lu et al. In Sect. 6.1, we propose further (although slight) improvements and compare our results and Lu et al.

We note that the restriction $\eta \geq \tau$ comes from the fact that we can obtain better results than $\eta < \tau$ for small secret exponent attacks on the prime power RSA for $r \geq 2$. As we claimed, the algorithm construction fully generalizes the weaker Boneh-Durfee. That means the weaker Boneh-Durfee result can be obtained by setting $\eta < \tau$. The connection is hard to follow from Sarkar's proof [Sar15] and they did not claim it. As our previous proofs, the construction comes from our definition of sets of monomials S and M that play the same roles as those for Ernst et al. that is a partial key exposure extension of the weaker Boneh-Durfee. More concretely, each of our S for $\tilde{s} = \{z_2^a, z_1 z_2^a, z_1^2 z_2^a, \ldots, z_1^{r-1} z_2^a, z_1^{r-1} z_2^{a+1}\}$ play the same role as that for Ernst et al. and so do M. However, our n, s_X, s_Y, and s_Z do not become larger by a factor of $(r+1)$ of those of Ernst et al. for the asymmetry of p and q for the prime power RSA key generation. So far, the asymmetry made it difficult to exploit the connection between the standard RSA and the prime power RSA, and to generalize attacks on the standard RSA to the prime power RSA.

5.2 Partial Key Exposure Attack

In this section, we propose partial key exposure attacks on the prime power RSA that satisfy the following property.

Theorem 6. *Let $N = p^r q$ be a public modulus and let $e \approx N^\alpha$ and $d \approx N^\beta$ be public exponent and secret exponent of prime power RSA, respectively. When $(\beta - \delta) \log N$ bits of the most significant bits or the least significant bits are exposed, if*

$$0 < -r(r+1)^2(\alpha+\beta) + r(r+1)(1-\delta)((r+1)+3r\tau) + r(r+1)^2 - 1$$
$$- 3r\eta(1+r\eta) - r^3(1-\eta+\tau)^3 + r^2(\eta-\tau)^3 \text{ where}$$
$$\eta = \frac{r(r+1)(1-\delta)-1}{2r} \text{ and } \tau = \eta - \frac{r - \sqrt{-r+(r+1)^2(1-\delta)}}{r+1}$$
$$\text{for } 1 < \alpha+\beta \leq \frac{3r^3+r^2+5r-1}{4r(r+1)}, \text{ or}$$

$$\delta < 1 - \frac{r + \sqrt{12r^2(r+1)(\alpha+\beta) - r(9r^2 + 14r - 3)}}{3r(r+1)}$$

$$for \ \frac{3r^3 + r^2 + 5r - 1}{4r(r+1)} \le \alpha + \beta$$

holds, then prime power RSA modulus N can be factorized in polynomial time.
The result fully generalizes Ernst et al. [EJMW05] in the sense that it completely covers their attack, i.e., $\beta < \left(5 - 2\sqrt{-5 + 6(\alpha + \beta)}\right)/6$ for $r = 1$. Moreover, we exploit the exact connection between the algorithm constructions of Theorem 6 and the Ernst et al.

Proof of Theorem 6. Looking at a key generation for prime power RSA with the exposed bits (regardless of the MSBs or the LSBs); $e(\tilde{d} + (d - \tilde{d})) = 1 + \ell p^{r-1}(p-1)$ $(q-1)$ with some integer $|\ell| \approx N^{\alpha + \beta - 1}$. To recover unknown parts $d - \tilde{d}$, we use the following polynomial

$$f_{PP.PKE.i}(x, y, z_1, z_2) = 1 - e\tilde{d} + eMx + yz_1^{r-1}(z_1 - 1)(z_2 - 1)$$

where $M = 1$ (resp. $M \lfloor 2^{\lfloor (\beta - \delta) \log N \rfloor} \rfloor$) with the exposed MSBs (resp. LSBs) whose roots over the integers are $(x, y, z_1, z_2) = (-(d - \tilde{d}), \ell, p, q)$. The absolute values are bounded by $X := N^{\delta}, Y := N^{\alpha + \beta - 1}, Z_1 := 2N^{1/(r+1)}, Z_2 := 2N^{1/(r+1)}$. We also use a notation $Z = Z_1 = Z_2$ for simplicity.

These formulations and that for small secret exponent attacks in Sect. 5.1 are essentially the same when we use the Jochemsz-May strategy. That means the Newton polygons of polynomials $f_{PP.PKE.i}(x, y, z_1, z_2)$ and $f_{PP.PKE.i}(x, y, z_1, z_2)$ are the same, e.g., there are six monomials for variables $1, x, yz_1^{r-1}, yz_1^r, yz_1^{r-1}z_2$, and y. Hence, we use almost the same algorithm construction. We set an (possibly large) integer W such that $W < N^{\alpha + \beta}$ since $\|f_{PP.PKE.i}(xX, yY, z_1Z_1, z_2Z_2)\|_\infty \ge \max\{|1 - e\tilde{d}|, |eMX|\} \approx N^{\alpha + \beta}$. Next, we set an integer $R := W(XY)^{m-1} \cdot Z^{r(m-1-a+t)}$ with some integers $m = \omega(r)$ and $t = \tau m$ where $\tau \ge 0$ such that $\gcd(R, 1 - e\tilde{d}) = 1$. We compute $c = (1 - e\tilde{d})^{-1}$ mod R and $f'_{PP.PKE.i}(x, y, z_1, z_2) := c \cdot f_{PP.PKE.i}(x, y, z_1, z_2)$ mod R. We define shift-polynomials $g_{PP.PKE.i}$ and $g'_{PP.PKE.i}$ as

$$g_{PP.PKE.i} : x^{i_X} y^{i_Y} z_1^{i_{Z_1}} z_2^{i_{Z_2}} \cdot f'_{PP.PKE.i} \cdot X^{m-1-i_X} Y^{m-1-i_Y} Z^{r(m-1-a+t)-i_{Z_1}-i_{Z_2}}$$

$$\text{for } x^{i_X} y^{i_Y} z_1^{i_{Z_1}} z_2^{i_{Z_2}} \in S,$$

$$g'_{PP.PKE.i} : x^{i_X} y^{i_Y} z_1^{i_{Z_1}} z_2^{i_{Z_2}} \cdot R \quad \text{for } x^{i_X} y^{i_Y} z_1^{i_{Z_1}} z_2^{i_{Z_2}} \in M \backslash S,$$

for sets of monomials S and M that are the same as in Sect. 5.1 where $f_{PP.SSE.i}$ is replaced by $f_{PP.PKE.i}$. All these shift-polynomials $g_{PP.PKE.i}$ and $g'_{PP.PKE.i}$ modulo R have the roots $(x, y, z_1, z_2) = (-(d - \tilde{d}), \ell, -p, -q)$ that are the same as $f_{PP.PKE.i}(x, y, z_1, z_2)$. Hence, based on the Jochemsz-May strategy [JM06], LLL outputs short lattice vectors that satisfy Lemma 1 when the inequality (2) holds. For partial key exposure attacks (regardless of the MSBs or the LSBs are exposed), the inequality leads to

$$0 < -r(r+1)^2(\alpha + \beta) + r(r+1)(1 - \delta)((r+1) + 3r\tau) + r(r+1)^2$$

$$-1 - 3r\eta(1 + r\eta) - r^3(1 - \eta + \tau)^3 + r^2(\eta - \tau)^3.$$

To maximize the right hand side of the inequality, we set parameters $\eta = \frac{r(r+1)(1-\delta)-1}{2r}$ and $\tau = \eta - \frac{r - \sqrt{-r+(r+1)^2(1-\delta)}}{r+1}$ that results in the first condition of Theorem 6. To satisfy the restriction $\eta \geq \tau$, the condition $\delta \geq \frac{1}{r+1}$ should hold. The condition results in $\alpha + \beta \leq \frac{3r^3 + r^2 + 5r - 1}{4r(r+1)}$. Notice that other restrictions $\tau \geq 0$ and $\eta \geq 0$ always hold.

For smaller $\alpha + \beta$, we use the other lattice construction that fully generalizes Ernst et al. However, the construction is essentially the same as previous one as we noted in the proof of Theorem 5. Indeed, we use the same shift-polynomials $g_{PP.PKE.i}$ and $g'_{PP.PKE.i}$ with the same sets of monomials S and M. The only difference is a restriction of parameters $\eta \leq \tau$. Hence, by definition, it follows that

$$
\begin{aligned}
x^{i_X} y^{i_Y} z_1^{i_{Z_1}} z_2^{i_{Z_2}} \in S \Leftrightarrow{}& i_X = 0, 1, \ldots, m - a + t - 1; \\
& i_Y = a - t, a - t + 1, \ldots, m - 1 - i_X; \\
& i_{Z_1} = 0, 1, \ldots, r(i_Y - a + t); i_{Z_2} = 0, \text{ and} \\
& i_X = 0, 1, \ldots, m - 1; i_Y = 0, 1, \ldots, m - 1 - i_X; \\
& i_{Z_1} = \max\{0, r - i_Y + r(i_{Z_2} - 1 - a)\}, \ldots, r - 1; \\
& i_{Z_2} = a + 1, a + 2, \ldots, a + \lceil (i_Y + 1)/r \rceil, \text{ and} \\
& i_X = 0, 1, \ldots, m - 1; i_Y = 0, 1, \ldots, m - 1 - i_X; \\
& i_{Z_1} = 0, 1, \ldots, r - 1; \\
& i_{Z_2} = \max\{0, -i_Y + a - t\}, \ldots, a, \\
x^{i_X} y^{i_Y} z_1^{i_{Z_1}} z_2^{i_{Z_2}} \in M \Leftrightarrow{}& i_X = 0, 1, \ldots, m - a + t; \\
& i_Y = a - t, a - t + 1, \ldots, m - i_X; \\
& i_{Z_1} = 0, 1, \ldots, r(i_Y - a + t); i_{Z_2} = 0, \\
& i_X = 0, 1, \ldots, m; i_Y = 0, 1, \ldots, m - i_X; \\
& i_{Z_1} = \max\{0, r - i_Y + r(i_{Z_2} - 1 - a)\}, \ldots, r - 1; \\
& i_{Z_2} = a + 1, a + 2, \ldots, a + \lceil (i_Y + 1)/r \rceil, \text{ and} \\
& i_X = 0, 1, \ldots, m; i_Y = 0, 1, \ldots, m - i_X; \\
& i_{Z_1} = 0, 1, \ldots, r - 1; \\
& i_{Z_2} = \max\{0, -i_Y + a - t\}, \ldots, a.
\end{aligned}
$$

All these shift-polynomials $g_{PP.PKE.i}$ and $g'_{PP.PKE.i}$ modulo R have the roots $(x, y, z_1, z_2) = (-d, \ell, -p, -q)$ that are the same as $f_{PP.PKE.i}(x, y, z_1, z_2)$. We replace each occurrence of $z_1^r z_2$ by N and construct a lattice with coefficients of $g_{PP.PKE.i}(xX, yY, z_1 Z_1, z_2 Z_2)$ and $g'_{PP.SSE.i}(xX, yY, z_1 Z_1, z_2 Z_2)$ as the bases. The shift-polynomials generate a triangular basis matrix.

Ignoring low order terms of m, based on the Jochemsz-May strategy [JM06], LLL outputs short vectors that satisfy Lemma 1 when

$$X^{\left(\frac{r+1}{6}+\frac{r}{2}\tau\right)m^3}Y^{\left(\frac{r+1}{3}+\frac{r}{2}\tau\right)m^3}Z_1^{\left(\frac{r^2(1+\tau-\eta)^3}{6}-\frac{r^2(\tau-\eta)^3}{6}\right)m^3}Z_2^{\left(\frac{1}{6r}+\frac{1}{2}\eta+\frac{r}{2}\eta^2\right)m^3}$$

$$< W^{\left(\frac{r+1}{6}+\frac{r}{2}\tau\right)m^3}$$

that leads to

$$0 < -(r+1)^2(\alpha+\beta) + (2(r+1)^2 + 3r(r+1)\tau) - \delta((r+1)^2 + 3r(r+1)\tau)$$
$$- r^2(1+\tau-\eta)^3 + r^2(\tau-\eta)^3 - \frac{1}{r} - 3\eta - 3r\eta^2.$$

To maximize the right hand side of the inequality, we set parameters $\eta = \frac{r(r+1)(1-\delta)-1}{2r}$ and $\tau = \eta + \frac{(r+1)(1-\delta)-r}{2r}$ and the condition becomes

$$\delta < 1 - \frac{r + \sqrt{12r^2(r+1)(\alpha+\beta) - r(9r^2+14r-3)}}{3r(r+1)}$$

as required. To satisfy the restriction $\eta \leq \tau$, the condition $\delta \leq \frac{1}{r+1}$ should hold. The condition results in $\frac{3r^3+r^2+5r-1}{4r(r+1)} \leq \alpha + \beta$. Notice that other restrictions $\tau \geq 0$ and $\eta \geq 0$ always hold. $\square$

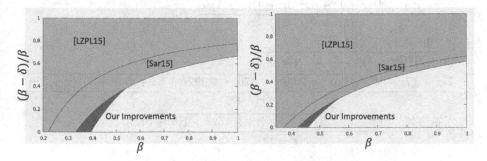

Fig. 3. Comparisons of partial key exposure attacks on the prime power RSA when the MSBs are exposed for $\alpha = 1$. We compare how much portions of d should be exposed for β between the attack of Lu et al. [LZPL15], Sarkar [Sar15], and our Theorem 6. The left figure is for $r = 2$ and the right figure is for $r = 3$.

When the MSBs are exposed, our attack is better than that of Sarkar when $\alpha+\beta$ is small and is better than that of Lu et al. when r is small. Figure 3 compare Theorem 6 and those of Lu et al. and Sarkar for $r = 2$ and 3. Our attack is the better for small β, e.g., our attack works with less partial information.

In Sect. 6.2, we propose an improved attack with the LSBs. However, it seems that our Theorem 6 with the exposed MSBs also has room for improvements.

As opposed to the Takagi RSA, and as the standard RSA, we can compute the MSBs of ℓ since we know the MSBs of $p^{r-1}(p-1)(q-1)$. Indeed, the result of Sarkar makes use of the fact and generalize the other attack of Ernst et al. In addition, there exists better attacks by Takayasu and Kunihiro for small β. To generalize the attack to the prime power RSA remains as a future work.

6   Attacks on the Prime Power RSA by Solving Modular Equations

In this section, we analyze the security of prime power RSA by solving modular equations. In Sect. 6.1, we propose a small secret exponent attack that (almost) fully generalizes the stronger Boneh-Durfee result [BD00]. In Sect. 6.2, we propose a partial key exposure attack that (almost) fully generalizes Takayasu and Kunihiro's result [TK14].

6.1   Small Secret Exponent Attack

In this section, we propose small secret exponent attacks on the prime power RSA that satisfy the following property.

Theorem 7. *Let $N = p^r q$ be a public modulus and let $e \approx N^\alpha$ and $d \approx N^\beta$ be public exponent and secret exponent of prime power RSA, respectively. If*

$$\beta < 1 - \frac{-r + \sqrt{4r(r+1) + 4r^2(3r+4)(r+1)^2\alpha}}{r(3r+4)(r+1)} \ for$$

$$\alpha \geq \frac{9(r+1)^2}{(r+2)^2(3r+4)} - \frac{1}{r(r+1)(3r+4)}, \ or$$

$$\beta < \frac{7r^2 + 17r + 9 - \sqrt{36r^4 + 204r^3 + 376r^2 + 292r + 84 + 4r(r+1)^2(r+3)\alpha}}{r(r+1)}$$

$$for \ \alpha > \frac{-4r^2 - 8r - 3 + 2\sqrt{(r+1)(4r^3 + 15r^2 + 10r + 3)}}{r(r+1)}$$

holds, then prime power RSA modulus N can be factorized in polynomial time.

The result (almost) fully generalizes the stronger Boneh-Durfee [BD00] in the sense that it is better than the weaker Boneh-Durfee and weaker than the stronger Boneh-Durfee for $r = 1$, i.e., $\beta < (15 - 2\sqrt{30})/14 = 0.28896\cdots$. Since the results of Theorem 7 are better than those of Theorem 5, they are outperforming the Jochemsz-May.

Proof of Theorem 7. Looking at a key generation for the prime power RSA; $ed = 1 + \ell p^{r-1}(p-1)(q-1)$ with some integer $|\ell| \approx N^{\alpha+\beta-1}$. To recover the secret exponent d, we use the following polynomial

$$f_{PP.SSE.m}(x, y_1, y_2) = 1 + xy_1^{r-1}(y_1 - 1)(y_2 - 1).$$

The polynomial modulo e has roots $(x, y_1, y_2) = (\ell, p, q)$. The absolute values are bounded by $X := N^{\alpha+\beta-1}, Y_1 = Y_2 := 2N^{1/(r+1)}$. Let $m = \omega(r)$ and $a = \eta m$ be integers. To solve a modular equation $f_{PP.SSE.m}(x, y_1, y_2) = 0 \mod e$, we use shift-polynomials

$$g_{PP.SSE.m}(x, y_1, y_2) = x^{i_X} y_1^{i_{Y_1}} y_2^{a+i_{Y_2}} f_{PP.SSE.m}^u(x, y_1, y_2) e^{m-u}$$

with indices in

$$\mathcal{I}_{x1} \Leftrightarrow u = 0, 1, \ldots, m; i_X = 0, 1, \ldots, m - u; i_{Y_1} = 0, 1, \ldots, r - 1; i_{Y_2} = 0,$$
$$\mathcal{I}_{x2} \Leftrightarrow u = 0, 1, \ldots, m; i_X = 0, 1, \ldots, m - u; i_{Y_1} = r - 1; i_{Y_2} = 1,$$
$$\mathcal{I}_y \Leftrightarrow u = 0, 1, \ldots, m; i_X = 0; i_{Y_1} = 1, 2, \ldots, \lfloor (1 - (r+1)\beta)u \rfloor + ra; i_{Y_2} = 0.$$

All these shift-polynomials $g_{PP.SSE.m}$ modulo e^m have the roots $(x, y_1, y_2) = (\ell, -p, -q)$ that are the same as $f_{PP.sse.m}(x, y_1, y_2)$. We replace each occurrence of $y_1^r y_2$ by N and construct a lattice with coefficients of $g_{PP.SSE.m}(xX, y_1Y_1, y_2Y_2)$ as the bases.

As in the proof of Theorem 5, the shift-polynomials $g_{PP.SSE.m}$ with indices in $\mathcal{I}_{x1}$ for $i_{Y_1} = 0, 1, \ldots, r - 1$ and $\mathcal{I}_{x2}$ play the same role as x-shifts of the stronger Boneh-Durfee by a factor of $(r + 1)$. Although $g_{PP.SSE.m}$ with indices in $\mathcal{I}_y$ plays the same role as y-shifts of the stronger Boneh-Durfee by a factor of r since i_{Y_1} is upper bounded by $\lfloor (1 - (r+1)\beta)u \rfloor + ra$ that depends on u. However, there are no additional y-shifts which play the same role as the stronger Boneh-Durfee. Notice that all polynomials are multiplied by y_2^a and the operation plays the same role as the y-shifts of the weaker Boneh-Durfee. Hence, our Theorem 7 (almost) fully generalizes the stronger Boneh-Durfee and is always better than Theorem 5. We do not know how to fully generalize the stronger Boneh-Durfee and we think there may be room for improvements.

Assume that $\lfloor (1 - (r + 1)\beta)u \rfloor + ra \geq 0$, e.g., $\eta \geq ((r+1)\beta - 1)/r$, and the shift-polynomials generate triangular basis matrix with diagonals

$- X^{u+i_X} Y_1^{\max\{0, r(u-a)+i_{Y_1}\}} Y_2^{\max\{a - \lfloor u+i_{Y_1}/r \rfloor, 0\}} e^{m-u}$ for indices in $\mathcal{I}_{x1}$,
$- X^{u+i_X} Y_2^{a+\lceil (u+1)/r \rceil} e^{m-u}$ for indices in $\mathcal{I}_{x2}$,
$- X^u Y_1^{ru+i_{Y_1}} e^{m-u}$ for indices in $\mathcal{I}_y$.

In $\mathcal{I}_y$, i_{Y_1} is upper bounded by $\lfloor (1 - (r + 1)\beta)u \rfloor + ra$. The definition follows from the fact that the shift-polynomials reduce norms of outputs by the LLL algorithm, e.g., the diagonals for the shift-polynomials are smaller than e^m.

Ignoring low order terms of m, the LLL algorithm outputs short lattice vectors that satisfy Lemma 1 when $(\det(L))^{1/n} < e^m$ that leads to

$$0 < -r(r + 1)^2\alpha - 1 - 3r\eta(1 + r\eta)$$
$$+ r(r + 1)(2 + 3r\eta)(1 - \delta) + r(r + 1)^2(1 - \delta)^2.$$

To maximize the right hand side of the inequality, we set the parameter $\eta = \frac{r(r+1)(1-\beta)-1}{2r}$ and the condition becomes

$$\beta < 1 - \frac{-r + \sqrt{4r(r + 1) + 4r^2(3r + 4)(r + 1)^2\alpha}}{r(3r + 4)(r + 1)}$$

as required. To satisfy the restriction $\eta \geq ((r+1)\beta - 1)/r$, the condition $\beta < \frac{r(r+1)+1}{(r+2)(r+1)}$ should hold. The condition results in $\frac{9(r+1)^2}{(r+2)^2(3r+4)} - \frac{1}{r(r+1)(3r+4)} \leq \alpha$.

For smaller α, we propose an alternative lattice construction. We use the same shift-polynomials $g_{PP.SSE.m}(x, y_1, y_2)$ with indices in

$$\mathcal{I}_{x1} \Leftrightarrow u = 0, 1, \ldots, m; i_X = 0, 1, \ldots, m - u; i_{Y_1} = 0, 1, \ldots, r - 1; i_{Y_2} = 0,$$
$$\mathcal{I}_{x2} \Leftrightarrow u = 0, 1, \ldots, m; i_X = 0, 1, \ldots, m - u; i_{Y_1} = r - 1; i_{Y_2} = 1,$$
$$\mathcal{I}_y' \Leftrightarrow u = 0, 1, \ldots, m; i_X = 0; i_{Y_1} = 1, 2, \ldots, \lfloor r(a - \eta u) \rfloor; i_{Y_2} = 0.$$

We replace each occurrence of $y_1^r y_2$ by N and construct a lattice with coefficients of $g_{PP.SSE.m}(xX, y_1Y_1, y_2Y_2)$ as the bases. Assume $0 \leq \eta$ and the shift-polynomials generate a triangular basis matrix with the same diagonals as previous ones.

As previous cases, we should define $\mathcal{I}_y'$ such that the shift-polynomials reduce norms of outputs by the LLL algorithm, e.g., the diagonals for the shift-polynomials are smaller than e^m. However, that is not the case and the definition is a suboptimal. Therefore, we think there may be room for improvements.

Ignoring low order terms of m, the LLL algorithm outputs short vectors that satisfy Lemma 1 when $(\det(L))^{1/n} < e^m$ that leads to

$$0 < -r(r+1)^2\alpha + r(1-\beta)\left(2(r+1)^2 + r(r+1)\eta\right) - r^3(1-\eta)^2 - 1 - 3r\eta(1+r\eta).$$

To maximize the right hand side of the inequality, we set the parameter $\eta = \frac{r(r+1)(1-\beta)+2r^2-3}{2r^2+6r}$ and the condition becomes

$$\beta < \frac{7r^2 + 17r + 9 - \sqrt{36r^4 + 204r^3 + 376r^2 + 292r + 84 + 4r(r+1)^2(r+3)\alpha}}{r(r+1)}$$

as required. To satisfy $\alpha + \beta > 1$, the condition $\alpha > \frac{-4r^2 - 8r - 3 + 2\sqrt{(r+1)(4r^3 + 15r^2 + 10r + 3)}}{r(r+1)}$ should hold. The restriction $\eta \geq 0$ always holds.   □

Since Theorem 7 works when $\alpha > \frac{-4r^2 - 8r - 3 + 2\sqrt{(r+1)(4r^3 + 15r^2 + 10r + 3)}}{r(r+1)}$, it works for smaller α than Theorem 5. Indeed, Theorem 7 is (although slightly) always better than Theorem 5. Figure 4 compare Theorem 7 and Lu et al. for $r = 2$ and 3. Theorem 7 is the better for all α and the differences become larger for smaller α. Moreover, Table 1 compare Lu et al., Theorems 5 and 7 for $r = 5$ and 6. When $\alpha = 1$, Lu et al. is the best. However, our attack becomes the better for smaller α.

6.2   Partial Key Exposure Attack

In this section, we propose small secret exponent attacks on the prime power RSA that satisfy the following property.

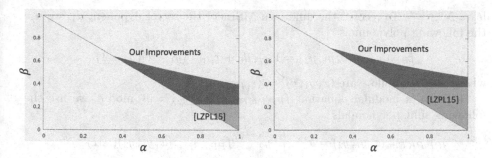

Fig. 4. Comparisons of small secret exponent attacks on the prime power RSA. We compare recoverable values β for α between the attack of Lu et al. [LZPL15] and our Theorem 7. The left figure is for $r = 2$ and the right figure is for $r = 3$.

Table 1. Comparisons of small secret exponent attacks on the prime power RSA. We compare recoverable values β for α between the attack of Lu et al. [LZPL15], our Theorem 5, and Theorem 7. The left table is for $r = 5$ and the right table is for $r = 6$.

α	[LZPL15]	Theorem 5	Theorem 7
1	0.5555	0.5442	0.5495
0.9	0.5555	0.5670	0.5730
0.8	0.5555	0.5911	0.5979
0.7	0.5555	0.6167	0.6244
0.6	0.5555	0.6442	0.6528
0.5	0.5555	0.6741	0.6837
0.4	–	0.7073	0.7179
0.3	–	0.7452	0.7561

α	[LZPL15]	Theorem 5	Theorem 7
1	0.6122	0.5738	0.5798
0.9	0.6122	0.5950	0.6017
0.8	0.6122	0.6174	0.6248
0.7	0.6122	0.6412	0.6494
0.6	0.6122	0.6668	0.6759
0.5	0.6122	0.6946	0.7046
0.4	0.6122	0.7254	0.7364
0.3	–	0.7607	0.7724
0.2	–	0.8036	0.8106

Theorem 8. *Let $N = p^r q$ be a public modulus and let $e \approx N^\alpha$ and $d \approx N^\beta$ be public exponent and secret exponent of prime power RSA, respectively. When $(\beta - \delta) \log N$ bits of the least significant bits are exposed, if*

$$\delta < 1 - \frac{r(2r+1) + 2\sqrt{r(r+1)(r(r+1)(3r+4)(\alpha+\beta) - 3r^3 - 6r^2 - 4r + 1)}}{r(r+1)(3r+4)}$$

$$for \quad \frac{30r^3 + 51r^2 + 25r - 4}{4r(r+1)(3r+4)} \le \alpha + \beta$$

holds, then prime power RSA modulus N can be factorized in polynomial time.

As Theorem 7, the result (only almost) fully generalizes Takayasu and Kunihiro's attack. However, the result is better than Theorem 6 with the exposed LSBs.

Proof of Theorem 8. Looking at a key generation for prime power RSA with the exposed LSBs; $e(d_1 M + d_0) = 1 + \ell p^{r-1}(p-1)(q-1)$ with some integer

$|\ell| \approx N^{\alpha+\beta-1}$. To recover the unknown MSBs of the secret exponent d_1, we use the following polynomials

$$f_{PP.PKE.m}(x, y_1, y_2) = 1 - ed_0 + xy_1^{r-1}(y_1 - 1)(y_2 - 1)$$

whose roots modulo e are $(x, y_1, y_2) = (\ell, p, q)$.

To solve a modular equation $f_{PP.PKE.m}(x, y_1, y_2) = 0 \mod e$, we use the following shift-polynomials

$$g_{PP.PKE.m}(x, y_1, y_2) = x^{i_X} y_1^{i_{Y_1}} y_2^{a+i_{Y_2}} f_{PP.SSE.m}^u(x, y_1, y_2)(eM)^{m-u}$$

with indices in

$$\mathcal{I}_{x1} \Leftrightarrow u = 0, 1, \ldots, m; i_X = 0, 1, \ldots, m - u; i_{Y_1} = 0, 1, \ldots, r - 1; i_{Y_2} = 0,$$
$$\mathcal{I}_{x2} \Leftrightarrow u = 0, 1, \ldots, m; i_X = 0, 1, \ldots, m - u; i_{Y_1} = r - 1; i_{Y_2} = 1,$$
$$\mathcal{I}_y \Leftrightarrow u = 0, 1, \ldots, m; i_X = 0; i_{Y_1} = 1, 2, \ldots, \lfloor((r+1)(1-\delta) - 1)u\rfloor + ra; i_{Y_2} = 0.$$

All these shift-polynomials modulo $(eM)^m$ have roots $(x, y_1, y_2) = (\ell, p, q)$ that are the same as $g_{PP.PKE.m}$. We replace each occurrence of $y_1^r y_2$ by N and construct a lattice with coefficients of $g_{PP.PKE.m}(xX, y_1Y_1, y_2Y_2)$ as the bases. The shift-polynomials generate a triangular basis matrix with diagonals

- $X^{u+i_X} Y_1^{\max\{0, r(u-a)+i_{Y_1}\}} Y_2^{\max\{a-\lfloor u+i_{Y_1}/r\rfloor, 0\}} (eM)^{m-u}$ with indices in $\mathcal{I}_{x1}$,
- $X^{u+i_X} Y_2^{a+\lceil(u+1)/r\rceil} (eM)^{m-u}$ with indices in $\mathcal{I}_{x2}$,
- $X^u Y_1^{ru+i_{Y_1}} (eM)^{m-u}$ with indices in $\mathcal{I}_y$.

In $\mathcal{I}_y$, i_{Y_1} is upper bounded by $\lfloor((r + 1)(1 - \delta) - 1)u\rfloor + ra$. The definition follows from the fact that the shift-polynomials reduce norms of outputs by the LLL algorithm, e.g., the diagonals for the shift-polynomials are smaller than the modulus $(eM)^m$.

Ignoring low order terms of m, the LLL algorithm outputs short vectors that satisfy Lemma 1 when $(\det(L))^{1/n} < (eM)^m$ that leads to

$$0 < -r(r+1)^2(\alpha + \beta - 1) - 1 - 3r\eta(1 + r\eta)$$
$$- r(r+1)(r - 1 - 3r\eta)(1 - \delta) + r(r+1)^2(1 - \delta)^2.$$

To maximize the right hand side of the inequality, we set the parameter $\eta = \frac{r(r+1)(1-\delta)-1}{2r}$ and the condition becomes

$$\delta < 1 - \frac{r(2r+1) + 2\sqrt{r(r+1)(r(r+1)(3r+4)(\alpha+\beta) - 3r^3 - 6r^2 - 4r + 1)}}{r(r+1)(3r+4)}$$

as required. To satisfy the restriction $\eta \geq 0$, $\delta \leq 1 - \frac{1}{r(r+1)}$ should hold. The condition results in $\frac{30r^3+51r^2+25r-4}{4r(r+1)(3r+4)} \leq \alpha + \beta$.   □

When the LSBs are exposed, our attack is better than that of Lu et al. when r is small. Figure 5 compare Theorem 8 and Lu et al. for $r = 2$ and 3. Our attack is the better for all β, e.g., our attack works with less partial information.

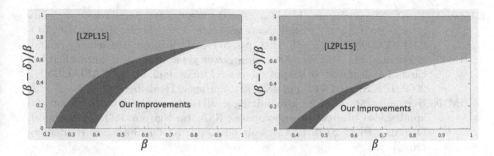

Fig. 5. Comparisons of partial key exposure attacks on the prime power RSA for $\alpha = 1$ when the least significant bits are exposed. We compare how much portions of d should be exposed for β between the attack of Lu et al. [LZPL15] and our Theorem 8. The left figure is for $r = 2$ and the right figure is for $r = 3$.

Acknowledgement. We would like to thank Shuichi Katsumata for their helpful comments. The first author is supported by a JSPS Fellowship for Young Scientists. This research was supported by CREST, JST and supported by JSPS KAKENHI Grant Number 25280001 and 26·8237.

References

[BD00] Boneh, D., Durfee, G.: Cryptanalysis of RSA with private key d less than $N^{0.292}$. IEEE Trans. Inf. Theory **46**(4), 1339–1349 (2000). (Proceedings of Eurocrypt 1999, LNCS, vol. 1592, pp. 1–11. Springer, Heidelberg (1999))

[BDH99] Boneh, D., Durfee, G., Howgrave-Graham, N.: Factoring tex2html_wrap_inline127 for Large r. In: Wiener, M. (ed.) CRYPTO 1999. LNCS, vol. 1666, pp. 326–337. Springer, Heidelberg (1999)

[BM03] Blömer, J., May, A.: New partial key exposure attacks on RSA. In: Boneh, D. (ed.) CRYPTO 2003. LNCS, vol. 2729, pp. 27–43. Springer, Heidelberg (2003)

[Cop96a] Coppersmith, D.: Finding a small root of a univariate modular equation. In: Maurer, U.M. (ed.) EUROCRYPT 1996. LNCS, vol. 1070, pp. 155–165. Springer, Heidelberg (1996)

[Cop96b] Coppersmith, D.: Finding a small root of a bivariate integer equation; factoring with high bits known. In: Maurer, U.M. (ed.) EUROCRYPT 1996. LNCS, vol. 1070, pp. 178–189. Springer, Heidelberg (1996)

[Cop97] Coppersmith, D.: Small solutions to polynomial equations, and low exponent RSA vulnerabilities. J. Cryptol. **10**(4), 233–260 (1997)

[Cop01] Coppersmith, D.: Finding small solutions to small degree polynomials. In: Silverman, J.H. (ed.) CaLC 2001. LNCS, vol. 2146, pp. 20–31. Springer, Heidelberg (2001)

[Cor04] Coron, J.-S.: Finding small roots of bivariate integer polynomial equations revisited. In: Cachin, C., Camenisch, J.L. (eds.) EUROCRYPT 2004. LNCS, vol. 3027, pp. 492–505. Springer, Heidelberg (2004)

[Cor07] Coron, J.-S.: Finding small roots of bivariate integer polynomial equations: a direct approach. In: Menezes, A. (ed.) CRYPTO 2007. LNCS, vol. 4622, pp. 379–394. Springer, Heidelberg (2007)

[EJMW05] Ernst, M., Jochemsz, E., May, A., de Weger, B.: Partial key exposure attacks on RSA up to full size exponents. In: Cramer, R. (ed.) EURO-CRYPT 2005. LNCS, vol. 3494, pp. 371–386. Springer, Heidelberg (2005)

[HM09] Herrmann, M., May, A.: Attacking power generators using unravelled linearization: when do we output too much? In: Matsui, M. (ed.) ASIACRYPT 2009. LNCS, vol. 5912, pp. 487–504. Springer, Heidelberg (2009)

[HM10] Herrmann, M., May, A.: Maximizing small root bounds by linearization and applications to small secret exponent RSA. In: Nguyen, P.Q., Pointcheval, D. (eds.) PKC 2010. LNCS, vol. 6056, pp. 53–69. Springer, Heidelberg (2010)

[How97] Howgrave-Graham, N.: Finding small roots of univariate modular equations. In: Michael, D. (ed.) Cryptography and Coding 1997. LNCS, vol. 1355, pp. 131–142. Springer, Heidelberg (1997)

[HHX+14] Huang, Z., Hu, L., Xu, J., Peng, L., Xie, Y.: Partial key exposure attacks on Takagi's variant of RSA. In: Boureanu, I., Owesarski, P., Vaudenay, S. (eds.) ACNS 2014. LNCS, vol. 8479, pp. 134–150. Springer, Heidelberg (2014)

[IKK08] Itoh, K., Kunihiro, N., Kurosawa, K.: Small secret key attack on a variant of RSA (due to Takagi). In: Malkin, T. (ed.) CT-RSA 2008. LNCS, vol. 4964, pp. 387–406. Springer, Heidelberg (2008)

[JM06] Jochemsz, E., May, A.: A strategy for finding roots of multivariate polynomials with new applications in attacking RSA variants. In: Lai, X., Chen, K. (eds.) ASIACRYPT 2006. LNCS, vol. 4284, pp. 267–282. Springer, Heidelberg (2006)

[Len87] Lenstra, H.W.: Factoring integers with elliptic curves. Ann. Math. **126**, 649–673 (1987)

[LLL82] Lenstra, A.K., Lenstra, H.W., Lovasz, L.: Factoring polynomials with rational coefficients. Math. Ann. **261**, 515–534 (1982)

[LZPL15] Lu, Y., Zhang, R., Peng, L., Lin, D.: Solving linear equations modulo unknown divisors: revisited. In: Iwata, T., Cheon, J.H. (eds.) ASIACRYPT 2015. LNCS, vol. 9452, pp. 189–213. Springer, Heidelberg (2015)

[May03] May, A.: New RSA vulnerabilities using lattice reduction methods. Ph.D thesis, University of Paderborn (2003)

[May04] May, A.: Secret exponent attacks on RSA-type schemes with moduli $N = p^r q$. In: Bao, F., Deng, R., Zhou, J. (eds.) PKC 2004. LNCS, vol. 2947, pp. 218–230. Springer, Heidelberg (2004)

[May10] May, A.: Using LLL-reduction for solving RSA and factorization problems: a survey (2010). http://www.cits.rub.de/permonen/may.html

[NS01] Nguyên, P.Q., Stern, J.: The two faces of lattices in cryptology. In: Silverman, J.H. (ed.) CaLC 2001. LNCS, vol. 2146, pp. 146–180. Springer, Heidelberg (2001)

[RSA78] Rivest, R.L., Shamir, A., Adleman, L.M.: A method for obtaining digital signatures and public-key cryptosystems. Commun. ACM **21**(2), 120–126 (1978)

[Sar14] Sarkar, S.: Small secret exponent attack on RSA variant with modulus $N = p^r q$. Des. Codes Cryptogr. **73**(2), 383–392 (2014)

[Sar15] Sarkar, S.: Revisiting prime power RSA. Available from IACR Cryptology ePrint Archive, Report 2015/774 (2015)

[SGM10] Sarkar, S., Sen Gupta, S., Maitra, S.: Partial key exposure attack on RSA –
         improvements for limited lattice dimensions. In: Gong, G., Gupta, K.C.
         (eds.) INDOCRYPT 2010. LNCS, vol. 6498, pp. 2–16. Springer, Heidelberg
         (2010)

[Tak98] Takagi, T.: Fast RSA-type cryptosystem modulo $p^k q$. In: Krawczyk, H.
         (ed.) CRYPTO 1998. LNCS, vol. 1462, pp. 318–326. Springer, Heidelberg
         (1998)

[TK14]   Takayasu, A., Kunihiro, N.: Partial key exposure attacks on RSA: achieving
         the Boneh-Durfee bound. In: Joux, A., Youssef, A. (eds.) SAC 2014. LNCS,
         vol. 8781, pp. 345–362. Springer, Heidelberg (2014)

[Wie90] Wiener, M.J.: Cryptanalysis of short RSA secret exponents. IEEE Trans.
         Inf. Theor. **36**(3), 553–558 (1990)

Leakage-Resilient and Circularly Secure Encryption

Leakage-Resilient Public-Key Encryption from Obfuscation

Dana Dachman-Soled[1]([✉]), S. Dov Gordon[2], Feng-Hao Liu[3], Adam O'Neill[4], and Hong-Sheng Zhou[5]

[1] University of Maryland, College Park, USA
danadach@ece.umd.edu
[2] George Mason University, Fairfax, USA
crypto@dovgordon.com
[3] Florida Atlantic University, Boca Raton, USA
fenghao.liu@fau.edu
[4] Georgetown University, Washington, D.C., USA
adam@cs.georgetown.edu
[5] Virginia Commonwealth University, Richmond, USA
hszhou@vcu.edu

Abstract. The literature on leakage-resilient cryptography contains various leakage models that provide different levels of security. In this work, we consider the *bounded leakage* and the *continual leakage* models. In the bounded leakage model (Akavia et al. – TCC 2009), it is assumed that there is a fixed upper bound L on the number of bits the attacker may leak on the secret key in the entire lifetime of the scheme. Alternatively, in the continual leakage model (Brakerski et al. – FOCS 2010, Dodis et al. – FOCS 2010), the lifetime of a cryptographic scheme is divided into "time periods" between which the scheme's secret key is updated. Furthermore, in its attack the adversary is allowed to obtain some bounded amount of leakage on the current secret key during each time period.

In the continual leakage model, a challenging problem has been to provide security against *leakage on key updates*, that is, leakage that is a function not only of the current secret key but also the *randomness used to update it*. We propose a new, modular approach to overcome this problem. Namely, we present a compiler that transforms any public-key encryption or signature scheme that achieves a slight strengthening of continual leakage resilience, which we call *consecutive continual leakage resilience*, to one that is continual leakage resilient with leakage on key updates, assuming *indistinguishability obfuscation*

D. Dachman-Soled—This work was done in part while the author was visiting the Simons Institute for the Theory of Computing, supported by the Simons Foundation and by the DIMACS/Simons Collaboration in Cryptography through NSF grant #CNS-1523467.

S. Dov Gordon—This work was done when the author was a research scientist at Applied Communication Sciences.

F.-H. Liu—This work was done when the author was a postdoc at the University of Maryland.

© International Association for Cryptologic Research 2016
C.-M. Cheng et al. (Eds.): PKC 2016, Part II, LNCS 9615, pp. 101–128, 2016.
DOI: 10.1007/978-3-662-49387-8_5

(Barak et al. – CRYPTO 2001, Garg et al. – FOCS 2013). Under the stronger assumption of *public-coin differing-inputs obfuscation* (Ishai et al. – TCC 2015) the leakage rate tolerated by our compiled scheme is essentially as good as that of the starting scheme. Our compiler is obtained by making a new connection between the problems of leakage on key updates and so-called "sender-deniable" encryption (Canetti et al. – CRYPTO 1997). In particular, our compiler adapts and optimizes recent techniques of Sahai and Waters (STOC 2014) that make any encryption scheme sender-deniable. We then show that prior continual leakage resilient schemes can be upgraded to security against consecutive continual leakage without introducing new assumptions.

In the bounded leakage model, we develop an entirely new approach to constructing leakage-resilient encryption from obfuscation directly, based upon the public-key encryption scheme from iO and punctured pseudo-random functions due to Sahai and Waters (STOC 2014). In particular, we achieve (1) leakage-resilient public key encryption tolerating L bits of leakage for any L from iO and one-way functions, (2) leakage-resilient public key encryption with optimal leakage rate of $1 - o(1)$ based on public-coin differing-inputs obfuscation and collision-resistant hash functions.

1   Introduction

1.1   Background and Motivation

In recent years, researchers have uncovered a variety of ways to capture cryptographic keys through *side-channel attacks*: physical measurements, such as break execution time, power consumption, and even sound waves generated by the processor. This has prompted cryptographers to build models for these attacks and to construct *leakage resilient* schemes that remain secure in the face of such attacks. Of course, if the adversary can leak the entire secret key, security becomes impossible, and so the *bounded leakage model* was introduced (cf. [1,4,19,22]). Here, it is assumed that there is a fixed upper bound, L on the number of bits the attacker may leak, regardless of the parameters of the scheme, or, alternatively, it is assumed that the attacker is allowed to leak $L = \lambda \cdot |\text{sk}|$ total number of bits, where the amount of leakage increases as the size of the secret key increases. Various works constructed public key encryption and signature schemes with optimal leakage rate of $\lambda = 1 - o(1)$, from specific assumptions (cf. [4,22]). Hazay et al. [17] constructed a leakage resilient public key encryption scheme in this model, assuming only the existence of some standard public key encryption scheme; the tradeoff is that they tolerate a leakage rate of only $O(\log(\kappa)/|sk|)$, where $|sk|$ is the size of the secret key when using security parameter κ.

Surprisingly, it is possible to do better; an interesting strengthening of the model — the *continual leakage model*[1] — allows the adversary to request

---

[1] Here "continual" refers to the fact that the total amount of leakage obtained by the adversary is unbounded. Additionally, the model is more accurately called the continual *memory* leakage model to contrast with schemes constructed under an assumption that "only computation leaks" [21].

unbounded leakage. This model was introduced by Brakerski et al. [5] and Dodis et al. [11], who constructed continual-leakage resilient (CLR) public-key encryption and signature schemes. Intuitively, the CLR model divides the lifetime of the attack, which may be unbounded, into time periods and: (1) allows the adversary to obtain the output of a "bounded" leakage function in each time period, and (2) allows the secret key (but not the public key!) to be updated between time periods. So, while the adversary's leakage in each round is bounded, the total leakage is unbounded.

Note that the algorithm used by any CLR scheme to update the current secret key to the next one must be *randomized*, since otherwise the adversary can obtain some future secret key, bit-by-bit, via its leakage in each time period. While the CLR schemes of [5,11] were able to tolerate a remarkable $1 - o(1)$ leakage rate (the ratio of the allowed number of bits leaked per time period to the length of the secret key) handling leakage *during the update procedure itself* — that is, produced as a function of the randomness used by the update algorithm as well as the current secret key — proved to be much more challenging. The first substantial progress on this problem of "leakage on key updates" was made by Lewko et al. [20], with their techniques being considerably refined and generalized by Dodis et al. [12]. In particular, they give encryption and signature schemes that are CLR with leakage on key updates tolerating a constant leakage rate, using "dual-system" techniques (cf. [24]) in bilinear groups.

1.2 Overview of Our Results

Our first main contribution is to show how to compile *any* public-key encryption or signature scheme that satisfies a slight strengthening of CLR (which we call "consecutive" CLR or 2CLR) *without* leakage on key updates to one that is CLR *with* leakage on key updates. Our compiler is based on a new connection we make between the problems of leakage on key updates and "sender-deniability" [6] for encryption schemes. In particular, our compiler uses program obfuscation — either indistinguishability obfuscation (iO) [2,14] or the public-coin differing-inputs obfuscation [18][2] — and adapts and extends techniques recently developed by Sahai and Waters [23] to achieve sender-deniable encryption. This demonstrates the applicability of the techniques of [23] to other seemingly unrelated contexts.[3] We then show that the existing CLR encryption scheme of Brakerski et al. [5] can be extended to meet the stronger notion of 2CLR that we require for our compiler. Additionally, we show all our results carry over to signatures as well. In particular, we show that 2CLR PKE implies 2CLR signatures (via the intermediate notion of CLR "one-way relations" of Dodis et al. [11]), and

---

[2] To the best of our knowledge, no impossibility results are known for public-coin differing-inputs obfuscation. Indeed, the impossibility results of Garg et al. [15] do not apply to this setting.

[3] We note that the techniques of [23] have been shown useful in adaptively secure two-party and multiparty computation [7,9,16] and "only computation leaks" (OCL) circuits without trusted hardware [10]. We note that this work precedes the work of [9].

observe that our compiler also upgrades 2CLR signatures to ones that are CLR with leak on updates.

Our second main contributions concerns constructions of leakage-resilient public-key encryption directly from obfuscation. In particular, we show that the approach of Sahai and Waters to achieve public-key encryption from iO and punctured pseudorandom functions [23] can be extended to achieve leakage-resilience in the bounded-leakage model. Specifically, we achieve (1) leakage-resilient public key encryption tolerating L bits of leakage for any L from iO and one-way functions, (2) leakage-resilient public key encryption with optimal leakage rate of $1 - o(1)$ based on public-coin differing-inputs obfuscation and collision-resistant hash functions. Extending these constructions to continual leakage-resilience (without introducing additional assumptions) is an interesting open problem.

In summary, we provide a thorough study of the connection between program obfuscation and leakage resilience. We define a new notion of leakage-resilience (2CLR), and demonstrate new constructions of 2CLR secure encryption and signature schemes from program obfuscation. Also using program obfuscation, we construct a compiler that lifts 2CLR-secure schemes to CLR with leakage on updates; together with our new constructions, this provides a unified and modular method for constructing CLR with leakage on key updates. Under appropriate assumptions (namely, the ones used by Brakerski et al. [5] in their construction), this approach allows us to achieve a leakage rate of $1/4 - o(1)$, a large improvement over prior work, where the best leakage rate was $1/258 - o(1)$ [20]. Our result nearly matches the trivial upper-bound of $1/2 - o(1)$.[4] In the bounded leakage model, we show that it is possible to achieve optimal-rate leakage-resilient public key encryption from obfuscation and generic assumptions. As we have mentioned above, Hazay et al. [17] constructed leakage resilient public key encryption in this model from a far weaker generic assumption, albeit with a far worse leakage rate. In addition to offering a tradeoff between the strength of the assumption and the leakage rate, the value of our result in the bounded leakage model is that it provides direct insight into the connection between program obfuscation and leakage resilience. We are hopeful that our techniques might lead to future improvements in the continual-leakage models.

1.3 Details and Techniques

Part I: The Leak-on-Update Compiler. As described above, in the model of continual leakage-resilience (CLR) [5,11] for public-key encryption or signature schemes, the secret key can be updated periodically (according to some algorithm

---

[4] Unlike the case of CLR without leakage on key updates, observe that any scheme that is CLR with leakage on key updates can leak at most $1/2 \cdot |\mathsf{sk}|$-bits per time period, since otherwise the adversary can recover an entire secret key. As a consequence, the optimal leakage rate for a scheme that is CLR with leakage on key updates is at most $\frac{1/2 \cdot |\mathsf{sk}|}{|\mathsf{sk}| + |r_{up}|} < 1/2$, where $|\mathsf{sk}|$ is the secret key length and $|r_{up}|$ is the length of the randomness needed by the update algorithm.

Update) and the adversary can obtain bounded leakage between any two updates. Our compiler applies to schemes that satisfy a slight strengthening of CLR we call *consecutive* CLR, where the adversary can obtain bounded leakage as a *joint* function of any two consecutive keys. More formally, let $\mathsf{sk}_0, \mathsf{sk}_1, \mathsf{sk}_2, \ldots, \mathsf{sk}_t, \ldots$ be the secret keys at each time period, where $\mathsf{sk}_i = \mathsf{Update}(\mathsf{sk}_{i-1}, r_i)$, and each r_i denotes fresh random coins used at that round. For leakage functions $f_1, \ldots, f_t, \ldots$ (chosen adaptively by the adversary), consider the following two leakage models:

(1) For **consecutive CLR (2CLR)**, the adversary obtains leakage

$$f_1(\mathsf{sk}_0, \mathsf{sk}_1), f_2(\mathsf{sk}_1, \mathsf{sk}_2), \ldots, f_t(\mathsf{sk}_{t-1}, \mathsf{sk}_t), \ldots .$$

(2) For **CLR with leakage on key updates**, the adversary obtains leakage

$$f_1(\mathsf{sk}_0, r_1), f_2(\mathsf{sk}_1, r_2), \ldots, f_t(\mathsf{sk}_{t-1}, r_t), \ldots .$$

Our compiler from 2CLR to CLR with leakage on key updates produces a slightly different Update algorithm for the compiled scheme depending on whether we assume indistinguishability-obfuscation (iO) [2,14] or public-coin differing-inputs obfuscation [18]. In both cases, if we start with an underlying scheme that is consecutive two-key CLR while allowing μ-bits of leakage, then our compiled scheme is CLR with leakage on key updates with leakage rate

$$\frac{\mu}{|\mathsf{sk}| + |r_{up}|},$$

where $|r_{up}|$ is the length of the randomness required by Update. When using iO, we obtain $|r_{up}| = 6|\mathsf{sk}|$, where $|\mathsf{sk}|$ is the secret key length for the underlying 2CLR scheme, whereas using public-coin differing-input obfuscation we obtain $|r_{up}| = |\mathsf{sk}|$. Thus:

- Assuming iO, the compiled scheme is CLR with leakage on key updates with leakage rate $\frac{\mu}{7 \cdot |\mathsf{sk}|}$.
- Assuming public-coin differing-input obfuscation, the compiled scheme is CLR with leakage on key updates with leakage rate $\frac{\mu}{2 \cdot |\mathsf{sk}|}$.

Thus, if the underlying 2CLR scheme tolerates the optimal number of bits of leakage ($\approx 1/2 \cdot |\mathsf{sk}|$), then our resulting public-coin differing-inputs based scheme achieves leakage rate $1/4 - o(1)$.

Our compiler is obtained by adapting and extending the techniques developed by [23] to achieve sender-deniable PKE from any PKE scheme. In sender-deniable PKE, a sender, given a ciphertext and *any* message, is able to produce coins that make it appear that the ciphertext is an encryption of that message. Intuitively, the connection we make to leakage on key updates is that the simulator in the security proof faces a similar predicament to the coerced sender in the case of deniable encryption; it needs to come up with some randomness that "explains" a current secret key as the update of an old one. Our compiler makes any two such keys explainable in a way that is similar to how Sahai and Waters make any ciphertext and message explainable. Intuitively, this is done by "encoding" a secret key in the explained randomness in a special way that can be detected only by the (obfuscated) Update algorithm. Once detected, the Update algorithm outputs the encoded secret key, instead of running the normal procedure.

However, in our context, naïvely applying their techniques would result in the randomness required by our Update algorithm being very long, which, as described above, affects the leakage rate of our resulting CLR scheme with leakage on key updates in a crucial way (we would not even be able to get a constant leakage rate). We decrease the length of this randomness in two steps. First, we note that the sender-deniable encryption scheme of Sahai and Waters encrypts a message bit-by-bit and "explains" each message-bit individually. This appears to be necessary in their context in order to allow the adversary to choose its challenge messages *adaptively* depending on the public key. For our setting, this is not the case, since the secret key is chosen honestly (not by the adversary), so "non-adaptive" security is in fact sufficient in our context and we can "explain" a secret key all at once. This gets us to $|r_{up}| = 6 \cdot |\mathsf{sk}|$ and thus $1/14 - o(1)$ leakage rate assuming the underlying 2CLR scheme can tolerate the optimal leakage. Second, we observe that by switching assumptions from iO to the public-coin differing-inputs obfuscation we can replace some instances of sk in the explained randomness with its value under a collision-resistant hash, which gets us to $|r_{up}| = \mathsf{sk}$ and thus $1/4 - o(1)$ leakage rate in this case.

A natural question is whether the upper bound of $1/2 - o(1)$ leakage rate for CLR with leakage on key updates, can be attained via our techniques (if at all). We leave this as an intriguing open question, but note that the *only* way to do so would be to further decrease $|r_{up}|$ so that $|r_{up}| < |\mathsf{sk}|$.

Part II: Constructions Against Two-Key Consecutive Continual Leakage. We revisit the existing CLR public-key encryption scheme of [5] and show that a suitable modification of it achieves 2CLR[5] with optimal $1/4 - o(1)$ leakage rate[6], under the same assumption used by [5] to achieve optimal leakage rate in the basic CLR setting (namely the symmetric external Diffie-Hellman (SXDH) assumption in bilinear groups; smaller leakage rates can be obtained under weaker assumptions). Our main technical tool here is a new generalization of the Crooked Leftover Hash Lemma [3,13] that generalizes the result of [5], which shows that "random subspaces are leakage resilient," showing that random subspaces are in fact resilient to "consecutive leakage." Our claim also leads to a simpler analysis of the scheme than appears in [5].

Finally, we also show (via techniques from learning theory) that 2CLR public-key encryption generically implies 2CLR one-way relations. Via a transformation of Dodis et al. [11], this then yields 2CLR signatures with the same leakage rate

---

[5] Note that [5] also constructs such a signature scheme, but, as discussed below, such a signature scheme can in fact be generically obtained, and therefore for simplicity we do not consider their direct construction here.

[6] In the 2CLR model, the maximum amount of leakage is roughly $1/2 \cdot |\mathsf{sk}|$, so the optimal rate is roughly $\frac{1/2 \cdot |\mathsf{sk}|}{|\mathsf{sk}| + |\mathsf{sk}|} = 1/4$.

as the starting encryption scheme. Therefore, all the above results translate to the signature setting as well. We also show a direct approach to constructing 2CLR one-way relations following [11] based on the SXDH assumption in bilinear groups, although we are not able to achieve as good of a leakage rate this way (only $1/8 - o(1)$).

Part III: Exploring the Relationship Between Bounded Leakage Resilience and Obfuscation. Note that, interestingly, even the strong notion of VBB obfuscation does not immediately lead to constructions of leakage resilient public-key encryption. In particular, if we replace the secret key of a public key encryption scheme with a VBB obfuscation of the decryption algorithm, it is not clear that we gain anything: E.g., the VBB obfuscation may output a circuit of size $|C|$, where only $\sqrt{|C|}$ number of the gates are "meaningful" and the remaining gates are simply "dummy" gates, in which case we cannot hope to get a leakage bound better than $L = \sqrt{|C|}$, and a leakage rate of $1/\sqrt{|C|}$. Nevertheless, we are able to show that the PKE scheme of Sahai and Waters (SW) [23], which is built from iO and "punctured pseudorandom functions (PRFs)," can naturally be made leakage resilient. To give some brief intuition, a ciphertext in our construction is of the form $(r, w, \mathsf{Ext}(\mathsf{PRF}(k; r), w) \oplus m)$, where Ext is a strong extractor, r and w are random values[7], and the PRF key k is embedded in obfuscated programs that are used in both encryption and decryption. In the security proof, we "puncture" the key k at the challenge point, t^*, and hardcode the mapping $t^* \to y$, where $y = \mathsf{PRF}(k; t^*)$, in order to preserve the input/output behavior. As in SW, we switch the mapping to $t^* \to y^*$ for a random y^* via security of the puncturable PRF. But now observe we have that the min-entropy of y^* is high even after leakage, so the output of the extractor is close to uniform. To achieve optimal leakage rate, we further modify the scheme to separate $t^* \to y^*$ from the obfuscated program and store only an encryption of $t^* \to y^*$ in the secret key.

2   Compiler from 2CLR to Leakage on Key Updates

In this section, we present a compiler that upgrades any scheme for public key encryption (PKE), digital signature (SIG), or one-way relation (OWR) that is consecutive two-key leakage resilient, into one that is secure against leak on update. We first introduce a notion of *explainable update transformation*, which is a generalization of the idea of universal deniable encryption by Sahai and Waters [23]. We show how to use such a transformation to upgrade a scheme (PKE, SIG, or OWR) that is secure in the consecutive two-key leakage model to one that is secure in the leak-on-update model (Sect. 2.2). Finally, we show two instantiations of the explainable update transformation: one based on indistinguishability obfuscation, and the other on differing-inputs obfuscation (Sect. 2.3). For clarity of exposition, the following sections will focus on constructions of PKE, but we remark that the same results can be translated to SIG and OWR.

---

[7] Technically, we actually use pseudo-random value r, just as SW do. We omit this here to make the explanation a little more clear.

2.1 Consecutive Continual Leakage Resilience (2CLR)

In this section, we present a new notion of *consecutive continual leakage resilience* for public-key encryption (PKE). We remark that this notion can be easily extended to different cases, such as signatures, leakage resilient one-way relations [11]. We only present the PKE version for simplicity and concreteness. Let κ denote the security parameter, and μ be the leakage bound between two updates. Let $\mathsf{PKE} = \{\mathsf{Gen}, \mathsf{Enc}, \mathsf{Dec}, \mathsf{Update}\}$ be an encryption scheme with update.

Setup Phase. The game begins with a setup phase. The challenger calls $\mathsf{PKE.Gen}(1^{\kappa})$ to create the initial secret key sk_0 and public key pk. It gives pk to the attacker. No leakage is allowed in this phase.

Query Phase. The attacker specifies an efficiently computable leakage function f_1, whose output is at most μ bits. The challenger updates the secret key (changing it from sk_0 to sk_1), and then gives the attacker $f_1(\mathsf{sk}_0, \mathsf{sk}_1)$. The attacker then repeats this a polynomial number of times, each time supplying an efficiently computable leakage function f_i whose output is at most μ bits. Each time, the challenger updates the secret key from sk_{i-1} to sk_i according to $\mathsf{Update}(\cdot)$, and gives the attacker $f_i(\mathsf{sk}_{i-1}, \mathsf{sk}_i)$.

Challenge Phase. The attacker chooses two messages m_0, m_1 which it gives to the challenger. The challenger chooses a random bit $b \in \{0, 1\}$, encrypts m_b, and gives the resulting ciphertext to the attacker. The attacker then outputs a guess b' for b. The attacker wins the game if $b = b'$. We define the advantage of the attacker in this game as $|\frac{1}{2} - \Pr[b' = b]|$.

Definition 1 (Continual Consecutive Leakage Resilience). *We say a public-key encryption scheme is μ-leakage resilient against consecutive continual leakage (or μ-2CLR) if any probabilistic polynomial time attacker only has a negligible advantage (negligible in κ) in the above game.*

2.2 Explainable Key-Update Transformation

Now we introduce a notion of *explainable key-update transformation*, and show how it can be used to upgrade security of a PKE scheme from 2CLR to CLR with leakage on key updates. Informally, an encryption scheme has an "explainable" update procedure if given both sk_{i-1} and $\mathsf{sk}_i = \mathsf{Update}(\mathsf{sk}_{i-1}, r_i)$, there is an efficient way to come up with some explained random coins $\hat{r}_i$ such that no adversary can distinguish the real coins r_i from the explained coins $\hat{r}_i$. Intuitively, this gives a way to handle leakage on random coins given just leakage on two consecutive keys.

We start with any encryption scheme PKE that has some key update procedure, and we introduce a transformation that produces a scheme PKE′ with an *explainable* key update procedure.

Definition 2 (Explainable Key Update Transformation). *Let* $\mathsf{PKE} = \mathsf{PKE}.\{\mathsf{Gen}, \mathsf{Enc}, \mathsf{Dec}, \mathsf{Update}\}$ *be an encryption scheme with key update. An explainable key update transformation for* PKE *is a* PPT *algorithm* TransformGen

that takes input security parameter 1^κ, an update circuit C_{Update} (that implements the key update algorithm $\mathsf{PKE.Update}(1^\kappa, \cdot; \cdot)$), a public key pk of PKE, and outputs two programs $\mathcal{P}_{\mathsf{update}}, \mathcal{P}_{\mathsf{explain}}$ with the following syntax:
  Let $(\mathsf{pk}, \mathsf{sk})$ be a pair of public and secret keys of the encryption scheme

- *$\mathcal{P}_{\mathsf{update}}$ takes inputs sk, random coins r, and $\mathcal{P}_{\mathsf{update}}(\mathsf{sk}; r)$ outputs a updated secret key sk';*
- *$\mathcal{P}_{\mathsf{explain}}$ takes inputs $(\mathsf{sk}, \mathsf{sk}')$, random coins $\bar{v}$, and $\mathcal{P}_{\mathsf{explain}}(\mathsf{sk}, \mathsf{sk}'; \bar{v})$ outputs a string r.*

  Given a public key pk, we define $\Pi_{\mathsf{pk}} = \bigcup_{j=0}^{\mathrm{poly}(\kappa)} \Pi_j$, where $\Pi_0 = \{\mathsf{sk} : (\mathsf{pk}, \mathsf{sk}) \in \mathsf{PKE.Gen}\}$, $\Pi_i = \{\mathsf{sk} : \exists \mathsf{sk}' \in \Pi_{i-1}, \mathsf{sk} \in \mathsf{Update}(\mathsf{sk}')\}$ for $i = 1, 2, \ldots, \mathrm{poly}(\kappa)$. In words, Π_{pk} is the set of all secret keys sk such that either $(\mathsf{pk}, \mathsf{sk})$ is in the support of $\mathsf{PKE.Gen}$ or sk can be obtained by the update procedure Update (up to polynomially many times) with an initial $(\mathsf{pk}, \mathsf{sk}') \in \mathsf{PKE.Gen}$.
  We say the transformation is secure if:

(a) *For any pk, all $\mathsf{sk} \in \Pi_{\mathsf{pk}}$, any $\mathcal{P}_{\mathsf{update}} \in \mathsf{TransformGen}(1^\kappa, \mathsf{PKE.Update}, \mathsf{pk})$, the following two distributions are statistically close: $\{\mathcal{P}_{\mathsf{update}}(\mathsf{sk})\} \approx \{\mathsf{PKE.Update}(\mathsf{sk})\}$. Note that the circuit $\mathcal{P}_{\mathsf{update}}$ and the update algorithm $\mathsf{PKE.Update}$ might have different spaces for random coins, but the distributions can still be statistically close.*
(b) *For any public key pk and secret key $\mathsf{sk} \in \Pi_{\mathsf{pk}}$, the following two distributions are computationally indistinguishable:*

$$\{(\mathcal{P}_{\mathsf{update}}, \mathcal{P}_{\mathsf{explain}}, \mathsf{pk}, \mathsf{sk}, u)\} \approx \{(\mathcal{P}_{\mathsf{update}}, \mathcal{P}_{\mathsf{explain}}, \mathsf{pk}, \mathsf{sk}, e)\},$$

where $(\mathcal{P}_{\mathsf{update}}, \mathcal{P}_{\mathsf{explain}}) \leftarrow \mathsf{TransformGen}(1^\kappa, \mathsf{PKE.Update}, \mathsf{pk})$, $u \leftarrow U_{\mathrm{poly}(\kappa)}$, $\mathsf{sk}' = \mathcal{P}_{\mathsf{update}}(\mathsf{sk}; u)$,
$e \leftarrow \mathcal{P}_{\mathsf{explain}}(\mathsf{sk}, \mathsf{sk}')$, and $U_{\mathrm{poly}(\kappa)}$ denotes the uniform distribution over a polynomial number of bits.

Let $\mathsf{PKE} = \mathsf{PKE}.\{\mathsf{Gen}, \mathsf{Enc}, \mathsf{Dec}, \mathsf{Update}\}$ be a public key encryption scheme and $\mathsf{TransformGen}$ be an explainable key update transformation for PKE as above. We define the following transformed scheme $\mathsf{PKE}' = \mathsf{PKE}'.\{\mathsf{Gen}, \mathsf{Enc}, \mathsf{Dec}, \mathsf{Update}\}$ as follows:

- $\mathsf{PKE}'.\mathsf{Gen}(1^\kappa)$: compute $(\mathsf{pk}, \mathsf{sk}) \leftarrow \mathsf{PKE.Gen}(1^\kappa)$.
  Then compute $(\mathcal{P}_{\mathsf{update}}, \mathcal{P}_{\mathsf{explain}}) \leftarrow \mathsf{TransformGen}(1^\kappa, \mathsf{PKE.Update}, \mathsf{pk})$.
  Finally, output $\mathsf{pk}' = (\mathsf{pk}, \mathcal{P}_{\mathsf{update}}, \mathcal{P}_{\mathsf{explain}})$ and $\mathsf{sk}' = \mathsf{sk}$.
- $\mathsf{PKE}'.\mathsf{Enc}(\mathsf{pk}', m)$: parse $\mathsf{pk}' = (\mathsf{pk}, \mathcal{P}_{\mathsf{update}}, \mathcal{P}_{\mathsf{explain}})$. Then output $c \leftarrow \mathsf{PKE.Enc}(\mathsf{pk}, m)$.
- $\mathsf{PKE}'.\mathsf{Dec}(\mathsf{sk}', c)$: output $m = \mathsf{PKE.Dec}(\mathsf{sk}', c)$.
- $\mathsf{PKE}'.\mathsf{Update}(\mathsf{sk}')$: sample $\mathsf{sk}'' \leftarrow \mathcal{P}_{\mathsf{update}}(\mathsf{sk}')$ and overwrite the old key, i.e. $\mathsf{sk}' := \mathsf{sk}''$.

Then we are able to show the following theorem for the upgraded scheme PKE'.

Theorem 1. *Let* PKE = PKE.{Gen, Enc, Dec, Update} *be a public key encryption scheme that is μ-2CLR (without leakage on update), and* TransformGen *a secure explainable key update transformation for* PKE. *Then the transformed scheme* PKE' = PKE'.{Gen, Enc, Dec, Update} *described above is μ-CLR with leakage on key updates.*

Proof. Assume towards contradiction that there is a PPT adversary $\mathcal{A}$ and a non-negligible $\epsilon(\cdot)$ such that for infinitely many values of κ, $\mathsf{Adv}_{\mathcal{A},\mathsf{PKE}'} \geq \epsilon(\kappa)$ in the leak-on-update model. Then we show that there exists $\mathcal{B}$ that breaks the security of the underlying PKE (in the consecutive two-key leakage model) with probability $\epsilon(\kappa) - \mathsf{negl}(\kappa)$. This is a contradiction.

For notionally simplicity, we will use $\mathsf{Adv}_{\mathcal{A},\mathsf{PKE}'}$ to denote the advantage of the adversary $\mathcal{A}$ attacking the scheme PKE' (according to leak-on-update attacks), and $\mathsf{Adv}_{\mathcal{B},\mathsf{PKE}}$ to denote the advantage of the adversary $\mathcal{B}$ attacking the scheme PKE (according to consecutive two-key leakage attacks).

We define $\mathcal{B}$ in the following way: $\mathcal{B}$ internally instantiates $\mathcal{A}$ and participates externally in a continual consecutive two-key leakage experiment on public key encryption scheme PKE'. Specifically, $\mathcal{B}$ does the following:

- Upon receiving pk^* externally, $\mathcal{B}$ runs
  $(\mathcal{P}_{\mathsf{update}}, \mathcal{P}_{\mathsf{explain}}) \leftarrow$ TransformGen$(1^\kappa, \mathsf{PKE.Update}, \mathsf{pk}^*)$. Note that by the properties of the transformation, this can be done given only pk^*. $\mathcal{B}$ sets $\mathsf{pk}' = (\mathsf{pk}^*, \mathcal{P}_{\mathsf{update}}, \mathcal{P}_{\mathsf{explain}})$ to be the public key for the PKE' scheme and forwards pk' to $\mathcal{A}$.
- When $\mathcal{A}$ asks for a leakage query $f(\mathsf{sk}'_{i-1}, r_i)$, $\mathcal{B}$ asks for the following leakage query on $(\mathsf{sk}_{i-1}, \mathsf{sk}_i)$: $f'(\mathsf{sk}_{i-1}, \mathsf{sk}_i) = f(\mathsf{sk}_{i-1}, \mathcal{P}_{\mathsf{explain}}(\mathsf{sk}_{i-1}, \mathsf{sk}_i))$ and forwards the response to $\mathcal{A}$. Note that the output lengths of f and f' are the same.
- At some point $\mathcal{A}$ submits m_0, m_1 and $\mathcal{B}$ forwards them to its external experiment.
- Upon receiving the challenge ciphertext c^*, $\mathcal{B}$ forwards it to $\mathcal{A}$ and outputs whatever $\mathcal{A}$ outputs.

Now we would like to analyze the advantage of $\mathcal{B}$. It is easy to see that $\mathcal{B}$ has the same advantage as $\mathcal{A}$, however there is a subtlety such that $\mathcal{A}$ does not necessarily have advantage $\epsilon(\kappa)$: the simulation of leakage queries provided by $\mathcal{B}$ is not identical to the distribution in the real game that $\mathcal{A}$ would expect. Recall that in the security experiment of the scheme PKE', the secret keys are updated according to $\mathcal{P}_{\mathsf{update}}$. In the above experiment (where $\mathcal{B}$ set up), the secret keys were updated using the Update externally, and the random coins were simulated by the $\mathcal{P}_{\mathsf{explain}}$ algorithm.

Our goal is to show that actually $\mathcal{A}$ has essentially the same advantage in this modified experiment as in the original experiment. We show this by the following lemma:

Lemma 1. *For any polynomial n, the following two distributions are computationally indistinguishable.*

$$D_1 \equiv (\mathcal{P}_{\mathsf{update}}, \mathcal{P}_{\mathsf{explain}}, \mathsf{pk}, \mathsf{sk}_0, r_1, \mathsf{sk}_1, \ldots, \mathsf{sk}_{n-1}, r_n, \mathsf{sk}_n) \approx$$
$$D_2 \equiv (\mathcal{P}_{\mathsf{update}}, \mathcal{P}_{\mathsf{explain}}, \mathsf{pk}, \mathsf{sk}_0, \widehat{r}_1, \widehat{\mathsf{sk}}_1, \ldots, \widehat{\mathsf{sk}}_{n-1}, \widehat{r}_n, \widehat{\mathsf{sk}}_n),$$

where the initial $\mathsf{pk}, \mathsf{sk}_0$ *and* $\mathsf{TransformGen}(1^\kappa, \mathsf{pk})$ *are sampled identically in both experiment; in* D_1 $\mathsf{sk}_{i+1} = \mathcal{P}_{\mathsf{update}}(\mathsf{sk}_i; r_{i+1})$, *and* r_{i+1}*'s are uniformly random; in* D_2, $\widehat{\mathsf{sk}}_{i+1} \leftarrow \mathsf{Update}(\widehat{\mathsf{sk}}_i)$, $\widehat{r}_{i+1} \leftarrow \mathcal{P}_{\mathsf{explain}}(\widehat{\mathsf{sk}}_i, \widehat{\mathsf{sk}}_{i+1})$. *(Note* $\widehat{\mathsf{sk}}_0 = \mathsf{sk}_0$*).*

Proof. To show the lemma, we consider the following hybrids: for $i \in [n]$ define

$$H^{(i)} = (\mathcal{P}_{\mathsf{update}}, \mathcal{P}_{\mathsf{explain}}, \mathsf{pk}, \mathsf{sk}_0, \widehat{r}_1, \widehat{\mathsf{sk}}_1, \ldots, \widehat{\mathsf{sk}}_{i-1}, r_i, \mathsf{sk}_i, r_{i+1}, \mathsf{sk}_{i+1}, r_{i+2}, \ldots, \mathsf{sk}_n),$$

where the experiment is identical to D_2 for up to $\widehat{\mathsf{sk}}_{i-1}$. Then it samples a uniformly random r_i, sets $\mathsf{sk}_i = \mathcal{P}_{\mathsf{update}}(\widehat{\mathsf{sk}}_{i-1}; r_i)$, and proceeds as D_1.

$$H^{(i.5)} = (\mathcal{P}_{\mathsf{update}}, \mathcal{P}_{\mathsf{explain}}, \mathsf{pk}, \mathsf{sk}_0, \widehat{r}_1, \widehat{\mathsf{sk}}_1, \ldots, \widehat{\mathsf{sk}}_{i-1}, \widehat{r}_i, \mathsf{sk}_i, r_{i+1}, \mathsf{sk}_{i+1}, r_{i+2}, \ldots, \mathsf{sk}_n),$$

where the experiment is identical to $H^{(i)}$ for up to $\widehat{\mathsf{sk}}_{i-1}$, and then it samples $\mathsf{sk}_i \leftarrow \mathcal{P}_{\mathsf{update}}(\widehat{\mathsf{sk}}_{i-1})$, and $\widehat{r}_i \leftarrow \mathcal{P}_{\mathsf{explain}}(\widehat{\mathsf{sk}}_{i-1}, \mathsf{sk}_i)$. The experiment is identical to D_1 for the rest.

Then we establish the following lemmas, and the lemma follows directly.

Lemma 2. *For* $i \in [n-1]$, $H^{(i.5)}$ *is statistically close to* $H^{(i+1)}$.

Lemma 3. *For* $i \in [n]$, $H^{(i)}$ *is computationally indistinguishable from* $H^{(i.5)}$.

This first lemma follows directly from the property (a) of Definition 2. We now prove Lemma 3.

Proof. Suppose there exists a (polysized) distinguisher $\mathcal{D}$ that distinguishes $H^{(i)}$ from $H^{(i.5)}$ with non-negligible probability, then there exist $\mathsf{pk}^*, \mathsf{sk}^*$, and another $\mathcal{D}'$ that can break the property (b).

From the definition of the experiments, we know that $\mathcal{P}_{\mathsf{update}}, \mathcal{P}_{\mathsf{explain}}$ are independent of the public key and the first i secret keys, i.e. $\boldsymbol{p} = (\mathsf{pk}, \mathsf{sk}_0, \widehat{\mathsf{sk}}_1, \ldots, \widehat{\mathsf{sk}}_{i-1})$. By an average argument, there exists a fixed

$$\boldsymbol{p}^* = (\mathsf{pk}^*, \mathsf{sk}_0^*, \widehat{\mathsf{sk}}_1^*, \ldots, \widehat{\mathsf{sk}}_{i-1}^*)$$

such that $\mathcal{D}$ can distinguish $H^{(i)}$ from $H^{(i.5)}$ conditioned on $\boldsymbol{p}^*$ with non-negligible probability (the probability is over the randomness of the rest experiment). Then we are going to argue that there exist a polysized distinguisher $\mathcal{D}'$, a key pair $\mathsf{pk}', \mathsf{sk}'$ such that $\mathcal{D}'$ can distinguish $(\mathcal{P}_{\mathsf{update}}, \mathcal{P}_{\mathsf{explain}}, \mathsf{pk}', \mathsf{sk}', u)$ from $(\mathcal{P}_{\mathsf{update}}, \mathcal{P}_{\mathsf{explain}}, \mathsf{pk}', \mathsf{sk}', e)$ where u is from the uniform distribution, $\mathsf{sk}'' = \mathcal{P}_{\mathsf{update}}(\mathsf{sk}'; u)$, and $e \leftarrow \mathcal{P}_{\mathsf{explain}}(\mathsf{sk}', \mathsf{sk}'')$.

Let $\mathsf{pk}' = \mathsf{pk}^*$, $\mathsf{sk}' = \widehat{\mathsf{sk}}_{i-1}^*$, and we define $\mathcal{D}'$ (with the prefix $\boldsymbol{p}^*$ hardwired) who on the challenge input $(\mathcal{P}_{\mathsf{update}}, \mathcal{P}_{\mathsf{explain}}, \mathsf{pk}', \mathsf{sk}', z)$ does the following:

- For $j \in [i-1]$, $\mathcal{D}'$ samples $\widehat{r}_j = \mathcal{P}_{\mathsf{explain}}(\mathsf{sk}_{j-1}^*, \mathsf{sk}_j^*)$.
- Set $\mathsf{sk}_{i-1} = \mathsf{sk}'$ and $r_i = z$, $\mathsf{sk}_i = \mathcal{P}_{\mathsf{update}}(\mathsf{sk}_{i-1}, z)$.

- For $j \geq i+1$, $\mathcal{D}'$ samples r_j from the uniform distribution and sets $\mathsf{sk}_j = \mathcal{P}_{\mathsf{update}}(\mathsf{sk}_{j-1}; r_j)$.
- Finally, $\mathcal{D}'$ outputs $\mathcal{D}(\mathcal{P}_{\mathsf{update}}, \mathcal{P}_{\mathsf{explain}}, \mathsf{pk}', \mathsf{sk}_0^*, \widehat{r}_1, \mathsf{sk}_1^*, \ldots, \mathsf{sk}_{i-1}, r_i, \mathsf{sk}_i, r_{i+1}, \ldots, \mathsf{sk}_n)$.

Clearly, if the challenge z was sampled according to uniformly random (as u), then $\mathcal{D}'$ will output according to $\mathcal{D}(H^{(i)}|_{p*})$. On the other hand, suppose it was sampled according to $\mathcal{P}_{\mathsf{explain}}$ (as e), then $\mathcal{D}'$ will output according to $\mathcal{D}(H^{i.5}|_{p*})$. This completes the proof of the lemma.

Remark. The non-uniform argument above is not necessary. We present in this way for simplicity. The uniform reduction can be obtained using a standard Markov type argument, which we omit here.

Now, we are ready to analyze the advantage of $\mathcal{B}$ (and $\mathcal{A}$). Denote $\mathsf{Adv}_{\mathcal{A},\mathsf{PKE}';D}$ as the advantage of $\mathcal{A}$ in the experiment where the leakage queries are answered according to the distribution D. By assumption, we know that $\mathsf{Adv}_{\mathcal{A},\mathsf{PKE}';D_1} = \epsilon(\kappa)$, and by definition the leakage queries are answered according to D_1. By the above lemma, we know that $|\mathsf{Adv}_{\mathcal{A},\mathsf{PKE}';D_1} - \mathsf{Adv}_{\mathcal{A},\mathsf{PKE}';D_2}| \leq \mathsf{negl}(\kappa)$, otherwise D_1 and D_2 are distinguishable. Thus, we know $\mathsf{Adv}_{\mathcal{A},\mathsf{PKE}';D_2} \geq \epsilon(\kappa) - \mathsf{negl}(\kappa)$. It is not hard to see that $\mathsf{Adv}_{\mathcal{B},\mathsf{PKE}} = \mathsf{Adv}_{\mathcal{A},\mathsf{PKE}';D_2}$, since $\mathcal{B}$ answers $\mathcal{A}$'s the leakage queries exactly according to the distribution D_2. Thus, $\mathsf{Adv}_{\mathcal{B},\mathsf{PKE}} \geq \epsilon(\kappa) - \mathsf{negl}(\kappa)$, which is a contradiction. This completes the proof of the theorem.

2.3   Instantiations via Obfuscation

In this section, we show how to build an explainable key update transformation from program obfuscation. Our best parameters are achieved using public-coin differing-inputs obfuscation [18] (rather than the weaker indistinguishability obfuscation (iO) [2,14]), so we present this version here.

Let $\mathsf{PKE} = (\mathsf{Gen}, \mathsf{Enc}, \mathsf{Dec}, \mathsf{Update})$ be a public-key encryption scheme (or a signature scheme with algorithms $\mathsf{Verify}, \mathsf{Sign}$) with key-update, and diO be a public-coin differing-inputs obfuscator (for some class defined later). Let κ be a security parameter. Let L_{sk} be the length of secret keys in PKE and L_r be the length of randomness used by Update. For ease of notation, we suppress the dependence of these lengths on κ. We note that in the 2CLR case, it is without loss of generality to assume $L_r \ll L_{\mathsf{sk}}$, because we can always use pseudorandom coins (e.g. the output of a PRG) to do the update. Since only the two consecutive keys are leaked (not the randomness, e.g. the seed to the PRG), the update with the pseudorandom coins remains secure, assuming the PRG is secure.

Let $\mathcal{H}$ be a family of public-coin collision resistant hash functions, as well as a family of $(2\kappa, \epsilon)$-good unseeded extractors[8], mapping $2L_{\mathsf{sk}} + 2\kappa$ bits to κ bits. Let F_1 and F_2 be families of puncturable pseudo-random functions, where F_1

---

[8] The extractor outputs a distribution that is ϵ close to the uniform distribution if the source has min-entropy 2κ. Here we set ϵ to be some negligible. The hash function is chosen from a family of functions, and once chosen, it is a deterministic function.

has input length $2L_{sk} + 3\kappa$ bits and output length L_r bits, and it is as well an $(L_r + \kappa, \epsilon)$-good unseeded extractor; F_2 has input length κ and output length $L_{sk} + 2\kappa$. Here $|u_1| = \kappa$ and $|u_2| = L_{sk} + 2\kappa$, $|r'| = 2\kappa$.

Define the algorithm TransformGen$(1^\kappa, \text{pk})$ that on input the security parameter, a public key pk and a circuit that implements PKE.Update$(\cdot)$ as follows:

– TransformGen samples K_1, K_2 as keys for the puncturable PRF as above, and $h \leftarrow \mathcal{H}$. Let P_1 be the program as Fig. 1, and P_2 as Fig. 2.
– Then it samples $\mathcal{P}_{update} \leftarrow \text{diO}(P_1)$, and $\mathcal{P}_{explain} \leftarrow \text{diO}(P_2)$. It outputs $(\mathcal{P}_{update}, \mathcal{P}_{explain})$.

Internal (hardcoded) state: Public key pk, keys K_1, K_2, and h.

On input secret key sk_1; randomness $u = (u_1, u_2)$.

  – If $F_2(K_2, u_1) \oplus u_2 = (\text{sk}_2, r')$ for (proper length) strings sk_2, r' and $u_1 = h(\text{sk}_1, \text{sk}_2, r')$, then output sk_2.
  – Else let $x = F_1(K_1, (\text{sk}_1, u))$. Output $\text{sk}_2 = \text{PKE.Update}(\text{pk}, \text{sk}_1; x)$.

Fig. 1. Program update

Internal (hardcoded) state: key K_2.

On input secret keys sk_1, sk_2; randomness $r \in \{0, 1\}^\kappa$

  – Set $u_1 = h(\text{sk}_1, \text{sk}_2, r)$. Set $u_2 = F_2(K_2, u_1) \oplus (\text{sk}_2, r)$. Output $e = (u_1, u_2)$.

Fig. 2. Program explain

Then we can establish the following theorem.

Theorem 2. *Let* PKE *be any public key encryption scheme with key update. Assume* diO *is a secure* public-coin *differing-inputs indistinguishable obfuscator for the circuits required by the construction,* F_1, F_2 *are puncturable pseudorandom functions with the additional properties stated above, and* $\mathcal{H}$ *is a family of public-coin collision resistant hash function with the extraction property as above. Then the transformation* TransformGen *defined above is a secure explainable update transformation for* PKE *as defined in Definition 2.*

Proof. Recall we need to demonstrate that for any public key pk^* and secret key $\text{sk}^* \in \Pi_{pk}$, the following two distributions are computationally indistinguishable:

$$\{(\mathcal{P}_{update}, \mathcal{P}_{explain}, \text{pk}^*, \text{sk}^*, u^*)\} \approx \{(\mathcal{P}_{update}, \mathcal{P}_{explain}, \text{pk}^*, \text{sk}^*, e^*)\},$$

where these values are generated by

1. $(\mathcal{P}_{\mathsf{update}}, \mathcal{P}_{\mathsf{explain}}) \leftarrow \mathsf{TransformGen}(1^\kappa, \mathsf{PKE.Update}, \mathsf{pk}^*)$,
2. $u^* = (u_1^*, u_2^*) \leftarrow \{0,1\}^{L_{\mathsf{sk}}+3\kappa}$,
3. Set $x^* = F_1(K_1, \mathsf{sk}^*||u^*)$, $\mathsf{sk}' = \mathcal{P}_{\mathsf{update}}(\mathsf{sk}^*; u^*)$. Then choose uniformly random r^* of length κ, and set $e_1^* = h(\mathsf{sk}^*, \mathsf{sk}', r^*)$ and $e_2^* = F_2(K_2, e_1^*) \oplus (\mathsf{sk}', r^*)$.

We prove this through the following sequence of hybrid steps.

Hybrid 1: In this hybrid step, we change Step 3 of the above challenge. Instead of computing $\mathsf{sk}' = \mathcal{P}_{\mathsf{update}}(\mathsf{sk}^*; u^*)$, we compute $\mathsf{sk}' = \mathsf{PKE.Update}(\mathsf{pk}^*, \mathsf{sk}^*; x^*)$:

1. $(\mathcal{P}_{\mathsf{update}}, \mathcal{P}_{\mathsf{explain}}) \leftarrow \mathsf{TransformGen}(1^\kappa, \mathsf{PKE.Update}, \mathsf{pk}^*)$,
2. $u^* = (u_1^*, u_2^*) \leftarrow \{0,1\}^{L_{\mathsf{sk}}+3\kappa}$,
3. Set $x^* = F_1(K_1, \mathsf{sk}^*||u^*)$, $\mathsf{sk}' = \mathsf{PKE.Update}(\mathsf{pk}^*, \mathsf{sk}^*; x^*)$, and choose uniformly random r^* of length κ. Then, $e_1^* = h(\mathsf{sk}^*, \mathsf{sk}', r^*)$ and $e_2^* = F_2(K_2, e_1^*) \oplus (\mathsf{sk}', r^*)$.

Note that the only time in which this changes the experiment is when the values $(u_1^*, u_2^*) \leftarrow \{0,1\}^{2L_{\mathsf{sk}}+3\kappa}$ happen to satisfy $F_2(K_2, u_1^*) \oplus u_2^* = (\mathsf{sk}', r')$ such that $u_1^* = h(\mathsf{sk}^*, \mathsf{sk}', r')$. For any fixed $u_1^*, \mathsf{sk}^*, \mathsf{sk}'$, and a random u_{2^*}, we know the marginal probability of r' is still uniform given $u_1^*, \mathsf{sk}^*, \mathsf{sk}'$. Therefore, we have $\Pr_{u_{2^*}}[h(\mathsf{sk}^*, \mathsf{sk}', r') = u_1^*] = \Pr_{r'}[h(\mathsf{sk}^*, \mathsf{sk}', r') = u_1^*] < 2^{-\kappa} + \epsilon$. This is because h is a $(2\kappa, \epsilon)$-extractor, so the output of h is ϵ-close to uniform over $\{0,1\}^\kappa$, and a uniform distribution hits a particular string with probability $2^{-\kappa}$. Since we set ϵ to be some negligible, the two distributions are only different with the negligible quantity.

Hybrid 2: In this hybrid step, we modify the program in Fig. 1, puncturing key K_1 at points $\{\mathsf{sk}_1||u^*\}$ and $\{\mathsf{sk}_1||e^*\}$, and adding a line of code at the beginning of the program to ensure that the PRF is never evaluated at these two points. See Fig. 3. We claim that with overwhelming probability over the choice of u^*, this modified program has identical input/output as the program that was used in Hybrid 1 (Fig. 1). Note that on input (sk^*, e^*) the output of the original program was already sk' as defined in Hybrid 1, so the outputs of the two programs are identical on this input. (This follows because e^* anyway encodes sk', so when the "Else if" statement is triggered in the program of Fig. 1, the output is sk'.) As long as u_1^* and u_2^* do not have the property that $u_1^* = h(\mathsf{sk}^*, F_2(K_2, u_1^*) \oplus u_2^*)$, then the programs have identical output on input (sk^*, u^*) as well. (This follows because sk' is defined as $\mathsf{sk}' = \mathcal{P}_{\mathsf{update}}(\mathsf{sk}^*; F_1(K_1, \mathsf{sk}^*||u^*))$ in the challenge game, which is also the output of the program in Fig. 1 when u_1^* and u_2^* fail this condition.) As we argued in Hybrid 1, with very high probability, u^* does not have this property. (We stress that u^* is fixed *before* we construct the obfuscated program described in Fig. 3, so with overwhelming probability over the choice of u^*, the two programs have identical input output behavior.) Indistinguishability of Hybrids 1 and 2 follows from the security of the obfuscation.

Hybrid 3: In this Hybrid we change the challenge game to use truly random x^* when computing $\mathsf{sk}' = \mathsf{PKE.Update}(\mathsf{pk}^*, \mathsf{sk}^*; x^*)$, (instead of $x^* = F_1(K_1; \mathsf{sk}^*||u^*)$). Security holds by a reduction to the pseudo-randomness of

---

Internal   (hardcoded)   state: Public   key pk^*,   keys $\widetilde{K}_1$ $=$ PRF.Punct$(K_1, \{\mathsf{sk}^*\|u^*\}, \{\mathsf{sk}^*\|e^*\})$, K_2, sk' (as defined in Hybrid 1) and h.

On input secret key sk_1; randomness $u = (u_1, u_2)$.

  – If $(\mathsf{sk}_1, u) = (\mathsf{sk}^*, u^*)$ or $(\mathsf{sk}_1, u) = (\mathsf{sk}^*, e^*)$ output the value sk'.
  – Else If $F_2(K_2; u_1) \oplus u_2 = (\mathsf{sk}_2, r')$ such that $u_1 = h(\mathsf{sk}_1, \mathsf{sk}_2, r')$, then output sk_2.
  – Else let $x = F_1(\widetilde{K}_1, \mathsf{sk}_1 \| u)$. Output $\mathsf{sk}_2 = \mathsf{PKE.Update}(\mathsf{pk}^*, \mathsf{sk}_1; x)$.

Fig. 3. Program update, as used in Hybrid 2

F_1 at the punctured point (sk^*, u^*). More specifically, given an adversary $\mathcal{A}$ that distinguishes Hybrid 2 from Hybrid 3 on values $\mathsf{pk}^*, \mathsf{sk}^*$, we describe an reduction $\mathcal{B}$ that attacks the security of the puncturable PRF, F_1. $\mathcal{B}$ generates u^* at random and submits (sk^*, u^*) to his challenger. He receives $\widetilde{K}_1 = \mathsf{PRF.Punct}(K_1, \{\mathsf{sk}^*\|u^*\})$, and a value x^* as a challenge. $\mathcal{B}$ computes $\mathsf{sk}' = \mathsf{PKE.Update}(\mathsf{pk}^*, \mathsf{sk}^*; x^*)$, chooses r^* at random, and computes e^* as in the original challenge game. He creates $\mathcal{P}_{\mathsf{update}}$ using $\widetilde{K}_1$ and sampling K_2 honestly. The same K_2 is used for creating $\mathcal{P}_{\mathsf{explain}}$. $\mathcal{B}$ obfuscates both circuits, which completes the simulation of $\mathcal{A}$'s view.

Hybrid 4: In this hybrid, we puncture K_2 at both u_1^* and e_1^*, and modify the Update program to output appropriate hardcoded values on these inputs. (See Fig. 4.) To prove that Hybrids 3 and 4 are indistinguishable, we rely on security of public-coin differing-inputs obfuscation and public-coin collision resistant hash function. In particular, we will show that suppose the Hybrids are distinguishable, then we can break the security of the collision resistant hash function.

Consider the following sampler $\mathsf{Samp}(1^\kappa)$: outputs C_0, C_1 as the two update programs as in Hybrids 3 and 4 respectively; and it outputs an auxiliary input $\mathsf{aux} = (\mathsf{pk}^*, \mathsf{sk}^*, \mathsf{sk}', u^*, e^*, K_2, h, r^*)$ sampled as in the both hybrids. Note that aux includes all the random coins of the sampler. Suppose there exists a distinguisher $\mathcal{D}$ for the two hybrids, then there exists a distinguished $\mathcal{D}'$ that distinguishes $(\mathsf{diO}(C_0), \mathsf{aux})$ from $(\mathsf{diO}(C_1), \mathsf{aux})$. This is because given the challenge input, $\mathcal{D}'$ can complete the rest of the experiment either according to Hybrid 3 or Hybrid 4. Then by security of the diO, we know there exists an adversary (extractor) $\mathcal{B}$ that given (C_0, C_1, aux) finds an input such that C_0 and C_1 evaluate differently. However, this contradicting the security of the public-coin collision resistant hash function. We establish this by the following lemma.

Lemma 4. *Assume h is sampled from a family of public-coin collision resistant hash function, (and $(2\kappa, \epsilon)$-extracting) as above. Then for any PPT adversary, the probability is negligible to find a differing input given (C_0, C_1, aux) as above.*

Proof. By examining the two circuits, we observe that the differing inputs have the following two forms: $(\bar{\mathsf{sk}}, u_1^*, \bar{u}_2)$ such that $u_1^* = h(\bar{\mathsf{sk}}, F_2(K_2; u_1^*) \oplus \bar{u}_2)$, $(\bar{\mathsf{sk}}, \bar{u}_2) \neq (\mathsf{sk}^*, u_2^*)$; or $(\bar{\mathsf{sk}}, e_1^*, \bar{e}_2)$ such that $e_1^* = h(\bar{\mathsf{sk}}, F_2(K_2; e_1^*) \oplus \bar{e}_2)$, $(\bar{\mathsf{sk}}, \bar{e}_2) \neq (\mathsf{sk}^*, e_2^*)$. This is because they will run enter the first Else IF in Hybrid 3 (Fig. 3), but will enter the modified line (the first Else IF) in Hybrid 4 (Fig. 4). We argue that both cases happen with negligible probability; otherwise security of the hash function can be broken.

For the first case, we observe that the collision resistance and $(2\kappa, \epsilon)$ extracting guarantee that the probability of finding an pre-image of a random value u_1^* is small, even given aux; otherwise there is an adversary who can break collision resistance. For the second case, we know that $e_1^* = h(\mathsf{sk}^*, \mathsf{sk}', r^*) = h(\bar{\mathsf{sk}}, F_2(K_2; e_1^*) \oplus \bar{e}_2) = h(\bar{\mathsf{sk}}, e_2^* \oplus (\mathsf{sk}', r^*) \oplus \bar{e}_2)$. Since we know that $(\bar{\mathsf{sk}}, \bar{e}_2) \neq (\mathsf{sk}^*, e_2^*)$, we find a collision, which again remains hard even given aux.

Thus, suppose there exists a differing-input finder $\mathcal{A}$, we can define an adversary $\mathcal{B}$ to break the collision resistant hash function: on input h, $\mathcal{B}$ simulates the sampler Samp with the h. Then it runs $\mathcal{A}$ to find a differing input. Then according to the above argument, either of the two cases will lead to finding a collision.

Internal (hardcoded) state: Public key pk^*, keys $\widetilde{K}_1 =$ PRF.Punct$(K_1, \{\mathsf{sk}^*\|u^*\}, \{\mathsf{sk}^*\|e^*\})$, $\widetilde{K}_2 =$ PRF.Punct$(K_2, \{u_1^*\}, \{e_1^*\})$, sk' (as defined in Hybrid 3) and h.

On input secret key sk_1; randomness $u = (u_1, u_2)$.

- If $(\mathsf{sk}_1, u) = (\mathsf{sk}^*, u^*)$ or $(\mathsf{sk}_1, u) = (\mathsf{sk}^*, e^*)$ output value sk'.
- Else If $u_1 = u_1^*$ or $u_1 = e_1^*$, let $x = F_1(\widetilde{K}_1, \mathsf{sk}_1\|u)$. Output $\mathsf{sk}_2 =$ PKE.Update$(\mathsf{pk}^*, \mathsf{sk}_1; x)$.
- Else
  - If $F_2(K_2; u_1) \oplus u_2 = (\mathsf{sk}_2, r')$ such that $u_1 = h(\mathsf{sk}_1, \mathsf{sk}_2, r')$, then output sk_2.
  - Else let $x = F_1(\widetilde{K}_1, \mathsf{sk}_1\|u)$. Output $\mathsf{sk}_2 =$ PKE.Update$(\mathsf{pk}^*, \mathsf{sk}_1; x)$.

Fig. 4. Program update, as used in Hybrid 4

Hybrid 5: In this hybrid, we puncture K_2 at both u_1^* and e_1^*, and modify the Explain program to output appropriate hardcoded values on these inputs. (See Fig. 5.) Similar to the argument for the previous hybrids, we argue that Hybrids 4 and 5 are indistinguishable by security of the public-coin differing-inputs obfuscation and public-coin collision resistant hash function. Consider a sampler Samp(1^κ) : outputs C_0, C_1 as the two explain programs as in Hybrids 4 and 5 respectively; and it outputs an auxiliary input aux $= (\mathsf{pk}^*, \mathsf{sk}^*, \mathsf{sk}', u^*, e^*, \widetilde{K}_2, h, r^*)$ sampled as in the both hybrids (note that aux includes all the random coins of the sampler). Similar to the above argument: suppose there exists a distinguisher $\mathcal{D}$ that distinguishers Hybrids 4 and 5, then we can construct a distinguisher $\mathcal{D}'$ that distinguishes $(\mathsf{diO}(C_0), \mathsf{aux})$ from $(\mathsf{diO}(C_1), \mathsf{aux})$. This is because given the challenging input, $\mathcal{D}'$ can simulate the hybrids. Then by security of the diO, there exists an adversary (extractor) $\mathcal{B}$ that can find differing inputs. Now we want to argue that suppose the h comes from a public-coin collision resistant hash family, then no PPT adversary can find differing inputs. This leads to a contradiction.

Lemma 5. *Assume h is sampled from a family of public-coin collision resistant hash function, (and $(2\kappa, \epsilon)$-extracting) as above. Then for any* PPT *adversary, the probability is negligible to find a differing input given (C_0, C_1, aux) as above.*

Proof. The proof is almost identical to that of Lemma 4. We omit the details.

Internal (hardcoded) state: key $\widetilde{K}_2 = \mathsf{PRF.Punct}(K_2, \{u_1^*\}, \{e_1^*\})$, u^*, e^*.

On input secret keys $\mathsf{sk}_1, \mathsf{sk}_2$; randomness $r \in \{0,1\}^{\kappa}$

 - If $u_1^* = h(\mathsf{sk}_1, \mathsf{sk}_2, r)$, output u^*. Else If $e_1^* = h(\mathsf{sk}_1, \mathsf{sk}_2, r)$, output e^*.
 - Else, set $u_1 = h(\mathsf{sk}_1, \mathsf{sk}_2, r)$. Set $u_2 = F_2(K_2, u_1) \oplus (\mathsf{sk}_2, r)$. Output $e = (u_1, u_2)$.

Fig. 5. Program explain, as used in Hybrid 5

Hybrid 6: In this hybrid, we change both e_1^* and e_2^* to uniformly random. Hybrids 5 and 6 are indistinguishable by the security of the puncturable PRF F_2, and by the fact that h is $(2\kappa, \epsilon)$-extracting. Clearly in this hybrid, the distributions of $\{(\mathcal{P}_{\mathsf{update}}, \mathcal{P}_{\mathsf{explain}}, \mathsf{pk}^*, \mathsf{sk}^*, u^*)\}$ and $\{(\mathcal{P}_{\mathsf{update}}, \mathcal{P}_{\mathsf{explain}}, \mathsf{pk}^*, \mathsf{sk}^*, e^*)\}$ are identical. From the indistinguishable arguments that the original game and Hybrid 6 are indistinguishable, we can argue that the distributions in the original game are indistinguishable. This concludes the proof.

3 2CLR from "Leakage Resilient Subspaces"

We show that the PKE scheme of Brakerski et al. [5] (BKKV), which has been proven CLR, can achieve 2CLR (with a slight adjustment in the scheme's parameters). We note that our focus on PKE here is justified by the fact that we show generically in the full version [8] that any CLR (resp. 2CLR) PKE scheme implies a CLR "one-way relation" (OWR) [11]; to the best of our knowledge, such an implication was not previously known. Therefore, by the results of Dodis et al. [11], this translates all our results about PKE to the signature setting as well. In the full version [8] of the paper, we show that the approach of Dodis et al. [11] for constructing CLR OWRs can be extended to 2CLR one-way relations, but we achieve weaker parameters this way.

Recall that in the work [5], to prove that their scheme is CLR, they show *"random subspaces are leakage resilient"*. In particular, they show that for a random subspace X, the statistical difference between $(X, f(v))$ and $(X, f(u))$ is negligible, where f is an arbitrary length-bounded function, v is a random point in the subspace, and u is a random point in the whole space. Then by a simple hybrid argument, they show that $(X, f_1(v_0), f_2(v_1), \ldots, f_t(v_{t-1}))$ and $(X, f_1(u_0), f_2(u_1), \ldots, f_t(u_{t-1}))$ are indistinguishable, where $f_1, \ldots, f_t$ are arbitrary and adaptively chosen length-bounded functions, $v_0, v_1, \ldots, v_{t-1}$ are independent random points in the subspace, and $u_0, u_1, \ldots, u_{t-1}$ are independent random points in the whole space. This lemma plays the core role in their proof.

In order to show that their scheme satisfies the 2CLR security, we consider random subspaces under "consecutive" leakage. That is, we want to show:

$$(X, f_1(v_0, v_1), f_2(v_1, v_2), \ldots, f_t(v_{t-1}, v_t)) \approx (X, f_1(u_0, u_1), f_2(u_1, u_2), \ldots, f_t(u_{t-1}, u_t)),$$

for arbitrary and adaptively chosen f_i's, i.e. each f_i can be chosen after seeing the previous leakage values $f_1, \ldots, f_{i-1}$. However, this does not follow by a hybrid argument of $(X, f(v)) \approx (X, f(u))$, because in the 2CLR case each point is leaked twice. It is not clear how to embed a challenging instance of $(X, f(z))$ into the larger experiment while still being able to simulate the rest.

To handle this technical issue, we establish a new lemma showing *random subspaces are "consecutive" leakage resilient*. With the lemma and a hybrid argument, we can show that the above experiments are indistinguishable. Then we show how to use this fact to prove that the scheme of BKKV is 2CLR.

Lemma 6. *Let* $t, n, \ell, d \in \mathbb{N}$, $n \geq \ell \geq 3d$, *and* q *be a prime. Let* $(A, X) \leftarrow \mathbb{Z}_q^{t \times n} \times \mathbb{Z}_q^{n \times \ell}$ *such that* $A \cdot X = 0$, $T, T' \leftarrow \mathsf{Rk}_d(\mathbb{Z}_q^{\ell \times d})$, $U \leftarrow \mathbb{Z}_q^{n \times d}$ *such that* $A \cdot U = 0$, *(i.e.* U *is a random matrix in* $\mathsf{Ker}(A)$), *and* $f : \mathbb{Z}_q^{t \times n} \times \mathbb{Z}_q^{n \times 2d} \to W$ *be any function[9] . Then we have:*

$$\Delta\big((A, X, f(A, XT, XT'), XT'), (A, X, f(A, U, XT'), XT')\big) \leq \epsilon,$$

as long as $|W| \leq (1 - 1/q) \cdot q^{\ell - 3d + 1} \cdot \epsilon^2$.

Proof. We will actually prove something stronger, namely we will prove, under the assumptions of the Lemma 6, that

$$\Delta\Big(\big(A, X, f(A, X \cdot T, X \cdot T'), X \cdot T', T'\big), \big(A, X, f(A, U, X \cdot T'), X \cdot T', T'\big)\Big)$$

$$\leq \frac{1}{2}\sqrt{\frac{3|W|}{(1 - 1/q)q^{\ell - 3d + 1}}} < \epsilon.$$

Note that this implies the Lemma by solving for ϵ, after noting that ignoring the last component in each tuple can only decrease statistical difference.

For the proof, we will apply Lemma 7 as follows. We will take hash function H to be $H : \mathbb{Z}_q^{n \times \ell} \times \mathbb{Z}_q^{\ell \times d} \to \mathbb{Z}_q^{n \times d}$ where $H_K(D) = KD$ (matrix multiplication), and take the set $\mathcal{Z}$ to be $\mathbb{Z}_q^{n \times \ell} \times \mathbb{Z}_q^{\ell \times d}$. Next we take random variable K to be uniform on $\mathbb{Z}_q^{n \times \ell}$ (denoted as the matrix X), D to be uniform on $\mathsf{Rk}_d(\mathbb{Z}_q^{\ell \times d})$, and finally $Z = (A, XT', T')$ where A is uniform conditioned on $AX = 0$, $T' \in \mathsf{Rk}_d(\mathbb{Z}_q^{\ell \times d})$ is independent uniform. We define $U_{|Z}$ as the uniform distribution such that $AU = 0$. This also means that U is a random matrix in the kernel of A.

It remains to prove under these settings that

$$\Pr\big[(D, D', Z) \in \mathsf{BAD}\big] \leq \frac{1}{(1 - 1/q)q^{\ell - 3d + 1}}$$

---

[9] Note: Rk denotes rank. Here we use n as the dimension (different from [5] who used m) to avoid overloading notation.

with BAD defined as in Lemma 7. For this let us consider

$$\Delta\big((H_{K|z}(T_1), H_{K|z}(T_2)), (U_{|z}, U'_{|z})\big)$$

where $Z = (A, XT', T')$ as defined above. The above statistical distance is zero as long as the outcomes of T_1, T_2, T' are all linearly independent. This is so because $\ell \geq 3d$. Now, by a standard formula the probability that T_1, T_2, T' have a linear dependency is bounded by $\frac{1}{(1-1/q)q^{\ell-3d+1}}$, and we are done.

We note that this lemma is slightly different that the original lemma in the work [5]: the leakage function considered here also takes in a public matrix A, which is used as the public key in the system. We observe that both our work and [5] need this version of the lemma to prove security of the encryption scheme.

We actually prove Lemma 6 as a consequence of a new generalization of the Crooked Leftover Hash Lemma (LHL) [3,13] we introduce (to handle hash functions that are only pairwise independent if some bad event does not happen), as follows.

Lemma 7. *Let $H \colon \mathcal{K} \times \mathcal{D} \to \mathcal{R}$ be a hash function and (K, Z) be joint random variables over $(\mathcal{K}, \mathcal{Z})$ for the set $\mathcal{K}$ and some set $\mathcal{Z}$. Define the following set*

$$\mathsf{BAD} = \Big\{(d, d', z) \in \mathcal{D} \times \mathcal{D} \times \mathcal{Z} : \Delta\big((H_{K|Z=z}(d), H_{K|Z=z}(d')), (U_{|Z=z}, U'_{|Z=z})\big) > 0 \Big\}, \quad (1)$$

where $U_{|Z=z}, U'_{|Z=z}$ denote two independent uniform distributions over $\mathcal{R}$ conditioned on $Z = z$, and $K|_{Z=z}$ is the conditional distribution of K given $Z = z$. We note that $\mathcal{R}$ might depend on z, so when we describe a uniform distribution over $\mathcal{R}$, we need to specify the condition $Z = z$.

Suppose D and D' are i.i.d. random variables over $\mathcal{D}$, (K, Z) are random variables over $\mathcal{K} \times \mathcal{Z}$ satisfying $\Pr\big[(D, D', Z) \in \mathsf{BAD}\big] \leq \epsilon'$. Then for any set $\mathcal{S}$ and function $f \colon \mathcal{R} \times \mathcal{Z} \to \mathcal{S}$ it holds that

$$\Delta\big((K, Z, f(H_K(D), Z)), (K, Z, f(U_{|Z}, Z))\big) \leq \frac{1}{2}\sqrt{3\epsilon' |\mathcal{S}|} .$$

Proof. The proof is an extension of the proof of the Crooked LHL given in [3]. First, using Cauchy-Schwarz and Jensen's inequality we have

$$\Delta\big((K, Z, f(H_K(D), Z)), (K, Z, f(U_{|Z}, Z))\big)$$

$$\leq \frac{1}{2}\sqrt{|\mathcal{S}| \, \mathbf{E}_{k,z}\Big[\sum_s (\Pr\big[f(H_k(D), z) = s\big] - \Pr\big[f(U_{|Z=z}, z) = s\big])^2\Big]} ,$$

where $U_{|Z=z}$ is uniform on $\mathcal{R}$ conditioned on $Z = z$, and the expectation is over (k, z) drawn from (K, Z). Thus, to complete the proof it suffices to prove the following lemma.

Lemma 8.

$$\mathbf{E}_{k,z}\left[\sum_s\left(\Pr\left[f(H_k(D),z)=s\right]-\Pr\left[f(U_{|Z=z},z)=s\right]\right)^2\right]\le 3\epsilon'. \quad (2)$$

Proof. By the linearity of expectation, we can express Eq. 2 as:

$$\mathbf{E}_{k,z}\sum_s\Pr\left[f(H_k(D),z)=s\right]^2-2\mathbf{E}_{k,z}\sum_s\Pr\left[f(H_k(D),z)=s\right]\Pr\left[f(U_{|Z=z},z)=s\right]$$
$$+\mathbf{E}_z\mathsf{Col}(f(U_{|Z=z},z)), \quad (3)$$

where $U_{|Z=z}$ is uniform on $\mathcal{R}$ conditioned on $Z=z$, and Col is the collision probability of its input random variable. Note that since $f(U_{|Z=z},z)$ is independent of k, we can drop it in the third term. In the following, we are going to calculate bounds for the first two terms.

For any $s\in\mathcal{S}$, we can write $\Pr\left[f(H_k(D),z)=s\right]=\sum_d\Pr\left[D=d\right]$ $\delta_{f(H_k(d),z),s}$ where $\delta_{a,b}$ is 1 if $a=b$ and 0 otherwise, and thus

$$\sum_s\Pr\left[f(H_k(D),z)=s\right]^2=\sum_{d,d'}\Pr\left[D=d\right]\Pr\left[D=d'\right]\delta_{f(H_k(d),z),f(H_k(d'),z)}\ .$$

So we have

$$\mathbf{E}_{k,z}\sum_s\Pr\left[f(H_k(D),z)=s\right]^2=\mathbf{E}_{k,z}\left[\sum_{d,d'}\Pr\left[D=d\right]\Pr\left[D=d'\right]\delta_{f(H_k(d),z),f(H_k(d'),z)}\right]$$

$$=\mathbf{E}_z\left[\sum_{d,d'}\Pr\left[D=d\right]\Pr\left[D=d'\right]\mathbf{E}_k\left[\delta_{f(H_k(d),z),f(H_k(d'),z)}\right]\right]$$

$$\le\sum_{z,d,d'\notin\mathsf{BAD}}\Pr\left[Z=z\right]\Pr\left[D=d\right]\Pr\left[D=d'\right]\mathbf{E}_k\left[\delta_{f(H_k(d),z),f(H_k(d'),z)}\right]+\epsilon'$$

$$=\mathbf{E}_z\left[\mathsf{Col}(f(U_{|Z=z},z))\right]+\epsilon', \quad (4)$$

where BAD is defined as in Eq. (1) from Lemma 7. The inequality holds because, by our definition of BAD, if $(z,d,d')\notin\mathsf{BAD}$, $(H_k(d),H_k(d'))$ are distributed exactly as two uniformly chosen elements (conditioned on $Z=z$), and because $\Pr[(z,d,d')\in\mathsf{BAD}]\le\epsilon'$.

By a similar calculation, we have:

$$\mathbf{E}_{k,z}\sum_s\Pr\left[f(H_k(D),z)=s\right]\Pr\left[f(U_{|Z=z},z)=s\right]\ge\mathbf{E}_z\left[\mathsf{Col}(f(U_{|Z=z},z))\right]-\epsilon'\ .$$

$$(5)$$

For the same reason, $H_k(D)$ is uniformly random except for the bad event, whose probability is bounded by ϵ'.

Putting things together, the inequality in Eq. 2 follows immediately by plugging the bounds in Eqs. 4 and 5. This concludes the proof.

Here we describe the BKKV encryption scheme, and show it is 2CLR-secure. We begin by presenting the main scheme in BKKV, which uses the weaker linear assumption, but achieves a worse leakage rate (that can tolerate roughly $1/8 \cdot |\mathsf{sk}| - o(\kappa)$). In that work [5], it is also pointed out that under the stronger SXDH assumption, the rate can be improved to tolerate roughly $1/4 \cdot |\mathsf{sk}| - o(k)$, with essentially the same proof. The same argument also holds in the 2CLR setting. To avoid repetition, we just describe the original scheme in BKKV, and prove that it is actually 2CLR under the linear assumption.

- **Parameters.** Let G, G_T be two groups of prime order p such that there exists a bilinear map $e : G \times G \to G_T$. Let g be a generator of G (and so $e(g,g)$ is a generator of G_T). An additional parameter $\ell \geq 7$ is polynomial in the security parameter. (Setting different ℓ will enable a tradeoff between efficiency and the rate of tolerable leakage). For the scheme to be secure, we require that the linear assumption holds in the group G, which implies that the size of the group must be super-polynomial, i.e. $p = \kappa^{\omega(1)}$.
- **Key-generation.** The algorithm samples $A \leftarrow \mathbb{Z}_p^{2 \times \ell}$, and $Y \leftarrow \mathsf{Ker}^2(A)$, i.e. $Y \in \mathbb{Z}_p^{\ell \times 2}$ can be viewed as two random (linearly independent) points in the kernel of A. Then it sets $\mathsf{pk} = g^A$, $\mathsf{sk} = g^Y$. Note that since A is known, Y can be sampled efficiently.
- **Key-update.** Given a secret key $g^Y \in G^{\ell \times 2}$, the algorithm samples $R \leftarrow \mathsf{Rk}_2(\mathbb{Z}_p^{2 \times 2})$ and then sets $\mathsf{sk}' = g^{Y \cdot R}$.
- **Encryption.** Given a public key $\mathsf{pk} = g^A$, to encrypt 0, it samples a random $r \in \mathbb{Z}_p^2$ and outputs $c = g^{r^T \cdot A}$. To encrypt 1, it just outputs $c = g^{u^T}$ where $u \leftarrow \mathbb{Z}_p^\ell$ is a uniformly random vector.
- **Decryption.** Given a ciphertext $c = g^{v^T}$ and a secret key $\mathsf{sk} = g^Y$, the algorithm computes $e(g,g)^{v^T \cdot Y}$. If the result is $e(g,g)^0$, then it outputs 0; otherwise 1.

Then we are able to achieve the following theorem:

Theorem 3. *Under the linear assumption, for every $\ell \geq 7$, the encryption scheme above is μ-bit leakage resilient against two-key continual and consecutive leakage, where $\mu = \frac{(\ell-6) \cdot \log p}{2} - \omega(\kappa)$. Note that the leakage rate would be $\frac{\mu}{|\mathsf{sk}| + |\mathsf{sk}|} \approx 1/8$, as ℓ is chosen sufficiently large.*

Proof. The theorem follows directly from the following lemma:

Lemma 9. *For any $t \in \mathsf{poly}(\kappa)$, $r \leftarrow \mathbb{Z}_p^2$, $A \leftarrow \mathbb{Z}_p^{2 \times \ell}$, random $Y \in \mathsf{Ker}^2(A)$, and polynomial sized functions $f_1, f_2, \ldots, f_t$ where each $f_i : \mathbb{Z}_p^{\ell \times 2} \times \mathbb{Z}_p^{\ell \times 2} \to \{0,1\}^\mu$ and can be adaptively chosen (i.e. f_i can be chosen after seeing the leakage values of $f_1, \ldots, f_{i-1}$), the following two distributions, D_0 and D_1, are computationally indistinguishable:*

$$D_0 = (g, g^A, g^{r^T \cdot A}, f_1(\mathsf{sk}_0, \mathsf{sk}_1), \ldots f_t(\mathsf{sk}_{t-1}, \mathsf{sk}_t))$$

$$D_1 = (g, g^A, g^u, f_1(\mathsf{sk}_0, \mathsf{sk}_1), \ldots f_t(\mathsf{sk}_{t-1}, \mathsf{sk}_t)),$$

where $\mathsf{sk}_0 = g^Y$ and $\mathsf{sk}_{i+1} = (\mathsf{sk}_i)^{R_i}$ for R_i a random 2 by 2 matrix of rank 2.

Basically, the distribution D_0 is the view of the adversary when given an encryption of 0 as the challenge ciphertext and continual leakage of the secret keys; D_1 is the same except the challenge ciphertext is an encryption of 1. Our goal is to show that no polynomial sized adversary can distinguish between them.

We show the lemma in the following steps:

1. We first consider two modified experiment D_0' and D_1' where in these experiments, all the secret keys are sampled independently, i.e. $\mathsf{sk}_{i+1}' \leftarrow \mathsf{Ker}^2(A)$. In other words, instead of using a rotation of the current secret key, the update procedure resamples two random (linearly independent) points in the kernel of A. Denote $D_b' = (g, g^A, g^z, f_1(\mathsf{sk}_0', \mathsf{sk}_1'), \ldots f_t(\mathsf{sk}_{t-1}', \mathsf{sk}_t'))$ for g^z is sampled either from $g^{r^T \cdot A}$ or g^u depending on $b \in \{0,1\}$. Intuitively, the operations are computed in the exponent, so the adversary cannot distinguish between the modified experiments from the original ones. We formally prove this using the linear assumption.
2. Then we consider the following modified experiments: for $b \in \{0,1\}$, define

$$D_b'' = (g, g^A, g^z, f_1(g^{u_0}, g^{u_1}), f_2(g^{u_1}, g^{u_2}), \cdots, f_t(g^{u_{t-1}}, g^{u_t})),$$

where the distribution samples a random $X \in \mathbb{Z}_p^{\ell \times (\ell-3)}$ such that $A \cdot X = 0$; then it samples each $u_i = X \cdot T_i$ for $T_i \leftarrow \mathsf{Rk}_2(\mathbb{Z}_p^{(\ell-3) \times 2})$; finally it samples z either as $r^T \cdot A$ or uniformly random as in D_b'. We then show that D_b'' is indistinguishable from D_b' using the new geometric lemma.
3. Finally, we show that $D_0'' \approx D_1''$ under the linear assumption.

To implement the approach just described, we establish the following lemmas.

Lemma 10. *For both $b \in \{0,1\}$, D_b is computationally indistinguishable from D_b'.*

To show this lemma, we first establish a lemma:

Lemma 11. *Under the linear assumption, $(g, g^A, g^Y, g^{Y \cdot U}) \approx (g, g^A, g^Y, g^{Y'})$, where $A \leftarrow \mathbb{Z}_p^{2 \times \ell}$, Y, Y' $\mathsf{Ker}^2(A)$, and $U \leftarrow \mathsf{Rk}_2(\mathbb{Z}_p^{2 \times 2})$.*

Suppose there exists a distinguisher $\mathcal{A}$ that breaks the above statement with non-negligible probability, then we can construct $\mathcal{B}$ that can break the linear assumption (the matrix form). In particular, $\mathcal{B}$ distinguishes $(g, g^C, g^{C \cdot U})$ from $(g, g^C, g^{C'})$ where C and C' are two independent and uniformly random samples from $\mathbb{Z}_p^{(\ell-2) \times 2}$, and U is uniformly random matrix from $\mathbb{Z}_p^{2 \times 2}$. Note that when $p = \kappa^{\omega(1)}$ (this is required by the linear assumption), then with overwhelming probability, $(C||C')$ is a rank 4 matrix, and $(C||C \cdot U)$ is a rank 2 matrix. The linear assumption is that no polynomial time adversary can distinguish the two distributions when given in the exponent.

$\mathcal{B}$ does the following on input (g, g^C, g^Z), where Z is either $C \cdot U$ or a uniformly random matrix C':

- $\mathcal{B}$ samples a random rank 2 matrix $A \in \mathbb{Z}_p^{2 \times \ell}$. Then $\mathcal{B}$ computes an arbitrary basis of $\mathsf{Ker}(A)$ (note that $\mathsf{Ker}(A) = \{v \in \mathbb{Z}_p^\ell : A \cdot v = 0\}$), denoted as X. By the rank-nullity theorem (see any linear algebra textbook), the dimension of $\mathsf{Ker}(A)$ plus $\mathsf{Rk}(A)$ is ℓ. So we know that $X \in \mathbb{Z}_p^{\ell \times (\ell-2)}$, i.e. X contains $(\ell-2)$ vectors that are linearly independent.
- $\mathcal{B}$ computes $g^{X \cdot C}$ and $g^{X \cdot Z}$. This can be done efficiently given (g^C, g^Z) and X in the clear.
- $\mathcal{B}$ outputs $\mathcal{A}(g, g^A, g^{X \cdot C}, g^{X \cdot Z})$.

We observe that when $p = \kappa^{\omega(1)}$, the distribution of A is statistically close to a random matrix, and U is statistically close to a random rank 2 matrix. Then it is not hard to see that $g^{X \cdot C}$ is identically distributed to g^Y, and $g^{X \cdot Z}$ is distributed as $g^{(X \cdot C) \cdot U}$ if $Z = C \cdot U$, and otherwise as $g^{Y'}$. So $\mathcal{B}$ can break the linear assumption with probability essentially the same as that of $\mathcal{A}$. This completes the proof of the lemma.

Then Lemma 10 can be proven using the lemma via a standard hybrid argument. We show that $D_0 \approx D_0'$ and the other one can be shown by the same argument. For $i \in [t + 1]$, define hybrids H_i as the experiment as D_0 except the first i secret keys are sampled independently, as D_0'; the rest are sampled according to rotations, as D_0. It is not hard to see that $H_1 = D_0$, $H_{t+1} = D_0'$, and $H_i \approx H_{i+1}$ using the lemma. The argument is obvious and standard, so we omit the detail.

Then we recall the modified distribution D_b'': for $b \in \{0, 1\}$,

$$D_b'' = (g, g^A, g^z, f_1(g^{u_0}, g^{u_1}), f_2(g^{u_1}, g^{u_2}), \cdots, f_t(g^{u_{t-1}}, g^{u_t})),$$

where the distribution samples a random $X \in \mathbb{Z}_p^{\ell \times (\ell-2)}$ such that $A \cdot X = 0$; then it samples each $u_i = X \cdot T_i$ for $T_i \leftarrow \mathsf{Rk}_2(\mathbb{Z}_p^{(\ell-2) \times 2})$, and z is sampled either $r^T \cdot A$ or uniformly random. We then establish the following lemma.

Lemma 12. For $b \in \{0, 1\}$, D_b' is computationally indistinguishable from D_b''.

We prove the lemma using another hybrid argument. We prove that $D_0' \approx D_0''$, and the other follows from the same argument. We define hybrids Q_i for $i \in [t]$ where in Q_i, the first i secret keys (the exponents) are sampled randomly from $\mathsf{Ker}^2(A)$ (as D_0'), and the rest secret keys (the exponents) are sampled as $X \cdot T$ (as D_0''). Clearly, $Q_0 = D_0''$ and $Q_{t+1} = D_0'$. Then we want to show that Q_i is indistinguishable from Q_{i+1} using the extended geometric lemma (Lemma 6).

For any $i \in [t + 1]$, we argue that suppose there exists an (even unbounded) adversary that distinguishes Q_i from Q_{i+1} with probability better than ϵ, then there exist a leakage function L and an adversary $\mathcal{B}$ such that $\mathcal{B}$ can distinguish $\left(A, X, L(A, X \cdot T, X \cdot T'), X \cdot T' \right)$ from $\left(A, X, L(A, U, X \cdot T'), X \cdot T' \right)$ in Lemma 6 with probability better than $\epsilon - \mathsf{negl}(\kappa)$ (dimensions will be set later). We will set the parameters of Lemma 6 such that the two distributions have negligible statistical difference; thus ϵ can be at most a negligible quantity.

Now we formally set the dimensions: let X be a random matrix in $\mathbb{Z}_p^{\ell \times (\ell-3)}$; T, T' be two random rank 2 matrices in $\mathbb{Z}_p^{(\ell-3) \times 2}$, i.e. $\mathsf{Rk}_2\left(\mathbb{Z}_p^{(\ell-3) \times 2}\right)$; $L : \mathbb{Z}_p^{\ell \times 2} \times$

$\mathbb{Z}_p^{\ell \times 2} \to \{0, 1\}^{2\mu}$; recall that $2\mu = (\ell - 6) \cdot \log p - \omega(\kappa)$, and thus $|L| \leq p^{\ell-6} \cdot \kappa^{-\omega(1)}$. By Lemma 6, for any (even computationally unbounded) L, we have

$$\Delta\left(\left(A, X, L(A, X \cdot T, X \cdot T'), X \cdot T'\right), \left(A, X, L(A, U, X \cdot T'), X \cdot T'\right)\right) < \kappa^{-\omega(1)} = \mathsf{negl}(\kappa).$$

Let g be a random generator of G, and ω is some randomness chosen uniformly. We define a particular function L^*, with g, ω hardwired, as follows: $L^*(A, w, v)$ on input A, w, v does the following:

- It first samples $Y_0, \ldots, Y_{i-1} \leftarrow \mathsf{Ker}^2(A)$, using the random coins ω. Then it sets $\mathsf{sk}_j = g^{Y_j}$ for $j \in [i-1]$.
- It simulates the leakage functions, adaptively, obtains the values $f_1(\mathsf{sk}_0, \mathsf{sk}_1), \ldots, f_{i-1}(\mathsf{sk}_{i-2}, \mathsf{sk}_{i-1})$, and obtains the next leakage function f_i.
- It computes $f_i(\mathsf{sk}_{i-1}, g^w)$, and then obtains the next leakage function f_{i+1}.
- Finally it outputs $f_i(\mathsf{sk}_{i-1}, g^w) \| f_{i+1}(g^w, g^v)$.

Recall that f_i, f_{i+1} are two leakage functions with μ bits of output, so L^* has 2μ bits of output. Now we construct the adversary $\mathcal{B}$ as follows:

- Let g be the random generator, ω be the random coins as stated above, and L^* be the function defined above. Then $\mathcal{B}$ gets input $(A, X, L^*(A, Z, X \cdot T'), X \cdot T')$ where Z is either uniformly random or $X \cdot T$.
- $\mathcal{B}$ samples $Y_0, \ldots, Y_{i-1} \leftarrow \mathsf{Ker}^2(A)$, using the random coins ω. Then it sets $\mathsf{sk}_j = g^{Y_j}$ for $j \in [i-1]$. We note that the secret keys (in the first $i-1$ rounds) are consistent with the values used in the leakage function for they use the same randomness ω.
- $\mathcal{B}$ sets $\mathsf{sk}_{i+2} = g^{X \cdot T'}$.
- $\mathcal{B}$ samples $T_{i+3}, \ldots, T_{t+1} \leftarrow \mathsf{Rk}_2(\mathbb{Z}_p^{(\ell-3) \times 2})$ and sets $\mathsf{sk}_j = g^{X \cdot T_j}$ for $j \in \{i + 3, \ldots, t+1\}$.
- $\mathcal{B}$ outputs $\mathcal{A}\Big(g^A, g^z, f_1(\mathsf{sk}_0, \mathsf{sk}_1), f_2(\mathsf{sk}_1, \mathsf{sk}_2), \cdots, f_{i-1}(\mathsf{sk}_{i-2}, \mathsf{sk}_{i-1}), L^*(Z, X \cdot T'), f_{i+2}(\mathsf{sk}_{i+2}, \mathsf{sk}'_{i+3}), \ldots, f_t(\mathsf{sk}'_t, \mathsf{sk}'_{t+1})\Big)$.

Then it is not hard to see that if Z comes from the distribution XT, then the simulation of $\mathcal{B}$ and L^* distributes as Q_i, and otherwise Q_{i-1}. Thus, suppose $\mathcal{A}$ can distinguish Q_i from Q_{i+1} with non-negligible probability ϵ, then $\mathcal{B}$ can distinguish the two distributions with a non-negligible probability. This contradicts Lemma 6.

Finally, we show that D_0'' is computationally indistinguishable from D_1'' under the linear assumption.

Lemma 13. *Under the linear assumption, the distributions D_0'' and D_1'' are computationally indistinguishable.*

We use the same argument as the work [5]. In particular, we will prove that suppose there exists an adversary $\mathcal{A}$ that distinguishes D_0'' from D_1'', then there exists an adversary $\mathcal{B}$ that distinguishes the distributions $\{g^C : C \leftarrow \mathbb{Z}_p^{3\times3}\}$ and $\{g^C : C \leftarrow \mathsf{Rk}_2(\mathbb{Z}_p^{3\times3})\}$. We assume that the second distribution samples two random rows, and then sets the third row as a random linear combination of the first two rows. As argued in the work [5], this assumption is without loss of generality.

Now we describe the adversary $\mathcal{B}$. $\mathcal{B}$ on input g^C does the following.

- $\mathcal{B}$ samples a random matrix $X \leftarrow \mathbb{Z}_p^{\ell\times(\ell-3)}$, and a random matrix $B \leftarrow \mathbb{Z}_p^{3\times\ell}$ such that $B \cdot X = 0$.
- $\mathcal{B}$ computes g^{CB}, and sets its first two rows as g^A and the last row as g^z.
- $\mathcal{B}$ samples $T_1, \ldots, T_t \leftarrow \mathsf{Rk}_2(\mathbb{Z}_p^{(\ell-3)\times2})$, and sets $\mathsf{sk}_i = g^{XT_i}$ for $i \in [t]$.
- $\mathcal{B}$ outputs $\mathcal{A}(g, g^A, g^z, f_1(\mathsf{sk}_0, \mathsf{sk}_1), \ldots, f_t(\mathsf{sk}_{t-1}, \mathsf{sk}_t))$.

As argued in the work [5], if C is uniformly random, then (A, z) is distributed uniformly as D_1''. If C is of rank 2, then (A, z) is distributed as $(A, r^T A)$ for some random $r \in \mathbb{Z}_p^2$ as D_0''. Thus, suppose $\mathcal{A}$ can distinguish D_0'' from D_1'' with non-negligible probability, then $\mathcal{B}$ breaks the linear assumption with non-negligible probability.

Lemma 9 ($D_0 \approx D_1$) follows directly from Lemmas 10, 12, and 13. This suffices to prove the theorem. We present the proofs of Lemmas 10, 12, and 13.

4   Bounded Leakage-Resilient Encryption Schemes from Obfuscation

We show that by modifying the Sahai-Waters (SW) public key encryption scheme [23] in two simple ways, the scheme already becomes non-trivially leakage resilient in the one-time, bounded setting. Recall that in this setting, the adversary, after seeing the public key and before seeing the challenge ciphertext, may request a single leakage query of length L bits. We require that semantic security hold, even given this leakage.

Our scheme can tolerate an arbitrary amount of one-time leakage. Specifically, for any $L = L(\kappa) = \mathrm{poly}(\kappa)$, we can obtain a scheme which is L-leakage resilient by setting the parameter ρ in Fig. 6 depending on L. However, our leakage *rate* is not optimal, since the size of the secret key sk, grows with L. In the full version [8] of the paper, we will show how to further modify the construction to achieve optimal leakage rate.

On a high-level, we modify SW in the following ways: (1) Instead of following the general paradigm of encrypting a message m by xoring with the output of a PRF, we first apply a strong randomness extractor Ext to the output of the PRF and then xor with the message m; (2) We modify the secret key of the new scheme to be an iO of the underlying decryption circuit. Recall that in SW, decryption essentially consists of evaluating a puncturable PRF. In our scheme, sk consists of an iO of the puncturable PRF, padded with $\mathrm{poly}(L)$ bits.

We show that, even given L bits of leakage, the attacker cannot distinguish $\mathsf{Ext}(y)$ from random, where y is the output of the PRF on a fixed input t^*. This will be sufficient to prove security. We proceed by a sequence of hybrids: First, we switch sk to be an obfuscation of a circuit which has a PRF key punctured at t^* and a point function $t^* \to y$ hardcoded. On input $t \neq t^*$, the punctured PRF is used to compute the output, whereas on input t^*, the point function is used. Since the circuits compute the same function and—due to appropriate padding—they are both the same size, security of the iO implies that an adversary cannot distinguish the two scenarios. Next, just as in SW, we switch from $t^* \to y$ to $t^* \to y^*$, where y^* is uniformly random of length $L+L_{\mathsf{msg}}+2\log(1/\epsilon)$ bits; here we rely on the security of the punctured PRF. Now, observe that since y^* is uniform and since Ext is a strong extractor for inputs of min-entropy $L_{\mathsf{msg}} + 2\log(1/\epsilon)$ and output length L_{msg}, $\mathsf{Ext}(y^*)$ looks random, even under L bits of leakage.

The informal theorem statement is below. We present the formal theorem and proof in the full version (Figs. 7 and 8).

Encryption Scheme $\mathcal{E} = (\mathcal{E}.\mathsf{Gen}, \mathcal{E}.\mathsf{Enc}, \mathcal{E}.\mathsf{Dec})$

Key Generation: $(\mathsf{pk}, \mathsf{sk}_0) \leftarrow \mathcal{E}.\mathsf{Gen}(1^\kappa)$
  Compute $k \leftarrow \mathsf{PRF}.\mathsf{Gen}(1^\kappa)$, where $\mathsf{PRF} : \{0,1\}^\kappa \times \{0,1\}^\rho \to \{0,1\}^\rho$. Let C_k be the circuit described in Figure 7, and let $C_{\mathsf{Enc}} \leftarrow \mathsf{iO}(C_k)$.
  Let $C_{k,\kappa+\rho}$ be the circuit described in Figure 8, and let $C_{\mathsf{Dec}} \leftarrow \mathsf{iO}(C_{k,\kappa+\rho})$.
  Output $\mathsf{pk} = (C_{\mathsf{Enc}})$ and $\mathsf{sk} = (C_{\mathsf{Dec}})$.
Encryption: $c \leftarrow \mathcal{E}.\mathsf{Enc}(\mathsf{pk}, m)$
  On input message $m \in \{0,1\}^{L_{\mathsf{msg}}}$, sample $r \leftarrow \{0,1\}^\kappa, w \leftarrow \{0,1\}^d$, and output $c = (G(r), w, \mathsf{Ext}(C_{\mathsf{Enc}}(r), w) \oplus m)$, where PRG $G : \{0,1\}^\kappa \to \{0,1\}^\rho$, and Ext : $\{0,1\}^\rho \times \{0,1\}^d \to \{0,1\}^{L_{\mathsf{msg}}}$.
Decryption: $\hat{m} \leftarrow \mathcal{E}.\mathsf{Dec}(\mathsf{sk}, c)$
  On input ciphertext $c = (t, w, v)$, compute $y := C_{\mathsf{Dec}}(t)$.
  If $y \neq \bot$, output $\hat{m} = \mathsf{Ext}(y, w) \oplus v$. Otherwise, output $\hat{m} = \bot$.

Fig. 6. The one-time, bounded leakage encryption scheme, $\mathcal{E}$.

Internal (hardcoded) state: k.

On input: r

 – Output $z = \mathsf{PRF}.\mathsf{Eval}(k, G(r))$, where G is the same PRG used in $\mathcal{E}.\mathsf{Enc}$.

Fig. 7. This program C_k is obfuscated using iO and placed in the public key to be used for encryption.

Theorem 4 (Informal.). *Under appropriate assumptions, $\mathcal{E}$ is L-leakage resilient against one-time key leakage where $L = \rho - 2\log(1/\epsilon) - L_{\mathsf{msg}}$.*

> Internal (hardcoded) state: k.
>
> On input: t
>
> – Output $z = \mathsf{PRF.Eval}(k, t)$.

Fig. 8. The circuit above is padded with $\mathrm{poly}(\kappa + \rho)$ dummy gates to obtain the circuit $C_{k,\kappa+\rho}$. $C_{k,\kappa+\rho}$ is then obfuscated using iO and placed in the secret key.

References

1. Akavia, A., Goldwasser, S., Vaikuntanathan, V.: Simultaneous hardcore bits and cryptography against memory attacks. In: Reingold, O. (ed.) TCC 2009. LNCS, vol. 5444, pp. 474–495. Springer, Heidelberg (2009)
2. Barak, B., Goldreich, O., Impagliazzo, R., Rudich, S., Sahai, A., Vadhan, S.P., Yang, K.: On the (im)possibility of obfuscating programs. J. ACM **59**(2), 6 (2012)
3. Boldyreva, A., Fehr, S., O'Neill, A.: On notions of security for deterministic encryption, and efficient constructions without random oracles. In: Wagner, D. (ed.) CRYPTO 2008. LNCS, vol. 5157, pp. 335–359. Springer, Heidelberg (2008)
4. Boyle, E., Segev, G., Wichs, D.: Fully leakage-resilient signatures. In: Paterson, K.G. (ed.) EUROCRYPT 2011. LNCS, vol. 6632, pp. 89–108. Springer, Heidelberg (2011)
5. Brakerski, Z., Kalai, Y.T., Katz, J., Vaikuntanathan, V.: Overcoming the hole in the bucket: public-key cryptography resilient to continual memory leakage. In: 51st FOCS, pp. 501–510. IEEE Computer Society Press, October 2010
6. Canetti, R., Dwork, C., Naor, M., Ostrovsky, R.: Deniable encryption. In: Kaliski Jr., B.S. (ed.) CRYPTO 1997. LNCS, vol. 1294, pp. 90–104. Springer, Heidelberg (1997)
7. Canetti, R., Goldwasser, S., Poburinnaya, O.: Adaptively secure two-party computation from indistinguishability obfuscation. In: Dodis, Y., Nielsen, J.B. (eds.) TCC 2015, Part II. LNCS, vol. 9015, pp. 557–585. Springer, Heidelberg (2015)
8. Dachman-Soled, D., Gordon, S.D., Liu, F.-H., O'Neill, A., Zhou, H.-S.: Leakage-resilient public-key encryption from obfuscation. Full version (2016)
9. Dachman-Soled, D., Katz, J., Rao, V.: Adaptively secure, universally composable, multiparty computation in constant rounds. In: Dodis, Y., Nielsen, J.B. (eds.) TCC 2015, Part II. LNCS, vol. 9015, pp. 586–613. Springer, Heidelberg (2015)
10. Dachman-Soled, D., Liu, F.-H., Zhou, H.-S.: Leakage-resilient circuits revisited – optimal number of computing components without leak-free hardware. In: Oswald, E., Fischlin, M. (eds.) EUROCRYPT 2015. LNCS, vol. 9057, pp. 131–158. Springer, Heidelberg (2015)
11. Dodis, Y., Haralambiev, K., López-Alt, A., Wichs, D.: Cryptography against continuous memory attacks. In: 51st FOCS, pp. 511–520. IEEE Computer Society Press, October 2010
12. Dodis, Y., Lewko, A.B., Waters, B., Wichs, D.: Storing secrets on continually leaky devices. In: Ostrovsky, R. (ed.) 52nd FOCS, pp. 688–697. IEEE Computer Society Press, October 2011
13. Dodis, Y., Smith, A.: Correcting errors without leaking partial information. In: Gabow, H.N., Fagin, R. (eds.) 37th ACM STOC, pp. 654–663. ACM Press, May 2005

14. Garg, S., Gentry, C., Halevi, S., Raykova, M., Sahai, A., Waters, B.: Candidate indistinguishability obfuscation and functional encryption for all circuits. In: 54th FOCS, pp. 40–49. IEEE Computer Society Press, October 2013
15. Garg, S., Gentry, C., Halevi, S., Wichs, D.: On the implausibility of differing-inputs obfuscation and extractable witness encryption with auxiliary input. In: Garay, J.A., Gennaro, R. (eds.) CRYPTO 2014, Part I. LNCS, vol. 8616, pp. 518–535. Springer, Heidelberg (2014)
16. Garg, S., Polychroniadou, A.: Two-round adaptively secure MPC from indistinguishability obfuscation. In: Dodis, Y., Nielsen, J.B. (eds.) TCC 2015, Part II. LNCS, vol. 9015, pp. 614–637. Springer, Heidelberg (2015)
17. Hazay, C., López-Alt, A., Wee, H., Wichs, D.: Leakage-resilient cryptography from minimal assumptions. In: Johansson, T., Nguyen, P.Q. (eds.) EUROCRYPT 2013. LNCS, vol. 7881, pp. 160–176. Springer, Heidelberg (2013)
18. Ishai, Y., Pandey, O., Sahai, A.: Public-coin differing-inputs obfuscation and its applications. In: Dodis, Y., Nielsen, J.B. (eds.) TCC 2015, Part II. LNCS, vol. 9015, pp. 668–697. Springer, Heidelberg (2015)
19. Katz, J., Vaikuntanathan, V.: Signature schemes with bounded leakage resilience. In: Matsui, M. (ed.) ASIACRYPT 2009. LNCS, vol. 5912, pp. 703–720. Springer, Heidelberg (2009)
20. Lewko, A.B., Lewko, M., Waters, B.: How to leak on key updates. In: Fortnow, L., Vadhan, S.P. (eds.) 43rd ACM STOC, pp. 725–734. ACM Press, June 2011
21. Micali, S., Reyzin, L.: Physically observable cryptography. In: Naor, M. (ed.) TCC 2004. LNCS, vol. 2951, pp. 278–296. Springer, Heidelberg (2004)
22. Naor, M., Segev, G.: Public-key cryptosystems resilient to key leakage. In: Halevi, S. (ed.) CRYPTO 2009. LNCS, vol. 5677, pp. 18–35. Springer, Heidelberg (2009)
23. Sahai, A., Waters, B.: How to use indistinguishability obfuscation: deniable encryption, and more. In: Shmoys, D.B. (ed.) 46th ACM STOC, pp. 475–484. ACM Press, May/June 2014
24. Waters, B.: Dual system encryption: realizing fully secure IBE and HIBE under simple assumptions. In: Halevi, S. (ed.) CRYPTO 2009. LNCS, vol. 5677, pp. 619–636. Springer, Heidelberg (2009)

On Generic Constructions of Circularly-Secure, Leakage-Resilient Public-Key Encryption Schemes

Mohammad Hajiabadi$^{(\boxtimes)}$, Bruce M. Kapron, and Venkatesh Srinivasan

Department of Computer Science, University of Victoria, Victoria, Canada
{mhaji,bmkapron,srinivas}@uvic.ca

Abstract. We propose generic constructions of public-key encryption schemes, satisfying *key-dependent message (KDM) security for projections* and different forms of *key-leakage resilience*, from CPA-secure private-key encryption schemes with two main abstract properties: (1) a form of (additive) homomorphism with respect to both plaintexts and randomness, and (2) *reproducibility*, providing a means for reusing encryption randomness across independent secret keys. More precisely, our construction transforms a private-key scheme with the stated properties (and one more mild condition) into a public-key one, providing:

- KDM-projection security, an extension of circular security, where the adversary may also ask for encryptions of negated secret key bits;
- a $(1 - o(1))$ resilience rate in the bounded-memory leakage model of Akavia et al. (TCC 2009); and
- *Auxiliary-input security* against subexponentially-hard functions.

We introduce *homomorphic weak pseudorandom functions*, a homomorphic version of the weak PRFs proposed by Naor and Reingold (FOCS '95) and use them to realize our base encryption scheme. We in turn obtain homomorphic weak PRFs from *homomorphic hash-proof systems* (*HHPS*). We also show how the base encryption scheme may be realized using subgroup indistinguishability (implied, in particular, by quadratic residuosity (QR) and decisional composite residuosity (DCR)). As corollaries of our results, we obtain (1) the first multiple-key projection-secure bit-encryption scheme (as well as the first scheme with a $(1 - o(1))$ resilience rate) based solely on the HHPS assumption, and (2) a unifying approach explaining the results of Boneh et al. (CRYPTO '08) and Brakerski and Goldwasser (CRYPTO '10). Finally, by observing that Applebaum's KDM amplification method (EUROCRYPT '11) preserves both types of leakage resilience, we obtain schemes providing at the same time high leakage resilience and KDM security against any fixed polynomial-sized circuit family.

Work of the first two authors supported in part by an NSERC Discovery Grant, "Foundational studies in privacy and security", and the Simons Institute for the Theory of Computing program "Real analysis in computer science". Work of the second author was partly completed while a Visiting Member of the School of Mathematics at the Institute for Advanced Study. Part of this work was done while the third author was a Senior Visiting Research Fellow at the Centre for Quantum Technologies, NUS, Singapore.

C.-M. Cheng et al. (Eds.): PKC 2016, Part II, LNCS 9615, pp. 129–158, 2016.
DOI: 10.1007/978-3-662-49387-8_6

1   Introduction

A central goal in cryptography is to build a variety of cryptographic primitives with a high degree of versatility from assumptions that are as general as possible. Encryption in particular has been defined, starting with the seminal paper of Goldwasser and Micali [23], with respect to successively strong models of security. However, standard notions of encryption security (i.e., CPA and different forms of CCA security [17,23,36,38]) fall short in certain applications, in particular, where the adversary may obtain some side information about the internal secret parameters (e.g., the secret key) of the scheme. This leakage of side information may occur due to some unforeseen attacks on the scheme (*side-channel attacks*), or more fundamentally, when encryption is used as a primitive in a complex protocol which may inherently expose inside information. These observations have led to the definition and realization of stronger notions of encryption security, such as security against different forms of leakage [1,2,9,14,15,19,25,32,35], and key-dependent message (KDM) security [3–5,7–10,27,31]. Our goal is to construct schemes realizing these security properties from general assumptions. Our results concern a basic model of leakage, known as the *bounded-leakage model* [1] and a basic model of KDM security, known as *projection* security (which is slightly stronger than *circular* security). We will also consider a model of *auxiliary-input security* [14,15]. We first provide some background on these models and then describe our results.

For all definitions below (unless otherwise stated) we assume we are encrypting the secret key (or functions thereof) bit-by-bit, i.e., the scheme is either bit encryption, or there is a mapping from bits to two fixed plaintext messages.

KDM Security. KDM security is defined with respect to a function family F: informally, an encryption scheme (G, E, Dec) is F-KDM$^{(1)}$ secure if no adversary can distinguish between two oracles, where the first one, on input $f \in F$, returns $E_{pk}(f(sk))$ (for a random (pk, sk) chosen at the beginning), and the second one, regardless of the input, returns an encryption of a fixed message. A basic form of KDM$^{(1)}$ security is 1-circular security, allowing the adversary to obtain encryptions of any bit of the secret key. Another basic notion is projection security, which also allows the adversary to obtain encryptions of negations of secret key bits. KDM$^{(1)}$ security generalizes naturally to the case of multiple pairs of keys, giving rise to the notion of F-KDM$^{(n)}$-security, where in a system with the pairs of keys $(pk_1, sk_1), \ldots, (pk_n, sk_n)$ a chosen function $f \in F$ comes with an index j, and as a result $f(sk_1, \ldots, sk_n)$ is encrypted under pk_j. For example, n-projection security allows the adversary to see encryptions of any bit of any secret key or its negation under (possibly) any other public key.

KDM security was originally defined by Black et al. [7], who built a *fully-KDM*-secure scheme (i.e., KDM-security with respect to all functions) in the random oracle model. In [8] Boneh et al. gave the first construction in the standard model, based on the DDH assumption, of a public-key scheme that was proved KDM$^{(n)}$ secure with respect to *affine functions*. This positive result led to a series of subsequent works, focusing on building affine-KDM$^{(n)}$ security under alternate specific assumptions (i.e., LPN/LWE [4], and QR/DCR and more generally *subgroup indistinguishability (SG)* assumptions [9]), and on developing *KDM-amplification* methods for transforming schemes with basic forms of KDM security into schemes with more sophisticated forms of KDM security [3,5,10]. These amplification methods in turn employ techniques such as garbled circuits [5], *randomized encoding of functions* [3] and *entropic-KDM* security [10] to enable KDM transformations. Most relevant to our work are the results of Applebaum [3], showing that, informally speaking, projection security is sufficient to obtain KDM security with respect to any fixed circuit family whose size is poly-bounded. Thus, a fundamental question regarding KDM security is to study general assumptions sufficient for realizing projection security, which is one of the main goals in our paper.

It turns out that realizing even 1-circular security for bit encryption is considerably more difficult than the case where the secret-key space is a subset of the plaintext space (so one can encrypt the whole key at once). In the latter case, through simple modifications to the encryption algorithm, one can make any CPA-secure scheme 1-circularly secure. Currently, the only constructions that provide bitwise 1-circular security are those of [4,8,10], which are based on specific assumptions. Also, it was shown in [41] that the implication that "any CPA-secure bit encryption scheme is also 1-circularly secure" is not provable using reductions that use both the adversary and the scheme in a blackbox way.[1] Moreover, under widely-believed assumptions, there exist CPA-secure bit-encryption schemes that are not 1-circularly secure [30,41].

Leakage Resilience. Akavia et al. [1] introduce the notion of encryption security against bounded memory leakage, wherein an adversary (after seeing the public key) may obtain arbitrary information about the secret key, of the form $f(sk)$ for adaptively chosen f, as long as the total number of bits leaked does not exceed an a priori fixed quantity, ℓ. (We refer to the fraction $\ell/|sk|$ as the resilience rate.) They showed that Regev's scheme [39] and the identity based encryption scheme of [20], both under the LWE assumption, provide resilience rate $O(1/polylog(|sk|))$. Naor and Segev [35] showed how to obtain encryption schemes resilient to high leakage lengths (but with low resilience rates) from any hash-proof system [13] and how to obtain schemes with $(1 - o(1))$-resilience rates from d-linear assumptions; moreover, they showed that the circularly-secure scheme of [8] provides a $(1 - o(1))$ resilience rate. Brakerski and Goldwasser [9], under the subgroup indistinguishability assumption, implied in turn by the QR and DCR assumptions, showed how to obtain encryption schemes that are affine-KDM secure, with a $(1 - o(1))$ resilience rate.

Auxiliary-Input Security. In the auxiliary-input model [14,15] the adversary is given some side information of the form $h(pk, sk)$, and the goal is to guarantee security as long as recovering sk from $h(pk, sk)$ is sufficiently, computationally hard. For public-key encryption Dodis et al. [14] build schemes based on LWE

---

[1] Note that this is different from asking whether CPA-secure bit encryption implies the existence of circularly-secure bit encryption.

and DDH (where their DDH-based scheme is a variant of [8]) secure against *subexponentially-hard-to-invert* functions. Brakerski and Goldwasser [9] present schemes with the same level of auxiliary-input security under the subgroup indistinguishability assumption.

1.1 Our Results (Assumptions and Constructions)

As pointed our earlier, the only constructions of circularly-secure/projection-secure bit encryption (even 1-circular security) are based on specific assumptions [4,8,9]. Moreover, the schemes of [8,9], referred to as BHHO and BG henceforth, besides KDM security, also provide security against different forms of leakage (as shown in [9,14,35]). Therefore, a natural question is whether there exist more general constructions that encompass all these specific constructions.

We will try to answer these questions by building leakage-resilient, projection-secure encryption schemes from CPA-secure private-key schemes with some special properties, which we now informally describe. Then we will use this private-key encryption abstraction as a stepping stone toward obtaining our results under other primitives.

The first property is a generalized version of additive homomorphism, where homomorphism is required to hold also with respect to randomness (let Hom denote the associated function). The second property is what Bellare et al. [6] call *reproducibility*, requiring that given a message m_2, secret key sk_2 and ciphertext $c = E_{sk_1}(m_1; r)$, where sk_1, m_1 and r are unknown, one can efficiently obtain $E_{sk_2}(m_2; r)$, i.e., there is a way to efficiently transfer the randomness from one encryption to another, provided the secret key for the second encryption is known.[2] We denote this efficient computation by $Rep(c, m_2, sk_2)$. Note that if an encryption algorithm reveals its randomness in the clear, then reproducibility is trivially satisfied, e.g., the standard way of building CPA-secure private-key encryption from a pseudorandom function family F, defining encryption as $E_{sk}(m) = (r, F_{sk}(r) \oplus m)$, provides reproducibility. In fact, we will later use this idea to obtain our encryption primitive, based on the existence of *homomorphic weak pseudorandom functions*. Note that for homomorphism, we are assuming that the message and randomness spaces must form groups. For technical reasons, we will also require the following property: from any encryption $E_{sk}(b; r)$, for unknown sk, b, r, one can obtain $E_{sk}(1; 0)$, i.e., the encryption of bit 1 under key sk based on the identity element of the randomness group.[3] We see this as a form of *degenerate* homomorphism.

We introduce a construction C (formalized in Sect. 3 and sketched in Subsect. 1.4) that transforms a private-key scheme with the stated properties into a public-key one and show the following result.

---

[2] Both these conditions were used implicitly by Peikert and Waters as the main building blocks for their construction of lossy-trapdoor functions [37].

[3] The actual assumption we need is substantially weaker. However, we leave it this way for the sake of readability. In fact, under all concrete schemes we present, $E_{sk}(m; 0)$ depends only on m and is independent of sk.

Theorem (Informal). Assume that $\mathcal{E} = (G, E, Dec, Hom, Rep)$ is a CPA-secure private-key, bit-encryption scheme that is degenerate additively homomorphic and reproducible. Then the constructed scheme $\mathcal{E}' = C(\mathcal{E})$ is a public-key bit-encryption scheme that satisfies the following properties.

- For any integer n, by appropriately choosing the system parameters, $\mathcal{E}'$ is n-projection secure. (Formalized in Theorem 2)
- By appropriately choosing the system parameters, $\mathcal{E}'$ provides a $(1 - o(1))$-leakage resilience rate. (Formalized in Theorem 3)
- $\mathcal{E}'$ provides auxiliary-input leakage resilience against subexponentially-hard functions. (Formalized in Theorem 6 and Remark 1)

We will also discuss generalizations of the above construction to the case the base scheme is not bit-encryption.

1.2   Realizations

From Homomorphic Weak Pseudorandom Functions. Pseudorandom function families (PRFs) provide a convenient way of realizing reproducible CPA-secure private-key encryption via the standard PRF-based encryption construction. Towards providing homomorphism for a PRF-based scheme, we call a function family *homomorphic* if both the domain and range of the underlying functions form groups, and each function acts as a homomorphism. A standard PRF cannot, however, be homomorphic since with high probability a truly random function will not be homomorphic and an adversary with the power to (even) nonadaptively query a function oracle may easily exploit this fact. To prevent this type of attack, we work with *weak PRFs*, defined by Naor and Reingold [34], which allow an adversary to see values of the function only on a sequence of random inputs. Formally, f_k is *weakly pseudorandom* if no adversary can distinguish between $(d_1, f_k(d_1)), \ldots, (d_p, f_k(d_p))$ and $(d_1, r_1), \ldots, (d_p, r_p)$, where all d_i's and r_i's are chosen independently at random. As we see next, not only is the notion of homomorphic weak PRFs meaningful, it is naturally realizable under specific assumptions. We also note that the standard construction of private-key encryption from a PRF, when applied to homomorphic weak PRFs, results in a scheme that satisfies the properties we need from our base encryption primitive (Lemma 4).

For a DDH-hard group $\mathbb{G}$ with $o = |\mathbb{G}|$, define $F = \{f_k \colon \mathbb{G} \to \mathbb{G}\}_{k \in \mathbb{Z}_o}$ by $f_k(g) = g^k$. This function family was introduced and proved to be weakly pseudorandom by Naor, Pinkas and Reingold [33]; the proof of weak pseudorandomness uses standard techniques related to random-self-reducibility of DDH. The fact that f_k is homomorphic is clear. Interestingly, by plugging this PRF into our general construction, we obtain a scheme which is a close variant of the BHHO scheme. We also give a realization of weak homomorphic PRFs under *homomorphic hash-proof systems (HHPS)* [13]: here the PRF is simply the family of hash functions on *valid* points (Theorem 4). A corollary of our results is the following.

Corollary. Under the HHPS assumption and for any integer n, there exists a public-key encryption scheme that provides, at the same time, n-projection security and a $(1 - o(1))$-leakage resilience rate.

To the best of our knowledge, our results give the first HHPS-based encryption scheme that provides (even individually) n-projection security and a $(1 - o(1))$-leakage resilience rate. (See Subsect. 1.4 for a comparison of our results with those of the recent work of [42].) Naor and Segev [35] show how to construct schemes with high tolerated leakage lengths (but low *rates* of leakage resilience) from any hash-proof system, and also how to obtain schemes with $(1 - o(1))$ leakage-resilience rates from *k-linear assumptions*. Our results can be thought of as complementing those of [35], by saying that if we add homomorphism to a HPS, we obtain schemes with high resilience rates. Hazay et al. [26] show how to obtain schemes withstanding high leakage lengths from any CPA-secure public-key encryption (which is the minimal assumption). Their construction, however, produces a scheme with low leakage-resilience rates, and does not imply our leakage resilience result based on HHPS.

From Subgroup Indistinguishability. We show how to instantiate our encryption primitive under the subgroup indistinguishability (SG) assumption [9], of which QR and DCR are special cases (Lemma 5). Our current formulation of homomorphic weak PRFs does not seem to be realizable under the SG assumption. It is, however, possible to formulate a more relaxed version of such PRFs, one that is still sufficient for realizing our encryption assumptions and is also realizable under the SG assumption. We choose not to pursue this direction since there is already an easy way to realize our encryption primitive under the SG assumption.

We provide a summary of our results in Fig. 1.

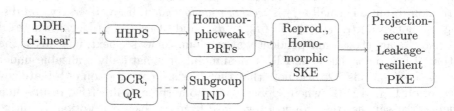

Fig. 1. Summary of results (dashed arrows indicate known implications)

1.3 KDM Amplification and Leakage Resilience

We prove that Applebaum's KDM amplification method [3] for obtaining KDM-security for any fixed family of bounded circuits from projection security also preserves both types of leakage resilience (Theorem 9). We were not, however, able to show this for the KDM amplification methods of [5,10]. Applebaum's transformation has the key property that it only modifies the encryption and decryption algorithms of the base scheme, by applying *randomized encoding and decoding*, which are fixed mappings constructed based on the target function family, inside the encryption and decryption algorithms. This property facilitates reducing leakage resilience and auxiliary input security of the constructed scheme to the same requirements (i.e., with the same parameters) on the base scheme. As a corollary, for any fixed bounded function family F and any integer n, assuming the existence of private-key schemes with the stated properties, we obtain schemes that at the same time provide (1) F-KDM$^{(n)}$ security, (2) a $(1 - o(1))$-leakage resilience rate, and (3) auxiliary-input security against subexponentially-hard functions (Corollary 1).

1.4   Construction Technique and Further Discussion

Construction and Proof Techniques. We now give a sketch of the construction, C, and proof techniques. Fix $\mathcal{E} = (G, E, D, Rep, Hom)$ to be a private-key bit-encryption scheme that provides reproducibility and the generalized homomorphism condition. The latter, using additive notation, states the following condition that $Hom(E_{sk}(b_1; r_1), E_{sk}(b_2; r_2)) = E_{sk}(b_1 + b_2; r_1 + r_2)$. (Note that because of our additive notation our message space is $\mathbb{Z}_2$, and 0 is the identity element of the randomness space.)

Under $\mathcal{E}' = C(\mathcal{E}) = (G', E', D')$, the secret key is a random string $\mathbf{s} \leftarrow \{0,1\}^l$ (for some poly l) and the public key is a tuple of ciphertexts

$$\mathbf{pk} = (E_{sk}(0; r_1), \ldots, E_{sk}(0; r_l), E_{sk}(0; \mathbf{s} \cdot \mathbf{r})),$$

where $sk, r_1, \ldots, r_l$ are generated randomly under $\mathcal{E}$ and $(\cdot)$ denotes the inner product of $\mathbf{s}$ and $\mathbf{r} = (r_1, \ldots, r_l)$. In words, $\mathbf{pk}$ consists of $l + 1$ $\mathcal{E}$-encryptions of zero, where the first l encryptions are produced independently, while the randomness value used for the last encryption is a "subset-sum" of the previous ones based on $\mathbf{s}$. To encrypt a bit b we sample $sk' \leftarrow G(1^\lambda)$ and output $(E_{sk'}(0; r_1), \ldots, E_{sk'}(0; r_l), E_{sk'}(b; \mathbf{s} \cdot \mathbf{r}))$, which can be computed from $\mathbf{pk}$ by applying Rep component-wise. To decrypt $(c_1, \ldots, c_l, c_{l+1})$ under $\mathbf{s}$, we return 0 iff $c_{l+1} = Hom_{\mathbf{s}}(c_1, \ldots, c_l)$, where $Hom_{\mathbf{s}}(c_1, \ldots, c_l)$ "sums" those ciphertexts c_i where $\mathbf{sk}_i = 1$. The correctness of decryption follows.

Some notes are in order. Firstly, under G', the secret key of the old scheme, sk, is used *only* to compute the encryptions needed to form $\mathbf{pk}$. Roughly, the fact that $\mathbf{s}$ is independent of sk underlies the circular security of $\mathcal{E}'$. Secondly, E' has the somewhat unusual property that it calls G, with the returned values comprising all the randomness used in encryption.

As a warm-up we first discuss CPA security of $\mathcal{E}'$. Consider a malformed public key $\mathbf{pk}_{mal}$ with r_{l+1} chosen independently at random (instead of being $\mathbf{s} \cdot \mathbf{r}$). CPA security under $\mathbf{pk}_{mal}$ reduces to showing $(\mathbf{pk}_{mal}, \mathbf{c}_0) \equiv^c (\mathbf{pk}_{mal}, \mathbf{c}_1)$, where $\equiv^c$ denotes computational indistinguishability, and

$$\mathbf{c}_b = (E_{sk'}(0; r_1), \ldots, E_{sk'}(0; r_l), E_{sk'}(b; r_{l+1}))$$

This in turn follows by appealing to the CPA security and reproducibility of $\mathcal{E}$. To complete the CPA-security proof, it would suffice to argue that a malformed public-key is indistinguishable from a valid one, which follows information theoretically (from the *leftover hash lemma*) if l is large enough. Below we extend the arguments given here to argue about KDM and leakage-resilience security of the scheme.

KDM Security. A main idea used in the proof of 1-circular security (for simplicity) is that if one possesses $\mathbf{s}$, then the encryption of a bit b may be equivalently computed as $\mathbf{c} = (c_1, \ldots, c_l, Hom(c_{i_1}, \ldots, c_{i_w}, c'))$, where $sk' \leftarrow G(1^\lambda)$, $c_j \leftarrow E_{sk'}(0)$ for $1 \leq j \leq l$, $(i_1, \ldots, i_w)$ are the indices of nonzero bits of $\mathbf{s}$ and $c' = E_{sk'}(b; 0)$ (i.e., c' is the encryption of b where the randomness value is fixed to the group identity 0.) Now we consider an intermediate hybrid, W_1, in which to encrypt the hth bit of $\mathbf{s}$, we return $(c_1, \ldots, c_l, Hom(c_{i_1}, \ldots, c_{i_w}, c'))$, where now c_h is an encryption of 1, but every other c_j is an encryption of 0 (and c' is an encryption of $\mathbf{s}_h$ under the identity randomness). We will show that W_1 provides a view computationally indistinguishable from the real view, W_0; the main idea is that any distinguisher between W_0 and W_1 can be reduced to an adversary $\mathcal{A}$ that wins in a special vector-encryption game (performed under $\mathcal{E}$), in which $\mathcal{A}$ may adaptively issue fixed-length vectors of bits (of a certain form), and in response to each vector query $\mathbf{v}$, either $\mathbf{v}$ or the all-zero vector (depending on the challenge bit) is component-wise encrypted under a fresh secret key, but by reusing randomness across each fixed component of vectors (that is the ith component of each vector is always encrypted under a fixed random r_i). In Lemma 3 we show any $\mathcal{A}$ has a negligible advantage under this game, and use this to prove the indistinguishability of W_0 and W_1. (It turns out this last step also requires us to use degenerate homomorphism to compute $E_{sk'}(1; 0)$ obliviously to sk'.) Having proved the indistinguishability of W_0 and W_1 we notice that under W_1 the reply to "encrypt the hth bit of $\mathbf{s}$" is indeed formed as $(E_{sk'}(0; r_1), \ldots, E_{sk'}(0; r_{h-1}), E_{sk'}(1; r_h), E_{sk'}(0; r_{h+1}), \ldots, E_{sk'}(0; r_l), E_{sk}(0; \mathbf{s} \cdot \mathbf{r}))$, and in particular is independent of $\mathbf{s}$ beyond $\mathbf{s} \cdot \mathbf{r}$, which makes the rest of the proof follow smoothly using ideas described for the CPA case.

The described techniques might be called *simulated KDM encryptions*, originally introduced in [8], used also in subsequent works [4,9], which show how to simulate KDM responses under public information. The main challenge in our setting is how to enable such properties under our general assumptions.

Leakage Resilience. For simplicity, we first outline the idea of the proof for the case of nonadaptive leakage resilience (that is, the function f is queried before the public key being published). To argue about nonadaptive leakage resilience, one has to show $D_0 \equiv^c D_1$, where $D_b = (\mathbf{pk}, \mathbf{c}_b, f(\mathbf{s}))$, and

$$\mathbf{c}_b = (E_{sk'}(0; r_1), \ldots, E_{sk'}(0; r_l), E_{sk'}(b; \mathbf{s} \cdot \mathbf{r}))$$

Now since f is chosen independently of $\mathbf{pk}$, it is also independent of $\mathbf{r}$, which allows us to apply the average-case version of the leftover hash lemma [16] (considering the inner product acts as a universal hash function) to replace $\mathbf{s} \cdot \mathbf{r}$ with a totally random r_{l+1}; the rest of the proof follows from the fact that $\mathcal{E}$ allows secure reuse of randomness. For the adaptive case, to handle the issue that f depends on **pk** (and so we cannot apply random extraction directly), we use similar techniques to those used by [35]: we consider a hybrid D_b', which is similar to D_b, but in which the first l bits encrypted under sk' are independently random bits $b_1, \ldots, b_l$ (as opposed to zeros) and that the last bit is $\mathbf{s} \cdot (b_1, \ldots, b_l) + b$. By proving $D_b' \equiv^c D_b$, for both $b \in \{0, 1\}$, (essentially using reproducibility and semantic security of $\mathcal{E}$) we can now apply the generalized leftover hash lemma by taking $(b_1, \ldots, b_l)$ as the seed, $\mathbf{s}$ as the source and considering that b_i's are chosen independently of f and $\mathbf{r}$; this allows us to replace $\mathbf{s} \cdot (b_1, \ldots, b_l)$ with a uniformly random bit, proving D_0' is statistically close to D_1'. The leakage resilience proof follows. The proof for the auxiliary-input case essentially follows the same line of arguments, except for replacing randomness extraction with pseudorandomness extraction [22]. We refer the reader to the full proof.

Final Remarks. Instantiating the above construction using homomorphic weak PRFs provides an improvement in efficiency, matching the same level of efficiency as [8] if the base PRF (in turn) is instantiated under the corresponding assumption. Technically, in this case, it would suffice to define the public key to be $(d_1, \ldots, d_l, \mathbf{s} \cdot (d_1, \ldots, d_l))$, i.e., instead of putting the whole ciphertext in each component, we only give the underlying randomness, which would have been given out by the ciphertext itself in the clear. Also, to encrypt m under $\mathbf{pk} = (d_1, \ldots, d_l, d_{l+1})$, we simply output $(F_{sk}(d_1), \ldots, F_{sk}(d_l), F_{sk}(d_{l+1}) + m)$, where sk is a fresh PRF key.

While our results enable us to explain those of [8,9,35], regarding KDM security and leakage resilience of the BHHO and BG schemes, they suffer from the same limitations as those of [9], in that, in order to achieve KDM$^{(n)}$ security, we must choose the parameters of our constructed scheme based on n. Boneh et al. [8] get around this dependency by using the *random self-reducibility* of DDH and strong key-homomorphism properties of DDH-based schemes. Similar dependencies for (even specific) non-DDH-based assumptions occur in other settings as well, e.g., [11]. We leave it as an open problem to resolve this dependency. We should also mention that the BHHO and BG schemes were proved affine-KDM secure; under the current assumptions, we were not able to extend our results to the affine-KDM setting. Finally, we note that just the fact that we can build a CPA-secure (as opposed to KDM secure) public-key scheme from our private-key assumptions is not unheard of since even weaker forms of homomorphism are known to be sufficient to bridge this gap [40].

Comparison with [42]. Concurrently with our work, Wee [42] recently showed that the original HHPS-based encryption scheme of Cramer and Shoup [13] provides F-KDM$^{(1)}$ security, where F is a function class defined based on the underlying hash functions. (Specifically, following notation in Subsect. 6.2, $F = \{f_{c,k} \colon \mathsf{SK} \mapsto \mathsf{K}\}$, where $f_{c,k}(sk) = \Lambda_{sk}(c) + k$.) We note that the basic KDM setting of [42] is different from ours in that we are concerned with KDM-security with respect to bit-projections of the secret key. Nevertheless, by instantiating that framework under specific DDH/SG-based HHPSs, [42] obtains schemes that are close variants of BHHO and BG. Moreover, the results of [42] also explain the bit-affine-security of BHHO and BG, while our results only explain the projection security. On the other hand, we obtain HHPS-based schemes that are n-projection secure, while the results of [42] do not seem to extend to the multiple-key setting (as noted there). Moreover, by using an encryption-based primitive as our base assumptions, we are able to obtain generic constructions under homomorphic weak PRFs, that is a weaker abstraction than the HHPS, as we show.

Other Related Work. Choi and Wee [12] show how to construct *lossy trapdoor functions* from homomorphic reproducible encryption by abstracting the matrix-based construction of Peikert and Waters [37]. This shows one more application of homomorphic weak PRFs as a general primitive. We mention, however, that the main difference between our constructions and those of [12,37] is that in [12, 37] the trapdoor key of the constructed schemes consists of secret keys produced under the base scheme, while in our setting, the main challenge (and novelty) is to come up with a construction whose encryption function still somehow calls that of the base scheme (in order to inherit its security), but in such a way that the secret keys of the base scheme are not included in the constructed secret key.

2   Definitions

2.1   Standard Notation and Definitions

For a finite set S we use $x \leftarrow S$ to denote sampling x uniformly at random from S and denote by U_S or $U(S)$ the uniform distribution on S. If D is a distribution then $x \leftarrow D$ denotes choosing x according to D. We denote the support set of a distribution D by $Sup(D)$, and write $x \in D$ to indicate $x \in Sup(D)$. The notions of computational indistinguishability and statistical indistinguishability are standard. We use $\equiv^c$ to refer to computational indistinguishability, $\equiv^s$ to statistical indistinguishability and $\equiv$ to *identity* of two distributions. We use the term PPT in this paper in the standard sense. We will often omit the adjective PPT/efficient when discussing functions – by default we assume all such functions are efficient.

We denote the length of $x \in \{0,1\}^*$ by $|x|$ and the ith bit of x, for $1 \leq i \leq |x|$, by x_i. We denote the n-th Cartesian power of a set S by S^n. We call $f : \mathbb{N} \to \mathbb{R}$ negligible if $f(\lambda) < 1/P(\lambda)$, for any poly P and sufficiently large λ.

All groups are assumed to admit efficient group operations, and to be commutative, but not necessarily cyclic, unless otherwise indicated.

2.2   Syntax of Encryption Schemes

We first start with some notation. We use $A(a_1, a_2, \ldots; r)$ to denote the deterministic output of randomized function A on inputs $a_1, a_2, \ldots$ and randomness r, and use $x \leftarrow A(a_1, a_2, \ldots)$ to denote the distribution formed by first choosing r uniformly at random and then outputting $A(a_1, a_2, \ldots; r)$.

We assume that all cryptographic primitives (encryption, PRFs, etc.) discussed in this paper, besides their usual algorithms, have a *parameter-generation* algorithm that produces *public parameters* (e.g., a group) used by all other algorithms. In situations where we talk about generating many keys it should be understood that all keys are sampled under the same public parameters, which were generated randomly at the beginning. We now give the syntax of encryption schemes.

A *public-key encryption scheme* $\mathcal{E}$ is given by algorithms $(Param, G, E, Dec)$, all taking as input a *security parameter* 1^λ (that we make it explicit for $Param$ and G and implicit for other algorithms.) $Param$ takes input 1^λ, and outputs a public parameter, par. The *key-generation* algorithm, takes 1^λ and par and outputs public/secret keys, $(pk, sk) \leftarrow G(1^\lambda, par)$. The *encryption* algorithm E, takes a public key pk, a plaintext $m \in \mathcal{M}_\lambda$ (where $\mathcal{M}_\lambda$ is the *plaintext space*) and randomness $r \in \mathcal{R}_\lambda$ (where $\mathcal{R}_\lambda$ is the *randomness space*), and deterministically produces ciphertext $c = E_{pk}(b; r)$. Finally, the *decryption* algorithm takes a secret key sk and ciphertext c, and deterministically outputs $m = Dec_{sk}(c)$. For correctness, we require, for every $par \in Param(1^\lambda)$, $(pk, sk) \in G(1^\lambda, param)$, every m and $c \in E_{pk}(m)$, that $Dec_{sk}(E_{pk}(m)) = m$. We typically use $\mathcal{PK}_\lambda$ and $\mathcal{SK}_\lambda$ to refer to the public-key and secret-key spaces. Formally, $(\mathcal{PK}_\lambda, \mathcal{SK}_\lambda) = Sup(G(1^\lambda))$. We make the inclusion of $Param$ implicit henceforth.

2.3   Key-Dependent-Message Security

In this paper we consider encryption schemes, whose generated secret keys are always bitstrings, but whose plaintext space may or may not be the single-bit space, e.g., it may be a group space. For the latter case, in order to make the notion of bitwise encryption of the secret key meaningful, we assume that a fixed mapping ($\{0, 1\} \rightarrow \mathcal{M}_\lambda$) is already in place. In the following, when we say $E_{pk}(b)$, where b is a bit, if E is a bit encryption algorithm, then we are encrypting the actual bit b, and otherwise, we are encrypting the element that b is mapped to. We now proceed to describe the notion of KDM$^{(n)}$ security for an arbitrary encryption scheme $\mathcal{E} = (G, E, Dec)$ (bit encryption or otherwise).

Assume that $F = \{F_\lambda\}_{\lambda \in \mathbb{N}}$ is an ensemble of sets of functions, where for each $f \in F_\lambda$, it holds that $f : \mathcal{SK}_\lambda^n \rightarrow \{0, 1\}$.

We define F-KDM$^{(n)}$ security through the following F-KDM$^{(n)}$ game, played between a challenger and an adversary. The challenger first chooses $b \leftarrow \{0, 1\}$, generates $(pk_1, sk_1), \ldots, (pk_n, sk_n) \leftarrow G(1^\lambda)$, and gives $pk_1, \ldots, pk_n$ to the adversary. The adversary $\mathcal{A}$, given pk_i's, can repeatedly and adaptively, for $1 \le i \le n$, make queries of the form (i, f), where $f \in F_\lambda$, or of the form (i, m), where $m \in \mathcal{M}_\lambda$, and in return,

- If $b = 0$, the challenger returns $E_{pk_i}(f(sk_1, \ldots, sk_n))$ in response to (i, f) and $E_{pk_i}(m)$ in response to (i, m); and
- If $b = 1$, the challenger returns $E_{pk_i}(0)$.

$\mathcal{A}$ finally outputs a bit b'. We define the F-KDM$^{(n)}$ *advantage of $\mathcal{A}$* as

$$Adv^{F\text{-KDM}^{(n)}}(\mathcal{A}) = |\Pr[b' = 1 | b = 0] - \Pr[b' = 1 | b = 1]| \, ,$$

where the probabilities are computed over the coins of $\mathcal{A}$ and of the challenger.

We say that $\mathcal{E}$ is F-KDM$^{(n)}$-secure if for any $\mathcal{A}$ in the above game, it holds that $Adv^{F\text{-}\mathrm{KDM}^{(n)}}(\mathcal{A}) = negl$.

Assume $\mathcal{SK}_\lambda = \{0,1\}^{l(\lambda)}$ and let $l = l(\lambda)$. For $1 \le i \le n$ and $1 \le j \le l$, define $Sel_{i,j}\colon \mathcal{SK}_\lambda^n \mapsto \{0,1\}$ to be the function that on input $(sk_1,\ldots,sk_n)$ returns the jth bit of sk_i. Similarly, define $NSel_{i,j}$ to be the function that on input $(sk_1,\ldots,sk_n)$ returns the negation of the jth bit of sk_i. Finally, define $S_\lambda = \{Sel_{i,j}\colon 1 \le i \le n, 1 \le j \le l\}$ and $\hat{S}_\lambda = \{NSel_{i,j}\colon 1 \le i \le n, 1 \le j \le l\}$. We now give the following definitions.

- We call $\mathcal{E}$ n-*circularly secure* if $\mathcal{E}$ is F-KDM$^{(n)}$ secure, where $F_\lambda = S_\lambda$.
- We call $\mathcal{E}$ n-*projection secure* if $\mathcal{E}$ is F-KDM$^{(n)}$ secure for $F_\lambda = S_\lambda \cup \hat{S}_\lambda$.

Semantic Security for Private-Key Encryption. For a private-key encryption scheme (G, E, Dec) it is convenient to work with the following definition of CPA security. (1) The challenger chooses $b \leftarrow \{0,1\}$ and private key $sk \leftarrow G(1^\lambda)$. (2) The adversary submits a sequence of messages $(m_1,\ldots,m_p)$, where $p = p(\lambda)$ is an arbitrary function. (3) The challenger returns $(E_{sk}(m_1),\ldots,E_{sk}(m_p))$ if $b = 0$, and $(E_{sk}(0),\ldots,E_{sk}(0))$, otherwise. (4) The adversary returns a bit b'. We define the CPA-security advantage of the adversary as

$$\left| \Pr[b' = 1 | b = 0] - \Pr[b' = 1 | b = 1] \right|,$$

and call the scheme CPA secure if all adversaries have negligible advantage.

2.4   Leakage Resilience

We define the notion of leakage resilience. For $\mathcal{L} = \mathcal{L}(\lambda)$, we say that the public-key encryption scheme $\mathcal{E} = (G, E, Dec)$ is $\mathcal{L}$-*length leakage resilient* if, for any adversary $\mathcal{A}$, the $\mathcal{L}$-leakage-advantage of $\mathcal{A}$, $Adv^{\mathcal{L}\text{-}leak}(\mathcal{A})$, defined via the following game, is negligible.

- Setup: The challenger generates $(pk, sk) \leftarrow G(1^\lambda)$ and gives pk to $\mathcal{A}$.
- Leakage queries: $\mathcal{A}$ sends function $f : \mathcal{SK}_\lambda \to \{0,1\}^*$ to the challenger, where $|f(sk)| \le \mathcal{L}$, and receives, in response, $f(sk)$.
- Challenge: $\mathcal{A}$ submits $(m_0, m_1) \in \mathcal{M}_\lambda^2$, and the challenger, samples $b \leftarrow \{0,1\}$, and returns $E_{pk}(m_b)$ to $\mathcal{A}$. Finally, $\mathcal{A}$ returns an output bit b'.

We define $Adv^{\mathcal{L}\text{-}leak}(\mathcal{A}) = \left| \Pr[b' = 1 | b = 0] - \Pr[b' = 1 | b = 1] \right|$. We say that $\mathcal{E}$ is r-*rate leakage resilient* (or has *resilience rate* r) if $\mathcal{E}$ is $r \cdot \log |\mathcal{SK}|$-length leakage resilient.

Finally, we note that restricting $\mathcal{A}$ in the above game to a single leakage query is without loss of generality. In particular, the security definition does not become stronger if $\mathcal{A}$ is allowed to adaptively make multiple leakage queries provided that the total length of the bits leaked is bounded by $\mathcal{L}(\lambda)$. The proof of this fact is straightforward; see [1] for a proof.

2.5 Properties of the Base Scheme

We give the definitions of the main properties that we need from the base private-key encryption scheme.

Definition 1. *A private-key encryption scheme* $\mathcal{E} = (G, E, Dec)$ *provides* reproducibility *(or is* reproducible*) if there is an efficient function Rep such that for any* $sk, sk' \in G(1^\lambda)$, $r \in \mathcal{R}_\lambda$ *and* $m_1, m_2 \in \mathcal{M}_\lambda$,

$$Rep(E_{sk}(m_1; r), m_2, sk') = E_{sk'}(m_2; r).$$

Definition 2. *Let* $\mathcal{E} = (G, E, Dec)$ *be a private key encryption scheme where both* $(\mathcal{R}_\lambda, +)$ *and* $(\mathcal{M}_\lambda, +)$ *form groups. Then* $\mathcal{E}$ *is* additively homomorphic with respect to plaintexts and randomness (PR-additively homomorphic) *if there is an efficient function Hom such that for every* $sk \in G(1^\lambda)$, $m_1, m_2 \in \mathcal{M}_\lambda$, *and* $r_1, r_2 \in \mathcal{R}_\lambda$,

$$Hom\left(E_{sk}(m_1; r_1), E_{sk}(m_2; r_2)\right) = E_{sk}(m_1 + m_2; r_1 + r_2).$$

We extend the notation of $Hom(\cdot)$ *to define* $Hom(c_1, \ldots, c_m)$ *in the straightforward way. For technical reasons, we also need the following condition: for any* sk, m, r *and* m', *given only* m' *and* $E_{sk}(m; r)$, *we can form the ciphertext* $E_{sk}(m', 0)$, *where 0 denotes the identity element of* $\mathcal{R}_\lambda$. *We sometimes refer to this property as the* degenerate condition.

Henceforth, when discussing encryption schemes, we will use "homomorphic" as shorthand for "PR-additively homomorphic."

3 Construction

We first fix some notation. Throughout this section we will be working with additive notation for groups with 0 denoting the identity element. For $\mathbf{g} = (g_1, \ldots, g_p) \in \mathbb{G}^p$ and $\mathbf{b} = (b_1, \ldots, b_p) \in \{0,1\}^p$ we define $\mathbf{b} \cdot \mathbf{g} = b_1 \cdot g_1 + \ldots + b_p \cdot g_p \in \mathbb{G}$, where, $0 \cdot g = 0$, and for $n \in \mathbb{N}$, we define $n \cdot g = g + (n-1) \cdot g$.

We present a generic construction that transforms a reproducible, homomorphic private-key encryption scheme into a public-key bit-encryption scheme. This always produces a bit-encryption scheme even if the base scheme is not. In the full version we show how to adjust the construction, to maintain the plaintext space, at the cost of additional syntactic assumptions (which are satisfied by our specific instantiations).

For simplicity, we present (and prove the security of) the bit-encryption construction for the case where the base scheme is also bit encryption.

Let $\mathcal{E} = (G, E, Dec, Hom, Rep)$ be a CPA-secure private-key bit-encryption scheme providing reproducibility (with the associated function Rep) and homomorphism (with the associated function Hom). Recall for homomorphism, both the message space, $\{0,1\}$, and the randomness space, $\mathcal{R}_\lambda$, form groups, which implies the plaintext group is just $\mathbb{Z}_2$. We now present the construction.

Construction 1 *(Single bit encryption): Let $\mathcal{E} = (G, E, Dec, Hom, Rep)$ be as above and let $l = l(\lambda)$ be a value that we instantiate later.*

- *Key generation G': Choose the secret key as $\mathbf{s} \leftarrow \{0,1\}^l$ and the public key as $(E_{sk}(0; r_1), \ldots, E_{sk}(0; r_l), E_{sk}(0; \mathbf{s} \cdot \mathbf{r}))$, where $sk \leftarrow G(1^\lambda)$, $r_1, \ldots, r_l \leftarrow \mathcal{R}_\lambda$ and $\mathbf{r} = (r_1, \ldots, r_l)$.*
- *Encryption E': To encrypt bit b under public key $(c_1, \ldots, c_l, c_{l+1})$, do the following: choose $sk' \leftarrow G(1^\lambda)$ and return $(c'_1, \ldots, c'_l, c'_{l+1})$, where $c'_i = Rep(c_i, 0, sk')$, for $1 \le i \le l$, and $c'_{l+1} = Rep(c_{l+1}, b, sk')$.*
- *Decryption Dec': To decrypt $(c'_1, \ldots, c'_l, c'_{l+1})$ under secret key $\mathbf{s}$, letting $(i_1, \ldots, i_w)$ be the indices of non-zero bits of s, output 0 if $c'_{l+1} = Hom\left(c'_{i_1}, \ldots, c'_{i_w}\right)$, and 1 otherwise.*

The completeness of the scheme follows immediately. A few comments are in order. First, the encryption algorithm of the constructed scheme uses that of the base scheme, but by reusing the randomness values of the ciphertexts given in the public key. Second, the constructed decryption function does not need any secret keys of the base scheme, e.g., sk, for its computation. Roughly, this is why proving circular security for the constructed scheme should not be much harder than proving CPA security. In our security proofs, we will rely on the fact that we may use the homomorphism properties of the base primitive to form public keys and encryptions in alternate, equivalent ways as described below.

Proposition 1   *1. The public key may be computed as $(c_1, \ldots, c_l, c_{l+1})$, where $c_i \leftarrow E_{sk}(0)$, for $1 \le i \le l$, and $c_{l+1} = Hom\left(c_{i_1}, \ldots, c_{i_w}\right)$, where $(i_1, \ldots, i_w)$ are the indices of non-zero bits of $\mathbf{s}$.*
  2. Let $\mathbf{s}$, sk' and $c'_1, \ldots, c'_l$ be as in the definition of encryption in Construction 1. Then, c'_{l+1} may be computed as $c'_{l+1} = Hom(c_{i_1}, \ldots, c_{i_w}, E_{sk'}(b; 0))$, where $(i_1, \ldots, i_w)$ are the indices of non-zero bits of $\mathbf{s}$.

4   Proof of Projection Security

In this section we give the proof of projection security of our constructed scheme. This section is organized as follows. In Subsect. 4.1 we reviews some facts related to entropy which are needed by our proofs. In Subsect. 4.2 we introduce an intermediate lemma that will be used in the proofs of our main theorems. Finally, in Subsect. 4.3 we give the proof for projection security.

4.1   Information-Theoretic Tools

We denote the *min-entropy* of a distribution D by $H_\infty(D)$, defined as $H_\infty(D) = \min_{d \in D} \left[\log(\frac{1}{\Pr[D=d]}) \right]$. We also need to work with the notion of *average min entropy*, formalized by Dodis et al. [16], which measures the expected unpredictability of X given a random value y of Y. Formally,

$$\tilde{H}_\infty(X|Y) = -\log\left(E_{y \leftarrow Y}(2^{-H_\infty(X|Y=y)}) \right) = -\log\left(E_{y \leftarrow Y}(\max_x \Pr[X=x|Y=y]) \right).$$

A well-known fact about average-min entropy is a special form of the *chain rule*, saying that conditioning on a random variable Y, the average min entropy decreases by at most the logarithm of the support size of Y.

Lemma 1 [16]. *For any (X, Y, Z) it holds that $\tilde{H}_\infty(X|Y, Z) \geq \tilde{H}_\infty(X|Z) - \log|Sup(Y)|$.*

A family of functions $\{h : D \to R\}_{h \in H}$ is called *universal* if for all $x_1, x_2 \in D$, with $x_1 \neq x_2$, it holds that

$$\Pr_{h \leftarrow H}[h(x_1) = h(x_2)] \leq \frac{1}{|R|}.$$

We typically denote a family of functions $\{h : D \to R\}_{h \in H}$ as a single function $\mathcal{H} : D \times H \to R$, where $\mathcal{H}(d, h) = h(d)$. We have the following fact, showing that universal hash functions are good *average-case extractors*.

Lemma 2 [16]. *If $Ext : \{0,1\}^n \times W \to W'$ is a family of universal hash functions, then for any pair of random variables (D, X), where D takes values in $\{0,1\}^n$, it holds that*

$$\Delta((Ext(D, S), S, X), (R, S, X)) \leq 1/2\sqrt{2^{-\tilde{H}_\infty(D|X)}|W'|},$$

where S is uniform over W, R is uniform over W' and Δ denotes statistical distance. We stress that S is independent of (D, X).

4.2   A Useful Lemma

We begin by introducing a game that will be used in proving our main results. Intuitively, the following experiment corresponds to a vector-encryption game, in which an adversary may interactively issue vectors of bits (of certain forms) to be encrypted, and each vector is component-wise encrypted under a fresh secret key while reusing randomness across each fixed component of vectors.

The Randomness-Sharing (RS) Game. Let (G, E, Dec) be a private-key bit-encryption scheme. As some notation, for $l \in \mathbb{N}$, we let $\mathbf{e}_i^l$, for $1 \leq i \leq l$, be the the vector of size l which has 1 in the ith position and 0 everywhere else, and $\mathbf{e'}_i^l$, for $1 \leq i \leq l$, be the vector of size l which has 1 in both its ith position and last position, and 0 everywhere else. We let $\mathbf{0}^l$ be the all-0 vector of size l. Finally, for $\mathbf{b} = (b_1, \ldots, b_l)$ and $\mathbf{r} = (r_1, \ldots, r_l)$, we define $E_{sk}(\mathbf{b}; \mathbf{r}) = (E_{sk}(b_1; r_1), \ldots, E_{sk}(b_l; r_l))$.

The game is parameterized over $l = l(\lambda)$ and is played as follows.

The challenger chooses $b \leftarrow \{0,1\}$ and it samples $\mathbf{r} = (r_1, \ldots, r_l) \leftarrow \mathcal{R}_\lambda^l$. Then the game proceeds as follows: the adversary repeatedly and adaptively makes queries of the form $\mathbf{e}$, for $\mathbf{e} \in \{\mathbf{0}^l\} \cup \{\mathbf{e}_1^l, \ldots, \mathbf{e}_l^l\} \cup \{\mathbf{e'}_1^l, \ldots, \mathbf{e'}_l^l\}$, and in response to each such query, the challenger samples $sk \leftarrow G(1^\lambda)$ (using fresh coins for each query) and returns $E_{sk}(\mathbf{e}; \mathbf{r})$ if $b = 0$, and $E_{sk}(\mathbf{0}^l; \mathbf{r})$, otherwise. Finally, the adversary outputs a bit b' and its advantage is defined as:

$$Adv^{p\text{-}rs}(\mathcal{A}) = \Pr[b' = 1 \mid b = 0] - \Pr[b' = 1 \mid b = 1].$$

The following lemma is used extensively in our subsequent proofs.

Lemma 3. *Assume $\mathcal{E} = (G, E, Dec, Rep)$ is a CPA-secure, private-key bit-encryption scheme that provides reproducibility. For any polynomial functions $l(\cdot)$, any adversary $\mathcal{A}$ in the l-RS game has a negligible advantage.*

Proof. First, we introduce the following notation. For $\mathbf{b} = (b_1, \ldots, b_l)$ and $\mathbf{c} = (c_1, \ldots, c_l)$, define

$$Rep(\mathbf{c}, \mathbf{b}, sk) = (Rep(c_1, b_1, sk), \ldots, Rep(c_l, b_l, sk)).$$

Assuming that $\mathcal{A}$ makes $t = t(\lambda)$ queries $\mathbf{q}_1, \ldots, \mathbf{q}_t$ we define the hybrid W_i, for $1 \le i \le t + 1$, as follows: first generate randomness vector $\mathbf{r} = (r_1, \ldots, r_l) \leftarrow \mathcal{R}^l$ and respond to queries as follows: in response to the j'th query, for $1 \le j < i$, generate $sk_j \leftarrow G(1^\lambda)$ and return $E_{sk_j}(\mathbf{q}_j; \mathbf{r})$ (i.e., encryption of the actual vector); and in response to the w'th query, for $w \ge i$, generate $sk_w \leftarrow G(1^\lambda)$ and return $E_{sk_w}(\mathbf{0}^l; \mathbf{r})$ (i.e., encryption of the all-zero vector). Note that W_1 and W_{t+1} match exactly the view of the adversary produced under the RS game when $b = 1$ and $b = 0$, respectively. Thus, for the rest of the proof, we show how to reduce an adversary that can distinguish between W_i and W_{i+1}, for some $1 \le i \le t$, to an adversary against the CPA security game; the whole proof then follows using a standard hybrid argument.

Assume that $\mathcal{A}'$ can distinguish between W_i and W_{i+1} with a non-negligible advantage. Noting that W_i and W_{i+1} only differ in the way that the answer to the ith query is made, and that each query vector can take at most $2l + 1$ different values, we guess the ith query vector (that is going to be issued by $\mathcal{A}'$), call the LOR-CPA oracle, which is parameterized over an unknown secret key, on the guessed vector to receive $\mathbf{c} = (c_1, \ldots, c_l)$, and start simulating $\mathcal{A}'$ as follows: in response to the j'th query, $\mathbf{q}_j$, for $1 \le j < i$, we generate $sk_j \leftarrow G(1^\lambda)$ and return $Rep(\mathbf{c}, \mathbf{q}_j, sk_j)$; in response to the ith query we return $\mathbf{c}$ (if our guess for $\mathbf{q}_i$ was incorrect, we stop and return a random bit); and in response to the w'th query, $\mathbf{q}_w$, for $w > i$, we generate $sk_w \leftarrow G(1^\lambda)$ and return $Rep(\mathbf{c}, \mathbf{0}^l, sk_w)$. Now it is easy to see that, if our guessing for the ith query was correct, depending on whether the CPA-challenge bit was zero or one, the resulting experiment matches exactly either W_i or W_{i+1}. This completes the proof. $\square$

4.3 Proof of Projection Security

We first give the proof of 1-projection security of our scheme, building on techniques from [9], which in turn generalize the DDH-based techniques of [8].

Theorem 1. *Let $\mathcal{E} = (G, E, Dec, Hom, Rep)$ be a CPA-secure private-key bit-encryption scheme providing degenerate homomorphism and reproducibility. Then, by taking $l = l(\lambda) = \omega(\log \lambda) + \log(|\mathcal{R}_\lambda|)$, the scheme built in Construction 1 is 1-projection secure.*

Proof. To represent the 1-projection game more concisely, we denote:

– *enc-secret*(i) encrypt the ith bit of the secret key; and
– *enc-secret*$(\bar{i})$ encrypt the negation of the ith bit of the secret key.

We introduce a series of hybrid games and show no adversary can distinguish between any two adjacent games. The first game corresponds to the real-encryption circular-security game, while the last game is the one where we always encrypt 0. Letting x_i be the adversary's output in *Game-i*, we write *Game-i* $\equiv^G$ *Game-j* to indicate $|\Pr[x_i = 1] - \Pr[x_j = 1]| = negl$. In all these games, whenever we write, say, $sk' \leftarrow G(1^\lambda)$ we mean that sk' is chosen freshly, so we may keep using the same variable sk' inside each game whenever we are producing a new key. Let $\mathcal{R} = \mathcal{R}_\lambda$ for the following discussion. Also, recall the notation $E_{sk}(\mathbf{b}, \mathbf{r})$ introduced in Subsect. 4.2. Below we write $\mathbf{e}_i$ as shorthand for $\mathbf{e}_i^l$.

Game-0: Real Encryption. This game provides the adversary with a view that is identical to that under the projection security game in which the challenge bit is zero. The identical view is produced by using the algorithm *Hom* to produce the public key and to reply to encryption queries (See Proposition 1).

Generate $\mathbf{r} = (r_1, \ldots, r_l) \leftarrow \mathcal{R}^l$ and $\mathbf{s} \leftarrow \{0,1\}^l$ and let $(i_1, \ldots, i_w)$ be the indices of nonzero bits of $\mathbf{s}$. Then,

– the adversary is given $(c_1, \ldots, c_l, Hom(c_{i_1}, \ldots, c_{i_w}))$ as the public key, where

$$(c_1, \ldots, c_l) = E_{sk}(\mathbf{0}^l; \mathbf{r})$$

and $sk \leftarrow G(1^\lambda)$.
– In response to *enc-secret*(i) we return $(c'_1, \ldots, c'_l, Hom(c'_{i_1}, \ldots, c'_{i_w}, E_{sk'}(\mathbf{s}_i; 0)))$, where
$$(c'_1, \ldots, c'_l) = E_{sk'}(\mathbf{0}^l; \mathbf{r})$$

and $sk' \leftarrow G(1^\lambda)$. Again we emphasize sk' is chosen freshly for each query.
– In response to *enc-secret*$(\bar{i})$ we return $(c''_1, \ldots, c''_l, Hom(c''_{i_1}, \ldots, c''_{i_w}, E_{sk''}(\bar{\mathbf{s}}_i; 0)))$, where
$$(c''_1, \ldots, c''_l) = E_{sk''}(\mathbf{0}^l; \mathbf{r})$$

and $sk'' \leftarrow G(1^\lambda)$.

Game-1: In this game we handle key generation exactly as in *Game-0*, but we reply to *enc-secret* queries in a special way. Formally, generate $\mathbf{r} = (r_1, \ldots, r_l) \leftarrow \mathcal{R}^l$ and $\mathbf{s} \leftarrow \{0,1\}^l$ and let $(i_1, \ldots, i_w)$ be the indices of nonzero bits of $\mathbf{s}$. Then,

– the adversary is given $(c_1, \ldots, c_l, Hom(c_{i_1}, \ldots, c_{i_w}))$ as the public key, where $(c_1, \ldots, c_l) = E_{sk}(\mathbf{0}^l; \mathbf{r})$, for $sk \leftarrow G(1^\lambda)$.
– In response to *enc-secret*(i) we return $(c'_1, \ldots, c'_l, Hom(c'_{i_1}, \ldots, c'_{i_w}, E_{sk'}(\mathbf{s}_i; 0)))$, where $(c'_1, \ldots, c'_l) = E_{sk'}(\mathbf{e}_i; \mathbf{r})$ and $sk' \leftarrow G(1^\lambda)$.
– In response to *enc-secret*$(\bar{i})$ we return $(c''_1, \ldots, c''_l, Hom(c''_{i_1}, \ldots, c''_{i_w}, E_{sk''}(\bar{\mathbf{s}}_i; 0)))$, where $(c''_1, \ldots, c''_l) = E_{sk''}(\mathbf{e}_i; \mathbf{r})$ and $sk'' \leftarrow G(1^\lambda)$.

We claim that the difference between $Game$-0 and $Game$-1 can be simulated through the l-RS game. The reason is if we know $\mathbf{s}$, then we can compute $Hom(c'_{i_1}, \ldots, c'_{i_w}, E_{sk'}(\mathbf{s}_i; 0))$ from $(c'_1, \ldots, c'_l)$ even if we do not have sk': note that here we are using the degenerate condition of the homomorphism property. A similar argument holds with respect to c and c''. Moreover, for every $1 \leq j \leq l$, the ciphertexts c_j, c'_j and c''_j were formed under the same randomness. Thus, we can reduce any distinguisher between $Game$-0 and $Game$-1 to an l-RS game adversary $\mathcal{A}$ as follows: $\mathcal{A}$ samples $\mathbf{s} \leftarrow \{0,1\}^l$ and lets $(i_1, \ldots, i_w)$ be the indices of nonzero bits of $\mathbf{s}$; it calls its RS-oracle on $\mathbf{0}^l$ to receive $(c_1, \ldots, c_l)$ and then returns $(c_1, \ldots, c_l, Hom(c_{i_1}, \ldots, c_{i_w}))$ as the public key; it responds to enc-$secret(i)$ by first calling its oracle on $\mathbf{e}_i$ to get $(c'_1, \ldots, c'_l)$ and then returning $(c'_1, \ldots, c'_l, Hom(c'_{i_1}, \ldots, c'_{i_w}, E_{sk'}(\mathbf{s}_i; 0)))$; it responds to enc-$secret(\bar{i})$ in a similar way. Thus, by Lemma 3 we obtain that $Game$-$0 \equiv^G Game$-1.

Finally, note that under this game, the distribution of the public key and the distributions of responses to enc-$secret(i)$'s and to enc-$secret(\bar{i})$'s are:

$$
\begin{array}{ll}
\big(E_{sk}(\mathbf{0}^l; \mathbf{r}), E_{sk}(0; r_{l+1})\big) & \text{public key} \\
\big(E_{sk}(\mathbf{e}_i; \mathbf{r}), E_{sk'}(0; r_{l+1})\big) & enc\text{-}secret(i) \\
\big(E_{sk}(\mathbf{e}_i; \mathbf{r}), E_{sk''}(1; r_{l+1})\big) & enc\text{-}secret(\bar{i}),
\end{array} \tag{1}
$$

where $sk, sk', sk'' \leftarrow G(1^\lambda)$, $\mathbf{s} \leftarrow \{0,1\}^l$ and $\mathbf{r} = (r_1, \ldots, r_l) \leftarrow \mathcal{R}^l$ and $r_{l+1} = \mathbf{s} \cdot \mathbf{r}$. In particular, note that the bits of $\mathbf{s}$ never appear as a plaintext (under E) in Eq. 1, and the only place we use $\mathbf{s}$ is to form r_{l+1}.

$\underline{Game\text{-}2}$: This game proceeds exactly as in $Game$-1, except we now sample r_{l+1} independently of all other r_i's. Namely, we sample $(r_1, \ldots, r_l, r_{l+1}) \leftarrow \mathcal{R}^{l+1}$ and run the game by forming the public key and responses to the adversary's queries exactly as in Eq. 1. Notice that the entire game can be simulated by only knowing $(r_1, \ldots, r_l, r_{l+1})$: we generate the public key and we answer to enc-$secret$ queries by sampling sk, sk' and sk'' on our own and forming the outputs as spelled out by Eq. 1. (Here we are exploiting the fact that the bits of $\mathbf{s}$ never appear as a plaintext under E in Eq. 1.) Thus, since $l = \omega(\log \lambda) + \log(|\mathcal{R}|)$ and the inner product is a family of universal hash functions, by Lemma 2 (indeed by the Leftover Hash Lemma, which is a special case of Lemma 2) we obtain that the statistical distance between $(\mathbf{r}, \mathbf{s} \cdot \mathbf{r})$ and a tuple chosen uniformly at random from $\mathcal{R}^l_\lambda$ is at most $\sqrt{1/2^{\omega(\log \lambda)}} = negl(\lambda)$, and thus $Game$-$1 \equiv^G Game$-2.

$\underline{Game\text{-}3}$: In this game we again sample r_{l+1} independently of other r_i's, but reply to all queries as "encryptions" of zero. That is, we generate $(r_1, \ldots, r_l, r_{l+1}) \leftarrow \mathcal{R}^{l+1}$ and form the public key and responses to the adversary's queries as follows:

$$
\begin{array}{ll}
\big(E_{sk}(0; r_1), \ldots, E_{sk}(0; r_l), E_{sk}(0; r_{l+1})\big) & \text{public key} \\
\big(E_{sk'}(0; r_1), \ldots, E_{sk'}(0; r_l), E_{sk'}(0; r_{l+1})\big) & \text{response to all queries}
\end{array} \tag{2}
$$

where, again, sk' is sampled freshly for each query. Now using the fact that all r_i's are sampled independently, and also that sk' is generated using fresh coins each time, we obtain that any adversary that can distinguish between *Game*-2 and *Game*-3 can be reduced to break the $(l + 1)$-RS security of $\mathcal{E}$ (which is a contradiction by Lemma (3)). Thus, *Game*-2 $\equiv^G$ *Game*-3.

Game-4: In this game we change back the distributions of r_i's to the original, but answer to all the adversary's queries as encryptions of zero. That is, we generate $\mathbf{s} \leftarrow \{0,1\}^l$, $\mathbf{r} = (r_1, \ldots, r_l) \leftarrow \mathcal{R}^l$, let $r_{l+1} = \mathbf{s} \cdot \mathbf{r}$, and form the public key and responses to the adversary's queries as follows:

$$
\begin{array}{ll}
(E_{sk}(0; r_1), \ldots, E_{sk}(0; r_l), E_{sk}(0; r_{l+1})) & \text{public key} \\
(E_{sk'}(0; r_1), \ldots, E_{sk'}(0; r_l), E_{sk'}(0; r_{l+1})) & \text{responses to all queries}
\end{array}
\tag{3}
$$

Now, similarly to our proof of *Game*-1 $\equiv^G$ *Game*-2, since *Game*-3 and *Game*-4 differ only in the way that $(r_1, \ldots, r_l, r_{l+1})$ is generated, and again using the fact that $l = \omega(\log \lambda) + \log(|\mathcal{R}|)$, by applying Lemma 2, we conclude that *Game*-3 $\equiv^G$ *Game*-4. This completes the proof.   □

We give the statement of n-projection security below, and give the proof in the full version [24].

Theorem 2. *Let* $\mathcal{E} = (G, E, Dec, Hom, Rep)$ *be a CPA-secure private-key bit-encryption scheme providing degenerate homomorphism and reproducibility. For any constant* $c > 1$, *by taking* $l = n \log(|\mathcal{R}_\lambda|) + \omega(\log \lambda)$, *the scheme built in Construction 1 is* n-*projection secure.*

5 Proof of Leakage Resilience

The following theorem shows the leakage resilience property of our scheme.

Theorem 3. *Let* $\mathcal{E} = (G, E, Dec, Hom, Rep)$ *be a CPA-secure private-key bit-encryption scheme providing degenerate homomorphism and reproducibility. Then, the scheme built in Construction 1 is* $(l - \log |\mathcal{R}_\lambda| - u)$-*length leakage resilient, for any* $u \in \omega(\log \lambda)$. *Moreover, by taking* $l = \omega(\log |\mathcal{R}_\lambda| + u)$, *the constructed scheme achieves a* $(1 - o(1))$ *resilience rate.*

Proof. We first show the second statement of the theorem, assuming the first statement is true. Fix $u \in \omega(\log \lambda)$. We know that the scheme provides $(l - \log |\mathcal{R}_\lambda| - u)$-length leakage resilience, and so its resilience rate is

$$
\frac{\omega(\log |\mathcal{R}_\lambda| + u) - \log |\mathcal{R}_\lambda| - u}{\omega(\log |\mathcal{R}_\lambda| + u)} = 1 - \frac{\log |\mathcal{R}_\lambda| + u}{\omega(\log |\mathcal{R}_\lambda| + u)} = 1 - o(1). \tag{4}
$$

To prove the first statement, first we assume without loss of generality that the adversary always outputs $(0, 1)$ as its challenge query, since otherwise the challenge ciphertext can be simulated by the adversary itself. We prove the first statement through a series of games, where the first game matches the actual leakage game (under a fixed challenge bit b), and in the last game the view of the adversary is independent of the challenge bit b. We conclude the proof by showing that the views of the adversary under any two adjacent games under the same $b \in \{0,1\}$ are computationally indistinguishable. Thus, fix $b \in \{0,1\}$ for the rest of the proof. In all game below, we let f be the leakage query of the adversary.

Game-0: In this game we reply to the adversary's queries exactly as in the actual leakage game, where the challenge bit is b. Thus, at the end of the game, the view of the adversary is $(c_1, \ldots, c_l, c_{l+1}, f(\mathbf{s}), c_1', \ldots, c_l', c_{l+1}')$, produced as follows: $\mathbf{s} \leftarrow \{0,1\}^l$, $\mathbf{r} = (r_1, \ldots, r_l) \leftarrow \mathcal{R}_\lambda^l$, $r_{l+1} = \mathbf{s} \cdot \mathbf{r}$, $sk \leftarrow G(1^\lambda)$, $sk' \leftarrow G(1^\lambda)$, $c_i = E_{sk}(0; r_i)$, for $1 \leq i \leq l+1$, $c_j' = E_{sk'}(0; r_j)$, for $1 \leq j \leq l$, and $c_{l+1}' = E_{sk'}(b; r_{l+1})$.

Notice that the view of the adversary may identically be produced as

$$(c_1, \ldots, c_l, c_{l+1}'', f(\mathbf{s}), c_1', \ldots, c_l', c_{l+1}'''), \tag{5}$$

where all c_i's and c_i''s are produced as above, and $c_{l+1}'' = Hom(c_{h_1}, \ldots, c_{h_w})$ and $c_{l+1}''' = Hom(c_{h_1}', \ldots, c_{h_w}', E_{sk'}(b; 0))$ with $(h_1, \ldots, h_w)$ being the indices of non-zero bits of $\mathbf{s}$.

Game-1: In this game we generate the secret key, the public key and the response to the leakage query exactly as in *Game-0*, but we reply to the encryption challenge query in a special way. Formally, choose $\mathbf{s} \leftarrow \{0,1\}^l$, $\mathbf{r} = (r_1, \ldots, r_l) \leftarrow \mathcal{R}_\lambda^l$, let $(h_1, \ldots, h_w)$ be the indices of non-zero bits of $\mathbf{s}$, and

- form the public key as $(c_1, \ldots, c_l, c_{l+1}'')$, where $sk \leftarrow G(1^\lambda)$, $c_i = E_{sk}(0; r_i)$, for $1 \leq i \leq l$, and $c_{l+1}'' = Hom(c_{h_1}, \ldots, c_{h_w})$;
- reply to the leakage query f with $f(\mathbf{s})$;
- return $(c_1', \ldots, c_l', c_{l+1}''')$ as the challenge ciphertext, where $\mathbf{b} = (b_1, \ldots, b_l) \leftarrow \{0,1\}^l$, $sk' \leftarrow G(1^\lambda)$, $c_j' = E_{sk'}(b_j; r_j)$, for $1 \leq j \leq l$, and

$$c_{l+1}''' = Hom(c_{h_1}', \ldots, c_{h_w}', E_{sk'}(b; 0)).$$

To show *Game-0* $\equiv^G$ *Game-1*, note that both games can be simulated in exactly the same way by only having $\mathcal{D} = (c_1, \ldots, c_l, c_1', \ldots, c_l')$ (see Eq. 5); this can be done by sampling $\mathbf{s}$ by ourselves and forming c_{l+1}'' and c_{l+1}''' from, respectively, $(c_1, \ldots, c_l)$ and $(c_1', \ldots, c_l')$ by using the degenerate homomorphic property of $\mathcal{E}$. Further, since $\mathcal{E}$ is reproducible, in both games the distribution of $(c_1, \ldots, c_l)$ can be generated from $(c_1', \ldots, c_l')$ alone. Now since the distributions produced for $(c_1', \ldots, c_l')$ under the two games are computationally indistinguishable, which is followed by semantic security (recall that in *Game-0*, c_i''s are encryptions of zeros and in *Game-1*, they are encryptions of the bits of $\mathbf{b}$), we get that the distributions produced for $\mathcal{D}$ under the two games are computationally indistinguishable. Thus, we conclude *Game-0* $\equiv^G$ *Game-1*. Notice that, under Game-1, the view of the adversary is

$$\big(E_{sk}(0; r_1), \ldots, E_{sk}(0; r_l), E_{sk}(0; \mathbf{s} \cdot \mathbf{r}), f(\mathbf{s}), \tag{6}$$
$$E_{sk'}(b_1; r_1), \ldots, E_{sk'}(b_l; r_l), E_{sk'}(b_{l+1} + b; \mathbf{s} \cdot \mathbf{r})\big),$$

where $b_{l+1} = \mathbf{s} \cdot \mathbf{b}$.

Game-2: This game runs exactly as in _Game_-1 (Eq. 6), except that now we generate $b_{l+1} \leftarrow \{0,1\}$, i.e., independent of $\mathbf{b} = (b_1, \ldots, b_l)$. First, notice that both _Game_-1 and _Game_-2 can be simulated in exactly the same manner by only having

$$Dis = (\mathbf{r}, \mathbf{s} \cdot \mathbf{r}, \mathbf{b}, b_{l+1}, f(\mathbf{s})). \tag{7}$$

The only difference between Dis from _Game_-1 to _Game_-2 is that under _Game_-1 we set $b_{l+1} = \mathbf{s} \cdot \mathbf{b}$, while in _Game_-2 we sample b_{l+1} freshly; the other parts of Dis are generated in the same way under both games: that is, $\mathbf{s} \leftarrow \{0,1\}^l$ and $\mathbf{r} = (r_1, \ldots, r_l) \leftarrow \mathcal{R}_\lambda^l$. Thus, to show the indistinguishability between these two games, it suffices to show that the distributions of Dis under the two games are indistinguishable. We have,

$$\begin{aligned} \tilde{H}_\infty(\mathbf{s}|\mathbf{r}, \mathbf{s} \cdot \mathbf{r}, f(\mathbf{s})) &\geq \tilde{H}_\infty(\mathbf{s}|\mathbf{r}, f(\mathbf{s})) - log|\mathcal{R}_\lambda| \\ &= \tilde{H}_\infty(\mathbf{s}|f(\mathbf{s})) - log|\mathcal{R}_\lambda| \\ &\geq H_\infty(\mathbf{s}) - l + \log|\mathcal{R}_\lambda| + u - log|\mathcal{R}_\lambda| \\ &= u = \omega(\log \lambda). \end{aligned}$$

Now, since $\mathbf{r}$ is independent of $\mathbf{b}$, and also that f is independent of $\mathbf{b}$ (since f is queried before seeing the challenge ciphertext) we may use Lemma 2 to deduce that the distribution of Dis under _Game_-1 and _Game_-2 are statistically indistinguishable. To apply Lemma 2, take $D = \mathbf{s}$, $S = \mathbf{b}$ and $X = (\mathbf{r}, \mathbf{s} \cdot \mathbf{r}, f(\mathbf{s}))$. Notice that _Game_-2 produces the same views for the adversary under $b = 0$ and $b = 1$ (since b_{l+1} is chosen uniformly at random and hides the value of b), and hence the proof is complete. □

6 Realizations

We show how to realize our base encryption primitive under various number-theoretic assumptions. In Subsect. 6.1 we formulate an abstraction, called _homomorphic weak pseudorandom functions_, and use them to realize our encryption primitive. Then in Subsect. 6.2 we give realizations of such pseudorandom functions using _homomorphic hash-proof systems_. Finally, in Subsect. 6.3 we show how to realize our encryption primitive under _subgroup indistinguishably_.

6.1 Realizations from Homomorphic Weak PRFs

We introduce the notion of _homomorphic weak pseudorandom functions (PRFs)_, which is a homomorphic version of the notion of weak PRFs, introduced by Naor and Reingold [34].

Let $K = \{K_\lambda\}_{\lambda \in \mathbb{N}}$, $D = \{D_\lambda\}_{\lambda \in \mathbb{N}}$ and $R = \{R_\lambda\}_{\lambda \in \mathbb{N}}$ be ensembles of sets. For each security parameter λ and each $k \in K_\lambda$ we have an associated function $f_k : D_\lambda \to R_\lambda$. We let $F_\lambda = \{f_k \mid k \in K_\lambda\}$ and $F = \{F_\lambda\}_{\lambda \in \mathbb{N}}$. The following is the definition of weak pseudorandomness for a function family.

Definition 3. *[34] We call F a* weak pseudorandom function family *if for any polynomial function $p = p(\lambda)$, it holds that $\mathcal{DS}_1 \equiv^c \mathcal{DS}_2$, where*

$$\mathcal{DS}_1 \equiv (d_1, r_1), \ldots, (d_p, r_p)$$
$$\mathcal{DS}_2 \equiv (d_1, f_k(d_1)), \ldots, (d_p, f_k(d_p)),$$

for $k \leftarrow K_\lambda$, $d_1, \ldots, d_p \leftarrow D_\lambda$ and $r_1, \ldots, r_p \leftarrow R_\lambda$.[4]

Note that a PRF in the standard sense is trivially a weak PRF.

Let F be as above. We call F *homomorphic* if for every $\lambda \in \mathbb{N}$, both D_λ and R_λ are groups, and that for every $k \in K_\lambda$, the function f_k is a homomorphism from D_λ to R_λ.

Now we show that the standard method of constructing CPA-secure private-key encryption from a PRF, when applied to a homomorphic weak PRF, results in the kind of encryption primitive we need.

Lemma 4. *Assuming the existence of a homomorphic weak pseudorandom function family, there exists a CPA-secure private-key encryption scheme which is degenerately homomorphic and reproducible.*

Proof. Let F be a homomorphic weak PRF with the associated set parameters given above (i.e., K_λ, etc.). Construct $\mathcal{E} = (G, E, Dec)$, with plaintext space R_λ and randomness spaces D_λ as follows: $G(1^\lambda)$ returns $k \leftarrow K_\lambda$; $E_k(p_1; d_1)$ returns $(d_1, f_k(d_1) + p_1)$; and $Dec_k(d, r)$ returns $r - f_k(d)$. CPA-security, homomorphism and reproducibility of $\mathcal{E}$ are clear. Finally, note that since $f_k(0) = 0$, we have $E_k(p; 0) = (0, p)$, which verifies the degenerate case of homomorphism.   □

6.2   Homomorphic Hash-Proof Systems to Homomorphic Weak PRFs

We first review the notion of a *homomorphic hash-proof system* (HHPS), originally defined in [13]. Then we realize homomorphic weak PRFs using an HHPS.

A HHPS HHPS = (Param, Priv, Pub) is described as follows. The randomized *setup* algorithm Param($\cdot$) takes as input a security parameter 1^λ and outputs *public parameters* HP $= (C, C_v, W, K, SK, PK, \mu : SK \rightarrow PK, \Lambda : SK \times C \rightarrow K)$, where, C is called the set of *ciphertexts*, $C_v \subseteq C$ the set of *valid ciphertexts*, W the set of *witnesses*, K the set of *plaintexts*, SK the set of *secret keys* and PK the set of *public keys*. We should point out that all these aforementioned sets are indeed descriptions of their actual sets. Each $c \in C_v$ admits a witness $w \in W$ of its membership in C_v, meaning that there exists a PPT relation R such that

$$c \in C_v \Leftrightarrow \exists w \in W \text{ s.t. } R(c, w) = 1.$$

We assume it is efficiently possible to generate a uniform element from C_v along with a corresponding witness, and also to sample uniformly from SK and K.

---

[4] The domain and the key spaces may themselves come with an associated distribution, but we leave this point implicit for simplicity.

The efficient *private evaluation* algorithm Priv takes as input $sk \in SK$ and $c \in C$, and deterministically computes $Priv_{sk}(c) = \Lambda(sk, c)$. The efficient *public evaluation* algorithm Pub, takes as input $pk = \mu(sk)$, $c \in C_v$ and a witness w for c, and deterministically computes $Pub_{pk}(c, w_c) = \Lambda(sk, c)$. Finally, we require HHPS to satisfy the following properties.

Subset Membership: For every adversary $\mathcal{A}$, given all the public parameters of the scheme, it holds that

$$|\Pr\left[\mathcal{A}(c_v) = 1\right] - \Pr\left[\mathcal{A}(c_{inv}) = 1\right]| = negl(\lambda),$$

where, $c_v \leftarrow C_v$, $c_{inv} \leftarrow C \setminus C_v$ and the probabilities are computed over the random coins of the adversary and over the choices of c_v and c_{inv}, and also over the choices of C and C_v, which are taken from the output of $Param(1^\lambda)$.

Smoothness: It holds that $\Delta\left[(pk, Priv_{sk}(c), c), (pk, k, c)\right] = negl(\lambda)$, where $c \leftarrow C \setminus C_v$, $k \leftarrow K$, $sk \leftarrow SK$ and $pk = \mu(sk)$.

Homomorphism: $(C, +)$, $(C_v, +)$ and $(K, +)$ admit groups (with efficient group operations), and, for every sk, it holds that $\Lambda(sk, \cdot)$ constitutes a homomorphism, i.e., for every $sk \in SK$ and $c_1, c_2 \in C$, it holds that,[5]

$$\Lambda(sk, c_1) + \Lambda(sk, c_2) = \Lambda(sk, c_1 + c_2).$$

We now show how to construct a homomorphic weak PRF from a HHPS.

Theorem 4. *Assuming the existence of a HHPS, there exists a homomorphic weak PRF.*

Proof. Assume that HHPS = (Param, Priv, Pub) is a HHPS. Let

$$HP = (C, C_v, W, K, SK, PK, \mu : SK \to PK, \Lambda : SK \times C \to K)$$

be the public parameters of HHPS produced by running Param. The tuple HP will also be the public parameters of our PRF, F, constructed as follows. We set $K_\lambda = SK$, $D_\lambda = C_v$ and $R_\lambda = K$, and define $f_{sk}(c) = \Lambda_{sk}(c)$. We have that both C_v and K admit groups and that $f_{sk}(c_1) + f_{sk}(c_2) = f_{sk}(c_1 + c_2)$, which implies homomorphism for PRF F. To prove weak pseudorandomness for F we need to show that, for any $p = p(\lambda)$, it holds that $\mathcal{DS} \equiv^c \mathcal{DS}'$, where

$$\mathcal{DS} = (c_1, \Lambda_{sk}(c_1)), \dots, (c_p, \Lambda_{sk}(c_p))$$
$$\mathcal{DS}' = (c_1, k_1), \dots, (c_p, k_p),$$

---

[5] We remark that in many settings the homomorphism of C_v is implied by that of C: Especially in the standard setting, where the set of valid ciphertexts is defined as those, for which the value of $\Lambda(sk, \cdot)$, for any sk is determined solely from the ciphertexts itself and $\mu(sk)$. However, we put it as a separate condition just to be as general as possible.

for $c_1, \ldots, c_p \leftarrow C_v$, $k_1, \ldots, k_p \leftarrow K$ and $sk \leftarrow SK$. To this end, for $0 \leq i \leq p$, we define the hybrid $\mathcal{DS}_i$ as follows.

$$\mathcal{DS}_i = ((c_1, \Lambda_{sk}(c_1)), \ldots, (c_i, \Lambda_{sk}(c_i)), (c_{i+1}, k_{i+1}), \ldots, (c_p, k_p)), \qquad (8)$$

where $c_1, \ldots, c_p$, $k_1, \ldots, k_p$ and sk are sampled as above. Note that $\mathcal{DS}' = \mathcal{DS}_0$ and $\mathcal{DS} = \mathcal{DS}_p$. Now to conclude the proof for each $0i$ we show $\mathcal{DS}_i \equiv^c \mathcal{DS}_{i+1}$.

Note that we have $(pk, c_{i+1}, \Lambda_{sk}(c_{i+1})) \equiv^c (pk, c_{i+1}, k_{i+1})$. This follows by combining the subset membership and smoothness properties of HHPS. Now we claim that $\mathcal{DS}_i = \mathcal{DS}_{i+1}$ follows from the fact that was just given: to see this, given $(pk, c_{i+1}, *)$, where $*$ either corresponds to $\Lambda_{sk}(c_{i+1})$ or to k_{i+1}, we form

$$((c_1, \mathsf{Pub}_{pk}(c_1, w_1)), \ldots, (c_i, \mathsf{Pub}_{pk}(c_i, w_i)), (c_{i+1}, *), (c_{i+2}, k_{i+2}), \ldots, (c_p, k_p)), \qquad (9)$$

where, for $1 \leq j \leq i$, we sample $c_j \leftarrow C_v$ along with a witness w_j, and sample $c_{i+2}, \ldots, c_p \leftarrow C_v$ and $k_{i+2}, \ldots, k_p \leftarrow K$. The distribution given in Equation 9 would either correspond to $\mathcal{DS}_i$ or to $\mathcal{DS}_{i+1}$. $\square$

6.3 Realization Under Subgroup Indistinguishability Assumptions

For the sake of clarity, in this section we give an instantiation of our encryption primitive based only on the *quadratic residuosity* assumption, which is a special case of the subgroup indistinguishability (SG) assumption. We leave the general SG-based instantiation to the full version [24].

We first start by reviewing the *quadratic residuosity* assumption. For an *RSA number* N (i.e., $N = pq$, where p and q are distinct odd primes) we use $\mathcal{QR}_N$ to denote the subset of $\mathbb{Z}_N^*$ consisting of quadratic residues modulo N, and let $\mathcal{J}_N$ denote the set of elements in $\mathbb{Z}_N^*$ with Jacobi symbol one. Finally, we define $\mathcal{QNR}_N = \mathcal{J}_N \setminus \mathcal{QR}_N$.

Assume that $\mathsf{RSAGen}(1^\lambda)$ is a PPT algorithm that on input 1^λ generates a *Blum integer* N, i.e., $N = pq$ with p and q being distinct primes satisfying $p, q \equiv 3 \pmod 4$. We stress here that we do not need $\mathsf{RSAGen}(1^\lambda)$ to output the factorization of N as well. We say that the quadratic residuosity (QR) problem is hard under RSAGen if $\{N, U(\mathcal{QR}_N)\}_{\lambda \in \mathbb{N}}$ is computationally indistinguishable from $\{N, U(\mathcal{QNR}_N)\}_{\lambda \in \mathbb{N}}$, where N is generated according to $RSAGen(1^\lambda)$.

Theorem 5. *Assuming the quadratic residuosity assumption holds for* RSAGen *there exists a CPA-secure private-key bit encrypiton scheme that is both reproducible and homomorphic.*

Proof. We construct the private-key bit encryption scheme (G, E, Dec) as follows. The public parameter of the scheme is $N \leftarrow \mathsf{RSAGen}(1^\lambda)$, and the plaintext group and the randomness group of the scheme are, respectively, $\mathbb{Z}_2$ and $\mathcal{QR}_N$. The components of the encryption scheme are defined as follows. (All computations, if not otherwise stated, are done modulo N.)

- $G(1^\lambda)$: Choose the secret key as $x \leftarrow \mathbb{Z}_{N^2}$;

- $E_x(b; g)$: return $(g, (-1)^b g^x)$;
- $Dec_x(g_1, g_2)$: return $b \in \{0, 1\}$ if $g_2 = (-1)^b g_1^x$.

We first verify the syntactic properties required of the scheme. Notice that given an encryption $(g, (-1)^b g^{x_1})$ (of an arbitrary bit b) under x_1, we can efficiently obtain the encryption of an arbitrary bit b_1 under the same randomness, g, relative to a secret key x_2 by simply outputting $(g, (-1)^{b_1} g^{x_2})$. This verifies the reproducibility property. As for homomorphism, from $(g_1, (-1)^{b_1} g_1^x)$ and $(g_2, (-1)^{b_2} g_2^x)$, we can easily derive $(g_1 g_2, (-1)^{b_1 + b_2} (g_1 g_2)^x)$, which is the encryption of $b_1 + b_2$ under randomness $g_1 g_2$ (relative to the same unknown secret key x). Note that as the randomness group here is multiplicative, we will denote the identity element by 1. We then have that $F_x(h; 1) = (1, (-1)^b)$, independently of x. This verifies the degenerate case of homomorphism.

To show that the above scheme is CPA-secure, we need to show that for any $p = p(\lambda)$ and any sequence of bits $(b_1, \ldots, b_p)$, it holds that $\mathcal{DS}_0 \equiv^c \mathcal{DS}_1$, where

$$\mathcal{DS}_0 = \begin{bmatrix} g_1 & g_2 & \cdots & g_p \\ (-1)^{b_1} g_1^x & (-1)^{b_2} g_2^x & \cdots & (-1)^{b_p} g_p^x \end{bmatrix}, \text{ and} \tag{10}$$

$$\mathcal{DS}_1 = \begin{bmatrix} g_1 & g_2 & \cdots & g_p \\ g_1^x & g_2^x & \cdots & g_p^x \end{bmatrix}, \tag{11}$$

for $g_1, \ldots, g_p \leftarrow \mathcal{QR}_N$ and $x \leftarrow \mathbb{Z}_{N^2}$. The proof of the above indistinguishability is standard. (See, e.g., [13,29] for a simple proof and also [9, Lemma 5.1] for a stronger statement.)   □

7   Extensions

In this section we discuss some extensions and complementary results. In Subsect. 7.1 we show that our constructed scheme provides *auxiliary-input security*. In Subsect. 7.2 we show that an existing *KDM-amplification* construction preserves leakage resilience.

7.1   Auxiliary-Input Security

We first give the definitions related to auxiliary-input security.

Background. Let $\mathcal{E} = (G, E, Dec)$ be an encryption scheme with public-key, secret-key and message spaces, respectively, $\mathcal{PK}_\lambda$, $\mathcal{SK}_\lambda$ and $\mathcal{M}_\lambda$. Throughout this Section we use f to refer to a function with domain $(\mathcal{PK}_\lambda, \mathcal{SK}_\lambda)$ and range $\mathcal{SK}_\lambda$. We follow the notation of [9]. For $\mathcal{E} = (G, E, Dec)$ we define f-*weak inversion* and f-*strong inversion* as follows. We say that f is ϵ-*strongly-uninvertible* under $\mathcal{E}$ if for any adversary $\mathcal{A}$, the probability that $\mathcal{A}$ outputs sk when given $(f(pk, sk), pk)$ is at most $\epsilon(\lambda)$, where the probability is taken over $\mathcal{A}$'s random coins and $(pk, sk) \leftarrow G(1^\lambda)$. Also, we say that f is ϵ-*weakly-uninvertible* under $\mathcal{E}$ if for any adversary $\mathcal{A}$, the probability that $\mathcal{A}$ outputs sk when given $f(pk, sk)$ is at most $\epsilon(\lambda)$, where the probability is taken over $\mathcal{A}$'s random coins

and $(pk, sk) \leftarrow G(1^\lambda)$. Let Aux_ϵ^{st} be the class of all ϵ-strongly-uninvertible functions and Aux_ϵ^{wk} be the class of all ϵ-weakly-uninvertible functions. Note that
$Aux_\epsilon^{st} \subseteq Aux_\epsilon^{wk}$.

We say that $\mathcal{E}$ is f-auxiliary-input secure if any adversary $\mathcal{A}$ has a negligible
advantage in the following game: $\mathcal{A}$ is given $(pk, f(pk, sk))$, where $(pk, sk) \leftarrow$
$G(1^\lambda)$; $\mathcal{A}$ submits $(m_0, m_1) \in \mathcal{M}_\lambda^2$; $\mathcal{A}$ receives $E_{pk}(m_b)$, for $b \leftarrow \{0, 1\}$; finally,
$\mathcal{A}$ outputs bit b', and achieves the following advantage

$$|\Pr[b' = 1|b = 0] - \Pr[b' = 1|b = 1]|.$$

We say that $\mathcal{E}$ is ϵ-weakly-auxiliary-input secure (resp., ϵ-strongly-auxiliary-input
secure) if $\mathcal{E}$ is f-auxiliary-input secure for any $f \in Aux_\epsilon^{st}$ (resp., Aux_ϵ^{wk}). We
say $\mathcal{E}$ is auxiliary-input secure against subexponentially-hard functions if for some
$c > 0$, $\mathcal{E}$ is $1/(2^{\lambda^c})$-strongly-auxiliary-input secure.

We now show that the encryption scheme produced by Construction 1 provides auxiliary-input security. We first consider weak-auxiliary-input security
and then discuss the extension to the strong-auxiliary case.

Theorem 6. *Let $\mathcal{E} = (G, E, Dec, Hom, Rep)$ be a CPA-secure private-key bit-
encryption scheme providing degenerate homomorphism and reproducibility. Let
$\mathcal{E}'$ be the scheme constructed from $\mathcal{E}$ using Construction 1. For any poly-bounded
$l = l(\lambda)$ and negligible function $\epsilon = \epsilon(\lambda)$, it holds that $\mathcal{E}'$ is ϵ-weakly-auxiliary-
input secure.*[6]

The proof of Theorem 6 follows similarly to that of Theorem 3, except for
one step, where we replace real-randomness extraction with *pseudorandomness
extraction*. We first give the following theorem, due to Goldreich and Levin [22],
where we follow the presentation of [14], adapted to the binary field.

Theorem 7 [22]. *Assume that $l = l(\lambda)$ and $h \colon \{0, 1\}^l \to \{0, 1\}^*$ is a (possibly
randomized) function and $\mathcal{D}$ is a distinguisher, where*

$$|\Pr[D(\mathbf{b}, b, h(\mathbf{s})) = 1] - \Pr[D(\mathbf{b}, b', h(\mathbf{s})) = 1]| = \delta(l), \tag{12}$$

*where $\mathbf{s}, \mathbf{b} \leftarrow \{0, 1\}^l$, $b \leftarrow \{0, 1\}$ and $b' = \mathbf{s} \cdot \mathbf{b}$. Then there exists an inverter $\mathcal{A}$,
for which it holds that*

$$\Pr[\mathcal{A}(y) = \mathbf{s}] \in \Omega(\frac{\delta^3}{l}), \tag{13}$$

where $\mathbf{s} \leftarrow \{0, 1\}^l$ and $y \leftarrow h(\mathbf{s})$.

We now give the proof of Theorem 6, using ideas from [14].

Proof. The proof follows by introducing *Game*-0, *Game*-1 and *Game*-2 exactly
as in the proof of Theorem 3 (except that now the function f is applied to both
the secret key and the public key), and deriving *Game*-0 $\equiv^G$ *Game*-1 exactly as

---

[6] In order for statement to be useful, it should hold that $\frac{1}{2^l} \leq \epsilon$, because otherwise
the statement will be vacuously true, as $Aux_\epsilon^{st} = Aux_\epsilon^{wk} = \emptyset$.

in there. To prove $Game\text{-}1 \equiv^G Game\text{-}2$, however, we proceed as below. To prove $Game\text{-}1 \equiv^G Game\text{-}2$, it suffices to show that

$$(b_1,\ldots,b_l,b_{l+1},f(\overbrace{PK,\mathbf{s}), E_{sk}(0;r_1),\ldots, E_{sk}(0;r_l), E_{sk}(0;r_{l+1})}^{PK}) \equiv^c \qquad (14)$$
$$(b_1,\ldots,b_l,b'_{l+1},f(\underbrace{PK,\mathbf{s}), E_{sk}(0;r_1),\ldots, E_{sk}(0;r_l), E_{sk}(0;r_{l+1})}_{PK}),$$

where $\mathbf{s} \leftarrow \{0,1\}^l$, $b_1,\ldots,b_l,b_{l+1} \leftarrow \{0,1\}$, $b'_{l+1} = \mathbf{s} \cdot (b_1,\ldots,b_l)$, $\mathbf{r} = (r_1,\ldots,r_l) \leftarrow \mathcal{R}^l_\lambda$, $r_{l+1} = \mathbf{s} \cdot \mathbf{r}$ and $sk \leftarrow G(1^\lambda)$. The fact that proving Eq. 14 suffices to conclude $Game\text{-}1 \equiv^G Game\text{-}2$ can easily be verified by considering the descriptions of $Game\text{-}1$ and $Game\text{-}2$, taking into account the fact that the private-key scheme is reproducible.

By the assumption of the theorem, we know that it is ϵ-hard to recover $\mathbf{s}$ from $(PK, f(PK, \mathbf{s}))$. Now Eq. 14 follows from Theorem 7, by defining the randomized function $h(\mathbf{s}) = (PK, f(PK, \mathbf{s}))$, where all the variables are sampled as above. Formally, if there is an adversary that can distinguish between the distributions in Eq. 14 with a non-negligible probability, then there exists an adversary that, with a non-negligible probability, recovers $\mathbf{s}$ from $h(\mathbf{s}) = (PK, f(PK, \mathbf{s}))$, which is a contradiction to the first sentence of this paragraph.

Remark 1. As in previous work [9,14] we can prove strong auxiliary-input security for $\mathcal{E}'$ with respect to subexponentially-hard functions by working with a modification of Construction 1, letting $(c_1,\ldots,c_l) = (E_{sk}(0;r_1),\ldots, E_{sk}(0;r_l))$ be the public parameters of the scheme, and letting the public key be computed, under secret key $\mathbf{s}$, as $Hom(c_{i_1},\ldots,c_{i_w})$, where $(i_1,\ldots,i_w)$ are the indices of non-zero bits of $\mathbf{s}$. Now since a public key under the new scheme has at most $l' = |\mathcal{R}_\lambda|$ different values we can obtain $\frac{\epsilon}{l'}$-strong auxiliary-input security from ϵ-weak-auxiliary-input security. This last step follows since, for any scheme with l' different public keys, if recovering sk from $f(pk, sk)$ is ϵ/l'-hard (i.e., succeeds with a probability at most ϵ/l'), recovering sk from $(f(pk, sk), pk)$ is ϵ-hard. Finally, we mention that the proof of multiple-key circular security (Theorem 2) extends to the setting above which contains public parameters.

7.2 KDM Amplification

We show that Applebaum's KDM-amplification method [3], which, informally speaking, shows that projection security is sufficient for obtaining "rich-KDM" security, preserves both types of leakage resilience. For simplicity, we focus on the case of bit encryption and 1-KDM security.

As notation, we identify an efficiently computable function $f = \{f_\lambda \colon \{0,1\}^{l(\lambda)} \mapsto \{0,1\}\}_{\lambda \in \mathbb{N}}$ with an ensemble of circuits $\{c_\lambda\}_{\lambda \in \mathbb{N}}$, and say that f has size $p = p(\lambda)$ if, for any λ, the circuit c_λ has size at most p. We say an ensemble of sets of functions $F = \{F_\lambda\}_{\lambda \in \mathbb{N}}$ is p-bounded if for every λ and every $f \in F_\lambda$, f has size p. The following theorem is a special case of the results of [3].

Theorem 8 [3]. *Assume that $F = \{F_\lambda\}_\lambda$ is a fixed p-bounded ensemble of sets of functions and $\mathcal{E} = (G, E, Dec)$ is a 1-projection-secure public-key encryption scheme. The scheme $\mathcal{E}' = (G, E', D')$, constructed below, is $F\text{-}KDM^{(1)}$ secure: $E'_{pk}(b) = E_{pk}(Sim(b))$ and $D'_{sk}(C) = Rec(D_{sk}(C))$. Here Sim is a randomized function and Rec is a deterministic function, both of which are constructed based on F, through the procedure of randomized encoding of functions. The details of Sim and Rec are not important for our analysis, bu we refer the reader to [3] for further details.*

Theorem 9. *Let $\mathcal{E}$ and $\mathcal{E}'$ be as in Theorem 8. Then assuming that $\mathcal{E}$ is r-rate leakage resilient (resp., ϵ-auxiliary input secure) then $\mathcal{E}'$ is r-rate leakage resilient (resp., ϵ-auxiliary input secure).*

Proof. This follows by noting that the constructed scheme $\mathcal{E}'$ has the same key generation algorithm as that $\mathcal{E}$. We consider the leakage resilience case; the proof for the auxiliary-input case is entirely the same. Assume $\mathcal{A}'$ wins against ℓ-length leakage resilience of $\mathcal{E}'$; we build $\mathcal{A}$ that breaks the ℓ-length leakage resilience of $\mathcal{E}'$ by simulating $\mathcal{A}'$ as follows: $\mathcal{A}$ runs $\mathcal{A}'(pk)$, where pk is the public key that $\mathcal{A}$ receives; when $\mathcal{A}'$ sub,its the leakage query f, $\mathcal{A}$ makes the same query from its oracle and gives $f(sk)$ to $\mathcal{A}'$; finally, when $\mathcal{A}'$ submits (b_0, b_1), $\mathcal{A}$ submits $(Sim(b_0), Sim(b_1))$ to its oracle and gives the returned ciphertext to $\mathcal{A}'$. Thus, $\mathcal{A}$ achieves the same advantage as $\mathcal{A}'$ does, and the proof is complete.   □

We now obtain the following corollary, by combining Theorems 2, 3, 6 and 9.

Corollary 1. *Assuming the existence of a CPA-secure private-key scheme with reproducibility and degenerate homomorphism, for any poly p and any fixed p-bounded function family F, there exists a scheme $\mathcal{E}'$ which (at the same time) (1) is F-KDM secure, (2) achieves a $(1 - o(1))$ resilience rate, and (3) is auxiliary-input secure against subexponentially-hard functions.*

Acknowledgments. We would like to thank Josh Benaloh and Dan Boneh for helpful discussions.

References

1. Akavia, A., Goldwasser, S., Vaikuntanathan, V.: Simultaneous hardcore bits and cryptography against memory attacks. In: Reingold, O. (ed.) TCC 2009. LNCS, vol. 5444, pp. 474–495. Springer, Heidelberg (2009)
2. Alwen, J., Dodis, Y., Naor, M., Segev, G., Walfish, S., Wichs, D.: Public-key encryption in the bounded-retrieval model. In: Gilbert [21], pp. 113–134
3. Applebaum, B.: Key-dependent message security: generic amplification and completeness. In: Paterson, K.G. (ed.) EUROCRYPT 2011. LNCS, vol. 6632, pp. 527–546. Springer, Heidelberg (2011)
4. Applebaum, B., Cash, D., Peikert, C., Sahai, A.: Fast cryptographic primitives and circular-secure encryption based on hard learning problems. In: Halevi, S. (ed.) CRYPTO 2009. LNCS, vol. 5677, pp. 595–618. Springer, Heidelberg (2009)

5. Barak, B., Haitner, I., Hofheinz, D., Ishai, Y.: Bounded key-dependent message security. In: Gilbert [21], pp. 423–444
6. Bellare, M., Boldyreva, A., Staddon, J.: Randomness re-use in multi-recipient encryption schemeas. Public Key Crypt.-PKC **2003**, 85–99 (2003)
7. Black, J., Rogaway, P., Shrimpton, T.: Encryption-scheme security in the presence of key-dependent messages. In: Nyberg, K., Heys, H.M. (eds.) SAC 2002. LNCS, vol. 2595, pp. 62–75. Springer, Heidelberg (2002)
8. Boneh, D., Halevi, S., Hamburg, M., Ostrovsky, R.: Circular-secure encryption from decision diffie-hellman. In: Wagner, D. (ed.) CRYPTO 2008. LNCS, vol. 5157, pp. 108–125. Springer, Heidelberg (2008)
9. Brakerski, Z., Goldwasser, S.: Circular and leakage resilient public-key encryption under subgroup indistinguishability. In: Rabin, T. (ed.) CRYPTO 2010. LNCS, vol. 6223, pp. 1–20. Springer, Heidelberg (2010)
10. Brakerski, Z., Goldwasser, S., Kalai, Y.T.: Black-box circular-secure encryption beyond affine functions. In: Ishai [28], pp. 201–218
11. Brakerski, Z., Segev, G.: Better security for deterministic public-key encryption: the auxiliary-input setting. In: Rogaway, P. (ed.) CRYPTO 2011. LNCS, vol. 6841, pp. 543–560. Springer, Heidelberg (2011)
12. Choi, S.G., Wee, H.: Lossy trapdoor functions from homomorphic reproducible encryption. Inf. Process. Lett. **112**(20), 794–798 (2012)
13. Cramer, R., Shoup, V.: Universal hash proofs and a paradigm for adaptive chosen ciphertext secure public-key encryption. In: Knudsen, L.R. (ed.) EUROCRYPT 2002. LNCS, vol. 2332, pp. 45–64. Springer, Heidelberg (2002)
14. Dodis, Y., Goldwasser, S., Tauman Kalai, Y., Peikert, C., Vaikuntanathan, V.: Public-key encryption schemes with auxiliary inputs. In: Micciancio, D. (ed.) TCC 2010. LNCS, vol. 5978, pp. 361–381. Springer, Heidelberg (2010)
15. Dodis, Y., Kalai, Y.T., Lovett, S.: On cryptography with auxiliary input. In: STOC 2009, pp. 621–630 (2009)
16. Dodis, Y., Ostrovsky, R., Reyzin, L., Smith, A.: Fuzzy extractors: how to generate strong keys from biometrics and other noisy data. SIAM J. Comput. **38**(1), 97–139 (2008)
17. Dolev, D., Dwork, C., Naor, M.: Non-malleable cryptography (extended abstract). In: STOC 1991, pp. 542–552 (1991)
18. Dwork, C. (ed.): Proceedings of the 40th Annual ACM Symposium on Theory of Computing, Victoria, British Columbia, Canada. ACM, 17–20 May 2008
19. Dziembowski, S., Pietrzak, K.: Leakage-resilient cryptography. In: FOCS 2008, pp. 293–302 (2008)
20. Gentry, C., Peikert, C., Vaikuntanathan, V.: Trapdoors for hard lattices and new cryptographic constructions. In: Dwork [18], pp. 197–206
21. Gilbert, H. (ed.): EUROCRYPT 2010. LNCS, vol. 6110. Springer, Heidelberg (2010)
22. Goldreich, O., Levin, L.A.: A hard-core predicate for all one-way functions. In: Johnson, D.S. (ed.) Proceedings of the 21st Annual ACM Symposium on Theory of Computing, pp. 25–32, Seattle, Washigton, USA. ACM, 14–17 May 1989
23. Goldwasser, S., Micali, S.: Probabilistic encryption. J. Comput. Syst. Sci. **28**(2), 270–299 (1984)
24. Hajiabadi, M., Kapron, B.M., Srinivasan, V.: On generic constructions of circularly-secure, leakage-resilient public-key encryption schemes. IACR Cryptology ePrint Archive 2015, p. 741 (2015)
25. Halevi, S., Lin, H.: After-the-fact leakage in public-key encryption. In: Ishai [28], pp. 107–124

26. Hazay, C., López-Alt, A., Wee, H., Wichs, D.: Leakage-resilient cryptography from minimal assumptions. In: Johansson, T., Nguyen, P.Q. (eds.) EUROCRYPT 2013. LNCS, vol. 7881, pp. 160–176. Springer, Heidelberg (2013)

27. Hofheinz, D., Unruh, D.: Towards key-dependent message security in the standard model. In: Smart, N.P. (ed.) EUROCRYPT 2008. LNCS, vol. 4965, pp. 108–126. Springer, Heidelberg (2008)

28. Ishai, Y. (ed.): TCC 2011. LNCS, vol. 6597. Springer, Heidelberg (2011)

29. Kiltz, E., Pietrzak, K., Stam, M., Yung, M.: A new randomness extraction paradigm for hybrid encryption. In: Joux, A. (ed.) EUROCRYPT 2009. LNCS, vol. 5479, pp. 590–609. Springer, Heidelberg (2009)

30. Koppula, V., Ramchen, K., Waters, B.: Separations in circular security for arbitrary length key cycles. In: Dodis, Y., Nielsen, J.B. (eds.) TCC 2015, Part II. LNCS, vol. 9015, pp. 378–400. Springer, Heidelberg (2015)

31. Malkin, T., Teranishi, I., Yung, M.: Efficient circuit-size independent public key encryption with KDM security. In: Paterson, K.G. (ed.) EUROCRYPT 2011. LNCS, vol. 6632, pp. 507–526. Springer, Heidelberg (2011)

32. Micali, S., Reyzin, L.: Physically observable cryptography. In: Naor, M. (ed.) TCC 2004. LNCS, vol. 2951, pp. 278–296. Springer, Heidelberg (2004)

33. Naor, M., Pinkas, B., Reingold, O.: Distributed pseudo-random functions and KDCs. In: Stern, J. (ed.) EUROCRYPT 1999. LNCS, vol. 1592, pp. 327–346. Springer, Heidelberg (1999)

34. Naor, M., Reingold, O.: Synthesizers and their application to the parallel construction of pseudo-random functions. J. Comput. Syst. Sci. **58**(2) (1999)

35. Naor, M., Segev, G.: Public-key cryptosystems resilient to key leakage. SIAM J. Comput. **41**(4), 772–814 (2012)

36. Naor, M., Yung, M.: Public-key cryptosystems provably secure against chosen ciphertext attacks. In: STOC 1990, pp. 427–437 (1990)

37. Peikert, C., Waters, B.: Lossy trapdoor functions and their applications. In: Dwork [18], pp. 187–196

38. Rackoff, C., Simon, D.R.: Non-interactive zero-knowledge proof of knowledge and chosen ciphertext attack. In: Feigenbaum, J. (ed.) CRYPTO 1991. LNCS, vol. 576, pp. 433–444. Springer, Heidelberg (1992)

39. Regev, O.: On lattices, learning with errors, random linear codes, and cryptography. In: STOC 2005, pp. 84–93 (2005)

40. Rothblum, R.: Homomorphic encryption: from private-key to public-key. In: Ishai [28], pp. 219–234

41. Rothblum, R.D.: On the circular security of bit-encryption. In: Sahai, A. (ed.) TCC 2013. LNCS, vol. 7785, pp. 579–598. Springer, Heidelberg (2013)

42. Wee, H.: KDM-security via homomorphic smooth projective hashing. IACR Cryptology ePrint Archive 2015, p. 721 (2015)

KDM-Security via Homomorphic Smooth Projective Hashing

Hoeteck Wee[(✉)]

ENS, Paris, France
wee@di.ens.fr

Abstract. We present new frameworks for constructing public-key encryption schemes satisfying key-dependent message (KDM) security and that yield efficient, universally composable oblivious transfer (OT) protocols via the dual-mode cryptosystem framework of Peikert, Waters and Vaikuntanathan (Crypto 2008).

- Our first framework yields a conceptually simple and unified treatment of the KDM-secure schemes of Boneh et al. (Crypto 2008), Brakerski and Goldwasser (Crypto 2010) and Brakerski, Goldwasser and Kalai (TCC 2011) in the single-key setting.
- Using our second framework, we obtain new dual-mode cryptosystems based on the d-linear, quadratic residuocity and decisional composite residuocity assumptions.

Both of these frameworks build on the notion of smooth projective hashing introduced by Cramer and Shoup (Eurocrypt 2002), with the additional requirement that the hash function is homomorphic, as is the case for all known instantiations.

1 Introduction

The most basic security guarantee we require of a public key encryption scheme is that of semantic security against chosen-plaintext attacks (CPA) [21]: it is infeasible to learn anything about the plaintext from the ciphertext. However, a series of increasingly sophisticated use of encryption —both directly in the case of practical applications, and indirectly as a cryptographic building block in more theoretical work — call for encryption schemes with much stronger security guarantees. In this work, we consider two such security notions.

Key-Dependent Message (KDM) Security. The standard CPA security definition does not provide any guarantee where the plaintext depends on the secret key (as pointed out in [21]), as may be the case in disk encryption. It was later observed that this situation is not so unlikely and may sometimes even be desirable [1,12]. Black, Rogaway and Shrimpton [7] formally defined

CNRS, INRIA and Columbia University. Partially supported by ANR Project EnBiD (ANR-14-CE28-0003), NSF Award CNS-1445424 and the Alexander von Humboldt Foundation.

© International Association for Cryptologic Research 2016
C.-M. Cheng et al. (Eds.): PKC 2016, Part II, LNCS 9615, pp. 159–179, 2016.
DOI: 10.1007/978-3-662-49387-8_7

key-dependent message (KDM) security: roughly speaking, we want to guarantee semantic security even against an adversary that can obtain encryptions of (efficient) functions of its choosing, taken from some specified class of functions $\mathcal{F}$, applied to the secret key.

Several years ago, Boneh et al. (BHHO) [9] presented a public-key encryption scheme that is KDM-secure w.r.t. the class of affine functions under the decisional Diffie-Hellman (DDH) assumption. Since then, Applebaum et al. [4] presented a scheme under the LWE assumption (which is itself a variant of Regev's cryptosystem [33]) and Brakerski and Goldwasser [10] presented a BHHO-like scheme based on the quadratic residuocity (QR) and decisional composite residuocity (DCR) assumptions. All of these schemes achieve KDM-security w.r.t. the class of affine functions, which can in turn be "boosted" to the class of circuits of a-priori bounded size [3,5]. In spite of the fact that many of these schemes inherit the BHHO algebraic structure, there does not seem to be a general principle that explains the design or analysis of these schemes: the BHHO analysis uses an intermediate notion of an "expanded system", whereas that of Brakerski and Goldwasser rely on an incomparable "interactive vector" game.

Dual-Mode Cryptosystems. Dual-mode cryptosystems were put forth by Peikert et al. [32] as a tool for constructing efficient and universally composable oblivious transfer (OT) protocols. Oblivious transfer is a fundamental two-party cryptographic primitive for secure two-party and multi-party computation [20,28,35]: it allows one party, called the receiver, to obtain exactly one of two values from another party, called the sender. The receiver remains oblivious to the other value, and the sender is oblivious to which value was received.

A natural approach towards realizing OT is to have the receiver generate a pair of public keys, and have the sender encrypt both of its input values under the respective public keys [17,19]. In order to provide security against a malicious sender, we can simply generate a pair of "normal" public keys along with the corresponding secret keys and we can then decrypt the ciphertexts sent by the sender to extract both its inputs. On the other hand, if the receiver is malicious, we need to ensure that (at least) one of the two public keys be "messy", namely it carries no information about the ciphertext encrypted under the key.

A dual-mode cryptosystem provides exactly both of these guarantees in the common reference string (CRS) model. The cryptosystem admits two types of public keys, "normal" keys that enable correct decryption, and "messy" keys that carry no information statistically about the ciphertext. Moreover, a simulator can generate the CRS in one of two indistinguishable modes: a "messy" mode which ensures that amongst any pair of possibly adversarially chosen public keys, at least one must be "messy"; and a "decryption" mode which allows a simulator to generate a pair of "normal" keys.

Peikert et al. also presented three instantiations of dual-mode cryptosystems based on DDH, QR and LWE. However, there seems to be no overarching theme to the three constructions – the DDH-based scheme relies on a "re-randomization trick" from the earlier OT protocols of Naor and Pinkas [30] whereas the QR-based scheme relies on algebraic properties of Cocks' IBE scheme [14].

Our Results. We present new frameworks for constructing KDM-secure encryption schemes and dual-mode cryptosystems that admit a very simple and modular analysis. Both of these frameworks build on the notion of smooth projective hashing, introduced by Cramer and Shoup in the context of CCA-secure encryption [15,16], with the additional requirement that the hash function is homomorphic, as is the case for all known instantiations. Using our frameworks, we obtain:

– a unified treatment of the KDM-secure encryption schemes based on DDH, QR, and DCR given in [9,10] for affine functions of the secret key, as well as those for low-degree functions of the secret key in [11] (we focus here on the single-key setting, which already captures much of the difficulty in realizing KDM-security in prior works; see Sect. 2.1 for a discussion on multiple keys),
– new constructions of dual-mode cryptosystems: (i) a construction based on the d-linear assumption, generalizing the previous construction based on DDH; (ii) a simple construction based on QR, which does not rely on the Cocks IBE; (iii) a new construction based on DCR.

We regard our first construction for KDM security as our primary technical contribution. The second for dual-mode cryptosystems builds heavily upon existing constructions of OT from smooth project hashing in [23], although highlighting the role of the group structure and homomorphism for dual-mode cryptosystems appears to be novel to this work (c.f. comparison in Sect. 2.2).

Our high-level approach for KDM security is quite simple. Via the projective property, we will define ciphertexts via decryption with the secret key instead of encryption with the public key. Now, by feeding the decryption algorithm some "malformed" ciphertext, decryption leaks a function f of the secret key SK. In fact, we can design the malformed ciphertexts carefully so that they decrypt to $f($SK$)$; moreover, these malformed ciphertexts are indistinguishable from random encryptions of $f($SK$)$. It is important here that the distribution of the malformed ciphertext depends only on f and the public key PK. For this to work out, we require some algebraic structure for the decryption algorithm and the space of ciphertexts, as is captured by precisely by homomorphic projective hashing.

We note that in the proof of KDM security, we show that the simulated encryptions of $f($SK$)$ are computationally indistinguishable from honest encryptions of $f($SK$)$, even if the indistinguisher gets SK; this is necessary to enable a hybrid argument across the KDM queries. (As a side remark, we note that we cannot rely on smoothness at this step of the proof.) Projective hashing have the distinctive and extremely useful property in that it enables a computational assumption on the ciphertext space even against distinguishers that know the secret key; this property also played a crucial role in the original work on CCA-security [16], and the more recent work on leakage resilience [31].

2   Overview of Our Constructions

Smooth Projective Hashing. We begin with an informal overview of smooth projective hashing [15,16], since our constructions build on this framework. We consider a family of hash functions $\Lambda_{\text{HK}}(\cdot)$ indexed by a hashing key HK, whose input comes from a group $\mathcal{G}$. Let $\mathcal{G}_{\text{YES}}$ be a subgroup of $\mathcal{G}$ and let $\mu(\cdot)$ denote a projection map defined on the hashing key HK. We are interested in hash functions that satisfy the following properties:

- (projective) for $C \in \mathcal{G}_{\text{YES}}$, the value $\Lambda_{\text{HK}}(C)$ is uniquely determined by $\mu(\text{HK})$ and C. Moreover, there is an algorithm Pub that given $\mu(\text{HK})$ along with the randomness r used to sample C, outputs $\Lambda_{\text{HK}}(C)$.
- (smoothness) for $C \notin \mathcal{G}_{\text{YES}}$, the value $\Lambda_{\text{HK}}(C)$ is statistically close to random even given $\mu(\text{HK})$ and C.
- (homomorphic) for all $C_0, C_1 \in \mathcal{G}$, we have $\Lambda_{\text{HK}}(C_0 \cdot C_1) = \Lambda_{\text{HK}}(C_0) \cdot \Lambda_{\text{HK}}(C_1)$.

In addition, we require that the uniform distributions over $\mathcal{G}_{\text{YES}}$ and $\mathcal{G}$ be computationally indistinguishable, and that the uniform distributions over $\mathcal{G}_{\text{YES}}$ and $\mathcal{G}_{\text{NO}} := \mathcal{G} \setminus \mathcal{G}_{\text{YES}}$ are also computationally indistinguishable. (If $\mathcal{G}_{\text{YES}}$ has negligible density, then the former implies the latter.)

2.1   KDM-Security

Starting with a smooth projective hash function $\Lambda_{\text{HK}}(\cdot)$ defined on $\mathcal{G}$, we can build a CPA-secure encryption scheme —which we will refer to as the "Cramer-Shoup scheme"— as follows:

- Gen(1^k): Sample a uniform hashing key HK and output the key pair

$$\text{PK} := \mu(\text{HK}) \quad \text{and} \quad \text{SK} := \text{HK}$$

  Henceforth, we will use SK and HK interchangeably for this scheme.
- Enc(PK, m): To encrypt a message m, sample $C \leftarrow_{\text{R}} \mathcal{G}_{\text{YES}}$ with randomness r, output the ciphertext

$$(C, \Lambda_{\text{SK}}(C) \cdot m)$$

  where $\Lambda_{\text{SK}}(C)$ is computed via the projective property using Pub(PK, C, r).
- Dec(SK, (C, ψ)): On input a ciphertext (C, ψ), output the plaintext

$$(\Lambda_{\text{SK}}(C)^{-1} \cdot \psi)$$

A standard argument shows that this scheme is CPA-secure: we switch the distribution of C in the ciphertext to $C \leftarrow_{\text{R}} \mathcal{G}_{\text{NO}}$ and then by smoothness, the ciphertext statistically hides m. Moreover:

> **Theorem (informal).** Suppose in addition that $\Lambda_{\text{SK}}(\cdot)$ is homomorphic. Then this encryption scheme is KDM-secure w.r.t. the class of functions $\{\text{SK} \mapsto \Lambda_{\text{SK}}(e)\}$ for any $e \in \mathcal{G}$.

Once we have KDM-security for affine functions, we can "boost" to the class of circuits of a-priori bounded size [3,5].

Simulating KDM Queries. The core difficulty lies in simulating encryptions of $\Lambda_{\text{SK}}(e)$ given only the public key, which turns out to be really simple in our framework.

$$
\begin{aligned}
\mathsf{Enc}(\mathrm{PK}, \Lambda_{\mathrm{SK}}(e)) &\equiv (C, \mathsf{Pub}(\mathrm{PK}, C, r) \cdot \Lambda_{\mathrm{SK}}(e)) &&: C \leftarrow_{\mathrm{R}} \mathcal{G}_{\mathrm{YES}}, \text{randomness } r \\
&\equiv (C, \Lambda_{\mathrm{SK}}(C) \cdot \Lambda_{\mathrm{SK}}(e)) &&: C \leftarrow_{\mathrm{R}} \mathcal{G}_{\mathrm{YES}}, \text{via projective property} \\
&\approx_c (C, \Lambda_{\mathrm{SK}}(C) \cdot \Lambda_{\mathrm{SK}}(e)) &&: C \leftarrow_{\mathrm{R}} \mathcal{G}, \text{via subgroup membership} \\
&\equiv (C, \Lambda_{\mathrm{SK}}(C \cdot e)) &&: C \leftarrow_{\mathrm{R}} \mathcal{G}, \text{since } \Lambda_{\mathrm{SK}}(\cdot) \text{ is homomorphic} \\
&\equiv (C \cdot e^{-1}, \Lambda_{\mathrm{SK}}(C)) &&: C \leftarrow_{\mathrm{R}} \mathcal{G}, \text{since } e \in \mathcal{G} \\
&\approx_c (C \cdot e^{-1}, \Lambda_{\mathrm{SK}}(C)) &&: C \leftarrow_{\mathrm{R}} \mathcal{G}_{\mathrm{YES}} \\
&\equiv (C \cdot e^{-1}, \mathsf{Pub}(\mathrm{PK}, C, r)) &&: C \leftarrow_{\mathrm{R}} \mathcal{G}_{\mathrm{YES}}, \text{randomness } r, \text{via projective}
\end{aligned}
$$

Note that:

- we can sample from the final distribution given only PK;
- the above transition does not rely on smoothness, and therefore everything goes through even if we append SK to the view, namely $(\mathrm{SK}, \mathsf{Enc}(\Lambda_{\mathrm{SK}}(e))) \approx_c (\mathrm{SK}, (C \cdot e^{-1}, \mathsf{Pub}(\mathrm{PK}, C, r)))$, which allows us to carry out a hybrid argument over the KDM queries;
- the treatment of KDM queries relies on the projective and homomorphic properties of $\Lambda_{\mathrm{SK}}(\cdot)$ but not smoothness; instead, we will use smoothness for the normal encryption queries.

Again, we stress that the proof crucially exploits the projective property; the role of the projective property is not captured by any of the prior "expanded system", "interactive vector" or the "triple proofs" frameworks for KDM-security in [9, 10, 29].

An Instantiation. In the BHHO DDH-based KDM-secure encryption scheme, the underlying projective hash function is defined on a group $\mathcal{G} := \mathbb{G}^{\ell}$ where $\mathbb{G}$ is the DDH group with some generator g, and ℓ is a parameter. The hashing key (also the secret key) $\mathrm{SK} = (s_1, \ldots, s_\ell)$ lies in $\{0, 1\}^{\ell}$, and given an instance $C = (c_1, \ldots, c_\ell) \in \mathbb{G}^{\ell}$,

$$
\Lambda_{\mathrm{SK}}^{\mathsf{BHHO}}(C) = c_1^{s_1} \cdot c_2^{s_2} \cdots c_\ell^{s_\ell}
$$

This means that given any $(a_1, \ldots, a_\ell) \in \mathbb{Z}_q^{\ell}$,

$$
\Lambda_{\mathrm{SK}}^{\mathsf{BHHO}}((g^{a_1}, \ldots, g^{a_\ell})) = g^{a_1 s_1 + \cdots + a_\ell s_\ell}
$$

Average-case smoothness follows readily from the left-over hash lemma. Now, if we modify the underlying Cramer-Shoup scheme to encrypt the message in the exponent, this function corresponds precisely to linear functions of the bits of the secret key. To handle affine functions, we need to handle an additional offset as described in Sect. 4.

Moreover, we can further extend the hash proof system to handle KDM-security with respect to some fixed functions $f_1, \ldots, f_t$ for any polynomial t (for instance, constant-degree polynomials in the bits of the secret keys or uniform Turing machine computation of description at most $c \log k$ bits) as is the setting considered in Brakerski, Goldwasser and Kalai [11]. We now consider instances $C = (c_1, \ldots, c_{\ell+t}) \in \mathbb{G}^{\ell+t}$,

$$
\Lambda_{\mathrm{SK}}^{\mathsf{BHHO}}(C) = c_1^{s_1} \cdot c_2^{s_2} \cdots c_\ell^{s_\ell} \cdot c_{\ell+1}^{f_1(\mathrm{SK})} \cdots c_{\ell+t}^{f_t(\mathrm{SK})}
$$

Average-case smoothness follows as before from the left-over hash lemma. Then, $\Lambda_{\mathrm{SK}}^{\mathsf{BHHO}}(g^{e_{\ell+i}}) = g^{f_i(\mathrm{SK})}$ corresponds to an encryption of $f_i(\mathrm{SK})$. This provides a more direct construction of KDM-security with respect to $f_1, \ldots, f_t$ as opposed to the entropic-KDM framework in [11].

On KDM-Security with Multiple Keys. We clarify that we only address KDM-security in this paper with a single public/secret key, whereas the previous constructions in [9,10] address KDM-security with multiple public/secret key pairs. We note that simplifying KDM-security for a single public/secret key is still important in and of itself: (1) it suffices for some applications, e.g. disk encryption, (2) it already captures much of the technical difficulty in realizing KDM-security, (3) previous schemes in [4,9,10] first establish KDM-security for a single public/secret key, and then "bootstrap" to multiple keys (in a non-black-box way), (4) more recent schemes for RKA-KDM-security in [8] also reduces security to KDM-security for a single public/secret key. In particular, our framework clarifies the first step of the analysis for multiple key pairs; our framework is also the first to point out the role of the projective property for KDM-security (which is not covered in prior "expanded system", "interactive vector" or the "triple proofs" frameworks for KDM-security in [9,10,29]) and that captures the algebraic structure needed for the decryption algorithm and the space of ciphertexts via homomorphic projective hashing.

Connection to Leakage Resilience. Let us informally refer to a Cramer-Shoup scheme as "linear" if $\Lambda_{SK}(\cdot)$ computes a linear function of SK (possibly in the exponent), where the coefficients of the linear function are specified by the instance. From the preceding discussion, we see that (1) linear Cramer-Shoup schemes are KDM-secure w.r.t. linear functions, and (2) the BHHO scheme [9] along with the BHHO-like schemes given by Brakerski and Goldwasser [10] are examples of such schemes. Naor and Segev [31] also showed that linear Cramer-Shoup schemes are resilient to bounded key leakage; this follows from the fact that random linear functions are good strong extractors. This yields a simple explanation as to why the BHHO scheme and variants there-of are both KDM-secure and resilient to bounded key leakage.

2.2   Dual-Mode Encryption

Starting with a smooth projective hash function $\Lambda_{HK}(\cdot)$ defined on $\mathcal{G}$, we can build a different CPA-secure encryption scheme —which we will refer to as the "dual Cramer-Shoup scheme"— as follows:

- Gen(1^k): Sample $C \leftarrow_R \mathcal{G}_{YES}$ with randomness r and output the key pair

$$PK := C \quad \text{and} \quad SK := r$$

- Enc(PK, m): To encrypt a message m, sample a random HK and output the ciphertext

$$(\mu(HK), \Lambda_{HK}(C) \cdot m)$$

- Dec$(SK, (p, \psi))$: On input a ciphertext (p, ψ), compute $K := \Lambda_{HK}(C)$ using Pub on input p, C and r (via the projective property) and output

$$(K^{-1} \cdot \psi)$$

As observed in by Halevi and Kalai [23,24], if we sample the public key $C \leftarrow_R \mathcal{G}_{NO}$, smoothness tells us that we obtain a "messy" public key where the ciphertext carries no information about the message. This suggests the following natural construction of a dual-mode cryptosystem / OT protocol:

- the receiver generates a pair of public keys $C_0, C_1 \in \mathcal{G}$ subject to the constraint that $C_0 \cdot C_1$ is the CRS.
- in the normal mode, we pick $C_0, C_1 \leftarrow_R \mathcal{G}_{YES}$, and the CRS is chosen uniformly from $\mathcal{G}_{YES}$.
- in the messy mode, the CRS is chosen uniformly from $\mathcal{G}_{NO}$. Now, whenever a possibly malicious receiver sends a pair of public keys (C_0, C_1) such that $C_0 \cdot C_1 \in \mathcal{G}_{NO}$, then we know that one of C_0, C_1 lies in $\mathcal{G}_{NO}$ and is therefore messy. (Otherwise, if $C_0, C_1 \in \mathcal{G}_{YES}$, then $C_0 \cdot C_1 \in \mathcal{G}_{YES}$ by closure properties of the subgroup.)

We note that exploiting subgroup structure of $\mathcal{G}_{YES}$ appears to be novel to this work, and we use subgroup structure in two ways: first, to argue that if $C_0 \cdot C_1 \in \mathcal{G}_{NO}$, then one of C_0, C_1 lies in $\mathcal{G}_{NO}$; and second, randomizing $\mathcal{G}_{YES}$ in the CRS (which is necessary for reusability in the context of UC security) by adding another random $\mathcal{G}_{YES}$ instance. In contrast, the prior work [23] uses the fact that if two pairs of group elements agree on the first component and disagree on the second, then one of them is a non-DDH tuple, and there is no need for randomizing $\mathcal{G}_{YES}$ as it addresses stand-alone security.

2.3   Discussion

On Lattice-Based Instantiations. A natural question is whether our frameworks extend to LWE-based instantiations of KDM-secure encryption and dual-mode cryptosystems given in [2,4,32], while relying on an approximate notions of smooth projective hashing as given in [27]. In the LWE setting, the "yes" instances as given by valid LWE instances do not form a subgroup. We note that for KDM security, our proof does not rely on the fact that $\mathcal{G}_{YES}$ forms a subgroup. For dual-mode cryptosystems, we only require that the "product" of two instances in $\mathcal{G}_{YES}$ is "far" from $\mathcal{G}_{NO}$, which is indeed satisfied by LWE instances. However, in order to obtain an OT protocol where the same CRS can be reused for an a-priori unbounded number executions, it is crucial that we can statistically rerandomize instances in $\mathcal{G}_{YES}$. We do not know how to achieve the latter for LWE; indeed, the LWE-based OT in [32] only achieves security for an a-priori bounded number of OT executions. In particular, we do not know any LWE instantiations for the "full-fledged" notion of dual-mode cryptosystems.

Additional Related Work. Smooth projective hashing is an extremely versatile tool that has found many other applications beyond CCA-security – two-message oblivious transfer [23], password-authenticated key exchange [6,18], bounded leakage resilience [31], and encryption schemes secure against selective opening attacks [24]. The works of Barak et al. and Applebaum [3,5], Brakerski,

Goldwasser and Kalai [11], and Malkin, Teranishi and Yung [29] each presented general and different techniques to extend KDM-security to richer classes of functions with incomparable trade-offs. Haitner and Holenstein [22] presented black-box impossibility results for (single-key) KDM-security based on general assumptions. In subsequent work, Hofheinz [25] presented a KDM-CCA-secure scheme with compact ciphertexts, inspired in part by the connection between smooth projective hashing and KDM-security established in this work.

Organization. We present definition and results on KDM-secure public-key encryption in Sect. 4, and those for dual-mode encryption in Sect. 5. We present the instantiations in Sects. 6 and 7.

3   Preliminaries

Notation. We denote by $s \leftarrow_R S$ the fact that s is picked uniformly at random from a finite set S and by $x, y, z \leftarrow_R S$ that all x, y, z are picked independently and uniformly at random from S. By PPT, we denote a probabilistic polynomial-time algorithm. Throughout, we use 1^k as the security parameter. We use $\cdot$ to denote multiplication (or group operation) as well as component-wise multiplication. We use lower case boldface to denote (column) vectors and upper case boldface to denote matrices.

3.1   Smooth Projective Hashing

We present the notion of smooth projective hashing as introduced by Cramer and Shoup [16], in the context of group-theoretic languages.

Setup. Fix a family of groups $\mathcal{G}_{PP}$ indexed by a public parameter PP. We require that PP be efficiently samplable along with a secret parameter SP given a security parameter 1^k, and assume that all algorithms are given PP as part of its input. We omit PP henceforth whenever the context is clear. We consider subgroups $\mathcal{G}_{YES}$ of $\mathcal{G}$ and we use $\mathcal{G}_{NO}$ to denote $\mathcal{G} \setminus \mathcal{G}_{YES}$. We will require that each of these groups $\mathcal{G}, \mathcal{G}_{YES}, \mathcal{G}_{NO}$ be efficiently samplable given PP, and that given the secret parameter SP, we can efficiently verify membership in $\mathcal{G}_{YES}$. Observe that if $\mathcal{G}_{YES}$ has negligible density (as is the case for most instantiations), we may use the same sampling algorithm for both $\mathcal{G}$ and $\mathcal{G}_{NO}$ since both distributions are statistically indistinguishable.

Subgroup Membership Assumption. We will consider two related computational assumptions pertaining to the group $\mathcal{G}$, which we refer to collectively as the *subgroup membership assumption*. The first assumption states that the uniform distributions over $\mathcal{G}_{YES}$ and $\mathcal{G}$ are computationally indistinguishable, even given PP. The second assumption states that the uniform distributions over $\mathcal{G}_{YES}$ and $\mathcal{G}_{NO}$ are computationally indistinguishable, even given PP. Again, observe that if $\mathcal{G}_{YES}$ has negligible density, these two assumptions are equivalent, since the distributions over $\mathcal{G}$ and $\mathcal{G}_{NO}$ are then statistically indistinguishable.

Homomorphic Projective Hashing. Fix a public parameter PP. We consider a family of hash functions $\{\Lambda_{\mathrm{HK}} : \mathcal{G} \to \mathcal{K}\}$ indexed by a hashing key HK. We require that $\Lambda_{\mathrm{HK}}(\cdot)$ be efficiently computable (by a 'private evaluation' algorithm), and HK be efficiently samplable. In addition, we require that both $\mathcal{G}$ and $\mathcal{K}$ are groups, and that $\Lambda_{\mathrm{HK}}(\cdot)$ is a group *homomorphism*, that is, for all HK and all $C_0, C_1 \in \mathcal{G}$, we have $\Lambda_{\mathrm{HK}}(C_0) \cdot \Lambda_{\mathrm{HK}}(C_1) = \Lambda(C_0 \cdot C_1)$. We say that $\Lambda_{\mathrm{HK}}(\cdot)$ is *projective* if there exists a projection map $\mu(\cdot)$ defined on HK such that $\mu(\mathrm{HK})$ determines the behavior of Λ_{HK} on inputs from $\mathcal{G}_{\mathrm{YES}}$. Specifically, we require that there exists an efficient public evaluation algorithm Pub that on input $\mu(\mathrm{HK})$ and $C \in \mathcal{G}_{\mathrm{YES}}$ along with the randomness r used to sample C, outputs the value $\Lambda_{\mathrm{HK}}(C)$.

Smoothness. We say that $\Lambda_{\mathrm{HK}}(\cdot)$ is *smooth* if the behavior of Λ_{HK} on $\mathcal{G}_{\mathrm{NO}}$ is completely undetermined. That is, for all $C \in \mathcal{G}_{\mathrm{NO}}$, the following distributions are statistically close:

$$(\mathrm{PK}, \Lambda_{\mathrm{HK}}(C)) \quad \text{and} \quad (\mathrm{PK}, K)$$

where HK is random, $\mathrm{PK} = \mu(\mathrm{HK})$ and $K \leftarrow_{\mathrm{R}} \mathcal{K}$. (Looking ahead, we will also consider a relaxed notion in some of our instantiations where we choose K from the uniform distribution over some subset of $\mathcal{K}$; see Sect. 7.) We also say that $\Lambda_{\mathrm{HK}}(\cdot)$ is *average-case smooth* where we relax the requirement for smoothness to hold for a random $C \in \mathcal{G}$ [31]. That is, the following distributions are statistically close:

$$(C, \mathrm{PK}, \Lambda_{\mathrm{HK}}(C)) \quad \text{and} \quad (C, \mathrm{PK}, K)$$

where HK is random, $\mathrm{PK} = \mu(\mathrm{HK})$, $C \leftarrow_{\mathrm{R}} \mathcal{G}$ and $K \leftarrow_{\mathrm{R}} \mathcal{K}$.

4   KDM-Secure Encryption

Key-Dependent Message Security. We adopt a simulation-based variant of key-dependent message (KDM) security from [7,9], in the setting where there is only one public/secret key pair. Fix a public-key encryption scheme (Gen, Enc, Dec). For a stateful adversary $\mathcal{A}$, we define the advantage function

$$\mathsf{AdvKDM}^{\mathcal{A},\mathcal{F}}(k) := \Pr\left[\begin{matrix} (\mathrm{PK}, \mathrm{SK}) \leftarrow \mathsf{Gen}(1^k); \\ \mathcal{A}^{\mathsf{kdmEnc}(\cdot), \mathsf{Enc}(\mathrm{PK}, \cdot)}(\mathrm{PK}) = 1 \end{matrix} \right] - \Pr\left[\begin{matrix} (\mathrm{PK}, \mathrm{SK}) \leftarrow \mathsf{Gen}(1^k); \\ \mathcal{A}^{\mathsf{kdmEnc}^*(\mathrm{PK}, \cdot), \mathsf{Enc}^*(\mathrm{PK}, \cdot)}(\mathrm{PK}) = 1 \end{matrix} \right]$$

where

- $\mathsf{kdmEnc}(\cdot)$ is an oracle that on input $f \in \mathcal{F}$ returns a random encryption $\mathsf{Enc}(\mathrm{PK}, f(\mathrm{SK}))$;
- $\mathsf{kdmEnc}^*(\mathrm{PK}, \cdot)$ corresponds to a simulator that gets as input $f \in \mathcal{F}$;
- $\mathsf{Enc}^*(\mathrm{PK}, \cdot)$ is an oracle that on input m, returns $\mathsf{Enc}(\mathrm{PK}, 0^{|m|})$.

An encryption scheme is said to be *F-KDM secure* if there exists an efficient kdmEnc*() such that for all PPT $\mathcal{A}$, the advantage $|\mathsf{AdvKDM}^{\mathcal{A},\mathcal{F}}(k)|$ is a negligible function in k.

Construction. Starting with a projective hash function $\Lambda_{\mathrm{HK}} : \mathcal{G} \to \mathcal{K}$, we may derive a semantically secure public-key encryption scheme (Gen, Enc, Dec). The message space is $\mathcal{M}$, and we require an injective map $\phi : \mathcal{M} \to \mathcal{K}$ which is efficiently computable and invertible.

- Gen(1^k): Sample public parameters PP, a uniform hashing key HK and compute PK $:= (\mathrm{PP}, \mu(\mathrm{HK}))$. Output the key pair

$$\mathrm{PK} := (\mathrm{PP}, \mu(\mathrm{HK})) \quad \text{and} \quad \mathrm{SK} := \mathrm{HK}$$

- Enc(PK, m): Sample $C \leftarrow_{\mathrm{R}} \mathcal{G}_{\mathrm{YES}}$ with randomness r, output the ciphertext

$$(C, \mathsf{Pub}(\mathrm{PK}, C, r) \cdot \phi(m))$$

- Dec(SK, (C, ψ)): Output the plaintext

$$\phi^{-1}(\Lambda_{\mathrm{SK}}(C)^{-1} \cdot \psi)$$

Theorem 1. *Suppose $\Lambda_{\mathrm{HK}}(\cdot)$ is a projective hash function that is average-case smooth and homomorphic, and the subgroup membership problem is hard (w.r.t. $\mathcal{G}$ vs $\mathcal{G}_{\mathrm{YES}}$). Then, the encryption scheme (Gen, Enc, Dec) described above is F-KDM secure where $\mathcal{F} = \{f_{e,k} : \mathrm{SK} \mapsto \phi^{-1}(\Lambda_{\mathrm{SK}}(e) \cdot k) \mid e \in \mathcal{G}, k \in \mathcal{K}\}$.*

We do require that given a description of the function $f_{e,k}$, we can efficiently compute the corresponding $e \in \mathcal{G}, k \in \mathcal{K}$. Later on in the instantiations, the term e allows us to specify the coefficients in a linear function, whereas k corresponds to the constant off-set in an affine function. On the first reading, we suggest that the reader assume ϕ is the identity map.

Proof. Observe that correctness of the encryption scheme follows readily from the projective property. We proceed to establish KDM security. First, we describe kdmEnc*: on input PK, $f_{e,k}$ and randomness r, use r to sample $C \leftarrow_{\mathrm{R}} \mathcal{G}_{\mathrm{YES}}$ and output

$$(C \cdot e^{-1}, \mathsf{Pub}(\mathrm{PK}, C, r) \cdot k)$$

We proceed via a sequence of games. Fix a PPT adversary $\mathcal{A}$ that makes at most Q_0 queries to kdmEnc and Q_1 queries to Enc. We show that

$$|\mathsf{AdvKDM}^{\mathcal{A},\mathcal{F}}(k)| \leq (2Q_0 + 2Q_1) \cdot \epsilon$$

where ϵ is the advantage for the subgroup membership assumption. We start with Game 0, where the challenger proceeds like in the security game with kdmEnc, Enc oracles in the left experiment and kdmEnc*, Enc* oracles in the right experiment.

Game 1. We will run a hybrid argument over the Q_0 queries to kdmEnc. That is, for $i = 1, \ldots, Q_0$, in Game 1.i, we replace the i'th query $f_{e,k}$ to kdmEnc on the left with kdmEnc*, so that we answer the first i queries using kdmEnc* and the last $Q_0 - i$ queries using kdmEnc. It suffices to show that for each i,

$$(\text{PK}, \text{SK}, \text{Enc}(\text{PK}, f_{e,k}(\text{SK}))) \overset{2\epsilon}{\approx}_c (\text{PK}, \text{SK}, (C \cdot e^{-1}, \text{Pub}(\text{PK}, C, r) \cdot k)),$$

where we would use PK to simulate the Enc queries and the first $i-1$ kdmEnc* queries, and SK to simulate the remaining $Q_0 - i$ kdmEnc queries. For notational simplicity, we omit (PK, SK) in the hybrid transitions below:

$$
\begin{aligned}
&\text{Enc}(\text{PK}, f_{e,k}(\text{SK}); r) \\
= \ &(C, \text{Pub}(\text{PK}, C, r) \cdot \Lambda_{\text{SK}}(e) \cdot k) &&: C \leftarrow_{\text{R}} \mathcal{G}_{\text{YES}}, \text{randomness } r \\
\equiv \ &(C, \Lambda_{\text{SK}}(C) \cdot \Lambda_{\text{SK}}(e) \cdot k) &&: C \leftarrow_{\text{R}} \mathcal{G}_{\text{YES}}, \text{via projective property} \\
\approx_c \ &(C, \Lambda_{\text{SK}}(C) \cdot \Lambda_{\text{SK}}(e) \cdot k) &&: C \leftarrow_{\text{R}} \mathcal{G}, \text{via subgroup membership} \\
\equiv \ &(C, \Lambda_{\text{SK}}(C \cdot e) \cdot k) &&: C \leftarrow_{\text{R}} \mathcal{G}, \text{since } \Lambda_{\text{SK}}(\cdot) \text{ is homomorphic} \\
\equiv \ &(C \cdot e^{-1}, \Lambda_{\text{SK}}(C) \cdot k) &&: C \leftarrow_{\text{R}} \mathcal{G}, \text{since } e \in \mathcal{G} \\
\approx_c \ &(C \cdot e^{-1}, \Lambda_{\text{SK}}(C) \cdot k) &&: C \leftarrow_{\text{R}} \mathcal{G}_{\text{YES}} \\
\equiv \ &(C \cdot e^{-1}, \text{Pub}(\text{PK}, C, r) \cdot k) &&: C \leftarrow_{\text{R}} \mathcal{G}_{\text{YES}}, \text{randomness } r, \text{via projective}
\end{aligned}
$$

Note that the above transition does not rely on smoothness, and therefore everything goes through even if we append (PK, SK) to the view.

Game 2. For $i = 1, \ldots, Q_1$, replace the i'th query m to Enc on the left with Enc*. We will run a hybrid argument over the Q_1 queries, and thus it suffices to show that for each i,

$$(\text{PK}, \text{Enc}(\text{PK}, m)) \overset{2\epsilon}{\approx}_c (\text{PK}, \text{Enc}(\text{PK}, 0^{|m|})).$$

This is standard CPA-security of the Cramer-Shoup encryption. Observe that the view includes PK, which is sufficient to run kdmEnc*.

$$
\begin{aligned}
\text{Enc}(\text{PK}, m) \equiv \ &(C, \text{Pub}(\text{PK}, C, r) \cdot \phi(m)) &&: C \leftarrow_{\text{R}} \mathcal{G}_{\text{YES}}, \text{randomness } r \\
\equiv \ &(C, \Lambda_{\text{SK}}(C) \cdot \phi(m)) &&: C \leftarrow_{\text{R}} \mathcal{G}_{\text{YES}}, \text{via projective property} \\
\approx_c \ &(C, \Lambda_{\text{SK}}(C) \cdot \phi(m)) &&: C \leftarrow_{\text{R}} \mathcal{G}, \text{via subgroup membership} \\
\equiv \ &(C, K \cdot \phi(m)) &&: C \leftarrow_{\text{R}} \mathcal{G}, K \leftarrow_{\text{R}} \mathcal{K}, \text{via smoothness} \\
\equiv \ &(C, K \cdot \phi(0^{|m|})) &&: C \leftarrow_{\text{R}} \mathcal{G}, K \leftarrow_{\text{R}} \mathcal{K}, \text{via uniformity of } K \\
\approx_c \ &\text{Enc}(\text{PK}, 0^{|m|})) &&\text{by reversing the hybrids}
\end{aligned}
$$

We conclude by observing that in Game 2, the left and right experiments are identical (both use the kdmEnc*, Enc* oracles), and therefore the advantage is 0.

$\square$

5   Dual-Mode Encryption

In this section, we present the definition of a dual-mode cryptosystem from [32], and show a generic construction from smooth projective hashing. By [32, Theorem 4.1], once we have a dual-mode cryptosystem, we immediately obtain UC-secure two-message oblivious transfer in the CRS model.

Preliminaries. Most of this is copied verbatim from [32, Sect. 3].

- Setup($1^k, \mu$): given security parameter 1^k and mode $\mu \in \{0,1\}$, outputs (CRS, τ). The CRS is a common string for the remaining algorithms, and τ is a trapdoor value that enables either the FindMessy or TrapKeyGen algorithm, depending on the selected algorithm. We will also denote the messy setup algorithm using SetupMessy($\cdot$) := Setup($\cdot$, 0) and the decryption mode setup algorithm using SetupDec($\cdot$) := Setup($\cdot$, 1). All the remaining algorithms take CRS as their first input, but for notational clarity, we usually omit it from the list of arguments.
- KeyGen(σ): given a desired decryptable branch value $\sigma \in \{0,1\}$, outputs (PK, SK) where PK is a public encryption key and SK is a corresponding secret key for messages encrypted on branch σ.
- Enc(PK, b, m): given a public key PK, a branch value $b \in \{0,1\}$, and a message $m \in \{0,1\}^\ell$, outputs a ciphertext c encrypted on branch b.
- Dec(SK, ψ): given a secret key SK and a ciphertext ψ, outputs a message $m \in \{0,1\}^\ell$.
- FindMessy(τ, PK): given a trapdoor τ for CRS generated in messy mode and some (possibly malformed) public key PK, outputs a branch value $b \in \{0,1\}$ corresponding to a messy branch of PK.
- TrapKeyGen(τ): given a trapdoor τ for CRS generated in decryption mode, outputs (PK, SK_0, SK_1) where PK is a public encryption key and SK_0, SK_1 are corresponding secret decryption keys for branches 0 and 1 respectively.

We use SetupMessy$_1$, SetupDec$_1$ to denote the first output CRS of SetupMessy, SetupDec and KeyGen$_1$ to denote the first output PK of KeyGen.

Definition 1 (Dual-Mode Encryption). *A dual-mode cryptosystem is a tuple of algorithms described above that satisfy the following properties:*

1. *Completeness for decryptable branch: For every $\mu \in \{0,1\}$, every (CRS, τ) ← Setup($1^k, \mu$), every $\sigma \in \{0,1\}$, every (PK, SK) ← KeyGen(σ) and every $m \in \{0,1\}^\ell$, decryption is correct on branch σ, i.e. Dec(SK, Enc(PK, σ, m)) = m.*
2. *Indistinguishability of modes: the first outputs of SetupMessy and SetupDec are computationally indistinguishable, i.e. SetupMessy$_1(1^k) \approx_c$ SetupDec$_1(1^k)$.*
3. *(Messy Mode) Trapdoor identification of messy branch: For every (CRS, τ) ← SetupMessy(1^k) and every (possibly malformed) PK, FindMessy(τ, PK) outputs a branch value $b \in \{0,1\}$ such that Enc(PK, $b, \cdot$) is messy. Namely, for every $m_0, m_1 \in \{0,1\}^\ell$, Enc(PK, b, m_0) $\approx_s$ Enc(PK, b, m_1).*
4. *(Decryption Mode) Trapdoor generation of keys decryptable on both branches: For every (CRS, τ) ← SetupDec(1^k), TrapKeyGen(τ) outputs (PK, SK_0, SK_1) such that for every $\sigma \in \{0,1\}$: (PK) $\approx_s$ KeyGen$_1(\sigma)$ and (PK, SK_σ) $\in$ Supp(KeyGen(σ)).*

Remark 1. Our requirement for decryption mode is actually weaker than that in [32], which stipulates that for every $\sigma \in \{0,1\}$, (PK, SK_σ) $\approx_s$ KeyGen(σ). That is, we allow TrapKeyGen output any valid secret key SK_σ for branch σ, whereas the original requirement is that the distribution of SK_σ be close to that output by

KeyGen(σ). This weaker guarantee is nonetheless sufficient for UC-secure OT, since the decryption mode is used in the case of a corrupted sender. A corrupted sender sees only PK and not SK_0 or SK_1; moreover, as long as both SK_0 and SK_1 are valid, we will be able to extract both of its inputs.

Dual-Mode Encryption from Projective Hashing. We begin with the set-up algorithms:

- SetupMessy(1^k): Run Param(1^k) ← (PP, SP) and sample $C \leftarrow_R \mathcal{G}_{NO}$. Output

$$CRS := (PP, C) \quad \text{and} \quad \tau := SP$$

- SetupDec(1^k): Run Param(1^k) ← (PP, SP) and sample $C \leftarrow_R \mathcal{G}_{YES}$ with randomness r. Output

$$CRS := (PP, C) \quad \text{and} \quad \tau := r$$

All the remaining algorithms take CRS = (PP, C) where $C \in \mathcal{G}$ as their first input.

- KeyGen(σ): On input a branch value $\sigma \in \{0, 1\}$, sample $C_\sigma \leftarrow_R \mathcal{G}_{YES}$ with randomness r_σ. Set $C_{1-\sigma} := C \cdot C_\sigma^{-1}$. Output

$$PK := (C_0, C_1) \quad \text{and} \quad SK := (\sigma, r_\sigma)$$

- Enc(PK, b, m): On input PK = (C_0, C_1), sample a uniform hashing key HK and output

$$\psi := (\mu(HK), \Lambda_{HK}(C_b) \cdot m)$$

- Dec(SK, ψ): On input SK = (σ, r) and $\psi = (PK^*, \psi^*)$, output

$$m := \mathsf{Pub}(PK^*, C_\sigma, r)^{-1} \cdot \psi^*$$

- FindMessy(τ, PK): On input τ = SP and PK = (C_0, C_1), check that $C_0 \cdot C_1 = C$. Output

$$b := \begin{cases} 1 & \text{if } C_0 \in \mathcal{G}_{YES} \\ 0 & \text{otherwise} \end{cases}$$

- TrapKeyGen(τ): On input τ = r, sample $C_0 \leftarrow_R \mathcal{G}_{YES}$ with randomness r_0 and compute $C_1 \in \mathcal{G}_{YES}$ with randomness $r_1 := r - r_0$ (so that $C_0 \cdot C_1 = C$). Output

$$PK := (C_0, C_1) \quad \text{and} \quad (SK_0, SK_1) := (r_0, r_1)$$

Theorem 2. *Suppose $\Lambda_{HK}(\cdot)$ is a smooth projective hash function, and the subgroup membership problem is hard (w.r.t. $\mathcal{G}_{YES}$ vs $\mathcal{G}_{NO}$). Then, the above construction yields a dual-mode cryptosystem.*

We note here that our construction requires an additional property from underlying group, namely that given the respective randomness r_0, r_1 for sampling $C_0, C_1 \in \mathcal{G}_{YES}$, the value $r_0 + r_1$ is the randomness for sampling $C_0 \cdot C_1$ (that is, the sampling algorithm is also homomorphic). This requirement may be eliminated if we are willing to settle for the weaker guarantee where each CRS may only be used for a single (or a-priori bounded) instance of OT, as with the LWE-based instantiation in [32].

Proof. We verify that our construction satisfies all of the four properties in Definition 1:

1. Completeness for decryptable branch: This follows readily from the projective property.
2. Indistinguishability of modes: This follows readily from our subset membership assumption.
3. (Messy Mode) Trapdoor identification of messy branch: In the messy mode, we require that $C_0 \cdot C_1 = C \in \mathcal{G}_{NO}$. Therefore, (at least) one of $C_0, C_1 \in \mathcal{G}_{NO}$ (a subgroup is closed under multiplication, so if $C_0, C_1 \in \mathcal{G}_{YES}$, then $C_0 \cdot C_1 \in \mathcal{G}_{YES}$). Moreover, using the membership trapdoor, we can identify which of C_0 or C_1 is in $\mathcal{G}_{NO}$. The corresponding ciphertext must be messy by smoothness.
4. (Decryption Mode) Trapdoor generation of keys decryptable on both branches: It is clear that the distribution of each of C_0 and C_1 is the uniform distribution over $\mathcal{G}_{YES}$. Moreover, r_0 and r_1 are randomness used for sampling C_0 and C_1 respectively. Therefore, by the projective property, we can decrypt ciphertexts on both branches. □

6 Instantiations from DLIN

Let $\mathbb{G}$ be a group of prime order q specified using a generator g. The DDH assumption asserts that g^{ab} is pseudorandom given g, g^a, g^b where $g \leftarrow_R \mathbb{G}; a, b \leftarrow_R \mathbb{Z}_q$. The d-LIN assumption asserts that $g_{d+1}^{r_1 + \cdots + r_d}$ is pseudorandom given $g_1, \ldots, g_{d+1}, g_1^{r_1}, \ldots, g_d^{r_d}$ where $g_1, \ldots, g_{d+1} \leftarrow_R \mathbb{G}; r_1, \ldots, r_d \leftarrow_R \mathbb{Z}_q$. DDH is equivalent to 1-LIN.

6.1 Dual-Mode Encryption

For dual-mode encryption, we use the original Cramer-Shoup DDH-based hash proof system in [15,16] and its generalization to d-LIN [26,34].

Setup. Sample $\mathbf{P} \leftarrow_R \mathbb{Z}_q^{d \times (d+1)}$ along with a check vector $\mathbf{v} \neq \mathbf{0}$ so that $\mathbf{Pv} = \mathbf{0}$. Output

$$\text{PP} := (\mathbb{G}, q, g, g^{\mathbf{P}}) \quad \text{and} \quad \text{SP} := (\mathbf{v})$$

The subgroup indistinguishability problem is given by:

$$\mathcal{G}_{YES} := \left\{ g^{\mathbf{r}^\top \mathbf{P}} : \mathbf{r} \in \mathbb{Z}_q^d \right\} \quad \text{and} \quad \mathcal{G} := \left\{ g^{\mathbf{a}^\top} : \mathbf{a} \in \mathbb{Z}_q^{d+1} \right\}$$

where $\mathsf{SampR}(\mathbf{r}) = g^{\mathbf{r}^\top \mathbf{P}}$ and the group operation is the natural one given by entry-wise product. The uniform distributions over $\mathcal{G}_{YES}$ and $\mathcal{G}$ are computationally distinguishable under the d-LIN assumption as shown in [9,31]. Observe that we can efficiently verify membership in $\mathcal{G}_{YES}$ using $\mathbf{v}$ since:

$$g^{\mathbf{a}^\top} \in \mathcal{G}_{YES} \quad \Longleftrightarrow \quad g^{\mathbf{a}^\top \mathbf{v}} = 1$$

Hashing. The hashing key is given by a column vector $\mathbf{s} \leftarrow_R \mathbb{Z}_q^{d+1}$, with

$$\mu(g^{\mathbf{P}}, \mathbf{s}) := g^{\mathbf{Ps}} \in \mathbb{G}^{d \times 1}$$

Private and public evaluation are given by:

$$\Lambda_{\mathbf{s}}(g^{\mathbf{a}^{\top}}) := g^{\mathbf{a}^{\top}\mathbf{s}} \in \mathbb{G} \quad \text{and} \quad \mathsf{Pub}(g^{\mathbf{Ps}}, \mathbf{C}, \mathbf{r}) := g^{\mathbf{r}^{\top}(\mathbf{Ps})}$$

Clearly, $\Lambda_{\mathbf{s}}(\cdot)$ is a group homomorphism. For the projective property, observe that for $\mathbf{C} = g^{\mathbf{r}^{\top}\mathbf{P}} \in \mathcal{G}_{\text{YES}}$, we have

$$\Lambda_{\mathbf{s}}(\mathbf{C}) = g^{\mathbf{r}^{\top}\mathbf{Ps}} = \mathsf{Pub}(g^{\mathbf{Ps}}, \mathbf{C}, \mathbf{r})$$

Smoothness. Observe that for any $g^{\mathbf{a}^{\top}} \in \mathcal{G}_{\text{NO}}$ (and $\mathbf{a} \neq \mathbf{0}$), we have that $\mathbf{a}^{\top}$ is not in the row span of $\mathbf{P}$. This means that for a random $\mathbf{s} \leftarrow_R \mathbb{Z}_q^{d+1}$, $\mathbf{a}^{\top}\mathbf{s}$ is uniformly distributed over $\mathbb{Z}_q$ given $\mathbf{Ps}$. Smoothness follows readily.

6.2 KDM-security

We extend the d-LIN based hash proof system in [9,31], which are the vectorial analogues of the preceding constructions, augmented with t functions following [11]. This in turn captures the DDH-based KDM-secure encryption in [9] and the DLIN-based scheme in [13]. Fix $\ell \geq (d+2)\log q$ and suppose we have t additional (efficiently computable) functions $f_1, \ldots, f_t : \{0,1\}^{\ell} \to \{0,1\}$, where $t \geq 0$. For instance, these functions may be low-degree polynomials of the bits of the input, as considered in [11].

Setup. Sample $\mathbf{P} \leftarrow_R \mathbb{Z}_q^{d \times (\ell+t)}$. Output

$$\text{PP} := (\mathbb{G}, q, g, g^{\mathbf{P}})$$

The subgroup indistinguishability problem is given by:

$$\mathcal{G}_{\text{YES}} := \left\{ g^{\mathbf{r}^{\top}\mathbf{P}} : \mathbf{r} \in \mathbb{Z}_q^d \right\} \quad \text{and} \quad \mathcal{G} := \left\{ g^{\mathbf{a}^{\top}} : \mathbf{a} \in \mathbb{Z}_q^{\ell+t} \right\}$$

where the group operation is the natural one given by entry-wise product. The uniform distributions over $\mathcal{G}_{\text{YES}}$ and $\mathcal{G}$ are computationally distinguishable under the d-LIN assumption as shown in [9,31].

Hashing. The hashing key is given by a column vector $\mathbf{s} \leftarrow_R \{0,1\}^{\ell}$. We then set $\hat{\mathbf{s}} \in \{0,1\}^{\ell+t}$ to be the concatenation of $\mathbf{s}$ and $f_1(\mathbf{s}), \ldots, f_t(\mathbf{s})$.

$$\mu(g^{\mathbf{P}}, \mathbf{s}) := g^{\mathbf{P}\hat{\mathbf{s}}} \in \mathbb{G}^{d \times 1}$$

Private and public evaluation are given by:

$$\Lambda_{\mathbf{s}}(g^{\mathbf{a}}) := g^{\mathbf{a}^{\top}\hat{\mathbf{s}}} \in \mathbb{G} \quad \text{and} \quad \mathsf{Pub}(g^{\mathbf{P}\hat{\mathbf{s}}}, \mathbf{C}, \mathbf{r}) := g^{\mathbf{r}^{\top}(\mathbf{P}\hat{\mathbf{s}})}$$

Clearly, $\Lambda_{\mathbf{s}}(\cdot)$ is a group homomorphism and the projective property simply follows from the fact that $g^{(\mathbf{r}^{\top}\mathbf{P})\hat{\mathbf{s}}} = g^{\mathbf{r}^{\top}(\mathbf{P}\hat{\mathbf{s}})}$.

Smoothness. For average-case smoothness, the left-over hash lemma implies that for $\ell > (d+2)\log q$, the following distributions:

$$(\mathbf{P}, \mathbf{P}\hat{\mathbf{s}}, \mathbf{a}, \mathbf{a}^\top \hat{\mathbf{s}}) \quad \text{and} \quad (\mathbf{P}, \mathbf{P}\hat{\mathbf{s}}, \mathbf{a}, a')$$

are $1/q$-statistically close, where $\mathbf{s} \leftarrow_R \{0,1\}^\ell, \mathbf{a} \leftarrow_R \mathbb{Z}_q^\ell, a' \leftarrow_R \mathbb{Z}_q$. Note that $\hat{\mathbf{s}}$ has ℓ bits of min-entropy, so $\hat{\mathbf{s}}$ conditioned on $\mathbf{P}\hat{\mathbf{s}} \in \mathbb{Z}_q^{d\times 1}$ has roughly $\ell - d\log q \geq 2\log q$ bits of min-entropy.

Class $\mathcal{F}$. The message space $\mathcal{M} = \{0,1\}$ and $\phi(m) = g^m$.

- Observe that for all $\mathbf{a} \in \mathbb{Z}_q^\ell, c \in \mathbb{Z}_q$ (such that $\mathbf{a}^\top\mathbf{s} + c \in \{0,1\}$ for all $\mathbf{s} \in \{0,1\}^\ell$):

$$\Lambda_{\mathbf{s}}(g^{(\mathbf{a}\|\mathbf{0})^\top}) \cdot g^c = g^{(\mathbf{a}\|\mathbf{0})^\top\hat{\mathbf{s}}} \cdot g^c = \phi(\mathbf{a}^\top\mathbf{s} + c)$$

- Moreover, for all $i \in [t]$,

$$\Lambda_{\mathbf{s}}(g^{\mathbf{e}_{\ell+i}}) = g^{f_i(\mathbf{s})} = \phi(f_i(\mathbf{s}))$$

where $\mathbf{e}_{\ell+i} \in \{0,1\}^{\ell+t}$ is the unit vector with a 1 in the $(\ell+i)$'th index. That is, the resulting scheme is $\mathcal{F}$-KDM secure for $\mathcal{F} = \{\mathbf{s} \mapsto \mathbf{a}^\top\mathbf{s} + c \mid \mathbf{a} \in \mathbb{Z}_q^\ell, c \in \mathbb{Z}_q\} \cup \{f_1, \ldots, f_t\}$, i.e. affine functions of the bits of the secret key (which includes flipping the i'th bit of the key $\mathbf{s} \mapsto 1 - s_i$) plus the functions $f_1, \ldots, f_t$.

7   Instantiations from QR and DCR

We will rely on the subgroup indistinguishability framework of Brakerski and Goldwasser [10] (also [16, Sect. 7.4.2]). We consider a family of finite commutative groups $\mathbb{G}$ that is generated by two elements g, h of co-prime order (thus $|\mathbb{G}| = \mathrm{ord}(g) \cdot \mathrm{ord}(h)$); we use $\mathbb{G}_0$ to denote $\langle g \rangle$. We will require the following additional properties:

- given the public description of $\mathbb{G}$, we may compute $\mathrm{ord}(h)$ and a good approximation a for $\mathrm{ord}(g)$ (so that the uniform distributions over $[a]$ and over $[\mathrm{ord}(g)]$ are statistcally close).
- computing discrete log with respect to h is easy.
- the uniform distributions over $\mathbb{G}_0$ and over $\mathbb{G}$ are computationally indistinguishable, given g, h.
- given some trapdoor, deciding membership in $\langle g \rangle$ is easy.

For our instantiations here, the output of $\Lambda_{\mathrm{HK}}(\cdot)$ lies in $\mathbb{G}$. We will work with a relaxed notion of smoothness here in this section, where instead of requiring that $\Lambda_{\mathrm{HK}}(\cdot)$ be random over $\mathbb{G}$, we only require that $\Lambda_{\mathrm{HK}}(\cdot) \bmod \mathbb{G}_0$ be random over $\langle h \rangle$. More formally, smoothness states that for all $C \in \mathcal{G}_{\mathrm{NO}}$: $\Lambda_{\mathrm{HK}}(C) \bmod \mathbb{G}_0$ is statistically close to uniform over the subgroup $\langle h \rangle$ even given $\mu(\mathrm{HK})$. Similarly, average-case smoothness states that the following distributions are statistically close:

$$(\mu(\mathrm{HK}), C, \Lambda_{\mathrm{HK}}(C) \bmod \mathbb{G}_0) \quad \text{and} \quad (\mu(\mathrm{HK}), C, h')$$

where $C \leftarrow_R \mathcal{G}$ and $h' \leftarrow_R \langle h \rangle$. The relaxed notion of smoothness is sufficient for all of our applications as long as we will embed the message into the subgroup $\langle h \rangle$.

Instantiation from QR. Fix a Blum integer $N = PQ$ for k-bit safe primes $P, Q \equiv 3 \pmod 4$ (such that $P = 2p + 1$ and $Q = 2q + 1$ for primes p, q). Let $\mathbb{J}_N$ denote the subgroup of $\mathbb{Z}_N^*$ with Jacobi symbol $+1$, and let $\mathbb{QR}_N$ denote the subgroup of quadratic residues. The QR assumption states that the uniform distributions over $\mathbb{QR}_N$ and $\mathbb{J}_N \setminus \mathbb{QR}_N$ are computationally indistinguishable. That is, we may take $\mathbb{G}$ and $\mathbb{G}_0$ to be $\mathbb{J}_N$ and $\mathbb{QR}_N$ respectively. Observe that $\mathbb{J}_N$ is isomorphic to $\mathbb{QR}_N \times (\pm 1)$ and that $|\mathbb{J}_N| = 2pq = 2|\mathbb{QR}_N|$. We can then sample g by squaring a random element in $\mathbb{Z}_N^*$ and fix h to be -1. Note that $|\mathbb{QR}_N| = pq = N/4 - O(\sqrt{N})$, which we may approximate by $N/4$.

Instantiation from DCR. (See [16, Sect. 8.2]). Again, fix a Blum integer $N = PQ$ for k-bit safe primes $P, Q \equiv 3 \pmod 4$ (such that $P = 2p+1$ and $Q = 2q+1$ for primes p, q). Let $\mathbb{J}_{N^2}$ denote the subgroup of $\mathbb{Z}_{N^2}^*$ with Jacobi symbol $+1$, so $|\mathbb{J}_{N^2}| = N\phi(N)/2 = 2Npq$. Consider the cyclic subgroup $\mathbb{G}_0$ of $\mathbb{J}_{N^2}$ consisting of all N'th powers of elements of $\mathbb{J}_{N^2}$. Then, $\mathbb{J}_{N^2} = \mathbb{G}_0 \times \langle 1+N \rangle$. Roughly speaking, the DCR assumption states that the uniform distributions over $\mathbb{G}_0$ and $\mathbb{J}_{N^2}$ are computationally indistinguishable. We can sample a random generator g of $\mathbb{G}_0$ as follows: pick $x \leftarrow_R \mathbb{Z}_{N^2}^*$ and set $g := -x^N$. In addition, we can fix $h := 1 + N$. Note that $|\mathbb{G}_0| = Npq = N^2/4 - O(\sqrt{N})$, which we may approximate by $N^2/4$.

7.1   Dual-Mode Encryption

For dual-mode encryption, we use the Cramer-Shoup QR/DCR-based hash proof system in [16].

Setup. Sample a random group $\mathbb{G}$ along with generators g and h.

$$\text{PP} := (\mathbb{G}, g, h)$$

The subgroup indistinguishability problem is given by:

$$\mathcal{G}_{\text{YES}} := \left\{ g^r : r \in \mathbb{Z}_{\text{ord}(g)} \right\} = \mathbb{G}_0 \quad \text{and} \quad \mathcal{G} := \left\{ h^d \cdot g^r : d \in \mathbb{Z}_{\text{ord}(h)}, r \in \mathbb{Z}_{\text{ord}(g)} \right\} = \mathbb{G}$$

where $\text{SampR}(r) = g^r$. We also denote by SP the trapdoor that allows us to verify membership in $\mathcal{G}_{\text{YES}}$; for the instantiations from QR and DCR, this would be the factorization of N.

Hashing. The hashing key is given by $s \leftarrow_R \mathbb{Z}_{\text{ord}(\mathbb{G})}$.

$$\mu(\text{PP}, s) := g^s \in \mathbb{G}$$

Private and public evaluation are given by:

$$\Lambda_s(C) := C^s \in \mathbb{G} \quad \text{and} \quad \text{Pub}(g^s, g^r, r) := (g^s)^r = g^{rs}$$

Clearly, $\Lambda_s(\cdot)$ is a group homomorphism. The projective property follows from the fact that $(g^r)^s = (g^s)^r$. For smoothness, first observe that by the Chinese Remainder Theorem, $s \bmod \text{ord}(h)$ is random even given g^s. Hence, $\Lambda_s(h^d g^r) \bmod \mathbb{G}_0 = h^{ds}$ is random over $\langle h \rangle$ if $d \neq 0$.

7.2   KDM-security

The next construction is implicit in [10], and is the vectorial analogue of the preceding construction, augmented with t functions following [11]. Let $\ell > 3 \log |\mathbb{G}|$. Suppose we have t additional (efficiently computable) functions $f_1, \ldots, f_t : \{0,1\}^\ell \to \mathbb{Z}_{\mathrm{ord}(h)}$, where $t \geq 0$.

Setup. Sample a random group $\mathbb{G}$ along with generators g and h. In addition, sample $\mathbf{p} \leftarrow_{\mathrm{R}} \mathbb{Z}_{\mathrm{ord}(g)}^{\ell+t}$. Output

$$\mathrm{PP} := (\mathbb{G}, g^{\mathbf{P}}, h)$$

The subgroup indistinguishability problem is given by:

$$\mathcal{G}_{\mathrm{YES}} := \left\{ g^{r\mathbf{P}} : r \in \mathbb{Z}_{\mathrm{ord}(g)} \right\} \subseteq \mathbb{G}_0^{\ell+t} \quad \text{and} \quad \mathcal{G} := \left\{ h^{\mathbf{d}} \cdot g^{r\mathbf{P}} : \mathbf{d} \in \mathbb{Z}_{\mathrm{ord}(h)}^{\ell+t}, r \in \mathbb{Z}_{\mathrm{ord}(g)} \right\} \subseteq \mathbb{G}^{\ell+t}$$

where the group operation over $\mathbb{G}^{\ell+t}$ is the natural one given by coordinate-wise product. The uniform distributions over $\mathcal{G}_{\mathrm{YES}}$ and $\mathcal{G}$ are computationally distinguishable under subgroup indistinguishability as shown in [10]. (The reduction is fairly straight-forward: it essentially takes the challenge (x, g, h) where either $x \leftarrow_{\mathrm{R}} \mathbb{G}_0$ or $x \leftarrow_{\mathrm{R}} \mathbb{G}$ and computes $(g^{\mathbf{p}'}, x^{\mathbf{p}'})$ where $\mathbf{p}' \leftarrow_{\mathrm{R}} \mathbb{Z}_{|\mathbb{G}|}^{\ell+t}$.)

Hashing. The hashing key is given by a column vector $\mathbf{s} \leftarrow_{\mathrm{R}} \mathbb{Z}_{\mathrm{ord}(h)}^{\ell}$. We then set $\hat{\mathbf{s}} \in \mathbb{Z}_{\mathrm{ord}(h)}^{\ell+t}$ to be the concatenation of $\mathbf{s}$ and $f_1(\mathbf{s}), \ldots, f_t(\mathbf{s})$.

$$\mu(g^{\mathbf{P}}, \mathbf{s}) := g^{\mathbf{p}^\top \hat{\mathbf{s}}} \in \mathbb{G}$$

Private and public evaluation are given by:

$$\Lambda_{\mathbf{s}}(\mathbf{c}) := \mathbf{c}^{\hat{\mathbf{s}}} \in \mathbb{G} \quad \text{and} \quad \mathsf{Pub}(g^{\mathbf{p}^\top \hat{\mathbf{s}}}, \mathbf{c}, r) := (g^{\mathbf{p}^\top \hat{\mathbf{s}}})^r$$

where $\mathbf{c}^{\hat{\mathbf{s}}} := \sum_{i=1}^{\ell+t} \mathbf{c}_i^{\hat{\mathbf{s}}_i}$. Clearly, $\Lambda_{\mathbf{s}}(\cdot)$ is a group homomorphism. The projective property simply follows from the fact that $g^{(r\mathbf{p})^\top \hat{\mathbf{s}}} = g^{r\mathbf{p}^\top \hat{\mathbf{s}}} = (g^{\mathbf{p}^\top \hat{\mathbf{s}}})^r$.

Smoothness. To establish average-case smoothness, first observe that:

$$\Lambda_{\hat{\mathbf{s}}}(h^{\mathbf{d}} \cdot g^{r\mathbf{P}}) \bmod \mathbb{G}_0 = h^{\mathbf{d}^\top \hat{\mathbf{s}}}$$

The left-over hash lemma tells us that $\mathbf{d}^\top \hat{\mathbf{s}}$ is statistically close to uniform over $\mathbb{Z}_{\mathrm{ord}(h)}$. More precisely, for $\ell > 3 \log |\mathbb{G}|$, the following distributions:

$$(\mathbf{p}, \mathbf{p}^\top \hat{\mathbf{s}} \bmod |\mathbb{G}_0|, \mathbf{d}, \mathbf{d}^\top \hat{\mathbf{s}} \bmod \mathrm{ord}(h)) \quad \text{and} \quad \langle \mathbf{p}, \mathbf{p}^\top \hat{\mathbf{s}} \bmod |\mathbb{G}_0|, \mathbf{d}, d' \rangle$$

are statistically close, where $\mathbf{s} \leftarrow_{\mathrm{R}} \mathbb{Z}_{\mathrm{ord}(h)}^{\ell}, \mathbf{d} \leftarrow_{\mathrm{R}} \mathbb{Z}_{\mathrm{ord}(h)}^{\ell+t}, d' \leftarrow_{\mathrm{R}} \mathbb{Z}_{\mathrm{ord}(h)}$. Average-case smoothness follows readily, since $g^{\mathbf{p}^\top \hat{\mathbf{s}}}$ is completely determined by $\mathbf{p}^\top \hat{\mathbf{s}} \bmod |\mathbb{G}_0|$.

Class $\mathcal{F}$. The message space $\mathcal{M} = \mathbb{Z}_{\mathrm{ord}(h)}$ and $\phi(m) = h^m$.

  – Observe that for all $\mathbf{a} \in \mathbb{Z}^\ell, c \in \mathbb{Z}$ (such that $\mathbf{a}^\top \mathbf{s} + c \in \mathbb{Z}_{\mathrm{ord}(h)}$ for all $\mathbf{s} \in \mathbb{Z}_{\mathrm{ord}(h)}^\ell$):

$$\Lambda_{\mathbf{s}}(h^{\mathbf{a}||0}) \cdot h^c = h^{\mathbf{a}^\top \mathbf{s} + c} = \phi(\mathbf{a}^\top \mathbf{s} + c)$$

– Moreover, for all $i \in [t]$,

$$\Lambda_{\mathbf{s}}(h^{\mathbf{e}_{\ell+i}}) = h^{f_i(\mathbf{s})} = \phi(f_i(\mathbf{s}))$$

where $\mathbf{e}_{\ell+i} \in \{0,1\}^{\ell+t}$ is the unit vector with a 1 in the $(\ell + i)$'th index. That is, the resulting scheme is $\mathcal{F}$-KDM secure for $\mathcal{F} = \{\mathbf{s} \mapsto \mathbf{a}^\top \mathbf{s} + c \mid \mathbf{a} \in \mathbb{Z}^\ell, c \in \mathbb{Z}\} \cup \{f_1, \ldots, f_t\}$, i.e. affine functions of the bits of the secret key, plus the functions $f_1, \ldots, f_t$.

Acknowledgments. I would like to thank David Cash, Kai-Min Chung and Dennis Hofheinz for helpful discussions.

References

1. Adão, P., Bana, G., Herzog, J.C., Scedrov, A.: Soundness of formal encryption in the presence of key-cycles. In: di Vimercati, S.C., Syverson, P.F., Gollmann, D. (eds.) ESORICS 2005. LNCS, vol. 3679, pp. 374–396. Springer, Heidelberg (2005)
2. Alperin-Sheriff, J., Peikert, C.: Circular and KDM security for identity-based encryption. In: Fischlin, M., Buchmann, J., Manulis, M. (eds.) PKC 2012. LNCS, vol. 7293, pp. 334–352. Springer, Heidelberg (2012)
3. Applebaum, B.: Key-dependent message security: generic amplification and completeness. In: Paterson, K.G. (ed.) EUROCRYPT 2011. LNCS, vol. 6632, pp. 527–546. Springer, Heidelberg (2011)
4. Applebaum, B., Cash, D., Peikert, C., Sahai, A.: Fast cryptographic primitives and circular-secure encryption based on hard learning problems. In: Halevi, S. (ed.) CRYPTO 2009. LNCS, vol. 5677, pp. 595–618. Springer, Heidelberg (2009)
5. Barak, B., Haitner, I., Hofheinz, D., Ishai, Y.: Bounded key-dependent message security. In: Gilbert, H. (ed.) EUROCRYPT 2010. LNCS, vol. 6110, pp. 423–444. Springer, Heidelberg (2010)
6. Benhamouda, F., Blazy, O., Chevalier, C., Pointcheval, D., Vergnaud, D.: New techniques for SPHFs and efficient one-round PAKE protocols. In: Canetti, R., Garay, J.A. (eds.) CRYPTO 2013, Part I. LNCS, vol. 8042, pp. 449–475. Springer, Heidelberg (2013)
7. Black, J., Rogaway, P., Shrimpton, T.: Encryption-scheme security in the presence of key-dependent messages. In: Nyberg, K., Heys, H.M. (eds.) SAC 2002. LNCS, vol. 2595, pp. 62–75. Springer, Heidelberg (2003)
8. Böhl, F., Davies, G.T., Hofheinz, D.: Encryption schemes secure under related-key and key-dependent message attacks. In: Krawczyk, H. (ed.) PKC 2014. LNCS, vol. 8383, pp. 483–500. Springer, Heidelberg (2014)
9. Boneh, D., Halevi, S., Hamburg, M., Ostrovsky, R.: Circular-secure encryption from decision Diffie-Hellman. In: Wagner, D. (ed.) CRYPTO 2008. LNCS, vol. 5157, pp. 108–125. Springer, Heidelberg (2008)
10. Brakerski, Z., Goldwasser, S.: Circular and leakage resilient public-key encryption under subgroup indistinguishability. In: Rabin, T. (ed.) CRYPTO 2010. LNCS, vol. 6223, pp. 1–20. Springer, Heidelberg (2010)
11. Brakerski, Z., Goldwasser, S., Kalai, Y.T.: Black-box circular-secure encryption beyond affine functions. In: Ishai, Y. (ed.) TCC 2011. LNCS, vol. 6597, pp. 201–218. Springer, Heidelberg (2011)

12. Camenisch, J.L., Lysyanskaya, A.: An efficient system for non-transferable anonymous credentials with optional anonymity revocation. In: Pfitzmann, B. (ed.) EUROCRYPT 2001. LNCS, vol. 2045, pp. 93–118. Springer, Heidelberg (2001)
13. Camenisch, J., Chandran, N., Shoup, V.: A public key encryption scheme secure against key dependent chosen plaintext and adaptive chosen ciphertext attacks. In: Joux, A. (ed.) EUROCRYPT 2009. LNCS, vol. 5479, pp. 351–368. Springer, Heidelberg (2009)
14. Cocks, C.: An identity based encryption scheme based on quadratic residues. In: Honary, B. (ed.) Cryptography and Coding 2001. LNCS, vol. 2260, pp. 360–363. Springer, Heidelberg (2001)
15. Cramer, R., Shoup, V.: A practical public key cryptosystem provably secure against adaptive chosen ciphertext attack. In: Krawczyk, H. (ed.) CRYPTO 1998. LNCS, vol. 1462, pp. 13–25. Springer, Heidelberg (1998)
16. Cramer, R., Shoup, V.: Universal hash proofs and a paradigm for adaptive chosen ciphertext secure public-key encryption. In: Knudsen, L.R. (ed.) EUROCRYPT 2002. LNCS, vol. 2332, p. 45. Springer, Heidelberg (2002)
17. Even, S., Goldreich, O., Lempel, A.: A randomized protocol for signing contracts. In: Chaum, D., Rivest, R.L., Sherman, A.T. (eds.) CRYPTO, pp. 205–210. Springer, Heidelberg (1982)
18. Gennaro, R., Lindell, Y.: A framework for password-based authenticated key exchange. ACM Trans. Inf. Syst. Secur. 9(2), 181–234 (2006)
19. Gertner, Y., Kannan, S., Malkin, T., Reingold, O., Viswanathan, M.: The relationship between public key encryption and oblivious transfer. In: FOCS, pp. 325–335 (2000)
20. Goldreich, O., Micali, S., Wigderson, A.: How to play any mental game or a completeness theorem for protocols with honest majority. In: STOC, pp. 218–229 (1987)
21. Goldwasser, S., Micali, S.: Probabilistic encryption. J. Comput. Syst. Sci. 28(2), 270–299 (1984)
22. Haitner, I., Holenstein, T.: On the (im)possibility of key dependent encryption. In: Reingold, O. (ed.) TCC 2009. LNCS, vol. 5444, pp. 202–219. Springer, Heidelberg (2009)
23. Halevi, S., Kalai, Y.T.: Smooth projective hashing and two-message oblivious transfer. J. Cryptol. 25(1), 158–193 (2012)
24. Hemenway, B., Libert, B., Ostrovsky, R., Vergnaud, D.: Lossy encryption: constructions from general assumptions and efficient selective opening chosen ciphertext security. In: Lee, D.H., Wang, X. (eds.) ASIACRYPT 2011. LNCS, vol. 7073, pp. 70–88. Springer, Heidelberg (2011)
25. Hofheinz, D.: Circular chosen-ciphertext security with compact ciphertexts. In: Johansson, T., Nguyen, P.Q. (eds.) EUROCRYPT 2013. LNCS, vol. 7881, pp. 520–536. Springer, Heidelberg (2013)
26. Hofheinz, D., Kiltz, E.: Secure hybrid encryption from weakened key encapsulation. In: Menezes, A. (ed.) CRYPTO 2007. LNCS, vol. 4622, pp. 553–571. Springer, Heidelberg (2007)
27. Katz, J., Vaikuntanathan, V.: Smooth projective hashing and password-based authenticated key exchange from lattices. In: Matsui, M. (ed.) ASIACRYPT 2009. LNCS, vol. 5912, pp. 636–652. Springer, Heidelberg (2009)
28. Kilian, J.: Founding cryptography on oblivious transfer. In: STOC, pp. 20–31 (1988)

29. Malkin, T., Teranishi, I., Yung, M.: Efficient circuit-size independent public key encryption with KDM security. In: Paterson, K.G. (ed.) EUROCRYPT 2011. LNCS, vol. 6632, pp. 507–526. Springer, Heidelberg (2011)
30. Naor, M., Pinkas, B.: Efficient oblivious transfer protocols. In: SODA, pp. 448–457 (2001)
31. Naor, M., Segev, G.: Public-key cryptosystems resilient to key leakage. In: Halevi, S. (ed.) CRYPTO 2009. LNCS, vol. 5677, pp. 18–35. Springer, Heidelberg (2009)
32. Peikert, C., Vaikuntanathan, V., Waters, B.: A framework for efficient and composable oblivious transfer. In: Wagner, D. (ed.) CRYPTO 2008. LNCS, vol. 5157, pp. 554–571. Springer, Heidelberg (2008)
33. Regev, O.: On lattices, learning with errors, random linear codes, and cryptography. In: STOC, pp. 84–93 (2005)
34. Shacham, H · A Cramer-Shoup encryption scheme from the linear assumption and from progressively weaker linear variants. Cryptology ePrint Archive, Report /074, 2007 (2007)
35. Yao, A.C.-C.: How to generate and exchange secrets. In: FOCS, pp. 162–167 (1986)

Protocols

Asynchronous Secure Multiparty Computation in Constant Time

Ran Cohen[✉]

Department of Computer Science, Bar-Ilan University, Ramat Gan, Israel
cohenrb@cs.biu.ac.il

Abstract. In the setting of secure multiparty computation, a set of mutually distrusting parties wish to securely compute a joint function. It is well known that if the communication model is asynchronous, meaning that messages can be arbitrarily delayed by an unbounded (yet finite) amount of time, secure computation is feasible if and only if at least two-thirds of the parties are honest, as was shown by Ben-Or, Canetti, and Goldreich [STOC'93] and by Ben-Or, Kelmer, and Rabin [PODC'94]. The running-time of all currently known protocols depends on the function to evaluate. In this work we present the first asynchronous MPC protocol that runs in constant time.

Our starting point is the asynchronous MPC protocol of Hirt, Nielsen, and Przydatek [Eurocrypt'05, ICALP'08]. We integrate *threshold fully homomorphic encryption* in order to reduce the interactions between the parties, thus completely removing the need for the expensive *king-slaves* approach taken by Hirt et al.. Initially, assuming an honest majority, we construct a constant-time protocol in the asynchronous Byzantine agreement (ABA) hybrid model. Using a concurrent ABA protocol that runs in constant expected time, we obtain a constant expected time asynchronous MPC protocol, secure facing static malicious adversaries, assuming $t < n/3$.

Keywords: Multiparty computation · Asynchronous communication · Threshold FHE · Constant-time protocols · Byzantine agreement.

1 Introduction

1.1 Background

In the setting of secure multiparty computation, a set of mutually distrusting parties wish to jointly and securely compute a function of their inputs. This computation should be such that each party receives its correct output, and none of the parties learn anything beyond their prescribed output. The standard definition today [14,26] formalizes the above requirements (and others) in the

R. Cohen—Work supported by THE ISRAEL SCIENCE FOUNDATION (grant No. 189/11), the Ministry of Science, Technology and Space and by the National Cyber Bureau of Israel.

© International Association for Cryptologic Research 2016
C.-M. Cheng et al. (Eds.): PKC 2016, Part II, LNCS 9615, pp. 183–207, 2016.
DOI: 10.1007/978-3-662-49387-8_8

following general way. Consider an ideal world in which an external trusted party is willing to help the parties carry out their computation. An ideal computation takes place in this ideal world by having the parties simply send their inputs to the trusted party, who then computes the desired function and passes each party its prescribed output. The security of a real protocol is established by comparing the outcome of the protocol to the outcome of an ideal computation. Specifically, a real protocol that is run by the parties is secure, if an adversary controlling a coalition of corrupted parties can do no more harm in a real execution than in the ideal execution.

One of the most important parameters for designing a protocol is the communication model. In the *synchronous* communication model, messages that are sent are guaranteed to be delivered within a *known* and finite time frame. As a result, the computation can proceed in *rounds*, such that if a party failed to receive a particular message in some round, within the expected time frame, the receiver knows that the sender did not transmit the message. Impressive feasibility results are known in this model [8,17,27,38], stating that every functionality can be securely computed, assuming that a majority of the parties are honest. Furthermore, under suitable cryptographic assumptions, the computation can be done using constant-round protocols [2,4,24,28,31,33].

The *asynchronous* model of communication is arguably more appropriate for modeling the real world. In this model the adversary has a stronger control over the communication channels and can impose an arbitrary unbounded (yet finite) delay on the arrival of each message. In particular, an honest party cannot distinguish between a corrupted party that refuses to send messages and an honest party whose messages are delayed.

This inherent limitation was taken into account by Ben-Or et al. [9] by adjusting the ideal-world computation. Since messages from t parties might never be delivered during the execution of the protocol, the trusted party cannot compute the function on *all* inputs. Therefore, the ideal-world adversary gets to decide on a *core set* of $n - t$ input providers (t of which might be corrupted) and the trusted party computes the function on their inputs (and default values for the rest). Next, the trusted party sends to each party the output of the computation along with the identities of the parties in the core set. It immediately follows that a secure protocol implies agreement in the asynchronous setting, since the core set must be agreed upon as part of the protocol, and therefore is feasible in the standard model if and only if $t < n/3$ [9,10]. Asynchronous protocols that are secure assuming $t < n/2$ are only known in weaker models that assume either a synchronous broadcast round [6] or some form of non-equivocation [3]. Moreover, the running-time[1] of all currently known asynchronous protocols depends on the function to be computed and no constant-time protocols were known.

In this work we study the following question.

Do there exist asynchronous secure multiparty protocols which run in constant time?

---

[1] The running time is measured by the elapsed time of the protocol while normalizing the maximal delay imposed on a message to 1.

1.2 Our Result

Our main result is a feasibility result of an asynchronous secure multiparty protocol that runs in constant time in a hybrid model where the parties have access to an ideal *asynchronous Byzantine agreement (ABA)* functionality.

The main tools that we use are *threshold fully homomorphic encryption* (TFHE) and *threshold signatures* (TSIG). A fully homomorphic encryption scheme (FHE) is an encryption scheme that enables an evaluation of a function over a tuple of ciphertexts to obtain an encrypted result. TFHE is essentially a distributed version of FHE, where the decryption key is secret shared amongst the parties. In order to decrypt a ciphertext, each party locally uses its share of the decryption key and computes a share of the plaintext. The plaintext can then be reconstructed given $t + 1$ decryption shares. Similarly, in a threshold signature scheme, the signing key is secret shared and $t + 1$ shares are required in order to sign a message. We note that both of these computational assumption can be based on the standard *learning with errors* (LWE) problem, see Asharov et al. [2], Bendlin and Damgård [11] and Bendlin et al. [12].

Theorem 1 (informal). *Assume that TFHE and TSIG schemes exist, and that the cryptographic keys have been pre-distributed. Then any efficiently computable function f can be securely computed in the asynchronous setting facing static malicious adversaries, assuming an honest majority and given access to an ABA ideal functionality. The time complexity of the protocol is $O(1)$, the communication complexity is independent of the multiplication-depth of the circuit representing f and the number of (concurrent) invocations of the ABA ideal functionality is n.*

Using the concurrent ABA protocol of Ben-Or and El-Yaniv [7], which runs in constant expected time[2] and is resilient for $t < n/3$, we obtain the following corollary.

Corollary 1 (informal). *Assume that TFHE and TSIG schemes exist, then any function can be securely computed in the asynchronous setting using a constant expected time protocol, in the presence of static malicious adversaries, for $t < n/3$.*

1.3 Overview of the Protocol

The basis of our technique is the protocol of Cramer et al. [20] (designed for the *synchronous* setting), which is based on *threshold additively homomorphic encryption* (TAHE)[3] and is designed in a hybrid model where the encryption keys are pre-distributed before the protocol begins. Initially, each party encrypts its input and broadcasts the ciphertext. Next, the circuit is homomorphically evaluated, where addition gates are computed locally and multiplication gates

---

[2] Following the impossibility result of [22], asynchronous agreement protocols cannot be computed in constant time.

[3] Which essentially means that ciphertexts can be added but not multiplied.

are computed interactively. Finally, a threshold decryption protocol is executed, and the parties learn the output.

Hirt et al. [29,30] adopted the protocol of [20] into the asynchronous setting by introducing the *king-slaves paradigm*. Initially, each party sends its encrypted input to all the parties, and the core set is decided upon using an *agreement on a common subset* (ACS) protocol, which incorporates n instances of ABA. Next, n copies of the circuit are interactively evaluated. In each evaluation one of the parties acts as king while all other parties act as slaves. The role of the slaves is to help the king with the computation of multiplication gates. At the end of each such evaluation, the slaves send their decryption shares to the king which recovers the output. The evaluations of the circuit are executed asynchronously, i.e., one king may finish its computation while another king hasn't started yet, therefore each party must hold a state for each evaluation of the circuit.

The time complexity of the protocols of Hirt et al. [29,30] depends on the depth of the circuit to compute. In this work, we use a TFHE instead of TAHE in order to reduce the running time. This adjustment not only yields better time complexity and better communication complexity, but also enables a design *without* the expensive king-slave paradigm, since each party can locally and non-interactively evaluate the entire circuit. As a consequence, the description of the new protocol is greatly simplified, and also results with a better memory complexity compared to [29,30], since the parties do not need to store a local state for each of the n evaluations of the circuit.

Our protocol consists of three stages. The *input stage*, in which the core set of input providers is determined, follows in the lines of Hirt et al. [29,30]. In the *computation and threshold decryption stage*, each party homomorphically evaluates the circuit non-interactively and obtains an encrypted output $\tilde{c}$. Next, the party uses its share of the decryption key to compute a decryption share and send it to all other parties. Once a party receives $t + 1$ valid decryption shares it can recover the output. During these stages, the validity of each message sent by some party must be proven. This is done by running a sub-protocol which produces a *certificate* for the message (which is essentially a signature produced by $n - t$ parties). Therefore, a party must remain active and assist in constructions of certificates even *after* it obtained its output. The *termination stage* ensures a safe termination of all the parties and follows Bracha [13]. Once a party obtained its output it sends it to all other parties. When a party receives $t + 1$ consisting values it can safely set its output to this value (even if it did not complete the computation and threshold decryption stage) and once receiving outputs from $n - t$ parties, terminate.

1.4   Additional Related Work

Ben-Or et al. [9] were the first to define asynchronous secure multiparty computation. They constructed a BGW-alike [8] asynchronous protocol that is secure in the presence of malicious adversaries when $t < n/4$; the authors showed that this threshold is tight when considering *perfect* correctness. Ben-Or et al. [10] constructed a protocol with *statistical* correctness that is secure in the presence of malicious adversaries, for $t < n/3$. This threshold is also tight following the lower bound of Toueg [41], stating that asynchronous Byzantine agreement is impossible if $t \geq n/3$, even in the PKI model.

Following the feasibility results of [9,10] great improvements have been made regarding the communication complexity. Two main approaches have been used, the first is in the information-theoretic model and does not rely on cryptographic assumptions [5,19,35–37,40] while the second is in the computational model and is based on threshold additively homomorphic encryption, these protocols appear in [18,29,30] and rely on a preprocessing phase for key distribution.

In order to achieve security for an honest majority, the model must be weakened in some sense. Beerliová-Trubíniová et al. [6] allowed a limited usage of synchronous Byzantine agreement and adjusted the protocol from [30] to the case where $t < n/2$. Backes et al. [3] augmented the model with a non-equivocation oracle, and constructed a protocol that is secure assuming an honest majority.

In an independent work, Choudhury and Patra [18] suggested using TFHE in order to reduce the time complexity, but did not proceed in this route since they considered concrete efficiency. We note that in this work we focus on feasibility results rather than concrete efficiency of the protocols.

A comparison of the asynchronous MPC protocols appears in Table 1.

Paper Organization

The cryptographic primitives are defined in Sect. 2 and followed by the description of the UC security model in Sect. 3. Certificates are defined in Sect. 4 and then in Sect. 5 we present our asynchronous MPC protocol. The security proof is given in Sect. 6.

2   Preliminaries

In this section we present the definitions of the cryptographic schemes that are used in our protocol.

2.1   Threshold Fully Homomorphic Encryption

Definition 1. *A homomorphic encryption (HE) scheme consists of 4 PPT algorithms:*

- **Key generation:** $(dk, ek) \leftarrow \text{Gen}(1^\kappa)$; *outputs a pair of keys: the secret decryption key dk and the public encryption (and evaluation) key ek.*
- **Encryption:** $c \leftarrow \text{Enc}_{ek}(m)$; *using ek, encrypt a plaintext m into a ciphertext c.*
- **Decryption:** $m = \text{Dec}_{dk}(c)$; *using dk, decrypt the ciphertext c to into a plaintext m.*
- **Homomorphic evaluation:** $c = \text{Eval}_{ek}(C, c_1, \ldots, c_\ell)$; *using ek, evaluate a circuit C over a tuple of ciphertexts $(c_1, \ldots, c_\ell)$ to produce a ciphertext c.*

Table 1. Comparison of asynchronous MPC protocols.

Paper	Resilience	Correctness	Time[a]	Communication[b]	Assumptions[c]	Hybrid Model[d]
[9]	$t < n/4$	Perfect	$O(c_M)$	$O(c_M \cdot n^6)$		
[10]	$t < n/3$	Statistical	$O(c_M)$	$\Omega(c_M \cdot n^{11})$		
[40]	$t < n/4$	Perfect	$O(c_M)$	$\Omega(c_M \cdot n^5)$		
[37]	$t < n/4$	Statistical	$O(c_M)$	$O(c_M \cdot n^4 + n^5)$		
[29]	$t < n/3$	Computational	$O(c_M)$	$O(c_M \cdot n^3 \kappa)$	TAHE, TSIG	KeyDist
[5]	$t < n/4$	Perfect	$O(c_M)$	$O(c_M \cdot n^3)$		
[30]	$t < n/3$	Computational	$O(c_M)$	$O(c_M \cdot n^2 \kappa + n^3 \kappa)$	TAHE, TSIG	KeyDist
[35]	$t < n/3$	Statistical	$O(c_M)$	$O(c_M \cdot n^5)$		
[36]	$t < n/4$	Statistical	$O(c_M)$	$O(c_M \cdot n^2 + n^4)$		
[36]	$t < n/4$	Perfect	$O(c_M)$	$O(c_M \cdot n^2 + n^3)$		
[6]	$t < n/2$	Computational	$O(c_M)$	$O(c_M \cdot n^4 \kappa)$	TAHE, TSIG	KeyDist, Bcast
[19]	$t < n/4$	Statistical	$O(c_M)$	$O(c_M \cdot n + n^3)$		
[3]	$t < n/2$	Computational	$O(c_M)$	$O(c_M \cdot n^3 \kappa)$	AHE, TSIG	KeyDist, NEQ
[3]	$t < n/2$	Computational	$O(c_M)$	$O(c_M \cdot n^2 \kappa + n^3 \kappa)$	TAHE, TSIG	KeyDist, NEQ
[18]	$t < n/3$	Computational	$O(c_M)$	$O(c_M \cdot n \kappa + n^3 \kappa)$	TSHE	KeyDist
This work	$t < n/3$	Computational	$O(1)$	$O(n^3 \kappa)$	TFHE, TSIG	KeyDist

[a]Time complexity is measured in the ABA-hybrid model.
[b]c_M denotes the number of multiplication gates. Input, output and addition gates are ignored.
[c]TSIG is a threshold digital signature scheme, AHE is an additively homomorphic encryption scheme, TAHE is a threshold additively homomorphic encryption scheme, TSHE is a threshold somewhat homomorphic encryption scheme, TFHE is a threshold fully homomorphic encryption scheme.
[d]KeyDist stands for key distribution for a threshold cryptosystem, NEQ stands for transferable non-equivocation mechanism, Bcast stands for *synchronous* broadcast.

We say that a HE scheme is correct for circuits in a circuit class $\mathcal{C}$ if for every $C \in \mathcal{C}$ and every series of inputs $m_1, \ldots, m_\ell \in \{0,1\}^*$ it holds that

$$\Pr\left[\text{Dec}_{dk}\left(\text{Eval}_{ek}\left(C, \text{Enc}_{ek}(m_1), \ldots, \text{Enc}_{ek}(m_\ell)\right)\right) \neq C\left(m_1, \ldots, m_\ell\right)\right] \leq \text{negl}(\kappa).$$

Semantic security of HE schemes is defined in the standard way, see [25].

Definition 2. *A family of HE schemes* $\{\Pi^{(d)} = (\text{Gen}^{(d)}, \text{Enc}^{(d)}, \text{Dec}, \text{Eval}^{(d)}) \mid d \in \mathbb{N}^+\}$ *is* leveled fully homomorphic *if for every* $d \in \mathbb{N}^+$, *the following holds:*

- **Correctness:** $\Pi^{(d)}$ *correctly evaluates the set of all boolean circuits of depth at most* d.
- **Compactness:** *There exists a polynomial s such that the common decryption algorithm can be expressed as a circuit of size at most $s(\kappa)$ and is independent of d.*

In our protocol for computing a function f, the depth d of the circuit C representing f is known in advance. We remove the notation (d) from the schemes throughout the paper for clarity. We also require the FHE scheme to have a threshold decryption, informally this means that Gen generates the public key ek as well as a t_e-secret sharing of the secret key $(dk_1, \ldots, dk_n)$, such that decrypting c using dk_i produces a share m_i of the plaintext m. We will use $t_e = t + 1$.

Definition 3. *A* threshold homomorphic encryption scheme *is a homomorphic encryption scheme augmented with the following properties:*

- *The key generation algorithm is parameterized by (t_e, n) and outputs $(dk, ek) \leftarrow \mathrm{Gen}_{(t_e, n)}(1^\kappa)$, where dk is represented using a (t_e, n)-threshold secret sharing of the secret key $(dk_1, \ldots, dk_n)$.*
- *Given a ciphertext c and a share of the secret key dk_i, the share-decryption algorithm outputs $d_i = \mathrm{DecShare}_{dk_i}(c)$ such that $(d_1, \ldots, d_n)$ forms a (t_e, n)-threshold secret sharing of the plaintext $m = \mathrm{Dec}_{dk}(c)$. We denote the reconstruction algorithm that receives t_e decryption shares $\{d_i\}$ by $m = \mathrm{DecRecon}(\{d_i\})$.*

2.2 Threshold Signatures

A threshold signature scheme is a signature scheme in which the signing key is shared amongst n parties using a t_s-threshold secret-sharing scheme. Using t_s shares of the signing key it is possible to sign on any message, however using less than t_s shares it is infeasible to forge a signature. We will use $t_s = n - t$.

Definition 4 (Threshold Signature Scheme). *A* threshold signature scheme *is a signature scheme* (SigGen, Sign, Vrfy) *augmented with the following properties*

- *The signature key generation algorithm is parameterized by (t_s, n) and outputs $(sk, vk) \leftarrow \mathrm{SigGen}_{(t_s, n)}(1^\kappa)$, where sk is represented using a (t_s, n)-threshold secret sharing of the secret signing key $(sk_1, \ldots, sk_n)$.*
- *Given a plaintext m and a share of the secret key sk_i, the share-signing algorithm outputs $\sigma_i \leftarrow \mathrm{SignShare}_{sk_i}(m)$ such that $(\sigma_1, \ldots, \sigma_n)$ forms a (t_s, n)-threshold secret sharing of the signature $\sigma \leftarrow \mathrm{Sign}_{sk}(m)$.*

For a security definition of threshold signatures see, for example, [1].

3 The Security Model

3.1 The UC Framework

In this section we present a high-level description of the security model. We follow the UC framework of Canetti [14], which is based on the *real/ideal paradigm*, i.e., comparing what an adversary can do in the real execution of the protocol to what it can do in an ideal model where an uncorrupted trusted party (an ideal functionality) assists the parties. Informally, a protocol is secure if whatever an adversary can do in the real protocol (where no trusted party exists) can be done in the ideal computation.

The Real World. An execution of a protocol π in the real model consists of n *interactive Turing machines* (ITMs) $P_1, \ldots, P_n$ representing the parties, along with two additional ITMs, an *adversary* $\mathcal{A}$, describing the behavior of the corrupted parties and an *environment* $\mathcal{Z}$, representing the external environment in which the protocol operates. The environment gives inputs to the honest parties, receives their outputs, and can communicate with the adversary at any point during the execution. The adversary controls the operations of the corrupted parties and the delivery of messages between the parties.

In more details, each ITM is initialized with the security parameter κ and random coins, where the environment may receive an additional auxiliary input. We consider *static* corruptions, meaning that the set of corrupted parties is fixed before the protocol begins and is known to $\mathcal{A}$ and $\mathcal{Z}$. The protocol proceeds by a sequence of *activations*, where the environment is activated first and at each point a single ITM is active. The environment can either activate one of the parties with input or activate the adversary by sending it a message. Once a party is activated it can perform a local computation, write on its output tape or send messages to other parties. After the party completes its operations the control is returned to the environment. Once the adversary is activated it can send messages on behalf of the corrupted parties or send a message to the environment. In addition, $\mathcal{A}$ controls the communication between the parties, and so it can read the content of the messages sent between the parties and is responsible for delivering each message to its recipient. Once $\mathcal{A}$ delivers a message to some party, this party is activated. We assume that the adversary cannot omit, change or inject messages, however it can decide *which* message will be delivered and *when*.[4] The protocol completes once $\mathcal{Z}$ stops activating other parties and outputs a single bit.

If the adversary is fail-stop, it always instructs the corrupted parties to follow the protocol, with the exception that they can halt prematurely and stop sending messages. If the adversary is malicious, it may instruct the corrupted parties to deviate from the protocol arbitrarily.

Let $\text{REAL}_{\pi,\mathcal{A},\mathcal{Z}}(\kappa, z, \boldsymbol{r})$ denote $\mathcal{Z}$'s output on input z and security parameter κ, after interacting with adversary $\mathcal{A}$ and parties $P_1, \ldots, P_n$ running protocol π with random tapes $\boldsymbol{r} = (r_1, \ldots, r_n, r_{\mathcal{A}}, r_{\mathcal{Z}})$ as described above. Let $\text{REAL}_{\pi,\mathcal{A},\mathcal{Z}}(\kappa, z)$ denote the random variable $\text{REAL}_{\pi,\mathcal{A},\mathcal{Z}}(\kappa, z, \boldsymbol{r})$, when the vector $\boldsymbol{r}$ is uniformly chosen.

The Ideal Model. A computation in the ideal model consists of n *dummy* parties $P_1, \ldots, P_n$, an *ideal adversary* (simulator) $\mathcal{S}$, an *environment* $\mathcal{Z}$, and an *ideal functionality* $\mathcal{F}$. The environment gives inputs to the honest (dummy) parties, receives their outputs, and can communicate with the ideal adversary at any point during the execution. The dummy parties act as channels between the environment and the ideal functionality, meaning that they send the inputs received from $\mathcal{Z}$ to $\mathcal{F}$, and transfer the output they receive from $\mathcal{F}$ to $\mathcal{Z}$. We

---

[4] This behaviour is formally modeled using the *eventual-delivery secure message transmission* ideal functionality in [32].

consider static corruptions, and so the set of corrupted parties is fixed before the computations, and is known to $\mathcal{Z}$, $\mathcal{S}$ and $\mathcal{F}$. As before, the computation completes once $\mathcal{Z}$ stops activating other parties and outputs a single bit.

The ideal functionality defines the desired behaviour of the computation. $\mathcal{F}$ receives the inputs from the dummy parties, executes the desired computation and sends the output to the parties. The ideal adversary does not see and cannot delay the communication between the parties and the ideal functionality, however, $\mathcal{S}$ can communicate with $\mathcal{F}$. As we consider asynchronous protocols in the real model, ideal functionalities must consider some inherent limitations, for instance, the ability of the adversary to decide when each honest party learns the output. Since the UC framework has no notion of time, we follow [32,34] and model time by number of activations. Once $\mathcal{F}$ prepares an output for some party it does not ask permission from the adversary to deliver it to the party, instead the party must request the functionality for the output, and this can only be done when the party is active. Furthermore, the adversary can instruct $\mathcal{F}$ to delay the output for each party by ignoring the requests for a polynomial number of activations. If the environment activates the party sufficiently many times, the party will eventually receive the output from the ideal functionality. It follows that the ideal computation will terminate, i.e., all honest parties will obtain their output, in case the environment will allocate enough resources to the parties. We use the term $\mathcal{F}$ *sends a request-based delayed output to P_i* to describe the above interaction between the $\mathcal{F}$, $\mathcal{S}$ and P_i.

Let $\text{IDEAL}_{\mathcal{F},\mathcal{S},\mathcal{Z}}(\kappa, z, \boldsymbol{r})$ denote $\mathcal{Z}$'s output on input z and security parameter κ, after interacting with ideal adversary $\mathcal{S}$ and dummy parties $P_1, \ldots, P_n$ which interact with ideal functionality $\mathcal{F}$ with random tapes $\boldsymbol{r} = (r_\mathcal{S}, r_\mathcal{Z})$ as described above. Let $\text{IDEAL}_{\mathcal{F},\mathcal{S},\mathcal{Z}}(\kappa, z)$ denote the random variable $\text{IDEAL}_{\mathcal{F},\mathcal{S},\mathcal{Z}}(\kappa, z, \boldsymbol{r})$, when the vector $\boldsymbol{r}$ is uniformly chosen.

Definition 5. *We say that a protocol π t-securely UC realizes an ideal functionality $\mathcal{F}$ in the presence of static malicious (resp., fail-stop) adversaries, if for any PPT malicious (resp., fail-stop) real model adversary $\mathcal{A}$, controlling a subset of up to t parties, and any PPT environment $\mathcal{Z}$, there exists a PPT ideal model adversary $\mathcal{S}$ such that following two distribution ensembles are computationally indistinguishable*

$$\left\{\text{REAL}_{\pi,\mathcal{A},\mathcal{Z}}(\kappa, z)\right\}_{\kappa \in \mathbb{N}, z \in \{0,1\}^*} \overset{c}{\equiv} \left\{\text{IDEAL}_{\mathcal{F},\mathcal{S},\mathcal{Z}}(\kappa, z)\right\}_{\kappa \in \mathbb{N}, z \in \{0,1\}^*}.$$

The Hybrid Model. In a $\mathcal{G}$-hybrid model, the execution of the protocol proceeds as in the real model, however, the parties have access to an ideal functionality $\mathcal{G}$ for some specific operations. The communication of the parties with the ideal functionality $\mathcal{G}$ is performed as in the ideal model. An important property of the UC framework is that an ideal functionality in a hybrid model can be replaced with a protocol that securely UC realizes $\mathcal{G}$. We informally state the composition theorem from Canetti [14].

Theorem 2 [14]. *Let π be a protocol that t-securely UC realizes $\mathcal{F}$ in the $\mathcal{G}$-hybrid model and let ρ be a protocol that t-securely UC realizes $\mathcal{G}$. Then the* *protocol π^ρ that is obtained from π by replacing every ideal call to $\mathcal{G}$ with the protocol ρ, t-securely UC realizes $\mathcal{F}$ in the model without ideal functionality $\mathcal{G}$.*

3.2 Some Ideal Functionalities

We now present the asynchronous SFE and asynchronous BA functionalities.

Asynchronous Secure Function Evaluation. *Secure function evaluation (SFE)* is a multiparty primitive where a set of n parties wish to compute a (possibly randomized) function $f\colon (\{0,1\}^*)^n \times \{0,1\}^* \to (\{0,1\}^*)^n$, where $f = (f_1, \ldots, f_n)$. That is, for a vector of inputs $\boldsymbol{x} = (x_1, \ldots, x_n) \in (\{0,1\}^*)^n$ and random coins $r \in_R \{0,1\}^*$, the output vector is $(f_1(\boldsymbol{x}; r), \ldots, f_n(\boldsymbol{x}; r))$. The output for the i'th party (with input x_i) is defined to be $f_i(\boldsymbol{x}; r)$. The function f has public output, if all parties output the same value, i.e., $f_1 = \ldots = f_n$, otherwise f has private output.

In an asynchronous protocol for computing secure function evaluation, the adversary can always delay messages from t parties, and so t input values might not take part in the computation. Therefore, in the definition of the ideal functionality for asynchronous SFE, the ideal-model adversary is given the power to determine a *core set* of $n - t$ input providers (t of which might be corrupted) that will contribute input values for the computation. The asynchronous secure function evaluation functionality, $\mathcal{F}^f_{\mathsf{ASFE}}$, is presented in Fig. 1.

Functionality $\mathcal{F}^f_{\mathsf{ASFE}}$

$\mathcal{F}^f_{\mathsf{ASFE}}$ proceeds as follows, running with parties $P_1, \ldots, P_n$ and an adversary $\mathcal{S}$, and parameterized by an n-party function $f\colon (\{0,1\}^*)^n \times \{0,1\}^* \to (\{0,1\}^*)^n$. For each party P_i initialize an input value $x_i = \bot$ an output value $y_i = \bot$.

- Upon receiving a message (input, sid, v) from some party P_i, if CoreSet has not been recorded yet or if $P_i \in$ CoreSet, set $x_i = v$. Next, send a message (input, sid, P_i) to $\mathcal{S}$.
- Upon receiving a message (coreset, sid, CoreSet) from $\mathcal{S}$, verify that CoreSet is a subset of $\{P_1, \ldots, P_n\}$ of size $n - t$; else ignore the message. If CoreSet has not been recorded yet, record CoreSet and for every P_i not in CoreSet, set x_i to some default input value $x_i = \tilde{x}_i$.
- Upon receiving a message (output, sid) from some party P_i, do:
  1. If CoreSet has not been recorded yet or if x_j has not been recorded for some $P_j \in$ CoreSet, ignore the message.
  2. Otherwise, if $y_1, \ldots, y_n$ have not been set yet, then choose $r \in_R \{0,1\}^*$ and compute $(y_1, \ldots, y_n) = f(x_1, \ldots, x_n; r)$.
  3. Generate a request-based delayed output (output, sid, (CoreSet, y_i)) to P_i and send (output, sid, P_i) to $\mathcal{S}$.

Fig. 1. The asynchronous secure function evaluation functionality

Asynchronous Byzantine Agreement. In a *synchronous* Byzantine agreement, each party has an input bit and outputs a bit. Three properties are required: *agreement*, meaning that all honest parties agree on the same bit, *validity*, meaning that if all honest parties have the same input bit then this will be the common output and *termination*, meaning that the protocol eventually terminates. When considering *asynchronous* Byzantine agreement (ABA), the definition must be weakened, since t input values may be delayed and not effect the result. We adopt the ABA functionality as defined in [34]. The asynchronous Byzantine agreement functionality, $\mathcal{F}_{\mathsf{ABA}}$, is presented in Fig. 2.

Functionality $\mathcal{F}_{\mathsf{ABA}}$

$\mathcal{F}_{\mathsf{ABA}}$ proceeds as follows, running with parties $P_1, \ldots, P_n$ and an adversary $\mathcal{S}$:

- Upon receiving a message (vote, sid, b), where $b \in \{0, 1\}$ from party P_i, send a message (vote, sid, P_i, b) to the adversary. The adversary is also allowed to vote.
- The result is computed using one of the following rules:
  - If $n - t$ parties voted, and $t + 1$ voted b and $\mathcal{S}$ voted b, then set the result to be b.
  - If $n - t$ parties voted b, then set the result to be b.
  - If $n - t$ parties voted, but do not agree, then the result is set by the vote of $\mathcal{S}$.

  When the result of voting sid has been decided to be v, the functionality sends (decide, sid, v) as a request-based delayed output to all parties.

Fig. 2. The asynchronous Byzantine agreement functionality

4   Zero-Knowledge Proofs and Certificates

In order to ensure security against malicious behaviour, the parties must prove their actions using zero-knowledge proofs during the protocol. The zero-knowledge functionality $\mathcal{F}_{\mathsf{ZK}}$ and its one-to-many extension $\mathcal{F}_{\mathsf{ZK}}^{1:M}$ are defined in Sect. 4.1 and the notion of certificates in Sect. 4.2.

4.1   Zero-Knowledge Proofs

In the *zero-knowledge functionality*, parameterized by a relation R, the prover sends the functionality a statement x to be proven along with a witness w. In response, the functionality forwards the statement x to the verifier if and only if $R(x, w) = 1$ (i.e., if and only if x a correct statement and w is a witness for x). Thus, in actuality, this is a proof of knowledge in that the verifier is assured that the prover actually knows w (and has explicitly sent w to the

---

Functionality $\mathcal{F}_{ZK}$

$\mathcal{F}_{ZK}$ proceeds as follows, running with prover P, a verifier V and an adversary $\mathcal{S}$, and parameterized with a relation R:

- Upon receiving (ZK-prover, sid, x, w) from P, do: if $R(x,w) = 1$, then send (ZK-proof, sid, x) to $\mathcal{S}$, send a request-based delayed output (ZK-proof, sid, x) to V and halt. Otherwise, halt.

Fig. 3. The zero-knowledge functionality

functionality), rather than just being assured that such a w exists. The zero-knowledge functionality, $\mathcal{F}_{ZK}$, is presented in Fig. 3.[5]

The zero-knowledge functionality, as defined in Fig. 3, is parameterized by a single relation R (and thus a different copy of $\mathcal{F}_{ZK}$ is needed for every different relation required). In this work we require zero-knowledge proofs for several relations, therefore, we use standard techniques by considering the relation R index several predetermined relations. This can be implemented by separating the statement x into two parts: x_1 that indexes the relation to be used and x_2 that is the actual statement. Then, define $R((x_1, x_2), w)$ as $R_{x_1}(x_2, w)$.

We now define the *one-to-many extension* of the zero-knowledge functionality, where one party proves a statement to some subset of parties. The definition of the one-to-many zero-knowledge functionality, denoted $\mathcal{F}_{ZK}^{1:M}$, is presented in Fig. 4.

Functionality $\mathcal{F}_{ZK}^{1:M}$

$\mathcal{F}_{ZK}^{1:M}$ proceeds as follows, running with parties $P_1, \ldots, P_n$ and an adversary $\mathcal{S}$, and parameterized with a relation R:

- Upon receiving (ZK-prover, sid, $\mathcal{P}$, x, w) from party P_i, where $\mathcal{P} \subseteq \{P_1, \ldots, P_n\}$ do: if $R(x, w) = 1$, then send (ZK-proof, sid, P_i, $\mathcal{P}$, x) to $\mathcal{S}$, a request-based delayed output (ZK-proof, sid, P_i, $\mathcal{P}$, x) to all parties in $\mathcal{P}$ and halt. Otherwise, halt.

Fig. 4. The one-to-many zero-knowledge functionality

4.2 Certificates

As we consider static corruptions, there exists efficient constant-round zero-knowledge protocols in the $\mathcal{F}_{CRS}$-hybrid model, e.g., omega protocols [23], and

---

[5] For simplicity, we concentrate on the single-session version of $\mathcal{F}_{ZK}$, which requires a separate common reference string for each protocol that realizes $\mathcal{F}_{ZK}$. The protocols realizing $\mathcal{F}_{ZK}$ will later be composed, using the universal composition with joint state of Canetti and Rabin [16], to obtain protocols that use only a single copy of the common reference string when realizing all the copies of $\mathcal{F}_{ZK}$.

even non-interactive zero-knowledge proofs [21]. These protocols would suffice for realizing $\mathcal{F}_{\mathsf{ZK}}$ as it is a two-party functionality. However, when considering the multiparty functionality $\mathcal{F}_{\mathsf{ZK}}^{1:M}$, some problems may arise. The reason is that the statement that needs to be proven is not public, and a malicious prover may prove different statements to different parties.

This problem is resolved using *certificates*, introduced by Hirt et al. [30]. Certificates are generated by an interactive protocols among the parties such that at the end of the execution, one party can non-interactively prove correctness of some statement to each other party, without revealing additional information. The protocol for issuing a certificate is based on threshold signatures and involves two stages. First, a signature proving the statement is computed interactively with all the parties — it is essential that all the parties are active during this stage, otherwise the prover might not receive enough shares to reconstruct the signature. Next, the prover can send the signature as a non-interactive proof of the statement and every other party can validate it.

During out main protocol, in Sect. 5, we consider three relations:

- **Proof of Plaintext Knowledge.** The relations is parameterized by a TFHE scheme. The statement consists of a public encryption key ek and a ciphertext c and the witness consists of the plaintext x and random coins r, explaining c as an encryption of x under ek. That is

$$R_{\mathsf{PoPK}} = \{((ek, c), (x, r)) \mid c = \mathrm{Enc}_{ek}(x; r)\}.$$

- **Proof of Correct Decryption.** The relations is parameterized by a TFHE scheme. The statement consists of a public encryption key ek, a ciphertext c and a decryption share d and the witness consists of the decryption key dk. That is

$$R_{\mathsf{PoCD}} = \{((ek, c, d), dk) \mid d = \mathrm{DecShare}_{dk}(c)\}.$$

- **Proof of Correct Signature.** The relations is parameterized by a TSIG scheme. The statement consists of a public verification key vk, a message msg and a signature share σ and the witness consists of the signing key sk. That is

$$R_{\mathsf{PoCS}} = \{((vk, \mathsf{msg}, \sigma), sk) \mid \sigma = \mathrm{SignShare}_{sk}(\mathsf{msg})\}$$

Lemma 1. *Let $n > 2t + 1$ and let R_{x_1} be a binary relation. Assuming the existence of threshold signature schemes, $\mathcal{F}_{\mathsf{ZK}}^{1:M}$ can be UC realized in the $\mathcal{F}_{\mathsf{ZK}}$-hybrid model in the presence of static malicious adversaries.*

Proof. Consider a party P_i, holding a witness w, that wishes to prove a statement x to all other parties. The high-level idea is for P_i to prove x to each other P_j using a two-party zero-knowledge proof. If all parties are active and P_i is honest, it is guaranteed that eventually at least $n - t$ proofs will successfully terminate. Once a verifier P_j accepts the proof, it produces a share σ_j of a signature approving x, sends the share back to P_i and proves the validity of σ_j to P_i using another two-party zero-knowledge proof. After P_i obtains $n - t$ valid signature shares, it can reconstruct the signature σ which serves as its certificate.

Assuming that $n > 2t+1$, it holds that $(n-t)-t \geq 1$, and so it is guaranteed that at least one honest party accepted the proof of the statement x; it follows that the corrupted parties cannot falsely certify invalid statements. Furthermore, assuming the two-parties zero-knowledge proofs are constant round, certifying a statement takes constant time.

Protocol 3 shows how to compute $\mathcal{F}_{\mathsf{ZK}}^{1:\mathsf{M}}$ in the $\mathcal{F}_{\mathsf{ZK}}$-hybrid model. During the protocol, two instances of $\mathcal{F}_{\mathsf{ZK}}$ are used; the first is for proving statements for the relation R_{x_1} and the second for the relation R_{PoCS}. We use the notation sid_j^k for the string $\mathsf{sid} \circ k \circ j$.

Protocol 3 ($\mathcal{F}_{\mathsf{ZK}}^{1:\mathsf{M}}$ protocol, in the $\mathcal{F}_{\mathsf{ZK}}$-hybrid model)

Offline setup:
    For every $j \in [n]$, party P_j is initialized with keys for a threshold signature scheme (vk, sk_j), where $(sk, vk) \leftarrow \mathsf{SigGen}_{(n-t,n)}(1^\kappa)$, and $sk = (sk_1, \ldots, sk_n)$.

Code for sender P_i:
- Upon receiving $(\mathsf{ZK\text{-}prover}, \mathsf{sid}, \mathcal{P}, (x_1, x_2), w)$ from the environment, party P_i sends $(\mathsf{ZK\text{-}prover}, \mathsf{sid}_j^1, (x_1, x_2), w)$ to $\mathcal{F}_{\mathsf{ZK}}$ where P_i acts as the prover and P_j acts as the verifier (for every $j \in [n] \setminus \{i\}$). In addition, send $(\mathsf{sid}, \mathcal{P})$ to every party.
- Request output from $\mathcal{F}_{\mathsf{ZK}}$ until receiving $(\mathsf{ZK\text{-}proof}, \mathsf{sid}_j^2, (\mathsf{PoCS}, vk, \mathsf{msg}, \sigma))$, with $\mathsf{msg} = \langle (x_1, x_2)$ is a valid statement, for $(\mathsf{sid}, \mathcal{P}) \rangle$ (for every $j \in [n] \setminus \{i\}$), until receiving $n - t$ signature shares $\{\sigma_j\}$.
- Compute $\mathsf{cert} = \mathsf{SignRecon}(\{\sigma_j\})$, send $(\mathsf{sid}, (x_1, x_2), \mathsf{cert})$ to every party in $\mathcal{P}$ and halt.

Code for receiver P_j (for $j \neq i$):
- Requests output from $\mathcal{F}_{\mathsf{ZK}}$ until receiving $(\mathsf{ZK\text{-}proof}, \mathsf{sid}_j^1, (x_1, x_2))$. Next, upon receiving the message $(\mathsf{sid}, \mathcal{P})$ from P_i, set $\mathsf{msg} = \langle (x_1, x_2)$ is a valid statement, for $(\mathsf{sid}, \mathcal{P}) \rangle$, compute $\sigma_j = \mathsf{SignShare}_{sk_j}(\mathsf{msg})$ and send $(\mathsf{ZK\text{-}prover}, \mathsf{sid}_j^2, (\mathsf{PoCS}, vk, \mathsf{msg}, \sigma_j), sk_j)$ to $\mathcal{F}_{\mathsf{ZK}}$ where P_j acts as the prover and P_i acts as the verifier.
- Upon receiving the first message $(\mathsf{sid}, (x_1, x_2), \mathsf{cert})$ from P_i set $\mathsf{msg} = \langle (x_1, x_2)$ is a valid statement, for $(\mathsf{sid}, \mathcal{P}) \rangle$ and verify that $\mathsf{Vrfy}_{vk}(\mathsf{msg}, \mathsf{cert}) = 1$. If so output $(\mathsf{ZK\text{-}proof}, \mathsf{sid}, P_i, \mathcal{P}, (x_1, x_2))$ and halt.

The one-to-many zero-knowledge protocol

Let $\mathcal{A}$ be an adversary attacking Protocol 3 and let $\mathcal{Z}$ be an environment. We construct a simulator $\mathcal{S}$ as follows. $\mathcal{S}$ runs the adversary $\mathcal{A}$ and simulates the environment, the honest parties and the ideal functionality $\mathcal{F}_{\mathsf{ZK}}$ towards $\mathcal{A}$. In order to simulate $\mathcal{Z}$, $\mathcal{S}$ forwards every message it receives from $\mathcal{Z}$ to $\mathcal{A}$ and vice-versa. $\mathcal{S}$ simulates the honest parties towards $\mathcal{A}$. In case P_i is corrupted, $\mathcal{S}$ receives $((x_1, x_2), w)$ by simulating $\mathcal{F}_{\mathsf{ZK}}$ and in addition receives $\mathcal{P}$ from $\mathcal{A}$. Next, $\mathcal{S}$ sends $(\mathsf{ZK\text{-}prover}, \mathsf{sid}, \mathcal{P}, (x_1, x_2), w)$ to $\mathcal{F}_{\mathsf{ZK}}^{1:\mathsf{M}}$ and continues simulating the honest parties and $\mathcal{F}_{\mathsf{ZK}}$ to $\mathcal{A}$. In case P_i is not corrupted, it first receives $(\mathsf{ZK\text{-}proof}, \mathsf{sid}, P_i, \mathcal{P}, (x_1, x_2))$ from $\mathcal{F}_{\mathsf{ZK}}^{1:M}$. Next, whenever $\mathcal{A}$ requests output from $\mathcal{F}_{\mathsf{ZK}}$ with sid_j^1 for $j \in \mathcal{I}$, $\mathcal{S}$ replies with $(\mathsf{ZK\text{-}proof}, \mathsf{sid}, (x_1, x_2))$. The rest of the simulation follows the protocol. It is straight-forward to see that the view of $\mathcal{A}$ is indistinguishable when interacting with $\mathcal{S}$ and when attacking the execution of Protocol 3, and the proof follows.

5 Asynchronous MPC Protocol

Following the spirit of [29, 30], the protocol consists of an offline key-distribution stage (preprocessing) followed three online stages: the input stage, the computation and threshold-decryption stage and the termination stage. We present the protocol for *public-output* functionalities, and a variant for *private-output* functionalities can be obtained using the technique of [29].

5.1 Key-Distribution Stage

The *key-distribution stage* can be computed once for multiple instances of the protocol and essentially distributes the keys for threshold schemes amongst the parties. We will describe the protocol in a hybrid model where the key-distribution is done by an ideal functionality $\mathcal{F}_{\mathsf{KeyDist}}$. This ideal functionality can be realized using any asynchronous MPC protocol that does not require preprocessing, e.g., [35]. We emphasize that the time complexity of the protocol realizing the key-distribution stage is *independent* of the function to compute.

$\mathcal{F}_{\mathsf{KeyDist}}$ generates the public and secret keys for the TFHE and the TSIG schemes and sends to each party its corresponding keys. The key-distribution functionality is described in Fig. 5.

5.2 Input Stage

In the input stage, as described in Protocol 4, each party encrypts its input and sends it to all the other parties along with certificates proving that the party knows the plaintext (and so independence of inputs is retained) and that $n - t$ parties have obtained it. Next, the parties jointly agree on a common subset of input providers, CoreSet, which consists of $n - t$ parties whose encrypted input has been obtained by all the parties. This stage proceeds in a similar manner to [29] with the difference that the plaintexts are encrypted using TFHE rather than TAHE.

In more details, each party P_i starts by encrypting its input $c_i \leftarrow \mathrm{Enc}_{ek}(x_i)$, and proving to each other party knowledge of the plaintext. Once a party P_j accepts the proof, it sends P_i a signature share for the statement $\mathsf{msg} = \langle n - t$ parties hold the input c_i of $P_i \rangle$. After P_i obtains $n - t$ signature shares, it can reconstruct and distribute the certificate $\mathsf{cert}_i^{\mathsf{input}}$, which is essentially a signature on msg.

Functionality $\mathcal{F}_{\mathsf{KeyDist}}$

$\mathcal{F}_{\mathsf{KeyDist}}$ proceeds as follows, interacting with parties $P_1, \ldots, P_n$ and an adversary $\mathcal{S}$, and parameterized by TFHE and TSIG schemes.

- Upon receiving a message (keydist, sid) from party P_i, do:
  1. If there is no value (sid, dk, ek, sk, vk) recorded, compute $(dk, ek) \leftarrow \mathrm{Gen}_{(t,n)}(1^\kappa)$, where $dk = (dk_1, \ldots, dk_n)$, and $(sk, vk) \leftarrow \mathrm{SigGen}_{(n-t,n)}(1^\kappa)$, where $sk = (sk_1, \ldots, sk_n)$ and record (sid, dk, ek, sk, vk).
  2. Send (sid, P_i, ek, vk) to $\mathcal{S}$ and a request-based delayed output[a] (sid, dk_i, ek, sk_i, vk) to P_i.

---

[a] This is the standard formalization of the asynchronous setting in the UC framework, see Section 3; P_i must request the output from $\mathcal{F}_{\mathsf{KeyDist}}$, and $\mathcal{S}$ can continuously instruct $\mathcal{F}_{\mathsf{KeyDist}}$ to arbitrarily delay the answer.

Fig. 5. The key-distribution functionality

When a party collects $n - t$ certificates it knows that at least $n - t$ parties have their certified inputs distributed to at least $n - t$ parties. Since $n \geq 2t + 1$, by assumption, this means that at least $(n - t) - t \geq 1$ *honest* parties obtained certified inputs from at least $n - t$ parties. Hence, if the honest parties echo the certified inputs they receive and collect $n - t$ echoes, then all honest parties will end up holding the certified inputs of the $n - t$ parties which had their certified inputs distributed to at least one honest party. These $n - t$ parties will eventually be the input providers. To determine who they are, the asynchronous Byzantine agreements functionality $\mathcal{F}_{\mathsf{ABA}}$ is invoked (concurrently) n times. During the protocol description we use the notation sid_j^k for the string $\mathsf{sid} \circ k \circ j$.

5.3   Computation and Threshold Decryption Stage

In the computation and threshold-decryption stage, as described in Protocol 5, each party locally prepares the circuit $\mathsf{Circ}(\mathsf{CoreSet})$ (with hard-wired default input values for parties outside $\mathsf{CoreSet}$) and evaluates it over the encrypted input ciphertexts that were agreed upon in the input stage. Since the encryption scheme is fully homomorphic, this part is done without interaction between the parties. Once the encrypted output $\tilde{c}_i$ is obtained, P_i computes a decryption share d_i and interactively certifies it. Next, P_i sends the certified decryption share to all other parties and waits until it receives $t + 1$ certified decryption shares, from which it can reconstruct the output y_i.

Once P_i obtains the output, it should send it to all other parties in order to trigger the termination stage. This is done by first computing a signature share $\sigma_i^{\mathsf{output}}$ for the statement that y_i is the output value, interactively certify $\sigma_i^{\mathsf{output}}$ and send it to all parties. Once P_i receives $n - t$ signature shares it can

Protocol 4 (The input stage, in the $(\mathcal{F}_{\mathsf{KeyDist}}, \mathcal{F}_{\mathsf{ZK}}, \mathcal{F}_{\mathsf{ZK}}^{1:M}, \mathcal{F}_{\mathsf{ABA}})$-hybrid)

Setup: Upon receiving input $(\mathsf{input}, \mathsf{sid}, x_i)$ from the environment, proceed as follows:

1. Send $(\mathsf{keydist}, \mathsf{sid})$ to $\mathcal{F}_{\mathsf{KeyDist}}$.
2. Request the output from $\mathcal{F}_{\mathsf{KeyDist}}$ until receiving $(\mathsf{sid}, dk_i, ek, sk_i, vk)$.
3. Initialize the following sets to $\emptyset$: $\mathsf{VerProv}_i$ (verified input providers), $\mathsf{VerDistProv}_i$ (verified distributed input providers), $\mathsf{GlobalProv}_i$ (globally verified distributed input providers), $\mathsf{CertInputs}_i$ (certified inputs) and $\mathsf{GlobalInputs}_i$ (globally certified inputs).

Distribution of Encrypted Input:

1. Compute $c_i = \mathrm{Enc}_{ek}(x_i; r_i)$ (for uniformly distributed r_i).
2. Send $(\mathsf{ZK\text{-}prover}, \mathsf{sid}_i^1, \{P_1, \ldots, P_n\} \setminus \{P_i\}, (\mathsf{PoPK}, ek, c_i), (x_i, r_i))$ to $\mathcal{F}_{\mathsf{ZK}}^{1:M}$.
3. Request output from $\mathcal{F}_{\mathsf{ZK}}$ (with $\mathsf{sid}_{i,j}^2$ for every $j \in [n] \setminus \{i\}$) until receiving $(\mathsf{ZK\text{-}proof}, \mathsf{sid}_{i,j}^2, (\mathsf{PoCS}, vk, \mathsf{msg}, \sigma_j^{\mathsf{input}_i}))$, where P_i acts as the verifier and P_j acts as the prover, with $\mathsf{msg} = \langle n - t$ parties hold the input c_i of $P_i \rangle$, until receiving $n - t$ signature shares $\{\sigma_j^{\mathsf{input}_i}\}$.
4. Compute the certificate $\mathsf{cert}_i^{\mathsf{input}} = \mathrm{SignRecon}(\{\sigma_j^{\mathsf{input}_i}\})$ (which equals $\mathrm{Sign}_{sk}(\mathsf{msg})$). Send $(\mathsf{sid}, \mathsf{msg}, c_i, \mathsf{cert}_i^{\mathsf{input}})$ to all the parties.

Grant Certificate:

Request the output from $\mathcal{F}_{\mathsf{ZK}}^{1:M}$ (with sid_j^1 for every $j \in [n] \setminus \{i\}$). Upon receiving $(\mathsf{ZK\text{-}proof}, \mathsf{sid}_j^1, P_j, \{P_1, \ldots, P_n\} \setminus \{P_j\}, (\mathsf{PoPK}, ek, c_j))$, add j to $\mathsf{VerProv}_i$. Next, set the message $\mathsf{msg} = \langle n - t$ parties hold the input c_j of $P_j \rangle$, compute $\sigma_i^{\mathsf{input}_j} = \mathrm{SignShare}_{sk_i}(\mathsf{msg})$, and send $(\mathsf{ZK\text{-}prover}, \mathsf{sid}_{j,i}^2, (\mathsf{PoCS}, vk, \mathsf{msg}, \sigma_i^{\mathsf{input}_j}), sk_i)$ to $\mathcal{F}_{\mathsf{ZK}}$, where P_i acts as the prover and P_j as the verifier.

Echo Certificate:

Upon receiving $(\mathsf{sid}, \mathsf{msg}, c_j, \mathsf{cert}_j^{\mathsf{input}})$ with the message $\mathsf{msg} = \langle n - t$ parties hold the input c_j of $P_j \rangle$ and $\mathrm{Vrfy}_{vk}(\mathsf{msg}, \mathsf{cert}_j^{\mathsf{input}}) = 1$, check if $j \notin \mathsf{VerDistProv}_i$. If so, add j to $\mathsf{VerDistProv}_i$, add $(c_j, \mathsf{cert}_j^{\mathsf{input}})$ to $\mathsf{CertInputs}_i$ and forward $(\mathsf{sid}, \mathsf{msg}, c_j, \mathsf{cert}_j^{\mathsf{input}})$ to all the parties.

Select Input Providers:

When $|\mathsf{VerDistProv}_i| \geq n - t$, stop executing the above rules and proceed as follows:

1. Send $(\mathsf{sid}, \mathsf{VerProv}_i, \mathsf{CertInputs}_i)$ to all the parties.
2. Collect a set of $\left\{(\mathsf{VerProv}_j, \mathsf{CertInputs}_j)\right\}_{j \in J}$ of $n - t$ pairs.
3. Let $\mathsf{GlobalProv}_i = \cup_{j \in J} \mathsf{VerProv}_j$ and $\mathsf{GlobalInputs}_i = \cup_{j \in J} \mathsf{CertInputs}_j$.
4. For $j \in [n]$, send $(\mathsf{vote}, \mathsf{sid}_j^3, v_j)$ to $\mathcal{F}_{\mathsf{ABA}}$, where $v_j = 1$ iff $j \in \mathsf{GlobalProv}_i$.
5. Request the outputs from $\mathcal{F}_{\mathsf{ABA}}$ until receiving $(\mathsf{decide}, \mathsf{sid}_j^3, w_j)$ for every $j \in [n]$.
6. Denote $\mathsf{CoreSet} = \{j \in [n] \mid w_j = 1\}$.
7. For each $j \in \mathsf{GlobalProv}_i \cap \mathsf{CoreSet}$, send $(\mathsf{sid}, c_j, \mathsf{cert}_j^{\mathsf{input}})$ to all the parties (note that $(c_j, \mathsf{cert}_j^{\mathsf{input}}) \in \mathsf{GlobalInputs}_i$).
8. Wait until receiving $(c_j, \mathsf{cert}_j^{\mathsf{input}})$ for every $j \in \mathsf{CoreSet}$.

The input stage code for P_i

reconstruct a certificate proving that y_i is indeed the output value. Finally P_i sends y_i along with the certificate to all the parties.

Protocol 5 (The computation and threshold-decryption stage)

Wait until input stage is completed, resulting with a core set CoreSet and input ciphertexts $\{c_j \mid j \in \mathsf{CoreSet}\}$.

Circuit Evaluation:
1. For each $j \notin \mathsf{CoreSet}$, hard-wire the default value $\tilde{x}_j$ for P_j into the circuit Circ, denote the new circuit by $\mathsf{Circ}(\mathsf{CoreSet})$.
2. Locally compute the homomorphic evaluation of the circuit

$$\tilde{c}_i = \mathsf{Eval}_{ek}\left(\mathsf{Circ}(\mathsf{CoreSet}), c_{j_1}, \ldots, c_{j_{|\mathsf{CoreSet}|}}\right).$$

Threshold Decryption:
1. Compute the decryption share $d_i = \mathsf{DecShare}_{dk_i}(\tilde{c}_i)$.
2. Send $(\mathsf{ZK\text{-}prover}, \mathsf{sid}_i^4, \{P_1, \ldots, P_n\} \setminus \{P_i\}, ((\mathsf{PoCD}, ek, \tilde{c}_i, d_i), dk_i)$ to $\mathcal{F}_{\mathsf{ZK}}^{1:M}$.
3. Request the output from $\mathcal{F}_{\mathsf{ZK}}^{1:M}$ (for every $j \in [n] \setminus \{i\}$). Upon receiving $(\mathsf{ZK\text{-}proof}, \mathsf{sid}_j^4, P_j, \{P_1, \ldots, P_n\} \setminus \{P_j\}, (\mathsf{PoCD}, ek, \tilde{c}_j, d_j))$, accept the proof if $\tilde{c}_i = \tilde{c}_j$.
4. Once $t+1$ decryption shares with accepted proofs $\{(ek, \tilde{c}_i, d_j)\}$ have arrived, reconstruct the output $y_i = \mathsf{DecRecon}(\{d_j\})$.
5. Set $\mathsf{msg} = \langle y_i \text{ is the output value}\rangle$ and compute $\sigma_i^{\mathsf{output}} = \mathsf{SignShare}_{sk_i}(\mathsf{msg})$.
6. Send $(\mathsf{ZK\text{-}prover}, \mathsf{sid}_i^5, \{P_1, \ldots, P_n\} \setminus \{P_i\}, (\mathsf{PoCS}, vk, \mathsf{msg}, \sigma_i^{\mathsf{output}}), sk_i)$ to $\mathcal{F}_{\mathsf{ZK}}^{1:M}$.
7. Request output from $\mathcal{F}_{\mathsf{ZK}}^{1:M}$ (for $j \in [n] \setminus \{i\}$) until receiving $(\mathsf{ZK\text{-}proof}, \mathsf{sid}_j^5, P_j, \{P_1, \ldots, P_n\} \setminus \{P_j\}, (\mathsf{PoCS}, vk, \mathsf{msg}, \sigma_j^{\mathsf{output}}))$, with $\mathsf{msg} = \langle y_i \text{ is the output value}\rangle$.
8. Compute the certificate $\mathsf{cert}_i^{\mathsf{output\text{-}verified}} = \mathsf{SignRecon}(\{\sigma_j^{\mathsf{output}_i}\})$ (which equals $\mathsf{Sign}_{sk}(\mathsf{msg})$ with $\mathsf{msg} = \langle y_i \text{ is the output value}\rangle$). Send $(\mathsf{sid}, \mathsf{msg}, \mathsf{cert}_i^{\mathsf{output\text{-}verified}})$ to all the parties.

The computation and threshold-decryption stage code for P_i

5.4   Termination Stage

The termination stage, as described in Protocol 6, ensures that all honest parties will eventually terminate the protocol, and will do so with the same output. Recall that the computation and threshold-decryption stage is concluded when a party sends a certified output value to all the parties. The party cannot terminate at this point since it might be required to assist in certifying statements for other parties. Therefore, during the entire course of the protocol the termination code is run concurrently. The termination stage follows the technique of Bracha [13].

In this stage, each party continuously collects certified outputs sent by other parties. Once it receives $t + 1$ certified outputs of the same value it knows that this is the correct output value for the computation (since at least one honest party sent it). The party then adopts this certified output as its own output (in case it did not obtain the output value earlier) and echoes it to all other parties. Once the party receives $n - t$ certified outputs of the same value, it can terminate.

Protocol 6 (The termination stage)

During the protocol, concurrently executes the following rule:

Collecting Output Values:

When receiving for the first time from party P_j the value $(\mathsf{sid}, \mathsf{msg}, \mathsf{cert}_j^{\mathsf{output\text{-}verified}})$, with $\mathsf{msg} = \langle y_j \text{ is the output value}\rangle$ and $\mathsf{Vrfy}_{vk}(\mathsf{msg}, \mathsf{cert}_j^{\mathsf{output\text{-}verified}}) = 1$.

1. If the value y_j has arrived from $t + 1$ parties and the output of P_i is not set to be y_j, then set the output y_i to be y_j and echo $(\mathsf{sid}, \mathsf{msg}, \mathsf{cert}_j^{\mathsf{output\text{-}verified}})$ to all the parties.
2. If the value y_j has arrived from $n - t$ parties, then terminate with output $(\mathsf{output}, \mathsf{sid}, (\mathsf{CoreSet}, y_i))$.

The termination stage code for P_i

6   Proof of Security

Lemma 2. *Let f be an n-party functionality and assume the existence of TFHE and TSIG schemes. Then the protocol π described in Protocols 4, 5 and 6 UC realizes $\mathcal{F}_{\mathsf{ASFE}}^{f}$ in the $(\mathcal{F}_{\mathsf{KeyDist}}, \mathcal{F}_{\mathsf{ZK}}, \mathcal{F}_{\mathsf{ZK}}^{1:M}, \mathcal{F}_{\mathsf{ABA}})$-hybrid model, in constant time, in the presence of static malicious adversaries corrupting at most t parties, for $t < n/2$.*

Proof. Let $\mathcal{A}$ be a static malicious adversary against the execution of π and let $\mathcal{Z}$ be an environment. Denote by $\mathcal{I}$ the set of indices of the corrupted parties. We construct an ideal-process adversary $\mathcal{S}$, interacting with the environment $\mathcal{Z}$ and with the ideal functionality $\mathcal{F}_{\mathsf{ASFE}}^{f}$. $\mathcal{S}$ constructs virtual real-model honest parties and runs the real-model adversary $\mathcal{A}$. $\mathcal{S}$ must simulate the view of $\mathcal{A}$, i.e., its communication with $\mathcal{Z}$, the messages sent by the uncorrupted parties, and the interactions with the functionalities $(\mathcal{F}_{\mathsf{KeyDist}}, \mathcal{F}_{\mathsf{ZK}}, \mathcal{F}_{\mathsf{ZK}}^{1:M}, \mathcal{F}_{\mathsf{ABA}})$.

In order to simulate the communication with $\mathcal{Z}$, every message that $\mathcal{S}$ receives from $\mathcal{Z}$ is sent to $\mathcal{A}$, and likewise, every message sent from $\mathcal{A}$ sends to $\mathcal{Z}$ is forwarded by $\mathcal{S}$.

Simulating the Input Stage. $\mathcal{S}$ starts by simulating $\mathcal{F}_{\mathsf{KeyDist}}$ and generates the cryptographic keys by computing $(dk, ek) \leftarrow \mathrm{Gen}_{(t,n)}(1^\kappa)$, where $dk = (dk_1, \ldots, dk_n)$, and $(sk, vk) \leftarrow \mathrm{SigGen}_{(n-t,n)}(1^\kappa)$, where $sk = (sk_1, \ldots, sk_n)$, and recording (dk, ek, sk, vk). Upon request from $\mathcal{A}$, $\mathcal{S}$ sends the corresponding keys (dk_i, ek, sk_i, vk) for each corrupted party P_i $(i \in \mathcal{I})$.

Next, $\mathcal{S}$ simulates the operations of all honest parties in the input stage (Protocol 4). During the *Distribution of Encrypted Input* phase, $\mathcal{S}$ sets every ciphertext of an honest party to be an encryption of zero, that is for every $j \notin \mathcal{I}$, compute $c_j \leftarrow \mathrm{Enc}_{ek}(0)$. When the adversary send a request to $\mathcal{F}_{\mathsf{ZK}}^{1:M}$ with sid_j^1 (for $j \notin \mathcal{I}$) on behalf of a corrupted party, $\mathcal{S}$ responds with a confirmation of the validity of the ciphertext c_j, i.e., with $(\mathsf{ZK\text{-}proof}, \mathsf{sid}_j^1, P_j, \{P_1, \ldots, P_n\} \setminus \{P_j\}, (\mathsf{PoPK}, ek, c_j))$. When a corrupted party P_i $(i \in \mathcal{I})$ sends $(\mathsf{ZK\text{-}prover}, \mathsf{sid}_i^1, \{P_1, \ldots, P_n\} \setminus \{P_i\}, (\mathsf{PoPK}, ek, c_i), (x_i, r_i))$ to $\mathcal{F}_{\mathsf{ZK}}^{1:M}$, $\mathcal{S}$ confirms that indeed $c_i = \mathrm{Enc}_{ek}(x_i; r_i)$ and if so records the input x_i. $\mathcal{S}$ continues to simulate the honest parties by following the protocol; in all other calls to $\mathcal{F}_{\mathsf{ZK}}$, $\mathcal{S}$ responds according to the ideal functionality. When the simulation reaches the *Select Input Providers* phase, $\mathcal{S}$ simulates the interface to $\mathcal{F}_{\mathsf{ABA}}$ to $\mathcal{A}$. When the first honest party completes the simulated input stage, $\mathcal{S}$ learns the set CoreSet.

Note that $\mathcal{S}$ learned the input values that were used by the adversary $\mathcal{A}$ on behalf of the corrupted parties that were selected to be input providers. This follows since for every $i \in \mathcal{I} \cap \mathsf{CoreSet}$, there exists an honest party that confirmed the ciphertext c_i and sent a signature share to P_i (except for the negligible probability that $\mathcal{A}$ managed to forge a signature). It follows that the corrupted party must have sent its input to $\mathcal{F}_{\mathsf{ZK}}^{1:M}$ during the *Distribution of Encrypted Input* phase, and so its input value x_i was recorded by $\mathcal{S}$.

Interacting with $\mathcal{F}_{\mathsf{ASFE}}^{f}$. Once $\mathcal{S}$ learns CoreSet, it sends to $\mathcal{F}_{\mathsf{ASFE}}^{f}$ the input value x_i that was recorded for each $i \in \mathcal{I} \cap \mathsf{CoreSet}$, the input value $x_i = 0$ for each $i \in \mathcal{I} \setminus \mathsf{CoreSet}$ and the set CoreSet as the set of input providers. Once $\mathcal{S}$ receives back the output value y, it starts the simulation of the computation and threshold-decryption stage.

Simulating the Computation and Threshold-Decryption Stage. In order to simulate the honest parties in this stage (Protocol 5), $\mathcal{S}$ proceeds as follows. Initially, $\mathcal{S}$ computes the evaluated ciphertext $\tilde{c}$ based on the input ciphertexts of the input providers, i.e., $\tilde{c} = \mathrm{Eval}_{ek}(\mathsf{Circ}(\mathsf{CoreSet}), c_{j_1}, \ldots, c_{j_{|\mathsf{CoreSet}|}})$. Next, for every $i \in \mathcal{I}$, use the share of the decryption key dk_i to compute the decryption share $d_i = \mathrm{DecShare}_{dk_i}(\tilde{c})$. $\mathcal{S}$ then sets the decryption share d_j, for every $j \notin \mathcal{I}$, such that $(d_1, \ldots, d_n)$ form a secret sharing of the output value y. When the adversary sends a request to $\mathcal{F}_{\mathsf{ZK}}^{1:M}$ with sid_j^4 (for $j \notin \mathcal{I}$) on behalf of a corrupted party, $\mathcal{S}$ responds with a confirmation of the validity of the decryption share d_j, i.e., with $(\mathsf{ZK\text{-}proof}, \mathsf{sid}_j^4, P_j, \{P_1, \ldots, P_n\} \setminus \{P_j\}, (\mathsf{PoCD}, ek, \tilde{c}, d_j))$. $\mathcal{S}$ continues to simulate the honest parties by following the protocol; in all other calls to $\mathcal{F}_{\mathsf{ZK}}^{1:M}$, $\mathcal{S}$ responds according to the ideal functionality.

Simulating the Termination Stage. $\mathcal{S}$ simulates the honest parties in the termination stage (Protocol 6) by following the protocol;

We now define a series of hybrid games that will be used to prove the indistinguishability of the real and ideal worlds. The output of each game is the output of the environment.

The Game REAL$_{\pi,\mathcal{A},\mathcal{Z}}$. This is exactly the execution of the protocol π in the real-model with environment $\mathcal{Z}$ and adversary $\mathcal{A}$ (and ideal functionalities $(\mathcal{F}_{\mathsf{KeyDist}}, \mathcal{F}_{\mathsf{ZK}}, \mathcal{F}_{\mathsf{ZK}}^{1:M}, \mathcal{F}_{\mathsf{ABA}}))$.

The Game HYB$_{\pi,\mathcal{A},\mathcal{Z}}^{1}$. In this game, we modify the real-model experiment in the computation stage as follows. Whenever a corrupted party requests output from $\mathcal{F}_{\mathsf{ZK}}^{1:M}$ with sid_j^4 (for $j \notin \mathcal{I}$), the response from $\mathcal{F}_{\mathsf{ZK}}^{1:M}$ is (ZK-proof, $\mathsf{sid}_j^4, P_j, \{P_1, \ldots, P_n\} \setminus \{P_j\}, (\mathsf{PoCD}, ek, \tilde{c}, d_j))$, without checking if P_j sent a valid witness.

Claim 7. REAL$_{\pi,\mathcal{A},\mathcal{Z}} \equiv$ HYB$_{\pi,\mathcal{A},\mathcal{Z}}^{1}$.

Proof. This follows since in the execution of π, honest parties always send a valid witness to $\mathcal{F}_{\mathsf{ZK}}^{1:M}$, and so the response from $\mathcal{F}_{\mathsf{ZK}}^{1:M}$ is the same in both games.

The Game HYB$_{\pi,\mathcal{A},\mathcal{Z}}^{2}$. This game is just like an execution of HYB^1 except for the computation of the decryption shares of honest parties during the computation stage. Let y be the output of f, let $\tilde{c}$ be the evaluated ciphertext, let dk_i (for $i \in \mathcal{I}$) be the shares of the decryption key held by the corrupted parties, and let $d_i = \mathsf{DecShare}_{dk_i}(\tilde{c})$ be the corresponding decryption shares. Then, instead of computing the decryption share of the honest parties as $d_j = \mathsf{DecShare}_{dk_j}(\tilde{c})$ (for $j \notin \mathcal{I}$), the decryption shares are computed such that $(d_1, \ldots, d_n)$ form a secret sharing of the output value y.

Claim 8. HYB$_{\pi,\mathcal{A},\mathcal{Z}}^{1} \overset{c}{\equiv}$ HYB$_{\pi,\mathcal{A},\mathcal{Z}}^{2}$.

Proof. The ability to compute the decryption shares of the honest parties follows from the properties of the secret sharing scheme.[6] Computational indistinguishability follows from the semantic security of the TFHE scheme.

The Game HYB$_{\pi,\mathcal{A},\mathcal{Z}}^{3}$. This game is just like an execution of HYB^2 except for the following difference. Whenever a corrupted party requests output from $\mathcal{F}_{\mathsf{ZK}}^{1:M}$ with sid_j^1 (for $j \notin \mathcal{I}$), the response from $\mathcal{F}_{\mathsf{ZK}}^{1:M}$ is (ZK-proof, $\mathsf{sid}_j^1, P_j, \{P_1, \ldots, P_n\} \setminus \{P_j\}, (\mathsf{PoPK}, ek, c_j))$, without checking if P_j sent a valid witness.

Claim 9. HYB$_{\pi,\mathcal{A},\mathcal{Z}}^{2} \equiv$ HYB$_{\pi,\mathcal{A},\mathcal{Z}}^{3}$.

Proof. This follows since in the execution of π, honest parties always send a valid witness to $\mathcal{F}_{\mathsf{ZK}}^{1:M}$, and so the response from $\mathcal{F}_{\mathsf{ZK}}^{1:M}$ is the same in both games.

---

[6] In the scheme of Shamir [39], fix the points corresponding to the shares d_i (for $i \in \mathcal{I}$) and the secret y, create a degree t polynomial interpolating these points, and compute the shares d_j (for $j \notin \mathcal{I}$) accordingly.

The Game $\text{HYB}^{4,\ell}_{\pi,\mathcal{A},\mathcal{Z}}$.. This game is just like an execution of HYB^3 with the following difference. In the input stage, in case $i \leq \ell$ honest party P_i encrypts its actual input $c_i \leftarrow \text{Enc}_{ek}(x_i)$, whereas in case $i > \ell$ P_i encrypts zeros $c_i \leftarrow \text{Enc}_{ek}(0)$. (Note that $\text{HYB}^{4,n}$ is exactly HYB^3.)

Claim 10. For every $\ell \in \{0, \ldots, n-1\}$, $\text{HYB}^{4,\ell}_{\pi,\mathcal{A},\mathcal{Z}} \overset{c}{\equiv} \text{HYB}^{4,\ell+1}_{\pi,\mathcal{A},\mathcal{Z}}$.

Proof. This follows from the semantic security of the encryption scheme.

Claim 11. $\text{HYB}^{4,0}_{\pi,\mathcal{A},\mathcal{Z}} \equiv \text{IDEAL}_{f,\mathcal{S},\mathcal{Z}}$.

Proof. This follows since the joint behaviour of ideal functionalities $(\mathcal{F}_{\text{KeyDist}}, \mathcal{F}_{\text{ZK}}, \mathcal{F}_{\text{ABA}})$, the modified behaviour of the ideal functionality $\mathcal{F}_{\text{ZK}}^{1:\text{M}}$ and the behaviour of the honest parties in $\text{HYB}^{4,0}$ is identical to the simulation done by $\mathcal{S}$.

Combining Claims 7–11, we conclude that $\text{REAL}_{\pi,\mathcal{A},\mathcal{Z}} \overset{c}{\equiv} \text{IDEAL}_{f,\mathcal{S},\mathcal{Z}}$.

7 Conclusions

By Lemma 1, $\mathcal{F}_{\text{ZK}}^{1:\text{M}}$ can be realized in the $\mathcal{F}_{\text{ZK}}$-hybrid model (assuming the existence of TSIG and an honest majority). Assuming the existence of enhanced trapdoor permutations, $\mathcal{F}_{\text{ZK}}$ can be UC realized in the $\mathcal{F}_{\text{CRS}}$-hybrid model non-interactively (meaning that the prover sends a single message to the verifier) [21]. Using universal composition with joint state [16], a multi-session version of $\mathcal{F}_{\text{ZK}}$ that requires a single copy of the CRS can be used. We thus obtain the following theorem from Lemma 2:

Theorem 12 (formal statement of Theorem 1). *Let f be an n-party function and assume that enhanced trapdoor permutations, TFHE schemes and TSIG schemes exist. Then $\mathcal{F}^f_{\text{ASFE}}$ can be UC realized in the $(\mathcal{F}_{\text{CRS}}, \mathcal{F}_{\text{KeyDist}}, \mathcal{F}_{\text{ABA}})$-hybrid model, in constant time, in the presence of static malicious adversaries corrupting at most t parties, for $t < n/2$.*

During the input stage (Protocol 4) the functionality $\mathcal{F}_{\text{ABA}}$ is concurrently invoked n times. If $\mathcal{F}_{\text{ABA}}$ is instantiated using a constant expected round protocol, e.g., the protocol of Canetti and Rabin [15], the time complexity of the concurrent composition will result with expectancy of $\log(n)$. Ben-Or and El-Yaniv [7] constructed a concurrent ABA protocol that runs in constant expected time, assuming that $t < n/3$.[7] We therefore conclude with the following corollary.

Corollary 2 (formal statement of Corollary 1). *Let f be an n-party function and assume that enhanced trapdoor permutations, TFHE schemes and TSIG schemes exist. Then $\mathcal{F}^f_{\text{ASFE}}$ can be UC realized in the $(\mathcal{F}_{\text{CRS}}, \mathcal{F}_{\text{KeyDist}})$-hybrid model, in constant expected time, in the presence of static malicious adversaries corrupting at most t parties, for $t < n/3$.*

---

[7] Although the protocol in [7] is proved based on the property-based definition of ABA, a simulation-based proof should follow as we consider static adversaries.

Acknowledgements. We would like to thank Yehuda Lindell and Ran Canetti for helpful discussions on modeling asynchronous MPC in the UC framework, and to Juan Garay for pointing us to the paper of Ben-Or and El-Yaniv [7].

References

1. Almansa, J.F., Damgård, I.B., Nielsen, J.B.: Simplified threshold RSA with adaptive and proactive security. In: Vaudenay, S. (ed.) EUROCRYPT 2006. LNCS, vol. 4004, pp. 593–611. Springer, Heidelberg (2006)
2. Asharov, G., Jain, A., López-Alt, A., Tromer, E., Vaikuntanathan, V., Wichs, D.: Multiparty computation with low communication, computation and interaction via threshold FHE. In: Pointcheval, D., Johansson, T. (eds.) EUROCRYPT 2012. LNCS, vol. 7237, pp. 483–501. Springer, Heidelberg (2012)
3. Backes, M., Bendun, F., Choudhury, A., Kate, A.: Asynchronous MPC with a strict honest majority using non-equivocation. In: Proceedings of the 33rd Annual ACM Symposium on Principles of Distributed Computing (PODC), pp. 10–19 (2014)
4. Beaver, D., Micali, S., Rogaway, P.: The round complexity of secure protocols (Extended Abstract). In: Proceedings of the 22nd Annual ACM Symposium on Theory of Computing (STOC), pp. 503–513(1990)
5. Beerliová-Trubíniová, Z., Hirt, M.: Simple and efficient perfectly-secure asynchronous MPC. In: Kurosawa, K. (ed.) ASIACRYPT 2007. LNCS, vol. 4833, pp. 376–392. Springer, Heidelberg (2007)
6. Beerliová-Trubíniová, Z., Hirt, M., Nielsen, J.B.: On the theoretical gap between synchronous and asynchronous MPC protocols. In: Proceedings of the 29th Annual ACM Symposium on Principles of Distributed Computing (PODC), pp. 211–218 (2010)
7. Ben-Or, M., El-Yaniv, R.: Resilient-optimal interactive consistency in constant time. Distrib. Comput. **16**(4), 249–262 (2003)
8. Ben-Or, M., Goldwasser, S., Wigderson., A.: Completeness theorems for non-cryptographic fault-tolerant distributed computation (Extended Abstract). In: Proceedings of the 20th Annual ACM Symposium on Theory of Computing (STOC), pp. 1–10 (1988)
9. Ben-Or, M., Canetti, R., Goldreich, O.: Asynchronous secure computation. In: Proceedings of the 25th Annual ACM Symposium on Theory of Computing (STOC), pp. 52–61 (1993)
10. Ben-Or, M., Kelmer, B., Rabin, T.: Asynchronous secure computations with optimal resilience (Extended Abstract). In: Proceedings of the 13th Annual ACM Symposium on Principles of Distributed Computing (PODC), pp. 183–192 (1994)
11. Bendlin, R., Damgård, I.: Threshold decryption and zero-knowledge proofs for lattice-based cryptosystems. In: Micciancio, D. (ed.) TCC 2010. LNCS, vol. 5978, pp. 201–218. Springer, Heidelberg (2010)
12. Bendlin, R., Krehbiel, S., Peikert, C.: How to share a lattice trapdoor: threshold protocols for signatures and (H)IBE. In: Jacobson, M., Locasto, M., Mohassel, P., Safavi-Naini, R. (eds.) ACNS 2013. LNCS, vol. 7954, pp. 218–236. Springer, Heidelberg (2013)
13. Bracha, G.: An asynchronous [(n-1)/3]-resilient consensus protocol. In: Proceedings of the Third Annual ACM Symposium on Principles of Distributed Computing (PODC), pp. 154–162 (1984)

14. Canetti, R., Security, U.C.: A new paradigm for cryptographic protocols. In: Proceedings of the 42nd Annual Symposium on Foundations of Computer Science (FOCS), pp. 136–145 (2001)
15. Canetti, R., Rabin, T.: Fast asynchronous Byzantine agreement with optimal resilience. In: Proceedings of the 25th Annual ACM Symposium on Theory of Computing (STOC), pp. 42–51 (1993)
16. Canetti, R., Rabin, T.: Universal composition with joint state. In: Boneh, D. (ed.) CRYPTO 2003. LNCS, vol. 2729, pp. 265–281. Springer, Heidelberg (2003)
17. Chaum, D., Crépeau, C., Damgård, I.: Multiparty unconditionally secure protocols (Extended Abstract). In: Proceedings of the 20th Annual ACM Symposium on Theory of Computing (STOC), pp. 11–19 (1988)
18. Choudhury, A., Patra, A.: Optimally resilient asynchronous MPC with linear communication complexity. In: Proceedings of the 16th International Conference on Distributed Computing and Networking (ICDCN), p. 5 (2015)
19. Choudhury, A., Hirt, M., Patra, A.: Asynchronous multiparty computation with linear communication complexity. In: Afek, Y. (ed.) DISC 2013. LNCS, vol. 8205, pp. 388–402. Springer, Heidelberg (2013)
20. Cramer, R., Damgård, I.B., Nielsen, J.B.: Multiparty computation from threshold homomorphic encryption. In: Pfitzmann, B. (ed.) EUROCRYPT 2001. LNCS, vol. 2045, pp. 280–300. Springer, Heidelberg (2001)
21. De Santis, A., Di Crescenzo, G., Ostrovsky, R., Persiano, G., Sahai, A.: Robust non-interactive zero knowledge. In: Kilian, J. (ed.) CRYPTO 2001. LNCS, vol. 2139, pp. 566–598. Springer, Heidelberg (2001)
22. Fischer, M.J., Lynch, N.A., Paterson, M.: Impossibility of distributed consensus with one faulty process. J. ACM **32**(2), 374–382 (1985)
23. Garay, J.A., MacKenzie, P.D., Yang, K.: Strengthening zero-knowledge protocols using signatures. J. cryptol. **19**(2), 169–209 (2006)
24. Garg, S., Gentry, C., Halevi, S., Raykova, M.: Two-round secure MPC from indistinguishability obfuscation. In: Lindell, Y. (ed.) TCC 2014. LNCS, vol. 8349, pp. 74–94. Springer, Heidelberg (2014)
25. Gentry, C.: A fully homomorphic encryption scheme. Ph.D thesis
26. Goldreich, O.: The Foundations of Cryptography - Basic Applications, vol. 2. Cambridge University Press, Cambridge (2004)
27. Goldreich, O., Micali, S., Wigderson A.: How to play any mental game or a completeness theorem for protocols with honest majority. In: Proceedings of the 19th Annual ACM Symposium on Theory of Computing (STOC), pp. 218–229 (1987)
28. Dov Gordon, S., Liu, F.-H., Shi, E.: Constant-Round MPC with fairness and guarantee of output delivery. In: Gennaro, R., Robshaw, M. (eds.) CRYPTO 2015. LNCS, vol. 9216, pp. 63–82. Springer, Heidelberg (2015)
29. Hirt, M., Nielsen, J.B., Przydatek, B.: Cryptographic asynchronous multi-party computation with optimal resilience (Extended Abstract). In: Cramer, R. (ed.) EUROCRYPT 2005. LNCS, vol. 3494, pp. 322–340. Springer, Heidelberg (2005)
30. Hirt, M., Nielsen, J.B., Przydatek, B.: Asynchronous multi-party computation with quadratic communication. In: Aceto, L., Damgård, I., Goldberg, L.A., Halldórsson, M.M., Ingólfsdóttir, A., Walukiewicz, I. (eds.) ICALP 2008, Part II. LNCS, vol. 5126, pp. 473–485. Springer, Heidelberg (2008)
31. Ishai, Y., Prabhakaran, M., Sahai, A.: Founding cryptography on oblivious transfer – efficiently. In: Wagner, D. (ed.) CRYPTO 2008. LNCS, vol. 5157, pp. 572–591. Springer, Heidelberg (2008)

32. Katz, J., Maurer, U., Tackmann, B., Zikas, V.: Universally composable synchronous computation. In: Sahai, A. (ed.) TCC 2013. LNCS, vol. 7785, pp. 477–498. Springer, Heidelberg (2013)
33. Mukherjee, P., Wichs, D.: Two round MPC from LWE via Multi-Key FHE.Cryptology ePrint Archive, Report 2015/345 (2015). http://eprint.iacr.org/
34. Nielsen, J.B.: A threshold pseudorandom function construction and its applications. In: Yung, M. (ed.) CRYPTO 2002. LNCS, vol. 2442, pp. 401–416. Springer, Heidelberg (2002)
35. Patra, A., Choudhary, A., Rangan, C.P.: Communication efficient statistical asynchronous multiparty computation with optimal resilience. In: Bao, F., Yung, M., Lin, D., Jing, J. (eds.) Inscrypt 2009. LNCS, vol. 6151, pp. 179–197. Springer, Heidelberg (2010)
36. Patra, A., Choudhury, A., Rangan, C.P.: Efficient asynchronous verifiable secret sharing and multiparty computation. J. Cryptol. 28(1), 49–109 (2015)
37. Prabhu, B.S., Srinathan, K., Pandu Rangan, C.: Asynchronous unconditionally secure computation: an efficiency improvement. In: Menezes, A., Sarkar, P. (eds.) INDOCRYPT 2002. LNCS, vol. 2551, pp. 93–107. Springer, Heidelberg (2002)
38. Rabin, T., Ben-Or, M.: Verifiable secret sharing and multiparty protocols with honest majority (Extended Abstract). In: Proceedings of the 21st Annual ACM Symposium on Theory of Computing (STOC), pp. 73–85 (1989)
39. Shamir, A.: How to share a secret. Commun. ACM 22(11), 612–613 (1979)
40. Srinathan, K., Pandu Rangan, C.: Efficient asynchronous secure multiparty distributed computation. In: Roy, B., Okamoto, E. (eds.) INDOCRYPT 2000. LNCS, vol. 1977, pp. 117–129. Springer, Heidelberg (2000)
41. Toueg, S.: Randomized Byzantine agreements. In: Proceedings of the Third Annual ACM Symposium on Principles of Distributed Computing (PODC), pp. 163–178 (1984)

Adaptively Secure Multi-Party Computation from LWE (via Equivocal FHE)

Ivan Damgård[1], Antigoni Polychroniadou[1]([⊠]), and Vanishree Rao[2]

[1] Department of Computer Science, Aarhus University, Aarhus, Denmark
{ivan,antigoni}@cs.au.dk
[2] PARC, a Xerox Company, Palo Alto, USA
vhvanshvansh@gmail.com

Abstract. Adaptively secure Multi-Party Computation (MPC) is an essential and fundamental notion in cryptography. In this work, we construct Universally Composable (UC) MPC protocols that are adaptively secure against all-but-one corruptions based on LWE. Our protocols have a constant number of rounds and communication complexity dependant only on the length of the inputs and outputs (it is independent of the circuit size).

Such protocols were only known assuming an honest majority. Protocols in the dishonest majority setting, such as the work of Ishai et al. (CRYPTO 2008), require communication complexity proportional to the circuit size. In addition, constant-round adaptively secure protocols assuming dishonest majority are known to be impossible in the stand-alone setting with black-box proofs of security in the plain model. Here, we solve the problem in the UC setting using a set-up assumption which was shown necessary in order to achieve dishonest majority.

The problem of constructing adaptively secure constant-round MPC protocols against arbitrary corruptions is considered a notorious hard problem. A recent line of works based on indistinguishability obfuscation construct such protocols with near-optimal number of rounds against arbitrary corruptions. However, based on standard assumptions, adaptively secure protocols secure against even just all-but-one corruptions with near-optimal number of rounds are not known. However, in this work we provide a three-round solution based only on LWE and NIZK secure against all-but-one corruptions.

In addition, Asharov et al. (EUROCRYPT 2012) and more recently Mukherjee and Wichs (ePrint 2015) presented constant-round protocols based on LWE which are secure *only* in the presence of static adversaries. Assuming NIZK and LWE their static protocols run in two rounds where the latter one is only based on a common random string. Assuming adaptively secure UC NIZK, proposed by Groth et al. (ACM 2012), and LWE as mentioned above our adaptive protocols run in three rounds.

Our protocols are constructed based on a special type of cryptosystem we call equivocal FHE from LWE. We also build adaptively secure UC commitments and UC zero-knowledge proofs (of knowledge) from LWE.

This is an extended abstract. Further details can be found in the full version [DPR14].

© International Association for Cryptologic Research 2016
C.-M. Cheng et al. (Eds.): PKC 2016, Part II, LNCS 9615, pp. 208–233, 2016.
DOI: 10.1007/978-3-662-49387-8_9

Moreover, in the decryption phase using an AMD code mechanism we avoid the use of ZK and achieve communication complexity that does not scale with the decryption circuit.

1 Introduction

Secure multi-party computation is an extremely strong and important tool for making distributed computing more secure. General solutions to the problem allows us to carry out any desired computation among a set of players, without compromising, the privacy of their inputs or the correctness of the outputs. This should even hold if some of the players have been corrupted by an adversary. An important issue in this connection is how the adversary chooses which players to target. In the static model, the adversary must choose who to corrupt before the protocol starts. A more general and also more realistic model is adaptive corruption where the adversary may corrupt new players during the protocol.

Of course efficiency of the protocol is also important, and important measures in this respect are the number of rounds we need to do, as well as the communication complexity (the total number of bits sent). Obviously, achieving a constant number of rounds and small communication complexity, while still getting the best possible security, is an important research goal.

Unconditionally secure protocols such as [BGW88] are typically adaptively secure. But these protocols are not constant round, and it is a major open problem if it is even possible to have unconditional security and constant number of rounds for secure computation of any function, see [DNP15] for a detailed discussion.

If we are willing to make computational assumptions, we can achieve constant round protocols, the first example of this is Yao's garbled circuits for two players, but on the other hand this does not give us adaptive security. Another class of protocols based on Fully Homomorphic Encryption (FHE) also naturally leads to constant round protocols, where we can tolerate that a majority of players are corrupted. Here we also get low communication complexity, that depends only on the lenght of inputs and outputs. But again, these protocols achieve only static security (see for instance [Gen09, AJLA+12, LTV12]). More recently, the work of Mukherjee and Wichs [MW15] achieve a two-round static protocol assuming LWE and NIZK where additionally the protocol only assumes a random reference string (as opposed to being sampled form a specific distribution).

We can in fact get adaptive security in the computational setting, as shown in [CFGN96] by introducing the notion of Non-Commiting Encryption (NCE). Moreover, in [DN03], adaptive security was obtained as well, but much more efficiently using additively homomorphic encryption. However, neither [CFGN96] nor [DN03] run in a constant number of rounds.

If we assume honest majority we can get both constant round and adaptive security but the communication complexity will be propositional to the size of the evaluated circuit. This was shown in several papers [DI05, DI06, DIK+08, IPS08]. The idea here is to use an unconditionally secure protocol to compute, for instance, a Yao garbled circuit, that is then used to compute the desired function in a constant number of rounds. Since the computation leading to the Yao circuit is easy to parallelise, this can be constant round as well and we inherit adaptive security from the unconditionally secure "preprocessing". On the other hand, as mentioned this requires communication that is proportional to the size of circuit to be securely evaluated. One may apply the IPS compiler to one of these protocols to get a solution for dishonest majority. This preserves the adaptive security and the constant number of rounds, but unfortunately also preserves the dependence of the communication complexity on the circuit size. Therefore, the question becomes:

Is it possible to construct constant round MPC protocols secure against an adaptive adversary that may corrupt all but one parties with communication complexity independent of the circuit size?

1.1   Contributions

We answer this in the affirmative. More specifically, we achieve an adaptive UC-secure protocol that tolerates corruption of $n-1$ of the n players with UC secure composition with protocols secure against $n-1$ corruptions. Our protocol requires a constant number of rounds and its communication complexity depends only on the length of inputs and outputs (and the security parameter), and not on the size of the evaluated circuit and the decryption circuit. The protocol is secure if the LWE problem is hard. Moreover, we *do not* consider the weaker model of secure erasures.

Theorem 1 (informal). *Assuming hardness of LWE, we show that arbitrary functions can be UC-securely computed in the presence of adaptive, active corruption of all-but-one parties within a constant number of rounds.*

Assuming adaptively secure UC NIZK, proposed by Groth et al. [GOS12], and LWE our adaptive protocols run in three rounds.

Theorem 2 (informal). *Assuming hardness of LWE and the existence of adaptively secure UC NIZK, we show that arbitrary functions can be UC-securely computed in the presence of adaptive, active corruption of all-but-one parties in three rounds of broadcast.*

In our construction we assume a broadcast channel where encryption is performed using what we call Equivocal FHE, a notion weaker than non-commiting encryption, presented in Sect. 3 which can be of independent interest. For example, using our equivocal scheme we also build adaptively secure UC commitment and UC zero-knowledge proofs (of knowledge) based on hardness of LWE (see Sect. 4).

Last but not least, in the standard ZK-based decryption used by approaches based on FHE, all the parties need to append a ZK proof, to prove that they decrypted correctly, whose communication complexity grows with the size of the decryption circuit. In this work using an AMD code mechanism [CDF+08] we avoid the use of ZK and achieve communication complexity that does not scale with the decryption circuit. In particular, the total communication complexity of the decryption phase of our concrete protocol is $\mathcal{O}(n^2\lambda)$ where λ is the security parameter.

1.2   Technical Difficulties and New Ideas

To construct our adaptively secure protocol, we start from the well known blueprint for FHE-based MPC: players encrypt their inputs under a common public key, evaluate the desired function locally and then jointly decrypt the result. This is possible under an appropriate set-up assumption, which is always needed for UC security and dishonest majority. Namely, we assume that a public key has been distributed, and players have been given shares of the corresponding secret key.

This approach has been used before and usually leads to static security. One reason for this is that encryptions are usually committing, so we are in trouble if the sender of a ciphertext is corrupted later. This can be solved using a cryptosystem with equivocal properties and this would mean that the input and the evaluation phase of the protocol can be simulated, even for adaptive corruptions. Players need, of course, to prove that they know the inputs they contribute, but this can be done once we construct constant round adaptively secure UC commitment and ZK proofs from LWE.

An important tool we would like to get in order to achieve constant-round adaptively secure MPC protocols may be a Fully Homomorphic Encryption (FHE) scheme with equivocal properties.

Starting Point – Fully Homomorphic NCE. It is tempting to consider a generic solution from FHE and Non-Commiting Encryption (NCE). In particular, in such a hypothetical construction, the secret key would be a secret key for an FHE scheme, the public key an FHE encryption of the NCE secret key and the NCE public key. Encryption would be performed using the NCE, and homomorphic evaluation and decryption would be performed as expected. However, there are fundamental caveats with this approach.

It does not seem to buy us any efficiency at all. In particular, NCE schemes are interactive, in that the receiver must send fresh (public-)key material for each new message to be encrypted. There is even a result by Nielsen saying that this is inherent for NCE [Nie02]. It will be hard for an interactive scheme to fit the above suggestion. Indeed, the public key material would run out after encrypting some number of inputs. Therefore, in generic NCE the public-key cannot be reused, and has to be updated for each new message. Moreover, one may go around this issue by having an NCE public-key for each party where the FHE encryption in the public key will include all the public keys. However, such a solution is highly inefficient since it is not the number of parties that matter but the amount of data to be encrypted. The amount of public-key material has to be proportional to size of the plaintext data. For instance, if only a constant number of parties had input, but a lot of, we would have a significant problem.

Another suggestion is to always regenerate this setup afresh using a constant round adaptive protocol prior to each new execution. This might work but unfortunately set-up data are considered reasonable if its size does not depend on the function to be computed (otherwise we are in the preprocessing model which is a completely different ball game). Hence, one would in fact always need this key regeneration step per execution.

It turns out that the motivation of considering NCE in this context is very weak.

Our Approach - Starting Afresh. Towards minimising the above caveat we propose a scheme we call Equivocal FHE. An equivocal FHE scheme is a fully homomorphic encryption scheme with additional properties. Most importantly, it is possible to generate "fake" public keys that look like normal keys but where encryption leads to ciphertexts that contain no information on the plaintext. This is similar to the known notion of meaningful/meaningless keys, but in addition we want that fake public keys come with a trapdoor that allows to "explain" (equivocate) a ciphertext as an encryption of any desired plaintext. This is similar to (but not the same as) what is required for NCE: for NCE one needs to equivocate a ciphertext even if the decryption key is also given (say, by corrupting the receiver), here we only need to give the adversary valid looking randomness for the encryption. In order to achieve such a cryptosystem the main properties we require from an FHE scheme is formula privacy, invertible sampling and homomorphishm over the randomness. Given this, we managed to obtain the required equivocation directly with much less overhead compared to a possible NCE solution.

We give a concrete instantiation of equivocal FHE based on LWE, starting from the FHE scheme by Brakerski et al. [BV11].

Adaptive UC Commitments and ZK from LWE. A second tool we need is constant-round UC-secure commitments and zero-knowledge proofs. For the commitments we start from a basic construction appeared in [CLOS02], which was originally based on claw-free trapdoor permutations (CFTP). We show that it can be instantiated based on LWE (which is not known to imply CFTP). Zero-knowledge then follows quite easily from known techniques.

Achieving a Simulatable Protocol. A harder problem is how to simulate the output phase in which ciphertexts containing the outputs are decrypted. In the simulation we cannot expect that these ciphertexts are correctly formed and hold the actual outputs, so the simulator needs to "cheat". However, each player holds a share of the secret key which we have to give to the adversary if he is corrupted. If this happens after some executions of the decryption protocol, we (the simulator) may already be committed to this share. It is therefore not clear how the simulator can achieve the desired decryption results by adjusting the shares of the secret key. To get around this, we adapt an idea from Damgård and Nielsen [DN03], who proposed an adaptively secure protocol based on additively homomorphic threshold encryption but in the honest majority scenario. The idea is to add a step to the protocol where each ciphertext is re-randomised just before decryption. This gives the simulator a chance to cheat and turn the ciphertext into one that contains the correct result, and one can therefore simulate the decryption without having to modify the shares of the secret key. The re-randomisation from [DN03] only works for honest majority, we show a different method that works for dishonest majority and augment our Equivocal FHE scheme with the *ciphertext randomisation* property to achieve our goal.

General Purpose Equivocal FHE. We mention for completeness that there is also a more generic approach which will give us adaptive security based only on our Equivocal FHE: namely, we follow the same blueprint as before, with input, evaluation and output phases. However, we implement the verification of cipher-texts in the input phase and the decryptions in the output phase using generic adaptively secure MPC a la [CLOS02, IPS08]. This way, the communication and the number of rounds do not depend on the size of circuit to be computed securely. However, it would not be genuinely constant round, and the communi-cation complexity would depend on the circuits computing the encryption and decryption functions of the underlying cryptosystem. Hence, unlike our proto-col, any such solution would have communication complexity proportional to the Boolean circuit complexity of the decryption function (which seems inherent since one needs Yao garbling underneath). We measure the round and commu-nication complexity of such a possible solution based on the IPS compiler. The bottom line is that using IPS generically would yield a larger (constant) num-ber of rounds (20–30 rounds) and worse dependence on the security parameter. A concise estimate can be found in Appendix A. Clearly the above estimate should be taken with large grains of salt. We have tried to be optimistic on the part of IPS, to not give our concrete protocol an unfair advantage. Thus, actual numbers could be larger. On the other hand, we propose a three-round solution.

AMD Code Solution to Replace ZK. However, contrary to the above generic IPS solution, our approach allows for significant optimization of the decryption as follows. Instead of using ZK proofs to prove that the player's evaluation shares to the decryption phase are correct, we change the evaluation phase of the protocol. In particular, instead of having ciphertexts containing the desired output z, the evaluation phase computes encryptions containing a codeword $c = (z, \alpha)$ in an algebraic manipulation detection code, where z is the data and α is the key/randomness. In the decryption stage, players commit to their decryption shares (recall that we have UC commitment available), and then all shares are opened. If decryption fails, or decoding the codeword fails, we abort, else we output the decoded z. If z and α are thought of as elements in a (large) finite field, then the codeword can just be $(z, \alpha, \alpha z)$. According to our optimization, the communication complexity of our protocol is not only independent of the size of the evaluated circuit but also independent of the circuit size of the decryption circuit.

Impossibility Results? In the following we mention two impossibility results which apply to adaptively secure MPC and mention why they do not apply in our setting.

Motivated by ruling out one possible approach to achieving adaptive security, Katz et al. [KTZ13] showed that FHE with security against adaptive corruption of the receiver is impossible. In our setting, we distribute the private key of an FHE scheme among n parties; since we allow only $n-1$ of the parties to be corrupted, the impossibility result from [KTZ13] does not apply. Note that if an FHE scheme is to be of use in MPC, it seems to be necessary that the players are able to decrypt, if not by themselves, then at least by collaborating. But if corruption of all n players was allowed, the adversary would necessarily learn all secret keys, and then the impossibility result from [KTZ13] would apply. This suggests that our result with $n-1$ corruptions is the best we can achieve based only on FHE.

We note that in [GS12], adaptive security in constant number of rounds in the plain model was obtained using a non-blackbox proof in the stand-alone setting. Also a solution with a blackbox proof was shown to be impossible, but this does not, of course, apply to our case, where we go for UC security, and therefore require a set-up assumption.

Security Against Arbitrary Corruptions: Round complexity of all known adaptively secure protocols secure against n corruptions grows (see, e.g. [CLOS02, KO04, GS12, DMRV13]) linearly in the depth of the evaluated circuit. Recent independent works [GP15, CGP15, DKR15], have been shown that MPC protocols with security against n corruptions in a constant number of rounds can be achieved using indistinguishability obfuscation (IO) [GGH+13].

While the above results on constant round MPC using IO are exciting, the focus of this work is to avoid indistinguishability obfuscation altogether and to achieve adaptive security against corruption of $n-1$ of the n players, (with communication complexity depended only on the length of inputs and outputs and not on the size of the circuit to be computed securely), using simpler tools with simple standard assumptions involving them. In particular, our construction only requires FHE based on the hardness of LWE and avoids the use of IO which also incurs a cost in efficiency. Also as we have already mentioned, our result with $n-1$ corruptions is the best we can achieve based only on FHE.

Roadmap. In Sect. 3 we define our *Equivocal fully homomorphic encryption* scheme and its properties. A concrete instantiation based on the scheme of [BV11] is given in the full version. In Sect. 4 we give our construction for UC commitments and ZKPoK. Next in Sect. 5, we proceed by presenting our MPC protocol. The simulator and the security proof of our protocol can be found in the full version. In Sect. 6 we show how AMD codes can be used in order to avoid the use of ZK.

2   Notation

Throughout the paper $\lambda \in \mathbb{N}$ will denote the security parameter. We use $d \leftarrow \mathcal{D}$ to denote the process of sampling d from the distribution $\mathcal{D}$ or, if $\mathcal{D}$ is a set, a uniform choice from it. We say that a function $f : \mathbb{N} \to \mathbb{R}$ is negligible if $\forall c \; \exists n_c$

s.t. if $n > n_c$ then $f(n) < n^{-c}$. We will use negl$(\cdot)$ to denote an unspecified negligible function. We often use $[n]$ to denote the set $\{1, ..., n\}$. We write $\boxplus$ and $\boxdot$ to denote operations over encrypted data including multiplication of a ciphertext with a non encrypted string. If $\mathcal{D}_1$ and $\mathcal{D}_2$ are two distributions, then we denote that they are statistically close by $\mathcal{D}_1 \approx_s \mathcal{D}_2$; we denote that they are computationally indistinguishable by $\mathcal{D}_1 \approx_c \mathcal{D}_2$; and we denote that they are identical by $\mathcal{D}_1 \equiv \mathcal{D}_2$. For a randomized algorithm A, we use $a \leftarrow A(x; r)$ to denote running A on input x and uniformly random bits $r \in \{0,1\}^*$, producing output a.

Invertible Sampling [OPW11]: We recall the notion of invertible sampling, which is closely connected to adaptive security in simulation models where erasures are not allowed. We say that an algorithm A with input space X has invertible sampling if there exists a PPT inverting algorithm, denoted by Inv_A, such that for all input $x \in X$, the outputs of the following two experiments are either computationally, or statistically indistinguishable:

$$
\begin{array}{c|c}
y \leftarrow A(x, r) & y \leftarrow A(x, r) \\
 & r' \leftarrow \mathsf{Inv}_A(y, x) \\
\text{Return } (x, y, r) & \text{Return } (x, y, r')
\end{array}
$$

3   Equivocal Fully Homomorphic Encryption Scheme

We start by recalling the notions of (fully) homomorphic encryption. Next we define the new notion of Equivocal FHE and we specify the properties needed for such an instantiation. We give a concrete instantiation of our Equicocal FHE scheme from the LWE assumption, based on Brakerski and Vaikutanathan [BV11] FHE scheme, in the full version.

3.1   Homomorphic Encryption

A homomorphic encryption scheme $\mathsf{HE} = (\mathsf{KeyGen}, \mathsf{Enc}, \mathsf{Eval}, \mathsf{Dec})$ is a quadruple of PPT algorithms. In this work, the message space M of the encryption schemes will be some (modulo 2) ring, and the functions to be evaluated will be represented as arithmetic circuits over this ring, composed of addition and multiplication gates. The syntax of these algorithms is given as follows.

- *Key-Generation.* The algorithm KeyGen, on input the security parameter 1^λ, outputs $(\mathsf{pk}, \mathsf{sk}) \leftarrow \mathsf{KeyGen}(1^\lambda)$, where pk is a public encryption key and sk is a secret decryption key.
- *Encryption.* The algorithm Enc, on input pk and a message $m \in M$, outputs a ciphertext $\mathsf{ct} \leftarrow \mathsf{Enc}_{\mathsf{pk}}(m)$.
- *Decryption.* The algorithm Dec on input sk and a ciphertext ct, outputs a message $\tilde{m} \leftarrow \mathsf{Dec}_{\mathsf{sk}}(\mathsf{ct})$.
- *Homomorphic-Evaluation.* The algorithm Eval, on input pk, an arithmetic circuit ckt, and a tuple of ℓ ciphertexts $(\mathsf{ct}_1, \ldots, \mathsf{ct}_\ell)$, outputs a ciphertext $\mathsf{ct}' \leftarrow \mathsf{Eval}_{\mathsf{pk}}(\mathsf{ckt}(\mathsf{ct}_1, \ldots, \mathsf{ct}_\ell))$.

We note that we can treat the evaluation key as a part of the public key. The security notion needed in this work is security against chosen plaintext attacks (IND-CPA security), defined as follows.

Definition 1 (IND-CPA security). *A scheme* HE *is IND-CPA secure if for any PPT adversary* $\mathcal{A}$ *it holds that:*

$$\mathsf{Adv}_{\mathsf{HE}}^{\mathsf{CPA}}[\lambda] := |Pr[\mathcal{A}(\mathsf{pk}, \mathsf{Enc}_{\mathsf{pk}}(0)) = 1] - Pr[\mathcal{A}(\mathsf{pk}, \mathsf{Enc}_{\mathsf{pk}}(1)) = 1]| = \mathrm{negl}(\lambda),$$

where, $(\mathsf{pk}, \mathsf{sk}) \leftarrow \mathsf{KeyGen}(1^\lambda)$.

3.2 Fully Homomorphic Encryption

A scheme HE is fully homomorphic if it is both compact and homomorphic with respect to a class of circuits. More formally:

Definition 2 (Fully homomorphic encryption). *A homomorphic encryption scheme* FHE = (KeyGen, Enc, Eval, Dec) *is fully homomorphic if it satisfies the following properties:*

1. Homomorphism: *Let* $\mathcal{C} = \{\mathcal{C}_\lambda\}_{\lambda \in \mathbb{N}}$ *be the set of all polynomial sized arithmetic circuits.* $(\mathsf{sk}, \mathsf{pk}) \leftarrow \mathsf{KeyGen}(1^\lambda)$, $\forall \mathsf{ckt} \in \mathcal{C}_\lambda$, $\forall (m_1, \ldots, m_\ell) \in M^\ell$ *where* $\ell = \ell(\lambda)$, $\forall (\mathsf{ct}_1, \ldots, \mathsf{ct}_\ell)$ *where* $\mathsf{ct}_i \leftarrow \mathsf{Enc}_{\mathsf{pk}}(m_i)$, *it holds that:*

$$Pr[\mathsf{Dec}_{\mathsf{sk}}(\mathsf{Eval}_{\mathsf{pk}}(\mathsf{ckt}, \mathsf{ct}_1, \ldots, \mathsf{ct}_\ell)) \neq \mathsf{ckt}(m_1, \ldots, m_\ell)] = \mathrm{negl}(\lambda)$$

2. Compactness: *There exists a polynomial* $\mu = \mu(\lambda)$ *such that the output length of* Eval *is at most* μ *bits long regardless of the input circuit* ckt *and the number of its inputs.*

3.3 Equivocal Fully Homomorphic Encryption Scheme

Our *Equivocal fully homomorphic encryption scheme* consists of a tuple (KeyGen, KeyGen*, QEnc, Rand, Eval, Dec, Equiv) of algorithms where the syntax of the procedures (KeyGen, QEnc, Eval, Dec) is defined as in the above FHE scheme. Our scheme is augmented with two algorithms (KeyGen*, Equiv) used for equivocation. Jumping ahead, in this paper we are interested in building adaptively secure n-party protocols generically using an equivocal QFHE scheme and gain in terms of round and communication efficiency. Two extra properties needed for the MPC purpose, are distributed decryption and ciphertext randomisation where the latter one guarantees simulatable decryption[1]. If the purpose of our Equivocal scheme is not MPC then these properties are not required, see Sect. 4 for QFHE based UC commitment schemes. In the sequel, we will use blue color to stress whether a part is relevant to the ciphertext randomisation property.

---

[1] Ciphertext randomisation is needed in order to force the output in the simulation.

Definition 3 (Equivocal fully homomorphic encryption). *An Equivocal fully homomorphic encryption scheme* $\mathsf{QFHE} = (\mathsf{KeyGen}, \mathsf{KeyGen}^*, \mathsf{QEnc}, \mathsf{Rand}, \mathsf{Eval}, \mathsf{Dec}, \mathsf{Equiv})$ *with message space M is made up of the following PPT algorithms:*

- $(\mathsf{KeyGen}, \mathsf{QEnc}, \mathsf{Eval}, \mathsf{Dec})$ *is an FHE scheme with the same syntax as in Sect. 3.1.*
- *The* Equivocal *key generation algorithm* $\mathsf{KeyGen}^*(1^\lambda)$, *outputs an equivocal public-key secret-key pair* $(\widetilde{\mathsf{PK}}, \widetilde{\mathsf{SK}})$.
- *The* Equivocation *algorithm* $\mathsf{Equiv}(\widetilde{\mathsf{PK}}, \widetilde{\mathsf{SK}}, \mathrm{ct}, r_{\mathrm{ct}}, m)$, *given* $\widetilde{\mathsf{PK}}$, $\widetilde{\mathsf{SK}}$, *a plaintext m, a ciphertext ct and random coins r_{ct}, outputs a value e in the randomness space.*
- *The* Ciphertext Randomisation *algorithm* $\mathsf{Rand}(\mathrm{ct}, \mathrm{ct}'_1, \ldots, \mathrm{ct}'_n)$, *given ciphertexts $\mathrm{ct}, \mathrm{ct}'_1, \ldots, \mathrm{ct}'_n$ generated by the procedure QEnc outputs a ciphertext CT.*

We require the following properties:
  1. Indistinguishability of equivocal keys. *We say that the scheme has indistinguishability of equivocal keys if the distributions of PK and $\widetilde{\mathsf{PK}}$ are computationally indistinguishable, where $(\mathsf{PK}, \cdot) \leftarrow \mathsf{KeyGen}(1^\lambda)$ and $(\widetilde{\mathsf{PK}}, \cdot) \leftarrow \mathsf{KeyGen}^*(1^\lambda)$.*
  2. Indistinguishability of equivocation. *Let $\mathcal{D}_{rand}(1^\lambda)$ denote the distribution of randomness used by QEnc. Let $\mathcal{O}(\widetilde{\mathsf{PK}}, m)$ and $\mathcal{O}'(\widetilde{\mathsf{PK}}, \widetilde{\mathsf{SK}}, m)$ be the following oracles:*

Let $\mathcal{O}(\widetilde{\mathsf{PK}}, m):$	Let $\mathcal{O}'(\widetilde{\mathsf{PK}}, \widetilde{\mathsf{SK}}, m):$
$r_{\mathrm{ct}} \leftarrow \mathcal{D}_{rand}(1^\lambda)$	$r_{\mathrm{ct}} \leftarrow \mathcal{D}_{rand}(1^\lambda)$
$\mathrm{ct} = \mathsf{QEnc}_{\widetilde{\mathsf{PK}}}, (m; r_{\mathrm{ct}})$	$\mathrm{ct} = \mathsf{QEnc}_{\widetilde{\mathsf{PK}}}(\widetilde{m}; r_{\mathrm{ct}})$
	$e = \mathsf{Equiv}(\widetilde{\mathsf{PK}}, \widetilde{\mathsf{SK}}, \mathrm{ct}, r_{\mathrm{ct}}, m)$
Output $(\widetilde{\mathsf{PK}}, \mathrm{ct}, r_{\mathrm{ct}})$	Output $(\widetilde{\mathsf{PK}}, \mathrm{ct}, e)$

There exists $\widetilde{m} \in M$ such that for any PPT adversary $\mathcal{A}$ with oracle access to $\mathcal{O}(\widetilde{\mathsf{PK}}, \cdot)$ and $\mathcal{O}'(\widetilde{\mathsf{PK}}, \widetilde{\mathsf{SK}}, \cdot)$ the following holds.

$$\left| \Pr \left[\begin{array}{l} (\widetilde{\mathsf{PK}}, \widetilde{\mathsf{SK}}) \leftarrow \mathsf{KeyGen}^*(1^\lambda) \\ 1 \leftarrow \mathcal{A}^{\mathcal{O}(\widetilde{\mathsf{PK}}, \cdot)} \end{array} \right] - \Pr \left[\begin{array}{l} (\widetilde{\mathsf{PK}}, \widetilde{\mathsf{SK}}) \leftarrow \mathsf{KeyGen}^*(1^\lambda) \\ 1 \leftarrow \mathcal{A}^{\mathcal{O}'(\widetilde{\mathsf{PK}}, \widetilde{\mathsf{SK}}, \cdot)} \end{array} \right] \right| \leq \mathrm{negl}(\lambda)$$

  3. <u>Ciphertext Randomisation.</u> *Let PK be the public key used in the procedure QEnc for generating ciphertexts $\mathrm{ct}, \mathrm{ct}'_1 \ldots \mathrm{ct}'_n$ from the plaintexts $m, m'_1, \ldots, m'_n \in M$, respectevely. If $Pr[\mathsf{Dec}_{\mathsf{sk}}(\mathrm{ct}) = m] = 1 - \mathrm{negl}(\lambda)$ and for all $i \in [n]$, $Pr[\mathsf{Dec}_{\mathsf{sk}}(\mathrm{ct}'_i) = m'_i] = 1 - \mathrm{negl}(\lambda)$ then it holds that*
$$Pr[\mathsf{Dec}_{\mathsf{sk}}(\mathsf{Rand}(\mathrm{ct}, \mathrm{ct}'_1 \ldots \mathrm{ct}'_n)) = m] = 1 - \mathrm{negl}(\lambda).$$

On the other hand, let $\widetilde{\mathsf{PK}}$ be the public key used in the procedure QEnc for generating ciphertexts $\mathrm{ct}, \mathrm{ct}'_1 \ldots \mathrm{ct}'_n$, respectevely. If $Pr[\mathsf{Dec}_{\mathsf{sk}}(\mathrm{ct}) = m] = 1 - \mathrm{negl}(\lambda)$ and for all $i \in [n]$, $Pr[\mathsf{Dec}_{\mathsf{sk}}(\mathrm{ct}'_i) = m'_i] = 1 - \mathrm{negl}(\lambda)$ then it holds that
$$Pr[\mathsf{Dec}_{\mathsf{sk}}(\mathsf{Rand}(\mathrm{ct}, \mathrm{ct}'_1 \ldots \mathrm{ct}'_n)) = m'_1 + \ldots + m'_n] = 1 - \mathrm{negl}(\lambda).$$

In the sequel for simplicity of exposition, we call the ciphertexts $ct_1' \ldots ct_n'$ **redundant** in case they are generated by $QEnc_{PK}$ and $\mathbf{non-redundant}$ if they are generated by $QEnc_{\widetilde{PK}}$. Analogously, we call the ciphetext ct $\mathbf{non-redundant}$ or **redundant** if it is generated by $QEnc_{PK}$ or $QEnc_{\widetilde{PK}}$, respectively[2].

In order to construct our equivocal QFHE scheme we use the following *special* FHE scheme with some additional properties.

Definition 4. *[Special fully homomorphic encryption] We call a fully homomorphic encryption scheme* $FHE = (KeyGen, Enc, Eval, Dec)$ *a special FHE scheme, if it is IND-CPA secure and satisfies the following properties: Let* $\mathcal{D}_{rand}(1^\lambda)$ *denote the distribution of randomness used by* Enc.

1. Additive homomorphism over random coins: $\forall r_1, r_2 \in \mathsf{Supp}(\mathcal{D}_{rand}(1^\lambda))$ and $\forall m \in M$, it holds that $\big(m \boxdot \mathsf{Enc}_{pk}(0; r_1)\big) \boxplus \mathsf{Enc}_{pk}(0; r_2) = \mathsf{Enc}_{pk}(0; m \cdot r_1 + r_2)$.
2. E-Hiding: There exists $\mathcal{D}'_{rand}(1^\lambda)$ such that $\forall m \in M$, if $r^{blind} \leftarrow \mathcal{D}_{rand}(1^\lambda)$ and $r^K \leftarrow \mathcal{D}'_{rand}(1^\lambda)$ then the distribution of $(r^{blind} - m \cdot r^K)$ is statistically close to $\mathcal{D}_{rand}(1^\lambda)$.[3]
3. Invertible Sampling: The distribution $\mathcal{D}_{rand}(1^\lambda)$, has invertible sampling via the algorithm $\mathsf{Inv}_{\mathcal{D}_{rand}}$.

Recall that we defined an invertible sampler of an algorithm A in Sect. 2 as an algorithm Inv_A that takes as inputs the input x and output y with consistent random coins. In our case, $x = 1^\lambda$ and y is a sample from the range of $\mathcal{D}_{rand}$. Next, in Fig. 1, we show how to build an equivocal FHE scheme using a special FHE scheme. The high level intuition is as follows. In order to achieve equivocality we modify an FHE scheme satisfying the properties of Definition 4 as follows: The public key contains an encryption of 1 and an encryption of 0. More specifically, $PK = (pk, K = \mathsf{Enc}_{pk}(1), R = \mathsf{Enc}_{pk}(0))$ where pk is the public key of an FHE scheme. An encryption of a message m in the real world is computed using K as $(m \boxdot K \boxplus \mathsf{Enc}_{pk}(0))$ and encryption for re-randomisation is computed using R as $(z \boxdot R \boxplus \mathsf{Enc}_{pk}(0))$ for a random value z. In the simulation, the values encrypted in K and R are switched, in particular, $K = \mathsf{Enc}_{pk}(0)$ and $R = \mathsf{Enc}_{pk}(1)$. Therefore, normal encryption leads to encryption of 0 with the guarantee of equivocation. However, encryption for re-randomisation actually encrypts non-zero values i.e., z, in order to force the output.

Theorem 3. *Let* FHE *be a special fully homomorphic encryption scheme. Then* $QFHE = (KeyGen, KeyGen^*, QEnc, Rand, Eval, Dec, Equiv)$ *in Fig. 1 is an equivocal QFHE scheme.*

---

[2] By the ciphertext randomisation property, the reader can think of the **redundant** messages as encryptions of zeros.

[3] Intuitively, E-Hiding can be argued in the same way as formula privacy for some FHE schemes. This requires *dwarfing* in the sense that r^{blind} should be *large* enough to dwarf mr^K where $\mathcal{D}_{rand}(1^\lambda)$ and $\mathcal{D}'_{rand}(1^\lambda)$ are Gaussian distributions. Hence, $r^K \leftarrow \mathcal{D}'_{rand}(1^\lambda)$ and $r^{blind} \leftarrow \mathcal{D}_{rand}(1^\lambda)$ such that the noise of $\mathcal{D}_{rand}(1^\lambda)$ is super-polynomially larger than the noise of $\mathcal{D}'_{rand}(1^\lambda)$.

QFHE

Let $\mathsf{FHE} = (\mathsf{KeyGen}_{\mathsf{FHE}}, \mathsf{Enc}, \mathsf{Eval}, \mathsf{Dec})$ be a *special* fully homomorphic encryption scheme. $\mathsf{QFHE} = (\mathsf{KeyGen}, \mathsf{KeyGen}^*, \mathsf{QEnc}, \mathsf{Eval}, \mathsf{Rand}, \mathsf{Dec}, \mathsf{Equiv})$ is defined as follows:

$\mathsf{KeyGen}(1^\lambda)$:

1. $(\mathsf{pk}, \mathsf{sk}) \leftarrow \mathsf{KeyGen}_{\mathsf{FHE}}(1^\lambda)$.
2. $K = \mathsf{Enc}_{\mathsf{pk}}(1; r^K)$ where $r^K \leftarrow \mathcal{D}'_{rand}(1^\lambda)$ and $R = \mathsf{Enc}_{\mathsf{pk}}(0; r^R)$ where $r^R \leftarrow \mathcal{D}'_{rand}(1^\lambda)$
3. Return as public key $\mathsf{PK} = (\mathsf{pk}, K, R)$ and secret key $\mathsf{SK} = \mathsf{sk}$.[a]

$\mathsf{KeyGen}^*(1^\lambda)$:

1. $(\mathsf{pk}, \mathsf{sk}) \leftarrow \mathsf{KeyGen}_{\mathsf{FHE}}(1^\lambda)$.
2. $\widetilde{K} = \mathsf{Enc}_{\mathsf{pk}}(0; r^{\widetilde{K}})$ where $r^{\widetilde{K}} \leftarrow \mathcal{D}'_{rand}(1^\lambda)$ and $\widetilde{R} = \mathsf{Enc}_{\mathsf{pk}}(1; r^{\widetilde{R}})$ where $r^{\widetilde{R}} \leftarrow \mathcal{D}'_{rand}(1^\lambda)$.
3. Return as public key $\widetilde{\mathsf{PK}} = (\mathsf{pk}, \widetilde{K}, \widetilde{R})$ and secret key $\widetilde{\mathsf{SK}} = (\mathsf{sk}, r^{\widetilde{K}}, r^{\widetilde{R}})$.

$\mathsf{QEnc}_{\mathsf{PK}}(b, m)$:

1. Compute $\mathsf{ct}^{\mathsf{blind}} = \mathsf{Enc}_{\mathsf{pk}}(0; r^{\mathsf{blind}})$ where $r^{\mathsf{blind}} \leftarrow \mathcal{D}_{rand}(1^\lambda)$.
2. If $b \notin \{0, 1\}$ then output $\perp$.
3. If $b = 0$ then output $\mathsf{ct} = (m \boxdot K) \boxplus \mathsf{ct}^{\mathsf{blind}}$ *otherwise* output $\mathsf{ct} = (m \boxdot R) \boxplus \mathsf{ct}^{\mathsf{blind}}$.

$\mathsf{QEnc}_{\widetilde{\mathsf{PK}}}(b, \widetilde{m})$:

1. Compute $\widetilde{\mathsf{ct}}^{\mathsf{blind}} = \mathsf{Enc}_{\mathsf{pk}}(0; \widetilde{r}^{\mathsf{blind}})$ where $\widetilde{r}^{\mathsf{blind}} \leftarrow \mathcal{D}_{rand}(1^\lambda)$.
2. If $b \notin \{0, 1\}$ then output $\perp$.
3. If $b = 0$ then output $\widetilde{\mathsf{ct}} = (\widetilde{m} \boxdot \widetilde{K}) \boxplus \widetilde{\mathsf{ct}}^{\mathsf{blind}}$ *otherwise* output $\widetilde{\mathsf{ct}} = (\widetilde{m} \boxdot \widetilde{R}) \boxplus \widetilde{\mathsf{ct}}^{\mathsf{blind}}$.

$\mathsf{Equiv}(b, \widetilde{\mathsf{PK}}, \widetilde{\mathsf{SK}}, \widetilde{\mathsf{ct}}, \widetilde{r}^{\mathsf{blind}}, m, \widetilde{m})$:

1. If $b = 0$ compute $r^{\mathsf{blind}} := \widetilde{r}^{\mathsf{blind}} + (\widetilde{m} - m) \cdot r^{\widetilde{K}}$ *otherwise* $r^{\mathsf{blind}} := \widetilde{r}^{\mathsf{blind}} + (\widetilde{m} - m) \cdot r^{\widetilde{R}}$
2. Run $r_{state} \leftarrow \mathsf{Inv}_{\mathcal{D}_{rand}}(r^{\mathsf{blind}})$ and output r_{state}.

$\mathsf{Rand}(\mathsf{ct}, \mathsf{ct}'_1 \ldots, \mathsf{ct}'_n)$: Output $\mathsf{CT} = \mathsf{ct} \boxplus \mathsf{ct}'_1 \boxplus \ldots \boxplus \mathsf{ct}'_n$.

Procedures $(\mathsf{Eval}, \mathsf{Dec})$ are as defined in normal FHE schemes.

---

[a] Note that procedure Dec, given sk, runs as in normal FHE schemes (see Section 3.1), so there is no need to provide r^K in SK. We also enhance the notation of QEnc to include a bit b which indicates whether the encryption is performed using the key K or R, respectively. In addition, the plaintext $\widetilde{m}$ is usually set to zero.

Fig. 1. Description of QFHE scheme

Proof. Indistinguishability of equivocal keys. Let $(\mathsf{PK}, \mathsf{SK}) \leftarrow \mathsf{KeyGen}(1^\lambda)$ and $(\widetilde{\mathsf{PK}}, \widetilde{\mathsf{SK}}) \leftarrow \mathsf{KeyGen}^*(1^\lambda)$, then the indistinguishability of the two pairs of public keys follows from the IND-CPA security of the FHE scheme.

Indistinguishability of equivocation. Without loss of generality, we will show that indistinguishability of equivocation holds for $\tilde{m} = 0$. Let $\mathcal{A}$ be an adversary that breaks indistinguishability of equivocation; then we construct a PPT algorithm R such that $R^{\mathcal{A}}$ breaks *E-hiding*. R simulates the oracle for every query m_i as follows. R invokes $\mathcal{A}$ and receives some message m_i and forwards it to the *E-hiding* challenger. Next it receives the challenge r_{ct_i} and computes $\text{ct}_i = \text{QEnc}_{\widetilde{\text{PK}}}(0, m_i; r_{\text{ct}_i})$ and forwards $(r_{\text{ct}_i}, \text{ct}_i)$ to $\mathcal{A}$ and outputs whatever $\mathcal{A}$ does. Now, if $r_{\text{ct}_i} \leftarrow \mathcal{D}_{rand}(1^\lambda)$ then $\text{ct}_i \leftarrow \text{QEnc}_{\widetilde{\text{PK}}}(0, m_i; r_{\text{ct}_i})$, namely, the view of $\mathcal{A}$ follows the distribution which corresponds to the left game in Definition 3 of indistinguishability of equivocation. On the other hand, if $r_{\text{ct}_i} = (r_i^{blind} - m_i \cdot r^{\widetilde{K}})$; then $\text{ct}_i = (m_i \boxdot \widetilde{K}) \boxplus \text{Enc}_{\text{pk}}(0; r_i^{blind} - m_i \cdot r^{\widetilde{K}}) = \text{Enc}_{\text{pk}}(0; r_i^{blind}) = \text{QEnc}_{\widetilde{\text{PK}}}(0, 0; r_i^{blind})$ which implies that in this case the view of $\mathcal{A}$ follows the distribution of the right game in Definition 3 of indistinguishability of equivocation. This means that the distinguishing advantage of R is the same as that of $\mathcal{A}$ which leads to a contradiction.

Ciphertext Randomisation. The algorithm Rand adds the ciphertexts $(\text{ct}, \text{ct}_1', \ldots, \text{ct}_n')$. If ct is a ciphertext generated by QEnc_{PK} for $b = 0$ and $(\text{ct}_1' \ldots \text{ct}_n')$ are ciphertexts generated by QEnc_{PK} for $b = 1$ then

$$Pr[\text{Dec}_{\text{sk}}(\text{Rand}(\text{ct}, \text{ct}_1' \ldots \text{ct}_n')) = m] = 1 - \text{negl}(\lambda)$$

since it is easy to see that the ciphertexts $(\text{ct}_1' \ldots \text{ct}_n')$ contain encryptions of zeros due to the fact that $R = \text{Enc}_{\text{pk}}(0)$. An analogous argument holds for ct and $\text{ct}_1' \ldots \text{ct}_n'$ generated by $\text{QEnc}_{\widetilde{\text{PK}}}$ for $b = 0$ and $b = 1$, respectively, since in this case the ciphertext ct contain an encryption of a zero (because in this case $\widetilde{K} = \text{Enc}_{\text{pk}}(0)$) and ciphertexts $(\text{ct}_1' \ldots \text{ct}_n')$ contain encryptions of the corresponding m_i' since $\widetilde{R} = \text{Enc}_{\text{pk}}(1)$.

$\square$

Distributed Decryption: As we mentioned above, we need distributed decryption to implement our MPC protocol. To this end, we assume that the common public key pk has been set up where the secret key sk has been secret-shared among the players in such a way that they can collaborate to decrypt. Notice that some setup assumption is always required to show UC security in the dishonest majority setting. Roughly, we assume that a functionality is available which generates a key pair and secret-shares the secret key among the players using a secret-sharing scheme that is assumed to be given as part of the specification of the cryptosystem. Since we allow corruption of all but one player, the maximal unqualified sets must be all sets of $n - 1$ players. We point out that we could make a weaker set-up assumption, such as a common reference string, and using a general UC secure multiparty computation protocol for the common reference string model to implement the above functionality. While this may not be very efficient, one only needs to run this protocol once in the life-time of the system. The properties needed for the distributed decryption and its protocol are specified later.

4   UC Adaptive Commitments and ZKPoK from LWE

Commitment schemes that satisfy both equivocality and extractability form useful tools in achieving adaptive security. In this section, we show how using a QFHE scheme, one can build equivocal and extractable commitments. Having realized a QFHE scheme based on the LWE assumption, we consequently get equivocal and extractable commitments assuming the hardness of LWE. Note that such commitments based on LWE can be of independent interest. We remark that any encryption scheme that satisfies the properties specified in Definition 4 would have sufficed for our purposes in this section – the multiplicative homomorphic property of our QFHE scheme will not be of use here; however, since we are using our commitment scheme as a tool in our adaptive MPC protocol based on LWE, we use the same QFHE scheme in our commitment scheme too.

Since we are interested in UC security against adaptive adversaries, our commitment scheme is in the CRS model. The scheme must satisfy the following two properties, polynomial equivocality and simulation extractability. The former guarantees that the simulator S needs to be able to produce polynomially many equivocal commitments using the same CRS. More specifically, S can open the equivocal commitments to any value of its choice and give consistent randomness to adversary A. The latter property says that the simulator S needs to be able to extract the contents of any valid commitment generated by adversary A, even after A obtains polynomially many equivocal commitments generated by S. Note that there is only an apparent conflict between equivocality and the binding property and between the extractability and the hiding property, as the simulator is endowed with additional power (trapdoors) in comparison with the parties in the real world execution. In the following we elaborate how our commitment scheme satisfies the above properties.

Our Construction. Equivocation in our scheme is achieved via QFHE. In particular, the commitment algorithm is the algorithm QEnc, defined in Fig. 1. In order to add extractability we must enhance our scheme in such a way that we do not sacrifice equivocality. A failed attempt is to include a public key for an encryption scheme secure against CCA2 attacks in the CRS. In this case, the committer will send an encryption of the decommitment information along with the commitment itself. Then, as the simulator has the associated decryption key, it can decrypt the decommitment information and hence extract the committed value from any adversarially prepared commitment. However, notice that such an encryption is binding even to the simulator, so equivocality cannot be achieved.

The solution to the problem is to send the commitment along with two pseudorandom ciphertexts. One ciphertext is an encryption of the decommitment information and the other ciphertext is a uniformly random string. In this way, the simulator can encrypt both decommitment values and later show that it only knows the decryption to one and that the other was uniformly chosen.

For the security of our construction, the encryption scheme used to encrypt the decommitment information has to be a CCA2-secure encryption scheme with the property that any produced ciphertext is pseudorandom and has deterministic decryption. To this end, the CCA2 encryption scheme of Micciancio and Peikert [MP12] based on LWE satisfies the above properties. They obtain their result via relatively generic assumptions using either strongly unforgeable one-time signatures [DDN00], or a message authentication code and a weak form of commitment [BCHK07]. The first assumption does not yield pseudorandom ciphertexts, thus another encryption producing pseudorandom ciphertexts on top of the scheme of [MP12] could have been used, resulting in a double encryption scheme. However, it turns out that their construction with the latter set of assumptions has pseudorandom ciphertexts.

The reader might have observed that this bears some resemblance with the trick used in the seminal work of [CLOS02], referred to as CLOS hereafter, to achieve extractability. Their scheme is based on enhanced trapdoor permutations, also needed in order to get double encryption CCA2 security. Moreover, in order to build equivocal commitments they need an NP reduction to graph Hamiltonicity since the CRS of their commitment scheme consists of a graph G sampled from a distribution such that it is computationally hard to tell if G has a Hamiltonian cycle. Interestingly, the CLOS commitment scheme does not give an instantiation based on LWE and to begin with, there are no known trapdoor permutations based on LWE. On the other hand, assuming the hardness of LWE, we propose an extractable and equivocal commitment *with no need of an NP reduction*, leading to a huge improvement in efficiency.

More formally, given a $\mathsf{QFHE} = (\mathsf{KeyGen}, \mathsf{KeyGen}^*, \mathsf{QEnc}, \mathsf{Eval}, \mathsf{Dec}, \mathsf{Equiv})$[4] scheme, a CCA2-secure scheme $\mathsf{E_{CCA}}$ with encryption algorithm $\mathsf{ENC_{CCA}}$ based on LWE [MP12], with the property that any ciphertext is pseudorandom and has deterministic decryption, we construct the following equivocal and extractable UC bit-commitment scheme Π_{COM}. For simplicity of exposition, we will use $\mathsf{E_{CCA}}$ in a black box manner. We note that the scheme naturally extends to a setting where commitments are defined over strings instead of just bits.

Common Reference String: The CRS consists of the public key (PK) of the QFHE scheme and the public key for the encryption scheme $\mathsf{ENC_{CCA}}$.

Commit Phase:

1. On input (Commit, $sid, ssid, P_i, P_j, b$) where $b \in \{0,1\}$, party P_i computes $z = \mathsf{QEnc_{PK}}(b; r)$ where $r \leftarrow \mathcal{D}_{rand}(1^\lambda)$. Next, P_i computes $C_b = \mathsf{ENC_{CCA}}(P_i, P_j, sid, ssid, r; s)$ using random coins s, and sets C_{1-b} to a random string of length $|C_b|$. Then, P_i records $(sid, ssid, P_j, r, s, b)$, and sends $c = (sid, ssid, P_i, z, C_0, C_1)$ to P_j.
2. P_j receives and records c, and outputs (Receipt, $sid, ssid, P_i, P_j$). P_j ignores any later commit messages from P_i with the same $(sid, ssid)$.

Reveal Phase:

1. On input (Reveal, $sid, ssid$), party P_i retrieves $(sid, ssid, P_j, r, s, b)$ and sends $(sid, ssid, r, s, b)$ to P_j.

---

[4] Algorithms $\mathsf{QEnc'}$, Rand are not necessary for the construction of UC Commitments.

2. Upon receiving $(sid, ssid, r, s, b)$ from P_i, P_j checks that it has a tuple $(sid, ssid, P_i, z, C_0, C_1)$. If yes, then it checks that $z = \mathsf{QEnc_{PK}}(b; r)$ and that $C_b = \mathsf{ENC_{CCA}}(P_i, P_j, sid, ssid, r; s)$. If both these checks succeed, then P_j outputs (Reveal, $sid, ssid, P_i, P_j, b$). Otherwise, it ignores the message.

Proposition 1. *Assuming hardness of LWE, Protocol* Π_{COM} *UC realizes* $\mathcal{F}_{\mathrm{MCOM}}$ *in the* $\mathcal{F}_{\mathrm{CRS}}$*-hybrid model.*

The above commitment scheme UC realizes the multi-session ideal commitment functionality $\mathcal{F}_{\mathrm{MCOM}}$, described in Fig. 2, which reuses the public string for multiple commitments. The proof can be found in the full version. Next, we show how our UC commitment scheme serves towards the realization of a commit-and-prove functionality $\mathcal{F}_{\mathrm{COM-ZK}}$ based on LWE.

Functionality $\mathcal{F}_{\mathrm{MCOM}}$

The functionality $\mathcal{F}_{\mathrm{MCOM}}$ runs with parties $P_1, \ldots, P_n$ and an adversary $\mathcal{S}$. It proceeds as follows:

Commit Phase:

Upon receiving a message (Commit, $sid, ssid, P_i, P_j, b$) from Pi, where $b \in \{0, 1\}$, record the tuple $(ssid, P_i, P_j, b)$ and send the message (Receipt, $sid, ssid, P_i, P_j$) to P_j and $\mathcal{S}$. Ignore any future commit messages with the same ssid from P_i to P_j.

Prove Phase:

Upon receiving a message (Reveal, $sid, ssid$) from P_i: If a tuple $(ssid, P_i, P_j, b)$ was previously recorded, then send the message (Reveal, $sid, ssid, P_i, P_j, b$) to Pj and $\mathcal{S}$. Otherwise, ignore.

Fig. 2. The ideal functionality $\mathcal{F}_{\mathrm{MCOM}}$.

4.1 Adaptive UC ZKPoK from LWE

Our UC commitment scheme serves towards the realization of a commit-and-prove functionality $\mathcal{F}_{\mathrm{COM-ZK}}$ based on LWE. Such a functionality is generic and hence is quite useful – it allows a party to prove NP statements relative to its commitment value in the setting where parties commit to their inputs but they never decommit. The functionality $\mathcal{F}_{\mathrm{COM-ZK}}$ is presented in Fig. 3 and is comprised of two phases. In the first phase, a party commits to a specific value. In the second phase, this party proves NP statements in zero-knowledge relative to the committed value. It allows the committer to commit to multiple secret values w_i, and then have the relation $\mathcal{R}$ depend on all these values in a single proof. In addition, the committer may ask to prove multiple statements with respect to the same set of secret values. Hence, once a committer gives a new (Commit, sid, w) command, $\mathcal{F}_{\mathrm{COM-ZK}}$ adds the current w to the already existing list $\overline{w}$ of committed values. Then, on receiving a (Proof, $sid, \mathcal{R}, x$) request, $\mathcal{F}_{\mathrm{COM-ZK}}$ evaluates $\mathcal{R}$ on x and the current list $\overline{w}$.

Functionality $\mathcal{F}_{\text{COM-ZK}}$

The functionality $\mathcal{F}_{\text{COM-ZK}}$ runs with parties $P_1, \ldots, P_n$ and an adversary $\mathcal{S}$. It proceeds as follows:

Commit Phase:

Upon receiving a message $(\text{Commit}, sid, cid, \mathcal{P}, w)^a$ from P_i where $\mathcal{P}$ is a set of parties and $w \in \{0,1\}^*$, append the value w to the existing list $\overline{w}$, record $\mathcal{P}$, and send the message $(\text{Receipt}, sid, cid, P_i, \mathcal{P})$ to the parties in $\mathcal{P}$ and $\mathcal{S}$. (Initially, the list $\overline{w}$ is empty. Also, if a commit message has already been received, then check that the recorded set of parties is $\mathcal{P}$. If it is a different set, then ignore this message.)

Prove Phase:

Upon receiving a message $(\text{Prover}, sid, \mathcal{R}, x)$ from P_i, where $x \in \{0,1\}^{poly(k)}$, compute $\mathcal{R}(x, w)$: If $\mathcal{R}(x, w) = 1$, then send the message $(\text{Proof}, sid, \mathcal{R}, x)$ to the parties in $\mathcal{P}$ and $\mathcal{S}$. Otherwise, ignore.

---

^{a} Note that in the protocol we use one command for two cid's. In particular we use cid_1 to commit to the encrypted value and cid_2 to commit to the randomness used for the corresponding encryption

---

Fig. 3. Ideal functionality $\mathcal{F}_{\text{COM-ZK}}$.

Using the power of the UC commitment scheme we constructed in Sect. 4, we show how it can be used to first construct UC Zero-Knowledge protocols from LWE. Canetti and Fischlin [CF01, Theorem 5], show that in the $\mathcal{F}_{\text{COM}}$-hybrid model there exists a 3-round protocol that securely realizes $\mathcal{F}_{\text{ZK}}$ with respect to any NP relation without any computational assumptions. Using the composition theorem and [CF01, Theorem 5], we can instantate $\mathcal{F}_{\text{COM}}$ with the UC commitment protocol from LWE (see Sect. 4) in the CRS model and realize $\mathcal{F}_{\text{ZK}}$ from LWE. Also, as it is noted by [CF01] we can replace $\mathcal{F}_{\text{COM}}$ by the functionality $\mathcal{F}_{\text{MCOM}}$.

We next obtain a protocol for UC realizing functionality $\mathcal{F}_{\text{COM-ZK}}$ in the $\mathcal{F}_{\text{ZK}}$-hybrid model, in the presence of adaptive adversaries. In [CLOS02, Proposition 7.2], a protocol for UC realizing $\mathcal{F}_{\text{COM-ZK}}$ in the $\mathcal{F}_{\text{ZK}}$-hybrid model, based on any one-way function is proposed. To guarantee security against adaptive adversaries, they need equivocal and extractable commitments which they instantiate assuming the existence of enhanced trapdoor permutations. Using [CLOS02, Proposition 7.2] we can get such an instantiation assuming the hardness of LWE via our extractable and equivocal commitment scheme described above and instantiation of the $\mathcal{F}_{\text{ZK}}$ functionality from LWE.

5   Our Protocol

Since we established all the primitives needed we are ready to present our MPC protocol. Our protocol is based on any equivocal QFHE scheme which comes together with a statistically secure distributed function sharing scheme. In addition, the protocol assumes access to the $\mathcal{F}_{\text{COM-ZK}}$ functionality which we build from any equivocal QFHE, see Sect. 4. In Fig. 4 we describe our protocol Π_{MPC} realizing the functionality $\mathcal{F}_{\text{AMPC}}$ in Fig. 6, in the $(\mathcal{F}_{\text{BROADCAST}}, \mathcal{F}_{\text{KEY-DIST}}, \mathcal{F}_{\text{COM-ZK}})$-hybrid model. The functionality $\mathcal{F}_{\text{KEY-DIST}}$ is described in Fig. 5 and the functionality $\mathcal{F}_{\text{COM-ZK}}$ is described in Fig. 3.

During the Load phase, players encrypt their inputs x_i under a common public key PK and give a ZKPoK. In the evaluation phase, players evaluate the desired function locally and obtain the ciphertext $\text{enc}(z)$. In the output phase they jointly decrypt the result calling the decryption protocol Π_{DDEC} together with the ciphertext randomisation technique as is abstracted by the algorithm Rand of the QFHE, see Sect. 3.

In the protocol Π_{DDEC} parties use ZK to prove that their evaluation shares are correct. However, as discussed in the introduction we optimise the output phase avoiding the expensive use of ZK proofs to prove that the player's evaluation shares to the decryption protocol are correct, changing the evaluation phase of the protocol and avoiding the ZK proofs. For details see Sect. 6.

5.1 Distributed Function Evaluation

In order to achieve distributed decryption, we assume, as a set up assumption, that a common public key pk has been set up where the secret key sk has been secret-shared between n parties in such a way that they can compute their corresponding decryption evaluation shares and then collaborate to decrypt while the sk is kept secret. We also need to enforce honest computation of the evaluation shares of a ciphertext. Commitments to the shares of the secret key are also made public, along with pk. Using these commitments, when parties are distributedly decrypting a ciphertext, they can then prove (via $\mathcal{F}_{\text{COM-ZK}}$) that the evaluation shares were computed honestly using the secret-key shares initially delegated to them.

To this end, the functionality $\mathcal{F}_{\text{KEY-DIST}}$ generates a key pair (pk, sk)[5] and secret-shares the secret key sk among the players using a secret-sharing scheme that is assumed to be given as part of the specification of the cryptosystem. The validity of the evaluation shares is tested inside the protocol Π_{DDEC} calling the functionality $\mathcal{F}_{\text{COM-ZK}}$. In order to describe our protocol Π_{DDEC}, we next define the following distributed sharing scheme.

Definition 5. *We call* (ShareSK, ShareEval, Combine) *a distributed function sharing scheme for an encryption scheme* $(\text{KeyGen}_{\text{FHE}}, \text{Enc}, \text{Dec})$, *with construction threshold* c *and privacy threshold* t, *if for a triple* (ShareSK, ShareEval, Combine) *of PPT algorithms the following hold:*

Key sharing: *The algorithm* ShareSK *on input* $(\text{pk}, \text{sk}) \leftarrow \text{KeyGen}_{\text{FHE}}(1^\lambda)$ *and a construction threshold* c, *outputs a tuple* $(\text{sk}_1, \ldots, \text{sk}_n) \leftarrow \text{ShareSK}(\text{sk})$.

---

[5] In the description of our protocol we choose to explicitly refer to the keys (pk, sk) since it helps in the description of the decryption protocol.

Protocol Π_{MPC}

Protocol Π_{MPC} uses an equivocal $\mathsf{QFHE} = (\mathsf{KeyGen}, \mathsf{KeyGen}^*, \mathsf{QEnc}, \mathsf{Rand}, \mathsf{Eval}, \mathsf{Dec}, \mathsf{Equiv})$ scheme and runs in the $(\mathcal{F}_{\text{BROADCAST}}{}^a, \mathcal{F}_{\text{KEY-DIST}}, \mathcal{F}_{\text{COM-ZK}})$-hybrid model with parties $(P_1, \ldots, P_n)$. It proceeds as follows:

Initialize:

On input $(\mathsf{init}, 1^\lambda)$ from all parties, invoke the functionalities $\mathcal{F}_{\text{BROADCAST}}$, $\mathcal{F}_{\text{KEY-DIST}}$ and $\mathcal{F}_{\text{COM-ZK}}$. The invocation of $\mathcal{F}_{\text{KEY-DIST}}$ results in every party P_i receiving $\big((\mathsf{PK}, c_1, \ldots, c_n), (\mathsf{sk}_i, r_i)\big)$.

Load:

To encrypt its input x_i, P_i does the following:
- P_i computes $X_i = \mathsf{QEnc}_{\mathsf{PK}}(0, x_i; r_{x_i})$, where $r_{x_i} \leftarrow \mathcal{D}_{rand}(1^\lambda)$, and broadcasts X_i via $\mathcal{F}_{\text{BROADCAST}}$.
- For $i \neq j$, P_i sends $(\mathsf{Commit}, sid, cid_1, cid_2, P_i, P_j, x_i, r_{x_i})$ to $\mathcal{F}_{\text{COM-ZK}}$. At this point all other parties P_j receive message $(\mathsf{Receipt}, sid, cid_1, cid_2, P_i, P_j)$ from $\mathcal{F}_{\text{COM-ZK}}$.
- For $j \neq i$, P_i sends $(\mathsf{Prover}, sid, (cid_1, cid_2), \mathcal{R}_{eq}, X_i)$ to $\mathcal{F}_{\text{COM-ZK}}$ for the relation

$$\mathcal{R}_{eq} = \{((\mathsf{PK}, X_i), (x_i, r_{x_i})) : X_i = \mathsf{QEnc}_{\mathsf{PK}}(0, x_i; r_{x_i})\}$$

whereupon P_j receives $(\mathsf{Proof}, sid, P_i, \mathcal{R}_{eq}, (\mathsf{PK}, X_i))$.
- If all the proofs are accepted then the parties define $\mathsf{enc}(x_i) = X_i$, otherwise output $\perp$.

Evaluation Phase:

Let ckt be the arithmetic circuit to be computed on inputs $(x_1, \ldots, x_n)$ by n parties. Every party executes the deterministic algorithm Eval and obtains $\mathsf{enc}(z) \leftarrow \mathsf{Eval}_{\mathsf{pk}}(\mathsf{ckt}, \mathsf{enc}(x_1), \ldots, \mathsf{enc}(x_n))$.

Output Phase:

- P_i generates $y_i \leftarrow \mathcal{D}_{rand}(1^\lambda)$ and **Load**s it into variable $\mathsf{enc}(y_i)$ via $\mathsf{QEnc}_{\mathsf{PK}}$ for $b = 0$. Let cid_1 and cid_2 be the identifiers of the commitment phase of this **Load**.
- P_i computes $\widetilde{\mathsf{enc}(y_i)} = \mathsf{QEnc}_{\mathsf{PK}}(1, y_i; \tilde{r}_{y_i})$, where $\tilde{r}_{y_i} \leftarrow \mathcal{D}_{rand}(1^\lambda)$, and broadcasts $\widetilde{\mathsf{enc}(y_i)}$ via $\mathcal{F}_{\text{BROADCAST}}$.
  Next, for $j \neq i$ party P_i sends $(\mathsf{Commit}, sid, cid_3, P_i, P_j, \tilde{r}_{y_i})$ to $\mathcal{F}_{\text{COM-ZK}}$ and $(\mathsf{Prover}, sid, (cid_1, cid_3), \mathcal{R}_{eq}, \widetilde{\mathsf{enc}(y_i)})$ to $\mathcal{F}_{\text{COM-ZK}}$, where cid_1 is the identifier of the commitment phase of the **Load** of the above Step 1, where P_i commits to y_i.
- Let J be the set of indices of P_j's having defined $\mathsf{enc}(y_i)$ and $\widetilde{\mathsf{enc}(y_i)}$. Then compute $\mathsf{CT} = \mathsf{Rand}(\mathsf{enc}(z), \{\mathsf{enc}(y_i)\}_{i \in J})$.
- Every party P_i runs $\Pi_{\text{DDEC}}{}^b$ with the rest of the parties to decrypt CT.

---

^{a} Since we have (potential) dishonest majority, note that we cannot guarantee termination. For a concrete implementation of the broadcast functionality we refer to [DPSZ12].

^{b} The protocol Π_{DDEC} is described in Subsetion 5.1 and Figure 7.

Fig. 4. Π_{MPC} Protocol.

Functionality $\mathcal{F}_{\text{KEY-DIST}}$

The functionality $\mathcal{F}_{\text{KEY-DIST}}$ runs with parties $P_1, \ldots, P_n$ and is parameterized by a statistically hiding commitment scheme with commitment function Com. It proceeds as follows:

Generate:

On input $(\text{init}, 1^\lambda)$ from all honest parties, run $\text{KeyGen}(1^\lambda)$ of the QFHE scheme and obtain PK, SK and then additively secret-share sk to obtain $(\text{sk}_1, \ldots, \text{sk}_n)$.

1. For $i = 1, \ldots, n$, commits to the share sk_i by computing $c_i = \text{Com}(\text{sk}_i; r_i)$ where $r_i \leftarrow \mathcal{D}_{rand}(1^\lambda)$.
2. In a round specified by the adversary, output $((\text{PK}, c_1, \ldots, c_n), (\text{sk}_i, r_i))$ to P_i.

Incorrect inputs:

If in the first round an honest party inputs a non-trivial value and does not input init, abort. Moreover, abort if an honest party inputs init twice or any other value than init.

Fig. 5. Ideal functionality $\mathcal{F}_{\text{KEY-DIST}}$.

Functionality $\mathcal{F}_{\text{AMPC}}$

The functionality $\mathcal{F}_{\text{AMPC}}$ runs with parties $P_1, \ldots, P_n$ and an adversary $\mathcal{S}$ and is parametrised by an arithmetic circuit ckt. It proceeds as follows.

Initialize:

On input $(\text{init}, 1^\lambda)$ from all parties, the functionality generates a random FHE key (SK, PK). It outputs PK to all parties.

Load Phase:

On input $(\text{Input}, P_i, varid, x)$ from P_i and $(\text{Input}, P_i, varid, ?)$ from all other parties, with $varid$ a fresh identifier, the functionality stores $(varid, x)$ and outputs $(cid, varid, \text{Defined})$ to all parties. If P_i is corrupted before $(cid, varid, \text{Defined})$ is output, and if the adversary outputs $(cid, varid, \text{Fail})$, then output $(cid, varid, \text{Fail})$ to all parties.

Evaluation Phase:

On input $(\text{Evaluation}, varid_1, \ldots, varid_n, varid_{n+1})$ from all parties (if $varid_1, \ldots, varid_n$ are present in memory and $varid_{n+1}$ is not), the functionality retrieves $(varid_1, x_1), \ldots, (varid_n, x_n)$ and stores $(varid_{n+1}, \text{ckt}(x_1, \ldots, x_n))$.

Output Phase:

On input $(\text{Output}, varid_{n+1})$ from all honest parties (if $varid_{n+1}$ is present in memory), the functionality retrieves $(varid_{n+1}, x)$ and outputs it to the environment. If the environment inputs OK then x is output to all players. Otherwise $\perp$ is output to all players.

Fig. 6. Ideal functionality for Arithmetic MPC.

Evaluation sharing: *The evaluation function* ShareEval *on input* (pk, sk_i) *and a ciphertext* $\text{Enc}_{\text{pk}}(z)$, *outputs an evaluation share*

$$ev_i = \text{ShareEval}(\text{pk}, \text{sk}_i, \text{Enc}_{\text{pk}}(z); r_{ev_i})$$

for $i \in [n]$ *where* $r_{ev_i} \leftarrow \mathcal{D}_{rand}(1^\lambda)$.

228 I. Damgård et al.

Share combining: *The algorithm* Combine *on input correctly computed evaluation shares* $\{ev_i\}_{i\in[n]}$ *of the same ciphertext* $\mathsf{Enc}_{pk}(z)$, *constructs the output* $\mathsf{Dec}_{sk}(\mathsf{Enc}_{pk}(z)) = \mathsf{Combine}(\{ev_i\}_{i\in[n]})$.

For our purposes, the construction threshold $\mathsf{c} = n$ and the corruption threshold $\mathsf{t} = n - 1$. In Fig. 7, we describe our protocol Π_{DDEC}, parameterized by (ShareSK, ShareEval, Combine).

Protocol Π_{DDEC}

The protocol runs in the $(\mathcal{F}_{\mathrm{BROADCAST}}, \mathcal{F}_{\mathrm{KEY\text{-}DIST}}, \mathcal{F}_{\mathrm{COM\text{-}ZK}})$-hybrid model with parties $P_1, \ldots, P_n$ and it is parametrized by (ShareEval, Combine), as defined in Definition 5. It proceeds as follows:

Key Sharing: On input $(\mathrm{init}, 1^\lambda)$ from all parties, invoke the functionalities $\mathcal{F}_{\mathrm{BROADCAST}}, \mathcal{F}_{\mathrm{KEY\text{-}DIST}}$ and $\mathcal{F}_{\mathrm{COM\text{-}ZK}}$. The invocation of $\mathcal{F}_{\mathrm{KEY\text{-}DIST}}$ results in every party P_i receiving $((\mathsf{PK}, c_1, \ldots, c_n), (\mathsf{sk}_i, r_i))$.

Evaluation Sharing:

1. For $i \neq j$, P_i samples $r_{ev_i} \leftarrow \mathcal{D}_{rand}(1^\lambda)$ and sends $(\mathsf{Commit}, sid, cid, P_i, P_j, r_{ev_i})$ to $\mathcal{F}_{\mathrm{COM\text{-}ZK}}$. At this point all other parties P_j receive message $(\mathsf{Receipt}, sid, P_i, P_j)$ from $\mathcal{F}_{\mathrm{COM\text{-}ZK}}$.

2. Party P_i, on input ciphertext CT, computes its evaluation share $ev_i \leftarrow \mathsf{ShareEval}(\mathsf{PK}, \mathsf{sk}_i, \mathrm{CT}; r_{ev_i})$ and broadcasts ev_i via $\mathcal{F}_{\mathrm{BROADCAST}}$.

3. For $j \neq i$, P_i sends $(\mathsf{Prover}, sid, P_i, P_j, \mathcal{R}_{eval}, (c_i, \mathsf{PK}, \mathsf{enc}(z), ev_i))$ to $\mathcal{F}_{\mathrm{COM\text{-}ZK}}$ for the relation

$$\mathcal{R}_{eval} = \{((c_i, \mathsf{PK}, \mathrm{CT}, ev_i), (\mathsf{sk}_i, r_i, r_{ev_i})) : c_i = \mathsf{Com}(\mathsf{sk}_i; r_i) \wedge$$

$$ev_i = \mathsf{ShareEval}(\mathsf{PK}, \mathsf{sk}_i, \mathrm{CT}; r_{ev_i})\}$$

where Com is the commitment scheme used in $\mathcal{F}_{\mathrm{KEY\text{-}DIST}}$.

4. For $i \neq j$, P_j sends the message $(\mathsf{Proof}, sid, \mathcal{R}_{eval}, (c_i, \mathsf{PK}, \mathrm{CT}, ev_i))$.

Share Combining: If any party P_i outputs reject for a proof given by any party P_j, then output Abort. Otherwise, output $\mathsf{Combine}(\{ev_i\}_{i\in[n]})$.

A concrete instantiation of the protocol Π_{DDEC} based on LWE is given in the full version.

Fig. 7. Distributed decryption protocol.

Theorem 4. *Let* $\mathsf{QFHE} = (\mathsf{KeyGen}, \mathsf{KeyGen}^*, \mathsf{QEnc}, \mathsf{Eval}, \mathsf{Rand}, \mathsf{Dec}, \mathsf{Equiv})$ *be an equivocal fully homomorphic encryption scheme; let it be associated with a distributed function sharing scheme* (ShareSK, ShareEval, Combine). *Then the constant-round protocol* Π_{MPC} *UC-securely realises the ideal functionality* $\mathcal{F}_{\mathrm{AMPC}}$ *in the* $(\mathcal{F}_{\mathrm{BROADCAST}}, \mathcal{F}_{\mathrm{KEY\text{-}DIST}}, \mathcal{F}_{\mathrm{COM\text{-}ZK}})$-*hybrid model with computational security against any adaptive, active adversary corrupting at most all-but-one parties.*

For the proof of Theorem 4 see the full version. Replacing *UC* ZK with *UC* NIZK yields a three-round protocol.

High Level Idea of the Security Proof. Our simulator uses the properties of the QFHE scheme such as the indistingusability of equivocation, according to Definition 3. Furthermore, as we discussed in Sect. 1, the simulator will not be able to cheat in the distributed decryption protocol by decrypting a given ciphertext to any desired value. The key setup for the decryption protocol fixes the shares of the private key even in the simulation. Thus, a ciphertext can only be decrypted to the value it actually contains. Of course, when decrypting the outputs, the correct results should be produced both in simulation and real life, and so we have a problem since all ciphertexts in the simulation generated with respect to the honest parties will contain encryptions of 0. For this issue we use the ciphertext randomisation property. Notice that the ciphertext ct in the ciphertext randomization property as per Definition 3 corresponds to the real output $\mathsf{enc}(z)$ of the protocol Π_{MPC} and the ciphertexts $\mathsf{ct}'_1, \ldots, \mathsf{ct}'_n$ correspond to the ciphertexts $\{\mathsf{enc}(y_i)\}_{i \in J}$. In the real-world the ciphertexts $\{\mathsf{enc}(y_i)\}_{i \in J}$ are **redundant**. On the other hand, in the ideal-world the final ciphertext CT decrypts to a value contributed only by the ciphertexts $\{\mathsf{enc}(y_i)\}_{i \in J}$. In this case we will call the ciphertexts $\{\mathsf{enc}(y_i)\}_{i \in J}$ **non − redundant**. This implies that an honest execution of the **Output** stage is not possible with the ciphertexts of $\{\mathsf{enc}(y_i)\}_{i \in J}$ being **non − redundant**. Analogously, the ciphertext $\mathsf{enc}(z)$ can be either **redundant** or **non − redundant**. In other words, it is pertinent that before we get to a hybrid where the **Output** stage is performed honestly, we need a hybrid where $\{\mathsf{enc}(y_i)\}_{i \in J}$ turn to **redundant** ciphertexts. However, with both ciphertexts $\{\mathsf{enc}(y_i)\}_{i \in J}$ and $\mathsf{enc}(z)$ **redundant**, we can not hope to get the final output CT to decrypt to the actual output value. Thus, even before turning $\{\mathsf{enc}(y_i)\}_{i \in J}$ to **redundant** ciphertexts, we need a hybrid where we can cheat in the final decryption. That is, we first need to have a hybrid that, instead of running the distributed decryption protocol, runs what we abstract as the simulator for the distributed decryption. Moreover, we also based on the semantic security of the FHE scheme in interchangeably switching the keys K and R to encryptions of 0 and 1, respectively. A full proof is given in the full version.

6   On the Communication Complexity of Distributed Decryption

Our protocol as described in Sect. 5 assumes that the QFHE scheme comes with a semi-honest secure distributed decryption protocol: from the ciphertext and shares of the secret key players can compute decryption shares which, if correct, allow the reconstruction of the plaintext. We then augment the distributed decryption with ZK proofs so that players prove that their contributions to the decryption are correct. This solution has communication complexity proportional to the circuit complexity of the decryption function.

However, our approach allows for a significant optimization of the decryption procedure compared to generic solutions. More specifically, we tweak our protocol

Π_{MPC} such that the communication complexity of the decryption becomes independent of its circuit complexity.

To this end, we modify the evaluation phase of our protocol presented in Sect. 5. Note that our original protocol allows us to securely compute any (randomized) function. In particular, any randomized function allows the parties to encrypt randomized shares and then add up them together. Therefore, instead of computing the original function, we compute a new function, which for each output z of the original function also outputs α and $w = \alpha z$ where α is randomly chosen in some large field, and where the multiplication αz also takes place in that field. Of course if we can compute this function securely then we can also compute the original function securely. Observe that this new function comes along with an extra property which allows to check if the output is correct or not based on whether $w = \alpha z$.

In order to incorporate the above, the modification to the protocol is as follows. Instead of having a single ciphertext $\text{enc}(z)$ containing z, we will have two extra ciphertexts, namely $\text{enc}(\alpha)$ and $\text{enc}(w)$. The ciphertext $\text{enc}(\alpha)$ is computed as follows. Each party randomly selects a one-time a_i and encrypts it according to the Load phase of our protocol Π_{MPC} in Fig. 5. Once each party has loaded and broadcasted $\text{enc}(a_i)$, each party computes $\text{enc}(\alpha) = \text{enc}(a_1) \boxplus \ldots \boxplus \text{enc}(a_n)$ and $\text{enc}(w) = \text{enc}(\alpha) \boxdot \text{enc}(z)$. Thus, instead of calling the output phase of our protocol only on input $\text{enc}(z)$ we call it on three different ciphertexts $\text{enc}(z), \text{enc}(\alpha), \text{enc}(w)$. This means that now the decryption protocol will generate three sets of evaluation shares.

The modification in the decryption protocol is as follows. Before we first broadcast the shares and then we prove in ZK that they were correct. Instead, we are *not* going to broadcast all the evaluation shares immediately due to the adversary who may see the contributions from the honest parties to α before his broadcast enabling him to forge. We need to guarantee that the adversary cannot forge the output by making sure that he should output his share before he sees α. In order to avoid the above complication, we first commit to the evaluation shares and then we open them. In particular, all players compute their evaluation shares for z, α and w and commit to them. If opening fails or if the decrypted values do not satisfy $\alpha z = w$, we abort. This solution avoids the use of ZK proofs yielding a solution which is independent of the circuit complexity of the decryption.

Since there is an encryption of α available, the new aspect in the proof is to show that this does not help the adversary to learn α unless he can break CPA security. We can argue this in the proof in the full version where we turn the ciphertext $\text{enc}(z)$ to **redundant**. Therefore, the same proof still applies but instead we will have three **redundant** ciphetexts $\text{enc}(\alpha z), \text{enc}(\alpha), \text{enc}(w)$. In this hybrid the outputs cannot be forged since the ciphertext $\text{enc}(\alpha)$ is **redundant** and it does not contain information about α. Thus, an advesary that he cannot forge he cannot distinguish in the real world and break CPA-security.

Acknowledgements. The authors would like to thank Nico Döttling, Yuval Ishai and Chris Peikert for helpful discussions. We also thank Jonathan Katz for pointing out his result [KTZ13]. Ivan Damgård and Antigoni Polychriniadou acknowledge support from the Danish National Research Foundation and the National Science Foundation of China (under the grant 61361136003) for the Sino-Danish Center for the Theory of Interactive Computation and from the Center for Research in Foundations of Electronic Markets (CFEM), supported by the Danish Strategic Research Council. In addition, the research was supported by the MPCPRO project funded by the ERC.

A   Performance of General Solution Based on the IPS Compiler

The following should be taken with large grains of salt. We have tried to be optimistic on the part of the IPS compiler, to not give our concrete protocol an unfair advantage. Thus, actual numbers could be larger.

We estimate that using the best known outer and inner protocols in the IPS compiler, one invocation of IPS would require 10–15 rounds. For the generic suggestion one needs two invocations, one to generate key material for NCE (see below) and one for decryption. On top of that one needs a few rounds for distributing inputs and proving knowledge of them in ZK or NIZK. So we estimate at least 30 rounds for the complete protocol.

The computation and communication overhead is even harder to estimate. We looked at communication since that is a lower bound on computation and made a crude estimate that equates statistical and computational security parameters. To do the FHE decryption generically, one needs to write it as a binary circuit, say of size s and then use the IPS compiler. For n players and security parameter λ, we get communication $\Omega(n^4\lambda^2 s)$ where s depends on the FHE scheme but can be expected to be at least quadratic in λ. This is based on a very optimistic assumption on what the outer protocol can do while also minimizing the number of rounds. If this is not true, then such a protocol yields an $\Omega(n^6\lambda^3 s)$ overhead.

In comparison the total communication of the decryption phase of our concrete protocol is $O(n^2\lambda)$. We used the IPS paper and there are likely ways to optimize, but it does seem that the difference is very significant nevertheless.

References

[AJLA+12] Asharov, G., Jain, A., López-Alt, A., Tromer, E., Vaikuntanathan, V., Wichs, D.: Multiparty computation with low communication, computation and interaction via threshold FHE. In: Pointcheval, D., Johansson, T. (eds.) EUROCRYPT 2012. LNCS, vol. 7237, pp. 483–501. Springer, Heidelberg (2012)

[BCHK07] Boneh, D., Canetti, R., Halevi, S., Katz, J.: Chosen-ciphertext security from identity-based encryption. SIAM J. Comput. **36**(5), 1301–1328 (2007)

[BGW88] Ben-Or, M., Goldwasser, S., Wigderson. A.: Completeness theorems for non-cryptographic fault-tolerant distributed computation (extended abstract). In: STOC, pp. 1–10 (1988)

[BV11] Brakerski, Z., Vaikuntanathan, V.: Fully homomorphic encryption from ring-LWE and security for key dependent messages. In: Rogaway, P. (ed.) CRYPTO 2011. LNCS, vol. 6841, pp. 505–524. Springer, Heidelberg (2011)

[CDF+08] Cramer, R., Dodis, Y., Fehr, S., Padró, C., Wichs, D.: Detection of algebraic manipulation with applications to robust secret sharing and fuzzy extractors. In: Smart, N.P. (ed.) EUROCRYPT 2008. LNCS, vol. 4965, pp. 471–488. Springer, Heidelberg (2008)

[CF01] Canetti, R., Fischlin, M.: Universally composable commitments. In: Kilian, J. (ed.) CRYPTO 2001. LNCS, vol. 2139, pp. 19–40. Springer, Heidelberg (2001)

[CFGN96] Canetti, R., Feige, U., Goldreich, O., Naor, M.: Adaptively secure multiparty computation. In: STOC, pp. 639–648 (1996)

[CGP15] Canetti, R., Goldwasser, S., Poburinnaya, O.: Adaptively secure two-party computation from indistinguishability obfuscation. In: Dodis, Y., Nielsen, J.B. (eds.) TCC 2015, Part II. LNCS, vol. 9015, pp. 557–585. Springer, Heidelberg (2015)

[CLOS02] Canetti, R., Lindell, Y., Ostrovsky, R., Sahai, A.: Universally composable two-party and multi-party secure computation. In: Proceedings of the Thiry-fourth Annual ACM Symposium on Theory of Computing, STOC 2002, pp. 494–503 (2002)

[DDN00] Dolev, D., Dwork, C., Naor, M.: Non-malleable cryptography. SIAM J. Comput. 30, 542–552 (2000)

[DI05] Damgård, I.B., Ishai, Y.: Constant-round multiparty computation using a black-box pseudorandom generator. In: Shoup, V. (ed.) CRYPTO 2005. LNCS, vol. 3621, pp. 378–394. Springer, Heidelberg (2005)

[DI06] Damgård, I.B., Ishai, Y.: Scalable secure multiparty computation. In: Dwork, C. (ed.) CRYPTO 2006. LNCS, vol. 4117, pp. 501–520. Springer, Heidelberg (2006)

[DIK+08] Damgård, I., Ishai, Y., Krøigaard, M., Nielsen, J.B., Smith, A.: Scalable multiparty computation with nearly optimal work and resilience. In: Wagner, D. (ed.) CRYPTO 2008. LNCS, vol. 5157, pp. 241–261. Springer, Heidelberg (2008)

[DKR15] Dachman-Soled, D., Katz, J., Rao, V.: Adaptively secure, universally composable, multiparty computation in constant rounds. In: Dodis, Y., Nielsen, J.B. (eds.) TCC 2015, Part II. LNCS, vol. 9015, pp. 586–613. Springer, Heidelberg (2015)

[DMRV13] Dachman-Soled, D., Malkin, T., Raykova, M., Venkitasubramaniam, M.: Adaptive and concurrent secure computation from new adaptive, nonmalleable commitments. In: Sako, K., Sarkar, P. (eds.) ASIACRYPT 2013, Part I. LNCS, vol. 8269, pp. 316–336. Springer, Heidelberg (2013)

[DN03] Damgård, I.B., Nielsen, J.B.: Universally composable efficient multiparty computation from threshold homomorphic encryption. In: Boneh, D. (ed.) CRYPTO 2003. LNCS, vol. 2729, pp. 247–264. Springer, Heidelberg (2003)

[DNP15] Damgård, I., Nielsen, J.B., Polychroniadou, A.: On the communication required for unconditionally secure multiplication. Cryptology ePrint Archive, Report 2015/1097 (2015). http://eprint.iacr.org/

[DPR14]   Damgård, I., Polychroniadou, A., Rao, V.: Adaptively secure multi-party computation from lwe (via equivocal fhe). Cryptology ePrint Archive, Report 2014/830 (2014). http://eprint.iacr.org/

[DPSZ12] Damgård, I., Pastro, V., Smart, N., Zakarias, S.: Multiparty computation from somewhat homomorphic encryption. In: Safavi-Naini, R., Canetti, R. (eds.) CRYPTO 2012. LNCS, vol. 7417, pp. 643–662. Springer, Heidelberg (2012)

[Gen09]   Gentry, C.: A fully homomorphic encryption scheme. Ph.D. thesis, Stanford University (2009). crypto.stanford.edu/craig

[GGH+13] Garg, S., Gentry, C., Halevi, S., Raykova, M., Sahai, A., Waters, B.: Candidate indistinguishability obfuscation and functional encryption for all circuits. In: 54th Annual Symposium on Foundations of Computer Science, Berkeley, CA, USA, IEEE Computer Society Press, 26–29 October, pp. 40–49 (2013)

[GOS12]   Groth, J., Ostrovsky, R., Sahai, A.: New techniques for noninteractive zero-knowledge. J. ACM **59**(3), 11 (2012)

[GP15]   Garg, S., Polychroniadou, A.: Two-round adaptively secure MPC from indistinguishability obfuscation. In: Dodis, Y., Nielsen, J.B. (eds.) TCC 2015, Part II. LNCS, vol. 9015, pp. 614–637. Springer, Heidelberg (2015)

[GS12]   Garg, S., Sahai, A.: Adaptively secure multi-party computation with dishonest majority. In: Safavi-Naini, R., Canetti, R. (eds.) CRYPTO 2012. LNCS, vol. 7417, pp. 105–123. Springer, Heidelberg (2012)

[IPS08]   Ishai, Y., Prabhakaran, M., Sahai, A.: Founding cryptography on oblivious transfer – efficiently. In: Wagner, D. (ed.) CRYPTO 2008. LNCS, vol. 5157, pp. 572–591. Springer, Heidelberg (2008)

[KO04]   Katz, J., Ostrovsky, R.: Round-optimal secure two-party computation. In: Franklin, M. (ed.) CRYPTO 2004. LNCS, vol. 3152, pp. 335–354. Springer, Heidelberg (2004)

[KTZ13]   Katz, J., Thiruvengadam, A., Zhou, H.-S.: Feasibility and infeasibility of adaptively secure fully homomorphic encryption. In: Hanaoka, G., Kurosawa, K. (eds.) PKC 2013. LNCS, vol. 7778, pp. 14–31. Springer, Heidelberg (2013)

[LTV12]   López-Alt, A., Tromer, E., Vaikuntanathan, V.: On-the-fly multiparty computation on the cloud via multikey fully homomorphic encryption. In: Proceedings of the 44th Symposium on Theory of Computing Conference, STOC 2012, New York, NY, USA, 19–22 May 2012, pp. 1219–1234 (2012)

[MP12]   Micciancio, D., Peikert, C.: Trapdoors for lattices: simpler, tighter, faster, smaller. In: Pointcheval, D., Johansson, T. (eds.) EUROCRYPT 2012. LNCS, vol. 7237, pp. 700–718. Springer, Heidelberg (2012)

[MW15]   Mukherjee, P., Wichs, D.: Two round mutliparty computation via multikey FHE. Cryptology ePrint Archive, Report 2015/345 (2015). http://eprint.iacr.org/

[Nie02]   Nielsen, J.B.: Separating random oracle proofs from complexity theoretic proofs: the non-committing encryption case. In: Yung, M. (ed.) CRYPTO 2002. LNCS, vol. 2442, pp. 111–126. Springer, Heidelberg (2002)

[OPW11]   O'Neill, A., Peikert, C., Waters, B.: Bi-deniable public-key encryption. In: Rogaway, P. (ed.) CRYPTO 2011. LNCS, vol. 6841, pp. 525–542. Springer, Heidelberg (2011)

Universally Composable Direct Anonymous Attestation

Jan Camenisch[1]([✉]), Manu Drijvers[1,2], and Anja Lehmann[1]

[1] IBM Research – Zurich, Säumerstrasse 4, 8803 Rüschlikon, Switzerland
{jca,mdr,anj}@zurich.ibm.com
[2] Department of Computer Science, ETH Zürich, 8092 Zürich, Switzerland

Abstract. Direct Anonymous Attestation (DAA) is one of the most complex cryptographic algorithms that has been deployed in practice. In spite of this and the long body of work on the subject, there is still no fully satisfactory security definition for DAA. This was already acknowledged by Bernard et al. (IJIC'13) who showed that in existing models insecure protocols can be proved secure. Bernard et al. therefore proposed an extensive set of security games which, however, aim only at a simplified setting termed pre-DAA. In pre-DAA, the host platform that runs the TPM is assumed to be trusted. Consequently, their notion does not guarantee any security if the TPM is embedded in a potentially corrupt host which is a significant restriction. In this paper, we give a comprehensive security definition for full DAA in the form of an ideal functionality in the Universal Composability model. Our definition considers the host and TPM to be separate entities that can be in different corruption states. None of the existing DAA schemes satisfy our strong security notion. We therefore propose a realization that is based on a DAA scheme supported by the TPM 2.0 standard and prove it secure in our model.

1 Introduction

Direct Anonymous Attestation (DAA) allows a small chip, the Trusted Platform Module (TPM), that is embedded in a host computer to create attestations about the state of the host system. Such attestations, which can be seen as signatures on the current state under the TPM's secret key, convince a remote verifier that the system is running on top of a certified hardware module and is using the correct software. A crucial feature of DAA is that it performs such attestations in a privacy-friendly manner. That is, the user of the host system can choose to create attestations anonymously ensuring that her transactions are unlinkable and do not leak any information about the particular TPM being used. User-controlled linkability is also allowed and is steered by a basename bsn: attestations under a fresh or empty basename can not be linked whereas the repeated use of the same basename makes the corresponding transactions linkable.

DAA is one of the most complex cryptographic protocols deployed in practice. The Trusted Computing Group (TCG), the industry standardization group

C.-M. Cheng et al. (Eds.): PKC 2016, Part II, LNCS 9615, pp. 234–264, 2016.
DOI: 10.1007/978-3-662-49387-8_10

that designed the TPM, standardized the first DAA protocol in the TPM 1.2 specification in 2004 [23] and included support for multiple DAA schemes in the TPM 2.0 specification in 2014 [24]. Over 500 million computers with TPM chips have been sold[1], making DAA one of the largest deployments of such a complex cryptographic scheme. This sparked a strong interest in the research community in the security and efficiency of DAA schemes [3,5–7,14–18].

Direct Anonymous Attestation has recently also gained the attention of the FIDO alliance which aims at basing online authentication on strong cryptography rather than passwords. The FIDO approach is to choose a fresh key pair for every user account, to provide the public key to the service provider, and to re-authenticate via the corresponding secret key. Adding DAA to this approach allows one to prove that the secret key is properly stored on and protected by a trusted platform.

Existing Security Models. Interestingly, in spite of the large scale deployment and the long body of work on the subject, DAA still lacks a sound and comprehensive security model. There exist a number of security definitions using the simulation-based and property-based paradigms. Unfortunately all have rather severe shortcomings such as allowing completely broken schemes to be proven secure. This was recently discussed by Bernard et al. [3] who provided an analysis of existing security notions and also proposed a new DAA model. In a nutshell, the existing simulation-based models that capture the desired security properties in form of an ideal functionality either miss to treat signatures as concrete objects that can be output or stored by the verifier [5] or are unrealizable by any instantiation [14,17]. The difficulty in defining a proper ideal functionality for the complex DAA setting might not be all that surprising considering the numerous (failed) attempts in modeling the much simpler standard signature scheme in the universal-composability framework [1,13].

Another line of work therefore aimed at capturing the DAA requirements in the form of property-based security games [3,7,15] as a more intuitive way of modeling. However, the first attempts [7,15] have missed to cover some of the expected security properties and also have made unconventional choices when defining unforgeability (the latter resulting in schemes being secure that use a *constant* value as signatures).

Realizing that the previous models were not sufficient, Bernard et al. [3] provided an extensive set of property-based security games. The authors consider only a simplified setting which they call pre-DAA. The simplification is that the host and the TPM are considered as single entity (the platform), thus they are both either corrupt or honest. For properties such as anonymity and non-frameability this is sufficient as they protect against a corrupt issuer and assume both the TPM and host to be honest. Unforgeability of a TPM attestation, however, should rely only on the TPM being honest but allow the host to be corrupt. This cannot be captured in their model. In fact, shifting the load of the computational work to the host without affecting security in case the host is

---

[1] http://www.trustedcomputinggroup.org/solutions/authentication.

corrupted is one of the main challenges when designing a DAA scheme. There-fore, a DAA security model should be able to formally analyze this setting of an honest TPM and a corrupt host.

This is also acknowledged by Bernard et al. [3] who, after proposing a pre-DAA secure protocol, argue how to obtain security in the full DAA context. Unfortunately, due to the absence of a full DAA security model, this argumen-tation is done only informally. We show that this argumentation is actually somewhat flawed: the given proof for unforgeability of the given pre-DAA proof can not be lifted (under the same assumptions) to the full DAA setting. This highlights the fact that an "almost matching" security model together with an informal argument of how to achieve the actually desired security does not pro-vide sound guarantees beyond what is formally proved.

Thus still no satisfying security model for DAA exists to date. This lack of a sound security definition is not only a theoretic problem but it in fact has resulted in insecure schemes being deployed in practice. A DAA scheme that allows anyone to forge attestations (as it does not exclude the "trivial" TPM credential $(1, 1, 1, 1)$) has even been ISO standardized [18,20].

Our Contributions. We tackle the challenge of formally defining Direct Anony-mous Attestation and provide an ideal functionality for DAA in the Univer-sal Composability (UC) framework [12]. Our functionality models the host and TPM as individual parties who can be in different corruption states and com-prises all expected security properties such as unforgeability, anonymity, and non-frameability. The model also includes verifier-local revocation where a veri-fier, when checking the validity of a signature, can specify corrupted TPMs from which he no longer accepts signatures.

We choose to define a new model rather than addressing the weaknesses of one of the existing models. The latest DAA security model by Bernard et al. [3] seem to be the best starting point. However, as this model covers pre-DAA only, changing all these definitions to full DAA would require changes to almost every aspect of them. Furthermore, given the complexity of DAA, we believe that the simulation-based approach is more natural as one has a lower risk of overlooking some security properties. A functionality provides a full description of security and no oracles have to be defined as the adversary simply gets full control over corrupt parties. Furthermore, the UC framework comes with strong composability guarantees that allow for protocols to be analyzed individually and preserve that security when being composed with other protocols.

None of the existing DAA constructions [3,6,7,16,18] satisfy our security model. Therefore, we also propose a modified version of recent DAA schemes [3, 18] that are built from pairing-based Camenisch-Lysyanskaya signatures [9] and zero-knowledge proofs. We then rigorously prove that our scheme realizes our new functionality. By the universal composition theorem, this proves that our scheme can be composed in arbitrary ways without losing security.

Organization. The rest of this paper is structured as follows. We start with a detailed discussion of existing DAA models in Sect. 2, with a focus on the latest model by Bernard et al. [3]. Section 3 then presents our new definition in the form of an ideal functionality in the UC framework. Section 4 introduces the building blocks required for our DAA scheme, which is presented in Sect. 5. The latter section also contains a discussion why the existing DAA schemes could not be proven secure in our model. The proof that the new DAA scheme fulfills our definition of security is sketched in Sect. 6 (the complete proof is given in the full version of this paper).

2   Issues in Existing Security Models

In this section we briefly discuss why current security models do not properly capture the security properties one would expect from a DAA scheme. Some of the arguments were already pointed out by Bernard et al. [3], who provide a thorough analysis of the existing DAA security notions and also propose a new set of definitions. For the sake of completeness, we summarize and extend their findings and also give an assessment of the latest model by Bernard et al.

Before discussing the various security models and their limitation, we informally describe how DAA works and what are the desired security properties. In a DAA scheme, we have four main entities: a number of trusted platform module (TPM), a number of hosts, an issuer, and a number of verifiers. A TPM and a host together form a platform which performs the *join protocol* with the issuer who decides if the platform is allowed to become a member. After becoming a member, the TPM and host together can *sign* messages with respect to base-names bsn. If a platform signs with bsn $= \perp$ or a fresh basename, the signature must be anonymous and unlinkable. That is, any verifier can check that the signature stems from a legitimate platform via a deterministic *verify* algorithm, but the signature does not leak any information about the identity of the signer. Only when the platform signs repeatedly with the same basename bsn $\neq \perp$, it will be clear that the resulting signatures were created by the same platform, which can be publicly tested via a (deterministic) *link* algorithm.

As usual one requires the typical completeness properties for signatures created by honest parties:

Completeness: When an honest platform successfully creates a signature on a message m w.r.t. a basename bsn, an honest verifier will accept the signature.

Correctness of Link: When an honest platform successfully creates two signatures, σ_1 and σ_2, w.r.t. the same basename bsn $\neq \perp$, an honest verifier running a link algorithm on σ_1 and σ_2 will output 1. To an honest verifier, it also does not matter in which order two signatures are supplied when testing linkability between the two signatures.

The more difficult part is to define the security properties that a DAA scheme should provide in the presence of malicious parties. These properties can be informally described as follows:

Unforgeability-1: When the issuer and all TPMs are honest, no adversary can create a signature on a message m w.r.t. basename bsn when no platform signed m w.r.t. bsn.

Unforgeability-2: When the issuer is honest, an adversary can only sign in the name of corrupt TPMs. More precisely, if n TPMs are corrupt, the adversary can at most create n unlinkable signatures for the same basename bsn $\neq \perp$.

Anonymity: An adversary that is given two signatures, w.r.t. two different basenames or bsn $= \perp$, cannot distinguish whether both signatures were created by one honest platform, or whether two different honest platforms created the signatures.

Non-frameability: No adversary can create signatures on a message m w.r.t. basename bsn that links to a signature created by an honest platform, when this honest platform never signed m w.r.t. bsn. We require this property to hold even when the issuer is corrupt.

2.1   Simulation-Based Models

A simulation-based security notion defines an ideal functionality, which can be seen as a central trusted party that receives inputs from all parties and provides outputs to them. Roughly, a protocol is called secure if its behavior is indistinguishable from the functionality.

The Brickell, Camenisch, and Chen Model [5]. DAA was first introduced by Brickell, Camenisch, and Chen [5] along with a simulation-based security model. This model has one procedure for signature generation and verification, meaning that a signature is generated for a specific verifier and will immediately be verified by that verifier. As the signature is never output to the verifier, he only learns that a message was correctly signed, but can neither forward signatures or verify them again. Clearly this limits the scenarios in which DAA can be applied.

Furthermore, linkability of signatures was not defined explicitly in the security model. In the instantiation it is handled by attaching pseudonyms to signatures, and when two signatures have the same pseudonym, they must have been created by the same platform.

The Chen, Morissey, and Smart Models [14, 17]. An extension to the model by Brickell et al. was later proposed by Chen, Morissey, and Smart [17]. It aims at providing linkability as an explicit feature in the functionality. To this end, the functionality is extended with a link interface that takes as input two signatures and determines whether they link or not. However, as discussed before, the sign and verify interfaces are interactive and thus signatures are never sent as output to parties, so it is not possible to provide them as input either. This was realized by the authors who thus proposed a new simulation-based model [14] that now separates the generation of signatures from their verification by outputting signatures. Unfortunately, the functionality models the signature generation in a too simplistic way: signatures are simply random values, even when the TPM is corrupt. Furthermore, the verify interface refuses all requests when the issuer is corrupt. Clearly, both these behaviours are not realizable by any protocol.

2.2 Property-Based Models

Given the difficulties in properly modeling signature-based ideal functionalities, there is also a line of work that captures DAA features via property-based definitions.

The Brickell, Chen, and Li Model [7]. The first paper is by Brickell, Chen, and Li [7], who define security games for anonymity, and "user-controlled traceability". The latter aims to capture our unforgeability-1 and unforgeability-2 requirements. Unfortunately, this model has several major shortcomings that were already discussed in detail by Bernard et al. [3].

The first problem is that the game for unforgeability-1 allows insecure schemes to be considered secure. The adversary in the unforgeability-1 game has oracle access to the honest parties from whom he can request signatures on messages and basenames of his choice. The adversary then wins if he can come up with a valid signature that is not a previous oracle response. This last requirement allows trivially insecure schemes to pass the security game: assume a DAA scheme that outputs the hash of the TPM's secret key gsk as signature, i.e., the signature is independent of the message. Clearly, this should be an insecure scheme as the adversary, after having seen one signature can provide valid signatures on arbitrary messages of his choice. However, it would actually be secure according to the unforgeability-1 game, as there reused signatures are not considered a forgery.

Another issue is that the game for unforgeability-2 is not well defined. The goal of the adversary is to supply a signature σ, message m, basename $\mathsf{bsn} \neq \bot$, and a signer's identity ID. The adversary wins if another signature "associated with the same ID" exists, but the signatures do not link. Firstly, there is no check on the validity of the supplied signature, which makes winning trivial for the adversary. Secondly, "another signature associated with the same ID" is not precisely defined, but we assume it to mean that the signature was the result of a signing query with that ID. However, then the adversary is limited to tamper with at most one of the signatures, whereas the second one is enforced to be honestly generated and unmodified. Thirdly, there is no check on the relation between the signature and the supplied ID. We expect that the intended behavior is that the supplied signature uses the key of ID, but there is no way to enforce this. Now an adversary can simply make a signing query with (m, bsn, ID_1) giving σ, and win the game with $(\sigma, m, \mathsf{bsn}, ID_2)$.

The model further lacks a security game that captures the non-frameability requirement. This means a scheme with a link algorithm that always outputs 1 can be proven secure. Chen [15] extends the model to add non-frameability, but this extension inherits all the aforementioned problems from [7].

The Bernard et al. Model [3]. Realizing that the previous models are not sufficient, Bernard et al. [3] provide an extensive set of property-based security definitions covering all expected security requirements.

The main improvement is the way signatures are identified. An identify algorithm is introduced that takes a signature and TPM key, and outputs whether the key was used to create the signature, which is possible as signatures are uniquely identifiable if the secret key is known. In the game definitions, the keys of honest TPMs are known, allowing the challenger to identify which key was used to create the signature, solving the problems related to the imprecisely defined ID in the Brickell, Chen, and Li model.

However, the security games make a simplifying assumption, namely that the platform, consisting of a host and a TPM, is considered as *one* party. This approach, termed "pre-DAA", suffices for anonymity and non-frameability, as there both the TPM and host have to be honest. However, for the unforgeability requirements it is crucial that the host does *not* have to be trusted. In fact, distributing the computational work between the TPM and the host, such that the load on the TPM is as small as possible and at the same time security does not require an honest host, is the main challenge in designing a DAA scheme. Therefore, a DAA security model must be able to formally analyze this setting of an honest TPM working with a corrupt host.

The importance of such full DAA security is also acknowledged by Bernard et al. [3]. After formally proving a proposed scheme secure in the pre-DAA model, the authors bring the scheme to the full DAA setting where the TPM and host are considered as separate parties. To obtain full DAA security, the host randomizes the issuer's credential on the TPM's public key. Bernard et al. then argue that this has no impact on the proven pre-DAA security guarantees, as the host does not perform any action involving the TPM secret key. While this is intuitively correct, it gives no guarantees whether the security properties are *provably* preserved in the full DAA setting.

Indeed, the proof of unforgeability of the pre-DAA scheme, which is proven under the DL assumption, does not hold in the full DAA setting as a corrupt host could notice the simulation used in the security proof. More precisely, in the Bernard et al. scheme, the host sends values (b, d) to the TPM which are the re-randomized part of the issuers credential and are supposed to have the form $b^{gsk} = d$ with gsk being the TPM's secret key. The TPM then provides a signature proof of knowledge (SPK) of gsk to the host. The pre-DAA proof relies on the DL assumption and places the unknown discrete logarithm of the challenge DL instance as the TPM key gsk. In the pre-DAA setting, the TPM then simulates the proof of knowledge of gsk for any input (b, d). This, however, is no longer possible in the full DAA setting. If the host is corrupt, he can send arbitrary values (b, d) with $b^{gsk} \neq d$ to the TPM, but would expect the TPM to respond with a SPK only if (b, d) are properly set. Relying only on the DL assumption does not allow the TPM to check whether (b, d) are well-formed though, such that he would provide correct proofs for false statements. Thus, the unforgeability can no longer be proven under the DL assumption. Note that the scheme could still be proven secure using the stronger static DH assumption, but the point is that a proof of pre-DAA security and a seemingly convincing but informal argument to transfer the scheme to the full DAA setting does not guarantee security in the full DAA setting.

Another peculiarity of the Bernard et al. model is that it makes some rather strong yet somewhat hidden assumptions on the adversaries behavior. For instance, in the traceability game showing unforgeability of the credentials, the adversary must not only output the claimed forgery but also the secret keys of all TPMs. For a DAA protocol this implicitly assumes that the TPM secret key can be extracted from every signature. Similarly, in games such as non-frameability or anonymity that capture security against a corrupt issuer, the issuer's key is generated honestly within the game, instead of being chosen by the adversary. For any realization this assumes either a trusted setup setting or an extractable proof of correctness of the issuer's secret key.

In the scheme proposed in [3], none of these implicit assumptions hold though: the generation of the issuer key is not extractable or assumed to be trusted, and the TPM's secret key cannot be extracted from every signature, as the rewinding would require exponential time. Note that these assumptions are indeed necessary to guarantee security for the proposed scheme. If the non-frameability game would allow the issuer to choose its own key, it could choose $y = 0$ and win the game. Ideally, a security model should not impose such assumptions or protocol details. If it is necessary though, then the required assumptions should be made more explicit to avoid pitfalls in the protocol design.

3 A New Security Model for DAA

In this section we present our security model for DAA, which is defined as an ideal functionality $\mathcal{F}_{daa}^l$ in the UC framework [12]. In UC, an environment $\mathcal{E}$ passes inputs and outputs to the protocol parties. The network is controlled by an adversary $\mathcal{A}$ that may communicate freely with $\mathcal{E}$. In the ideal world, the parties forward their inputs to the ideal functionality $\mathcal{F}$, which then (internally) performs the defined task and creates outputs that the parties forward to $\mathcal{E}$.

Roughly, a real-world protocol Π is said to securely realize a functionality $\mathcal{F}$, if the real world is indistinguishable from the ideal world, meaning for every adversary performing an attack in the real world, there is an ideal world adversary (often called simulator) $\mathcal{S}$ that performs the same attack in the ideal world. More precisely, a protocol Π is secure if for every adversary $\mathcal{A}$, there exists a simulator $\mathcal{S}$ such that no environment $\mathcal{E}$ can distinguish executing the real world with Π and $\mathcal{A}$, and executing the ideal world with $\mathcal{F}$ and $\mathcal{S}$.

3.1 Ideal Functionality $\mathcal{F}_{daa}^l$

We now formally define our ideal functionality $\mathcal{F}_{daa}^l$, for which we assume static corruptions, i.e., the adversary decides upfront which parties are corrupt and makes this information known to the functionality. The UC framework allows us to focus our analysis on a single protocol instance with a globally unique session identifier sid. Here we use session identifiers of the form $sid = (\mathcal{I}, sid')$ for some issuer $\mathcal{I}$ and a unique string sid'. To allow several sub-sessions for the join and sign related interfaces we use unique sub-session identifiers $jsid$ and *ssid*. Our ideal functionality $\mathcal{F}_{\mathsf{daa}}^l$ is further parametrized by a leakage function $l : \{0,1\}^* \to \{0,1\}^*$, that we need to model the information leakage that occurs in the communication between a host $\mathcal{H}_i$ and TPM $\mathcal{M}_j$.

We first briefly describe the main interfaces, then present the full functionality $\mathcal{F}_{\mathsf{daa}}^l$ and finally discuss in depth why $\mathcal{F}_{\mathsf{daa}}^l$ implements the desired security properties.

Setup. The SETUP interface on input $sid = (\mathcal{I}, sid')$ initiates a new DAA session for the issuer $\mathcal{I}$ and expects the adversary to provide a number of algorithms (ukgen, sig, ver, link, identify) that will be used inside the functionality.

- $gsk \xleftarrow{\$} \mathsf{ukgen}()$ will be used to generate keys gsk for honest TPMs.
- $\sigma \xleftarrow{\$} \mathsf{sig}(gsk, m, bsn)$ will also be used for honest TPMs and on input a key gsk, message m and basename bsn, it outputs a signature σ.
- $f \leftarrow \mathsf{ver}(\sigma, m, bsn)$ will be used in the verify interface. On input a signature σ, message m and basename bsn, it outputs $f = 1$ if the signature is valid, and $f = 0$ otherwise.
- $f \leftarrow \mathsf{link}(\sigma, m, \sigma', m', bsn)$ will be used in the link interface. It takes two tuples (σ, m), (σ', m'), a basename bsn and outputs $f = 1$ to indicate that both signature are generated by the same TPM and $f = 0$ otherwise.
- $f \leftarrow \mathsf{identify}(\sigma, m, bsn, gsk)$ outputs $f = 1$ if σ is a signature of m, bsn under key gsk, and $f = 0$ otherwise. We will use identify in several places to ensure consistency, e.g., whenever a new key gsk is generated or provided by the adversary.

Note that the ver and link algorithms only assist the functionality for signatures that are not generated by $\mathcal{F}_{\mathsf{daa}}^l$ itself. For signatures generated by the functionality, $\mathcal{F}_{\mathsf{daa}}^l$ will enforce correct verification and linkage using its internal records. While ukgen and sig are probabilistic algorithms, the other ones are required to be deterministic. The link algorithm also has to be symmetric, i.e., for all inputs it must hold that $\mathsf{link}(\sigma, m, \sigma', m', bsn) \leftrightarrow \mathsf{link}(\sigma', m', \sigma, m, bsn)$.

Join. When the setup is completed, a host $\mathcal{H}_j$ can request to join with a TPM $\mathcal{M}_i$ using the JOIN interface. Only if the issuer gives his approval through the JOINPROCEED interface, the join will complete and $\mathcal{F}_{\mathsf{daa}}^l$ stores $\langle \mathcal{M}_i, \mathcal{H}_j, gsk \rangle$ in an internal list Members. If the host or TPM are corrupt, gsk has to be provided by the adversary. If both are honest, $\mathcal{F}_{\mathsf{daa}}^l$ stores $gsk \leftarrow \bot$.

On the first glance, it might seem a bit surprising that we let the adversary also provide gsk when the host is corrupt but the TPM is honest. However we use gsk inside the functionality only to reflect the anonymity properties according to the set of corrupted parties. Only if the entire platform if honest, one can guarantee anonymity and then we enforce $gsk \leftarrow \bot$. Note that gsk has in particular no impact on the unforgeability guarantees that are always enforced by $\mathcal{F}_{\mathsf{daa}}^l$ if $\mathcal{M}_i$ is honest.

Sign. Once a platform joined, the host $\mathcal{H}_j$ can call the SIGN interface to request a DAA signature from a TPM $\mathcal{M}_i$ for message m with respect to basename bsn. If the issuer is honest, only platforms $\langle \mathcal{M}_i, \mathcal{H}_j, gsk \rangle \in$ Members can sign. Then, the TPM is notified and has to give its explicit approval through the SIGNPROCEED interface. If the host or TPM are corrupt, the signature σ has to be input by the adversary. When both are honest, the signature is generated via the sig algorithm. Thereby, $\mathcal{F}_{\mathsf{daa}}^l$ first chooses a fresh key gsk whenever an honest platform (honest host and honest TPM) wishes to sign under a *new* basename, which naturally enforces unlinkability and anonymity of those signatures. Every newly generated key is stored as $\langle \mathcal{M}_i, \mathsf{bsn}, gsk \rangle$ in a list DomainKeys and will be re-used whenever the honest platform wants to sign under the same bsn again. For honest platforms, the generated or adversarial provided signature is also stored as $\langle \sigma, m, \mathsf{bsn}, \mathcal{M}_i \rangle$ in a list Signed.

Verify. The verify interface VERIFY allows any party $\mathcal{V}$ to check whether σ is a valid signature on m with respect to bsn. The functionality will use its internal records to determine whether σ is a proper signature. Here we also use the helper algorithm identify to determine which of the gsk values stored by $\mathcal{F}_{\mathsf{daa}}^l$ belongs to that signature. If the key belongs to an honest TPM, then an entry $\langle \sigma, m, \mathsf{bsn}, \mathcal{M}_i \rangle \in$ Signed must exist. For signatures of corrupt TPMs, $\mathcal{F}_{\mathsf{daa}}^l$ checks that a valid signature would not violate any of the expected properties, e.g., whether the signature links to another signature by an honest TPM.

The interface also provides verifier-local revocation, as it excepts a revocations list RL as additional input which is a list of gsk's from which the verifier does not accept signatures anymore. To ensure that this does not harm the anonymity of honest TPMs, $\mathcal{F}_{\mathsf{daa}}^l$ ignores all honest $gsk's$ for the revocation check.

If the $\mathcal{F}_{\mathsf{daa}}^l$ did find some reason why the signature should *not* be valid, it sets the output to $f \leftarrow 0$. Otherwise, it determines the verification result f using the ver algorithm. Finally, the functionality keeps track of this result by adding $\langle \sigma, m, \mathsf{bsn}, \mathsf{RL}, f \rangle$ to a list VerResults.

Link. Any party $\mathcal{V}$ can use the LINK interface to learn whether two signature $(\sigma, m), (\sigma', m')$ generated for the same basename bsn originate from the same TPM or not. Similarly as for verification, $\mathcal{F}_{\mathsf{daa}}^l$ then first uses its internal records and helper functions to determine if there is any evidence for linkage or non-linkage. If such evidence is found, then the output bit f is set accordingly to 0 or 1. When the functionality has no evidence that the signatures must or must not belong together, it determines the linking result via the link algorithm.

The full definition of $\mathcal{F}_{\mathsf{daa}}^l$ is given in Figs. 1 and 2. To save on repeating and non-essential notation, we use the following conventions in our definition:

- All requests other than the SETUP are ignored until setup phase is completed. For such requests, $\mathcal{F}$ outputs $\perp$ to the caller immediately.
- Whenever the functionality performs a check that fails, it outputs $\perp$ directly to the caller of the respective interface.

- We require the link algorithm to be symmetric: $\text{link}(\sigma, m, \sigma', m', \text{bsn}) \leftrightarrow \text{link}(\sigma', m', \sigma, m, \text{bsn})$. To guarantee this, whenever we write that $\mathcal{F}$ runs $\text{link}(\sigma, m, \sigma', m', \text{bsn})$, it runs $\text{link}(\sigma, m, \sigma', m', \text{bsn})$ and $\text{link}(\sigma', m', \sigma, m, \text{bsn})$. If the results are equal, it continues as normal with the result, and otherwise $\mathcal{F}$ outputs $\bot$ to the adversary.
- When $\mathcal{F}$ runs algorithms $\text{sig}, \text{ver}, \text{identify}, \text{link}, \text{ukgen}$, it does so without maintaining state. This means all user keys have the same distribution, signatures are equally distributed for the same input, and $\text{ver}, \text{identify}$, and link invocations only depend on the current input, not on previous inputs.

We will further use two "macros" to determine if a gsk is consistent with the functionalities records or not. This is checked at several places in our functionality and also depends on whether the gsk belongs to an honest or corrupt TPM. The first macro CheckGskHonest is used when the functionality stores a new TPM key gsk that belongs to an honest TPM, and checks that none of the existing valid signatures are identified as belonging to this TPM key. The second macro CheckGskCorrupt is used when storing a new gsk that belongs to a corrupt TPM, and checks that the new gsk does not break the identifiability of signatures, i.e., it checks that there is no other known TPM key gsk', unequal to gsk, such that both keys are identified as the owner of a signature. Both functions output a bit b where $b = 1$ indicates that the new gsk is consistent with the stored information, whereas $b = 0$ signals an invalid key. Formally, the two macros are defined as follows.

$\text{CheckGskHonest}(gsk) =$

$\qquad \forall \langle \sigma, m, \text{bsn}, \mathcal{M} \rangle \in \texttt{Signed} : \text{identify}(\sigma, m, \text{bsn}, gsk) = 0 \ \land$

$\qquad\qquad \forall \langle \sigma, m, \text{bsn}, *, 1 \rangle \in \texttt{VerResults} : \text{identify}(\sigma, m, \text{bsn}, gsk) = 0$

$\text{CheckGskCorrupt}(gsk) =$

$\neg \exists \sigma, m, \text{bsn} : \big((\langle \sigma, m, \text{bsn}, * \rangle \in \texttt{Signed} \lor \langle \sigma, m, \text{bsn}, *, 1 \rangle \in \texttt{VerResults}) \ \land$

$\exists gsk' : (gsk \neq gsk' \land (\langle *, *, gsk' \rangle \in \texttt{Members} \lor \langle *, *, gsk' \rangle \in \texttt{DomainKeys}) \ \land$

$\qquad\qquad \text{identify}(\sigma, m, \text{bsn}, gsk) = \text{identify}(\sigma, m, \text{bsn}, gsk') = 1) \big)$

3.2 Detailed Analysis of $\mathcal{F}_{\text{daa}}^{l}$

We now argue that our functionality enforces the desired unforgeability, anonymity and non-frameability properties we informally introduced in Sect. 2.

In terms of completeness and correctness, we further have to add to three more properties: consistency of verify and link, and consistency of link. These properties are trivially achieved for property-based definitions, where one simply requires the algorithms to be deterministic, and the link algorithm to be symmetric. In a simulation-based definition, however, the behavior of a functionality may depend on its state, which is why we explicitly show that we achieve these properties.

We start with the security related properties unforgeability, anonymity and non-frameability, and then discuss the correctness and consistency properties.

Setup

1. **Issuer Setup.** On input (SETUP, sid) from issuer $\mathcal{I}$
   - Verify that $sid = (\mathcal{I}, sid')$ and output (SETUP, sid) to $\mathcal{S}$.
2. **Set Algorithms.** On input (ALG, sid, sig, ver, link, identify, ukgen) from $\mathcal{S}$
   - Check that ver, link and identify are deterministic **(i)**.
   - Store $(sid, \text{sig}, \text{ver}, \text{link}, \text{identify}, \text{ukgen})$ and output (SETUPDONE, sid) to $\mathcal{I}$.

Join

3. **Join Request.** On input (JOIN, sid, $jsid$, $\mathcal{M}_i$) from host $\mathcal{H}_j$
   - Create a join session record $\langle jsid, \mathcal{M}_i, \mathcal{H}_j, status \rangle$ with $status \leftarrow request$.
   - Output (JOINSTART, sid, $jsid$, $\mathcal{M}_i$, $\mathcal{H}_j$) to $\mathcal{S}$.
4. **Join Request Delivery.** On input (JOINSTART, sid, $jsid$) from $\mathcal{S}$
   - Update the session record $\langle jsid, \mathcal{M}_i, \mathcal{H}_j, status \rangle$ to $status \leftarrow delivered$.
   - Abort if $\mathcal{I}$ or $\mathcal{M}_i$ is honest and a record $\langle \mathcal{M}_i, *, * \rangle \in$ Members already exists **(ii)**.
   - Output (JOINPROCEED, sid, $jsid$, $\mathcal{M}_i$) to $\mathcal{I}$.
5. **Join Proceed.** On input (JOINPROCEED, sid, $jsid$) from $\mathcal{I}$
   - Update the session record $\langle jsid, \mathcal{M}_i, \mathcal{H}_j, status \rangle$ to $status \leftarrow complete$.
   - Output (JOINCOMPLETE, sid, $jsid$) to $\mathcal{S}$.
6. **Platform Key Generation.** On input (JOINCOMPLETE, sid, $jsid$, gsk) from $\mathcal{S}$.
   - Look up record $\langle jsid, \mathcal{M}_i, \mathcal{H}_j, status \rangle$ with $status = complete$.
   - If $\mathcal{M}_i$ and $\mathcal{H}_j$ are honest, set $gsk \leftarrow \perp$.
   - Else, verify that the provided gsk is eligible by checking
     - CheckGskHonest(gsk) = 1 **(iii)** if $\mathcal{H}_j$ is corrupt and $\mathcal{M}_i$ is honest, or
     - CheckGskCorrupt(gsk) = 1 **(iv)** if $\mathcal{M}_i$ is corrupt.
   - Insert $\langle \mathcal{M}_i, \mathcal{H}_j, gsk \rangle$ into Members and output (JOINED, sid, $jsid$) to $\mathcal{H}_j$.

Fig. 1. The setup and join related interfaces of $\mathcal{F}_{\text{daa}}^l$. *(The roman numbers are labels for the different checks made within the functionality and will be used as references in the detailed analysis in Sect. 3.2)*

Unforgeability. We consider two unforgeability properties, depending on all TPMs being honest or some of them being corrupt. The issuer is of course always honest when aiming at unforgeability. Firstly, if all TPMs are honest, an adversary cannot create a signature on a message m with respect to basename bsn when no honest TPM signed m with respect to bsn. By Check **(x)**, the signature must trace to some TPMs gsk. As we assumed all TPMs to be honest, Check **(xi)** will reject any signature on messages not signed by that TPM.

Secondly, when some TPMs are corrupt, an adversary cannot forge signatures with more distinct 'identities' than there are corrupt TPMs. More precisely, when the adversary corrupted n TPMs, he cannot create more than n unlinkable signatures for the same bsn $\neq \perp$, and when no honest TPM signed under bsn too. We show that for any $n + 1$ signatures $\{\sigma_i, m_i, \text{bsn}\}_{0 \geq i \geq n}$, we cannot have that all signatures verify, m_i was not signed with respect to bsn by an honest TPMs, and every pair of signatures is unlinkable.

If all signatures verify, by Check **(x)**, each of the $n+1$ signatures must trace to exactly one pair $(\mathcal{M}_i, gsk_i)$. Given the fact that no honest TPM signed m_i with respect to bsn, by Check **(xi)**, we must have that every TPM in the list of tracing $(\mathcal{M}_i, gsk_i)$ pairs is corrupt. Furthermore, we know that all $(\mathcal{M}_i, gsk_i)$ come from

Sign

7. **Sign Request.** On input (SIGN, $sid, ssid, \mathcal{M}_i, m, \mathsf{bsn}$) from host $\mathcal{H}_j$.
   - If $\mathcal{I}$ is honest and no entry $\langle \mathcal{M}_i, \mathcal{H}_j, * \rangle$ exists in Members, abort.
   - Create a sign session record $\langle ssid, \mathcal{M}_i, \mathcal{H}_j, m, \mathsf{bsn}, status \rangle$ with $status \leftarrow request$.
   - Output (SIGNSTART, $sid, ssid, l(m, \mathsf{bsn}), \mathcal{M}_i, \mathcal{H}_j$) to $\mathcal{S}$.
8. **Sign Request Delivery.** On input (SIGNSTART, $sid, ssid$) from $\mathcal{S}$.
   - Update the session record $\langle ssid, \mathcal{M}_i, \mathcal{H}_j, m, \mathsf{bsn}, status \rangle$ to $status \leftarrow delivered$.
   - Output (SIGNPROCEED, $sid, ssid, m, \mathsf{bsn}$) to $\mathcal{M}_i$.
9. **Sign Proceed.** On input (SIGNPROCEED, $sid, ssid$) from $\mathcal{M}_i$.
   - Look up record $\langle ssid, \mathcal{M}_i, \mathcal{H}_j, m, \mathsf{bsn}, status \rangle$ with $status = delivered$.
   - Output (SIGNCOMPLETE, $sid, ssid$) to $\mathcal{S}$.
10. **Signature Generation.** On input (SIGNCOMPLETE, $sid, ssid, \sigma$) from $\mathcal{S}$.
    - If $\mathcal{M}_i$ and $\mathcal{H}_j$ are honest, ignore the adversary's signature and internally generate the signature for a fresh or established gsk:
      - If $\mathsf{bsn} \neq \perp$, retrieve gsk from $\langle \mathcal{M}_i, \mathsf{bsn}, gsk \rangle \in$ DomainKeys for $(\mathcal{M}_i, \mathsf{bsn})$. If no such gsk exists or $\mathsf{bsn} = \perp$, set $gsk \leftarrow \mathsf{ukgen}()$. Check CheckGskHonest$(gsk) = 1$ **(v)** and store $\langle \mathcal{M}_i, \mathsf{bsn}, gsk \rangle$ in DomainKeys.
      - Compute signature as $\sigma \leftarrow \mathsf{sig}(gsk, m, \mathsf{bsn})$ and check $\mathsf{ver}(\sigma, m, \mathsf{bsn}) = 1$ **(vi)**.
      - Check $\mathsf{identify}(\sigma, m, \mathsf{bsn}, gsk) = 1$ **(vii)** and check that there is no $\mathcal{M}_i' \neq \mathcal{M}_i$ with key gsk' registered in Members or DomainKeys with $\mathsf{identify}(\sigma, m, \mathsf{bsn}, gsk') = 1$ **(viii)**.
    - If $\mathcal{M}_i$ is honest, store $\langle \sigma, m, \mathsf{bsn}, \mathcal{M}_i \rangle$ in Signed.
    - Output (SIGNATURE, $sid, ssid, \sigma$) to $\mathcal{H}_j$.

Verify

11. **Verify.** On input (VERIFY, $sid, m, \mathsf{bsn}, \sigma, \mathsf{RL}$) from some party $\mathcal{V}$.
    - Retrieve all pairs $(gsk_i, \mathcal{M}_i)$ from $\langle \mathcal{M}_i, *, gsk_i \rangle \in$ Members and $\langle \mathcal{M}_i, *, gsk_i \rangle \in$ DomainKeys where $\mathsf{identify}(\sigma, m, \mathsf{bsn}, gsk_i) = 1$. Set $f \leftarrow 0$ if at least one of the following conditions hold:
      - More than one key gsk_i was found **(ix)**.
      - $\mathcal{I}$ is honest and no pair $(gsk_i, \mathcal{M}_i)$ was found **(x)**.
      - There is an honest $\mathcal{M}_i$ but no entry $\langle *, m, \mathsf{bsn}, \mathcal{M}_i \rangle \in$ Signed exists **(xi)**.
      - There is a $gsk' \in \mathsf{RL}$ where $\mathsf{identify}(\sigma, m, \mathsf{bsn}, gsk') = 1$ and no pair $(gsk_i, \mathcal{M}_i)$ for an honest $\mathcal{M}_i$ was found **(xii)**.
    - If $f \neq 0$, set $f \leftarrow \mathsf{ver}(\sigma, m, \mathsf{bsn})$ **(xiii)**.
    - Add $\langle \sigma, m, \mathsf{bsn}, \mathsf{RL}, f \rangle$ to VerResults, output (VERIFIED, sid, f) to $\mathcal{V}$.

Link

12. **Link.** On input (LINK, $sid, \sigma, m, \sigma', m', \mathsf{bsn}$) from some party $\mathcal{V}$ with $\mathsf{bsn} \neq \perp$.
    - Output $\perp$ to $\mathcal{V}$ if at least one signature tuple $(\sigma, m, \mathsf{bsn})$ or $(\sigma', m', \mathsf{bsn})$ is not valid (verified via the verify interface with $\mathsf{RL} = \emptyset$) **(xiv)**.
    - For each gsk_i in Members and DomainKeys compute $b_i \leftarrow \mathsf{identify}(\sigma, m, \mathsf{bsn}, gsk_i)$ and $b_i' \leftarrow \mathsf{identify}(\sigma', m', \mathsf{bsn}, gsk_i)$ and do the following:
      - Set $f \leftarrow 0$ if $b_i \neq b_i'$ for some i **(xv)**.
      - Set $f \leftarrow 1$ if $b_i = b_i' = 1$ for some i **(xvi)**.
    - If f is not defined yet, set $f \leftarrow \mathsf{link}(\sigma, m, \sigma', m', \mathsf{bsn})$.
    - Output (LINK, sid, f) to $\mathcal{V}$.

Fig. 2. The sign, verify, and link related interfaces of $\mathcal{F}_{\mathsf{daa}}^l$

Members, as only honest TPMs occur in **DomainKeys**. Since the issuer is honest, Check (ii) enforces that every TPM can join at most once, i.e., there can be at most n pairs $(\mathcal{M}_i, gsk_i)$ of corrupt TPMs in **Members**. Thus, the traced list of $(\mathcal{M}_i, gsk_i)$ pairs must contain at least one duplicate entry. By Check (xvi), the two signatures that trace to the same gsk must link, showing that the adversary cannot forge more than n unlinkable signatures with a single **bsn** $\neq \perp$.

Anonymity. Anonymity of signatures created by an honest TPM $\mathcal{M}_i$ and host $\mathcal{H}_j$ is guaranteed by $\mathcal{F}_{\mathsf{daa}}^l$ due to the random choice of gsk for every signature. More precisely, if the platform is honest, our functionality does not store any unique gsk for the pair $(\mathcal{M}_i, \mathcal{H}_j)$ in **Members**, but leaves the key unassigned. Whenever a new signature is requested for an unused basename **bsn**, $\mathcal{F}_{\mathsf{daa}}^l$ first draws a fresh key $gsk \leftarrow$ ukgen under which it then creates the signature using the **sig** algorithm. The combination of basename and key is stored as $\langle \mathcal{M}_i, \mathsf{bsn}, gsk \rangle$ in a list **DomainKeys**, and gsk is re-used whenever $\mathcal{M}_i$ wishes to sign under the same **bsn** $\neq \perp$ again.

That is, two signatures with different basenames or with basename **bsn** $= \perp$ are distributed in exactly the same way for all honest platforms, independent of whether the signatures are created for the same platform or for two distinct platforms.

Verifier-local revocation is enabled via the revocation list attribute **RL** in the **VERIFY** interface and allows to "block" signatures of exposed gsk's. This revocation feature should not be exploitable to trace honest users, though, as that would clearly break anonymity. To this end, $\mathcal{F}_{\mathsf{daa}}^l$ ignores $gsk \in$ **RL** in the revocation test when the key belongs to an honest TPM (Check (xii)).

Note that the anonymity property dictated the use of the **sig** algorithm in $\mathcal{F}_{\mathsf{daa}}^l$. We only use the algorithm if the platform is honest though, whereas for corrupt platforms the simulator is allowed to provide the signature (which then could depend on the identity of the signer). This immediately reflects that anonymity is only guaranteed if both the TPM and host are honest.

Non-frameability. An honest platform $(\mathcal{M}_i, \mathcal{H}_j)$ cannot be framed, meaning that no one can create signatures on messages that the platform never signed but that link to signatures the platform did create. Note that this definition also crucially relies on both $\mathcal{M}_i, \mathcal{H}_j$ being honest. Intuitively, one might expect that only the TPM $\mathcal{M}_i$ is required to be honest, and the host could be corrupt. However, that would be unachievable. We can never control the signatures that a corrupt $\mathcal{H}_j$ outputs. In particular, the host could additionally run a corrupt TPM that joined as well, and create signatures using the corrupt TPM's key instead of using $\mathcal{M}_i$'s contribution. The resulting signature can not be protected from framing, as it uses a corrupt TPM's key. Thus, for a meaningful non-frameability guarantee, the host has to be honest too. The issuer can of course be corrupt.

We now show that when an honest platform $(\mathcal{M}_i, \mathcal{H}_j)$ created a signature σ on message m and under basename **bsn**, then no other signature σ' on some m' links to σ when $(\mathcal{M}_i, \mathcal{H}_j)$ never signed m' with respect to **bsn**. The first requirement in **LINK** is that both signatures must be valid (Check (xiv)). By completeness (discussed below) we know that σ, m, bsn generated by the honest platform is valid, and that it traces to some key gsk. If the second signature $\sigma', m', \mathsf{bsn}$ is valid too, we know by the Check (xi) in the VERIFY interface that the signature cannot trace to the same gsk, because $(\mathcal{M}_i, \mathcal{H}_j)$ has never signed m', bsn'. Finally, by Check (xv) that ensures that the output of identify must be consistent for *all* used keys, the output of LINK is set to $f \leftarrow 0$.

Completeness. The functionality guarantees completeness, i.e., when an honest platform successfully creates a signature, this signature will be accepted by honest verifiers. More precisely, when honest TPM $\mathcal{M}_i$ with honest host $\mathcal{H}_j$ signs m with respect to bsn resulting in a signature σ, a verifier will accept $(\sigma, m, \mathsf{bsn})$. To show this, we argue that the four checks the functionality makes (Check (ix), Check (x), Check (xi), and Check (xii)) do not set f to 0, and that ver will accept the signature.

Check (ix) will not trigger, as by Check (viii) there was no honest TPM other than $\mathcal{M}_i$ with a key matching this signature yet and, by Check (iv), Check (iv), and Check (v), gsk values matching σ cannot be added to Members and DomainKeys.

Check (x) will not trigger as we have an entry $\langle \mathcal{M}_i, \mathsf{bsn}, gsk \rangle \in$ DomainKeys, and by Check (vii) we know this one matches σ.

In Check (xi), $\mathcal{F}_{\mathsf{daa}}^l$ finds all honest TPMs that have a key matching this signature, and checks whether they signed m with respect to bsn. By Check (viii), at the time of signing there were no other TPMs with keys matching this signature and, by Check (iii) and Check (v), no honest TPM can get a key matching this signature. The only honest TPM with a matching key is $\mathcal{M}_i$, but as he honestly signed m with respect to bsn, we have an entry $\langle \sigma, m, \mathsf{bsn}, \mathcal{M}_i \rangle \in$ Signed ensuring that the check does not trigger.

The revocation test Check (xii) does not trigger as by Check (vii) we know that honest TPM $\mathcal{M}_i$ has a key matching this signature.

As all previous checks did not apply, $\mathcal{F}_{\mathsf{daa}}^l$ sets the verification outcome using the ver algorithm, we now show that ver will accept the signature. $\mathcal{F}_{\mathsf{daa}}^l$ checked that ver accepts the signature in Check (vi), and by Check (i) and the fact that $\mathcal{F}_{\mathsf{daa}}^l$ does not maintain state for the algorithms, the verification algorithm output only depends on its input, so ver outputs 1 and $\mathcal{F}_{\mathsf{daa}}^l$ accepts the signature.

Correctness of Link. If an honest platform signs multiple times with the same basename, the resulting signatures will link. Let platform $(\mathcal{M}_i, \mathcal{H}_j)$ sign messages m_1 and m_2 with basename $\mathsf{bsn} \neq \perp$, resulting in signatures σ_1 and σ_2 respectively. By completeness, both signatures verify, so Check (xiv) does not trigger. By Check (vii), both signatures identify to some gsk, which results in Check (xvi) setting the signatures as linked.

Consistency of Verify. This property ensures that calling the VERIFY interface with the same input multiple times gives the same result every time. To prevent the functionality from becoming unnecessarily complex, we only enforce consistency for valid signatures. That is, whenever a signature was accepted, it will remain valid, whereas an invalid signature could become valid at a later time.

Suppose a signature σ on message m with basename bsn was verified success-fully with revocation list RL. We now show that in any future verification with the same RL will lead to the same result. To show this, we argue that the four checks the functionality makes (Check (ix), Check (x), Check (xi), and Check (xii)) do not set f to 0, and that ver will accept the signature.

Check (ix) makes sure that at most one key gsk matches the signature σ, meaning that for at most one gsk we have identify$(\sigma, m, \text{bsn}, gsk) = 1$. This check does not cause rejection of the signature, as the signature previously verified, and by Check (ix) we have that at most one gsk matched the signature at that time. After that, the signature was placed in VerResults, which means Check (iii), Check (iv), and Check (v) prevent adding gsk values that match σ, so the number of matching gsk values has not changed and Check (ix) still passes.

Check (x) does not apply. If $\mathcal{I}$ is corrupt, the check trivially does not trigger. If $\mathcal{I}$ is honest, from the previous verification we have that there was precisely one key matching, and as argued for the previous check, no matching gsk values can be added, so we must still have precisely one matching gsk.

To show that Check (xi) does not apply, we must show that for every honest TPM that has a key matching this signature, that TPM has signed m with respect to bsn. As the check previously passed, so we know that at that point for any matching $\mathcal{M}_i$ there is a satisfying entry in Signed. No new TPMs matching this signature can be found, as Check (iii) and Check (v) prevent honest TPMs from registering a key that matches an existing signature.

Check (xii), the revocation check, did not reject σ in the previous verifica-tion. By the fact that identify is deterministic Check (i) and executed without maintaining state, it will not do so now.

As the four checks $\mathcal{F}_{\text{daa}}^l$ makes did not apply, $\mathcal{F}_{\text{daa}}^l$ uses the verification algo-rithm ver. Since the signature was previously accepted, by Check (xiii) ver must have accepted the signature. By the fact that ver is deterministic (Check (i)) and executed without maintaining state, it will also accept now.

Consistency of Link. We also want to ensure that calling the LINK interface with the same input multiple times gives the same result every time. Here we guarantee consistency for both outputs $f \in \{0, 1\}$ i.e., if LINK outputs f for some input $(\sigma, m, \sigma', m', \text{bsn})$, the result will always be f.

Suppose we have signatures σ and σ' on messages m and m' respectively, both with respect to basename bsn, that have been linked with output $f \in \{0, 1\}$ before. We now show that the same result f will be given in future queries, by showing that Check (xiv) will not cause an output of $\bot$, and by showing that Check (xv), Check (xvi), and the link algorithm are consistent.

$\mathcal{F}_{\text{daa}}^l$ will not output $\bot$, as by the previous output $f \neq \bot$ we know that the verification of both signatures must have passed. As VERIFY is consistent for valid signatures, this test in Check (xiv) will pass again.

Check (xv) and Check (xvi) are consistent. They depend on the gsk values in Members and DomainKeys that match the signatures and are retrieved via the deterministic identify algorithm. The matching gsk values cannot have changed as Check (iii), Check (iv), and Check (v) prevent conflicting gsk values to be added to these lists. The link algorithm used to in the final step is deterministic by Check (i). Thus, Link will consistently generate the same output bit f.

Symmetry of Link. The link interface is symmetric, i.e., it does not matter whether one gives input $(\mathsf{LINK}, \sigma, m, \sigma', m', \mathtt{bsn})$ or $(\mathsf{LINK}, \sigma', m', \sigma, m, \mathtt{bsn})$. Both signatures are verified, the order in which this happens does not change the outcome. Next $\mathcal{F}_{\mathsf{daa}}^l$ finds matching keys for the signatures, and as identify is executed without state, it does not matter whether it first tries to match σ or σ'. The next checks are based on the equality of the b_i and b_i' values, which clearly is symmetric. Finally $\mathcal{F}_{\mathsf{daa}}^l$ uses the link algorithm, which is enforced to be symmetric as $\mathcal{F}_{\mathsf{daa}}^l$ will abort as soon as it detects link not being symmetric.

4 Building Blocks

In this section we introduce the building blocks for our construction. Apart from standard building blocks such as pairing-based CL-signatures [9] and zero-knowledge proofs, we also provide a new functionality $\mathcal{F}_{\mathsf{auth}*}$ that captures the semi-authenticated channel that is present in the DAA setting.

4.1 Bilinear Maps

Let $\mathbb{G}_1$, $\mathbb{G}_2$ and $\mathbb{G}_T$ be groups of prime order q. A map $e : \mathbb{G}_1 \times \mathbb{G}_2 \to \mathbb{G}_T$ must satisfy bilinearity, i.e., $e(g_1^x, g_2^y) = e(g_1, g_2)^{xy}$; non-degeneracy, i.e., for all generators $g_1 \in \mathbb{G}_1$ and $g_2 \in \mathbb{G}_2$, $e(g_1, g_2)$ generates $\mathbb{G}_T$; and efficiency, i.e., there exists an efficient algorithm $\mathcal{G}(1^\tau)$ that outputs the bilinear group $(q, \mathbb{G}_1, \mathbb{G}_2, \mathbb{G}_T, e, g_1, g_2)$ and an efficient algorithm to compute $e(a, b)$ for any $a \in \mathbb{G}_1, b \in \mathbb{G}_2$. If $\mathbb{G}_1 = \mathbb{G}_2$ the map is called symmetric, otherwise the map is called asymmetric.

4.2 Camenisch-Lysyanskaya Signature

We now recall the pairing-based Camenisch-Lysyanskaya (CL) signature scheme [9] that allows for efficient proofs of signature possession and is the basis for the DAA scheme we extend. The scheme uses a bilinear group $(q, \mathbb{G}_1, \mathbb{G}_2, \mathbb{G}_T, e, g_1, g_2)$ that is available to all algorithms.

Key generation. The key generation algorithm chooses $x \xleftarrow{\$} \mathbb{Z}_q$ and $y \xleftarrow{\$} \mathbb{Z}_q$, and sets $sk \leftarrow (x, y)$, $pk \leftarrow (X, Y)$, where $X \leftarrow g_2^x$ and $Y \leftarrow g_2^y$.

Signature. On input a message m and secret key $sk = (x, y)$, choose a random $a \xleftarrow{\$} \mathbb{G}_1$, and output the signature $\sigma \leftarrow (a, a^y, a^{x+mxy})$.

Verification. On input a public key $pk = (X, Y)$, message m, and purported signature $\sigma = (a, b, c)$, output 1 if the following verification equations hold, and 0 otherwise: $a \neq 1_{\mathbb{G}_1}$, $e(a, Y) = e(g_1, b)$ and $e(X, a) \cdot e(X, b)^m = e(g_1, c)$.

This signature scheme is existentially unforgeable against a chosen-message attack (EUF-CMA) under the LRSW assumption [21], which is proven in [9]. Certain schemes [3, 18], including ours, add a fourth element $d = b^m$ to the signature, which allows more efficient proofs of knowledge of a message signed by a signature. This extended CL signature is as secure as the original CL signature: Any adversary that can create a standard CL forgery (a, b, c) on message m can forge an extended CL signature by adding $d = b^m$. Any adversary that can create an extended CL forgery (a, b, c, d) on m can forge a standard CL signature, by adding $d = b^m$ to the signing oracle outputs, and omitting d from the final forgery.

4.3 Proof Protocols

When referring to the zero-knowledge proofs of knowledge of discrete logarithms and statements about them, we will follow the notation introduced by Camenisch and Stadler [11] and formally defined by Camenisch, Kiayias, and Yung [8].

For instance, $PK\{(a, b, c) : y = g^a h^b \wedge \tilde{y} = \tilde{g}^a \tilde{h}^c\}$ denotes a *"zero-knowledge Proof of Knowledge of integers a, b and c such that $y = g^a h^b$ and $\tilde{y} = \tilde{g}^a \tilde{h}^c$ holds,"* where $y, g, h, \tilde{y}, \tilde{g}$ and $\tilde{h}$ are elements of some groups $\mathbb{G} = \langle g \rangle = \langle h \rangle$ and $\tilde{\mathbb{G}} = \langle \tilde{g} \rangle = \langle \tilde{h} \rangle$. Given a protocol in this notation, it is straightforward to derive an actual protocol implementing the proof [8]. Indeed, the computational complexities of the proof protocol can be easily derived from this notation: for each term $y = g^a h^b$, the prover and the verifier have to perform an equivalent computation, and to transmit one group element and one response value for each exponent.

SPK denotes a signature proof of knowledge, that is a non-interactive transformation of a proof with the Fiat-Shamir heuristic [19] in the random oracle model [2]. From these non-interactive proofs, the witness can be extracted by rewinding the prover and programming the random oracle. Alternatively, these proofs can be extended to be online-extractable, by verifiably encrypting the witness to a public key defined in the common reference string (CRS). Now a simulator controlling the CRS can extract the witness without rewinding by decrypting the ciphertext. A practical instantiation is given by Camenisch and Shoup [10] using Paillier encryption, secure under the DCR assumption [22].

4.4 Semi-Authenticated Channels via $\mathcal{F}_{\mathsf{auth}*}$

In the join protocol of DAA, it is crucial that the TPM and issuer authenticate to each other, such that only authentic TPMs can create signatures. This is not an ordinary authenticated channel, as all communication is channeled via the host, that can read the messages, block the communication, or append messages. There exist several sub-protocols and setup settings in the DAA context that provide this type of special authenticated channels, of which an overview is given by Bernard et al. [3]. These constructions require the TPM to have a key pair, the endorsement key, of which the public part is known to the issuer. In practice, the TPM manufacturer certifies the public key using traditional PKI, allowing an issuer to verify that this public key indeed belongs to a certain TPM. If the endorsement key is a key for a signature scheme, the TPM can send an authenticated message to the issuer by signing the message. If a public key encryption key is used, this can be used to exchange a MAC key to authenticate later messages.

We design a functionality $\mathcal{F}_{\mathsf{auth}*}$ modeling the desired channel, which allows us to rather use the abstract functionality in the protocol design instead of a concrete sub-protocol. Then, any protocol that securely realizes $\mathcal{F}_{\mathsf{auth}*}$ can be used for the initial authentication.

The functionality must capture the fact that the sender S sends a message containing an authenticated and an unauthenticated part to the receiver R, while giving some forwarder F (this role will be played by the host) the power to block the message or replace the unauthenticated part, and giving the adversary the power to replace the forwarder's message and block the communication. We capture these requirements in $\mathcal{F}_{\mathsf{auth}*}$, defined in Fig. 3.

---

1. On input (SEND, $sid, ssid, m_1, m_2, F$) from S. Check that $sid = (S, R, sid')$ for some R an output (REPLACE1, $sid, ssid, m_1, m_2, F$) to S.
2. On input (REPLACE1, $sid, ssid, m_2'$) from S, output (APPEND, $sid, ssid, m_1, m_2'$) to F.
3. On input (APPEND, $sid, ssid, m_2''$) from F, output (REPLACE2, $sid, ssid, m_1, m_2''$) to S.
4. On input (REPLACE2, $sid, ssid, m_2'''$) from S, output (SENT, $sid, ssid, m_1, m_2'''$) to R.

Fig. 3. The special authenticated communication functionality $\mathcal{F}_{\mathsf{auth}*}$

Clearly we can realize this functionality using the endorsement key and a signature scheme or public key encryption scheme.

5   Construction

In this section, we present our DAA scheme that securely implements $\mathcal{F}_{\mathsf{daa}}^l$. While our scheme is similar to previous constructions [3,6,7,16,18], it required several modifications in order to fulfill all of our desired security guarantees. We give a detailed discussion of the changes with respect to previous versions in Sect. 5.2.

The high-level idea of our DAA scheme is as follows. In the join protocol, a platform, consisting of a TPM $\mathcal{M}_i$ and host $\mathcal{H}_j$, receives a credential (a, b, c, d) from the issuer $\mathcal{I}$ which is a Camenisch-Lysyanskaya signature [9] on some TPM chosen secret gsk. After joining, the platform can sign any message m w.r.t. some basename bsn. To this end, the host first randomizes the credential (a, b, c, d) to $(a' = a^r, b' = b^r, c' = c^r, d' = d^r)$ for a random r and then lets the TPM $\mathcal{M}_i$ create a signature proof of knowledge (SPK) on m showing that $b'^{gsk} = d'$. To obtain user-controlled linkability for basenames bsn $\neq \perp$, pseudonyms are attached to the signature. Pseudonyms are similar to BLS signatures [4] on the basename and have the form nym $= H_1(\mathsf{bsn})^{gsk}$ for some hash function H_1. Whenever a basename bsn $\neq \perp$ is used, the SPK generated by the TPM also proves that the pseudonym is well-formed.

5.1   Our DAA Protocol Π_{daa}

We now present our DAA scheme in detail, and also give a simplified overview of the join and sign protocols in Figs. 4 and 5 respectively.

We assume that a common reference string functionality $\mathcal{F}_{\mathsf{crs}}^D$ and a certificate authority functionality $\mathcal{F}_{\mathsf{ca}}$ are available to all parties. The later allows the issuer to register his public key, and $\mathcal{F}_{\mathsf{crs}}^D$ is used to provide all entities with the system parameters comprising a security parameter τ, a bilinear group $\mathbb{G}_1, \mathbb{G}_2, \mathbb{G}_T$ of prime order q with generators g_1, g_2 and bilinear map e, generated via $\mathcal{G}(1^\tau)$. We further use a random oracle $H_1 : \{0,1\}^* \to \mathbb{G}_1$.

For the communication between the TPM and issuer (via the host) in the join protocol, we use our semi-authenticated channel $\mathcal{F}_{\mathsf{auth}*}$ introduced in Sect. 4.4. For all communication between a host and TPM we assume the secure message transmission functionality $\mathcal{F}_{\mathsf{smt}}^l$ (enabling authenticated and encrypted communication). In practice, $\mathcal{F}_{\mathsf{smt}}^l$ is naturally guaranteed by the physical proximity of the host and TPM forming the platform, i.e., if both are honest an adversary can neither alter nor read their internal communication. To make the protocol more readable, we simply say that $\mathcal{H}_i$ sends a message to, or receives a message from $\mathcal{M}_j$, instead of explicitly calling $\mathcal{F}_{\mathsf{smt}}^l$ with sub-session IDs etc. For definitions of the standard functionalities $\mathcal{F}_{\mathsf{crs}}^D$, $\mathcal{F}_{\mathsf{ca}}$ and $\mathcal{F}_{\mathsf{smt}}^l$ we refer to [12,13].

TPM	Host	Issuer
	$\xrightarrow{\quad\text{JOIN}\quad}$	
		$n \xleftarrow{\$} \{0,1\}^{l_n}$
$\xleftarrow{\quad n \quad}$	$\xleftarrow{\quad n \quad}$	
$gsk \xleftarrow{\$} \mathbb{Z}_q$		
$Q \leftarrow g_1^{gsk}$		
$\pi_1 \xleftarrow{\$} SPK\{(\alpha) : g_1^\alpha\}$		
$\xrightarrow{\quad Q, \pi_1 \quad}$	$\xrightarrow{\quad Q, \pi_1 \quad}$	
		verify π_1
		$r \xleftarrow{\$} \mathbb{Z}_q$
		$a \leftarrow g_1^r$
		$b \leftarrow a^{x+y \cdot m}$
		$c \leftarrow a^x \cdot Q^{rxy}$
		$d \leftarrow Q^{ry}$
		$\pi_2 \xleftarrow{\$} SPK\{(t) : b = g_1^t \wedge d = Q^t\}$
		$\xleftarrow{\quad a, b, c, d, \pi_2 \quad}$
	$e(a, X)e(c, Y) \overset{?}{=} e(b, g_2)$	
$\xleftarrow{\quad b, d, \pi_2 \quad}$		
verify π_2		
store (gsk, b, d)	$\xrightarrow{\quad\text{JOINED}\quad}$ store (a, b, c, d)	

Fig. 4. Overview of the join protocol

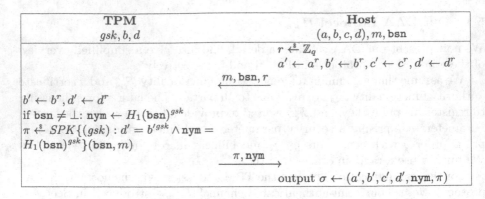

Fig. 5. Overview of the sign protocol

In the description of the protocol, we assume that parties call $\mathcal{F}_{crs}^D$ and $\mathcal{F}_{ca}$ to retrieve the necessary key material whenever they use a public key of another party. Further, if any of the checks in the protocol fails, the protocol ends with a failure message $\perp$. The protocol also outputs $\perp$ whenever a party receives an input or message it does not expect (e.g., protocol messages arriving in the wrong order.)

Setup. In the setup phase, the issuer $\mathcal{I}$ creates a key pair of the CL-signature scheme and registers the public key with $\mathcal{F}_{ca}$.

1. $\mathcal{I}$ upon input (SETUP, sid) generates his key pair:
   - Check that $sid = (\mathcal{I}, sid')$ for some sid'.
   - Choose $x, y \overset{\$}{\leftarrow} \mathbb{Z}_q$, and set $X \leftarrow g_2^x, Y \leftarrow g_2^y$. Initiate $\mathcal{L}_{\text{JOINED}} \leftarrow \emptyset$.
   - Prove that the key is well-formed in $\pi \overset{\$}{\leftarrow} SPK\{(x, y) : X = g_2^x \wedge Y = g_2^y\}$.
   - Register the public key (X, Y, π) at $\mathcal{F}_{ca}$, and store the secret key as (x, y).
   - Output (SETUPDONE, sid).

Join. The join protocol runs between the issuer $\mathcal{I}$ and a platform, consisting of a TPM $\mathcal{M}_i$ and a host $\mathcal{H}_j$. The platform authenticates to the issuer and, if the issuer allows, obtains a credential that subsequently enables the platform to create signatures. To distinguish several join sessions that might run in parallel, we use a unique sub-session identifier $jsid$ that is given as input to all parties.

1. $\mathcal{H}_j$ upon input (JOIN, sid, $jsid$, $\mathcal{M}_i$) parses $sid = (\mathcal{I}, sid')$ and sends the message (JOIN, sid, $jsid$) to $\mathcal{I}$.
2. $\mathcal{I}$ upon receiving (JOIN, sid, $jsid$) from a party $\mathcal{H}_j$ chooses a fresh nonce $n \leftarrow \{0, 1\}^\tau$ and sends $(sid, jsid, n)$ back to $\mathcal{H}_j$.
3. $\mathcal{H}_j$ upon receiving $(sid, jsid, n)$ from $\mathcal{I}$, sends $(sid, jsid, n)$ to $\mathcal{M}_i$.
4. $\mathcal{M}_i$ upon receiving $(sid, jsid, n)$ from $\mathcal{H}_j$, generates its secret key:
   - Check that no *completed* key record exists.
   - Choose $gsk \overset{\$}{\leftarrow} \mathbb{Z}_q$ and store the key as $(sid, \mathcal{H}_j, gsk, \perp)$.

- Set $Q \leftarrow g_1^{gsk}$ and compute $\pi_1 \overset{\$}{\leftarrow} SPK\{(gsk) : Q = g_1^{gsk}\}(n)$.
- Send (Q, π_1) via the host to $\mathcal{I}$ using $\mathcal{F}_{\text{auth*}}$, i.e., invoke $\mathcal{F}_{\text{auth*}}$ on input (SEND, $(\mathcal{M}_i, \mathcal{I}, sid), jsid, (Q, \pi_1), \mathcal{H}_j)$.

5. $\mathcal{H}_j$ upon receiving (APPEND, $(\mathcal{M}_i, \mathcal{I}, sid), jsid, Q, \pi_1)$ from $\mathcal{F}_{\text{auth*}}$, forwards the message to $\mathcal{I}$ by sending (APPEND, $(\mathcal{M}_i, \mathcal{I}, sid), jsid, \mathcal{H}_j)$ to $\mathcal{F}_{\text{auth*}}$. It also keeps state as $(jsid, Q)$.

6. $\mathcal{I}$ upon receiving (SENT, $(\mathcal{M}_i, \mathcal{I}, sid), jsid, (Q, \pi_1), \mathcal{H}_j)$ from $\mathcal{F}_{\text{auth*}}$ verifies π_1 and checks that $\mathcal{M}_i \notin \mathcal{L}_{\text{JOINED}}$. It stores $(jsid, Q, \mathcal{M}_i, \mathcal{H}_j)$ and outputs (JOINPROCEED, $sid, jsid, \mathcal{M}_i)$.

The join session is then completed when the issuer receives an explicit input telling him to proceed with join session $jsid$.

1. $\mathcal{I}$ upon input (JOINPROCEED, $sid, jsid$) generates the CL credential:
   - Retrieve the record $(jsid, Q, \mathcal{M}_i, \mathcal{H}_j)$ and add $\mathcal{M}_i$ to $\mathcal{L}_{\text{JOINED}}$.
   - Choose $r \leftarrow \mathbb{Z}_q$ and compute $a \leftarrow g_1^r$, $b \leftarrow a^y$, $c \leftarrow a^x \cdot Q^{rxy}$, $d \leftarrow Q^{ry}$.
   - Prove correctness of the signature in $\pi_2 \overset{\$}{\leftarrow} SPK\{(t) : b = g_1^t \wedge d = Q^t\}$.
   - Send the credential (a, b, c, d) to the host $\mathcal{H}_j$ by giving $\mathcal{F}_{\text{auth*}}$ input (SEND, $(\mathcal{I}, \mathcal{M}_i, sid), jsid, (b, d, \pi_2), (a, c), \mathcal{H}_j)$.

2. $\mathcal{H}_j$ upon receiving (APPEND, $(\mathcal{I}, \mathcal{M}_i, sid), jsid, (b, d, \pi_2), (a, c))$ from $\mathcal{F}_{\text{auth*}}$ verifies the credential (a, b, c, d) and forwards (b, d, π_2) to $\mathcal{M}_i$:
   - Retrieve $(jsid, Q)$ and verify π_2 w.r.t. Q.
   - Verify the credential as $a \neq 1$, $e(a, Y) = e(b, g_2)$, and $c(c, g_2) = e(a \cdot d, X)$.
   - Send (APPEND, $(\mathcal{I}, \mathcal{M}_i, sid), jsid, \perp)$ to $\mathcal{F}_{\text{auth*}}$.

3. $\mathcal{M}_i$ upon receiving (SENT, $(\mathcal{I}, \mathcal{M}_i, sid), jsid, (b, d, \pi_2), \perp)$ from $\mathcal{F}_{\text{auth*}}$, completes the join:
   - Retrieve the record $(sid, \mathcal{H}_j, gsk, \perp)$ and verify π_2 with respect to $Q \leftarrow g_1^{gsk}$.
   - Complete the record to $(sid, \mathcal{H}_j, gsk, (b, d))$ and send $(jsid, \text{JOINED})$ to $\mathcal{H}_j$.

4. $\mathcal{H}_j$ upon receiving $(jsid, \text{JOINED})$ from $\mathcal{M}_i$ stores $(sid, \mathcal{M}_i, (a, b, c, d))$ and outputs (JOINED, $sid, jsid$).

Sign. The sign protocol runs between a TPM $\mathcal{M}_i$ and a host $\mathcal{H}_j$. After joining, together they can sign a message m with respect to basename **bsn**. Again, we use a unique sub-session identifier $ssid$ to allow for multiple sign sessions.

1. $\mathcal{H}_j$ upon input (SIGN, $sid, ssid, \mathcal{M}_i, m, \text{bsn}$) re-randomizes the CL-credential:
   - Retrieve the join record $(sid, \mathcal{M}_i, (a, b, c, d))$.
   - Choose $r \overset{\$}{\leftarrow} \mathbb{Z}_q$ and set $(a', b', c', d') \leftarrow (a^r, b^r, c^r, d^r)$.
   - Send $(ssid, m, \text{bsn}, r)$ to $\mathcal{M}_i$ and store $(ssid, (a', b', c', d'))$

2. $\mathcal{M}_i$ upon receiving $(ssid, m, \text{bsn}, r)$ from $\mathcal{H}_j$ asks for permission to proceed.
   - Check that a complete join record $(sid, \mathcal{H}_j, gsk, (b, d))$ exists.
   - Store $(ssid, m, \text{bsn}, r)$ and output (SIGNPROCEED, $sid, ssid, m, \text{bsn}$).

The signature is completed when $\mathcal{M}_i$ gets permission to proceed for *ssid*.

1. $\mathcal{M}_i$ upon input (SIGNPROCEED, *sid*, *ssid*) computes the SPK and nym:
   - Retrieve records $(sid, \mathcal{H}_j, gsk, (b, d))$ and $(ssid, m, \mathbf{bsn}, r)$.
   - Compute $b' \leftarrow b^r, d' \leftarrow d^r$.
   - If $\mathbf{bsn} = \bot$, set $\mathtt{nym} = \bot$ and compute $\pi \overset{\$}{\leftarrow} SPK\{(gsk) : d' = b'^{gsk}\}(m, \mathbf{bsn})$.
   - If $\mathbf{bsn} \neq \bot$, set $\mathtt{nym} = H_1(\mathbf{bsn})^{gsk}$ and compute the SPK on (m,bsn) as $\pi \overset{\$}{\leftarrow} SPK\{(gsk) : \mathtt{nym} = H_1(\mathbf{bsn})^{gsk} \wedge d' = b'^{gsk}\}(m, \mathbf{bsn})$.
   - Send $(ssid, \pi, \mathtt{nym})$ to $\mathcal{H}_j$.
2. $\mathcal{H}_j$ upon receiving $(ssid, \pi, \mathtt{nym})$ from $\mathcal{H}_j$, retrieves $(ssid, (a', b', c', d'))$ and outputs (SIGNATURE, *sid*, *ssid*, $(a', b', c', d', \pi, \mathtt{nym})$).

Verify. The verify algorithm allows everyone to check whether signature σ on message m with respect to basename $\mathbf{bsn}$ is valid, i.e., stems from a certified TPM. To test whether the signature originates from a TPM that did get corrupted, the verifier can pass a revocation list RL to the algorithm. This list contains the keys of corrupted TPMs he no longer wishes to accept signatures from.

1. $\mathcal{V}$ upon input (VERIFY, *sid*, m, $\mathbf{bsn}$, σ, RL) verifies the signature:
   - Parse σ as $(a, b, c, d, \pi, \mathtt{nym})$.
   - Verify π with respect to $(m, \mathbf{bsn})$ and nym (if $\mathbf{bsn} \neq \bot$).
   - Check that $a \neq 1, b \neq 1, e(a, Y) = e(b, g_2)$ and $e(c, g_2) = e(a \cdot d, X)$.
   - For every $gsk_i \in$ RL, check that $b^{gsk_i} \neq d$.
   - If all tests pass, set $f \leftarrow 1$, otherwise $f \leftarrow 0$.
   - Output (VERIFIED, *sid*, f).

Link. With the link algorithm, anyone can test whether two signatures (σ, m), (σ', m') that were generated for the same basename $\mathbf{bsn} \neq \bot$, stem from the same TPM.

1. $\mathcal{V}$ upon input (LINK, *sid*, σ, m, σ', m', $\mathbf{bsn}$) verifies the signatures and compares the pseudonyms contained in σ, σ':
   - Check that $\mathbf{bsn} \neq \bot$ and that both signatures σ, σ' are valid.
   - Parse the signatures as $(a, b, c, d, \pi, \mathtt{nym}) \leftarrow \sigma, (a', b', c', d', \pi', \mathtt{nym}') \leftarrow \sigma'$.
   - If $\mathtt{nym} = \mathtt{nym}'$, set $f \leftarrow 1$, otherwise $f \leftarrow 0$.
   - Output (LINK, *sid*, f).

5.2 Differences with Previous Schemes

The proposed scheme is very similar to previous DAA schemes using the CL signature. For each part of the protocol, we now show the weaknesses of previous schemes and the way our solution overcomes them.

Setup. In our scheme, the issuer is required to prove knowledge of the issuer secret key. Previous works let the challenger generate the issuer key in the security game for anonymity, which allowed the simulator to use the issuer private key in the security reduction. This implicitly assumes that the issuer private key is extractable, but none of the schemes actually realized this. We therefore add a SPK proof π to the issuer's public key from which the simulator can extract the issuer secret key.

Join. In the join protocol, we reintroduced a proof π_1 by the TPM, that was present in many previous works but omitted in the scheme by Bernard et al. [3]. Additionally, our scheme contains the proof π_2 by the issuer, which was introduced by Bernard et al.

Many previous schemes [6,7,16,18] let the TPM prove knowledge of the discrete log of g^{gsk} in the join protocol. Bernard et al. removed this proof by reducing the forgery of a credential to the security of a blind signature scheme, and in the unforgeability game requiring the adversary to output all secret keys. This assumes that all these secrets are extractable which, if extraction by rewinding is used, would require exponential time. We realize efficient extraction by adding the TPM's proof of knowledge of gsk to the join protocol and allowing only a logarithmic number of simultaneous join sessions.

Bernard et al. let the issuer compute d and required the issuer to prove that he correctly formed the credential, which none of the previous works did. We also use this proof as it allows to simulate a TPM without knowing the secret key gsk. This is required in our reduction where we use the unknown discrete logarithm of a DL or DDH instance as the key of a TPM.

Sign. We change the communication between the TPM and host to prevent the TPM from leaking information about its secret key gsk to the host, and we only use pseudonyms when required.

Chen, Page, and Smart [18] let the host send a randomized b value of the credential to the TPM, which responded with $d = b^{gsk}$. This gives information to the host that cannot be simulated without knowing gsk, which prevents a proof of unforgeability under the DL assumption, and requires the stronger static DH assumption. The scheme by Bernard et al. [3] has a similar problem: The host sends (b, d) to the TPM, and the TPM responds with a proof proving that $b^{gsk} = d$. Now the TPM should only output a valid proof for valid inputs, i.e., when $b^{gsk} = d$. A simulator mimicking a TPM in the security proof, however, cannot decide this when reducing to the DL problem, a stronger assumption is required to prove unforgeability in their scheme.

We apply the fix by Xi et al. [25], in which the host sends the randomness r used to randomize the credential. This does not give the host any new information on gsk, which is why we can prove unforgeability under the DL assumption.

Some schemes [6,7,16,18] always attached a pseudonym to signatures to support revocation, even when the basename bsn was equal to $\bot$. However, we can perform the revocation check on the credential: $b^{gsk} \stackrel{?}{=} d$, so the pseudonym can be omitted when bsn $= \bot$ for a more efficient scheme.

Verify. We add a check $a \neq 1_{\mathbb{G}_1}$ to the verification algorithm, which many of the previous schemes [6,7,16,18] are lacking. Without this check, schemes tolerate a trivial issuer credential $(1_{\mathbb{G}_1}, 1_{\mathbb{G}_1}, 1_{\mathbb{G}_1}, 1_{\mathbb{G}_1})$ that allows anyone to create valid DAA signatures, which clearly breaks unforgeability. Note that [18] has been ISO standardized [20] with this flaw.

The verification algorithm also checks $b \neq 1_{\mathbb{G}_1}$, which is not present in any of the previous schemes. A credential with $b = 1_{\mathbb{G}_1}$ leads to $d = 1_{\mathbb{G}_1}$, and lets any gsk match the credential, which is undesirable as we no longer have a unique matching gsk. An adversarial issuer can create such credentials by choosing its secret key $y = 0$. This case is "excluded" by the non-frameability property of Bernard et al. [3] which assumes that even a corrupt issuer creates his keys honestly, so $y = 0$ will occur with negligible probability only. We avoid such an assumption and simply add the check $b \neq 1_{\mathbb{G}_1}$.

6   Security Proof Sketch

Theorem 1. *The protocol Π_{daa} presented in Sect. 5 securely realizes $\mathcal{F}_{daa}^l$ in the $(\mathcal{F}_{auth*}, \mathcal{F}_{ca}, \mathcal{F}_{smt}^l, \mathcal{F}_{crs}^D)$-hybrid model using random oracles and static corruptions, if the DL and DDH assumptions hold, the CL signature [9] is unforgeable, and the proofs-of-knowledge are online extractable.*

As CL signatures are unforgeable under the LRSW assumption [21], and we can instantiate the SPKs to be online extractable under the DCR assumption [22], we obtain the following corollary:

Corollary 1. *The protocol Π_{daa} presented in Sect. 5 instantiated with online extractable proofs securely realizes $\mathcal{F}_{daa}^l$ in the $(\mathcal{F}_{auth*}, \mathcal{F}_{ca}, \mathcal{F}_{smt}^l, \mathcal{F}_{crs}^D)$-hybrid model using random oracles and static corruptions under the DL, DDH, LRSW, and DCR assumptions.*

Instead of relying on *online extractable* SPKs one could also use extraction by rewinding, which would yield a more efficient scheme. However, one needs to take special care that the rewinding does not require exponential time in the security proof. The only SPK we constantly have to extract from in our security proof is π_1 used in the join protocol. Thus, we can avoid the exponential blow-up by letting the issuer limit the number of simultaneous join sessions to be logarithmic in the security parameter. Since we keep the way in which the simulator extracts witnesses abstract in the proof of Theorem 1, the very same simulator proves the scheme with extraction by rewinding secure. Note though, that the UC framework does not allow rewinding at all, i.e., this only proves the

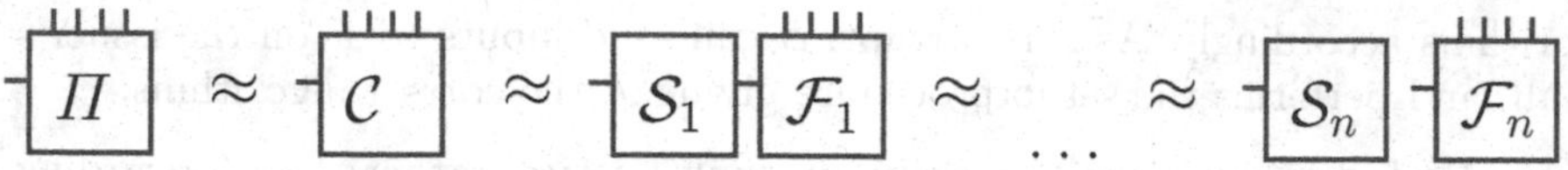

Fig. 6. Visualization of the proof strategy

instantiation using extraction by rewinding secure in a stand-alone fashion, but one cannot claim composability guarantees.

To show that no environment $\mathcal{E}$ can distinguish the real world, in which it is working with Π_{daa} and adversary $\mathcal{A}$, from the ideal world, in which it uses $\mathcal{F}^l_{\mathsf{daa}}$ with simulator $\mathcal{S}$, we use a sequence of games. We start with the real world protocol execution. In the next game we construct one entity $\mathcal{C}$ that runs the real world protocol for all honest parties. Then we split $\mathcal{C}$ into two pieces, a functionality $\mathcal{F}$ and a simulator $\mathcal{S}$, where $\mathcal{F}$ receives all inputs from honest parties and sends the outputs to honest parties. We start with a useless functionality, and gradually change $\mathcal{F}$ and update $\mathcal{S}$ accordingly, to end up with the full $\mathcal{F}^l_{\mathsf{daa}}$ and a satisfying simulator. This strategy is depicted in Fig. 6.

Due to space constraints, we present the complete security proof including all intermediate functionalities and simulators in the full paper. Here an overview of the game hops is given, along with an explanation how we can show indistinguishability between the games.

Game 1: This is the real world protocol.

Game 2: One entity $\mathcal{C}$ now receives all inputs and simulates the real world protocol for honest parties. Since $\mathcal{C}$ gets all inputs, it can simply run the real world protocol. It also simulates all hybrid functionalities, but does so honestly, so $\mathcal{E}$ does not see any difference. By construction, this is equivalent to the previous game.

Game 3: We now split $\mathcal{C}$ into $\mathcal{F}$ and $\mathcal{S}$. $\mathcal{F}$ receives all inputs, and simply forwards them to $\mathcal{S}$. $\mathcal{S}$ simulates the real world protocol and sends the outputs it generated to $\mathcal{F}$, who then outputs it to $\mathcal{E}$. This game only restructures the previous game.

Game 4: In the next step, we let the next intermediate $\mathcal{F}$ handle the setup related interfaces. $\mathcal{S}$ now has to give algorithms to $\mathcal{F}$, that will be used to verify, link, and identify signatures. Note that the sig algorithm must contain the issuer private key from the real world, so $\mathcal{S}$ must be able to get those values.

When $\mathcal{I}$ is honest, $\mathcal{S}$ will receive a message from $\mathcal{F}$ asking for the algorithms, which informs $\mathcal{S}$ what is happening and allows him to start simulating the issuer. Because $\mathcal{S}$ is simulating the issuer, it knows the secret keys, and can set the algorithms accordingly.

When $\mathcal{I}$ is corrupt, $\mathcal{S}$ knows when to simulate the setup as it simulates $\mathcal{F}_{\mathsf{ca}}$ and it notices the issuer registering a key. Because the public key includes a proof of knowledge of the secret key, $\mathcal{S}$ can extract the secret key and define the algorithms accordingly. As $\mathcal{I}$ is corrupt, $\mathcal{S}$ can send inputs to $\mathcal{F}$ on the issuer's behalf, and performs the setup procedure giving $\mathcal{F}$ the correct algorithms.

Game 5: $\mathcal{F}$ now performs the verify and link queries, rather than forwarding them to $\mathcal{S}$. Because verify and link do not involve network traffic, the simulator does not have to simulate network traffic, we must only make sure the output does not change.

$\mathcal{F}$ executes the algorithms that $\mathcal{S}$ supplied, and $\mathcal{S}$ supplied them in such a way that they are equivalent to the real world algorithms. $\mathcal{F}$ does not perform checks yet, so the outcome will clearly be equivalent.

Game 6: In this step we change $\mathcal{F}$ to handle to join-related interfaces, meaning it will receive the inputs and generate the outputs. We must make sure that $\mathcal{F}$ outputs the same values as the real world did. As the join interfaces do not output crypto values, but only output messages like start and complete, we only have to make sure that whenever the real world protocol would reach a certain output the functionality also allows that output, and vice versa. The first direction we achieve by removing all checks from $\mathcal{F}$, such that it will always proceed. We introduce these checks further on in the proof. The other direction we achieve as before every output, $\mathcal{F}$ sends a message to $\mathcal{S}$ and requires a response. When the real world protocol would not proceed, $\mathcal{S}$ simply does not respond to $\mathcal{F}$, such that $\mathcal{F}$ will also not proceed.

Furthermore, as $\mathcal{A}$ and $\mathcal{E}$ can communicate freely, $\mathcal{S}$ must make sure that $\mathcal{A}$ sees the right messages between every input and output. $\mathcal{S}$ is activated before every output, and in that activation must simulate the network traffic $\mathcal{A}$ expects to see. If $\mathcal{S}$ can figure out which inputs were send to $\mathcal{F}$, it can do so by simulating the real world protocol with the same input. When the host is honest, $\mathcal{F}$ upon receiving the first input from the host informs $\mathcal{S}$ of the full input, making the simulation easy. When the host is corrupt but the TPM is honest, $\mathcal{S}$ simulating the TPM will receive a message over a secure channel from the host, by which it learns that host wants to join with the TPM, again giving $\mathcal{S}$ the full input. Only when the TPM and host are corrupt and the issuer is honest, $\mathcal{S}$ is missing information: It cannot determine the identity of the host, as the host does not authenticate towards the issuer in the real world. This does not matter for the real world simulation, as $\mathcal{S}$ only has to simulate the honest issuer, for which it does know the input.

Finally, $\mathcal{S}$ must call $\mathcal{F}$ on behalf of corrupt parties. For inputs it can derive, $\mathcal{S}$ simply sends the input on behalf of the corrupt party to $\mathcal{F}$. The only input it cannot derive is the identity of the host when only the issuer is honest. Then, $\mathcal{S}$ simply chooses an arbitrary corrupt host and uses that as input to $\mathcal{F}$. This will only result in a different host in Members, but $\mathcal{F}$ never uses this identity when the corresponding TPM is corrupt.

Later in the proof, we need to know the gsk value of every TPM when $\mathcal{I}$ is honest. $\mathcal{S}$ can extract the key from the proof π_1 and submits it to $\mathcal{F}$.

Game 7, 8, 9, 10: Over the next four game hops, we transform $\mathcal{F}$ such that it handles the signing queries instead of forwarding the inputs and outputs. As in the previous step, $\mathcal{S}$ receives a message from $\mathcal{F}$ before every output, such that it can block any output that would not happen in the real world. We remove all checks from $\mathcal{F}$ such that it does not block any output that could happen in the real world, and we add these checks later on in the proof.

$\mathcal{S}$ can easily simulate the network traffic when the TPM or the host is corrupt, as it sees the message and basename sent over a secure channel in the real world. When both the TPM and host are honest, $\mathcal{F}$ only informs $\mathcal{S}$ of the leakage of the message and basename, $l(m, \mathsf{bsn})$. In this scenario, $\mathcal{S}$ only has to simulate the network traffic, and as all messages between the TPM and host are sent over a secure channel, it picks a message and basename with the same leakage which is sufficient to simulate the messages.

When the TPM or the host is corrupt, $\mathcal{S}$ is allowed to supply the signature, which it can take from the real world simulation, making it output the same as the real world. When both the TPM and the host are honest, $\mathcal{F}$ creates the signatures anonymously: It chooses a new gsk per basename, or per signature when $\mathsf{bsn} = \perp$. This difference is indistinguishable under the DDH assumption.

The reduction uses the fact that we can simulate a TPM knowing only $h = g_1^{gsk}$, but not gsk itself. A TPM uses gsk to set Q in the join protocol, to do proofs π_1 in the join protocol and π in signing, and to compute pseudonyms. In simulation, we set $Q \leftarrow h$ and we simulate the proofs. For pseudonyms, the power over the random oracle is used. $\mathcal{S}$ chooses $H_1(\mathsf{bsn}) = g_1^r$ for $r \xleftarrow{\$} \mathbb{Z}_q$, and now it can set $\mathsf{nym} \leftarrow h^r = H_1(\mathsf{bsn})^{gsk}$ without knowing gsk. Note that the proof the issuer makes in the join protocol helps simulating the TPM without knowing gsk: With this proof the TPM does not have to use gsk to check $b^{gsk} \overset{?}{=} d$, it can simply verify the proof.

Suppose an environment can distinguish a signature by an honest party with the gsk it joined with from a signature by the same party but with a different gsk. Then we show we can break DDH instance α, β, γ by simulating the join and the first signature using the unknown $log_{g_1}(\alpha)$ as gsk, and for the second signature we use the unknown $log_\beta(\gamma)$ as gsk. If the environment notices a difference, we know that $log_{g_1}(\alpha) \neq log_\beta(\gamma)$, solving the DDH problem.

Game 11: In this game we let $\mathcal{F}$ additionally check the validity of every new gsk that is generated or received in the join and sign interface.

$\mathcal{F}$ now checks that $\mathsf{CheckGskCorrupt}(gsk) = 1$, which prevents the adversary from choosing keys that will lead to two distinct gsk values matching one signature. This will never fail, as in our protocol for every valid signature there exists only a single gsk with $\mathsf{identify}(\sigma, m, \mathsf{bsn}, gsk)$.

For keys of honest TPMs, $\mathcal{F}$ verifies that $\mathsf{CheckGskHonest}(gsk) = 1$, which prevents the registration of keys for which there already are matching signatures. Because keys for honest TPMs are chosen uniformly at random from an exponentially large group and every signature as one matching key, the chance that a signature using that key already exists is negligible.

Game 12: We now add checks on honestly generated signatures to $\mathcal{F}$. After creating a signature, $\mathcal{F}$ checks whether the signature verifies and matches the right key. As $\mathcal{S}$ supplied proper algorithms, these checks will obviously always succeed.

It also checks no one else already has a key that matches this signature. If this fails, we can solve the DL problem: We simulate a TPM using the unknown discrete logarithm of a DL instance as key like before. If a matching gsk is found, then we solve the DL problem.

Game 13, 14, 15, 16: In these four game hops, we let $\mathcal{F}$ perform the four checks that are done by $\mathcal{F}_{\mathsf{daa}}^l$ in the verification interface and show that this does not change the verification outcome.

The first check prevents multiple gsk values matching one signature, but as identify considers the discrete log relation between b and d from the credential, and $b \neq 1$, there exists only one $gsk \in \mathbb{Z}_q$ such that $b^{gsk} = d$.

If the issuer is honest, the second check prevents signing with credentials that were not issued by the issuer. We can reduce this to the unforgeability of the CL signature. The signing oracle is now used to create credentials, and when a credential is verified that was not signed by the issuer, it must be a forgery.

$\mathcal{F}$ prevents signatures that use the key and credential of an honest TPM, but are signing messages that this TPM never signed. We can reduce this to the DL problem. Again we simulate a TPM using the unknown discrete logarithm of the problem instance. When a signature is verified that signs a message that the TPM never signed, we know that the proof π is not simulated, so we can extract gsk from it, breaking the DL assumption.

The last check prevents revocation of honest TPMs. This too we can reduce to the DL problem. We simulate the TPM using the DL instance, and if a matching key is placed on the revocation list, this must be the discrete logarithm of the problem instance.

Game 17: We now let $\mathcal{F}$ perform all the checks $\mathcal{F}_{\mathsf{daa}}^l$ makes for link inputs. If it notices a key that matches one signature but not the other, $\mathcal{F}$ states the signatures are not linked. If it notices one key that matches both signatures, it outputs that the signatures are linked. This output is always the same as the output link gives: If there is a gsk that matches one signature but not the other, by soundness of π we have that the pseudonyms are not based on the same gsk. As $H_1(\mathsf{bsn})$ generates $\mathbb{G}_1$ with overwhelming probability, the pseudonyms differ and link would output 0. If there is a gsk that matches both signatures, by soundness of π we have that the pseudonyms are based on the same gsk and must be equal, resulting in link outputting 1.

Now $\mathcal{F}$ is equal to $\mathcal{F}_{\mathsf{daa}}^l$, concluding our proof sketch.

Acknowledgements. This work was supported by the European Commission through the Seventh Framework Programme, under grant agreements #321310 for the PERCY grant and #318424 for the project FutureID.

References

1. Backes, M., Hofheinz, D.: How to break and repair a universally composable signature functionality. In: Zhang, K., Zheng, Y. (eds.) ISC 2004. LNCS, vol. 3225, pp. 61–72. Springer, Heidelberg (2004)
2. Bellare, M., Rogaway, P.: Random oracles are practical: a paradigm for designing efficient protocols. In: ACM CCS (1993)
3. Bernhard, D., Fuchsbauer, G., Ghadafi, E., Smart, N., Warinschi, B.: Anonymous attestation with user-controlled linkability. Int. J. Inf. Secur. **12**(3), 219–249 (2013)
4. Boneh, D., Lynn, B., Shacham, H.: Short signatures from the weil pairing. In: Boyd, C. (ed.) ASIACRYPT 2001. LNCS, vol. 2248, pp. 514–532. Springer, Heidelberg (2001)
5. Brickell, E., Camenisch, J., Chen, L.: Direct anonymous attestation. In: ACM CCS (2004)
6. Brickell, E., Chen, L., Li, J.: A new direct anonymous attestation scheme from bilinear maps. In: Lipp, P., Sadeghi, A.-R., Koch, K.-M. (eds.) Trust 2008. LNCS, vol. 4968, pp. 166–178. Springer, Heidelberg (2008)
7. Brickell, E., Chen, L., Li, J.: Simplified security notions of direct anonymous attestation and a concrete scheme from pairings. Int. J. Inf. Secur. **8**(5), 315–330 (2009)
8. Camenisch, J., Kiayias, A., Yung, M.: On the portability of generalized schnorr proofs. In: Joux, A. (ed.) EUROCRYPT 2009. LNCS, vol. 5479, pp. 425–442. Springer, Heidelberg (2009)
9. Camenisch, J.L., Lysyanskaya, A.: Signature schemes and anonymous credentials from bilinear maps. In: Franklin, M. (ed.) CRYPTO 2004. LNCS, vol. 3152, pp. 56–72. Springer, Heidelberg (2004)
10. Camenisch, J.L., Shoup, V.: Practical verifiable encryption and decryption of discrete logarithms. In: Boneh, D. (ed.) CRYPTO 2003. LNCS, vol. 2729, pp. 126–144. Springer, Heidelberg (2003)
11. Camenisch, J.L., Stadler, M.A.: Efficient group signature schemes for large groups. In: Kaliski Jr., B.S. (ed.) CRYPTO 1997. LNCS, vol. 1294, pp. 410–424. Springer, Heidelberg (1997)
12. Canetti, R.: Universally composable security: a new paradigm for cryptographic protocols. ePrint Archive Report 2000/067 (2000)
13. Canetti, R.: Universally composable signatures, certification and authentication. ePrint Archive, Report 2003/239 (2003)
14. Chen, L., Morrissey, P., Smart, N.: DAA: fixing the pairing based protocols. ePrint Archive, Report 2009/198 (2009)
15. Chen, L.: A DAA scheme requiring less TPM resources. In: Bao, F., Yung, M., Lin, D., Jing, J. (eds.) Inscrypt 2009. LNCS, vol. 6151, pp. 350–365. Springer, Heidelberg (2010)
16. Chen, L., Morrissey, P., Smart, N.P.: Pairings in trusted computing (invited talk). PAIRING (2008)
17. Chen, L., Morrissey, P., Smart, N.P.: On proofs of security for DAA schemes. In: Baek, J., Bao, F., Chen, K., Lai, X. (eds.) ProvSec 2008. LNCS, vol. 5324, pp. 156–175. Springer, Heidelberg (2008)
18. Chen, L., Page, D., Smart, N.P.: On the design and implementation of an efficient DAA scheme. In: Gollmann, D., Lanet, J.-L., Iguchi-Cartigny, J. (eds.) CARDIS 2010. LNCS, vol. 6035, pp. 223–237. Springer, Heidelberg (2010)
19. Fiat, A., Shamir, A.: How to prove yourself: practical solutions to identification and signature problems. In: Odlyzko, A.M. (ed.) CRYPTO 1986. LNCS, vol. 263, pp. 186–194. Springer, Heidelberg (1987)

20. International Organization for Standardization: ISO/IEC 20008-2: Information technology - Security techniques - Anonymous digital signatures - Part 2: Mechanisms using a group public key (2013)
21. Lysyanskaya, A., Rivest, R.L., Sahai, A., Wolf, S.: Pseudonym systems (extended abstract). In: Heys, H.M., Adams, C.M. (eds.) SAC 1999. LNCS, vol. 1758, pp. 184–199. Springer, Heidelberg (2000)
22. Paillier, P.: Public-key cryptosystems based on composite degree residuosity classes. In: Stern, J. (ed.) EUROCRYPT 1999. LNCS, vol. 1592, pp. 223–238. Springer, Heidelberg (1999)
23. Trusted Computing Group: TPM main specification version 1.2 (2004)
24. Trusted Computing Group: Trusted platform module library specification, family "2.0" (2014)
25. Xi, L., Yang, K., Zhang, Z., Feng, D.: DAA-related APIs in TPM 2.0 revisited. In: Holz, T., Ioannidis, S. (eds.) Trust 2014. LNCS, vol. 8564, pp. 1–18. Springer, Heidelberg (2014)

Universally Composable Authentication and Key-Exchange with Global PKI

Ran Canetti[1,2]($\boxtimes$), Daniel Shahaf[1], and Margarita Vald[1]

[1] Tel-Aviv University, Tel-Aviv, Israel
canetti@tau.ac.il, {daniel.shahaf,margarita.vald}@cs.tau.ac.il
[2] Boston University, Boston, USA

Abstract. Message authentication and key exchange are two of the most basic tasks of cryptography and are often basic components in complex and security-sensitive protocols. Thus composable security analysis of these primitives is highly motivated. Still, the state of the art in composable security analysis of these primitives is somewhat unsatisfactory in the prevalent case where solutions are based on public-key infrastructure (PKI). Specifically, existing treatments either (a) make the unrealistic assumption that the PKI is accessible only within the confines of the protocol itself, thus failing to capture real-world PKI-based authentication, or (b) impose often-unnecessary requirements—such as strong on-line non-transferability—on candidate protocols, thus ruling out natural candidates.

We give a modular and universally composable analytical framework for PKI-based message authentication and key exchange protocols. This framework guarantees security even when the PKI is pre-existing and globally available, without being unnecessarily restrictive. Specifically, we model PKI as a global set-up functionality within the *Global UC* security model [Canetti et al., TCC 2007] and relax the ideal authentication and key exchange functionalities accordingly. We then demonstrate the security of basic signature-based authentication and key exchange protocols. Our modeling makes minimal security assumptions on the PKI in use; in particular, "knowledge of the secret key" is not needed. Furthermore, there is no requirement of uniqueness in this binding: an identity may be represented by multiple strings of public keys.

Keywords: Public-key infrastructure · Message authentication · Digital signatures · Key exchange · Deniability · Non-transferability · Universal composability

R. Canetti—Supported by the Check Point Institute for Information Security, ISF grant 1523/14, and NSF Frontier CNS1413920 and 1218461 grants.
D. Shahaf—Supported by the Check Point Institute for Information Security.
M. Vald—Supported by the Check Point Institute for Information Security and a Google Europe Doctoral Fellowship in Security.

C.-M. Cheng et al. (Eds.): PKC 2016, Part II, LNCS 9615, pp. 265–296, 2016.
DOI: 10.1007/978-3-662-49387-8_11

1   Introduction

Public-Key-Based Authentication. Authentication may be done in many different ways, such as biometric human identification, or via some pre-shared longer-term secret (such as a pre-shared key or a password). In this work we concentrate on public-key authentication, as put forth in the groundbreaking work of Diffie and Hellman [DH76]: The parties have no *á priori* shared secret information or other physical means for authentication. The only mechanism available for authenticating messages is a globally-accessible public database that allows actors to record arbitrary information; each record is made publicly available and linked to the public identity of the actor who created it. We call this setting the *global public-key infrastructure* (PKI) setting.

A simple and frequently-used message authentication protocol in this setting proceeds as follows. For Alice to send an authenticated message to Bob, Alice signs (using her private key) the message, together with her and Bob's identities and a session identifier that's unique to that message, and sends the message and the signature to Bob over an unauthenticated channel. Bob authenticates the message by obtaining Alice's public key from the PKI and verifying the signature.

An almost equally simple authenticated key exchange protocol is the following: Alice sends to Bob her Diffie-Hellman message g^a, bob responds by sending his Diffie-Hellman message g^b, together with g^a and a signature $s_B = \mathrm{Sig}_{\mathrm{Bob}}(g^a, g^b, \text{'Alice'})$. Alice responds by $s_A = \mathrm{Sig}_{\mathrm{Alice}}(g^a, g^b, \text{'Bob'})$. Both parties are assumed to have each other's verification key in advance, and verify the signatures to authenticate. (This is essentially the ISO 9798-3 key exchange standard.) For sake of illustration, we keep these two simple protocols, respectively denoted ϕ_{auth} and ϕ_{ke}, as running examples throughout this paper. Practical protocols that use ϕ_{auth} and ϕ_{ke} (or close variants thereof) to establish trust in the identity of an interlocutor or in data payloads are ubiquitous. For instance, they include the TLS standard, chip-and-pin debit cards [EMV11], end-to-end authentication of email contents [RFC 1847], and many others.

Since these protocols use signatures against a globally-available PKI, and send them in the clear over world-readable channels, anyone in the system can verify Alice's and Bob's signatures, even though they were intended only for each other. While we recognize this as an inherent property of signatures (namely, they provide *transferable* verifiability), in the context of authentication this is merely a side-effect which may or may not be desirable.

We know that faithfully analyzing the security of public-key based authentication and key exchange protocols turns out to be a difficult problem, mainly due to the intricate interactions among the various components of the actual protocols, the public-key infrastructure, and the systems they run in. So a natural question arises: Is ϕ_{auth} a good authentication protocol? Is ϕ_{ke} a good key exchange protocol? Should we keep using them? Should we treat them as broken and use more sophisticated protocols instead?

Modular Analysis. In light of the complexity and ubiquity of authentication protocols, it would be desirable to be able to analyze them in a modular fashion:

to abstract out an ideal authentication service for higher-level protocols to use, such that the security of the higher-level protocols would be independent of the details of its implementation. This approach allows consumers of authentication to dynamically replace their authentication implementations—for example, to base authentication on a different setup service or on a different hard problem—without affecting the security of the higher-level protocol. Conversely, modularity also encourages reuse of an authentication module by multiple higher-level protocols, discouraging local, *ad hoc* implementations.

Several efforts to model public-key based authentication within a composable security framework appear in the literature. Canetti and Krawczyk [CK01] and Shoup [Sho99] perhaps provide the first such guarantees in the context of authenticated key exchange, but their modeling of the public key infrastructure is quite rudimentary and does not allow analyzing the long-term signature and certification module separately from the rest of the protocol.

Other attempts at composable analysis were made in [CK02] and later in [Can04] within the Universally Composable (UC) security framework of [Can01]. (The second work is more directly focused at analyzing the simple ϕ_{auth}.)

However, these works have the following significant drawback: They treat the public-key infrastructure—namely, the public record with the public information provided by each actor—as a construct that is local to each specific protocol instance and unavailable for use outside that protocol instance. This modeling is inadequate for representing the PKI model as envisioned by Diffie and Hellman and used in practice—where the public information is *globally* available. Instead, this analysis guarantees security only when each instance of the analyzed protocol uses its own independent instance of a PKI.

This is the case even if the PKI is modeled as joint to a number of instances of the authentication protocol in question, and composition is argued via Universal Composition with Joint State (JUC) [CR03]. Indeed, even there the PKI is modeled not as a global entity but rather as an entity that is local to a specific collection of instances of some specific protocol.

The works of [MTC13, KMO+14], which are set in the Abstract Cryptography setting of [MR11], have a similar modeling shortcoming: the public key infrastructure is modeled as local to the protocol instance. Furthermore, as argued below, this discrepancy is not merely aesthetic; rather, it has real security implications.

Long-lived, global trusted information that is shared among all parties, protocols, and protocol instances in the system are addressed in the Global UC (GUC) framework [CDPW07]. That framework is similar to the ("basic") UC framework, but directly models trusted entities that are globally available throughout the system regardless of any specific protocol to be analyzed. Authentication protocols with global PKI are analyzed in [DKSW09, Wal08]. However, these works consider only authentication protocols that provide additional properties on top of authenticity: only protocols that provide the *non-transferability* (or, *deniability*) property are considered. This leaves us with the following fundamental question:

How to formulate the basic composable security requirements from plain PKI-based authentication and key exchange protocols? In particular, how to justify signature-based protocols such as ϕ_{auth} and ϕ_{ke}?

268   R. Canetti et al.

A Litmus Test: The Transferability Problem. The discrepancy between the
security modeling of [CK02, Can04, CR03, MTC13, KMO+14] and real implementations of PKI infrastructure is illustrated by the following issue: while real-life
PKI-based authentication is transferable (i.e., non-deniable), ideal authentication is not.[1]

In detail, ideal authentication is defined as a deniable task that leaves "no
trace"; it passes a message from the sender to the receiver, but the receiver is
unable to subsequently prove to a third party that the authentication had in
fact happened. In contrast, some PKI-based authentication protocols (and, in
particular, protocol ϕ_{auth}) allow the receiver to obtain a *transferable* and non-
repudiable proof of communication (e.g., a signature), which can be verified by
anyone against the global PKI. Hence, PKI-based authentication protocols are
transferable (non-deniable) whenever the PKI is globally available. Moreover,
this transferability gap is independent of the security model in use. This was
formalized by [DKSW09], which proves that no protocol based on a plain PKI
can realize the ideal authentication functionality. Still, in [Can04, CR03, MTC13,
KMO+14], protocol ϕ_{auth} (or variants thereof) securely realize an ideal process
that guarantees non-transferable authentication. (Note that moving to a stronger
modeling of PKI, where registering parties are required to prove knowledge of a
secret key associated with the registered public value, does not solve the problem.
Indeed, protocol ϕ_{auth} remains transferable even with such stronger PKI.)

We stress that transferability, or lack thereof, is not the main concern of
this work; it only serves an example of the inadequacy of the current models of composable security in capturing the security requirements of PKI-based
authentication and key exchange.

What About Game-Based Modeling? The above line of reasoning concen-
trates on models that provide composable security, more specifically models that
define security by way of emulating an ideal process. Can we avoid the difficulties described above by putting general composability aside and instead using
game-based modeling of authentication and key exchange? This is an interesting research direction. Indeed, we are not aware of any game-based modeling of
authentication and key exchange that directly considers global PKI that can be
used (and abused) by arbitrary other applications.

1.1 Our Results

We provide a framework for analyzing security of authentication and key
exchange protocols that use a globally-available PKI. Our framework adequately
represents global PKIs. Specifically, we concentrate on authentication and jus-
tifying the security of transferable protocols. To exemplify our framework, we
analyze protocols ϕ_{ke} and ϕ_{auth}, which previously could not be justified in a
realistic security model. In particular:

---

[1] We use the terms "transferability" and "deniability" interchangeably, where they
refer to properties of message authentication.

(a) We model global PKI as a globally-available bulletin-board that provides minimal guarantees of binding between strings and identities, without requiring or promising any knowledge or secrecy.

(b) We relax the UC authentication and key exchange functionalities of [CK02, Can04] to be non-deniable. Our functionalities $\mathcal{F}_{\text{cert}-\text{auth}}$ and $\mathcal{F}_{\text{cert}-\text{ke}}$ allow the adversary to obtain "global" certificates on messages that have the session id of $\mathcal{F}_{\text{cert}-\text{auth}}$ or $\mathcal{F}_{\text{cert}-\text{ke}}$ as a prefix. (A global certificate is one that can be verified by any entity in the system.) In particular, the adversary may obtain a global certificate on the message to be authenticated. This coupling eliminates the authentication functionality's deniability, without affecting authenticity.

We remark that the underlying technical trick in $\mathcal{F}_{\text{cert}-\text{auth}}$ is reminiscent of the one in the relaxed key exchange functionality of [DKSW09]. However, there, one needs a PKI that is only partially-global and a very specific non-deniable protocol to realize that functionality. In contrast, our goal in this work is to analyze basic protocols with a completely-global PKI.

(c) We prove security of the natural public-key-based protocols ϕ_{auth} and ϕ_{ke}. The protocols require no setup beyond a bulletin-board and GUC-securely realize the authentication and key exchange functionalities $\mathcal{F}_{\text{cert}-\text{auth}}$ and $\mathcal{F}_{\text{cert}-\text{ke}}$, respectively.

To the best of our knowledge, *this is the first treatment of authentication with a realistic modeling of PKI* as a global construct that can be used by arbitrary protocols.

While we concentrate on protocol ϕ_{auth} and ϕ_{ke} for simplicity and clarity, our treatment can be naturally extended to deal with other PKI-based authentication and key exchange protocols.

Review of UC and GUC. We first briefly review the UC and GUC frameworks. Informally, UC security is defined via a challenge to distinguish between actual attacks, performed by an adversary $\mathcal{A}$ on protocol π and simulated attacks, performed by a simulator $\mathcal{S}$ on protocol ϕ. The model allows the attacks to be orchestrated by an environment $\mathcal{Z}$ that has an I/O interface to the parties running the challenge protocol (π or ϕ) and is allowed to freely communicate with the attacker (without knowing whether it is $\mathcal{A}$ or $\mathcal{S}$). However, the environment $\mathcal{Z}$ is *constrained* to execute only a single instance of the challenge protocol. In this execution model, protocol π is said to *UC-emulate* the protocol ϕ if for any adversary $\mathcal{A}$ attacking a protocol π there exists a simulator $\mathcal{S}$ attacking protocol ϕ such that no environment can successfully distinguish these two possible scenarios.

The GUC challenge experiment is similar to the basic UC experiment, only with an *unconstrained* environment. In particular, now $\mathcal{Z}$ is allowed to invoke and interact with arbitrary protocols, and even multiple sessions of the challenge protocol. The protocols invoked by $\mathcal{Z}$ may share subroutines with challenge protocol instances. GUC emulation is defined analogously to basic UC emulation. The UC and GUC frameworks are presented more rigorously in Sect. 2.

Our Methods. We develop a general framework for analyzing PKI-based authentication and key-exchange protocols. Our framework consists of an ideal message authentication functionality (or ideal key-exchange functionality) coupled with a long-lived certificates functionality.

For simplicity we concentrate on the authentication protocol. The treatment of the key exchange protocol is analogous. We formulate an ideal authentication functionality that does not impose unnecessary requirements (such as deniability) on the implementing protocols. The functionality, denoted $\mathcal{F}_{\text{cert-auth}}$, is a sender-receiver functionality that on input m from the sender not only delivers m to the receiver but also allows the adversary to see legitimate signatures on messages of its choice, which $\mathcal{F}_{\text{cert-auth}}$ obtains from the ideal certificates functionality $\mathcal{G}_{\text{cert}}$. (This does not affect $\mathcal{F}_{\text{cert-auth}}$'s authenticity promises since $\mathcal{F}_{\text{cert-auth}}$ delivers the original m to the receiver.) This is done as follows:

The adversary determines the message to be signed and hands it to $\mathcal{F}_{\text{cert-auth}}$; then, $\mathcal{F}_{\text{cert-auth}}$ requests a signature (on behalf of the sender) on the message affixed with the session identifier. The signature obtained by the adversary is thus tied to a specific $\mathcal{F}_{\text{cert-auth}}$ session and cannot be used in other sessions. Since the signature seen by the adversary is correctly generated and can be successfully verified by any entity in the system, deniability (or, non-transferability) is no longer guaranteed. Nonetheless, the essence of authentication—binding an action to some long-lived entity—remains guaranteed. That is, $\mathcal{F}_{\text{cert-auth}}$ guarantees that if a receiver accepts a message from a given sender, then that sender sent that message to the receiver. Therefore, any protocol that GUC-realizes $\mathcal{F}_{\text{cert-auth}}$ guarantees authenticated message transmission in the same way.

Observe that $\mathcal{F}_{\text{cert-auth}}$ allows the adversary to obtain, as a side-effect, the sender's signature on almost any message. This might seem weak, and almost contradictory to authentication. We note however that (a) $\mathcal{F}_{\text{cert-auth}}$ still guarantees authenticity, as argued above, and (b) other standard definitions of security for authentication protocols (e.g., the definition of authentication based on a local PKI) also allow the same side effects. We simply make this point explicit.

We note that a somewhat similar mechanism is used by [DKSW09] to augment the key exchange functionality with the secret keys of the parties. However, there the secret keys are made unavailable beyond the key exchange protocol, which is the opposite of our purpose here. Indeed, the goal in [DKSW09] is close to diametrically opposite to the goal of this work: Dodis *et al.* study deniable protocols, whereas we study real-life, non-deniable protocols.

We also show that standard EU-CMA signatures together with a globally-available PKI precisely capture the guarantees provided by $\mathcal{G}_{\text{cert}}$, and can be used in its stead. That is:

(a) We define a global ideal certificate functionality $\mathcal{G}_{\text{cert}}$ that is parametrized by a party identity (PID). That is, $\mathcal{G}_{\text{cert}}$ is willing to provide certificates on chosen messages to any session of that PID. The verification service is provided to any PID in the system. The authentication functionality $\mathcal{F}_{\text{cert-auth}}$ will provide certificates generated by $\mathcal{G}_{\text{cert}}$ to the adversary.

(b) To realize $\mathcal{G}_{\text{cert}}$, we define a signing module $\mathcal{G}_{\Sigma}$, parametrized by a PID, that holds the secret key (of some signature scheme) and similarly to $\mathcal{G}_{\text{cert}}$ is willing to provide signing service to any session of that PID. Similarly to [CK01], our signing module enables modeling "key knowledge" and "signing capabilities" separately. Separation of long-term key handling and signing module from session module is an essential part of security modeling of key-exchange and secure sessions: it preserves security of sessions even when other sessions using the same public-key are compromised. This was not done previously in any UC-based framework.

(c) We show a GUC-secure realization of ideal certificates $\mathcal{G}_{\text{cert}}$ from standard EU-CMA signatures (where the secret key is kept in the signing module).

We exemplify the usability of our model by analyzing ϕ_{auth} and ϕ_{ke}, the signed key exchange protocol of Diffie-Hellman (ISO 9798-3), within it and showing they GUC-realize $\mathcal{F}_{\text{cert-auth}}$ and $\mathcal{F}_{\text{cert-ke}}$, respectively. (The complete realization of $\mathcal{F}_{\text{cert-auth}}$ within our framework is depicted in Fig. 1).

To this end, we formalize new composition theorems that allow reduction between global functionalities. The first theorem (in Sect. 3) shows that a secure realization of functionality $\mathcal{G}$ is sufficient for replacing any use of $\mathcal{G}$ (as a global functionality) with $\mathcal{G}$'s implementation:

Theorem 1 (informal statement). *Let π be a protocol with access to global functionality $\mathcal{G}$. If a functionality $\mathcal{F}$ GUC-realizes $\mathcal{G}$, then π using global $\mathcal{F}$ GUC-realizes π using global $\mathcal{G}$.*

Our second composition theorem presents the necessary conditions, required from a pair of global functionalities, such that any secure protocol GUC-realizing some task using globally one of the functionalities would remain equally secure using the other:

Theorem 2 (informal statement). *Let π and ϕ be protocols with access to global functionality $\mathcal{G}$. If π GUC-realizes ϕ, the functionality $\mathcal{F}$ GUC-realizes $\mathcal{G}$ and $\mathcal{G}$ GUC-realizes $\mathcal{F}$, then π GUC-realizes ϕ with access to global functionality $\mathcal{F}$.*

Since the operation of replacing one global functionality by another was not considered before, we extend the definition of GUC-emulation. The extended definition admits not only previous results, but also allows arguing these theorems formally. Although the composition proof is simple, the terminology is vital for our analysis.

1.2 Related Work

Due to the fundamentality of the problem, there has been a vast line of works on secure authentication and its equivalent problem of key exchange. PKI-based authentication can be examined from three different angles: the composability guarantees of the model, the modeling of the PKI, and the deniability guarantees of the ideal authentication. We concentrate on composable settings, where the

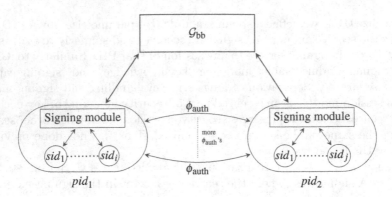

Fig. 1. A snapshot of an authentication in the system. The signing module together with $\mathcal{G}_{bb}$ is an instantiation of $\mathcal{G}_{cert}$. Each party participates in multiple executions of ϕ_{auth}, one per session. Each session may involve a different interlocutor (not limited to pid_1 and pid_2). The bulletin-board $\mathcal{G}_{bb}$ is shared with many other protocols executing in the system. The parties also obtain signatures from their local signing module instances upon demand.

authentication (or key exchange) maintains its security guarantees when used as a component in building complex protocols.

UC-Based Models. Many works [CK02, FAK08, CG10, AF10] analyze key agreement and key exchange protocols in the UC framework. However, like [Can04], they also model the PKI as local to the protocol instance. Another line of works in UC prohibit honest participants from engaging in multiple sessions concurrently [LBdM07, BLdMT09] or assume password-based security and erasures [DF12]. Likewise, here the PKI modeling does not allow external protocols to access the PKI.

Dodis *et al.* [DKSW09, Wal08] study deniable authentication in a GUC setting. They prove it impossible to securely realize standard message authentication in GUC with merely a standard PKI. To overcome this impossibility result, they present a non-transferable authentication protocol based on symmetric keys. The symmetric keys are obtained from a non-standard PKI. However, their protocol has two drawbacks: Its security proof requires a strong PKI (namely, key registration with proof of knowledge of the secret key) and their protocol is somewhat less efficient than ϕ_{auth}. Most importantly, that framework cannot be used to justify the security of ϕ_{auth} as a basic authentication protocol.

The Abstract Cryptography (AC) Model. Maurer *et al.* [MTC13] implement authenticated channels in the Abstract Cryptography setting of [MR11]. Their construction is composable, uses the canonical signature-based authentication protocol (ϕ_{auth}) and assumes a standard PKI. Still, similarly to Canetti [Can04], these works treat the PKI as a *local* functionality that services only a single instance of an authentication protocol. Indeed, their abstraction of an authentication channel is deniable, while their protocol is PKI-based.

Kohlweiss *et al.* [KMO+14] study the TLS protocol in the same setting and analyze three key exchange modes of TLS. Of them, one uses symmetric keys and two use a standard PKI. However, as with [Can04] and [MTC13], their PKI is private to the protocol. Thus, their modeling does not adequately capture global PKIs.

Game-Based Models. The work of [CK01] develops a game-based framework for analyzing the key exchange problem. Later, [BFS+13] proposed a framework with stronger composability guarantees to enable analysis of the TLS protocol. However, both frameworks allow only limited composition and model the PKI as a setup inaccessible by other protocols.

Other Models. Kidron and Lindell [KL07] study impossibility results in a number of public-key models. However, none of the considered public-key models are in a global setting, and thus do not address the issue at hand. Barak *et al.* [BCL+05] study what notion of security is achievable in a PKI-less setting. Their work does not address the setting of global PKI.

Invisible Adaptive Attacks. Nielsen and Strefler [NS14] point out a weakness in definitions of security in the GUC model, called *invisible adaptive attacks* and propose a general way to fix the weakness. We demonstrate in Sect. 6 that our protocols satisfy not only the [NS14] definition even a stronger (and simpler) definition proposed in this work.

2   Overview of Generalized UC Security

To provide the proper setting for the authentication, we now review the original UC [Can01, Can00] (referred to as basic UC) and Generalized UC [CDPW07] frameworks.[2] We will focus on the notion of protocol *emulation*, wherein the objective of a protocol π is to imitate another protocol ϕ. In this work, the entities and protocols we consider are polynomial-time bounded Interactive Turing Machines (ITMs), in the sense detailed in [Can01].

Systems of ITMs. To capture the mechanics of computation and communication among entities, the UC framework employs an extension of the ITM model [GMR89]. A computer program (such as run by a participant in a protocol, or by an adversary) is modeled in the form of an ITM. An execution experiment consists of a system of ITMs which are instantiated and executed, with multiple instances possibly sharing the same ITM code. A particular executing ITM instance running in the network is referred to as an ITI. Individual ITIs are parameterized by the program code of the ITM they instantiate, a party ID (pid) and a session ID (sid). We require that each ITI can be uniquely identified by the identity pair id = (pid,sid), irrespective of the code it may be running. All ITIs running with the same code and session ID are said to be a part of

---

[2] We relate to the 2013 version of [Can00] and explicitly mention in the text the relevant differences from previous versions.

the same protocol session, and the party IDs are used to distinguish among the various ITIs participating in a particular protocol session.

The Basic UC Framework. At a very high level, the intuition behind security in the basic UC framework is that any adversary $\mathcal{A}$ attacking a protocol π should learn no more information than could have been obtained via the use of a simulator $\mathcal{S}$ attacking protocol ϕ. Furthermore, we would like this guarantee to hold even if ϕ were to be used as a subroutine in arbitrary other protocols that may be running concurrently in the networked environment and after we substitute π for ϕ in all the instances where it is invoked. This requirement is captured by a challenge to distinguish between actual attacks on protocol ϕ and simulated attacks on protocol π. In the model, attacks are executed by an environment $\mathcal{Z}$ that also controls the inputs and outputs to the parties running the challenge protocol. The environment $\mathcal{Z}$ is *constrained* to execute only a single instance of the challenge protocol. In addition, the environment $\mathcal{Z}$ is allowed to interact freely with the attacker (without knowing whether it is $\mathcal{A}$ or $\mathcal{S}$). At the end of the experiment, the environment $\mathcal{Z}$ is tasked with distinguishing between adversarial attacks perpetrated by $\mathcal{A}$ on the challenge protocol π, and attack simulations conducted by $\mathcal{S}$ with protocol ϕ acting as the challenge protocol instead. If no environment can successfully distinguish these two possible scenarios, then protocol π is said to *UC-emulate* the protocol ϕ.

Balanced Environments. In order to keep the notion of protocol emulation from being unnecessarily restrictive, we consider only environments where the amount of resources given to the adversary (namely, the length of the adversary's input) is at least some fixed polynomial fraction of the amount of resources given to all protocols in the system. From now on, we only consider environments that are balanced.

Definition 1 (UC-emulation). *Let π and ϕ be multi-party protocols. We say that π UC-emulates ϕ if for any adversary $\mathcal{A}$ there exists an adversary $\mathcal{S}$ such that for any (constrained) environment $\mathcal{Z}$, we have:*

$$\mathrm{EXEC}_{\pi,\mathcal{A},\mathcal{Z}} \approx \mathrm{EXEC}_{\phi,\mathcal{S},\mathcal{Z}}$$

Defining protocol execution this way is sufficient to capture the entire range of network activity that is observable by the challenge protocol but may be under adversarial control. Therefore, the UC framework admits a very strong composition theorem, which guarantees that arbitrary instances of ϕ that may be running in the network can be safely substituted with any protocol π that UC-emulates it. More formally,

Definition 2 (Subroutine-respecting protocols; [Can00]). *We say that a protocol π is subroutine-respecting if the following properties hold with respect to every instance of π in any execution of any protocol ρ that makes subroutine calls to π:*

(a) No ITI which is a subsidiary of this instance passes inputs or outputs to an ITI which is not a party or subsidiary of this instance.

(b) At first activation, each ITI that is currently a subsidiary of this instance, or will ever become one, sends a special message to the adversary, notifying it of its own code and identity, as well as the code π and SID of this instance. We call this requirement subroutine publicness.[3]

Theorem 3 (UC-Composition). *Let ρ, π and ϕ be protocols such that ρ makes subroutine calls to ϕ. If π UC-emulates ϕ and both π and ϕ are subroutine-respecting, then protocol $\rho^{\pi/\phi}$ UC-emulates protocol ρ.*

The Generalized UC Framework. As mentioned above, the environment $\mathcal{Z}$ in the basic UC experiment is unable to invoke protocols that share state in any way with the challenge protocol. In many scenarios, the challenge protocol produces information that is shared by other network protocol sessions. For example, protocols may share information via a global setup such as a public Common Reference String (CRS) or a standard Public Key Infrastructure (PKI). The basic UC framework discussed above does not address this kind of shared state; moreover, the UC composition theorem does not hold for non-subroutine-respecting protocols (i.e., protocols that share state information with other protocol sessions). Still, we would like to analyze such protocols in a modular way. To overcome this limitation, [CDPW07] propose the Generalized UC (GUC) framework. The GUC challenge experiment is similar to the basic UC experiment, only with an *unconstrained* environment. In particular, now $\mathcal{Z}$ is allowed to invoke and interact with arbitrary protocols, and even multiple sessions of the challenge protocol. Some of the protocol sessions invoked by $\mathcal{Z}$ may even share state information with challenge protocol sessions, and indeed, those protocol sessions might provide $\mathcal{Z}$ with information related to the challenge protocol instances that it would have been unable to obtain otherwise. To distinguish this from the basic UC experiment, we denote the output of an unconstrained environment $\mathcal{Z}$, running with an adversary $\mathcal{A}$ and a challenge protocol π in the GUC protocol execution experiment, by $\text{GEXEC}_{\pi,\mathcal{A},\mathcal{Z}}$. GUC emulation is defined analogously to the definition of basic UC emulation outlined above:

Definition 3 (GUC-emulation). *Let π and ϕ be multi-party protocols. We say that π GUC-emulates ϕ if for any adversary $\mathcal{A}$ there exists an adversary $\mathcal{S}$ such that for any (unconstrained) environment $\mathcal{Z}$, we have:*

$$\text{GEXEC}_{\pi,\mathcal{A},\mathcal{Z}} \approx \text{GEXEC}_{\phi,\mathcal{S},\mathcal{Z}}.$$

The External-Subroutine UC Framework. The great generality provided by the GUC framework also raises difficulties in proving security of protocols in it. Observing real scenarios, it turns out to be sufficient to model shared state information via the use of "shared functionalities", which are simply functionalities that may interact with more than one protocol session (such as the PKI functionality). For clarity, we distinguish the notation for shared functionalities

---

[3] While natural, these properties are necessary for Theorem 4 and the composition to go through. The reader is referred to [Can00] for further details.

by adding a bar. We call a protocol π that only shares state information via a single global functionality $\bar{\mathcal{G}}$ a $\bar{\mathcal{G}}$-subroutine respecting protocol (Definition 2 is extended to allow communication with $\bar{\mathcal{G}}$). Moreover, a $\bar{\mathcal{G}}$-externally constrained environment is subject to the same constraints as the environment in the basic UC framework, only it is additionally allowed to invoke a single ITI that runs the code of $\bar{\mathcal{G}}$. Thus, any state information that will be shared by the challenge protocol must be shared via calls to $\bar{\mathcal{G}}$ (i.e., challenge protocols are $\bar{\mathcal{G}}$-subroutine respecting), and the environment is specifically allowed to access $\bar{\mathcal{G}}$. Although $\mathcal{Z}$ is once again constrained to invoking a single instance of the challenge protocol, it is now possible for $\mathcal{Z}$ to internally mimic the behavior of multiple sessions of the challenge protocol, or other arbitrary network protocols, by making use of calls to $\bar{\mathcal{G}}$ wherever shared state information is required. We allow the environment direct access to shared state information. This security notion is called External-subroutine UC (EUC) security. The EUC-security notion collapses to UC-security for subroutine-respecting protocols (Definition 2).

Given a $\bar{\mathcal{G}}$-subroutine respecting protocol π, we denote the output of the environment in the EUC protocol experiment by $\mathrm{EXEC}_{\pi,\bar{\mathcal{G}},\mathcal{D},\mathcal{Z}}$. The EUC-emulation definition presented here is an extension of the emulation definition appearing in [CDPW07]. The new definition allows a protocol π to emulate ϕ using a different shared functionality than ϕ uses. More formally,

Definition 4 (EUC-emulation). *Let π and ϕ be multi-party protocols, where π is $\bar{\mathcal{F}}$-subroutine respecting and ϕ is $\bar{\mathcal{G}}$-subroutine respecting. We say that π EUC-emulates ϕ if for any adversary $\mathcal{A}$ there exists a adversary $\mathcal{S}$ such that for any $\bar{\mathcal{F}}$-externally constrained environment $\mathcal{Z}$, we have:*

$$\mathrm{EXEC}_{\pi,\bar{\mathcal{F}},\mathcal{D},\mathcal{Z}} \approx \mathrm{EXEC}_{\phi,\bar{\mathcal{G}},\mathcal{S},\mathcal{Z}}.$$

Note that a $\bar{\mathcal{F}}$-subroutine respecting π communicates with the global functionality $\bar{\mathcal{F}}$ (similarly, ϕ with $\bar{\mathcal{G}}$). We remark that, in the underlying model, the substitution of $\bar{\mathcal{G}}$ for $\bar{\mathcal{F}}$ is done by changing the control function (so that messages addressed to $\bar{\mathcal{F}}$ are implicitly delivered to $\bar{\mathcal{G}}$ instead), in a similar manner to the changes effected thereto when substituting ϕ for π in UC or GUC.

Ideal Protocols ([Can01, Can00]). Let $\mathcal{F}$ be an ideal functionality and sid be its session ID. The ideal protocol $\mathsf{IDEAL}_{\mathcal{F}}$ for $\mathcal{F}$ is defined as follows: Whenever a dummy party is activated with input v, it writes v onto the input tape of the ideal functionality $\mathcal{F}_{(sid,\perp)}$ (recall that this message includes the extended identity of the calling ITI). Messages delivered by the adversaries, including corruption messages, are ignored. Whenever a dummy party receives a value v from $\mathcal{F}$ on its subroutine output tape, it writes this value on the subroutine output tape of an ITI instructed by $\mathcal{F}$. Specifying the output destination enables an ideal functionality $\mathcal{F}$ to communicate with another (shared) ideal functionality $\bar{\mathcal{Q}}$ via the dummy party. Such functionality $\mathcal{F}$ is called $\bar{\mathcal{Q}}$-subroutine respecting functionality. We say that a functionality $\mathcal{F}$ EUC-realizes an functionality $\mathcal{G}$ if $\mathsf{IDEAL}_{\mathcal{F}}$ EUC-emulates $\mathsf{IDEAL}_{\mathcal{G}}$. GUC-realization is defined analogously.

Since the class of $\bar{\mathcal{G}}$-subroutine respecting protocols captures a broad range of real-life protocols, we focus our attention on those. For this class of protocols, [CDPW07] shows that GUC-emulation is equivalent to EUC-emulation.

Theorem 4 ([CDPW07]). *Let $\mathcal{G}$ be some ideal functionality and let π and ϕ be $\bar{\mathcal{G}}$-subroutine respecting protocols. Then π GUC-emulates ϕ, if and only if π EUC-emulates ϕ.*

Although it is not stated in [CDPW07], subroutine publicness of ϕ, as described in Definition 2, is necessary for the equivalence to hold.

As a special case, if the challenge protocol does not share any state information (i.e., it is subroutine-respecting according to [Can01]), then Theorem 4 states that GUC- and UC-security are equivalent.

3   The Global Functionality Composition Theorem

Suppose a protocol ρ uses another protocol ϕ as a subroutine. Global UC [CDPW07] shows that we can replace the use of ϕ with any protocol π that GUC-emulates it. This replacement maintains the security of the composed protocol, even if both the calling protocol ρ and the subroutine protocol (ϕ or π) have access to the same instance of a global ideal functionality. However, it is unknown whether it is safe to replace the global functionality with something "equivalent". Such a replacement would be useful, for example, for designing protocols using an efficient signatures scheme (with keys that can be used concurrently by any other protocols) and analyzing their security using an ideal signatures functionality.

In this section we provide a new composition theorem that handles security of global functionality replacement. Informally, the theorem states that a protocol that shares state via a global functionality $\bar{\mathcal{G}}$ remains secure if we replace this functionality with a different (presumably weaker) global functionality $\bar{\mathcal{F}}$, provided that $\mathcal{F}$ is a secure implementation of $\mathcal{G}$. The theorem holds even if the global functionalities share state via a third global functionality. (In Sect. 4, this theorem is used to substitute an ideal certification functionality, which shares state via a global PKI functionality, by EU-CMA signatures.)

Theorem 5 (Generalized Functionality Composition). *Let $\mathcal{G}, \mathcal{F}$ be $\bar{\mathcal{Q}}$-subroutine respecting functionalities, for some ideal functionality $\mathcal{Q}$. Let π be a $\bar{\mathcal{G}}$-subroutine respecting protocol. If $\mathcal{F}$ EUC-realizes $\mathcal{G}$, then $\pi^{\bar{\mathcal{F}}/\bar{\mathcal{G}}}$ GUC-emulates π.*

Proof. We denote by π and π' the protocols $\pi^{\bar{\mathcal{G}}}$ and $\pi^{\bar{\mathcal{F}}/\bar{\mathcal{G}}}$ respectively. We first prove that π' EUC-emulates π and then show that GUC-emulation follows. We make use of an equivalent formulation of emulation with respect to dummy adversaries. Thus, denoting the dummy adversary by $\mathcal{D}$, we wish to construct an adversary $\mathcal{S}$ such that:

$$\text{EXEC}_{\pi', \bar{\mathcal{F}}, \mathcal{D}, \mathcal{Z}} \approx \text{EXEC}_{\pi, \bar{\mathcal{G}}, \mathcal{S}, \mathcal{Z}}$$

for any $(\bar{\mathcal{F}}, \bar{\mathcal{Q}})$-constrained environment $\mathcal{Z}$. Since $\mathcal{F}$ EUC-realizes $\mathcal{G}$ there is an adversary $\mathcal{S}_{\mathcal{F}}$ such that

$$\mathrm{EXEC}_{\mathcal{F}, \bar{\mathcal{Q}}, \mathcal{D}, \mathcal{Z}_{\mathcal{F}}} \approx \mathrm{EXEC}_{\mathcal{G}, \bar{\mathcal{Q}}, \mathcal{S}_{\mathcal{F}}, \mathcal{Z}_{\mathcal{F}}} \tag{1}$$

for any $\bar{\mathcal{Q}}$-constrained environment $\mathcal{Z}_{\mathcal{F}}$. That is, $\mathcal{S}_{\mathcal{F}}$ expects to interact with $\mathcal{G}$ and $\bar{\mathcal{Q}}$, and translates it to mimic the action of the corresponding execution of $\mathcal{F}$ and $\bar{\mathcal{Q}}$ from the viewpoint of any environment $\mathcal{Z}_{\mathcal{F}}$. We present and analyze $\mathcal{S}$. (We note that the construction of $\mathcal{S}$ and the proof of its validity are reminiscent of the treatment in [CDPW07]. Still, the context is quite different.) The construction idea is to internally run a single copy $\mathcal{S}_{\mathcal{F}}$ to mimic all the calls to $\mathcal{F}$ and route all relevant messages through this adversary. In addition, the adversary $\mathcal{S}$ behaves as follows:

(a) forwarding all messages intended for $\bar{\mathcal{F}}$ sent by the environment $\mathcal{Z}$ to its internal simulation of $\mathcal{S}_{\mathcal{F}}$, as well as forwarding any messages from $\mathcal{S}_{\mathcal{F}}$ back to $\mathcal{Z}$ as appropriate.
(b) forwarding all other messages sent by the environment $\mathcal{Z}$ to the external participants of π or to $\bar{\mathcal{Q}}$, as well as forwarding any incoming messages from π and $\bar{\mathcal{Q}}$ (and other protocols in the system) back to $\mathcal{Z}$ as appropriate.
(c) forwarding all messages of $\mathcal{S}_{\mathcal{F}}$ to the functionality $\bar{\mathcal{G}}$ and back, as appropriate. This is done using the subroutine publicness property, as explained in Definition 2).

A graphical description of $\mathcal{S}$ can be found in Fig. 2(a).

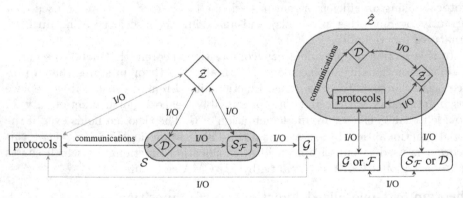

(a) The simulator $\mathcal{S}$ interacting with the protocol π and the global functionality $\mathcal{G}$.

(b) The environment $\hat{\mathcal{Z}}$ constructed out of $\mathcal{Z}$. The entire system is executed inside $\hat{\mathcal{Z}}$ except for the interaction with the global functionality, which is either $\mathcal{F}$ or $\mathcal{G}$.

Fig. 2. The simulator $\mathcal{S}$ and the distinguishing environment $\hat{\mathcal{Z}}$ constructed in the proof.

In order to prove that $\mathcal{S}$ satisfies the required, we perform a standard proof by contradiction. Assume there exists an environment $\mathcal{Z}$ capable of distinguishing the interaction with S and π from the interaction with $\mathcal{D}$ and π'. We show how to construct an environment $\hat{\mathcal{Z}}$ such that

$$\text{EXEC}_{\pi,\bar{\mathcal{G}},S,\mathcal{Z}} = \text{EXEC}_{\mathcal{G},\bar{\mathcal{Q}},S_{\mathcal{F}},\hat{\mathcal{Z}}}$$

and

$$\text{EXEC}_{\pi',\bar{\mathcal{F}},\mathcal{D},\mathcal{Z}} = \text{EXEC}_{\mathcal{F},\bar{\mathcal{Q}},\mathcal{D},\hat{\mathcal{Z}}}.$$

The environment $\hat{\mathcal{Z}}$ will internally run $\mathcal{Z}$ and behave as follows: Any message from $\mathcal{Z}$ to $\mathcal{F}$ is forwarded to the external adversary. Any output from the external adversary is forwarded back to $\mathcal{Z}$. Any other message from $\mathcal{Z}$ is internally simulated. That is, $\hat{\mathcal{Z}}$ internally executes the dummy adversary $\mathcal{D}$ and honestly simulates any uncorrupted entity in the execution (i.e., parties of π and parties of other protocols). Whenever an internally simulated honest party provides an input to $\mathcal{F}$ or $\bar{\mathcal{Q}}$, the environment $\hat{\mathcal{Z}}$ forwards it externally and the response is forwarded back to the internal honest party. Eventually, the environment $\hat{\mathcal{Z}}$ outputs whatever $\mathcal{Z}$ outputs. The environment $\hat{\mathcal{Z}}$ is depicted in Fig. 2(b).

It follows from the construction that if the external adversary is $\mathcal{D}$ then $\mathcal{Z}$ interacts with the dummy adversary $\mathcal{D}$, the protocol π' and functionality $\mathcal{F}$. If the external adversary is $S_{\mathcal{F}}$ then $\mathcal{Z}$ interacts with $\mathcal{D}$ where all of its accesses to $\mathcal{F}$ are replaced with accesses to $\mathcal{G}$ via $S_{\mathcal{F}}$. This is exactly the execution of $\mathcal{Z}$ with the adversary S and the protocol π with access to $\mathcal{G}$. Hence, existence of such distinguishing environment $\mathcal{Z}$ contradicts Eq. 1 as desired.

Note that the components of S (i.e., the dummy adversary $\mathcal{D}$ and simulator $S_{\mathcal{F}}$) can handle multiple instances of π and therefore S can simulate π' with unconstrained environment as well. In other words,

$$\text{GEXEC}_{\pi',\mathcal{D},\mathcal{Z}} \approx \text{GEXEC}_{\pi,S,\mathcal{Z}}.$$

for any unconstrained environment $\mathcal{Z}$.

Informally, secure realization allows replacing any use of an idealized task by an implementation of the task, in a localized manner (that is, without having to consider the rest of the system). In particular, if a protocol π securely implements another protocol ϕ, where $\bar{\mathcal{G}}$ exists in the system, then we intuitively expect π to continue to securely implement ϕ after we replace $\bar{\mathcal{G}}$ with some $\bar{\mathcal{F}}$ that securely implements $\bar{\mathcal{G}}$. However, this intuition is misleading. Consider, for example, some functionality $\mathcal{F}$ and let $\mathcal{G}$ be as $\mathcal{F}$ but with extra capabilities granted to the adversary. The functionality $\mathcal{F}$ (trivially) securely implements $\mathcal{G}$, since it is a restriction of $\mathcal{G}$. However, the simulation of π might be such that it uses the extra adversarial capabilities given him by $\bar{\mathcal{G}}$. Thus, once we replace $\bar{\mathcal{G}}$ with $\bar{\mathcal{F}}$ the simulation becomes invalid, and moreover, the extra capabilities might be essential to the simulation ability. This hints that in order for the intuition to hold, it must be the case that $\bar{\mathcal{F}}$ and $\bar{\mathcal{G}}$ must have "similar" adversarial interfaces. This is formally captured as follows:

Theorem 6. *Let $\mathcal{G}$, $\mathcal{F}$ be $\bar{\mathcal{Q}}$-subroutine respecting functionalities, for some ideal functionality $\mathcal{Q}$. Let π, ϕ be $\bar{\mathcal{G}}$-subroutine respecting protocols. If the following holds:*

(a) π GUC-emulates ϕ.
(b) $\mathcal{F}$ EUC-realizes $\mathcal{G}$ and vice versa.

Then $\pi^{\bar{\mathcal{F}}/\bar{\mathcal{G}}}$ GUC-emulates $\phi^{\bar{\mathcal{F}}/\bar{\mathcal{G}}}$.

Proof. The theorem fully follows from Theorem 5. We denote by π and ϕ the protocols $\pi^{\bar{\mathcal{G}}}$ and $\phi^{\bar{\mathcal{G}}}$ respectively. More formally, by Theorem 5 and Item (2) we obtain that $\pi^{\bar{\mathcal{F}}/\bar{\mathcal{G}}}$ GUC-emulates π. Combining this with Item (1) we obtain that $\pi^{\bar{\mathcal{F}}/\bar{\mathcal{G}}}$ GUC-emulates ϕ. Next, using again Theorem 5 with Item (2) we infer that ϕ GUC-emulates $\phi^{\bar{\mathcal{F}}/\bar{\mathcal{G}}}$ and conclude that $\pi^{\bar{\mathcal{F}}/\bar{\mathcal{G}}}$ GUC-emulates $\phi^{\bar{\mathcal{F}}/\bar{\mathcal{G}}}$ as desired.

Such composition enables the GUC-framework to offer full modularity in analyzing protocols.

4 Secure Authentication Using Signatures

As discussed in the introduction, the standard authentication functionality $\mathcal{F}_{\text{cert-auth}}$ is unimplementable in a GUC setting with fully global PKI since it requires non-transferability (deniability). However, this *de jure* impossibility does not prevent people from using digital signatures in day-to-day communications to achieve an authentication guarantee.

In this section, we bridge the gap between practical and provably secure authentication. We show that the classic, signature-based authentication protocol implements (transferable) authentication using standard public key infrastructure (PKI). That is, we formalize the "Authentication via signatures" paradigm in a GUC setting and present a functionality which encapsulates it.

This has two benefits: it allows for analyzing in the modular setting of GUC real-life protocols that use digital signatures as a building block, and it increases the trust in the signature-based authentication protocol by proving it secure under GUC's strong composition operation.

The proof details are similar to [Can04]; however, the formulation and analysis are done in the GUC framework. Section 4.1 presents a formulation of ideal certificate and ideal signature functionalities ($\bar{\mathcal{G}}_{\text{cert}}$ and $\bar{\mathcal{G}}_{\text{cwk}}$), and shows their equivalence. Section 4.2 shows that EU-CMA signatures provide the same security guarantees as the ideal signature functionality $\bar{\mathcal{G}}_{\text{cwk}}$. Section 4.3 presents and implements the relaxed, non-deniable message authentication functionality $\mathcal{F}_{\text{cert-auth}}$.

4.1 Signatures and Certificates

We formulate a global ideal functionality, $\bar{\mathcal{G}}_{\text{cert}}$, that provides ideal binding of messages to party identities. The key difference in our setting is that $\bar{\mathcal{G}}_{\text{cert}}$ is accessible at any time, by any party, no matter which protocols it participates in. Another important difference from previous formulations is that the public key lives in a global bulletin-board, to capture the fact that a principal has a single keypair ("secret") which she uses in multiple protocols. Then, we formulate

---

Global Functionality $\bar{\mathcal{G}}_{bb}$

Report: Upon receiving a message (Register, v) from party P, send (Registered, P, v) to the adversary; upon receiving OK from the adversary, and if this is the first request from P, then record the pair (P, v). Otherwise, ignore the new message.

Retrieve: Upon receiving a message (Retrieve, P_i) from some party P_j (or the adversary S), generate a public delayed output (Retrieve, P_i, v) to P_j, where $v = \bot$ if no record (P_i, v) exists.

Fig. 3. The bulletin-board certificate authority (CA) functionality. Any ITI can register a single key that would be associated with its identity. Any ITI in the system can request the key of any other ITI.

a global signature functionality $\bar{\mathcal{G}}_{cwk}$ that realizes $\bar{\mathcal{G}}_{cert}$ given a public bulletin-board $\bar{\mathcal{G}}_{bb}$.

The Bulletin Board Functionality. The global bulletin board functionality, $\bar{\mathcal{G}}_{bb}$, is presented in Fig. 3. The bulletin board accepts only the first registered value, and does not allow to modify or delete it.[4] The bulletin board is authenticated in a sense that it records the value along with the identity of the publisher, but does not perform any checks on the registered value; it simply publicly records the value. Nonetheless, as we will show later, the present minimal formulation suffices for authentication.

The Certification Functionality. The ideal certification functionality, $\bar{\mathcal{G}}_{cert}$, is presented in Fig. 4. The session ID names a distinguished principal, the 'signer'. The functionality provides direct binding between a message and the identity of the signer. (In contrast, $\mathcal{F}_{sig}$, which appears in Fig. 5, binds a message only to a verification key.) Using common terminology, this corresponds to providing signatures accompanied by "certificates" that bind the verification process to the signer's identity. The functionality generates a key for each new signer; however, the key is used only to register in the bulletin-board. That is, neither signing nor verification is done with respect to this key. Verification (and signing) requests are processed only if the signer is registered in the bulletin-board, however, they are indifferent to the registered value. Lastly, corrupted signers are allowed to dictate the verification result. We note that $\bar{\mathcal{G}}_{cert}$ is a $\bar{\mathcal{G}}_{bb}$-subroutine respecting functionality as defined in Sect. 2.

We model the certificate authority in a simplistic way, by associating each $\bar{\mathcal{G}}_{cert}$ with an owner PID, and providing certificates to any session of the owner. A more sophisticated modeling could have the certificate authority provide certificates according to some policy provided by the owner. For example, policies that allow sessions of other PIDs to generate certificates would capture a more refined notion of trust ("delegated signers").

---

[4] The modeling of PKI that allows a single public key per identity has been chosen for simplicity of the modeling and presentation. It can be extended in a natural way to handle the case where an entity may register and be authenticated via multiple public keys.

Global Functionality $\bar{\mathcal{G}}_{\text{cert}}^{pid}$

Parameterized by a party identity pid, global functionality $\bar{\mathcal{G}}_{\text{cert}}^{pid}$ proceeds as follows:

Signature Generation: Upon receiving a value (Sign, sid, m) from P_{pid} do:

    (a) Verify that $sid = (pid, sid')$ for some sid'. If not, then ignore the request.

    (b) If this is the first request then do:

        (i) If P_{pid} is honest then generate a verification key (i.e., run the Key Generation procedure described in Figure 5). Upon receiving (Verification Key, sid, v) from the adversary, send (Register, pid, v) to $\bar{\mathcal{G}}_{\text{bb}}$ (done via an output to P_{pid}).

        (ii) Else, check that P_{pid} is registered in the $\bar{\mathcal{G}}_{\text{bb}}$ (i.e., send (Retrieve, pid) and verifying that $v \neq \perp$). If not, then ignore the request.

    (c) Send (Sign, sid, m) to the adversary. Upon receiving (Signature, sid, m, σ) from the adversary, verify that no entry $(m, \sigma, 0)$ is recorded. If it is, then output an error message to P_{pid}. Else, output (Signature, sid, m, σ) to P_{pid}, and record the entry $(m, \sigma, 1)$.

Signature Verification: Upon receiving a value (Verify, sid, m, σ) from some party P, where $sid = (pid, sid')$ for some sid', check whether a pair (pid, v) is recorded. If not, send (Retrieve, pid) to $\bar{\mathcal{G}}_{\text{bb}}$, and obtain a response (Retrieve, pid, v). If $v = \perp$ then output (Verified, $sid, m, 0$). Else, record (pid, v) and hand (Verify, sid, m, σ) to the adversary. Upon receiving (Verified, sid, m, ϕ) from the adversary do:

    (a) If (m, σ, b') is recorded then set $f = b'$.

    (b) Else, if the signer is not corrupted, and no entry $(m, \sigma', 1)$ for any σ' is recorded, then set $f = 0$ and record the entry $(m, \sigma, 0)$.

    (c) Else, set $f = \phi$, and record the entry (m, σ, ϕ).

    Output (Verified, sid, m, f) to P.

Corruption: Upon receiving a value (Corrupt, sid) from the adversary, if $sid = (pid, sid')$ mark the party P_{pid} as corrupt.

Fig. 4. The certification functionality. The certification functionality is parametrized by a party identity, referred to as the *owner*, and allows only that party to sign messages. The functionality generates a key for the owner when the first signing request arrives. This is done to advertise that party's existence; neither signature nor verification is done with respect to that key.

The Certification with Keys Functionality. The functionality $\bar{\mathcal{G}}_{\text{cwk}}$ is a GUC adaptation of the ideal signature functionality $\mathcal{F}_{\text{sig}}$ of [Can04] (formal description of $\mathcal{F}_{\text{sig}}$ can be found in Fig. 5); it is used to realize the certification functionality. For an uncorrupted party it offers the capabilities of signing a message (reserved for the owner PID) and verifying a signature. It also captures the ways in which a corrupted party may deviate: as a signer, a corrupted party may refrain from registering the generated key in the bulletin-board, and as a verifier it may request verification of messages with respect to keys of its choice (instead of the key registered in the bulletin-board). The only difference between the two formulations is the inability of a corrupted signer to generate a signing key without providing a message to be signed. Nonetheless, the capabilities of the attacker with respect to the formulations are equivalent. A formal

---

Functionality $\mathcal{F}_{\text{sig}}^{pid}$

Parameterized by a party identity pid, functionality $\mathcal{F}_{\text{sig}}^{pid}$ proceeds as follows:

Key Generation: Upon receiving a value (KeyGen, sid) from some party P_{pid} verify that this is the first request and $sid = (pid, sid')$ for some sid'. If not, then ignore the request. Else, hand (KeyGen, sid) to the adversary. Upon receiving (Verification Key, sid, v) from the adversary, output (Verification Key, sid, v) to P_{pid}.

Signature Generation: Upon receiving a value (Sign, sid, m) from P_{pid}, verify that $sid = (pid, sid')$ for some sid'. If not, then ignore the request. Else, send (Sign, sid, m) to the adversary. Upon receiving (Signature, sid, m, σ) from the adversary, verify that no entry $(m, \sigma, v, 0)$ is recorded. If it is, then output an error message to P_{pid} and halt. Else, output (Signature, sid, m, σ) to P_{pid}, and record the entry $(m, \sigma, v, 1)$.

Signature Verification: Upon receiving a value (Verify, sid, m, σ, v') from party P, where $sid = (pid, sid')$ for some sid' verify that a pair (pid, v) is recorded. If not, output (Verified, $sid, m, 0$) to P. Else, hand (Verify, sid, m, σ, v') to the adversary. Upon receiving (Verified, sid, m, ϕ) from the adversary do:

(a) If $v' = v$ and the entry $(m, \sigma, v, 1)$ is recorded, then set $f = 1$. (This condition guarantees completeness: If the verification key v' is the registered one and σ is a legitimately generated signature for m, then the verification succeeds.)

(b) Else, if $v' = v$, the signer is not corrupted, and no entry $(m, \sigma', v, 1)$ for any σ' is recorded, then set $f = 0$ and record the entry $(m, \sigma, v, 0)$. (This condition guarantees unforgeability: If v' is the registered one, the signer is not corrupted, and never signed m, then the verification fails.)

(c) Else, if there is an entry (m, σ, v', f') recorded, then let $f = f'$. (This condition guarantees consistency: All verification requests with identical parameters will result in the same answer.)

(d) Else, let $f = \phi$ and record the entry (m, σ, v', ϕ)

Output (Verified, sid, m, f) to P.

Corruption: Upon receiving a value (Corrupt, sid) from the adversary, if $sid = (pid, sid')$ then mark the party P_{pid} as corrupt.

Fig. 5. The basic signature functionality [Can04]. The signature functionality is parametrized by a party identity and allows only this party to generate a key and sign messages. The owner can generate only a single key and sign only with respect to this key. Verifying a signature is done with respect to the signing key generated by the signature functionality. The functionality accepts verification requests from any ITI in the system. The signature functionality lets the adversary determine the signing key, the legitimate signatures, and the results of verifications that use an incorrect key or a different signature. When the signer is corrupted, the functionality allows the verification process to succeed, even if the message was never signed.

description appears in Fig. 6. We note that $\bar{\mathcal{G}}_{\text{cwk}}$ is a $\bar{\mathcal{G}}_{\text{bb}}$-subroutine respecting functionality, as defined in Sect. 2.

Lemma 1. *The functionality $\mathcal{G}_{\text{cwk}}$ EUC-realizes functionality $\mathcal{G}_{\text{cert}}$ and vice versa, with respect to adaptive corruptions.*

Global functionality $\bar{\mathcal{G}}_{\text{cwk}}^{pid}$ for realizing $\bar{\mathcal{G}}_{\text{cert}}$

The functionality $\bar{\mathcal{G}}_{\text{cwk}}^{pid}$ internally runs the code of $\mathcal{F}_{\text{sig}}$ and proceeds as follows:

Signature Generation: Upon receiving a value (Sign, sid, m) from P_{pid}, do:
   (a) Verify that $sid = (pid, sid')$ for some sid'. If not, then ignore the request. (That is, verify that it is the legitimate signer for this sid.)
   (b) If this is the first request then do:
      (i) If P_{pid} is corrupted, then verify that P_{pid} is registered in $\bar{\mathcal{G}}_{\text{bb}}$ (otherwise, then ignore the request).
      (ii) Generate a verification key, i.e., send (KeyGen, sid) to $\mathcal{F}_{\text{sig}}$. Upon receiving (Verification Key, sid, v), send (Register, pid, v) to $\bar{\mathcal{G}}_{\text{bb}}$ (done via an output to P_{pid}).
   (c) Send (Sign, sid, m) to $\mathcal{F}_{\text{sig}}$. Upon receiving (Signature, sid, m, σ) from $\mathcal{F}_{\text{sig}}$, output (Signature, sid, m, σ) to P_{pid}.

Signature Verification: Upon receiving a value (Verify, sid, m, σ), where $sid = (pid, sid')$ for some sid', check whether a pair (pid, v) is recorded. If not, send (Retrieve, pid) to $\bar{\mathcal{G}}_{\text{bb}}$, and obtain a response (Retrieve, pid, v). If $v = \bot$ then output (Verified, $sid, m, 0$). Else record (pid, v). Next, send (Verify, sid, m, σ, v) to $\mathcal{F}_{\text{sig}}$, and output the response (Verified, sid, m, f).

Corrupted Signature Verification: Upon receiving a value (Verify, sid, m, σ, v') from the adversary, where $sid = (pid, sid')$ for some sid', send (Verify, sid, m, σ, v') to $\mathcal{F}_{\text{sig}}$, and output the response (Verified, sid, m, f).

Corruption: Upon receiving a value (Corrupt, sid) from the adversary, forward it to $\mathcal{F}_{\text{sig}}$.

Fig. 6. The certification with keys functionality. The functionality $\bar{\mathcal{G}}_{\text{cwk}}$ is parametrized by a party identity and internally executes the code of the basic signature functionality $\mathcal{F}_{\text{sig}}$. The functionality does not allow generating a key without signing a message. Key generation is done internally by the functionality. Note that keys of corrupted parties registered with $\bar{\mathcal{G}}_{\text{bb}}$ do not have to match the keys generated by $\mathcal{F}_{\text{sig}}$.

Proof. First we observe that as long as verification requests are done with the actual verification key, the functionalities are equivalent. To handle the other scenarios, we use the simulator's ability to postpone signature requests of corrupted signers up to the verification moment.

We begin by showing that $\mathcal{G}_{\text{cwk}}$ GUC-realizes functionality $\mathcal{G}_{\text{cert}}$. The simulation here is even simpler than in [Can04] due to the existence of $\bar{\mathcal{G}}_{\text{bb}}$ also in the ideal execution. We make use of an equivalent formulation of GUC-emulation with respect to dummy adversaries. Thus, denoting the dummy adversary by $\mathcal{D}$, we wish to construct an adversary $\mathcal{S}$ such that:

$$\text{GEXEC}_{\mathcal{G}_{\text{cwk}}, \mathcal{D}, \mathcal{Z}} \approx \text{GEXEC}_{\mathcal{G}_{\text{cert}}, \mathcal{S}, \mathcal{Z}} \tag{2}$$

The adversary $\mathcal{S}$ is specified as follows. For signature generation, if the signer is honest then behave as the dummy adversary $\mathcal{D}$. That is, any output of $\mathcal{G}_{\text{cert}}$ and $\bar{\mathcal{G}}_{\text{bb}}$ is forwarded to $\mathcal{Z}$ and any input of $\mathcal{Z}$ is forwarded to $\mathcal{G}_{\text{cert}}$ or $\bar{\mathcal{G}}_{\text{bb}}$, in an appropriate manner. It also records the generated key v. If the signer is corrupted, $\mathcal{S}$ behaves as follows: for the first sign request it verifies that the signer is registered in $\bar{\mathcal{G}}_{bb}$ (if not it ignores the sign request) and simulates the key generation procedure. After recording the generated key v it simulates the signature generation process, without involving $\mathcal{G}_{cert}$, and records the tuple $(m, \sigma, v, 1)$ where σ is the signature chosen by $\mathcal{Z}$ (except when a record $(m, \sigma, v, 0)$ exists, in which case it outputs an error message). Note that $\mathcal{G}_{cert}$ does not receive any sign requests from a corrupted signer during the simulation of signature generation. Signing using $\mathcal{G}_{cert}$ is postponed, and executed only if a verification request is received for this record.

For signature verification, we simulate differently depending on the integrity of the signer and the key used by the verifier. If the signer is honest and some uncorrupted party makes a verification request (or a corrupted party that is using the key registered in $\mathcal{G}_{bb}$) then do the following:

(a) behave as a dummy adversary $\mathcal{D}$ in the retrieve process (if executed).
(b) Once (Verify, sid, m, σ) received, append the verification key, which is recorded in $\bar{\mathcal{G}}_{bb}$, and forward it to the environment $\mathcal{Z}$. The response of $\mathcal{Z}$ is forwarded back to $\mathcal{G}_{cert}$. If in the output $f = 0$ then record $(m, \sigma, v', 0)$.

For corrupted signer, upon receiving a verification request from a honest verifier (or a corrupted verifier that is using the key registered in $\bar{\mathcal{G}}_{bb}$) do the following:

(a) behave as a dummy adversary $\mathcal{D}$ in the retrieve process (if executed).
(b) if a record $(m, \sigma, v', 1)$ exists, where v' is the key registered in $\bar{\mathcal{G}}_{bb}$, forward a sign request on m to $\mathcal{G}_{cert}$, pick σ to be the signature and delete the record.
(c) behave exactly as in the honest signer honest verifier scenario to emulate the communication with $\mathcal{Z}$. That is, append the verification key, which is recorded in $\bar{\mathcal{G}}_{bb}$, and forward it to the environment $\mathcal{Z}$. The response of $\mathcal{Z}$ is forwarded back to $\mathcal{G}_{cert}$.

In case a verification request is made with a key that does not match the key registered in $\bar{\mathcal{G}}_{bb}$, independently of the signer's integrity, then simulate the verification process by giving $\mathcal{Z}$ the appropriate (Verify, sid, m, σ, v'') and obtaining its response ϕ. Next, if the tuple (m, σ, v'', b') is recorded, set $\phi = b'$, else record (m, σ, v'', ϕ). In any case, output (Verified, sid, m, ϕ). It is important to note that verification requests with $v'' \neq v$ are simulated without involving $\mathcal{G}_{cert}$.

Since the simulator does nor perform any cheating, the simulation is perfect. That is, the environment $\mathcal{Z}$'s view of an interaction with $\mathcal{S}$ and $\mathcal{G}_{cert}$ is distributed identically to its view of an interaction with parties running protocol $\mathcal{G}_{cwk}$ in the $\bar{\mathcal{G}}_{bb}$-hybrid model, even if $\mathcal{Z}$ is computationally unbounded.

Now we show the other direction: $\mathcal{G}_{cert}$ GUC-realizes functionality $\mathcal{G}_{cwk}$. Signature generation for a honest signer is simulated by behaving as a dummy adversary $\mathcal{D}$. If the signer is corrupted, we forward the signing request to $\mathcal{G}_{cwk}$ and pick the key for $\mathcal{F}_{sig}$ to be the key registered in $\bar{\mathcal{G}}_{bb}$. In the verification process, as before, retrieve is simulated by behaving as a dummy adversary. Upon receiving (Verify, sid, m, σ, v) from $\mathcal{G}_{cwk}$, the simulator drops v and forwards the modified message to $\mathcal{Z}$. The response (Verified, sid, m, ϕ) of $\mathcal{Z}$ is forwarded to $\mathcal{G}_{cwk}$. Note that the simulator ensures that the key in $\bar{\mathcal{G}}_{bb}$ is the same as the key registered in $\mathcal{F}_{\text{sig}}$. Therefore, all simulated verification requests are made with respect to the correct key, and hence answered exactly as in the real execution. This follows from the functionalities being identical when the verification is done with the key recorded in $\mathcal{F}_{\text{sig}}$.

4.2 Using EU-CMA Signatures for Certification

[Can04] shows that realizing $\mathcal{F}_{\text{sig}}$ is equivalent to being EU-CMA secure (existential unforgeability against chosen message attacks; [GMR88]). However, his theorem does not apply to a setting where the keys are reused by arbitrary protocols. This section extends the connection between ideal signatures and EU-CMA security to the GUC setting. Specifically, we show its equivalence to $\bar{\mathcal{G}}_{\text{cwk}}$.

Unforgeable Signatures. A signature scheme is a triple of PPT algorithms $\Sigma = (\text{gen}, \text{sig}, \text{ver})$, where sig may maintain local state between activations.

Definition 5 ([GMR88]). *A signature scheme* $\Sigma = (\text{gen}, \text{sig}, \text{ver})$ *is called EU-CMA if the following properties hold for any negligible function* ν *and all large enough values of the security parameter* κ.

Completeness: For any message m, $\Pr[(s,v) \leftarrow \text{gen}(1^\kappa); \sigma \leftarrow \text{sig}(s,m); 0 \leftarrow \text{ver}(m, \sigma, v)] < \nu(\kappa)$.

Consistency: For any m, *the probability that* $\text{gen}(1^\kappa)$ *generates* (s,v) *and* $\text{ver}(m, \sigma, v)$ *generates two different outputs in two independent invocations is smaller than* $\nu(\kappa)$.

Unforgeability: For any PPT forger F, $\Pr[(s,v) \leftarrow \text{gen}(1^\kappa); (m, \sigma) \leftarrow F^{\text{sig}(s,\cdot)}(v); 1 \leftarrow \text{ver}(m, \sigma, v)$ *and* F *never asked* sig *to sign* $m] < \nu(\kappa)$.

Signing Module. To capture re-usability of keys within different protocols, we describe a signing module that accepts sign requests from its owner PID. This module can be thought of as a *local* service process, physically running on some local machine, providing signing service to all authorized processes on this machine. This is formally described as an ideal functionality, denoted $\bar{\mathcal{G}}_\Sigma^{pid}$, parametrized by a signature scheme $\Sigma = (\text{gen}, \text{sig}, \text{ver})$ and some party ID. The keys' re-usability is modeled by having the functionality be shared among different SIDs, as long as they are owned by the same PID. That is, the functionality $\bar{\mathcal{G}}_\Sigma^{pid}$ is a "local" subroutine of this PID and is not accessible by anyone else.

The signing module separates the signing capability from secret key knowledge, and hence allows greater flexibility in terms of corruptions. Corrupting the module captures the scenario of complete privacy loss; corrupting a principal in a single session that uses the module captures a weaker privacy loss, allowing the adversary to sign some messages but not arbitrary messages. In particular, corrupting a session that uses the module does not provide the adversary with the secret key or with the ability to sign messages of other SIDs. The signing module could be generalized to be selective about which sign requests it honors (for example, as a function of the session id and message contents). For our purpose, it suffices to consider the basic module. Formal description of $\bar{\mathcal{G}}_\Sigma^{pid}$ appears in Fig. 7.

Functionality $\bar{\mathcal{G}}_\Sigma^{pid}$

Parameterized by a security parameter κ, a key generation and sign functions gen and sign respectively, global functionality $\bar{\mathcal{G}}_\Sigma^{pid}$ proceeds thusly when running with party P_{pid}:

Signature Generation: Upon receiving a value (Sign, sid, m) from P_{pid}, do:

    (a) Verify that $sid = (pid, sid')$ for some sid'. If not, then ignore the request.

    (b) If this is the first request run $(s, v) \leftarrow \text{gen}(1^\kappa)$, record (s, v).
        In any case, output (Signature, $sid, m, \text{sig}(s, m), v$).

Corruption-module: Upon receiving a value Corrupt-module from the adversary, output s if recorded, otherwise ignore.

Fig. 7. The signing module. The functionality $\bar{\mathcal{G}}_\Sigma^{pid}$ is parametrized by a party identity and some signature scheme. The functionality generates a signing and verification keypair. The signing key is kept inside $\bar{\mathcal{G}}_\Sigma$ and used to handle signing requests. The verification key is given outside, similarly to $\bar{\mathcal{G}}_{\text{cwk}}$.

To our knowledge, this is the first modeling of authentication in a composable setting to feature SID-wise corruption; prior works used PID-wise corruptions exclusively.

The Equivalence. A signature scheme $\Sigma = (\text{gen}, \text{sig}, \text{ver})$ may be translated into a per-PID protocol π_Σ^{pid} that "locally" uses $\mathcal{G}_\Sigma^{pid}$. This protocol localizes the signing/verification process and reduces trust in the setup. That is, it is no longer required to trust a global, accessible by many parties, signing functionality; instead, each party can trust merely his local signing module, which is running on his computer.

The protocol π_Σ^{pid} proceeds as follows:

(a) When party P receives an input (Sign, sid, m), it verifies that $sid = (P, sid')$ for some sid'. If not, it ignores the input. Next, it forwards (Sign, sid, m) to $\mathcal{G}_\Sigma^{pid}$. It obtains a verification key v and a signature σ on message m. If no key is registered, then forward v to $\mathcal{G}_{\text{bb}}$ and outputs (Signature, sid, m, σ).

(b) When party P receives an input (Verify, $\widehat{sid}, m, \sigma$), where $\widehat{sid} = (\widehat{pid}, sid')$, it checks whether a pair $(\widehat{pid}, v)$ is recorded. If not, send (Retrieve, $\widehat{pid}$) to $\mathcal{G}_{\text{bb}}$ and obtain a response (Retrieve, $\widehat{pid}, v$). If $v = \perp$ then output (Verified, $\widehat{sid}, m, 0$). Else record $(\widehat{pid}, v)$. Next output (Verified, $\widehat{sid}, m, \text{ver}(m, \sigma, v)$).

Lemma 2. *Let $\Sigma = (\text{gen}, \text{sig}, \text{ver})$ be a signature scheme. If Σ is EU-CMA, then π_Σ^{pid} EUC-realizes $\mathcal{G}_{\text{cwk}}^{pid}$ with respect to adaptive corruptions.*

Functionality $\mathcal{F}_{\text{cert-auth}}$

(a) Upon receiving an input $(\mathsf{Send}, S, R, sid, m)$ from ITI S, output $(\mathsf{Sent}, S, R, sid, m)$ to the adversary, and, after a delay, provide the same output to R and halt.

(b) Upon receiving a value $(\mathsf{Corrupt}, S, sid)$ from the adversary, mark S as corrupted.

(c) Upon receiving a value $(\mathsf{Corrupt\text{-}send}, S, R, sid, m')$ from the adversary, if S is marked as corrupted and an output was not yet delivered to R, then output $(\mathsf{Sent}, S, R, sid, m')$ to R and halt.

(d) Upon receiving $(\mathsf{External\text{-}info}, S, R, sid, m')$ from the adversary, if an output was not yet delivered to R, then output $\big(\mathsf{Sign}, (S, (R, sid)), (m', sid, R)\big)$ to $\bar{\mathcal{G}}_{\text{cert}}^{S}$ (on behalf of S) and forward the response to the adversary.

(e) Upon receiving $(\mathsf{Corrupt\text{-}sign}, S, R, sid, m')$ from the adversary, if S is marked as corrupted then output $\big(\mathsf{Sign}, (S, R, sid), (m', sid, R)\big)$ to $\bar{\mathcal{G}}_{\text{cert}}$ and forward the response to the adversary.

Fig. 8. The non-deniable authentication functionality. The adversarial ability to obtain legitimate signatures on messages of its choice makes the authentication non-deniable. Signatures are obtained by instructing the dummy party S to communicate with $\bar{\mathcal{G}}_{\text{cert}}$.

4.3   Defining and Realizing Non-deniable Message Authentication

This section shows that the most basic PKI, i.e., bulletin-board, suffices for secure authentication, even if the keys are reused in other arbitrary protocols. This is similar to the last step of [Can04]'s construction, except that we use a weaker authentication functionality—one that lets the adversary obtain a signature of the 'authentication transaction' —to capture non-deniability. (The signature serves as a *transferable* 'proof of transaction'.)

We first formulate a non-deniable ideal authentication functionality $\mathcal{F}_{\text{cert-auth}}$. The non-deniability property is obtained via the usage of ideal certificates. Then, we show that the classic signature-based authentication protocol (presented in Fig. 9) GUC-securely realizes this relaxed authentication functionality. Finally, using the composition theorem and the results of Sects. 4.1 and 4.2, we obtain an authentication protocol using merely existentially-unforgeable signatures and a global bulletin-board.

On Capturing Transferability. Since the essence of transferability is that "anyone" may become convinced of the message that was authenticated, one might attempt to capture transferability by having $\mathcal{F}_{\text{auth}}$ disclose to any principal in the system, upon request, that an authentication took place; the identities of the originator and recipient; and the contents of the authenticated message. This modeling allows any principal in the system to become convinced in the contents of the authenticated message and the identities of its originator and recipient. However, this modeling of authentication poses unnecessary requirements on the implementing protocol, such as supporting inquiries by third parties in an authenticated manner.

The Non-Deniable Authentication Functionality. The functionality $\mathcal{F}_{\text{cert-auth}}$, presented in Fig. 8, is a non-deniable version of the authentication functionality of [Can04]. The non-deniability of the functionality is captured by allowing the adversary to request signatures on messages affixed with $\mathcal{F}_{\text{cert-auth}}$'s session id (SID). Including the SID in the signed message binds the signature to the execution at hand, and prevents the adversary from reusing the signatures in other sessions. Later, any entity can verify this signature and be convinced that this message was indeed sent from S to R. Our $\mathcal{F}_{\text{cert-auth}}$ is a $\bar{\mathcal{G}}_{\text{cert}}$-subroutine-respecting functionality. We highlight that the signature provided during the authentication process includes the identity of the intended recipient and the session identifier. This has two consequences: it does not guarantee the receiver deniability since it allows to publicly verify not only that a specific message was sent by some ITI, but also the intended recipient's identity; and it also prevents the adversary from relaying signatures between different sessions. The authentication functionality enables a corrupted sender to produce many signature on messages of its choice. This enables corrupting parties without corrupting their signing module. One could define, and realize by a similar protocol, a receiver-deniable version of $\mathcal{F}_{\text{cert-auth}}$. However, receiver-deniable authentication enables the adversary to reroute messages to a destination of its choice.

Protocol ϕ_{auth} for realizing $\mathcal{F}_{\text{cert-auth}}$

(a) Upon receiving an input (Send, A, B, sid, m), party A sets $sid' = (A, B, sid)$, sets $m' = (m, sid, B)$, sends (Sign, sid', m') to $\bar{\mathcal{G}}_{\text{cert}}$, obtains the response (Signature, sid', m', σ), and sends (sid, A, m, σ) to B.

(b) Upon receiving (sid, A, m, σ), party B sets $sid' = (A, B, sid)$, sets $m' = (m, sid, B)$, sends (Verify, sid', m', σ) to $\bar{\mathcal{G}}_{\text{cert}}$, and obtains a response (Verified, sid', m', f). If $f = 1$ then B outputs (Sent, A, B, sid, m) and halts. Else B halts with no output.

Fig. 9. The signature-based authentication protocol.

Lemma 3. *The protocol ϕ_{auth} GUC-emulates functionality $\mathcal{F}_{\text{cert-auth}}$ with respect to adaptive corruptions.*

Proof. The proof here is simpler than the proof of [Can04] due to having the certificate functionality in both the ideal and real executions.

Let $\mathcal{D}$ be the dummy adversary that interacts with parties running ϕ_{auth} in the $\bar{\mathcal{G}}_{\text{cert}}$-hybrid model. We construct an ideal-process adversary (simulator) $\mathcal{S}$ such that the view of any environment $\mathcal{Z}$ from an interaction with $\mathcal{D}$ and ϕ_{auth} is distributed identically to its view of an interaction with $\mathcal{S}$ in the ideal process for $\mathcal{F}_{\text{cert-auth}}$. The simulator $\mathcal{S}$ proceeds as follows.

Simulating the Sender. When an uncorrupted party A is activated with input (Send, sid, B), $\mathcal{S}$ obtains this value from $\mathcal{F}_{\text{cert-auth}}$. Then, $\mathcal{S}$ replies with (External-info, A, B, sid, m) and behaves as $\mathcal{D}$ in the interaction with $\bar{\mathcal{G}}_{\text{cert}}$. That is, $\mathcal{S}$ forwards to $\mathcal{Z}$ the message (Sign, $(A, B, sid), (m, sid, B)$) from $\bar{\mathcal{G}}_{\text{cert}}$, and forwards back to $\bar{\mathcal{G}}_{\text{cert}}$ the obtained signature σ. Next, $\mathcal{S}$ hands $\mathcal{Z}$ the message

(sid, A, m, s) sent from A to B. If the sender is corrupted, then all that $\mathcal{S}$ has to do is to behave as the dummy party $\mathcal{D}$ in the interaction with $\bar{\mathcal{G}}_{cert}$.

Simulating the Verifier. When $\mathcal{Z}$ instructs to deliver a message $(sid, A, \bar{m}, \sigma)$ to an uncorrupted party B, $\mathcal{S}$ first sends $(\mathsf{Verify}, (A, B, sid), (\bar{m}, sid, B), \sigma)$ to $\bar{\mathcal{G}}_{cert}$. If $\bar{\mathcal{G}}_{cert}$ outputs $(\mathsf{Verified}, (A, B, sid), (\bar{m}, sid, B), \sigma, f = 1)$ then do the following: if the sender is honest, then allow $\mathcal{F}_{cert-auth}$ to deliver the message which was sent in the ideal process to B. If the sender is corrupted, then forward $(\mathsf{Corrupt\text{-}send}, sid, \bar{m})$ to $\mathcal{F}_{cert-auth}$. In case $f = 0$ do nothing.

It is readily seen that the combined view of $\mathcal{Z}$ and $\mathcal{D}$ in an execution of ϕ_{auth} is distributed identically to the combined view of $\mathcal{Z}$ and $\mathcal{S}$ in the ideal process. Indeed, the only case where the two views may potentially differ is if the receiver obtains $(\mathsf{Verified}, sid', m', \sigma, f = 1)$ from $\mathcal{F}_{cert-auth}$ for an incoming message (sid, A, m, σ), while A is honest and never sent this message. However, if A never sent (sid, A, m, σ), then the message $m' = (m, sid, B)$ was never signed by $\bar{\mathcal{G}}_{cert}$ with session id (A, B, sid); thus, according to the logic of $\bar{\mathcal{G}}_{cert}$, B would always obtain $(\mathsf{Verified}, sid', m', \sigma, f = 0)$ from $\bar{\mathcal{G}}_{cert}$.

Now we are ready to fully instantiate the ideal functionalities used for authentication. The resulting authentication protocol is the signature protocol used in practice, which is depicted in Fig. 1 along with the minimal PKI required for this task.

Corollary 1. *If EU-CMA signatures exist then protocol $\phi_{auth}^{\bar{\pi}_\Sigma / \bar{\mathcal{G}}_{cert}}$ GUC-realizes functionality $\mathcal{F}_{cert-auth}$ with respect to adaptive corruptions.*

Proof. By combining Lemma 1 with Theorem 2 we manage to reduce the security of $\mathcal{G}_{cert}$ to the security of π_Σ. This allows us to combine Lemma 3 with Theorem 5 and conclude that ϕ_{auth} GUC-realizes $\mathcal{F}_{cert-auth}$, where ϕ_{auth} uses $\bar{\pi}_\Sigma$ with $\bar{\mathcal{G}}_\Sigma$ instead of $\bar{\mathcal{G}}_{cert}$.

5   Non-deniable Key Exchange

We present a non-deniable key exchange functionality $\mathcal{F}_{cert-ke}$ and show that the classic signed-Diffie-Hellman protocol ϕ_{ke} (see ISO 9798-3, [CK01]), realizes it. The protocol ϕ_{ke} is presented in Fig. 10.

The Non-Deniable Key Exchange Functionality. The functionality, presented in Fig. 11, is a key exchange functionality coupled with $\bar{\mathcal{G}}_{cert}$, similarly to $\mathcal{F}_{cert-auth}$. The main difference between our functionality and [DKSW09] is that we do not guarantee mutual authentication. That is, $\mathcal{F}_{cert-ke}$ allows a party to have a key also if the other party aborted before establishing a shared key.

Lemma 4. *Under the Decisional Diffie-Hellman (DDH) assumption, the protocol ϕ_{ke} GUC-emulates functionality $\mathcal{F}_{cert-ke}$ with respect to adaptive corruptions.*

Protocol ϕ_{ke}

Parametrized by primes p and q such that $q \mid p - 1$, and an element g of order q in $\mathbb{Z}_p^*$, protocol ϕ_{ke} proceeds as follows:

(a) Upon receiving an input (keyexchange, sid, A, B), party A samples $x \xleftarrow{\$} \mathbb{Z}_q$, and sends $(sid, A, \alpha = g^x)$ to B.

(b) Upon receiving (sid, A, α), party B samples $y \xleftarrow{\$} \mathbb{Z}_q$, sets $sid' = (A, (B, sid))$, sets $m' = (\alpha, \beta = g^y, sid, A, B)$, and sends (Sign, sid', m') to $\bar{\mathcal{G}}_{cert}^B$, obtains the response (Signature, sid', m', σ_B), sends $(sid, B, \beta, \sigma_B)$ to A; computes the key $k = \alpha^y$; and erases y.

(c) Upon receiving $(sid, B, \beta, \sigma_B)$, party A sets $sid' = (A, (B, sid))$, sets $m' = (\alpha, \beta, sid, A, B)$, and sends (Verify, sid', m', σ_B) to $\bar{\mathcal{G}}_{cert}^B$, obtains the response (Verified, sid', m', f). If $f = 1$ then A sends (Sign, sid', m') to $\bar{\mathcal{G}}_{cert}^A$, obtains the response (Signature, sid', m', σ_A), sends (sid, A, σ_A) to B; computes the key $k = \beta^x$; erases x; and outputs (setkey, sid, A, B, k) and halts. Else A halts with no output.

(d) Upon receiving (sid, A, σ_A), party B sends (Verify, sid', m', σ_A) to $\bar{\mathcal{G}}_{cert}^B$, obtains the response (Verified, sid', m', f). If $f = 1$ then B outputs (setkey, sid, A, B, k) and halts. Else B halts with no output.

Fig. 10. The non-deniable-authentication-based key exchange protocol.

Proof. Let p, q, g be as in ϕ_{ke} and let $D = \{g^z\}_{z \in \mathbb{Z}_q^*}$. We construct a simulator $\mathcal{S}$ that simulates the execution of the protocol with the dummy adversary $\mathcal{D}$ and environment $\mathcal{Z}$. The simulation of uncorrupted parties is done by honestly executing the protocol. That is, the simulator honestly generates the share of the secret key, and obtains the necessary certificates via $\bar{\mathcal{G}}_{cert}$ of the appropriate party. Once the simulation reaches the output step of party A, the simulator provides $\mathcal{F}_{cert-ke}$ with (setkey, sid, S, R, k') where k' is set to be the simulated key. More formally,

(a) The simulator samples $x \xleftarrow{\$} \mathbb{Z}_q$ and outputs $(sid, A, \alpha = g^x)$ to $\mathcal{Z}$ as if it was sent by A.

(b) Upon receiving (sid, A, α') from $\mathcal{Z}$ as a message to be delivered to $\{0, 1\}$ (recall that the channels are unauthenticated and hence $\mathcal{Z}$ can instruct $\mathcal{D}$ to deliver a different message instead). $\mathcal{S}$ samples $y \xleftarrow{\$} \mathbb{Z}_q$, sets $sid' = (A, (B, sid))$, sets $m' = (\alpha', \beta = g^y, sid, A, B)$, and sends (External-info, B, sid', m') to $\mathcal{F}_{cert-ke}$, obtains the response (Signature, sid', m', σ_B), sends $(sid, B, \beta, \sigma_B)$ to $\mathcal{Z}$ as if this message was sent by B.

(c) Upon receiving $(sid, B, \beta', \sigma_B')$ from $\mathcal{Z}$, the simulator verifies the signature on $m' = (\alpha, \beta', sid, A, B)$ by sending an appropriate input to $\bar{\mathcal{G}}_{cert}^B$. If the signature is not verified, the simulation of A stops. Otherwise, it sends (External-info, B, sid', m') to $\mathcal{F}_{cert-ke}$, obtains the response (Signature, sid', m', σ_A), and outputs (sid, A, σ_A) to $\mathcal{Z}$. It also computes the key $k' = (\beta')^x$, gives input (setkey, sid, A, B, k') to $\mathcal{F}_{cert-ke}$, and instructs $\mathcal{F}_{cert-ke}$ to give output to A.

(d) Upon receiving (sid, A, σ'_A) the simulator verifies the signature on $m' = (\alpha', \beta, sid, A, B)$ by sending an appropriate input to $\bar{\mathcal{G}}^A_{cert}$. If the signature is not verified, the simulator halts. Otherwise, it instructs $\mathcal{F}_{cert-ke}$ to give output to B.

Upon corruption, the simulator reveals the secret information (if any) associated with the simulated transcript of the newly corrupted party. More concretely, if the environment requests to corrupt party A or party B before A outputs the key, then $\mathcal{S}$ reveals the share x or the simulated key k' respectively; in any other case, it reveals the secret key k provided to it by $\mathcal{F}_{cert-ke}$.

The analysis of $\mathcal{S}$ considers three possible scenarios:

(a) *No corruption case:* correctness can be violated by $\mathcal{Z}$ only with negligible probability. That is, the only way to have parties in the real execution output different keys is by forging a signature, which can happen negligibly often. In the ideal execution, correctness always holds and thence indistinguishability follows. Conditioned on $\mathcal{Z}$ not forging any signature, the view of $\mathcal{Z}$ in the real execution consists of $\{g^x, g^y, g^{xy}\}$ while in the simulated execution the view is $\{g^x, g^y, g^r\}$ for random r. If $\mathcal{Z}$ can distinguish the two executions with non-negligible advantage, then we can construct an adversary $\mathcal{A}$ that internally runs $\mathcal{Z}$ and breaks the DDH assumption.

(b) *Corruption after A produced an output:* this is similar to the no corruption case. After party A produced an output, there is no secret information avail-

---

Functionality $\mathcal{F}_{cert-ke}$

The functionality $\mathcal{F}_{cert-ke}$ parametrized by a domain D proceeds as follows:

(a) Upon receiving message of the form $(\mathsf{keyexchange}, sid, S, R)$ from some ITI S, if this is the first activation, set $k = \perp$ and send $(\mathsf{keyexchange}, sid, S, R)$ to S. (Otherwise, ignore the message).

(b) Upon receiving a value $(\mathsf{Corrupt}, sid, P)$ from $\mathcal{S}$, mark $P \in \{S, R\}$ as corrupted and output k to $\mathcal{S}$.

(c) Upon receiving a message of the form $(\mathsf{setkey}, sid, S, R, k')$ from the adversary, if either S or R is corrupt, then set key $k = k'$, else set $k \stackrel{\$}{\leftarrow} D$. Output a delayed message $(\mathsf{setkey}, sid, S, R, k)$ to S and R and halt.

(d) Upon receiving $(\mathsf{External\text{-}info}, P, sid, m')$ from the adversary, where $P \in \{S, R\}$, if $k \neq \perp$ and an output was not yet delivered to either party, output $\big(\mathsf{Sign}, (P, (P', sid)), (m', sid, P)\big)$ to $\bar{\mathcal{G}}^P_{cert}$ (where P' is the other party), and forward the response to the adversary.

(e) Upon receiving $(\mathsf{Corrupt\text{-}sign}, sid, P, m')$ from the adversary, where $P \in \{S, R\}$, if P is marked as corrupted then output $\big(\mathsf{Sign}, (P, (P', sid)), (m', sid, P)\big)$ to $\bar{\mathcal{G}}^P_{cert}$ and forward the response to the adversary.

Fig. 11. The non-deniable key exchange functionality $\mathcal{F}_{cert-ke}$. The functionality allows the adversary to request signatures on messages of its choice, together with the session and parties id. This behavior is allowed as long as the key it not outputted, to prevent the functionality from being used beyond the lifetime of the protocol.

able (it is erased beforehand) and hence indistinguishability follows as in the no corruption case.

(c) *Corruption before A produced an output:* in both executions the outputted key is distributed identically, since in the ideal execution the uncorrupted party is honestly simulated and the output is set to be the simulated key. Moreover, the secret share x of A (revealed in case $\mathcal{Z}$ requests to corrupt party A after the first message is sent) is distributed identically in both executions.   □

6 Capturing Invisible Adaptive Attacks

Recently, Nielsen and Strefler [NS14] introduced a concept called Invisible Adaptive Attacks (IAA), which the GUC framework fails to capture, and showed how to immune the GUC model from such attacks, for CRS-style setup assumptions. An IAA is an attack wherein a protocol behave insecurely with respect to some specific values of the global setup, but continues to behave securely under other values of the setup. Since the setup is long-lived and fixed for the lifetime of the system, such protocols should be rejected by the security definition. However, at present, the security definition accepts such protocols, since it examines candidate protocols' behavior only with respect to the average case of the setup-generating algorithm.

The approach of [NS14] for capturing such attacks is to consider worst-case security, i.e., guarantee security with respect to any setup. This is incorporated in the GUC model by letting the environment pick the random coins the setup (e.g. a CRS) uses. For our protocols, IAA security boils down to letting the environment determine the random coins of $\bar{\mathcal{G}}_{\Sigma}^{pid}$. This additional power does not influence the security and the analysis of ϕ_{auth} and ϕ_{ke}, since the only possible way to distinguish ideal from real is to forge a signature. However, since the environment is oblivious to the secret keys, its forging ability remains negligible and security continues to hold.

An Alternative Definition. We also propose an alternative approach for defining security in a way that captures such "invisible attacks". Rather than defining security of a protocol against a worst-case choice of the set-up, we define security of a protocol *relative to a specific CRS,* or more generally *relative to a specific random input for the set-up functionality.* This way, it is possible o capture a setting where the same protocol is considered (or, believed to be) secure with respect to some setup values, and insecure with respect to others. The approach is similar to the definition of security of a fixed hash function by Rogaway [Rog06]. That is, security is captured by a reduction from knowing a distinguishing environment (with respect to a specific setup value) to breaking a hard problem. This implies that the designer of a protocol is in charge of specifying the hard problem P for the security reduction. The meaning of such reduction is that, as long as solving P is believed to be hard, coming up with a distinguishing environment must be hard as well. It is stressed that here the existence of a reduction is *part of the definition of security* rather than part of the security argument. Furthermore, P can relate either to properties of the set-up itself, or alternatively to other constructs. More formally, let P be some problem; denote by $G(P)$ the game corresponding to P; and let $B(P)$ be the probability bound on winning in $G(P)$. For a shared setup $\bar{\mathcal{G}}$ we denote by $str = (s, v)$ a value of $\bar{\mathcal{G}}$ with s and v being the secret and public parts respectively.

Definition 6 (Reduction-UC). *Let π and ϕ be $\bar{\mathcal{G}}$-subroutine respecting multi-party protocols. We say that π RUC-emulates ϕ with respect to a value $str = (s, v)$ of $\mathcal{G}$ and a problem P if there exist an adversary $\mathcal{S}$ and a reduction f such that for any environment $\mathcal{Z}$ such that if*

$$\mathrm{EXEC}_{\pi, \mathcal{D}, \mathcal{Z}}^{s\bar{t}r} \not\approx \mathrm{EXEC}_{\phi, \mathcal{S}, \mathcal{Z}}^{s\bar{t}r}$$

we have that $\Pr[f(\mathcal{Z}, v)$ wins in $G(P)] > B(P)$.

An important observation is that RUC-security implies GUC-security, and the composition theorem easily holds for RUC-security. More formally, the simulator is the same as in the composition theorem proof, the hard problem is the problem the subroutine is defined with respect to, and the reduction is done by running the composition proof to obtain a distinguishing environment for the subroutine protocol and applying to that environment the reduction guaranteed for the subroutine by the RUC security definition. Another important benefit of this definition is that it easily induces a standard GUC-security definition: all we need to do is consider a setup-generating algorithm instead of a specific fixed string. For example, for ACRS this would be the key-generation algorithm. It should be noted that all GUC secure protocols (that we are aware of) are already proven secure by the way of reduction to some hard problem, and therefore RUC-secure. For example, the proof of our authentication and key-exchange protocols is done by a reduction to EU-CMA signatures and the DDH assumption respectively.

References

[AF10] Armknecht, F., Furukawa, J.: On the minimum communication effort for secure group key exchange. In: Biryukov, A., Gong, G., Stinson, D.R. (eds.) SAC 2010. LNCS, vol. 6544, pp. 320–337. Springer, Heidelberg (2011)

[BCL+05] Barak, B., Canetti, R., Lindell, Y., Pass, R., Rabin, T.: Secure computation without authentication. In: Shoup, V. (ed.) CRYPTO 2005. LNCS, vol. 3621, pp. 361–377. Springer, Heidelberg (2005)

[BFS+13] Brzuska, C., Fischlin, M., Smart, N.P., Warinschi, B., Williams, S.C.: Less is more: relaxed yet composable security notions for key exchange. Int. J. Inf. Sec. **12**(4), 267–297 (2013)

[BLdMT09] Burmester, M., Van Le, T., de Medeiros, B., Tsudik, G.: Universally composable RFID identification and authentication protocols. ACM Trans. Inf. Syst. Secur. **12**(4), 1–33 (2009)

[Can00] Canetti, R.: Universally composable security: A new paradigm for cryptographic protocols. Cryptology ePrint Archive, Report 2000/067, December 2000. Revisededition, July 2013

[Can01] Canetti, R.: Universally composable security: a new paradigm for cryptographic protocols. In: FOCS, pp. 136–145. IEEE Computer Society (2001)

[Can04] Canetti, R.: Universally composable signature, certification, and authentication. In: CSFW, p. 219. IEEE Computer Society (2004)

[CDPW07] Canetti, R., Dodis, Y., Pass, R., Walfish, S.: Universally composable security with global setup. In: Vadhan, S.P. (ed.) TCC 2007. LNCS, vol. 4392, pp. 61–85. Springer, Heidelberg (2007)

[CG10] Canetti, R., Gajek, S.: Universally composable symbolic analysis of Diffie-Hellman based key exchange. IACR Crypt. ePrint Arch. 2010, 303 (2010)

[CK01] Canetti, R., Krawczyk, H.: Analysis of key-exchange protocols and their use for building secure channels. In: Pfitzmann, B. (ed.) EUROCRYPT 2001. LNCS, vol. 2045, pp. 453–474. Springer, Heidelberg (2001)

[CK02] Canetti, R., Krawczyk, H.: Universally composable notions of key exchange and secure channels. In: Knudsen, L.R. (ed.) EUROCRYPT 2002. LNCS, vol. 2332, pp. 337–351. Springer, Heidelberg (2002)

[CR03] Canetti, R., Rabin, T.: Universal composition with joint state. In: Boneh, D. (ed.) CRYPTO 2003. LNCS, vol. 2729, pp. 265–281. Springer, Heidelberg (2003)

[DF12] Dagdelen, Ö., Fischlin, M.: Intercepting tokens: the empire strikesback in the clone wars. Cryptology ePrint Archive, Report 2012/537 (2012). http://eprint.iacr.org/

[DH76] Diffie, W., Hellman, M.E.: New directions in cryptography. IEEE Trans. Inf. Theor. 22(6), 644–654 (1976)

[DKSW09] Dodis, Y., Katz, J., Smith, A., Walfish, S.: Composability and on-line deniability of authentication. In: Reingold, O. (ed.) TCC 2009. LNCS, vol. 5444, pp. 146–162. Springer, Heidelberg (2009)

[EMV11] EMVCo, LLC. Integrated Circuit Card Specifications for Payment Systems: Book 2: Security and Key Management, Version 4.3, November 2011

[FAK08] Furukawa, J., Armknecht, F., Kurosawa, K.: A universally composable group key exchange protocol with minimum communication effort. In: Ostrovsky, R., De Prisco, R., Visconti, I. (eds.) SCN 2008. LNCS, vol. 5229, pp. 392–408. Springer, Heidelberg (2008)

[GMR88] Goldwasser, S., Micali, S., Rivest, R.L.: A digital signature scheme secure against adaptive chosen-message attacks. SIAM J. Comput. 17(2), 281–308 (1988)

[GMR89] Goldwasser, S., Micali, S., Rackoff, C.: The knowledge complexity of interactive proof systems. SIAM J. Comput. 18(1), 186–208 (1989)

[KL07] Kidron, D., Lindell, Y.: Impossibility results for universal composability in public-key models and with fixed inputs. Cryptology ePrint Archive, Report 2007/478 (2007). http://eprint.iacr.org/

[KMO+14] Kohlweiss, M., Maurer, U., Onete, C., Tackmann, B., Venturi, D.: (De-)Constructing TLS. IACR Cryptology ePrint Archive, 2014:20 (2014)

[LBdM07] Van Le, T., Burmester, M., de Medeiros, B.: Universally composable and forward-secure RFID authentication and authenticated key exchange. In: Bao, F., Miller, S., (ed.) ASIACCS, pp. 242–252. ACM (2007)

[MR11] Maurer, U., Renner, R.: Abstract cryptography. In: Chazelle, B. (ed.) ICS, pp. 1–21. Tsinghua University Press, Beijing (2011)

[MTC13] Maurer, U., Tackmann, B., Coretti, S.: Key exchange with unilateral authentication: composable security definition and modular protocol design. IACR Crypt. ePrint Arch. 2013:555 (2013)

[NS14] Nielsen, J.B., Strefler, M.: Invisible adaptive attacks. Cryptology ePrint
        Archive, Report 2014/597 (2014). http://eprint.iacr.org/
[Rog06] Rogaway, P.: Formalizing human ignorance. In: Nguyên, P.Q. (ed.) VIET-
        CRYPT 2006. LNCS, vol. 4341, pp. 211–228. Springer, Heidelberg (2006)
[Sho99] Shoup, V.: On formal models for secure key exchange. RZ 3120, IBM
        Research, April 1999. Version 4, revised November 1999
[Wal08] Walfish, S.: Enhanced security models for network protocols. Ph.D. thesis,
        Courant Institute of Mathematical Sciences, New York University (2008)

Very-Efficient Simulatable Flipping
of Many Coins into a Well
(and a New Universally-Composable
Commitment Scheme)

Luís T. A. N. Brandão[1,2]([⊠])

[1] Department of Informatics, Faculty of Sciences,
University of Lisbon, Lisbon, Portugal
[2] Electrical & Computer Engineering Department,
Carnegie Mellon University, Pittsburgh, USA
luis.papers@gmail.com

Abstract. This paper presents new cryptographic protocols for a stand-alone simulatable two-party parallel coin-flipping (into a well) and a universally composable commitment scheme, with near optimal asymptotic communication rate, in the static and computational malicious model. The approach, denoted *expand-mask-hash*, uses in both protocols a pseudo-random generator (PRG) and a collision-resistant hash function (CR-Hash) to combine separate extractable commitments and equivocable commitments (associated with short bit-strings) into a unified extractable-and-equivocable property amplified to a larger target length, amortizing the cost of base commitments. The new stand-alone coin-flipping protocol is based on a simple augmentation of the traditional coin-flipping template. To the knowledge of the author, it is the first proposal shown to simultaneously be two-side-simulatable and have an asymptotic (as the target length increases) communication rate converging to two bits per flipped coin and computation rate per party converging to that of PRG-generating and CR-hashing a bit-string with the target length. The new universally composable commitment scheme has efficiency comparable to very recent state-of-the-art constructions – namely asymptotic communication rate as close to 1 as desired, for each phase (commit and open) – while following a distinct design approach. Notably it does not require explicit use of oblivious transfer and it uses an erasure encoding instead of stronger error correction codes.

Keywords: Coin-flipping · Commitments · Protocols · Simulatability · Extractability · Equivocability · Rewinding · Universal composability

Extended abstract. Full version is at the Cryptology ePrint Archive, Report 2015/640. The author was supported as a student at FCUL-DI & CMU-ECE by the Fundação para a Ciência e a Tecnologia (Portuguese Foundation for Science and Technology) through the Carnegie Mellon Portugal Program under Grant SFRH/BD/33770/2009.

C.-M. Cheng et al. (Eds.): PKC 2016, Part II, LNCS 9615, pp. 297–326, 2016.
DOI: 10.1007/978-3-662-49387-8_12

1   Introduction

Secure two-party parallel coin-flipping is a probabilistic functionality that allows two mutually distrustful parties to agree on a common random bit-string of a certain *target* length. Using a coin-flipping protocol, both parties provide and combine independent *contributions* so that the output bit-string of an honest party is indistinguishable from random even if at most one party is malicious. The coin-flipping is denoted *simulatable* if it can be proven secure within the ideal/real simulation paradigm, showing that it *emulates* a protocol in an ideal world where an *ideal functionality* would decide and deliver the random bit-string to the two parties. Achieving simulatability is useful for the design of larger protocols, as it guarantees security under some type of *composition* operation, e.g., non-concurrent modular self-composition [Can00] (a.k.a. the stand-alone setting) or *universal composability* (UC) [Can01], depending on the type of achievable simulation, namely *with-rewinding* or *one-pass*, respectively.

Motivation for this functionality can be found directly in the real-world usefulness of "coin-flipping," enabling parties to jointly make random decisions (e.g., "who gets the car" [Blu83]). A more-technical motivation for simulatability is the security enhancement of larger cryptographic protocols. An important application is the joint decision of a large *common reference string* needed as setup condition of one or several follow-up protocols [CR03]. It is also useful for protocols whose probabilistic output needs to directly depend on random bit-strings, such as in S2PC-with-commitments (e.g., [Bra13]), where both parties may want to jointly generate many random commitments.

1.1   Coin-Flipping and Primitives

A protocol for two-party coin-flipping ("by telephone") was early proposed by Blum [Blu83]. It uses the fundamental notion of commitment scheme, allowing one party (P_A) to *commit* her own contribution before knowing anything about the contribution of the other party (P_B), but *hiding* it until the contribution of P_B is revealed, and *binding* P_A to only being able to *open* the committed value. The solution, emulating a coin-flipping into a well, sets the basis for what is hereinafter denoted as the *traditional template*:

- **Step 1.** (*Commit* phase) P_A commits to a contribution, hiding it from P_B.
- **Step 2.** P_B selects and sends his random contribution to P_A.
- **Step 3.** (*Open* phase) P_A opens her contribution to P_B in a convincing way.
- **Step 4.** Each party outputs a combination of both random contributions.

The simulatability of a coin-flipping protocol within this template may depend on the number of coins flipped in parallel, i.e., the length of the contributions, and the type of commitment scheme. When flipping a single coin, any hiding and binding commitment scheme is enough if rewinding is allowed in the simulation [Gol04, Sect. 7.4.3.1]. Conversely, when doing parallel flipping of coins in number at least linear in the security parameter, or when considering a setting without rewinding, simulatability is facilitated by commitment (Com) schemes with special *extractable* (Ext) and *equivocable* (Equiv) properties. In an Ext-Com scheme [SCP00], a *simulator* is able to *extract* a contribution that has been committed by another party, in apparent conflict with the *hiding* property. In an Equiv-Com scheme [Bea96], a *simulator* is able to *equivocate* the opening to any contribution, namely to a value different from what had been committed, in apparent conflict with the *binding* property. The conflict is only apparent, as in comparison with a real party the simulator has extra power, such as capability to rewind the other party in the simulated execution, and/or knowledge of secret information (a trapdoor) obtained from some specially selected setup.

Traditionally, achieving simultaneous Ext and Equiv properties is costly as a function of the target length. For example: in the plain model and when allowing rewinding, by requiring zero-knowledge (ZK) proofs (or ZK proofs of knowledge) about elements of size or in number linear with the target length [Lin03], or cut-and-choose techniques with high communication cost [PW09]; or, in a model with setup assumptions but not allowing rewinding, by requiring Com-schemes based on computationally expensive operations (e.g., exponentiations) in number or size dependent on the target length [CF01,BCPV13].

This paper explores efficiency improvements in two ways: (i) augmenting the traditional template into a new structure that requires less sophisticated commitments (i.e., not necessarily Ext&Equiv); (ii) devising a more efficient Ext&Equiv-Com scheme that can be directly used within the traditional template. Both cases benefit from a *pseudo-random generator* (PRG) (naturally associated with the generation of bit-strings indistinguishable from random) and a *collision-resistant hash function* (CR-Hash) (naturally associated with compressing commitments). As the target length increases, the asymptotic communication rate: converges to 1 for each contribution of a party in the stand-alone coin-flipping; converges to a rate close to 1 (i.e., closer than any desired distance), for each phase (commit and open) of the UC-Com scheme. The computational complexity for each party approximates that of applying a PRG and a CR-Hash to produce an output and hash an input, respectively, with length expansion rate asymptotically as close as desired to 1. This is useful given the high efficiency of standardized PRG [BK15] (e.g., based on block or stream ciphers) and CR-Hash [Nat15] constructions. In the UC-Com scheme each party also uses an erasure code to encode a string of length approximately equal to the target length.

The initial (incomplete) intuition comes from the observation that: the Ext of a large string can be reduced to the Ext of one short seed, whose PRG-expansion is used to mask (with a one-time-pad) the large string; the Equiv of a large string can be reduced to the Equiv of a short hash of whatever large string (e.g., the mask) the simulator wants to equivocate. However, a simple triplet composed of a masking of a string, an Ext-but-not-Equiv-Com of the *seed* of the mask, and an Equiv-but-not-Ext-Com of a *hash* of the mask does not result in an Ext&Equiv-Com of the string. For example, opening the Ext-Com would disallow equivocability. This paper devises two ways in which to very-efficiently and securely combine the two separate properties, associated with a few commitments of short seeds and hashes (in number independent of the target length), into a unified property extended to a much larger string.

Contributions. In summary, two novel constant-round protocols are devised for two-party parallel coin-flipping (the second stemming from a new UC-Com scheme). They are proven secure in a *static*, *active* and *computational* model; i.e., at most one party is corrupted at the onset of the protocol execution, the corrupted party may deviate from the protocol specification, and both parties are limited to probabilistic polynomial time computations. For simplicity and generality, the protocols and proofs are defined in a hybrid model with access to ideal commitment functionalities $\mathcal{F}_X$ and $\mathcal{F}_Q$, from which the simulator only needs to use either the Ext or the Equiv property, respectively, but not the complementary property (Equiv or Ext, respectively).

1.2 Intuition and Overview of Protocol #1

The first protocol (Sect. 4) is simulatable-with-rewinding. It augments the traditional template with a simple preamble, in order to avoid a simulatability difficulty (related with unknown adversarial probabilities of abort) found in the protocol of Blum [Blu83], due to the use of an Equiv-but-not-Ext-Com scheme in the traditional template. The new solution also avoids a full-fledged Ext&Equiv-Com scheme, whose (older) constructions have a larger associated complexity: explicit ZK proof/argument sub-protocols about a committed long-contribution, as required in Lindell's protocol [Lin03]; a high communication cost, as incurred in Pass and Wee protocol [PW09].

P_A is still the first party to learn the final bit-string. However, the new protocol starts with P_B producing an Equiv-Com of his contribution and only then proceeds to the traditional template. This allows the simulator in the role of P_A in the simulated execution to *non-locally* extract the contribution of a malicious P_B (i.e., upon rewinding beyond the respective *commit* phase), because said value cannot change across rewinding attempts, namely because P_B commits to it before the contribution of P_A is committed, and because the decision to open it (vs. aborting) is done while the contribution of P_A is still semantically hidden. The significant benefit is that now the commitment by P_A no longer needs to be Equiv, but rather only Ext. Correspondingly, using the Ext property, the simulator in the role of P_B in the simulated execution can extract the contribution of a malicious P_A, without P_A opening it.

To the knowledge of the author: this construction has not been analyzed before (which is surprising given its simplicity), and in the mentioned simulatability setting it allows, asymptotically, the most efficient instantiation to date of two-side-simulatable coin-flipping in the plain model (assuming a PRG and CR-Hash instantiation with computational cost linear in the target length). The simulatability motivation to depart from the traditional template is subtle and the analysis is challenging for the case of corrupted P_B (the simulator is allowed expected-polynomial time). Asymptotically, the protocol requires communication of only *two bits per flipped coin*. Computationally, each party has to commit and open a short value, and compute a PRG and a CR-Hash of a string with the target length. Assuming intractability of the Decisional Diffie-Hellman (DDH) problem, an instantiation is possible with only five exponentiations per party in a setup phase (allowing the simulator to extract a trapdoor), and four (or six) exponentiations in the online phase. Exponentiations can be avoided altogether, by using PRG-based commitments of short strings or even just bit-commitments (e.g., as in [PW09] or others analyzed in the full version of this paper). In the later example, the simulator exercises Ext and Equiv over the Ext-Com and the Equiv-Com, respectively, using rewinding, and the construction requires more communication rounds and larger concrete communication complexity of the short commitments but is still amortizable.

1.3 Intuition and Overview of Protocol #2

The second protocol (Sect. 5) is a new UC-Com scheme (thus Ext&Equiv) for large bit-strings, with asymptotic communication rate as close to 1 as desired, and computational complexity linear in the string size. It is based on a *cut-and-choose* method, where the size of each instance in the cut-and-choose is (approximately) inversely proportional to the number of instances. Each instance is a triplet containing: the Ext-Com of a seed; a masking of an "authenticated" *fragment* (produced by an erasure code) of the string being committed; and an Equiv-Com of the hash of the mask. This allows the simulator to anticipate (before the actual open phase) whether each extracted fragment is correct or not, and reconstruct the original message using only correct fragments. The fragments are also equivocable because the respective pseudo-random masks are equivocable.

The ideal commitment functionalities used for separate Ext and Equiv simulatability properties can also be instantiated with a full-fledged Ext&Equiv-Com functionality. Assuming the existence of a PRG and a CR-Hash, this represents a UC-Com length extension, where a few (*commit* and *open*) calls to an Ext&Equiv-Com scheme for short bit-strings enable an Ext&Equiv-Com scheme for a string of a polynomially larger size. At the cost of more interactivity, the Equiv-Coms can be based on Ext-Coms.

Similar amortized asymptotic communication complexity is also achieved by very recent UC-Com scheme proposals [GIKW14, DDGN14, CDD+15]. They explicitly use oblivious transfer (OT), i.e., as an ideal functionality in a hybrid model. In contrast, the protocol in this paper avoids explicit use of OT, and instead uses base Ext-Com and Equiv-Com schemes (besides a PRG and a CR-Hash). Also, [GIKW14, DDGN14] rely on *secret sharing schemes* with error-correction or verifiability requirements ([CDD+15] works with any linear code), whereas this paper uses a simpler erasure code, facilitated by an *authenticator* mechanism, with corresponding benefits in terms of encoding parameters. A comparison of tradeoffs allowed by each design is left for future work.

1.4   Roadmap

The paper proceeds as follows: Sect. 2 reviews related work; Sect. 3 mentions background notions about the security model and ideal functionalities; Sect. 4 describes the new protocol for coin-flipping simulatable-with-rewinding; Sect. 5 specifies the new UC commitment scheme.

2   Related Work

2.1   Basic Primitives

One-way permutations or functions are enough in theory to achieve many useful cryptographic primitives, such as PRGs [HILL99, VZ12], one-way hash functions [NY89, Rom90], some types of commitment schemes [Nao91, DCO99] and ZK proofs of knowledge (ZKPoK) [FS90]. CR-Hash functions can also be built from other primitives [Sim98], such as claw-free sets of permutations [Dam88] or pseudo-permutations [Rus95]. Based on such primitives, coin-flipping can be achieved in different ways, e.g., based solely on one-way functions [Lin03, PW09] (with rewinding). In different simulatability settings, coin-flipping can be more directly based on higher level primitives, such as bit or multi-bit Ext&Equiv-Com schemes (e.g., [CF01, DN02, Cre03]) and even from coin-flipping protocols with weaker properties [HMQU06, LN11].

In the computational model (the one considered in this paper), there are known theoretical feasibility results about coin-flipping, covering the stand-alone and the UC security settings. For example, in the UC setting it is possible to achieve coin-flipping extension, i.e., coin-flip a large bit-string when having as basis a single invocation of an ideal functionality realizing coin-flipping of a shorter length [HMQU06]. This paper shares the concern of achieving properties in large strings based on functionalities associated with short strings, but focuses on a base of a few short commitments (not needing to be simultaneously Ext and Equiv) and has a motivation of improving efficiency. The paper does not delve into analyzing implications between different primitives (e.g., see [DNO10] for relations between OT and commitments, under several setup assumptions).

Only in very recent research works (including this one) have UC commitment schemes been devised with an amortized communication cost, with asymptotic rate close to 1. In contrast, similar attention has not been given to coin-flipping in the stand-alone setting, where the most efficient protocols known to be two-side simulatable would not be highly efficient for large strings. While the new results for UC-Com schemes are directly applicable to stand-alone secure coin-flipping, with a corresponding asymptotic efficiency benefit (3 bits per flipped coin), an yet different and more efficient approach (2 bits per flipped coin) is herein devised for the stand-alone setting, without requiring an explicit Ext&Equiv-Com scheme.

In spite of very-efficient realizations of OT-extension [ALSZ15] and free-XOR techniques [KS08] for garbled circuits, a coin-flipping based on a direct (generic) approach of S2PC of bit-wise-XOR would still induce, in communication and computation, a multiplicative cost proportional to the security parameter, by requiring one *minicrypt* block operation (e.g., block-cipher evaluation) per flipped coin. In contrast, in the approach in this paper each block of bits (e.g., equal to the security parameter) requires a unitary number of minicrypt block operations (e.g., close to 1 block-cipher for the PRG and 1 CR-Hash).

The idea of combining commitments with a CR-Hash (*hash then commit*) and commitments with a PRG for efficiency reasons is not new. The former resembles the *hash then sign* paradigm, and it also has applications to non-malleable commitments [DCKOS01]. The later resembles hybrid encryption, where a symmetric key (the analogous to the PRG seed) would be encrypted with a public key system (the analogous to the commitment) and then the message would be encrypted with a symmetric scheme (the analogous to the one-time-pad masking using the PRG expansion). This paper explores ways of combining both techniques, aimed at efficient simulatable coin-flipping and UC commitment schemes.

2.2   Parallel Coin-Flipping Simulatable-with-Rewinding

A parallel coin-flipping using the traditional template is simulatable if the base commitment scheme is Ext&Equiv. Lindell achieved this (in two variant protocols [Lin03, Sects. 5.3 and 6]) by augmenting the *commit* and *open* phases with ZK sub-protocols that enable the respective Ext and Equiv properties: an Ext-commit phase (step 1) is a regular commitment followed by a ZK argument of knowledge of the committed value, from which the simulator in the role of receiver can extract the value; an Equiv-open phase (step 3) consists on sending the intended (equivocated) contribution of P_A (which on its own cannot be verified against the respective commitment) and giving a *fake* ZK argument that it was the valid committed value. The solution provides a feasibility result for constant-round simulatable parallel coin-flipping. However, for a general commitment scheme applied to a long bit-string, either a ZK proof/argument of knowledge for *extraction* or a ZK proof/argument for *equivocation* is typically expensive, if not both. Note: the protocols by Lindell also address an augmented version of coin-flipping into a well, where P_A receives a random bit-string and P_B receives the result of applying a known function to such bit-string – the case of the identity function is the one considered in this paper.

In a different approach, Pass and Wee [PW09] use cut-and-choose techniques to achieve Ext and Equiv properties directly from regular commitment schemes (and thus from one-way functions). They show simulatability of coin-flipping in the traditional template, based on an Ext&Equiv-Com scheme constructed from regular commitments in number proportional to the target length multiplied by the statistical parameter. In contrast with the two above referred constructions, protocol #1 in this paper integrates separately the Ext and Equiv properties, in different commitments, in order to improve efficiency, amortizing the cost of base commitment schemes to that of a PRG and CR-Hash.

Goldreich and Kahan [GK96] also joined two types of commitment schemes in a protocol to achieve (what this paper calls) *non-local* extraction. Their application is *constant round ZK interactive proof systems*, rather than coin-flipping. They also augment the protocol by introducing an unconditional hiding commitment as preamble, but their goal is achieving statistical soundness in an interactive proof system, rather than providing *local* equivocability or achieving a communication complexity amortization as in protocol #1 in this paper. They define a simulator that estimates the probability of non-abort of the malicious party, in order to dynamically determine an upper bound on the number of rewindings that should be tried before giving up on obtaining a (second) non-abort by the malicious party. The estimation works because the commitments are used in a way that prevents the probability of abort from depending (i.e., up to a negligible variation) on the value committed by the honest party. This simulation strategy was also used by [Lin03, PW09] for the simulation of ZK sub-protocols, and can also be used to simulate the coin-flipping protocol #1 in this paper, with an expected polynomial number of rewindings. However, the technique is not applicable in the coin-flipping protocol of Blum [Blu83], because there the decision of abort by the party that produced the Equiv-Com (i.e., the decision to open her contribution vs. to abort without opening) is made once already knowing the contribution of the other party.

A similar subtle problem of simulatability derived from unknown probabilities of abort has also been addressed by Rosen [Ros04]. With the goal of simplifying the analysis of simulatability of ZK proofs, Rosen introduces a preamble stage involving an unconditionally-hiding Ext-Com, allowing a prover in a ZK proof system to initially (and locally) extract the challenge of the verifier. Such augmentation is different from the one in this paper. First, the preamble commitment in their ZK proof (Ext-)commits a value (the *challenge*) that does not influence the actual honest output bit (accept vs. reject) of the ZK. Conversely, herein the value (Equiv-)committed (by P_B) in the preamble is a *contribution* with direct impact in the bit-string outputted by the coin-flipping execution. Second, in their ZK application the use of the preamble with the Ext-Com by one party (the verifier) relieves the simulator in the role of the other party (the prover) from having to do non-local equivocation in the subsequent part of the execution. Conversely, herein the preamble (with an Equiv-Com by P_B) does not relieve the simulator in the role of the other party (P_A) from having to non-locally equivocate the contribution that it commits to in the remainder of the execution. Third, their proposed Ext-Com scheme is unconditionally hiding, whereas the PRG-based Ext-Com construction used in protocol #1 to commit the contribution of P_A is (motivated by efficiency) inherently non-unconditionally hiding.

2.3 UC Commitment Schemes

When rewinding is not possible, the simulatability of flipping even a single coin using the traditional template requires the underlying commitment scheme to be simultaneously Ext and Equiv [CR03]. Canetti and Fischlin [CF01] developed non-interactive UC commitments, requiring a unitary number of asymmetric operations per committed bit. The construction assumes a *common reference string* (CRS) setup and is based on the equivocable bit-commitment from Crescenzo, Ishai and Ostrovsky [DCIO98]. Canetti, Lindell, Ostrovsky, and Sahai [CLOS02] proposed other non-interactive schemes from general primitives, with adaptive security without erasures. Damgård and Nielsen [DN02] then improved with a construction denoted *mixed commitment scheme*, that is able to commit a linear number of bits using only a unitary number of asymmetric operations, and using a linear number of communicated bits. For some keys they are unconditionally-hiding and *equivocable*, whereas for other keys they are unconditionally-binding and *extractable*. Crescenzo [Cre03] devised two non-interactive Ext&Equiv-Com schemes for individual bits, in the public random string model. One construction is based on Equiv-Com schemes and NIZKs, the other is based on one Ext-Com and one Equiv-Com schemes. Damgård and Lunemann [DL09] consider UC in a quantum setting and solve the problem of flipping a single bit, based on UC-Coms from [CF01]. Lunemann and Nielsen [LN11] consider also the quantum setting and achieve secure flipping of a bit-string based on mixed commitments from [DN02]. They consider how to amplify security from weaker security notions of coin-flipping (uncontrollable, random) up to full simulatable (enforceable). The use of Ext-Com and Equiv-Com schemes, together with a cut-and-choose and encoding scheme has been previously considered by Damgård and Orlandi [DO10]. They combine these techniques to enhance security from the passive to the active model for secure computation of arithmetic circuits, in a model where a trusted dealer is able to generate correlated triplets. While they achieve efficient constructions for multiparty computation (also including more than two parties), the efficiency is not amortized to communication rate 1.

More efficient commitment schemes have been proposed for short strings, e.g., [Lin11, FLM11, BCPV13, Fuj14] achieving a *low* (but greater than one) constant number of group elements of communication and of exponentiations to commit to a group element. Still, the trivial extension of these protocols for larger strings would imply a linear increase in said number of asymmetric operations (modular exponentiations), without amortization. Some of these schemes achieve adaptive security, whereas this paper considers only static security.

Recent independent works achieve asymptotic communication rate 1: [GIKW14] additionally considers selective openings; [DDGN14, CDD+15] additionally consider homomorphic properties and verification of linear relations between committed values; [CDD+15] achieves, comparably to this paper, linear computational complexity. These protocols are based on a hybrid model with an ideal OT functionality. In contrast to OT, the cut-and-choose mechanism in protocol #2 in this paper does not hide from the sender the partition of (check) instances. Also, an *authenticator* mechanism allows the simulator to recover the fragmented message using an erasure code, thus allowing a cut-and-choose with less instances than what an error correction code would imply (e.g., see Table 1). A more recent concurrent result [FJNT16] improves the complexity of the OT-based protocols (also for additively homomorphic commitments), using an additional *consistency check* mechanism to also allow an erasure code.

A concrete comparison between different methods – qualitative (e.g., implications between primitives) and quantitative (actual instantiations and implementations) – is left for future work. For example, [GIKW14]) reports 640 exponentiations for a concrete instantiation of the OT setup phase. In this paper, a concrete instantiation of Ext or Equiv commitments has not been explored, though their complexity is naturally upper bounded by that of instantiations of full-fledged UC-Coms for short strings, e.g., requiring less than a dozen group elements per base commitment [BCPV13]. The overall number of commitments of short strings will depend on the erasure code parameters, defined to meet the goals of statistical security and communication rate.

In summary, this paper is focused on the design of protocols that explore the duality between Ext and Equiv commitments, without considering OT as a primitive. About OT only two notes are mentioned here from other work: it is known that UC-OT implies UC-Coms in myriad setup models [DNO10, Fig. 1], e.g., in the *uniform*, the *chosen* and the *any* CRS models (U/C/A-CRS), and in the *chosen* and the *any key registration authority* models (C/A-KRA), whereas the reverse implication is proven only in a narrower set of models (e.g., U/A-CRS, A-KRA) [DNO10, Table 1]; while [GIKW14] shows that "the existence of a semi-honest OT protocol is necessary (and sufficient) for UC-Com length extension," the UC scheme in this paper does not make explicit use of OT and can also be seen as a UC-Com length extension (if replacing the Ext-Com and Equiv-Com schemes with an Ext&Equiv-Com scheme) – these two results do not superpose, since [GIKW14] only allows a single call to the ideal Com-scheme, whereas the extension herein requires several calls.

3   Background Notions

It is here assumed that the reader is familiar with the ideal/real simulation paradigm, as developed in the work of Canetti on composability of protocols [Can00, Can01]. Familiarity is also assumed with the standard ideal functionalities of commitment schemes ($\mathcal{F}_{\text{MCOM}}$) and coin-flipping ($\mathcal{F}_{\text{MCF}}$), namely in the UC framework. For example, instances can be found in [CF01, Fig. 3] (multiple bit-commitments), [DN02, Sect. 4.2] (multiple message-commitments, there also considering homomorphic relations), [DL09, Fig. 2] (coin-flipping), [Lin03] (general S2PC). A background review of these standard notions and specification of ideal functionalities is given in full version of this paper. For convenience, this section simply states informal notions about extractable and equivocable commitments.

Definition 1 (Extractability). *An extractable commitment (Ext-Com) scheme is one whose* commit *phase in a simulated execution allows $\mathcal{S}$ in the role of* receiver, *indistinguishable from an honest receiver in the view of a possibly malicious sender, to extract (i.e., learn) the committed value, with probability equal to or larger than a value negligibly-close to the maximum probability with which the (possibly malicious) sender is able to successfully open said value.*

Definition 2 (Equivocability). *An equivocable commitment (Equiv-Com) scheme is one whose* open *phase in a simulated execution allows $\mathcal{S}$ in the role of* sender, *indistinguishable from an honest sender in the view of a possibly malicious receiver, to equivocate the opening to any intended value, in the domain of committable values and possibly decided only after the commit phase.*

Definition 3 (Locality of Ext and Equiv). *Within a protocol using commitments, namely with both* commit *and* open *phases, extraction is characterized as* local *if S can extract the committed value within the respective* commit *phase, i.e., without going beyond that phase in the protocol and without rewinding to a step before that phase. Local equivocation is defined analogously in relation to the* open *phase. The properties are characterized as* non-local *if they can be achieved but not locally, i.e., involving rewinding beyond the respective phase.*

The protocols hereinafter are described and proven secure in a hybrid model with access to ideal commitment functionalities $\mathcal{F}_X$ and $\mathcal{F}_Q$, with which S respectively only needs to take advantage of Ext and Equiv, but not both.

4   A New Coin-Flipping Simulatable-with-Rewinding

This section devises a new (constant round) parallel coin-flipping protocol, simulatable-with-rewinding. The intuition has already been given (Sect. 1.2); a textual description follows, along with a specification with succinct notation in Fig. 1.

4.1   Description of Protocol #1

The protocol implicitly depends on a computational security parameter (1) and a respectively secure PRG and CR-Hash function (2). The execution starts when

---

Implicit parameters.	$P_A : t_A \leftarrow^\$ \{0,1\}^\ell$ (contribution masking) (13)
Security parameters: 1^κ (1)	$P_A \rightarrow P_B : (\texttt{cf-masking-1}, ctx, t_A)$ (14)
Primitives: $(\text{PRG}, \kappa_{\text{PRG}})$, CR-Hash (2)	**3. Open contribution of P_B (equivocable).**
0. Initial input.	$P_B \rightarrow \mathcal{F}_Q : (\texttt{open-ask}, (ctx, Q))$ (15)
$ctx \equiv (sid, cfid, P_A, P_B)$ (3)	$\mathcal{F}_Q \rightarrow P_A : (\texttt{open-send}, (ctx, Q), h_B)$ (16)
$input_A \rightarrow P_A : (\texttt{cf-start-1}, ctx, \ell)$ (4)	$P_B \rightarrow P_A : (\texttt{cf-contrib-2}, ctx, \chi_B)$ (17)
$input_B \rightarrow P_B : (\texttt{cf-start-2}, ctx, \ell)$ (5)	$P_A :$ If CR-Hash$(\chi_B) \neq h_B$ then ABORT (18)
1. Commit contribution of P_B.	**4. Open contribution of P_A.**
$P_B : \chi_B \leftarrow^\$ \{0,1\}^\ell$ (contribution of P_B) (6)	$P_A \rightarrow \mathcal{F}_X : (\texttt{open-ask}, (ctx, X))$ (19)
$P_B : h_B = \text{CR-Hash}(\chi_B)$ (short hash) (7)	$\mathcal{F}_X \rightarrow P_B : (\texttt{open-send}, (ctx, X), s_A)$ (20)
$P_B \rightarrow \mathcal{F}_Q : (\texttt{commit}, (ctx, Q), h_B)$ (8)	$P_A, P_B : s_A' = \text{PRG}[s_A](\ell)$ (seed expansion $\equiv$ mask) (21)
$\mathcal{F}_Q \rightarrow P_A : (\texttt{receipt}, (ctx, Q), |h_B|)$ (9)	$P_A, P_B : \chi_A = t_A \oplus s_A'$ (contribution of P_A) (22)
2. Commit contribution of P_A (extractable).	**5. Final output (locally combine contributions).**
$P_A : s_A \leftarrow^\$ \{0,1\}^{\kappa_{\text{PRG}}}$ (short seed) (10)	$P_A, P_B : \chi = \chi_A \oplus \chi_B$ (23)
$P_A \rightarrow \mathcal{F}_X : (\texttt{commit}, (ctx, X), s_A)$ (11)	$P_A \rightarrow output_A : (\texttt{cf-output-1}, ctx, \chi)$ (24)
$\mathcal{F}_X \rightarrow P_B : (\texttt{receipt}, (ctx, X), |s_A|)$ (12)	$P_B \rightarrow output_B : (\texttt{cf-output-2}, ctx, \chi)$ (25)

Fig. 1. Protocol #1 (Parallel coin-flipping (simulatable-with-rewinding).
Legend: κ (cryptographic security parameter, e.g., $128 \equiv 1^{128}$); ℓ (target length, i.e., number of bits to coin-flip in parallel, e.g., 10^6, satisfying $\ell \in O(poly(\kappa))$); χ_p (contribution of P_p, for $p \in \{A, B\}$); PRG$[s](\ell)$ (expansion of seed s, using the PRG, into a bitstring of length ℓ); κ_{PRG} (length of PRG input-seed, consistent with κ); X, Q (indices denoting *extractable* and *equivocable*); (ctx, x) (abbreviation for $(sid, (cfid, x), P_A, P_B)$, where $x \in \{X, Q\}$ – by including X and Q in the *context* information exchanged with the respective ideal Com functionalities ($\mathcal{F}_X, \mathcal{F}_Q$), it is syntactically easier to replace them both by a single full-fledged ideal X&Q (multi-)Com functionality $\mathcal{F}_{X\&Q}$).

both parties are activated to initiate a coin-flipping of a certain *target length*, with an appropriate execution context (3), which in particular encodes the roles of the two parties – P_A will be the first to learn the final outcome ((4)–(5)) – and the target length. After a possibly implicit setup phase (e.g., in the plain model, to allow the simulator to obtain a trapdoor), P_B selects his contribution (6) with the target length, calculates its hash (7), and uses $\mathcal{F}_Q$ to commit to the hash ((8)–(9)). Then, P_A selects a seed (10) and *commits* to it using $\mathcal{F}_X$ ((11)–(12)). P_A also selects a random bit-string (denoted *contribution masking*) with the target length (13) and sends it to P_B (14). Then, P_B uses $\mathcal{F}_Q$ to open the committed hash to P_A ((15)–(16)) and sends his contribution to P_A (17). P_A checks that the hash of the contribution of P_B is equal to the *opened* hash (18). If not, it Aborts; otherwise it proceeds. Then, P_A uses $\mathcal{F}_X$ to *open* to P_B the committed seed ((19)–(20)). Finally, each party proceeds concurrently with local computations: expanding the seed of P_A into a bit-string of the target length (21) (i.e., the *mask*); computing the *bit-wise exclusive-OR* (XOR) combination of the *mask* and the *contribution masking*, thus determining the contribution of P_A (22); and locally computing the final outcome as the XOR of the two contributions (23), and deciding that as the final output ((24)–(25)).

4.2   Concrete Instantiations in the Plain Model

In the *plain* model, $\mathcal{F}_X$ and $\mathcal{F}_Q$ can be respectively replaced by actual Ext-Com and Equiv-Com schemes, agreed upon in a *setup* phase, with Ext-Com being non-malleable with respect to opening of Equiv-Com. An intuition is given here for possible concrete instantiations (more details in the full version).

Based on DDH Intractability Assumption. For the Ext-Com scheme: P_A commits to the seed by sending a simple El-Gamal encryption [ElG85] of the seed; the simulator can extract if it knows the encryption key (a discrete-log); P_A opens the seed by revealing the seed and the encryption randomness, thus letting P_B verify its correctness. For the Equiv-Com scheme: P_B commits by sending a simple Pedersen commitment [Ped92] of the hash; P_B opens the hash by revealing the hash and the commitment randomness. The simulator can equivocate the opening if it knows the trapdoor (a discrete-log). Interestingly, both Com-schemes can have the same trapdoor, because the seed extraction and the hash equivocation are needed by the same simulator (in the role of P_B, when interacting with P_A^*). The parameters can be agreed in a setup phase, with P_A^* proposing them (two generators in a multiplicative group where the DDH assumption holds) and giving a ZKPoK of their relation (the discrete-log between two generators). Basically, this can be a ZK adaptation of Schnorr's protocol [Sch91], e.g., as described in [LPS08, Fig. 3]. Overall, this requires only 9 exponentiations from each party (or 11, using more practical parameters), 5 of which are in the setup phase (amortizable across several coin-flippings).

A Concrete Application Example. The S2PC-with-BitComs protocol in [Bra13], simulatable-with-rewinding, requires a simulatable coin-flipping to sample a random group element for each bit of input and output of the regular S2PC.

(Improvements of the protocol can reduce the needed number and size of said group-elements.) There, the benchmark evaluation of S2PC-with-BitComs of AES-128 requires a simulatable flipping of about 1.18 million bits. As suggested therein, using a DDH assumption in groups over elliptic curves, an instantiation of the coin-flipping with the protocol of [Lin03] would require (for practical parameters) 7 exponentiations per party per block of 256 bits, and communication of about 12 blocks per block, i.e., overall about 32 thousand exponentiations and 14 megabits. In contrast, the new coin-flipping devised herein would overall require (with the instantiation suggested in the previous paragraph) less than a dozen exponentiations per party and slightly less than 2.5 megabits of communication, thus reducing the coin-flipping sub-protocol complexity by more than 3,000 fold in number of exponentiations and about 6 fold in communication.

Based on PRG-Based Commitments. It is possible to avoid exponentiations by building Ext-Com and Equiv-Com schemes based on more basic primitives, such as regular commitments (i.e., hiding and biding but possibly not Ext and not Equiv). For example, Pass and Wee [PW09] analyze cut-and-choose based constructions (the full version of this paper explores improvements, e.g., using a random-seed-checking type of technique [GMS08]). Comparatively, those constructions require more concrete communication than the DDH based one, but still amortizable because it only applies to two short elements (one seed and one hash), and more online interactivity.

4.3   Security Analysis

Proving security (i.e., simulatability) amounts to show a simulator ($\mathcal{S}$) that, with an expected number of rewindings at most polynomial in the security parameter, induces in the ideal world a *global* output whose distribution is indistinguishable from the one in the real world. In the role of each party in a simulation, $\mathcal{S}$ must be able (with overwhelming probability) to learn the contribution of the other possibly-malicious (black-box) party and still be in a position to *open* the *needed complementary contribution*, as if it was honestly random, and at the same time simulate the correct probability of early abort.

Theorem 1 (Security of Protocol #1).   *Assuming a cryptographically secure PRG and CR-Hash, protocol #1 securely-emulates (with computational indistinguishability) the ideal functionality $\mathcal{F}_{MCF}$ of long bit-string coin-flipping between two-parties, in a stand-alone setting and in the $(\mathcal{F}_X, \mathcal{F}_Q)$-hybrid model, in the presence of static and computationally active rewindable adversaries. For each (polynomially arbitrarily-long) bit-string coin-flipping execution, each phase (commit and open) of $\mathcal{F}_X$ and $\mathcal{F}_Q$ is invoked only once for a short string; simulation is possible: without rewinding in the case of a malicious P_A^*; with an expected polynomial number of rewindings in the case of a malicious P_B^*.*

One-Pass Simulation (i.e., Without Rewinding), for Malicious P_A^*. In the simulated execution, $\mathcal{S}$ (in the role of P_B) commits to a random hash value

(8). Then, S impersonates $\mathcal{F}_X$ to extract from P_A^* the seed committed by P_A^* (11). S computes the PRG expansion of the seed (as in (21)). Then, upon receiving the contribution masking of P_A^* (14), S combines it with the PRG-expansion of the extracted seed (as in (22)), in order to learn the contribution of P_A^*. Then, in the ideal world, S in the role of the ideal $\widehat{P}_A^*$ receives from the ideal coin-flipping functionality $\mathcal{F}_{\text{MCF}}$ the random target coin-flipping bit-string. S then computes the needed complementary contribution of P_B, as the XOR between the target outcome and the contribution of P_A^*. S computes the hash of this complementary contribution (as in (7)) and in the role of $\mathcal{F}_Q$ it equivocates its opening to be such hash value (16). Finally, S also sends the complementary contribution to P_A^* (17). Since the ideal $\mathcal{F}_X$ is impersonated by S (respectively, in the plain model, since Equiv-Com is non-malleable with respect to opening of Ext-Com), it follows that P_A^* can only either open the contribution (19) that has been extracted by S, or abort without successfully opening her contribution. In case of abort by P_A^*, S *emulates an abort*; otherwise, S lets $\mathcal{F}_{\text{MCF}}$ continue the execution in the ideal world (i.e., send the bit-string to the ideal $\widehat{P}_B$) and S outputs in the ideal world what P_A^* outputs in the simulation. (In the plain model, extractability of Ext-Com and/or equivocability of Equiv-Com may require either local rewinding or rewinding in a setup phase, but that is irrelevant in the hybrid model).

Simulation with Explicit Rewinding, for Malicious P_B^*.

- **First iteration.** In the simulated execution, S in the role of an honest P_A interacts until receiving the contribution of P_B^* and verifying its hash against the respective opening (18). If P_B^* aborts until this step (including by an invalid opening), then S emulates an abort, otherwise it proceeds.
- **Get target outcome.** S in the role of ideal $\widehat{P}_B^*$ receives from $\mathcal{F}_{\text{MCF}}$ in the ideal world the target outcome and uses it to compute the needed complementary contribution of P_A in the simulated execution, namely the XOR between the target outcome and the contribution of P_B^*.
- **Determine upper-bound of rewindings.** S determines an upper bound number of rewindings (#rw-bound) needed for the next simulation stage. This can be based on the strategy of Goldreich and Kahan [GK96], which involves rewinding, possibly a super-polynomial number of times, to repeat committing a random contribution of P_A ((11)–(14)) and expecting to obtain an opening of the contribution of P_B ((16)–(17)), until indeed obtaining a successful opening (18) an adequate polynomial (e.g., quadratic) number of times, and estimating therefrom an adequate probability of non-abort by P_A, and defining #rw-bound as the inverse of said estimate. An intuition for the expected polynomial number of rewindings is that a negligible probability of non-abort also implies a negligible probability that the simulation reaches this estimation stage. (Using a more involved argument about the hiding property of the PRG-based Ext-Com of the contribution of P_A, the full version of the paper explores the possibility of a different simulation strategy, with a static super-polynomial upper bound #rw-bound, i.e., not depending on a dynamic estimation of the non-abort probability).

- **Induce target outcome.** S rewinds and selects (10) and commits (11) to a new random seed of P_A. Then, S computes and sends to P_B^* a contribution masking of P_A (14), computed as the XOR combination of the needed complementary contribution and the PRG-expansion of the seed (instead of a random *contribution masking* (13)). Since the Ext-Com+PRG-based commitment of the contribution of P_A is semantically hiding, the probability of abort by P_B^* changes at most by a negligible amount in comparison with the previous stage. If P_B^* subsequently opens his contribution successfully ((16)–(18)), then S continues the simulation until the end and outputs in the ideal world whatever P_B^* outputs in the simulated execution, even P_B^* aborts before receiving the opening of the seed of P_A (20). Otherwise, if P_B^* aborts without successfully opening his contribution, S rewinds and replays again as just described, again and again until either obtaining a successful opening of the contribution of P_B^* (equal to the one already known by S) and in that case leading the simulation to an end, or until reaching the #rw-bound bound, and in that case it emulates an abort in the ideal world.

5 A New UC Commitment Scheme

This section devises a new UC commitment scheme, thus one-pass-simulatable and with local Ext and Equiv properties, usable in the traditional template of coin-flipping to *commit* and *open* the contribution of P_A.

5.1 More Intuition

Besides the Ext-Com, Equiv-Com, PRG and CR-Hash, the new protocol embeds three main ingredients, in a sequence of optimizations:

- a **cut-and-choose:** P_A builds several *instances* of short commitments and then P_B checks the correctness of some (the *check* instances) to gain *some* confidence that a majority of the others (the *evaluation* instances) is correct;
- **authenticators:** allow the simulator to anticipate whether individual *instances* are *good* or *bad*, thus gaining assurance about correct extraction;
- an **information dispersal algorithm** (IDA): allows *splitting* the target message m into smaller *fragments*, and allows *recovery* of the original message from a sufficient number of those fragments (essentially, based on a threshold erasure code); using an IDA enables the size of each *instance* of the cut-and-choose to be reduced proportionally to the number of instances.

5.1.1 Cut-and-Choose Warmup
A simple (yet innefficient) UC-Com scheme:

- **Commit phase.** P_A produces several seeds, builds an Ext-Com of each, and also an Equiv-Com of a CR-Hash (hereafter denoted *global hash*) of the sequence of PRG-expansions of all seeds. Then, P_B *cuts* the set of instances

of seed-commitments into two random complementary subsets, and *chooses* one for a *check* operation and the other for an *evaluation* operation. For each *evaluation* instance, P_A uses the respective PRG-expansion to XOR-mask the *target message*, and sends the respective *message masking* to P_B.
- **Open phase.** P_A reveals the message m, letting P_B compute all used masks, one for each *evaluation* instance, namely the XOR of the message with each respective masking. P_A also opens all *check* seeds, letting P_B compute the respective PRG-expansions. Finally, P_A opens the committed global hash, letting P_B verify that it is equal to the one that can be obtained from the learned masks and PRG-expansions. Otherwise, if the global hash verification fails, P_A rejects the opening of the message m.

This has the needed simulatability properties (though high communication complexity: target length ℓ multiplied by number e of *evaluation* instances):

- **Hiding.** In the *commit* phase, the maskings hide the message from P_B, due to the XOR one-time-pad between message and PRG-expansions (the masks).
- **Binding.** In the *open* phase, P_A is bound to open a single message: by collision resistance of CR-Hash, P_A can know at most one pre-image of the global hash, i.e., at most one sequence of valid masks (one mask per instance). Thus, P_A can at most successfully open the message that for all evaluation instances is equal to the XOR of the respective mask and *masking*.
- **Equivocation.** In the *open* phase, the equivocator-simulator (S^Q) in the role of P_A can open any desired fake message, by revealing the message, opening the correct seeds of check instances and then *equivocating* the needed fake global hash (without revealing the respective seeds of evaluation instances).
- **Extractability.** In the *commit* phase, the extractor-simulator (S^X) in the role of P_B *extracts* the seed of each evaluation instance, then uses its PRG-expansion to unmask the respective masking into a tentative message. If a majority of the tentative messages are equal, then S^X chooses their value as the correct one. Otherwise S^X guesses that P_A will not be able to successfully open any message in the later open phase. Conditioned on a future successful verification of the global hash, the probability that the majority of the extracted seeds are correct is, with adequate cut-and-choose parameters [SS11, Sect. A], overwhelming in the total number of instances. For example, slightly more than 40 bits of statistical security, i.e., a probability of wrong extraction less that two to the minus 40, is obtained using 123 instances, 74 of which for *check* and 49 of which for *evaluation* [Bra13, Table 2].

5.1.2   Authenticator Aid
Statistical security can be improved by giving S^X the ability to decide whether isolated evaluation instances are *good* or *bad*. This allows S^X to extract an incorrect message (or none at all) only if all *check* instances are *good* and all

evaluation instances are *bad*, i.e., only if a malicious P_A^* anticipates the exact cut-and-choose partition. The new rationale about probabilities is similar to that of the forge-and-lose type of technique recently devised for more general S2PC protocols based on a cut-and-choose of garbled-circuits [Bra13, Lin13, HKE13]. The success criterion changes from "at least a majority of correct instances" to "at least one correct instance." For example, 40 bits of statistical security can now be obtained with 41 or 123 instances, by respectively limiting *evaluation* instances to be at most 20 or 8. Since only evaluation instances are relevant in terms of communication, with 123 instances this corresponds to a 6-fold reduction in communication (i.e., vs. the previous method with 49 evaluation instances).

The intended verifiability is achieved by augmenting each *evaluation* instance with a short *authenticator* that allows S^X to verify whether or not each extracted seed is consistent with each respective anticipated tentative message. Specifically, when S^X extracts a seed and uses its seed-expansion to unmask the respective masking received from P_A, only two things may happen: either (i) S^X gets a correctly *authenticated* message, which must be the only one that P_A can later successfully open, i.e., this is a *good* instance; or (ii) S^X gets an incorrectly *authenticated* message, implying that a successful *opening* by a malicious P_A^* will reveal a mask different from the seed-expansion, i.e., this is a *bad* instance.

The authenticator is implemented as a function that relates the message and a *nonce* in a non-trivial way, to ensure that it is infeasible for P_A^* to produce a masking for which two different unmaskings yield authenticated messages. Also, in order to allow equivocation by S^Q (when in the role of P_A), the authenticator is masked by an equivocable mask. The authenticator cannot simply be a CR-Hash function (i.e., without an unpredictable input) of the masked fragment, lest P_A^* would in that case (by maliciously using a mask different from the seed-expansion) be able to induce a collision by crafting a special mask different from the seed-expansion. Instead, the authenticator can be achieved by means of a *universal hash family*, such that the probability of collision is independent of the choices of P_A^*. This can be implemented by introducing a random unpredictable value (a *nonce*) that P_B discloses to P_A^* only after P_A^* becomes bound to her choices, e.g., after committing to the seeds and global hash. This nonce acts like an identifier of the hash from the universal hash family.

In concrete, the authenticator can for example be an algebraic field-multiplication between the nonce and a CR-hash of the message. If the image space of the CR-Hash is the set of bit-strings of some fixed length (e.g., 256 bits), the nonce can be uniformly selected from the non-null elements of a Galois field with characteristic 2, modulo an irreducible polynomial of degree equal to the hash length. This ensures that the authenticators of any two known messages (which by assumption have different CR-Hash) would have an unpredictably offset. Conversely, a successful forgery by P_A^* would require guessing this offset, in order to make the real mask have such (bit-wise XOR) offset with the seed-expansion. (Optimizations are possible, requiring a more involved explanation and/or correlation-robust type of assumptions – details in the full version.)

5.1.3   IDA Support

Communication is drastically reduced by using a threshold *information dispersal algorithm* (IDA) [Rab89]. The IDA enables splitting (i.e., *dispersing*) the original message m into several (e) fragments, such that m can be reconstructed from any subset with at least a threshold number t of good fragments, each with a *reduced length* ($|m|e/t$). As $|m|$ increases, the asymptotic communication complexity is thus proportional to e/t, which can be made as close to 1 as desired.

Any t-out-of-e erasure-code can be used, e.g., based on XOR operations and with linear time encoding and somewhat efficient decoding. It does not need to hide the original message, as would a full-fledged secret-sharing scheme [Sha79, Kra94], because in the commit phase P_B receives maskings of (authenticated) fragments, instead of fragments in clear. It also does not need to support correction of semantic errors [RS60], because the *authenticator* mechanism gives S^X (in the role of P_B) the ability to detect errors and thus simply discard *bad* fragments. S^X *reconstructs* m from any subset of at least t *good* fragments.

It is interesting to notice that parties only need to encode; only the simulator needs to decode. A rateless code is also possible, with appropriate probabilistic considerations – there are very efficient instantiations, e.g., [Lub02,Sho06].

The statistical security is again changed, with the new criterion for successful extraction requiring a number of *good* evaluation instances at least as high as the recovery threshold. Furthermore, the fragmentation also reduces the sum of all PRG-expansion lengths, as well as the length of the sequence of masks whose hash needs to be calculated. Concrete parameters are given in Table 1.

5.2   Description of Protocol #2

The protocol is succinctly described in Fig. 2. For further intuition, a pictorial sketch is provided in Fig. 3. The parties agree on security parameters (computational and statistic) and other consistent elements: the cut-and-choose parameters (with a fixed number of *check* and *evaluation* instances) (26); a PRG and a CR-Hash functions (27); the IDA scheme and parameters (28); and an authenticator mode (29) (in Fig. 2, the STRICT mode corresponds to the description given in Sect. 5.1.2) and respective parameters (30). The LOOSE mode (discussed in the full version of the paper) allows removing some steps of the protocol (namely avoiding the Equiv-Com of the hash of the message being committed) but requires a stronger assumption about the authenticator function.

5.2.1   Commit Phase (P_A Commits a Message to P_B)

– **1.a. Commit instances.** Upon being initialized to commit a message m (31), P_A selects n random seeds (32) (e.g., 119) and uses $\mathcal{F}_X$ to commit individually to each of them ((33)–(34)). P_A uses the PRG to expand each seed s_j into a string s'_j with a *reduced-length* (equal to the target length ℓ divided by the IDA recovery-*threshold* t) extended by an *authenticator-length* ℓ_a (35). P_A calculates the *global hash* h as the CR-hash of the concatenation of all seed-expansions (36). P_A then uses $\mathcal{F}_Q$ to commit to h ((37)–(38)). If in the STRICT mode, P_A also computes the hash of the message m (39) and then uses $\mathcal{F}_Q$ to commit to said hash ((40)–(41)).

- **1.b. Cut-and-choose.** P_B decides a random cut-and-choose partition (42) (e.g., identifying 73 instances for *check* and 46 for *evaluation*) and a random nonce z (43) and sends them both to P_A (44).
- **1.c. Message masking.** P_A uses the threshold IDA to *split* her message into as many fragments as the number of *evaluation* instances (45), each with a *reduced length*. Then, P_A computes the authenticator a_j of each fragment m'_j

---

Implicit parameters.

Security parameters: $1^\kappa, (1^\sigma, n, v, e)$	(26)	IDA: $(t, \text{IDA}[t]_{\text{split}}, \text{IDA}[t]_{\text{recover}})$ (28)
Primitives: $(\text{PRG}, \kappa_{\text{PRG}}), \text{CR-Hash}$	(27)	$\text{AuthMode} \in \{\text{STRICT}, \text{LOOSE}\}$ (29)
		Authenticator parameters: $\{\alpha, \ell_a = |\alpha|, \ell_s\}$ (30)

---

1. X-Commit phase.

$input_A \to P_A : (\text{commit}, sid, cid, P_A, P_B, m)$ (31)

1.a. Commit instances. For $j \in [n]$:

$P_A : s_j \xleftarrow{\$} \{0,1\}^{\kappa_{\text{PRG}}}$ (seed) (32)

$P_A \to \mathcal{F}_X : (\text{commit}, (ctx, (X, j)), s_j)$ (33)

$\mathcal{F}_X \to P_B : (\text{receipt}, (ctx, (X, j)), |s_j|)$ (34)

$P_A : s'_j = \text{PRG}[s_j](\lceil |m|/t + \ell_a \rceil)$ (35)

$P_A : h = \text{CR-Hash}(||_{j \in [n]} s'_j)$ (global hash) (36)

$P_A \to \mathcal{F}_Q : (\text{commit}, (ctx, Q), h)$ (37)

$\mathcal{F}_Q \to P_B : (\text{receipt}, (ctx, Q), |h|)$ (38)

If $\text{AuthMode} =^? \text{STRICT}$, then:

$P_A : \eta = \text{CR-Hash}(m)$ (hash of message) (39)

$P_A \to \mathcal{F}_Q : (\text{commit}, (ctx, (Q, +)), \eta)$ (40)

$\mathcal{F}_Q \to P_B : (\text{receipt}, (ctx, (Q, +)), |\eta|)$ (41)

1.b. Cut-and-choose. $(n = e + v)$

$P_B : (J_V, J_E) \xleftarrow{\$} \text{Partition}[v, e](n)$ (42)

$P_B : z \xleftarrow{\$} \{0,1\}^{\ell_z}$ (nonce) (43)

$P_B \to P_A : (ckc, sid, cid, P_B, P_A, (J_V, J_E, z))$ (44)

[1e1]c. **Message masking.**

$P_A : \langle m'_j : j \in J_E \rangle \leftarrow \text{IDA}[t]_{\text{split}}(m, J_E)$ (45)

$P_A : a_j = \alpha(m'_j, z) : j \in J_E$ (authenticators) (46)

$P_A : t_j = (m'_j || a_j) \oplus s'_j : j \in J_E$ (maskings) (47)

$P_A \to P_B : (\text{maskings}, sid, cid, P_A, P_B, ||_{j \in J_E} t_j)$ (48)

---

2. Q-Open phase.

$input_A \to P_A : (\text{open}, sid, cid, P_A, P_B)$ (49)

2.a. Reveal message.

$P_A \to P_B : (\text{reveal}, sid, cid, P_A, P_B, m)$ (50)

If $\text{AuthMode} =^? \text{STRICT}$, then:

$P_A \to \mathcal{F}_Q : (\text{open-ask}, (ctx, (Q, +)))$ (51)

$\mathcal{F}_Q \to P_B : (\text{open-send}, (ctx, (Q, +)), \eta)$ (52)

$P_B : \text{If } \text{CR-Hash}(m) \neq \eta \text{ then ABORT}$ (53)

2.b. Obtain evaluation maskings.

$P_B : \langle m'_j : j \in J_E \rangle \leftarrow \text{IDA}[t]_{\text{split}}(m, J_E)$ (54)

$P_B : a_j = \alpha(m'_j, z) : j \in J_E$ (authenticator) (55)

$P_B : s'_j = t_j \oplus (m'_j || a_j) : j \in J_E$ (tentative masks) (56)

2.b. Obtain check maskings.

$P_A \to \mathcal{F}_X : (\text{open-ask}, (ctx, (X, j))) : j \in J_V$ (57)

$\mathcal{F}_X \to P_B : (\text{open-send}, (ctx, (X, j)), s_j) : j \in J_V$ (58)

$P_B : s'_j = \text{PRG}[s_j](\lceil |m|/t + \ell_a \rceil) : j \in J_V$ (59)

2.d. Verify global hash.

$P_A \to \mathcal{F}_Q : (\text{open-ask}, (ctx, Q))$ (60)

$\mathcal{F}_Q \to P_B : (\text{open-send}, (ctx, Q), h)$ (61)

$P_B : \text{If } \text{CR-Hash}(||_{j \in [n]} s'_j) \neq h \text{ then ABORT}$ (62)

$P_B \to output_B : (\text{accept}, sid, cid, P_A, P_B, m)$ (63)

Fig. 2. Protocol #2 (UC commitment scheme). Legend: legend of Fig. 1 also applies; σ (statistical security parameter, e.g., $40 \equiv 1^{40}$); n, v, e (numbers of *total* instances, *check* instances and *evaluation* instances); $[n]$ (set of the first n positive integers); $\text{Partition}[v, e](n)$ (set of possible partitions of $[n]$, into a pair of complementary subsets, the first with v elements, and the second with the remaining e). $\text{IDA}[t]$ (*information dispersal algorithm* (erasure code) with *recovery threshold* of t fragments; it has sub-algorithms *split* and *recover*; if e and v are fixed in a setup phase they must satisfy $((n - b)! e!) / ((e - b) s!) \leq 2^{-\sigma}$, where $b = e - t + 1$ is the number of *bad* instances in an optimal attack); α (authenticator function); ℓ_z (length of nonce); ℓ_a (length of authenticator output, e.g., 256 bits).

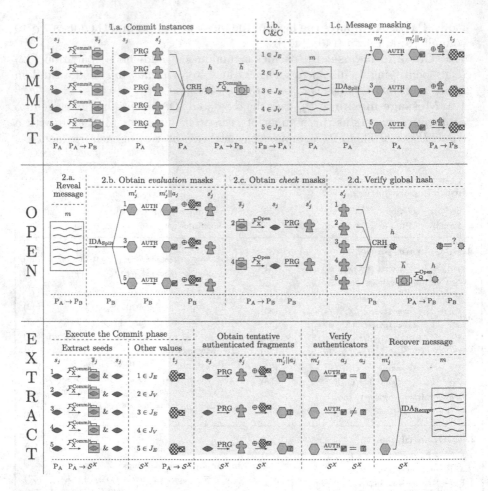

Fig. 3. Sketch of UC commitment scheme. Legend: ◆ (seed s_j); ▤ (Ext-Com $\overline{s}_j$ – like a vault with a single opening); ♟ (seed expansion s'_j – like a tree growing from a seed); ✿ (global hash – like a smashed paper); ▦ (Equiv-Com $\overline{h}$ – like a vault with several openings); ▤ (message m being committed – like a text file); ⬡ (message fragment m'_j – can be combined with other fragments to recover the initial message); ☑ (authenticator a_j – vouches for the correctness of the respective fragment); ▨ (masking t_j – the chess pattern represents something that is masked); AUTH (authenticator function); C&C (cut-and-choose); $\mathcal{F}_X$ (ideal extractable-commitment functionality); $\mathcal{F}_Q$ (ideal equivocable-commitment functionality); $\mathcal{S}^X$ (simulator with extraction goal). This is a toy example with a cut-and-choose with $n = 5$ instances, of which $v = 2$ are selected for *check* and $e = 3$ are selected for *evaluation*. In the *extraction* example, a malicious P_A^* constructed one *bad* instance ($j = 3$), selected for the *check* subset. $\mathcal{S}^X$ detects the bad instance and thus ignores it when using the IDA to reconstruct the message from only $t = 2$ (the recovery threshold) fragments.

as an appropriate function α of the fragment and the nonce (46); P_A then uses the extended mask s'_j to compute the masking t_j of the fragment concatenated with the authenticator (47). Finally, P_A sends to P_B the maskings associated with all *evaluation* instances (48).

5.2.2 Open Phase (P_A Opens a Message to P_B)

- **2.a. Reveal message.** Upon being initialized to open the committed message m (49), P_A sends m to P_B (50). If using the STRICT authenticator mode, then P_A also asks $\mathcal{F}_Q$ to open to P_B the hash of the message ((51)–(52)). P_B then verifies that it is consistent with the hash of the received message (53). If not, it Aborts; otherwise it proceeds.
- **2.b. Obtain *evaluation* masks.** P_B uses the IDA to obtain the same fragments that an honest P_A would (54). P_B computes the authenticator of the fragment in the same way that an honest P_A would have, based on the fragment and the nonce (55). Then, P_B concatenates the tentative fragment and the tentative authenticator, and computes the XOR combination of the resulting string with the extended masking, thus obtaining the tentative extended mask s'_j, supposedly used by P_A (56).
- **2.c. Obtain *check* masks.** P_A uses $\mathcal{F}_X$ to *open* to P_B the seeds of *check* instances (but not those of *evaluation* instances) ((57)–(58)). P_B locally computes the PRG-expansion (of appropriate length) of each *check* seed (59).
- **2.d. Verify global hash.** P_A uses $\mathcal{F}_Q$ to *open* to P_B the previously committed global hash ((60)–(61)). Then, P_B verifies that the global hash of all concatenated masks is equal to the one just opened by P_A (62). If some verification has failed, then P_B aborts, otherwise it accepts the message of P_A as a correct *opening* (63).

5.3 Concrete Configurations

Table 1 shows optimal configurations of the cut-and-choose and IDA parameters for 40 bits of statistical security and several goals of communication rate. Asymptotically as ℓ increases, it is possible to configure the parameters to yield arbitrary high levels of statistical security and reduce the expansion-rate to values arbitrarily close to 1. With $(n; e; t) = (119; 46; 23)$, the scheme achieves 40 bits of statistical security and an asymptotic communication expansion-rate $r = 2$ in the *commit* phase (the open phase always has an asymptotic rate 1). With $(n; e; t) = (775; 275; 250)$, the rate becomes $r = 1.1$, with the computed PRG output and the hash input being $r' = 3.1$ times the message length. Both r and r' can be brought arbitrarily close to 1. In comparison, for a communication expansion rate of $r = 1.1$, the protocol from [GIKW14] would require encoding m into 53,020 blocks, and using an error correcting code capable of correcting more than 1198 semantic errors. Table 1 also describes parameters for optimizations of [GIKW14], namely by using k-out-of-n OT instead of δ-Rabin OT, reducing the number of instances by up to a factor slightly larger than two.

Table 1. UC commitment scheme parameters for 40 bits of statistical security

A	B	C	D	E	F
Maximum allowed expansion rate	This work		[GIKW14] (original)	Variations of [GIKW14]	
	$r = e/t \leq r_{max}$	$r' = n/t \leq r_{max}$	$\delta = t_0/(2n')$ $r = n'/n$	Optimal δ $r = n'/n$	t_0-out-of-n' OT $r = n'/n$
$r_{max} \leq 2$	$n = 119$ $v = 73$ $e = 46$ $t = 23$ $r' \approx 5.17$ $r = 2$	$n = 324$ $v = 87$ $e = 237$ $t = 162$ $r' = 2$ $r \approx 1.46$	$n = 826$ $n' = 1652$ $t_0 = 428$ $t_{error} = \lfloor 399/2 \rfloor$ $\delta = 107/826 \approx 0.1295$ $r = 2$	$n = 577$ $n' = 1154$ $t_0 = 339$ $t_{error} = \lfloor 239/2 \rfloor$ $\delta \approx 0.2064$ $r = 2$	$n = 352$ $n' = 704$ $t_0 = 186$ $t_{error} = \lfloor 167/2 \rfloor$ $r = 2$
$r_{max} \leq 3/2$	$n = 193$ $v = 121$ $e = 72$ $t = 48$ $r' \approx 4.02$ $r = 1.5$	$n = 822$ $v = 144$ $e = 678$ $t = 548$ $r' = 1.5$ $r \approx 1.237$	$n = 2540$ $n' = 3810$ $t_0 = 650$ $t_{error} = \lfloor 621/2 \rfloor$ $\delta = 65/762 \approx 0.0853$ $r = 1.5$	$n = 1706$ $n' = 2559$ $t_0 = 481$ $t_{error} = \lfloor 373/2 \rfloor$ $\delta \approx 0.1379$ $r = 1.5$	$n = 1152$ $n' = 1728$ $t_0 = 296$ $t_{error} = \lfloor 281/2 \rfloor$ $r = 1.5$
$r_{max} \leq 11/10$	$n = 775$ $v = 500$ $e = 275$ $t = 250$ $r' = 3.1$ $r = 1.1$	$n = 12,793$ $v = 598$ $e = 12,195$ $t = 11,630$ $r' = 1.1$ $r \approx 1.0489$	$n = 48,200$ $n' = 53,020$ $t_0 = 2424$ $t_{error} = \lfloor 2397/2 \rfloor$ $\delta = \frac{303}{13255} \approx 0.0229$ $r = 1.1$	$n = 28,740$ $n' = 31,614$ $t_0 = 1498$ $t_{error} = \lfloor 1377/2 \rfloor$ $\delta \approx 0.03945$ $r = 1.1$	$n = 23,530$ $n' = 25,883$ $t_0 = 1185$ $t_{error} = \lfloor 1169/2 \rfloor$ $r = 1.1$
$r_{max} \leq 101/100$	$n = 7310$ $v = 4684$ $e = 2626$ $t = 2600$ $r' = 2.81$ $r = 1.01$	$n = 1,125,645$ $v = 5631$ $e = 1,120,014$ $t = 1,114,500$ $r' = 1.01$ $r \approx 1.00495$	$n = 4,474,600$ $n' = 4,519,346$ $t_0 = 22,388$ $t_{error} = \lfloor 22,359/2 \rfloor$ $\delta = \frac{5597}{2,259,673} \approx 0.00248$ $r = 1.01$	$n = 2,384,200$ $n' = 2,408,042$ $t_0 = 12,166$ $t_{error} = \lfloor 11,677/2 \rfloor$ $\delta \approx 0.004737$ $r = 1.01$	$n = 2,231,600$ $n' = 2,253,916$ $t_0 = 11,166$ $t_{error} = \lfloor 11,151/2 \rfloor$ $r = 1.01$

Common legend for columns B-F. r (communication expansion rate in the commit phase, relative to the target length, i.e., to the length of the value being committed – it is asymptotic in that it does not account with the base short commitments (columns B-C) or the OT implementation (columns D-F).

Legend for columns B-C ("This work"). r' (overall length of PRG output, divided by the target length (at P_A – it is smaller at P_B, because P_B does not evaluate the PRG for *evaluation* instances); also the overall length of CR-Hash input, divided by the target length); n (total number of instances in the cut-and-choose); e (number of evaluation instances = number of fragments); t (recovery threshold = number of fragments necessary to recover message). The parameters were chosen to minimize the total number of instances n, while satisfying the *maximum allowed rate* (r_{max}, identified in column A), as follows: in column B ("$r = e/t \leq r_{max}$"), the communication expansion rate r is limited to r_{max} (in this case the PRG and the CR-Hash can be applied to bigger lengths – see r'); in column C ($t = \lceil n/r \rceil$), the computation expansion rate r' determined by the length of PRG output and CR-Hash input are limited to r_{max} (and in this case the overall communication rate r is smaller). After minimizing n, the remaining parameters were chosen to minimize e.

Legend for columns D-F ("[GIKW14]" and variations). n (number of blocks before encoding, i.e., number of symbols in which the target message is partitioned); t_0 (0-info threshold (the original notation was t), i.e., number of blocks whose knowledge does not reveal anything about the original message); t_{error} (error-recovery threshold – the original notation is $\Delta/2$); δ (probability of message passing through the δ-Rabin-OT – the original version uses $t_0 = 2\delta n'$); n' (total number of blocks after encoding, satisfying $n' = t + n + \Delta - 1$). For each value $r = n'/n$, the values of other parameters were chosen to minimize n. In column F, where the equivocator-simulator can always equivocate, statistical security depends only on the probability that a malicious P_A can guess $t_{error} + 1$ positions that P_B will not select in the OT.

Remark (Interactivity Tradeoffs). The use of an Equiv-Com scheme with P_A as sender and P_B as receiver can be replaced by an Ext-Com scheme with P_B as sender and P_A as receiver, and a regular Com scheme (i.e., possibly neither Ext nor Equiv) and further interaction. Basically, the Ext of a short bit-string committed by P_B^* would allow S (in the role of P_A in the simulated execution) to decide (within the overall open phase of the UC scheme) any desired outcome of a (single-side simulatable) short coin-flipping played between P_A and P_B. Each bit of this short coin-flipping can be set to determine one-out-of-two positions to open from each pair of (supposedly) copies of a committed bit (and additional redundant checksum bits included to prevent malicious behavior). This allows S to equivocate the short-bit string because it could undetectably commit to two different bits in each position (instead of two copies of the same bit) and then open only the convenient ones. In a direction of less interaction, it is conceivably possible to let the cut-and-choose partition and nonce values be computed by P_A non-interactively, if willing to accept an assumption of a non-programmable random oracle model [Lin15]. This would make all interactivity of the commitment scheme (commit and open) become implicit in the instantiations of the base commitment schemes (Ext and Equiv). The cut-and-choose and IDA (erasure code) parameters would have to increase, letting the statistical security parameter become equal to the cryptographic security parameter, to mitigate the new possibility that P_A could computationally try a brute-force trial-and-error attempt to exploit the probability of error that would otherwise be negligible only in a low statistical parameter.

5.4   Security Analysis

Proving security amounts to show, without rewiding, that the new commitment scheme is Ext&Equiv, i.e., the *commit* phase is Ext and the *open* phase is Equiv. The analysis assumes that the PRG and CR-Hash are cryptographically secure and that the underlying Ext-Com and Equiv-Com schemes are realized (in a hybrid model) by respective ideal functionalities ($\mathcal{F}_X$, $\mathcal{F}_Q$). The proof of security is accomplished by defining respective simulators.

Theorem 2 (Security of Protocol #2). *Assuming a cryptographically secure PRG and CR-Hash, and an adequate authenticator, protocol #2 UC-realizes the ideal functionality $\mathcal{F}_{MCOM}$ of long bit-string commitments in the $(\mathcal{F}_X, \mathcal{F}_Q)$-hybrid model, in the presence of static and computationally active adversaries. Each phase of $\mathcal{F}_Q$ and $\mathcal{F}_X$ is invoked for short bit-strings only a number of times that is independent of the polynomial target length.*

5.4.1   Extractability – Simulatability with Corrupted P_A^*

The extractor-simulator S^X initiates a simulation, with black-box access to $\mathcal{A}$, letting it believes that it is in the real world controlling P_A^*.

Simulation of the Commit *Phase.* Once the protocol starts, S^X (in the role of honest P_B and also in the role of $\mathcal{F}_X$ in the simulated execution) extracts the seeds committed by P_A^* (33) and later receives from P_A^* the maskings of authenticated fragments of the message being committed (48). $\mathcal{S}^X$ then unmasks each masking, using the PRG-expansion of the respective extracted seed, obtaining from each a respective *tentative* authenticated fragment. $\mathcal{S}^X$ verifies whether the authentication is correct or not, thus identifying which instances are *good*. (The security of the described authenticator is statistically derived from the properties of a universal hash family.) If the number of good fragments is at least t (the recovery threshold) then $\mathcal{S}^X$ uses the IDA recovery algorithm to reconstruct the message from t (the recovery threshold) *good* fragments. Otherwise, if there are less than t good fragments, then $\mathcal{S}^X$ realizes that it cannot extract the message from P_A^*, but it does not complain. Instead, $\mathcal{S}^X$ computes a random message as the assumed extracted message, and in addition it memorizes that the extracted message is corrupted. Finally (in either of the two above cases), in the ideal world, $\mathcal{S}^X$ (in the role of the ideal $\widehat{P}_A^*$) sends the extracted message to the ideal functionality $\mathcal{F}_{\mathrm{MCOM}}$, thus committing to it.

***Simulation of the* Open Phase.** Once P_A^* opens the message to P_B in the simulated execution, $\mathcal{S}^X$ checks that the opening is successful and that it corresponds to the previously extracted message. If the opening is unsuccessful, e.g., if the global hash verification fails (62), then $\mathcal{S}^X$ emulates an abort, leading $\mathcal{F}_{\mathrm{MCOM}}$ to halt the execution associated with this commitment, consequently leading the ideal party $\widehat{P}_B$ to never receive any opening. If (with negligible probability) the opening is successful but different from the value previously extracted from $\mathcal{S}^X$, then $\mathcal{S}^X$ outputs `Fail` (i.e., in this case the simulation fails). Otherwise, if the opening of the expected message is done successfully, then $\mathcal{S}$ asks $\mathcal{F}_{\mathrm{MCOM}}$ in the ideal world to *open* the committed message.

Analysis of the Simulation (Statistical Security). In the commit phase, $\mathcal{S}$ makes a perfect emulation of the abort distribution, since it only aborts early if and only if P_A^* also aborts. Thus, distinguishability (by the environment) between real and simulated executions can only happen if P_A^* is able (with non-negligible probability) to successfully open a message different from the one $\mathcal{S}^X$ has extracted. However, this is not possible. Based on the (described) authenticator mechanism security (derived directly from the collision-resistance of a CR-Hash, and the statistical properties of a universal hash family), P_A^* cannot forge a bad authentication, i.e., lead $\mathcal{S}^X$ to believe that a *bad* fragment is actually *good*. Also, based on the default binding property of all underlying commitments, P_A^* is not able to equivocate any of the Ext-Com or Equiv-Com. It can thus be assumed impossible for $\mathcal{S}$ to unknowingly mark as *good* an evaluation fragment (i.e., the result upon unmasking) that is actually *bad*. Now, a malicious successful opening by P_A^* requires that all check instances are good selected and at least $n - t + 1$ evaluation instances are bad. However, the probability of this event can be made negligible for appropriate cut-and-choose and IDA parameters (see Table 1). As an example, in the trivial case where P_A^* would build all check and evaluation instances as bad, $\mathcal{S}^X$ in the ideal world would still commit to a random valid value, but later in the open phase it would never let the ideal functionality open the value to the honest P_B.

Remark. There is a subtle difference between two types of commitment schemes. There are those where the receiver is ensured that the committer is *technically able* to open the commitment (if it "wants" to). For example, this is the case when the commit phase includes a ZKPoK of the committed value. There are other schemes where the commit phase is not enough to let the receiver know about the actual ability of the committer to later open a value. It is possible that a maliciously played commit phase prevents the sender (P_A^*) in advance from being able to later open the commitment accepted by the receiver (P_B). Protocol #2 is of this second kind. Even if S detects, in a non-aborting commit phase, that P_A is unable to later open the commitment, S does not abort before a failed open phase. The protocol can be easily changed to become of the first type (if desired), at the cost of increasing the calls to the Equiv-Com functionality, namely one per instance of the cut-and-choose, while nonetheless retaining an amortized communication complexity. The idea is simple: instead of just producing one Equiv-Com of the global hash, P_A^* would produce one Equiv-Com for each possible mask (i.e., each PRG-expansion); then, after the cut-and-choose partition is determined, but still within the overall commit phase, P_A^* would open the check seeds and the check hashes. In this way, S immediately knows whether some bad check instance was bad. If any bad check instance is detected, then S can immediately emulate an abort; otherwise, S accepts an extracted message based on the verification of the authentication of extracted evaluation masks and the associated anticipated fragments. In this case there is a negligible probability that the number of good instances is less than the recovery threshold.

5.4.2 Equivocability – Simulatability with Corrupted P_B^*

The equivocator-simulator S^Q initiates a simulation, with black-box access to $\mathcal{A}$, letting it believe that it is in the real world controlling P_B^*.

Simulation of the Commit Phase. In the ideal world, S^Q in the role of $\widehat{P}_B^*$, waits to receive from $\mathcal{F}_{MCOM}$ a receipt of commitment done by the ideal $\widehat{P}_A$. Then, in the role of P_A in the simulated execution, S^Q plays the whole commit phase to commit a random message to P_B^*. This involves keeping state about the seeds (32) and their Ext-Coms (33), about the Equiv-Com of the global hash of masks (38), possibly about the Equiv-Com of the hash of the random message (41) (i.e., if in the STRICT mode), about the cut-and-choose partition and the nounce, and about the maskings of authenticated fragments (48). If P_B^* aborts at any point before the end of the overall *commit* phase, then S^Q emulates an abort, i.e., in the role of $\widehat{P}_B^*$ in the ideal world sends abort to $\mathcal{F}_{MCOM}$, thus making it ignore further actions related with this commitment sub-session.

Simulation of the Open Phase. S^Q waits in the ideal world to receive from $\mathcal{F}_{MCOM}$ the *opening* of the target message (i.e., the one committed by the ideal $\widehat{P}_A$). Then, S^Q, in the role of P_A and also in the role of $\mathcal{F}_Q$ in the simulated execution, sends to P_B^* the target message (50), instead of the previously committed random message. If in the STRICT mode, then $\mathcal{S}^Q$ in the role of $\mathcal{F}_Q$ equivocates the opening of the needed hash of the message (52). Then, $\mathcal{S}^Q$ computes what are the *alternative masks* s'_j needed to unmask (the maskings t_j previously sent) into the target message received from $\mathcal{F}_{\text{MCOM}}$. This is done in the exact same way that P_B does as receiver: $\mathcal{S}^Q$ computes the message fragments (54), then their authenticators (55), and then takes the XOR with the maskings t_j (56) that were transmitted in the commit phase. Finally, $\mathcal{S}^Q$ computes the global hash (as in (36), but now using the updated masks), and then impersonates $\mathcal{F}_Q$ and equivocates the opening of said global hash (61). This allows P_B^* to perform all verifications as if $\mathcal{S}^Q$ was in fact an honest P_A. Finally, $\mathcal{S}^Q$ outputs in the ideal world whatever P_B^* outputs in the simulated execution (63).

Analysis of the Simulation. The only difference between a real protocol execution and the simulated execution is that $\mathcal{S}^Q$ commits to a random message and later equivocates it. However, detection by P_B^* of equivocation would require differentiating the random masks from seed-expansions, which is contrary to the pseudo-randomness assumption of the PRG. Thus, in case of corrupted P_B^* the distributions between real and ideal world are computationally indistinguishable.

Remark. The cut-and-choose partition does not need to be decided via a simulatable coin-flipping, because equivocation is directly based on the assumed ability to equivocate the global hash (committed with an Equiv-Com), which directly allows equivocation of the masks of all evaluation instances. Thus, to P_B^*, the actions of $\mathcal{S}^Q$ "appear" as correct independently of the partition. $\mathcal{S}^Q$ simply produces all commitments of seeds and all maskings correctly (for a random value), so that later all check instances are consistent.

Acknowledgments

The author thanks the anonymous referees for their useful reviewing comments.

References

[ALSZ15] Asharov, G., Lindell, Y., Schneider, T., Zohner, M.: More efficient oblivious transfer extensions with security for malicious adversaries. In: Oswald, E., Fischlin, M. (eds.) EUROCRYPT 2015. LNCS, vol. 9056, pp. 673–701. Springer, Heidelberg (2015). doi:10.1007/978-3-662-46800-5_26. Also at ia.cr/2015/061

[BCPV13] Blazy, O., Chevalier, C., Pointcheval, D., Vergnaud, D.: Analysis and improvement of Lindell's uc-secure commitment schemes. In: Jacobson, M., Locasto, M., Mohassel, P., Safavi-Naini, R. (eds.) ACNS 2013. LNCS, vol. 7954, pp. 534–551. Springer, Heidelberg (2013). doi:10.1007/978-3-642-38980-1_34. Also at ia.cr/2013123

[Bea96] Beaver, D.: Adaptive zero knowledge and computational equivocation (extended abstract). In: STOC 1996, pp. 629–638. ACM, New York (1996). doi:10.1145/237814.238014

[BK15] Barker, E., Kelsey, J.: Recommendation for Random Number Generation Using Deterministic Random Bit Generators, NIST SP800-90A Rev. 1, NIST-ITL-CSD, U.S. Department of Commerce, June 2015. doi:10.6028/NIST.SP.800-90Ar1

[Blu83] Blum, M.: Coin flipping by telephone – a protocol for solving impossible problems. SIGACT News **15**, 23–27 (1983). doi:10.1145/1008908.1008911. Appeared also at CRYPTO 1981

[Bra13] Brandão, L.T.A.N.: Secure two-party computation with reusable bit-commitments, via a cut-and-choose with forge-and-lose technique. In: Sako, K., Sarkar, P. (eds.) ASIACRYPT 2013, Part II. LNCS, vol. 8270, pp. 441–463. Springer, Heidelberg (2013). doi:10.1007/978-3-642-42045-0_23. Also at ia.cr/2013/577

[Can00] Canetti, R.: Security and composition of multiparty cryptographic protocols. J. Cryptol. **13**(1), 143–202 (2000). doi:10.1007/s001459910006. Also at ia.cr/1998/018

[Can01] Canetti, R.: Universally composable security: a new paradigm for cryptographic protocols. In: FOCS 2001, pp. 136–145. IEEE (2001). doi:10.1109/SFCS.2001.959888, Also at ia.cr/2000/067

[CDD+15] Cascudo, I., Damgård, I., David, B., Giacomelli, I., Nielsen, J.B., Trifiletti, R.: Additively homomorphic UC commitments with optimal amortized overhead. In: Katz, J. (ed.) PKC 2015. LNCS, vol. 9020, pp. 495–515. Springer, Heidelberg (2015). doi:10.1007/978-3-662-46447-2_22. Also at ia.cr/2014/829

[CF01] Canetti, R., Fischlin, M.: Universally composable commitments. In: Kilian, J. (ed.) CRYPTO 2001. LNCS, vol. 2139, pp. 19–40. Springer, Heidelberg (2001). doi:10.1007/3-540-44647-8_2. Also at ia.cr/2001/055

[CLOS02] Canetti, R., Lindell, Y., Ostrovsky, R., Sahai, A.: Universally composable two-party and multi-party secure computation. In: STOC 2002, pp. 494–503. ACM, New York (2002). doi:10.1145/509907.509980, Also at ia.cr/2002/140

[CR03] Canetti, R., Rabin, T.: Universal composition with joint state. In: Boneh, D. (ed.) CRYPTO 2003. LNCS, vol. 2729, pp. 265–281. Springer, Heidelberg (2003). doi:10.1007/978-3-540-45146-4_16. Also at ia.cr/2002/047

[Cre03] Di Crescenzo, G.: Equivocable and extractable commitment schemes. In: Cimato, S., Galdi, C., Persiano, G. (eds.) SCN 2002. LNCS, vol. 2576, pp. 74–87. Springer, Heidelberg (2003). doi:10.1007/3-540-36413-7_6

[Dam88] Damgård, I.B.: Collision free hash functions and public key signature schemes. In: Price, W.L., Chaum, D. (eds.) EUROCRYPT 1987. LNCS, vol. 304, pp. 203–216. Springer, Heidelberg (1988). doi:10.1007/3-540-39118-5_19

[DCIO98] Di Crescenzo, G., Ishai, Y., Ostrovsky, R.: Non-interactive and non-malleable commitment. In: STOC 1998, pp. 141–150. ACM, New York (1998). doi:10.1145/276698.276722

[DCKOS01] Di Crescenzo, G., Katz, J., Ostrovsky, R., Smith, A.: Efficient and non-interactive non-malleable commitment. In: Pfitzmann, B. (ed.) EUROCRYPT 2001. LNCS, vol. 2045, pp. 40–59. Springer, Heidelberg (2001). doi:10.1007/3-540-44987-6_4. Also at ia.cr/2001/032

[DCO99] Di Crescenzo, G., Ostrovsky, R.: On concurrent zero-knowledge with pre-processing (extended abstract). In: Wiener, M. (ed.) CRYPTO 1999. LNCS, vol. 1666, pp. 485–502. Springer, Heidelberg (1999). doi:10.1007/3-540-48405-1_31

[DDGN14] Damgård, I., David, B., Giacomelli, I., Nielsen, J.B.: Compact VSS and efficient homomorphic UC commitments. In: Sarkar, P., Iwata, T. (eds.) ASIACRYPT 2014, Part II. LNCS, vol. 8874, pp. 213–232. Springer, Heidelberg (2014). doi:10.1007/978-3-662-45608-8_12. Also at ia.cr/2014/370

[DL09] Damgård, I., Lunemann, C.: Quantum-secure coin-flipping and applications. In: Matsui, M. (ed.) ASIACRYPT 2009. LNCS, vol. 5912, pp. 52–69. Springer, Heidelberg (2009). doi:10.1007/978-3-642-10366-7_4. Also at arXiv:0903.3118

[DN02] Damgård, I.B., Nielsen, J.B.: Perfect hiding and perfect binding universally composable commitment schemes with constant expansion factor. In: Yung, M. (ed.) CRYPTO 2002. LNCS, vol. 2442, pp. 581–596. Springer, Heidelberg (2002). doi:10.1007/3-540-45708-9_37. Also at ia.cr/2001/091

[DNO10] Damgård, I., Nielsen, J.B., Orlandi, C.: On the necessary and sufficient assumptions for UC computation. In: Micciancio, D. (ed.) TCC 2010. LNCS, vol. 5978, pp. 109–127. Springer, Heidelberg (2010). doi:10.1007/978-3-642-11799-2_8. Also at ia.cr/2009/247

[DO10] Damgård, I., Orlandi, C.: Multiparty computation for dishonest majority: from passive to active security at low cost. In: Rabin, T. (ed.) CRYPTO 2010. LNCS, vol. 6223, pp. 558–576. Springer, Heidelberg (2010). doi:10.1007/978-3-642-14623-7_30. Also at ia.cr/2010/318

[ElG85] El Gamal, T.: A public key cryptosystem and a signature scheme based on discrete logarithms. In: Blakely, G.R., Chaum, D. (eds.) CRYPTO 1984. LNCS, vol. 196, pp. 10–18. Springer, Heidelberg (1985). doi:10.1007/3-540-39568-7_2

[FJNT16] Frederiksen, T.K., Jakobsen, T.P., Nielsen, J.B., Trifiletti, R.: On the complexity of additively homomorphic UC commitments. In: Kushilevitz, E., Malkin, T. (eds.) TCC 2016-A. LNCS, vol. 9562, pp. 542–565. Springer, Heidelberg (2016). doi:10.1007/978-3-662-49096-9_23. Also at ia.cr/2015/694

[FLM11] Fischlin, M., Libert, B., Manulis, M.: Non-interactive and re-usable universally composable string commitments with adaptive security. In: Lee, D.H., Wang, X. (eds.) ASIACRYPT 2011. LNCS, vol. 7073, pp. 468–485. Springer, Heidelberg (2011). doi:10.1007/978-3-642-25385-0_25

[FS90] Feige, U., Shamir, A.: Zero knowledge proofs of knowledge in two rounds. In: Brassard, G. (ed.) CRYPTO 1989. LNCS, vol. 435, pp. 526–544. Springer, New York (1990). doi:10.1007/0-387-34805-0_46

[Fuj14] Fujisaki, E.: All-but-many encryption. In: Sarkar, P., Iwata, T. (eds.) ASIACRYPT 2014. LNCS, vol. 8874, pp. 426–447. Springer, Heidelberg (2014). doi:10.1007/978-3-662-45608-8_23. Also at ia.cr/2012/379

[GIKW14] Garay, J.A., Ishai, Y., Kumaresan, R., Wee, H.: On the complexity of UC commitments. In: Nguyen, P.Q., Oswald, E. (eds.) EUROCRYPT 2014. LNCS, vol. 8441, pp. 677–694. Springer, Heidelberg (2014). doi:10.1007/978-3-642-55220-5_37

[GK96] Goldreich, O., Kahan, A.: How to construct constant-round zero-knowledge proof systems for NP. J. Cryptol. 9(3), 167–189 (1996). doi:10.1007/BF00208001

[GMS08] Goyal, V., Mohassel, P., Smith, A.: Efficient two party and multi party computation against covert adversaries. In: Smart, N.P. (ed.) EUROCRYPT 2008. LNCS, vol. 4965, pp. 289–306. Springer, Heidelberg (2008). doi:10.1007/978-3-540-78967-3_17

[Gol04] Goldreich, O.: Foundations of Cryptography. Basic Applications, vol. 2. Cambridge University Press, New York (2004). doi:10.1017/CBO9780511721656. isbn: 9780521830843

[HILL99] Håstad, J., Impagliazzo, R., Levin, L.A., Luby, M.: A pseudorandom generator from any one-way function. SIAM J. Comput. **28**(4), 1364–1396 (1999). doi:10.1137/S0097539793244708

[HKE13] Huang, Y., Katz, J., Evans, D.: Efficient secure two-party computation using symmetric cut-and-choose. In: Canetti, R., Garay, J.A. (eds.) CRYPTO 2013, Part II. LNCS, vol. 8043, pp. 18–35. Springer, Heidelberg (2013). doi:10.1007/978-3-642-40084-1_2. Also at ia.cr/2013/081

[HMQU06] Hofheinz, D., Müller-Quade, J., Unruh, D.: On the (im-)possibility of extending coin toss. In: Vaudenay, S. (ed.) EUROCRYPT 2006. LNCS, vol. 4004, pp. 504–521. Springer, Heidelberg (2006). doi:10.1007/11761679_30. Also at ia.cr/2006/177

[Kra94] Krawczyk, H.: Secret sharing made short. In: Stinson, D.R. (ed.) CRYPTO 1993. LNCS, vol. 773, pp. 136–146. Springer, Heidelberg (1994). doi:10.1007/3-540-48329-2_12

[KS08] Kolesnikov, V., Schneider, T.: Improved garbled circuit: free XOR gates and applications. In: Aceto, L., Damgård, I., Goldberg, L.A., Halldórsson, M.M., Ingólfsdóttir, A., Walukiewicz, I. (eds.) ICALP 2008, Part II. LNCS, vol. 5126, pp. 486–498. Springer, Heidelberg (2008). doi:10.1007/978-3-540-70583-3_40

[Lin03] Lindell, Y.: Parallel coin-tossing and constant-round secure two-party computation. J. Cryptol. **16**(3), 143–184 (2003). doi:10.1007/s00145-002-0143-7. Also at ia.cr/2001/107

[Lin11] Lindell, Y.: Highly-efficient universally-composable commitments based on the DDH assumption. In: Paterson, K.G. (ed.) EUROCRYPT 2011. LNCS, vol. 6632, pp. 446–466. Springer, Heidelberg (2011). doi:10.1007/978-3-642-20465-4_25. Also at ia.cr/2011/180

[Lin13] Lindell, Y.: Fast cut-and-choose based protocols for malicious and covert adversaries. In: Canetti, R., Garay, J.A. (eds.) CRYPTO 2013, Part II. LNCS, vol. 8043, pp. 1–17. Springer, Heidelberg (2013). doi:10.1007/978-3-642-40084-1_1. Also at ia.cr/2013/079

[Lin15] Lindell, Y.: An efficient transform from sigma protocols to NIZK with a CRS and non-programmable random oracle. In: Dodis, Y., Nielsen, J.B. (eds.) TCC 2015, Part I. LNCS, vol. 9014, pp. 93–109. Springer, Heidelberg (2015). doi:10.1007/978-3-662-46494-6_5. Also at ia.cr/2014/710

[LN11] Lunemann, C., Nielsen, J.B.: Fully simulatable quantum-secure coin-flipping and applications. In: Nitaj, A., Pointcheval, D. (eds.) AFRICACRYPT 2011. LNCS, vol. 6737, pp. 21–40. Springer, Heidelberg (2011). doi:10.1007/978-3-642-21969-6_2. Also at ia.cr/2011/065

[LPS08] Lindell, Y., Pinkas, B., Smart, N.P.: Implementing two-party computation efficiently with security against malicious adversaries. In: Ostrovsky, R., De Prisco, R., Visconti, I. (eds.) SCN 2008. LNCS, vol. 5229, pp. 2–20. Springer, Heidelberg (2008). doi:10.1007/978-3-540-85855-3_2

[Lub02] Luby, M.: LT codes. In: FOCS 2002, pp. 271–280. IEEE (2002). doi:10.1109/SFCS.2002.1181950

[Nao91] Naor, M.: Bit commitment using pseudorandomness. J. Cryptol. **4**(2), 151–158 (1991). doi:10.1007/BF00196774

[Nat15] National Institute of Standards and Technology, SHA-3 Standard: Permutation-Based Hash and Extendable-Output Functions. FIPS Pub 202, NIST-ITL, U.S. Department of Commerce, August 2015. doi:10.6028/NIST.FIPS.202

[NY89] Naor, M., Yung, M.: Universal one-way hash functions and their cryptographic applications. In: STOC 1989, pp. 33–43. ACM, New York (1989). doi:10.1145/73007.73011

[Ped92] Pedersen, T.P.: Non-interactive and information-theoretic secure verifiable secret sharing. In: Feigenbaum, J. (ed.) CRYPTO 1991. LNCS, vol. 576, pp. 129–140. Springer, Heidelberg (1992). doi:10.1007/3-540-46766-1_9

[PW09] Pass, R., Wee, H.: Black-box constructions of two-party protocols from one-way functions. In: Reingold, O. (ed.) TCC 2009. LNCS, vol. 5444, pp. 403–418. Springer, Heidelberg (2009). doi:10.1007/978-3-642-00457-5_24

[Rab89] Rabin, M.O.: Efficient dispersal of information for security, load balancing, and fault tolerance. J. ACM 36(2), 335–348 (1989). doi:10.1145/62044.62050

[Rom90] Rompel, J.: One-way functions are necessary and sufficient for secure signatures. In: STOC 1990, pp. 387–394. ACM, New York (1990). doi:10.1145/100216.100269

[Ros04] Rosen, A.: A note on constant-round zero-knowledge proofs for NP. In: Naor, M. (ed.) TCC 2004. LNCS, vol. 2951, pp. 191–202. Springer, Heidelberg (2004). doi:10.1007/978-3-540-24638-1_11

[RS60] Reed, I.S., Solomon, G.: Polynomial codes over certain finite fields. J. SIAM 8(2), 300–304 (1960). doi:10.1137/0108018

[Rus95] Russell, A.: Necessary and sufficient conditions for collision-free hashing. J. Cryptol. 8(2), 87–99 (1995). doi:10.1007/BF00190757

[Sch91] Schnorr, C.: Efficient signature generation by smart cards. J. Cryptol. 4(3), 161–174 (1991). doi:10.1007/BF00196725

[SCP00] De Santis, A., Di Crescenzo, G., Persiano, G.: Necessary and sufficient assumptions for non-interactive zero-knowledge proofs of knowledge for all NP relations. In: Welzl, E., Montanari, U., Rolim, J.D.P. (eds.) ICALP 2000. LNCS, vol. 1853, pp. 451–462. Springer, Heidelberg (2000). doi:10.1007/3-540-45022-X_38

[Sha79] Shamir, A.: How to share a secret. Commun. ACM 22(11), 612–613 (1979). doi:10.1145/359168.359176

[Sho06] Shokrollahi, A.: Raptor codes. IEEE Trans. Inf. Theory 52(6), 2551–2567 (2006). doi:10.1109/TIT.2006.874390

[Sim98] Simon, D.R.: Findings collisions on a one-way street: can secure hash functions be based on general assumptions? In: Nyberg, K. (ed.) EUROCRYPT 1998. LNCS, vol. 1403, pp. 334–345. Springer, Heidelberg (1998). doi:10.1007/BFb0054137

[SS11] Shelat, A., Shen, C.: Two-output secure computation with malicious adversaries. In: Paterson, K.G. (ed.) EUROCRYPT 2011. LNCS, vol. 6632, pp. 386–405. Springer, Heidelberg (2011). doi:10.1007/978-3-642-20465-4_22. ia.cr/2011/533

[VZ12] Vadhan, S., Zheng, C.J.: Characterizing pseudoentropy and simplifying pseudorandom generator constructions. In: STOC 2012, pp. 817–836. ACM, New York (2012). doi:10.1145/2213977.2214051

Robust Secret Sharing Schemes
Against Local Adversaries

Allison Bishop[(✉)] and Valerio Pastro

Columbia University, New York, USA
{allison,valerio}@cs.columbia.edu

Abstract. We study robust secret sharing schemes in which between one third and one half of the players are corrupted. In this scenario, robust secret sharing is possible only with a share size larger than the secrets, and allowing a positive probability of reconstructing the wrong secret. We focus on the most challenging case where the number corruptions is just one less than the number of honest players. In the standard model, it is known that at least $m + k$ bits per share are needed to robustly share a secret of bit-length m with an error probability of 2^{-k}; however, to the best of our knowledge, no efficient scheme matches this lower bound: the one that gets closest has share size $m + \widetilde{O}(n+k)$, where n is the number of players in the scheme.

We show that it is possible to obtain schemes with close to minimal share size in a model of local adversaries, i.e. in which corrupt players cannot communicate between receiving their respective honest shares and submitting corrupted shares to the reconstruction procedure, but may coordinate before the execution of the protocol and can also gather information afterwards. In this limited adversarial model, we prove a lower bound of roughly $m + k$ bits on the minimal share size, which is (somewhat surprisingly) similar to the lower bound in the standard model, where much stronger adversaries are allowed. We then present efficient scheme that essentially meets our lower bound, and has shorter share size than any known efficient construction in the standard model for the same set of parameters. For our construction, we introduce a novel procedure that compiles an error correcting code into a new randomized one, with the following two properties: a single local portion of a codeword leaks no information on the encoded message itself, and any set of portions of a codeword reconstructs the message with error probability exponentially low in the set size.

1 Introduction

While many cryptographic primitives require computational hardness assumptions to leverage restrictions on an adversary's computing power, the fundamental primitive of secret sharing protects data information-theoretically. This is

A. Bishop—Research supported in part by NSF CNS 1413971 and NSF CCF 1423306.
V. Pastro—Research supported by NSF CNS 1413971.

C.-M. Cheng et al. (Eds.): PKC 2016, Part II, LNCS 9615, pp. 327–356, 2016.
DOI: 10.1007/978-3-662-49387-8_13

accomplished by dispersing a secret among several parties, a sufficient number of whom are trustworthy. In a classical secret sharing scheme (as introduced independently by Shamir [23] and Blakely [4]), a dealer shares a secret among n parties such that any $t+1$ of them can reconstruct the secret, but any coalition of at most t players cannot learn anything about the secret. This is an information-theoretic guarantee, requiring that the joint distribution of any t shares must be independent of the secret.

Applications of secret sharing schemes range widely from secure multiparty computation (MPC), secure storage, secure message transmission, and distributed algorithms. In some of these applications, particularly secure storage and message transmission, an additional feature of "robustness" is desirable. Robust secret sharing is defined to satisfy all the usual properties of secret sharing, while additionally requiring that when the reconstruction procedure receives at most t adversarially corrupted shares out of n, it still outputs the correct secret (with sufficiently high probability).

Prior works on robust secret sharing (e.g. [5,7,9,10,22]) have focused on robustness against a "monolithic" adversary, i.e. a (computationally unbounded) centralized adversary who maliciously corrupts t parties and submits arbitrary values for their shares to the reconstruction procedure, potentially using all of the joint information present in the t shares initially received by the corrupted parties. In this model, it is known that for $t < n/3$ robust secret sharing schemes can be perfect, i.e. for any admissible adversary the reconstruction procedure outputs the correct secret with probability one (e.g. Shamir secret sharing, with Reed-Solomon decoding achieves this property). Interestingly, for $n/3 \leq t < n/2$ robust secret sharing is possible, but only by allowing a positive reconstruction failure probability [8]. In this scenario, Cevallos et al. [9] presented a polynomial time robust secret sharing scheme over m-bit messages with share sizes of $m + \widetilde{O}(k + n)$ and reconstruction failure probability of 2^{-k}. This scheme has the lowest share size among efficient schemes in this model, but does not match the best known lower bound of $m + k$ [7]. Our work is motivated by the following question:

Can the share size be significantly reduced with additional, but reasonable, restrictions on the adversary?

We identify a very natural and realistic adversary for which we construct a scheme with considerably shorter shares – while still maintaining efficiency. In this new adversarial model, we also prove a lower bound of $m + k - 2 - \log_2(3)$ bits on the share size, which essentially matches our constructions' shares and is almost identical to the best known lower bound in the standard model, in which much stronger adversaries are allowed. By constructing a scheme that approximately attains our lower bound, we have a rather complete understanding of the share sizes that can be obtained for robust secret sharing schemes in this model, a degree of precision that has not yet been achieved against the standard monolithic adversary.

Our Adversarial Model. We consider a "local" adversary, meaning that the t corrupted players cannot communicate with each other during the execution of the protocol – but they may arbitrarily coordinate before and after (the latter to try to gain knowledge on the secret). This means that each of the corrupted parties must decide on his malicious share to submit to the reconstruction procedure based only on some pre-determined strategy and the one honest share it has received from the dealer. This model carries some similarities to the work of Lepinski et al. [18], in the context of collusion-free protocols. In the setting of secret sharing robust against local adversaries, it is still true that for $t < n/3$ schemes can be perfect, and for $n/3 \leq t < n/2$ robustness can be achieved only allowing a failure probability (the same proofs as the ones in the monolithic adversarial model still apply), but in this latter scenario, working with local adversaries allows us to construct schemes with optimal share sizes, still maintaining efficiency.

Motivation for Our Model. Local adversaries model several kinds of realistic limitations of adversarial power in many applications. For example, in a secure message transmission, data may travel quickly and realtime cooperation among corrupted nodes may be unlikely. In a large secure multiparty computation, the scale and pace of the computation may also make online coordination among adversarial parties unrealistic. Corrupted parties may also be mutually distrusting, unwilling to coordinate (e.g. if they have opposite goals), or they might not even know about the existence of each other (say in a large scale MPC over the Internet).

Similar adversary models have been well-studied in other subfields of computer science, such as the multi-prover setting for interactive proofs. In the classical result of $IP = PSPACE$ [24], a single, computationally unbounded and potentially duplicitous prover must convince a much less powerful verifier of the truth of a particular statement. As was shown in [3], considering two duplicitous but non-communicating provers greatly expands the class of statements that can be proved, as $MIP = NEXP$. Removing online communication between the provers is precisely what fuels this expanded power, and similar gains may be possible in other interactive scenarios, including secure multiparty computation and robust distributed algorithms.

In order to capture limited collusion among adversarial parties during the protocol, the locality model can be extended to allow small factions. More precisely, we could allow each adversarially submitted share to depend on the view of a certain bounded number of received shares. We do not address this extended model in this work, but we suspect that similar techniques can be applied to obtain such extensions.

More Details on Our Results. As mentioned earlier, we prove two complementary results on the share size of secret sharing schemes robust against a local adversary corrupting t of the n players, where $n/3 \leq t < n/2$, and where the reconstruction failure probability is 2^{-k}.

In the first part of the paper, we show a lower bound of $m + k - 2 - \log_2(3)$ on the minimal share size in this setting. This is somewhat surprising, since it is quantitatively comparable to the lower bound of $m + k$ proven in [7] in the case of a monolithic (and much stronger!) adversary. Our proof uses remarkably little adversarial power to obtain this lower bound: more precisely, we show that this lower bound holds against an oblivious adversary who completely ignores the honest shares given to corrupted parties and replaces them with either default values or fresh shares. We note that working with such little adversarial knowledge requires us to develop new lower bound techniques. In particular, the proof of the previous lower bound of [7] heavily leverages centralized adversarial knowledge of the true secret and all of the shares received by corrupted players. Their argument considers an adversary who maximizes its success conditioned on this knowledge – knowledge that our much weaker local adversary does not have.

In the second part, we construct a poly-time scheme robust against local adversaries whose share size is $m + O(k)$, which essentially meets our lower bound. Our core idea for shrinking the shares is to authenticate all honest shares with a single MAC key that is "hidden in plain sight" from a local adversary. To do so, while still ensuring that the key can be efficiently recovered by the reconstruction procedure, we develop a novel tool integrating error-correcting codes with "locally hiding" distributions, a rather general tool that may be of independent interest.

Compared to the scheme in the standard model with smallest share size [9], our scheme reduces the share size by removing the additive factor of n. Thus, we see that restricting to local adversaries allows us to considerably reduce share size down to approximately match a proven lower bound, removing any linear dependence on the number of players, while maintaining polynomial time efficiency. This yields a much tighter understanding of what is achievable against local adversaries than what is known against a monolithic adversary in the context of robust secret sharing.

Techniques for Our Construction. Previous constructions of robust secret sharing schemes use MACs to authenticate honest shares. Against a monolithic adversary who can view all of the shares received by corrupt players, it seems necessary to use many different MACs to prevent the adversary from compiling enough information about the keys to forge enough tags for corrupt shares. These many MAC keys and tags significantly increase the size of shares.

In the local adversary setting where each corrupt party can only act based upon a pre-determined strategy and its own received share, we can restrict to a single MAC key to be used on each share for authentication. Essentially, we will design our shares so that each party will be given a share that is distributed independently of the MAC key when considered on its own, but the joint distribution of just a constant number of honest shares reveals the key (hence allowing authentication of honest shares).

The basic idea is as follows: each share consists of a Shamir share of the secret, a tag on the Shamir share, and information on the global MAC key (used for the tag). This information has to be conveyed in a way that a single player obtains no information on the key itself (otherwise it could forge its tag), and the key is still retrievable even if nearly half of the shares are corrupt.

In our construction, the dealer embeds the key in a bit-matrix and distributes one row per player in such a way that each single row looks random, but the joint distribution of enough rows reveals the key. More specifically, each bit of the key is encoded as a column of such matrix, as follows: the bit 0 is encoded as a uniform bit-column, while the bit 1 is encoded as either the all-zero and the all-one column, and this choice is uniform. A single row in such matrix is a uniform string; no information on the key is revealed. On the other hand, looking across a bigger number of honest rows (and seeing them all agree at the positions corresponding to 1) allows us to invert the embedding with probability close to one – the failure probability decreases exponentially with the number of honest rows seen. In order to make the failure probability negligible when the number of inspected rows is constant, we encode the key via an asymptotically good error correcting code before the embedding procedure.

A secondary challenge is that looking at corrupt rows can lead to the wrong key. However, it is possible to detect a corrupt key by the fact that it verifies fewer than $t + 1$ tags with high probability (the honest shares are likely to be incompatible with a non-honest key).

Thus, we can iterate the procedure to invert the embedding of the key through all subsets of shares of a fixed constant size, attempt to reconstruct the MAC key from each set, and stop whenever we find one that authenticates properly. This computation is still polynomial in n and succeeds with sufficiently high probability. This comprises our construction of an efficient secret sharing scheme that is robust against local adversaries, with a significantly reduced share size compared to previous constructions in the standard model.

Techniques for the Lower Bound. To prove our lower bound on minimal share size in this setting, we consider very simple local adversary strategies. We suppose that a local adversary's goal is to cause a reconstruction failure when a challenger generates honest shares from a uniformly random secret. In particular, the adversary identifies a player with a share of minimal length and chooses to corrupt a random set of t of the remaining players and replaces the corrupt players' shares with freshly generated honest shares for a new uniformly chosen secret. Note that these t corrupted shares will be sampled from the same distribution as honest shares, but sampled independently from the true secret. For simplicity of illustration, suppose that this local adversary has replaced the first t shares with its own sample, while the remaining $t + 1$ shares are honest. Also suppose that the $t + 1$st share has minimal length (any scenario follows these assumptions, up to a relabeling of the players indices). Then, it is likely that the first t corrupted shares and the honest $t + 1$st share are also consistent with some honest sharing. At this point, the complete set of shares is ambiguous, in the sense that the first $t + 1$ shares define a (corrupt) secret, while the last $t + 1$ shares define another (honest) secret. Now, it is not clear whether running the reconstruction procedure on this set of shares will lead to one secret or the other: in particular, the probability that an honest sharing agrees with the first $t + 1$

shares could be different from the probability that an honest sharing agrees with the last $t+1$ shares – and the reconstruction procedure can take this into account when given an ambiguous set of shares as input (and, for example, output the secret defined by the shares that are more likely).

To address these subtleties, we parameterize the underlying probability space in terms of pairs of secrets and random strings chosen by the share generating algorithm. We group these pairs into various equivalence classes based on collisions of subsets of the resulting shares, and model these equivalences in a layered graph. Our analysis takes advantage of the fact that the adversary can produce the first t corrupted shares in a way that is consistent with the $t+1$st share without knowing what the reconstruction would output. This crucial property comes as a consequence of the privacy guarantee of the scheme: any first t shares are consistent with every secret, otherwise the adversary would get information on the secret after the protocol is over (and communication between corrupt players is allowed). This is a key source of the precision of our bound as compared to [7], where they capture adversary success by considering when the adversary correctly guesses an unknown share, making use of all the information on the t shares he is given. We manage to capture the adversarial success without requiring such guesses, and no knowledge on the honest shares given to the adversary.

Our lower bound proof holds for secret sharing schemes that are private, robust, and statistically correct (i.e. we are not requiring that $t+1$ shares determine the secret with probability one – however, even if this is the case, by the (t, δ)-robustness property for an $n = 2 \cdot t + 1$ player secret sharing scheme, we get that $t+1$ shares determine a secret with probability $1 - \delta$).

In summary, we obtain an extremely powerful lower bound, since it relies only upon (weak) local adversaries, and assumes only statistical correctness for the underlying scheme.

Additional Related Work. Robust secret sharing schemes are also considered in [11], which does not consider local adversaries, but relaxes the model by requiring a gap between privacy threshold and reconstruction threshold (this is commonly known as a ramp scheme). In this setting t/n must be less than $1/2 - \varepsilon$ for some positive ε. Moreover, ramp schemes can avoid the typical restriction that the size of individual shares must be at least as large as the secret size. In this model [11] achieves robust secret sharing with nearly constant sized shares.

Decentralized adversaries are also considered in [1,6], which provide frameworks for simulation-based security definitions for cryptographic primitives against local adversaries. Similarly, in the setting of leakage-resilient cryptography, various "local" adversarial models have been studied. For example, the "only computation leaks information" axiom of Micali and Reyzin [20] restricts an adversary to leakage that happens solely on whatever portion of a secret state is currently involved in a computation. Some other works, such as [13,14] consider secret state as divided among multiple devices and leaking independently. [2] also present a rather general study of various collusion restrictions on adversarial actors in multiparty protocols.

2   Preliminaries

In this section we list the classic tools and notation used in our paper.

We usually denote distributions by calligraphic letters (e.g. $\mathcal{D}$), random variables by capital letters (e.g. $D \sim \mathcal{D}$ reads as "D follows the distribution $\mathcal{D}$"), and samples by lowercase letters (e.g. $d \leftarrow D$ reads "d is sampled according to D"). Moreover, for any set X, we denote by $\mathcal{U}_X$ the uniform distribution on X.

Definition 1 (Projection). *For any integer n, for any set $X = X_1 \times \cdots \times X_n$, and for any $I \subseteq \{1, \ldots, n\}$, we write X_I to denote the set $\prod_{i \in I} X_i$. This notation is carried over to the elements of X.*

Definition 2 (Hamming Weight). *For a vector $v \in \mathbb{F}_2^c$, we define $w(v)$ to be the Hamming weight of v (i.e. the number of non-zero coordinates of v).*

We will use the following Chernoff Bound, which appears as Theorem 4.4 in [21].

Lemma 1. *Let $Y_1, \ldots, Y_m$ be independent random variables with $\Pr[Y_i = 1] = p$ and $\Pr[Y_i = 0] = 1 - p$. Let $Y = \sum_{i=1}^{m} Y_i$ and $\mu = p \cdot m$. Then for $0 < \beta \leq 1$,*

$$\Pr[Y \geq (1 + \beta) \cdot \mu] \leq e^{-\mu \beta^2 / 3}.$$

2.1   Message Authentication Codes

Definition 3 (MAC). *A (one time) ε-secure message authentication code (MAC) for messages in $\mathcal{M}$ is a function $\mathsf{MAC} : \mathcal{K} \times \mathcal{M} \to \mathcal{T}$, for some sets $\mathcal{K}$ (key space) and $\mathcal{T}$ (tag space) such that for all $m \neq m' \in \mathcal{M}$, for all $t, t' \in \mathcal{T}$, and for a uniform random variable $K \sim \mathcal{U}_\mathcal{K}$:*

$$\Pr[\mathsf{MAC}(K, m') = t' \mid \mathsf{MAC}(K, m) = t] \leq \varepsilon.$$

2.2   Error-Correcting Codes

An error-correcting code for messages that are bit strings of length h is a function $C : \mathbb{F}_2^h \to \mathbb{F}_2^c$, where c is called the block length. The distance d of the code is defined as

$$\min_{x \neq y \in \mathbb{F}_2^h} \{w(x - y)\}.$$

The number E of adversarial errors tolerated is $\lceil \frac{d}{2} - 1 \rceil$, while the fraction e of errors tolerated is $\frac{E}{c}$. The rate of the code r is defined to be h/c. A decoding procedure is a function $D : \mathbb{F}_2^c \to \mathbb{F}_2^h$ such that whenever z satisfies $w(z, C(x)) \leq E$, $D(z) = x$.

An infinite ensemble of codes for increasing block lengths c is said to be *asymptotically good* if the rate r and fraction of errors e are both lower bounded by positive constants. Such codes are known to exist, and with efficient encoding and decoding functions. For example, Justesen [17] gave an explicit family of asymptotically good codes with block lengths $h = 2m(2^m - 1)$ for each positive integer m with efficient encoding and decoding functions.

2.3   Robust Secret Sharing Schemes

Throughout the rest of the paper, we use the following notation:

- n is an integer that denotes the number of players in the scheme.
- $t \leq n$ denotes the maximum number of corruptible players in the scheme.
- $\mathcal{M}$ is the message space. We denote by m the integer such that $2^{m-1} < |\mathcal{M}| \leq 2^m$.
- $\mathcal{R}$ is a set that denotes the randomness space used by the scheme to share messages. We assume that the scheme samples uniform elements in $\mathcal{R}$ to produce sequences of shares.
- $\mathcal{S} = \mathcal{S}_1 \times \cdots \times \mathcal{S}_n$ is a set that denotes the ambient space of sequences of shares. For $i = 1, \ldots, n$ we denote by 0_i a default element in $\mathcal{S}_i$ (i.e. an element that any Turing machine can retrieve without any input). For example, if $\mathcal{S}_i$ is a group, 0_i could be the zero of $\mathcal{S}_i$ as a group.

Definition 4 (Secret Sharing Scheme). *A t-private, n-player secret sharing scheme over a message space $\mathcal{M}$ is a tuple* (Share, Rec) *of algorithms that run as follows:*

Share$(s, r) \rightarrow (s_1, \ldots, s_n)$: *this algorithm takes as input a message $s \in \mathcal{M}$ and randomness $r \in \mathcal{R}$ and outputs a sequence of shares $(s_1, \ldots, s_n) \in \mathcal{S}$.*

Rec$(s_1, \ldots, s_n) \rightarrow s'$: *this algorithm takes as input an element $(s_1, \ldots, s_n) \in \mathcal{S}$ (not necessarily output by* Share*) and outputs a message $s' \in \mathcal{M}$.*

Moreover, the following properties hold:

Privacy: *Any t out of n shares of a secret give no information on the secret itself. More formally, for any random variable S over $\mathcal{M}$ and uniform $R \sim \mathcal{U}_\mathcal{R}$:*

$$S = (S \mid \mathsf{Share}(S, R)_{C_1} = \mathsf{Share}(s, r)_{C_1}, \ldots, \mathsf{Share}(S, R)_{C_t} = \mathsf{Share}(s, r)_{C_t})$$

Perfect Correctness: *Reconstructing a sequence of shares generated by the sharing procedure leads to the original secret, even given $n - t - 1$ erasures. More formally, for any $I \subseteq \{1, \ldots, n\}$ with $|I| = t + 1$ let $\Delta(I) \in \{\bot, 1\}^n$ be the characteristic vector of I (i.e. for $i \in I$, $\Delta(I)_i = 1$; for $i \notin I$, $\Delta(I)_i = \bot$, where $\bot$ is a special symbol such that $\bot \cdot s_i = \bot$ for any share $s_i \in \mathcal{S}_i$). Then, for any $s \in \mathcal{M}$, $r \leftarrow \mathcal{U}_\mathcal{R}$:*

$$\Pr[\mathsf{Rec}(\mathsf{Share}(s, r) * \Delta(I)) = s] = 1,$$

where $*$ denotes the coordinate-wise product.

Remark 1. Jumping ahead, when defining (t, δ)-robust secret sharing, we relax perfect correctness to statistical correctness – i.e. correctness holds with probability $1 - \delta$ instead of 1.

Definition 5 (Merging Function). *Let $s \in \mathcal{M}, r \in \mathcal{R}$ and let $I \subseteq \{1, \ldots, n\}$. For $i \in I$, let $v_i \in \mathcal{S}_i$. We define the merging function of s, r with $I, (v_i)_{i \in I}$ as*

$$\mathsf{Merge}(s, r, I, (v_i)_{i \in I}) = S \in \mathcal{S}$$

where for $i \in I$ $S_i = v_i$, and for $i \notin I$ $S_i = \mathsf{Share}(s, r)_i$.

Definition 6 (Adversary). *For any t-private, n-player secret sharing scheme* (Share, Rec), *we define the experiment* $\mathbf{Exp}_{(\mathsf{Share},\mathsf{Rec})}(\mathcal{D}, \mathsf{Adv})$, *where $\mathcal{D}$ is a distribution over $\mathcal{M}$, and Adv is an interactive Turing machine, called the adversary.*

$\mathbf{Exp}_{(\mathsf{Share},\mathsf{Rec})}(\mathcal{D}, \mathsf{Adv})$ *is defined as follows:*

E.1. Send the public description (Share, Rec) *of the scheme and the distribution $\mathcal{D}$ to* Adv.

E.2. Adv *computes and outputs $I = \{i_1, \ldots, i_t\} \subseteq \{1, \ldots, n\}$, i.e. a subset of players whose size is less or equal to t.*

E.3. Sample $s \leftarrow \mathcal{D}$, and $r \leftarrow \mathcal{U}_\mathcal{R}$, compute $\mathsf{Share}(s, r)$ and send $\mathsf{Share}(s, r)_I$ to Adv.

E.4. Adv *outputs $(v_i)_{i \in I}$, where $v_i \leftarrow V_i$ and*

$$V_i = V_i(\mathsf{Share}, \mathsf{Rec}, \mathcal{D}, \mathsf{Share}(s, r)_{i_1}, \ldots, \mathsf{Share}(s, r)_{i_t})$$

is a random variable that may depend on the public information of the scheme, and the ensemble of shares indexed by I.

E.5. Return 1 if and only if $\mathsf{Rec}(\mathsf{Merge}(s, r, I, (v_i)_{i \in I})) \neq s$.

For $v \leq t$, we say that an adversary is v-local if for all $i \in I$,

$$V_i = V_i(\mathsf{Share}, \mathsf{Rec}, \mathcal{D}, \mathsf{Share}(s, r)_{i_1}, \ldots, \mathsf{Share}(s, r)_{i_v}),$$

i.e. V_i is a random variable that depends only on the public information of the scheme, and at most v elements of the ensemble of shares indexed by I.

Definition 7 (Robust Secret Sharing Scheme). *A t-private n-player secret sharing scheme* (Share, Rec) *over a message space $\mathcal{M}$ is (t, δ)-robust if the following property holds:*

Robustness: *With probability less or equal to δ the reconstruction procedure fails at outputing the correct shared value, even if t out of the n shares are corrupt by adversary. Formally, for any distribution $\mathcal{D}$, for any adversary* Adv*:*

$$\Pr[\mathbf{Exp}_{(\mathsf{Share},\mathsf{Rec})}(\mathcal{D}, \mathsf{Adv}) = 1] \leq \delta$$

We say that a scheme is (t, δ)-robust against v-local adversaries if robustness holds for any v-local adversary.

3   Lower Bound

We prove a lower bound for the share size of any secret sharing scheme that is robust against 0-local adversaries, which implies that this lower bound applies to any secret sharing scheme that is robust against v-local adversaries for any $v \geq 0$.

Theorem 1. *Let k, m, t be integers. Let $\delta = 2^{-k}$, $n = 2 \cdot t + 1$, $\mathcal{M}$ be a set with $2^{m-1} \leq |\mathcal{M}| \leq 2^m$. Let* (Share, Rec) *be an n-player secret sharing scheme over $\mathcal{M}$. If* (Share, Rec) *is (t, δ)-robust, then the minimum bit-length of any of its shares is at least $m + k - (2 + \log_2(3))$.*

3.1   Intuition for the Proof of Theorem 1

Here, we give a high level overview of our proof. Let P_{t+1} be a player associated with a share with the shortest size λ.

An Adversary. We relate the value λ to the security parameter k by analyzing the success probability of a (local) adversary that does the following:

1. "decide" whether to corrupt $I = \{P_1, \ldots, P_t\}$ or $J = \{P_{t+2}, \ldots, P_n\}$. An intuition about how this decision is made is given in the following.
2. sample a uniform message x and randomness r_x and compute $\mathsf{Share}(x, r_x)$
3. output $\mathsf{Share}(x, r_x)_i$ as the corrupt share of P_i, for all i in the set of corrupt players.

The decision made by the adversary in step 1 can be thought of simulating each choice (either corrupt I or J) and picking the one that leads to higher success probability. Studying this success probability is a bit tricky. A sufficient way to describe it is by analyzing the probability that:

- the $t + 1$st share is compatible with the corrupt shares *and*
- the reconstruction doesn't output the correct secret (this latter property alone would suffice, but it is easier to understand it in the presence of the former one)

Intuitively, in order to directly understand the above two properties, one has to understand the distribution induced by the sharing procedure on the *shares*, which may be cumbersome. It would be helpful to relate the success of the adversary solely on the distribution of *secrets* and *randomness* – the uniform distribution.

A Graph – Definition. We achieve this feature by relating the above two properties to a graph, constructed as follows: it is a 4-layered graph, where each vertex in a layer is a pair (s, r) for all possible messages s and randomness r. Edges are created according to the following rule:

(s, r) $\qquad\qquad$ (s^I, r^I) $\qquad\qquad$ (s^J, r^J) $\qquad\qquad$ (s', r')

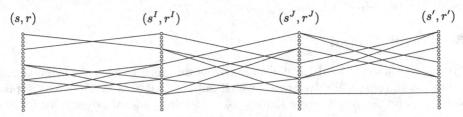

Edge if: $\mathsf{Share}(s, r)_I = \mathsf{Share}(s^I, r^I)_I$ $\mathsf{Share}(s^I, r^I)_{t+1} = \mathsf{Share}(s^J, r^J)_{t+1}$ $\mathsf{Share}(s^J, r^J)_J = \mathsf{Share}(s', r')_J$

A Graph – Properties. In order to make his decision, the adversary labels the edges between the second and third layer as follows:

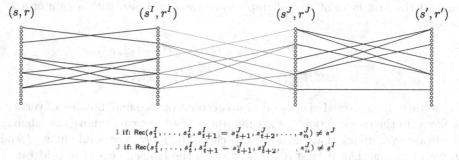

I if: $\mathrm{Rec}(s_1^I, \ldots, s_t^I, s_{t+1}^I = s_{t+1}^J, s_{t+2}^J, \ldots, s_n^J) \neq s^J$
J if: $\mathrm{Rec}(s_1^I, \ldots, s_t^I, s_{t+1}^I - s_{t+1}^J, s_{t+2}^J, \ldots, s_n^J) \neq s^I$

The decision he makes in step 1, is merely counting how many edges have a specific label:

Decide to corrupt I if $|I\text{-edges}| \geq |J\text{-edges}|$ (corrupt J otherwise)

Adversarial Success in the Graph. Without loss of generality, assume that the adversary chose to corrupt I. Then, the robustness experiment is equivalent to the following:

- choose a vertex (s^J, r^J) uniformly from the third layer of the graph
- choose a vertex (s, r) uniformly from the first layer of the graph

It turns out that the success probability of the adversary is equivalent to the probability that (s, r) and (s^J, r^J) are connected (this implies that the $t+1$st share is compatible with the corrupt shares), and there exists an I-edge in the connecting path (this implies that the reconstruction fails). In other words,

$$2^{-k} \geq \Pr[\mathbf{Exp}_{(\mathsf{Share},\mathsf{Rec})}(\mathcal{U}, \mathsf{Adv}) = 1]$$

$$= \Pr_{(s, r, s^J, r^J)}[\exists (s^I, r^I) \mid (s, r) \!-\! (s^I, r^I) \overset{I}{-\!\!\!-} (s^J, r^J)]$$

Refining, Analyzing Connectivity, and Concluding. Now, we can start an analysis of the above property which relates the security parameter to the size of the shortest share. Firstly, we define a subgraph with the specific connectivity property that the number of vertices at layer one connected by a path to a specific vertex at layer three is at least 2^m times the number of vertices at layer two connected to the same vertex at layer three. In other words,

$$|\{(s, r) \mid \exists (s^I, r^I) : (s, r)\!-\!(s^I, r^I)\!-\!(s^J, r^J)\}| \geq 2^m \cdot |(s^I, r^I) \mid (s, r)\!-\!(s^I, r^I)\!-\!(s^J, r^J)|$$

Somewhat surprisingly, this can be done by removing only a relatively small number $(2 \cdot 2^{-k}$ fraction$)$ of vertices to the second layer of the graph: among others, we remove all those vertices (s, r) such that $\mathsf{Rec}(\mathsf{Share}(s, r)) \neq s$ (there is most a 2^{-k} fraction of them, by statistical correctness), and then use perfect correctness and privacy on the induced graph to obtain the above.

We now use the graph properties to manipulate the resulting probability: the property of the refined graph allows us to essentially "move" the probability mass at the first layer of the subgraph to the second layer, with a gain of a 2^m factor:

$$\Pr{}_{(s,r,s^J,r^J)}[\exists (s^I, r^I) \mid (s,r)\text{---}(s^I, r^I)\overset{I}{\text{---}}(s^J, r^J)]$$
$$\approx 2^m \cdot \Pr{}_{(s^I, r^I, s^J, r^J)}[(s^I, r^I)\overset{I}{\text{---}}(s^J, r^J)]$$

(we write $\approx$ here instead of $=$ to take into account of the small number of vertices removed in the construction of the subgraph.) Then, we can remove the labeling condition by noticing that the adversary chose the more successful among I and J, which means that at least a $1/2$ fraction of the labeled edges are I-edges:

$$2^m \cdot \Pr{}_{(s^I, r^I, s^J, r^J)}[(s^I, r^I)\overset{I}{\text{---}}(s^J, r^J)] \geq 2^{m-1} \cdot \Pr{}_{(s^I, r^I, s^J, r^J)}[(s^I, r^I)\text{---}(s^J, r^J)]$$

The rest of the proof is an algebraic manipulation of the resulting probability which leads to the correct result by using standard probability tools, such as independence of random variables, union bounds, and the Cauchy-Schwarz inequality.

3.2   Proof of Theorem 1

Proof. We first note that it suffices to prove a lower bound of $m+k-(1+\log_2(3))$ for $|\mathcal{M}| = 2^m$, since a lower bound for the share size required to share a secret from a space of size 2^{m-1} certainly applies to sharing a secret from larger a space of size $|\mathcal{M}| \geq 2^{m-1}$. Throughout the proof, we will therefore assume that $|\mathcal{M}| = 2^m$.

Our proof will rely solely on very simple local adversary strategies. Namely, we will need to consider only two possible adversary strategies: one that replaces some subset of t shares with default values of (say) all zeros, and another that replaces them with shares generated with fresh randomness for a fresh (uniform) secret. These strategies are both 0-local because the adversary submits shares that are distributed independently of all the shares that the corrupted players receive. The key idea will be that if one share is very short, then it becomes more likely that the adversary submitting t freshly distributed shares will cause a "collision", meaning that the corrupted shares are consistent with the honestly generated short share. This will make it difficult for the reconstruction algorithm to tell which is the honestly shared secret. We also consider the adversary who submits default values for technical reasons within the argument, in order to prove that there are not too many honest sharings for differing secrets that agree in some set of at least $t + 1$ shares. If these were too common, the adversary submitting default values for the complement set would succeed in confusing the reconstruction algorithm with sufficient probability.

To carefully study the probability space of pairs (s,r) where s is a uniformly random secret and r is a random bit string used in the share generating procedure, we define a layered graph whose vertices at each layer correspond to these pairs (s, r), and edges between the layers represent agreeing shares for specified subsets of players. Essentially, our graph models various kinds of equivalence classes of values (s, r) corresponding to partial agreements of the resulting shares. To execute our proof, we will identify paths in our graph corresponding to the events of adversary success, and we will then lower bound the number of such edges and hence the success probability of the adversary.

A Graph. (For an intuitive description, see Sect. 3.1.) Let $P \in \{1, \dots, n\}$ be the index of a player, let $I \subset \{1, \dots, n\} \setminus \{P\}$ be a set of cardinality $|I| = t$, and let $J = \{1, \dots, n\} \setminus (\{P\} \cup I)$ be the set of size t corresponding to the players that are not in I and are not P. Let $G - G(P, I)$ be a graph defined as:

- Vertices$(G) = \{1, \dots, 4\} \times \mathcal{M} \times \mathcal{R}$, i.e. the vertex set consists of four layers of message and random value tuples.
- $((i, s, r), (i + 1, s', r')) \in$ Edges(G) if:
  - $i = 1$, and Share$(s, r)_I =$ Share$(s', r')_I$: i.e. a vertex at layer one is connected to a vertex at layer two if the tuples of shares they define agree on the shares at I.
  - $i = 2$, $s \neq s'$, and Share$(s, r)_P =$ Share$(s', r')_P$: i.e. a vertex at layer two is connected to a vertex at layer three if the vertices represent different secrets, and the tuples of shares they define agree on the share at P.
  - $i = 3$, and Share$(s, r)_J =$ Share$(s', r')_J$: i.e. a vertex at layer three is connected to a vertex at layer four if the tuples of shares they define agree on the shares at J.

Path Sets, Labeling, Balance. (For an intuitive description, see Sect. 3.1.) We want to construct a labeling system for paths from layer one to layer four, that will be useful to analyze certain reconstruction properties of the secret sharing scheme associated with the graph. Firstly, however, we need to construct a function that maps paths containing edges from layer two to layer three to sequences of shares. For $1 \leq i < j \leq 4$, let $\mathcal{E}_{i,j}$ be the set of paths successively connecting vertices at layer i to vertices at layer j; formally,

$$\mathcal{E}_{i,j} := \{((i, s_i, r_i), (i + 1, s_{i+1}, r_{i+1}), \dots, (j, s_j, r_j)) \mid$$
$$\text{for } i \leq k < j : ((k, s_k, r_k), (k + 1, s_{k+1}, r_{k+1})) \in \text{Edges}(G(P, I))\}.$$

We also define another set, $\mathcal{E}$, containing all paths with an edge between layer two and three; formally,

$$\mathcal{E} = \bigcup_{i \in \{1,2\}, j \in \{3,4\}} \mathcal{E}_{i,j}.$$

Now, we construct a *string function* S that assigns sequences of shares to paths in $\mathcal{E}$. Formally, for $\ell \in \mathcal{E}$, $\ell = (\dots, (2, s_2, r_2), (3, s_3, r_3), \dots)$, define $S(\ell)$ as the sequence of shares with the following properties:
- $S(\ell)_I :=$ Share$(s_2, r_2)_I$,

- $S(\ell)_P := \mathsf{Share}(s_2, r_2)_P = \mathsf{Share}(s_3, r_3)_P,$
- $S(\ell)_J := \mathsf{Share}(s_3, r_3)_J.$

Notice that the function S depends only on the edges between layer two and three, so any two paths in $\mathcal{E}$ sharing the same edge from layer two and three have the same image.

Now, for $i \in \{1, 2\}, j \in \{3, 4\}$, we define a *labeling relation* L as follows:

$$L : \mathcal{E} \longrightarrow \{I, J\}$$
$$\ell \longmapsto \begin{cases} I, & \text{if } \mathsf{Rec}(S(\ell)) \neq s_3, \\ J, & \text{if } \mathsf{Rec}(S(\ell)) \neq s_2 \end{cases}$$

Analogously to S, L depends only on the edges between layer two and three of a path. Also notice that L is not necessarily a function, as we do not exclude the existence of paths $\ell = (\dots, (2, s_2, r_2), (3, s_3, r_3), \dots)$ with $s_2 \neq \mathsf{Rec}(S(\ell)) \neq s_3$. Such paths would be labeled as both I and J.

Finally, we say that the graph G is *I-oriented* if there are at least as many edges in $\mathcal{E}_{2,3}$ labeled by I than J, i.e. if $|\{\ell \in \mathcal{E}_{2,3} \mid L(\ell) = I\}| \geq |\{\ell \in \mathcal{E}_{2,3} \mid L(\ell) = J\}|$.

Now that we introduced all the required tools and definitions, we are ready to begin our analysis.

Setup. Let λ be the minimal bit-length of any share of $(\mathsf{Share}, \mathsf{Rec})$. Without loss of generality, assume that P is a player associated with a share of $(\mathsf{Share}, \mathsf{Rec})$ of length λ.

Construction of an Adversary. (For an intuitive description, see Sect. 3.1.) Let Adv_A be the adversary who behaves as follows (during an execution of $\mathbf{Exp}_{(\mathsf{Share}, \mathsf{Rec})}(\mathcal{D}, \mathsf{Adv}_A)$):

1. Given the public information $(\mathsf{Share}, \mathsf{Rec})$, $\mathcal{D}$ in step E.1, sample $x \leftarrow \mathcal{U}_{\mathcal{M}}$, $r_x \leftarrow \mathcal{U}_{\mathcal{R}}$.
2. Compute $(v_1, \dots, v_n) \leftarrow \mathsf{Share}(x, r_x)$.
3. Sample a uniform set $I \subset \{1, \dots, n\} \setminus \{P\}$ with $|I| = t$.
4. Construct $G(P, I)$.
5. If $G(P, I)$ is I-oriented, output I at step E.2, and $(v_i)_{i \in I}$ at step E.4. Else, output J at step E.2, and $(v_j)_{j \in J}$ at step E.4.

Notice that Adv_A is a valid 0-local adversary, since all the computation Adv_A performs is independent of the values it is inputed at step E.3.

Representing Adversarial Success in the Graph. (For an intuitive description, see Sect. 3.1.) Assume that, if I is the set chosen by the adversary, the graph $G(P, I)$, induced by the given secret sharing scheme, is I-oriented. Let $z \in \mathcal{M}$, $r_z \leftarrow \mathcal{U}_{\mathcal{R}}$, let C be a sequence of shares defined as: for $i \in I$, $C_i = V_i = \mathsf{Share}(x, r_x)_i$; for $j \in J \cup \{P\}$, $C_j = \mathsf{Share}(z, r_z)_j$. Notice that C can be seen as a sharing of z corrupted at I by the above adversary, therefore, by the robustness property:

$$\Pr[\mathsf{Rec}(C) \neq z] \leq \delta = 2^{-k}, \tag{1}$$

where the probability is taken over uniform choices of $x, z \in \mathcal{M}$, $r_x, r_z \in \mathcal{R}$. Notice that if there exists (y, r_y) such that $\ell := ((1, x, r_x), (2, y, r_y), (3, z, r_z)) \in \mathcal{E}_{1,3}$ and $V(\ell) = I$ then $\mathsf{Rec}(C) \neq z$: in fact, if $\ell \in \mathcal{E}_{1,3}$, then $V(\ell) = I$ implies $\mathsf{Rec}(S(\ell)) \neq z$, by definition of V; and since $S(\ell) = C$ (by the following: $S(\ell)_I = \mathsf{Share}(y, r_y)_I = \mathsf{Share}(x, r_x)_I = C_I$, $S(\ell)_J = \mathsf{Share}(z, r_z)_J = C_J$ and $S(\ell)_P = \mathsf{Share}(y, r_y)_P = \mathsf{Share}(z, r_z)_P = C_P$) then $V(\ell) = I$ implies $\mathsf{Rec}(C) \neq z$. This means that

$$\Pr[\exists (y, r_y), \ell := ((1, x, r_x), (2, y, r_y), (3, z, r_z)) \in \mathcal{E}_{1,3}, V(\ell) = I]$$
$$\leq \Pr[\mathsf{Rec}(C) \neq z], \tag{2}$$

which implies

$$\Pr[\exists (y, r_y), \ell := ((1, x, r_x), (2, y, r_y), (3, z, r_z)) \in \mathcal{E}_{1,3}, V(\ell) = I] \leq 2^{-k}, \tag{3}$$

by combining Eqs. 1 and 2.

A More Refined Graph. (For an intuitive description, see Sect. 3.1.) In order to better analyze the left-hand side of Eq. 3, we introduce a subgraph $G'(P, I)$ of $G(P, I)$, defined by the following algorithm:

1. Initialize $G' \leftarrow G(P, I)$
2. For $a = (a_{i_1}, \ldots, a_{i_{t+1}}) \in \mathcal{S}_{I \cup \{P\}}$:
   (a) Define $H_a := \{(2, s, r) \in \mathsf{Vertices}(G) \mid \mathsf{Share}(s, r)_{I \cup \{P\}} = a\}$
   (b) Initialize $H'_a := H_a$
   (c) While there exist $(2, s, r), (2, s', r') \in H'_a$ such that $s \neq s'$:
       i. Update the graph G' by removing $(2, s, r)$ and $(2, s', r')$:
          – $\mathsf{Edges}(G') \leftarrow \mathsf{Edges}(G')_{|\mathsf{Vertices}(G') \setminus \{(2, s, r), (2, s', r')\}}$
          – $\mathsf{Vertices}(G') \leftarrow \mathsf{Vertices}(G') \setminus \{(2, s, r), (2, s', r')\}$
       ii. Update $H'_a \leftarrow \{(2, s, r) \in \mathsf{Vertices}(G') \mid \mathsf{Share}(s, r)_{I \cup \{P\}} = a\}$
3. Output $G'(P, I) \leftarrow G'$.

Notice that the vertices we are removing in this graph might exist, because we are allowing schemes where correctness is only statistical. In the following, we bound the number $V_R = |\mathsf{Vertices}(G(P, I)) \setminus \mathsf{Vertices}(G'(P, I))|$ of vertices removed from $G(P, I)$ by the above algorithm to obtain $G'(P, I)$. To do so, we relate V_R to $\Pr[\mathbf{Exp}_{(\mathsf{Share}, \mathsf{Rec})}(\mathcal{U}_{\mathcal{M}}, \mathsf{Adv}_B) = 1]$ where Adv_B is a specific adversary, defined as follows:

1. Let $b = (0_{j_1}, \ldots, 0_{j_t}) \in \mathcal{S}_J$
2. Output J at step E.2, b at step E.4.

Notice that Adv_B is a valid 0-local adversary, as b depends only on the public specifications $(\mathsf{Share}, \mathsf{Rec})$ of the scheme (and therefore it is independent of any value inputed to B at step E.3). Let

$$G_B := \{(s, r) \in \mathcal{M} \times \mathcal{R} \mid \mathsf{Rec}(\mathsf{Merge}(s, r, J, b)) \neq s\}$$

Notice that if any element (s, r) of G_B is sampled at step E.3 of $\mathbf{Exp}_{(\mathsf{Share},\mathsf{Rec})}(\mathcal{U}_{\mathcal{M}}, \mathsf{Adv}_B)$, then $\mathbf{Exp}_{(\mathsf{Share},\mathsf{Rec})}(\mathcal{U}_{\mathcal{M}}, \mathsf{Adv}_B)$ outputs 1, by definition of G_B. Notice also that the probability of sampling (s, r) in G_B at step E.3 is $|G_B|/|\mathcal{M} \times \mathcal{R}|$, as the experiment considers uniform messages (and randomness). Therefore, by the robustness of the scheme,

$$|G_B|/|\mathcal{M} \times \mathcal{R}| \leq 2^{-k} \tag{4}$$

Now, we want to relate G_B and V_R. Notice that any two vertices $(2, s, r)$, $(2, s', r')$, simultaneously removed in step 2(c)i, belong to the same set H_a for some a, which implies that

$$\mathsf{Share}(s, r)_{I \cup \{P\}} = a = \mathsf{Share}(s', r')_{I \cup \{P\}}, \tag{5}$$

by definition of H_a. Combining Eq. 5 with the fact that $\{1, \ldots, n\} \setminus J = I \cup \{P\}$, it follows that $\mathsf{Merge}(s, r, J, b) = S = \mathsf{Merge}(s', r', J, b)$. Now, let $s'' \leftarrow \mathsf{Rec}(S)$. Since $s \neq s'$ then at least one between s and s' differs from s'', which means that at least one between (s, r) and (s', r') lies in G_B. Therefore,

$$V_R \leq 2 \cdot |G_B| \tag{6}$$

In other words, at least half of the vertices $(2, s, r)$ removed in the construction of G' are such that to $(s, r) \in G_B$. Combining Eq. 6 with Eq. 4, we get

$$V_R \leq 2 \cdot 2^{-k} \cdot |\mathcal{M} \times \mathcal{R}| \tag{7}$$

General Facts About the Connectivity Between Layers. (For an intuitive description, see Sect. 3.1.) Now that we have a bound on the number of vertices removed from $G(P, I)$ to obtain $G'(P, I)$ we can proceed and study how some specific sets of vertices are connected between the layers of $G'(P, I)$. We are mostly interested in vertices on layer one and two. For any vertex $(2, s, r) \in \mathsf{Vertices}(G'(P, I))$, and for any secret $s' \in \mathcal{M}$, define

$$C_{s'}(2, s, r) := \{(1, s', r') \mid ((1, s', r'), (2, s, r)) \in \mathsf{Edges}(G'(P, I))\}$$

i.e. the set of vertices at layer one that represent secret s' and are connected to $(2, s, r)$. Notice that the set $\{C_{s'}(2, s, r)\}_{s' \in \mathcal{M}}$ is a partition of the set of vertices at layer one connected to $(2, s, r)$. We want to show that for any s', s'', $|C_{s'}(2, s, r)| = |C_{s''}(2, s, r)|$. For the sake of contradiction, assume this is not the case, so without loss of generality there exist $s' \neq s''$ such that $|C_{s'}(2, s, r)| > |C_{s''}(2, s, r)|$. By definition of $G'(P, I)$, this means that

$$|\{r' \in \mathcal{R} \mid \mathsf{Share}(s', r')_I = \mathsf{Share}(s, r)_I\}| > |\{r'' \in \mathcal{R} \mid \mathsf{Share}(s'', r'')_I$$
$$= \mathsf{Share}(s, r)_I\}|$$

which implies that

$$\text{Pr}[s' \mid \mathsf{Share}(s,r)_I] > \text{Pr}[s'' \mid \mathsf{Share}(s,r)_I]$$

and therefore violates the privacy of the scheme, as $\mathsf{Share}(s,r)_I$ would reveal that the secret is more likely to be s' than s'', but by privacy given any t shares the secret should look uniform. Therefore,

for any $s', s'' \in \mathcal{M}$, $(2, s, r) \in G'(P, I)$: $|C_{s'}(2, s, r)| = |C_{s''}(2, s, r)|$ (8)

This implies that any $(2, s, r) \in G'(P, I)$ is connected to $2^n \cdot |C_s(2, s, r)|$ vertices at layer one $(2^n \cdot |C_s(2, s, r)| = |\cup_{s' \in S} C_{s'}(2, s, r)|$, by the fact that $\{C_{s'}(2, s, r)\}_{s' \in \mathcal{M}}$ is a partition).

Particular Facts About the Connectivity Between Layers. (For an intuitive description, see Sect. 3.1.) Now, with a notation similar to the one in the construction of $G'(P, I)$, for $a \in \mathcal{S}_{I \cup \{P\}}$, let

$$H'_a := \{(2, s, r) \in \mathsf{Vertices}(G'(P, I)) \mid \mathsf{Share}(s, r)_{I \cup \{P\}} = a\}$$

Moreover, let

$$C'_a := \{(1, s, r) \in \mathsf{Vertices}(G'(P, I)) \mid \exists (2, s', r') \in H'_a : ((1, s, r), (2, s', r'))$$
$$\in \mathsf{Edges}(G'(P, I))\}$$

i.e. the set of vertices at layer one that are connected to H'_a. Notice that all vertices in H'_a represent the same secret: namely, if $(2, s, r), (2, s', r') \in H'_a$, then $s = s'$, by construction of $G'(P, I)$. Also, for any $(2, s, r) \in H'_a$, if $(2, s, r') \in H'_a$, then $((1, s, r'), (2, s, r)) \in \mathsf{Edges}(G'(P, I))$, again by construction of H'_a, and in particular from the fact that $\mathsf{Share}(s, r)_I = \mathsf{Share}(s, r')_I$. This implies that for any $(2, s, r) \in H'_a$, $|C_s(2, s, r)| \geq |H'_a|$. Using property 8, we get that any $(2, s, r) \in H'_a$ is connected to a set X of vertices at layer one of cardinality at least $2^m \cdot |H'_a|$. Since $|C'_a| \geq |X|$ (as $C'_a \supseteq X$), we get Therefore,

$$|C'_a| \geq 2^m \cdot |H'_a| \qquad (9)$$

Putting Things Together. (For an intuitive description, see Sect. 3.1.) We can now proceed and bound the left-hand side of Eq. 3 in terms of the size of $\mathcal{S}_P$. The following calculation starts with a probability space where (x, r_x) and (z, r_z) are independently and uniformly sampled form $\mathcal{M} \times \mathcal{R}$. We begin with some simple consequences of our definitions:

$$2^{-k} \geq \text{Pr}[\exists (y, r_y), \ell := ((1, x, r_x), (2, y, r_y), (3, z, r_z)) \in \mathcal{E}_{1,3}, V(\ell) = I]$$

$$= \sum_{a \in \mathcal{S}_{I \cup \{P\}}} \text{Pr} \begin{bmatrix} \exists (y, r_y), y \neq z, \mathsf{Share}(x, r_x)_I = a_I, \mathsf{Share}(y, r_y)_I = a_I, \\ \mathsf{Share}(y, r_y)_P = a_P, \mathsf{Share}(z, r_z)_P = a_P, V(\ell) = I \end{bmatrix}$$

(definition of $\mathcal{E}_{1,3}$)

$$= \sum_{a \in \mathcal{S}_{I \cup \{P\}}} \text{Pr} \begin{bmatrix} \mathsf{Share}(x, r_x)_I = a_I, \exists (2, y, r_y) \in \mathsf{Vertices}(G'(P, I)), y \neq z, \\ \mathsf{Share}(y, r_y)_{I \cup \{P\}} = a, \mathsf{Share}(z, r_z)_P = a_P, V(\ell) = I \end{bmatrix}$$

(Vertices$(G'(P, I)) \subseteq$ Vertices$(G(P, I))$)

Next we recall that the label of the ℓ can be determined without reference to (x, r_x). We will write $\ell_{2,3}$ as the edge connecting $(2, y, r_y)$ and $(3, z, r_z)$, and we note that $V(\ell) = V(\ell_{2,3})$. We note that the condition on x can now be written independently:

$$= \sum_{a \in \mathcal{S}_{I \cup \{P\}}} \Pr[(1, x, r_x) \in C_a'] \cdot \Pr \left[\begin{array}{l} \exists (2, y, r_y) \in \mathsf{Vertices}(G'(P, I)), \\ y \neq z, \mathsf{Share}(y, r_y)_{I \cup \{P\}} = a, \\ \mathsf{Share}(z, r_z)_P = a_P, V(\ell_{2,3}) = I \end{array} \right]$$
$$\text{(definition of } C_a')$$

$$= \sum_{a \in \mathcal{S}_{I \cup \{P\}}} \frac{|C_a'|}{|\mathcal{M} \times \mathcal{R}|} \cdot \Pr \left[\begin{array}{l} \exists (2, y, r_y) \in \mathsf{Vertices}(G'(P, I)), \\ y \neq z, \mathsf{Share}(y, r_y)_{I \cup \{P\}} = a, \\ \mathsf{Share}(z, r_z)_P = a_P, V(\ell_{2,3}) = I \end{array} \right]$$
$$\text{(unif. of } (x, r_x) \in \mathcal{M} \times \mathcal{R})$$

$$= \sum_{a \in \mathcal{S}_{I \cup \{P\}}} \frac{2^m \cdot |H_a'|}{|\mathcal{M} \times \mathcal{R}|} \cdot \Pr \left[\begin{array}{l} \exists (2, y, r_y) \in \mathsf{Vertices}(G'(P, I)), \\ y \neq z, \mathsf{Share}(y, r_y)_{I \cup \{P\}} = a, \\ \mathsf{Share}(z, r_z)_P = a_P, V(\ell_{2,3}) = I \end{array} \right] \quad \text{(Eq. 9)}$$

Now in order to express this in a more convenient form and then replace the existence condition on y with something easier to manipulate, we introduce a fresh random variable (Y, r_Y) sampled independently and uniformly from $\mathcal{M} \times \mathcal{R}$:

$$= 2^m \cdot \sum_{a \in \mathcal{S}_{I \cup \{P\}}} \Pr[(2, Y, r_Y) \in H_a'] \cdot \Pr \left[\begin{array}{l} \exists (2, y, r_y) \in \mathsf{Vertices}(G'(P, I)), \\ y \neq z, \mathsf{Share}(y, r_y)_{I \cup \{P\}} = a, \\ \mathsf{Share}(z, r_z)_P = a_P, V(\ell_{2,3}) = I \end{array} \right]$$
$$\text{(unif. of } (Y, r_Y) \in \mathcal{M} \times \mathcal{R})$$

$$\geq 2^m \cdot \sum_{a \in \mathcal{S}_{I \cup \{P\}}} \Pr \left[\begin{array}{l} (2, Y, r_Y) \in H_a', Y \neq z, \\ (2, Y, r_Y) \notin V_R, \mathsf{Share}(z, r_z)_P = a_P, V(\ell_{2,3}) = I \end{array} \right]$$

In this last expression, $\ell_{2,3}$ now denotes the edge between $(2, Y, r_Y)$ and $(3, z, r_z)$. Our labeling condition now applied to an edge between two uniformly sampled vertices at layer 2 and layer 3, hence we can directly apply our knowledge that the graph is I-oriented to conclude:

$$\geq \frac{2^m}{2} \cdot \sum_{a \in \mathcal{S}_{I \cup \{P\}}} \Pr \left[\begin{array}{l} (2, Y, r_Y) \in H_a', Y \neq z, \\ (2, Y, r_Y) \notin V_R, \mathsf{Share}(z, r_z)_P = a_P \end{array} \right]$$

We next observe that the events $Y \neq z$ and $\mathsf{Share}(z, r_z)_P = a_P$ are independent, by privacy. This allows us to proceed as:

$$\geq (1 - 2^{-m}) \cdot \frac{2^m}{2} \cdot \sum_{a \in \mathcal{S}_{I \cup \{P\}}} \Pr \begin{bmatrix} (2, Y, r_Y) \in H'_a, \\ (2, Y, r_Y) \notin V_R \end{bmatrix} \cdot \Pr[\mathsf{Share}(z, r_z)_P = a_P]$$

$$\text{(independence)}$$

$$= (1 - 2^{-m}) \cdot \frac{2^m}{2} \cdot \sum_{a \in \mathcal{S}_{I \cup \{P\}}} \Pr \begin{bmatrix} \mathsf{Share}(Y, r_Y)_I = a_I, \\ \mathsf{Share}(Y, r_Y)_P = a_P, \\ (2, Y, r_Y) \notin V_R \end{bmatrix} \cdot \Pr[\mathsf{Share}(z, r_z)_P = a_P]$$

$$\text{(definition of } H'_a)$$

We will next apply a union bound to remove the condition $(2, Y, r_Y) \notin V_R$, and then use our prior bound on the size of V_R:

$$\geq -\frac{|V_R|}{|\mathcal{M} \times \mathcal{R}|} + (1 - 2^{-m}) \cdot \frac{2^m}{2} \cdot$$
$$\cdot \sum_{a \in \mathcal{S}_{I \cup \{P\}}} \Pr \begin{bmatrix} \mathsf{Share}(Y, r_Y)_I = a_I, \\ \mathsf{Share}(Y, r_Y)_P = a_P \end{bmatrix} \cdot \Pr[\mathsf{Share}(z, r_z)_P = a_P]$$

$$\text{(union bound)}$$

$$\geq -2^{-k+1} + \frac{2^m}{2} \cdot$$
$$\cdot \sum_{a \in \mathcal{S}_{I \cup \{P\}}} \Pr \begin{bmatrix} \mathsf{Share}(Y, r_Y)_I = a_I, \\ \mathsf{Share}(Y, r_Y)_P = a_P \end{bmatrix} \cdot \Pr[\mathsf{Share}(z, r_z)_P = a_P] \quad \text{(Eq. 7)}$$

Next we reorganize our sum by looking at each a_P value and summing over all the values of a_I:

$$= -2^{-k+1} + \frac{2^m}{2} \cdot \sum_{a \in \mathcal{S}_P} \Pr[\mathsf{Share}(Y, r_Y)_P = a_P] \cdot \Pr[\mathsf{Share}(z, r_z)_P = a_P]$$

The remainder of the calculation is an application of the Cauchy-Schwarz inequality after exploiting the fact that (Y, r_Y) and (z, r_z) are identically distributed and now subject to the same condition:

$$= -2^{-k+1} + \frac{2^m}{2} \cdot \sum_{a \in \mathcal{S}_P} \Pr[\mathsf{Share}(Y, r_Y)_P = a_P]^2$$

$$\text{(identical random variables)}$$

$$= -2^{-k+1} + \frac{2^m}{2} \cdot \frac{1}{|\mathcal{S}_P|} \cdot \sum_{a \in \mathcal{S}_P} \Pr[\mathsf{Share}(Y, r_Y)_P = a_P]^2 \sum_{a \in \mathcal{S}_P} 1^2$$

$$\geq -2^{-k+1} + \frac{2^m}{2} \cdot \frac{1}{|\mathcal{S}_P|} \cdot \left(\sum_{a \in \mathcal{S}_{\{P\}}} \Pr[\mathsf{Share}(Y, r_Y)_P = a_P] \cdot 1 \right)^2$$

(Cauchy-Schwarz inequality)

$$= -2^{-k+1} + \frac{2^m}{2} \cdot \frac{1}{2^\lambda}$$

(definition of λ)

$$= 2^{m-\lambda-1} - 2^{-k+1}$$

Therefore, we must have

$$2^{m-\lambda-1} - 2^{-k+1} \leq 2^{-k},$$

which implies that

$$\lambda \geq m + k - (1 + \log_2(3)).$$

4 An Efficient Scheme

The main idea behind our efficient scheme is similar to many other robust secret sharing schemes in the standard model: in order to achieve robustness we use Shamir's secret sharing scheme and expand each share with some authentication data so that any adversary who submits a corrupt share cannot provide authentication data that matches it. Differently from previous work, however, we have more freedom in what authentication data we can add, since each corrupt share depends only on a single share sent by the dealer, instead of depending on all the shares assigned to the adversary. We use this property and embed the same MAC key into each share and add a tag to the share in such a way that the key is not recoverable by individual corrupt players, while it is recoverable by the reconstructor, who will then check the authenticity of each share.

More precisely, we will use our locally hiding transform developed in Appendix A to distribute a MAC key among the parties so that it cannot be learned by a local adversary but can be reliably extracted from a number of honest shares. Recovery of the key and authentication in the reconstruction procedure will be performed by iterating over constant subsets of shares, extracting a candidate key value, and then attempting to authenticate at least $t + 1$ shares. Since the local adversary cannot learn the real MAC key (during the execution of the protocol), we will prove that is it unlikely that a corrupted share will authenticate properly under the correct key. Similarly, we will prove it is unlikely for an incorrect candidate key to authenticate at least $t + 1$ shares. The error-correcting code in our locally hiding transform will ensure that when we attempt to extract a key from a subset of honest shares, we produce the correct key with very high probability. Putting this all together, we can argue that the correct key will be recovered and the correct secret will be reconstructed.

Remark 2. After the completion of this work, Daniel Wichs discovered a simplification of our construction, achieving similar parameters. Intuitively, to share a message s, the dealer does the following:

1. create Shamir secret shares s_i of s using a polynomial of degree t
2. choose a one-time MAC key z and compute a tag $t_i \leftarrow \mathsf{MAC}(z, s_i)$ on s_i via z
3. create Shamir secret shares z_i of z using a polynomial of degree 1
4. send (s_i, t_i, z_i) to P_i.

The reconstruction procedure recovers the correct key z from the z_i (this can be done via Reed-Solomon decoding and is correct against t corruption), checks it against each tag t_i and recovers the secret s from the shares s_i for which the check passes.

The key is unknown to the adversaries during the protocol, because they are local and the key is secret shared via a 1-private secret sharing. This means that the adversaries have no chance to forge their MACs during the protocol. Therefore, they cannot change their shares and make the test on the tags pass at the same time. Notice that *after* the protocol the adversaries can collude and reconstruct the key z, but at this point it is of no use for them, since the reconstructor already retrieved the correct secret s.

We feel that both constructions are of independent interest.

4.1 Construction

In the following, we use the MAC defined in Appendix B and the locally hiding transform defined in Appendix A. We let g denote the tag length of our MAC (the bit-length of its keys is then $h = 2 \cdot g$), and we define an additional parameter $d := m/g$, where m is the bit-length of messages. The security parameter for the MAC is $\varepsilon = d \cdot 2^{-g}$.

We give an explicit construction of our secret sharing scheme in Figs. 1 and 2.

The procedure Share:

Local computation: In the notation of Shamir secret sharing scheme, for $i = 1, \ldots, n$ let x_i be the evaluation point associated with P_i. On input $s \in \mathcal{M}$, the dealer does the following:

1. Choose a uniform polynomial $f \in \mathcal{M}[X]$ of degree t such that $f(0) = s$. Compute Shamir shares $s_1 = f(x_1), \ldots, s_n = f(x_n)$.
2. Choose a uniform MAC key $z = (a, b) \in \mathcal{K}$.
3. Define $M \in (\mathbb{F}_2)^{n \times c}$ as $M = \widehat{C}(z)$. (See Appendix A.3 for the definition of $\widehat{C}$)
4. For $i = 1, \ldots, t$, define $t_i = \mathsf{MAC}(z, s_i)$.

Share Distribution: For $i = 1, \ldots, n$, the dealer sends (M_i, s_i, t_i) to P_i.

Fig. 1. The sharing procedure Share.

The procedure Rec:

Communication: Every player P_i sends (M_i, s_i, t_i) to the reconstructor.
Default Check: For $y \in \{s_1, \ldots, s_n\}$ define I_y as $I_y = \{i \in \{1, \ldots, n\} \mid s_i = y\}$.
  Then:
  D1. If there exists y such that $|I_y| > t$, abort.
  D2. If there exists y such that $|I_y| = t$, define $G = \{1, \ldots, n\} \setminus I_y$, use Shamir
      reconstruction on $(s_i)_{i \in G}$ to obtain s and finish.
  D3. Else, proceed with the local computation.
Local computation: The reconstructor does the following, for each set $R \subseteq$
  $\{1, \ldots, n\}$ with $|R| = \alpha$:
  L1. Evaluate $\widehat{D}_R(M_R)$ to obtain $z = (a, b)$. (See Appendix A.3 for the definition
      of $\widehat{D}$)
  L2. Define $G_R = \{i \in \{1, \ldots, n\} \mid t_i = \mathsf{MAC}(z, s_i)\}$.
  L3. If $|G_R| \geq t + 1$, use Shamir reconstruction on $(s_i)_{i \in G_R}$ to obtain s and
      finish.

Fig. 2. The reconstruction procedure Rec.

Theorem 2. *For $n = 2 \cdot t + 1$, the scheme (Share, Rec) given in Figs. 1 and 2 is (t, δ)-robust against 1-local adversaries, where*

$$\delta = 2 \cdot (t+1) \cdot t/|\mathcal{M}| + \binom{n}{\alpha} \cdot (4 \cdot d \cdot \varepsilon + 5/|\mathcal{M}|) + e^{-\frac{c\beta^2}{3 \cdot 2^{\alpha-1}}}$$

The proof of Theorem 2 can be found in the full version of this work [19].

Corollary 1. *Given an error-correcting code C with block length $c = \Theta(g)$ and constant relative distance γ and $m = \Omega(g)$, there exists positive constants σ_1, σ_2 such that our construction in Figs. 1 and 2 is δ-robust for $\delta \leq 2^{-k}$ and share size is*

$$m + c + g = m + c + k \cdot \sigma_1^{-1} + \sigma_2 \cdot \sigma_1^{-1} \cdot (\log(n) + \log(d)) = m + O(k).$$

The proof of Corollary 1 can be found in the full version of this work [19].

Remark 3. Note that the restriction that $m = \Omega(g)$ can be removed, if one simply shares the shorter secrets in $\mathcal{M}$ with Shamir shares over a field of bit length g. In this case, the share size becomes $g + c + g = m + c + O(g)$ instead of precisely $m + c + g$.

A   New Tools for Scheme Construction

In this section, we develop some general tools that will be used in our efficient scheme construction. First, we will define a simple "locally hiding function" that generates two distributions $\mathcal{D}_0$ and $\mathcal{D}_1$. While any single bit of the output is distributed identically in $\mathcal{D}_0$ and $\mathcal{D}_1$, the joint distribution of a relatively small number of bits is sufficient to distinguish $\mathcal{D}_0$ from $\mathcal{D}_1$ with high probability.

A.1   Locally Hiding Function

Definition 8 (Locally Hiding Function). *Let* $\mathcal{D}_0 = \mathcal{U}_{\mathbb{F}_2^n}$ *be the uniform distribution over* $\mathbb{F}_2^n$, *and let* $\mathcal{D}_1 = \mathcal{U}_X$ *be the uniform distribution over* $X = \{0^n, 1^n\} \subseteq \mathbb{F}_2^n$. *The* n-*locally hiding function is a randomized function* $\eta : \mathbb{F}_2 \to \mathbb{F}_2^n$ *defined as:*

$$\eta : \mathbb{F}_2 \longrightarrow \mathbb{F}_2^n$$
$$v \longmapsto \mathcal{D}_v.$$

Lemma 2 (Properties). *The* n-*locally hiding function has the following properties:*

Local Hiding: *For any distribution* $\mathcal{D}$ *over* $\mathbb{F}_2$, *for any* $v \in \mathbb{F}_2$, *for any* $i \in \{1, \ldots, n\}$, *and for any* $w_i \in \mathbb{F}_2$, *if* $B \sim \mathcal{D}$,

$$\Pr[B = v] = \Pr[B = v \mid \eta(B)_i = w_i].$$

Local Almost Invertibility: *For any* $I \subseteq \{1, \ldots, n\}$, $|I| = \alpha$, *the function* $\iota_I : \mathbb{F}_2^\alpha \to \mathbb{F}_2$

$$\iota_I : \mathbb{F}_2^\alpha \longrightarrow \mathbb{F}_2$$
$$u \longmapsto \begin{cases} 1 \ \textit{if } u \in \{0^\alpha, 1^\alpha\} \\ 0 \ \textit{otherwise} \end{cases}$$

fails to invert η *with probability less or equal to* $2^{-\alpha+1}$. *More formally, for any* $v \in \mathbb{F}_2$,

$$\Pr[\iota_I(\eta(v)_I) \neq v] \leq 2^{-\alpha+1}.$$

Proof. To prove local hiding, notice that for any $i \in \{1, \ldots, n\}$

$$\eta(0)_i = \left(\mathcal{U}_{\mathbb{F}_2^n}\right)_i = \mathcal{U}_{\mathbb{F}_2} = \left(\mathcal{U}_{\{0^n, 1^n\}}\right)_i = \eta(1)_i,$$

which means that for any distribution $\mathcal{D}$ and $B \sim \mathcal{D}$, $\eta(B)_i$ is a uniform bit, independent of B. Therefore, for any $v, w_i \in \mathbb{F}_2$, we have $\Pr[B = v] = \Pr[B = v \mid \eta(B)_i = w_i]$.

To prove local almost invertibility, simple manipulation leads to the result:

$$
\begin{aligned}
\Pr[\iota_I(\eta(v)_I) \neq v] &= \Pr[\iota_I(\eta(v)_I) \neq v, v = 0] + \Pr[\iota_I(\eta(v)_I) \neq v, v = 1] \\
&\leq \Pr[\iota_I(\eta(0)_I) = 1] + \Pr[\iota_I(\eta(1)_I) = 0] \\
&\leq \Pr[\iota_I((\mathcal{U}_{\mathbb{F}_2^n})_I) = 1] + \Pr[\iota_I((\mathcal{U}_{\{0^n, 1^n\}})_I) = 0] \\
&\leq \Pr[S \in \{0^\alpha, 1^\alpha\} \mid S \sim (\mathcal{U}_{\mathbb{F}_2^n})_I] + \Pr[S \notin \{0^\alpha, 1^\alpha\} \mid S \sim (\mathcal{U}_{\{0^n, 1^n\}})_I]\} \\
&\leq \Pr[S \in \{0^\alpha, 1^\alpha\} \mid S \sim \mathcal{U}_{\mathbb{F}_2^\alpha}] + \Pr[S \notin \{0^\alpha, 1^\alpha\} \mid S \sim \mathcal{U}_{\{0^\alpha, 1^\alpha\}}] \\
&\leq 2 \cdot 2^{-\alpha} = 2^{-\alpha+1}.
\end{aligned}
$$

A.2   Extended Locally Hiding Function

Definition 9 (Extended Locally Hiding Function). *Let η be the n-locally hiding function. For any vector space $\mathbb{F}_2^c$, the extended n-locally hiding function is the coordinate-wise extension of η, as follows:*

$$\eta^c : \mathbb{F}_2^c \xrightarrow{\hspace{4cm}} \mathbb{F}_2^{n\times c}$$
$$v = (v_1, \ldots, v_c) \longmapsto (\eta(v_1), \ldots, \eta(v_c)).$$

Notice that the local hiding and invertibility properties are carried over as follows:

Lemma 3 (Properties). *The extended n-locally hiding function has the following properties:*

Local Hiding: *For any distribution $\mathcal{D}$ over $\mathbb{F}_2^c$, for any $v \in \mathbb{F}_2^c$, for any $i \in \{1, \ldots, n\}$, and for any $w_i \in \mathbb{F}_2^c$, if $B \sim \mathcal{D}$,*

$$\Pr[B = v] = \Pr[B = v \mid \eta^c(B)_i = w_i].$$

Local Almost Invertibility: *For any $I \subseteq \{1, \ldots, n\}$, $|I| = \alpha$, the function $\iota_I^c : \mathbb{F}_2^{\alpha\times c} \to \mathbb{F}_2^c$*

$$\iota_I^c : \mathbb{F}_2^{\alpha\times c} \xrightarrow{\hspace{4cm}} \mathbb{F}_2^c$$
$$u = (u_1, \ldots, u_c)^T \longmapsto (\iota_I(u_1), \ldots, \iota_I(u_c))$$

maps $u = \eta^c(v)$ "close to" v. More formally, for any $v \in \mathbb{F}_2^c$, $0 < \beta \le 1$:

$$\Pr[w(v - \iota_I^c(\eta^c(v)_I)) \ge (1+\beta) \cdot c2^{-\alpha+1}] \le e^{-\frac{c\beta^2}{3 \cdot 2^{\alpha-1}}}.$$

Proof. Similarly to the argument above, for all $v \in \mathbb{F}_2^c$, for all $i \in \{1, \ldots, n\}$:

$$\eta^c(v)_i = (\eta(v_1), \ldots, \eta(v_c))_i = (\eta(v_1)_i, \ldots, \eta(v_c)_i) = (\mathcal{U}_{\mathbb{F}_2}, \ldots, \mathcal{U}_{\mathbb{F}_2}) = \mathcal{U}_{\mathbb{F}_2}^c$$

which means that for any distribution $\mathcal{D}$ and $B \sim \mathcal{D}$, $\eta(B)_i$ is a uniform string of length c, independent of B. Therefore, for any $v, w_i \in \mathbb{F}_2^c$, we have $\Pr[B = v] = \Pr[B = v \mid \eta(B)_i = w_i]$.

To prove local almost invertibility, firstly for $i = 1, \ldots, c$ define the following (Bernoulli) random variable:

$$x_i := \begin{cases} 1 \text{ if } v_i - \iota_I(\eta(v_i)_I) \ne 0 \\ 0 \text{ otherwise} \end{cases}$$

By the local almost invertibility property of the (standard) locally hiding function, we have

$$\Pr[x_i = 1] \le 2^{-\alpha+1}$$

and applying the Chernoff bound in Lemma 1 on the x_i, for any $0 < \beta \leq 1 - 2^{-\alpha+1}$ we get

$$\Pr\left[\sum_{i=1}^{c} x_i \geq (1+\beta) \cdot c2^{-\alpha+1}\right] \leq e^{-\frac{c\beta^2}{3 \cdot 2^{\alpha-1}}}. \tag{10}$$

To conclude, notice that

$$(v - \iota_I^c(\eta^c(v)_I))_i = v_i - \iota_I^c(\eta^c(v)_I)_i = v_i - \iota_I(\eta(v_i)_I)$$

therefore $w(v - \iota_I^c(\eta^c(v)_I)) = \sum_{i=1}^{c} x_i$, by definition of x_i and Hamming weight. Combining this with Eq. 10, we get

$$\Pr\left[w(v - \iota_I^c(\eta^c(v)_I)) \geq (1+\beta) \cdot c2^{-\alpha+1}\right] \leq e^{-\frac{c\beta^2}{3 \cdot 2^{\alpha-1}}}.$$

A.3   Locally Hiding Transform

To use our locally hiding function inside an efficient robust secret sharing scheme, we would like it to be more resilient to inversion errors when we invert using a relatively small set of bits. This leads us to define the combined primitive of a locally hiding transform, a concatenation of an error-correcting code and our locally hiding function.

Definition 10 (Locally Hiding Transform). *Let* $C : \mathbb{F}_2^h \to \mathbb{F}_2^c$ *be a block (error-correcting) code over alphabet* $\mathbb{F}_2$, *with message length* h, *block length* c *and relative distance* γ. *Its* locally hiding transform *is a randomized function* $\widehat{C} : \mathbb{F}_2^h \to \mathbb{F}_2^{n \times c}$, *defined as* $\widehat{C} = \eta^c \circ C$:

$$
\begin{array}{ccccc}
 & & \overset{\widehat{C}}{\frown} & & \\
\mathbb{F}_2^h & \xrightarrow{\ C\ } & \mathbb{F}_2^c & \xrightarrow{\ \eta^c\ } & \mathbb{F}_2^{n \times c} \\
z = (z_1, \ldots, z_h) & \longmapsto & C(z) = (v_1, \ldots, v_c) & \longmapsto & (\eta(v_1), \ldots, \eta(v_c)).
\end{array}
$$

Moreover, for any $I \subseteq \{1, \ldots, n\}$ *with* $|I| = \alpha$, *define* $\widehat{D}_I = D \circ \iota_I$ *(where D is the decoding function for C):*

$$
\begin{array}{ccccc}
 & & \overset{\widehat{D}_I}{\frown} & & \\
\mathbb{F}_2^{\alpha \times c} & \xrightarrow{\ \iota_I^c\ } & \mathbb{F}_2^c & \xrightarrow{\ D\ } & \mathbb{F}_2^h \\
u = (u_1, \ldots, u_c)^T & \longmapsto & (\iota_I(u_1), \ldots, \iota_I(u_c)) = v & \longmapsto & D(v).
\end{array}
$$

Notice that the local hiding property of η^c is trivially translated to $\widehat{C}$. For local invertibility, if $\gamma > 2 \cdot (1+\beta)2^{-\alpha+1}$, then $\widehat{D}$ is locally inverts $\widehat{C}$ with error probability less or equal to $e^{-\frac{c\beta^2}{3 \cdot 2^{\alpha-1}}}$.

B   A Suitable MAC for Our Scheme

B.1   The MAC and Some of Its Algebraic Properties

Definition 11. *In the following, we assume that $h = 2 \cdot g$, $m = d \cdot g$, and use the following MAC, for $\mathcal{M} \subseteq \mathbb{F}_{2^m} \cong (\mathbb{F}_{2^g})^d$ (note that any set $\mathcal{M}$ can be thought of as a subset of $\mathbb{F}_{2^m}$, for large enough m), $\mathcal{K} = (\mathbb{F}_{2^g})^2$, and $\mathcal{T} = \mathbb{F}_{2^g}$:*

$$\mathrm{MAC} : (\mathbb{F}_{2^g})^2 \times (\mathbb{F}_{2^g})^d \longrightarrow \mathbb{F}_{2^g}$$

$$(a, b), (m_1, \ldots, m_d) \longmapsto \sum_{l=1}^{d} a^l \cdot m_l + b.$$

It is well known that the MAC described in Definition 11 is ε-secure for $\varepsilon = d \cdot 2^{-g}$, [12,16,25].

Lemma 4. *The MAC described in Definition 11 has the following properties:*

– *For any $m \in \mathcal{M}$ and $t \in \mathcal{T}$, there are at most 2^g different keys $z \in \mathcal{K}$ such that $\mathrm{MAC}(z, m) = t$.*
– *For $m_0, m_1 \in \mathcal{M}$, $m_0 \neq m_1$, and $t_0, t_1 \in \mathcal{T}$, there are at most d different keys $z \in \mathcal{K}$ such that $\mathrm{MAC}(z, m_0) = t_0$, $\mathrm{MAC}(z, m_1) = t_1$.*

Proof. For the first property, fix an arbitrary $m \in \mathcal{M}$ and $t \in \mathcal{T}$. Let define the set $K_{m,t} := \{z \in \mathcal{K} \mid \mathrm{MAC}(z, m) = t\}$ of keys that produce t as a tag of m. We want to study $|K_{m,t}|$. Using Definition 11, we have

$$K_{m,t} = \left\{ (a, b) \in \mathbb{F}_{2^g}^2 \mid \sum_{l=1}^{d} a^l \cdot m_l + b = t \right\}$$

This means that if $(a, b) \in K_{m,t}$, then $b = t - \sum_{l=1}^{d} a^l \cdot m_l$. Therefore,

$$K_{m,t} = \left\{ \left(a, t - \sum_{l=1}^{d} a^l \cdot m_l \right) \in \mathbb{F}_{2^g}^2 \right\}$$

Since the function $a \mapsto (a, t - \sum_{l=1}^{d} a^l \cdot m_l)$ is a bijection from $\mathbb{F}_{2^g}$ to $K_{m,t}$ (with inverse $(a, b) \mapsto a$), we have $|K_{m,t}| = |\mathbb{F}_{2^g}| = 2^g$.

For the second property, let $m_0, m_1 \in \mathcal{M}$, $m_0 \neq m_1$, and $t_0, t_1 \in \mathcal{T}$. We want to study the cardinality of the following set X

$$X := \{z \in \mathcal{K} \mid \mathrm{MAC}(z, m_0) = t_0, \mathrm{MAC}(z, m_1) = t_1\}$$

Again, using Definition 11,

$$X = \left\{ (a, b) \in \mathbb{F}_{2^g}^2 \mid \sum_{l=1}^{d} a^l \cdot m_{0,l} + b = t_0, \sum_{l=1}^{d} a^l \cdot m_{1,l} + b = t_1 \right\}$$

We can rewrite the above set as follows:

$$X = \left\{ \left(a, t_0 - \sum_{l=1}^{d} a^l \cdot m_{0,l} \right) \in \mathbb{F}_{2^g}^2 \mid \sum_{l=1}^{d} a^l \cdot (m_{0,l} - m_{1,l}) - t_0 + t_1 = 0 \right\} \quad (11)$$

Since $m_0 \neq m_1$, the polynomial $x \mapsto \sum_{l=1}^{d} x^l \cdot (m_{0,l} - m_{1,l}) - t_0 + t_1$ is a non-zero polynomial over $\mathbb{F}_{2^g}$ of degree at most d, which therefore has at most d roots. Since a is one of those roots, a can take only d values. From this, and the fact that for any $(a, b) \in X$ a completely defines b (by Eq. 11), we get that there are at most d pairs $(a, b) \in X$.

B.2 Behavior Towards Local Adversaries

We now prove another important property of the above MAC that will be useful for our construction of a robust secret sharing scheme. Intuitively, we want to study the probability that an honest message/tag pair is authenticated by any key that validates two distinct message/tag pairs, each of them chosen by a local adversary after seeing an honest message/tag pair. We also require that at least one between the two adversarially chosen pairs is not honest, otherwise the success probability of the adversaries would be trivially 1. To formalize this notion, we define the following game played between a challenger (who provides the honest message/tag pairs to the adversaries) and two, unbounded but non-communicating adversaries (whose target is to provide new message/tag pairs).

Game A:
1. The challenger samples uniform messages $m_0, m_1 \neq m_2 \in \mathcal{M}$.
2. The challenger samples a uniform key $z \in \mathcal{K}$.
3. For $i = 0, 1, 2$, the challenger computes $t_i = \mathsf{MAC}(z, m_i)$.
4. For $i = 1, 2$, the challenger sends m_i, t_i to adversary i.
5. For $i = 1, 2$, adversary i generates $\tilde{m}_i, \tilde{t}_i$ and sends them to the challenger.
6. The challenger checks and whether $\tilde{m}_2 \neq \tilde{m}_1 \neq m_1$ and whether there exists $\tilde{z}$ such that

$$t_0 = \mathsf{MAC}(\tilde{z}, m_0), \qquad \tilde{t}_1 = \mathsf{MAC}(\tilde{z}, \tilde{m}_1), \qquad \tilde{t}_2 = \mathsf{MAC}(\tilde{z}, \tilde{m}_2).$$

If so, the challenger sets $W = 1$; otherwise, it sets $W = 0$.

Lemma 5. *In the notation of* **Game A**,

$$\Pr[W = 1] \leq 2 \cdot d \cdot \varepsilon.$$

Proof. In order to analyze $\Pr[W = 1]$, we define another game which is equivalent to **Game A** – equivalent in the sense that the distribution of the random variables that are involved remains the same. First, since in **Game A** the value m_0, t_0 are never revealed to any adversary, they might as well be generated after the challenger receives $\tilde{m}_1, \tilde{t}_1$ from adversary 1 and $\tilde{m}_2, \tilde{t}_2$ from adversary 2. Therefore, **Game A** is equivalent to the following game

Game A1:

1. The challenger samples uniform messages $m_1 \neq m_2 \in \mathcal{M}$.
2. The challenger samples a uniform key $z \in \mathcal{K}$.
3. For $i = 1, 2$, the challenger computes $t_i = \mathsf{MAC}(z, m_i)$.
4. For $i = 1, 2$, the challenger sends m_i, t_i to adversary i.
5. For $i = 1, 2$, adversary i generates $\tilde{m}_i, \tilde{t}_i$ and sends them to the challenger.
6. The challenger samples a uniform $m_0 \in \mathcal{M}$ and computes $t_0 = \mathsf{MAC}(z, m_0)$.
7. The challenger checks whether $\tilde{m}_2 \neq \tilde{m}_1 \neq m_1$ and whether ther exists $\tilde{z}$ such that

$$t_0 = \mathsf{MAC}(\tilde{z}, m_0), \qquad \tilde{t}_1 = \mathsf{MAC}(\tilde{z}, \tilde{m}_1), \qquad \tilde{t}_2 = \mathsf{MAC}(\tilde{z}, \tilde{m}_2).$$

If so, the challenger sets $W = 1$; otherwise, it sets $W = 0$.

We are ready to analyze $\Pr[W = 1]$ in **Game A1**. First, define $\tilde{Z} \subseteq \mathcal{K}$ as the set of keys compatible with $\tilde{m}_1, \tilde{t}_1$ and $\tilde{m}_2, \tilde{t}_2$, i.e.

$$\tilde{Z} = \{\tilde{z} \in \mathcal{K} \mid \tilde{t}_1 = \mathsf{MAC}(\tilde{z}, \tilde{m}_1), \tilde{t}_2 = \mathsf{MAC}(\tilde{z}, \tilde{m}_2)\}.$$

We can rewrite $\Pr[W = 1]$ as follows:

$$\Pr[W = 1] = \Pr_{(z, m_0)}[\tilde{m}_2 \neq \tilde{m}_1 \neq m_1, \exists \tilde{z} \in \tilde{Z} : t_0 = \mathsf{MAC}(\tilde{z}, m_0)]$$

$$\leq \sum_{\tilde{z} \in \tilde{Z}} \Pr_{(z, m_0)}[\tilde{m}_2 \neq \tilde{m}_1 \neq m_1, t_0 = \mathsf{MAC}(\tilde{z}, m_0)]. \qquad (12)$$

Making the requirement $t_0 = \mathsf{MAC}(\tilde{z}, m_0)$ explicit, we obtain:

$$t_0 = \sum_{l=1}^{d} \tilde{a}^l \cdot m_{0,l} + \tilde{b}. \qquad (13)$$

Now, remember that m_0 is uniform, and t_0 is computed as follows, for $z = (a, b)$ sampled according to step 2:

$$t_0 = \sum_{l=1}^{d} a^l \cdot m_{0,l} + b. \qquad (14)$$

Subtracting Eq. 14 from Eq. 13, we get that any key $(\tilde{a}, \tilde{b})$ should satisfy

$$\sum_{l=1}^{d} \left(\tilde{a}^l - a^l\right) \cdot m_{0,l} + \tilde{b} - b = \left\langle \left(1, m_{0,1}, \ldots, m_{0,d}\right), \left(\tilde{b} - b, \tilde{a}^1 - a^1, \ldots, \tilde{a}^d - a^d\right)\right\rangle = 0. \qquad (15)$$

In Eq. 15, if $\tilde{a} = a$, then $\tilde{b} = b$. This means that $\tilde{m}_1, \tilde{t}_1$ is a valid message/tag pair for key (a, b), as it is valid for $(\tilde{a}, \tilde{b})$, since $(\tilde{a}, \tilde{b}) = (a, b)$. Since the MAC is ε-secure, and the adversaries are local (in particular adversary 1 only sees m_1, t_1 and provides $\tilde{m}_1, \tilde{t}_1$ with $m_1 \neq \tilde{m}_1$), then $\tilde{m}_1, \tilde{t}_1$ is a forgery for (a, b) –

since (a, b) is a uniform key, valid for both m_1, t_1 and $\widetilde{m}_1, \widetilde{t}_1$, with $\widetilde{m}_1 \neq m_1$. Therefore, for any $(\widetilde{a}, \widetilde{b}) = \widetilde{z} \in \widetilde{Z}$:

$$\Pr{}_{(z,m_0)}[\widetilde{m}_2 \neq \widetilde{m}_1 \neq m_1, t_0 = \mathsf{MAC}(\widetilde{z}, m_0), \widetilde{a} = a] \leq \varepsilon. \tag{16}$$

Now, If $\widetilde{a} \neq a$, then the vector $v = (\widetilde{b} - b, \widetilde{a}^1 - a^1, \ldots, \widetilde{a}^d - a^d) \in \mathbb{F}_2^{d+1}$ is non-zero, and Eq. 15 holds if and only if v is orthogonal to a uniformly chosen direction $u = (1, m_{0,1}, \ldots, m_{0,d})$, which happens with probability 2^{-g} for any non-zero v. Therefore,

$$\Pr{}_{(z,m_0)}[\widetilde{m}_2 \neq \widetilde{m}_1 \neq m_1, t_0 = \mathsf{MAC}(\widetilde{z}, m_0), \widetilde{a} \neq a] \leq 2^{-g} \leq \varepsilon. \tag{17}$$

Combining Eqs. 16 and 17 with inequality 12 we get:

$$\Pr[W = 1] \leq \sum_{\widetilde{z} \in \widetilde{Z}} \Pr{}_{(z,m_0)}[\widetilde{m}_2 \neq \widetilde{m}_1 \neq m_1, t_0 = \mathsf{MAC}(\widetilde{z}, m_0)] \leq \sum_{\widetilde{z} \in \widetilde{Z}} 2 \cdot \varepsilon \leq 2 \cdot d \cdot \varepsilon,$$

since $|\widetilde{Z}| = d$, from Lemma 4.

References

1. Alwen, J., Katz, J., Lindell, Y., Persiano, G., Shelat, A., Visconti, I.: Collusion-free multiparty computation in the mediated model. In: Halevi, S. (ed.) CRYPTO 2009. LNCS, vol. 5677, pp. 524–540. Springer, Heidelberg (2009)
2. Alwen, J., Katz, J., Maurer, U., Zikas, V.: Collusion-preserving computation. In: Safavi-Naini, R., Canetti, R. (eds.) CRYPTO 2012. LNCS, vol. 7417, pp. 124–143. Springer, Heidelberg (2012)
3. Babai, L., Fortnow, L., Lund, C.: Non-deterministic exponential time has two-prover interactive protocols. Comput. Complex. 1, 3–40 (1991)
4. Blakley, G.R.: Safeguarding cryptographic keys. In: International Workshop on Managing Requirements Knowledge, pp. 313–317. IEEE Computer Society (1979)
5. Blundo, C., De Santis, A.: Lower bounds for robust secret sharing schemes. Inf. Process. Lett. 63(6), 317–321 (1997)
6. Canetti, R., Vald, M.: Universally composable security with local adversaries. In: Visconti, I., De Prisco, R. (eds.) SCN 2012. LNCS, vol. 7485, pp. 281–301. Springer, Heidelberg (2012)
7. Carpentieri, M., De Santis, A., Vaccaro, U.: Size of shares and probability of cheating in threshold schemes. In: Helleseth [15], pp. 118–125
8. Cevallos, A.: Reducing the share size in robust secret sharing (2011). http://www.algant.eu/documents/theses/cevallos.pdf
9. Cevallos, A., Fehr, S., Ostrovsky, R., Rabani, Y.: Unconditionally-secure robust secret sharing with compact shares. In: Pointcheval, D., Johansson, T. (eds.) EUROCRYPT 2012. LNCS, vol. 7237, pp. 195–208. Springer, Heidelberg (2012)
10. Cramer, R., Damgård, I.B., Fehr, S.: On the cost of reconstructing a secret, or VSS with optimal reconstruction phase. In: Kilian, J. (ed.) CRYPTO 2001. LNCS, vol. 2139, pp. 503–523. Springer, Heidelberg (2001)
11. Cramer, R., Damgård, I.B., Döttling, N., Fehr, S., Spini, G.: Linear secret sharing schemes from error correcting codes and universal hash functions. In: Oswald, E., Fischlin, M. (eds.) EUROCRYPT 2015, Part II. LNCS, vol. 9057, pp. 313–336. Springer, Heidelberg (2015)

12. den Boer, B.: A simple and key-economical unconditional authentication scheme. J. Comput. Secur. **2**, 65–72 (1993)
13. Dodis, Y., Lewko, A.B., Waters, B., Wichs, D.: Storing secrets on continually leaky devices. In: Ostrovsky, R. (ed.) IEEE 52nd Annual Symposium on Foundations of Computer Science, FOCS 2011, Palm Springs, CA, USA, 22–25 October, 2011, pp. 688–697. IEEE (2011)
14. Dziembowski, S., Pietrzak, K.: Leakage-resilient cryptography. In: 49th Annual IEEE Symposium on Foundations of Computer Science, FOCS 2008, 25–28 October, 2008, Philadelphia, PA, USA, pp. 293–302. IEEE Computer Society (2008)
15. Helleseth, T. (ed.) EUROCRYPT 1993. LNCS, vol. 765. Springer, Heidelberg (1994)
16. Johansson, T., Kabatianskii, G., Smeets, B.J.M.: On the relation between a-codes and codes correcting independent errors. In: Helleseth [15], pp. 1–11
17. Justesen, J.: Class of constructive asymptotically good algebraic codes. IEEE Trans. Inf. Theor. **18**(5), 652–656 (1972)
18. Lepinski, M., Micali, S., Shelat, A.: Collusion-free protocols. In: Gabow, H.N., Fagin, R. (eds.) Proceedings of the 37th Annual ACM Symposium on Theory of Computing, Baltimore, MD, USA, 22–24 May, 2005, pp. 543–552. ACM (2005)
19. Lewko, A.B., Pastro, V.: Robust secret sharing schemes against local adversaries. IACR Cryptology ePrint Archive, 2014:909 (2014)
20. Micali, S., Reyzin, L.: Physically observable cryptography (extended abstract). In: Naor, M. (ed.) TCC 2004. LNCS, vol. 2951, pp. 278–296. Springer, Heidelberg (2004)
21. Mitzenmacher, M., Upfal, E.: Probability and Computing: Randomized Algorithms and Probabilistic Analysis. Cambridge University Press, New York (2005)
22. Rabin, T., Ben-Or, M.: Verifiable secret sharing and multiparty protocols with honest majority (extended abstract). In: Johnson, D.S. (ed.) Proceedings of the 21st Annual ACM Symposium on Theory of Computing, 14–17 May, 1989, Seattle, Washigton, USA, pp. 73–85. ACM (1989)
23. Shamir, A.: How to share a secret. Commun. ACM **22**(11), 612–613 (1979)
24. Shamir, A.: IP = PSPACE. J. ACM **39**(4), 869–877 (1992)
25. Taylor, R.: An Integrity Check Value Algorithm for Stream Ciphers. In: Stinson, D.R. (ed.) CRYPTO 1993. LNCS, vol. 773, pp. 40–48. Springer, Heidelberg (1994)

Primitives

Reducing Depth in Constrained PRFs: From Bit-Fixing to $\mathbf{NC}^1$

Nishanth Chandran[1]($\boxtimes$), Srinivasan Raghuraman[2],
and Dhinakaran Vinayagamurthy[3]

[1] Microsoft Research, Bengaluru, India
nichandr@microsoft.com
[2] CSAIL, Massachusetts Institute of Technology, Cambridge, USA
srirag@mit.edu
[3] University of Waterloo, Waterloo, Canada
dvinayag@uwaterloo.edu

Abstract. The candidate construction of multilinear maps by Garg, Gentry, and Halevi (Eurocrypt 2013) has lead to an explosion of new cryptographic constructions ranging from attribute-based encryption (ABE) for arbitrary polynomial size circuits, to program obfuscation, and to constrained pseudorandom functions (PRFs). Many of these constructions require κ-linear maps for large κ. In this work, we focus on the reduction of κ in certain constructions of access control primitives that are based on κ-linear maps; in particular, we consider the case of constrained PRFs and ABE. We construct the following objects:

- A constrained PRF for arbitrary circuit predicates based on $(n + \ell_{OR} - 1)$–linear maps (where n is the input length and ℓ_{OR} denotes the OR-depth of the circuit).
- For circuits with a specific structure, we also show how to construct such PRFs based on $(n + \ell_{AND} - 1)$–linear maps (where ℓ_{AND} denotes the AND-depth of the circuit).

We then give a black-box construction of a constrained PRF for $\mathbf{NC}^1$ predicates, from *any* bit-fixing constrained PRF that fixes only *one* of the input bits to 1; we only require that the bit-fixing PRF have certain key homomorphic properties. This construction is of independent interest as it sheds light on the hardness of constructing constrained PRFs even for "simple" predicates such as bit-fixing predicates.

Instantiating this construction with the bit-fixing constrained PRF from Boneh and Waters (Asiacrypt 2013) gives us a constrained PRF for $\mathbf{NC}^1$ predicates that is based only on n-linear maps, with no dependence on the predicate. In contrast, the previous constructions of constrained PRFs (Boneh and Waters, Asiacrypt 2013) required $(n + \ell + 1)$–linear maps for circuit predicates (where ℓ is the *total* depth of the circuit) and n-linear maps even for bit-fixing predicates.

We also show how to extend our techniques to obtain a similar improvement in the case of ABE and construct ABE for arbitrary circuits based on $(\ell_{OR} + 1)$–linear (respectively $(\ell_{AND} + 1)$–linear) maps.

Research done while all authors were at Microsoft Research, India.

© International Association for Cryptologic Research 2016
C.-M. Cheng et al. (Eds.): PKC 2016, Part II, LNCS 9615, pp. 359–385, 2016.
DOI: 10.1007/978-3-662-49387-8_14

1 Introduction

The breakthrough work on multilinear maps [GGH13a] has found tremendous applications in various areas of cryptography. It has lead to attribute-based encryption (ABE) for all polynomial size circuits [GGH+13c], indistinguishability obfuscation and functional encryption for general circuits [GGH+13b], constrained pseudorandom functions [BW13], and so on. Many of these constructions require κ-linear maps for large κ. Larger κ leads to more inefficient schemes and stronger hardness assumptions. In this work, we are interested in exploring the reduction of κ in such constructions – specifically, we consider the case of constrained PRFs and ABE.

Constrained Pseudorandom Functions. A pseudorandom function (PRF) is a keyed function, $F_k(x)$, that is computationally indistinguishable from a truly random function, even to an adversary who has oracle access to the function (but has no knowledge about the key k). Constrained PRFs (introduced in [BW13, BGI14, KPTZ13]), allow the owner of k to give out a constrained key k_f, for a predicate f, such that any user who has k_f can evaluate $F_k(x)$ iff $f(x) = 1$. The security requirement on all points x, such that $f(x) = 0$ is the same as that of standard PRFs.

Boneh and Waters [BW13] show how to construct constrained PRFs for bit-fixing predicates using an $n-$linear map (where n is the input length to the PRF), and also how to construct constrained PRFs for arbitrary circuit predicates using an $(n+\ell+1)-$linear map (where ℓ is the total depth of the circuit predicate). Constrained PRFs can be used to construct broadcast encryption with small ciphertext length, identity-based key exchange, and policy-based key distribution.

Attribute Based Encryption. Attribute based encryption (ABE) [SW05] allows a more fine-grained access policy to be embedded into public-key encryption. In more detail, in ABE schemes, there is a master authority who owns sk and publishes public parameters as well as a relation $R(x, y)$. A user who encrypts a message m, creates a ciphertext under some string x (that can specify some policy), to obtain $\mathsf{Enc}_{pk}(m, x)$. The master authority can give a user a secret key sk_y. Now, this user can use sk_y to decrypt $\mathsf{Enc}_{pk}(m, x)$ and obtain m iff $R(x, y) = 1$; otherwise, the user obtains no information about m. ABE, for the class of relations $R \in \mathbf{NC}^1$ can be constructed based on bilinear maps [GPSW06]. Recently, the work of [GGH+13c] shows how to construct ABE for arbitrary circuits based on $(\ell + 1)-$linear maps (where ℓ is the depth of the relation R when expressed as a boolean circuit), while [GVW13] also show how to construct ABE for arbitrary circuits based on the Learning with Errors (LWE) hardness problem.

1.1 Our Results

In this work, we show the following results:

- We construct constrained PRFs for arbitrary circuit predicates using an $(n + \ell_{\mathsf{OR}} - 1)$−linear map, where n is the input length to the PRF and ℓ_{OR} denotes the OR-depth of the constraint f when expressed as a boolean circuit (informally, the OR-depth of a circuit is defined to be the maximum number of OR gates from input wires to the output wire along any path in the circuit). We believe that the reduction in linearity is important even in cases when it is not an asymptotic improvement as lower linearity results in a weaker hardness assumption.
- Next, we construct constrained PRFs for circuit predicates using an $(n + \ell_{\mathsf{AND}} - 1)$−linear map, where ℓ_{AND} denotes the AND-depth of the constraint f (informally, the AND-depth of a circuit is defined to be the maximum number of AND gates from input wires to the output wire along any path in the circuit). Although in this construction, we require the circuit to be of a specific structure, we show that for several circuits, our construction reduces the number of levels of multilinear map needed.
- Then, we show (in a black-box manner) how to convert any bit-fixing constrained PRF that fixes only *one* bit[1] to 1 into a constrained PRF for $\mathbf{NC}^1$ circuits; we only require that the bit-fixing PRF have certain additive key-homomorphic properties. We believe this construction to be of independent interest as the only known (non-trivial) constructions of constrained PRFs are based on multilinear maps.

  By instantiating this construction with the bit-fixing constrained PRF of Boneh and Waters [BW13], we obtain a constrained PRF for all predicates $f \in \mathbf{NC}^1$ using an n−linear map. In particular, the number of levels in our construction has no dependence on f.
- Finally, we show how to extend our techniques to construct ABE schemes from lesser levels of multi-linear maps.

Similar to [BW13], all our constructions are based on the κ-Multilinear Decisional Diffie-Hellman (κ-MDDH) assumption and achieve selective security (i.e., the adversary must commit to the challenge query at the beginning of the security game); as in [BW13], we can achieve standard security via complexity leveraging. We remark that our techniques can be extended to the constructions of verifiable constrained PRFs [Fuc14, CRV14], thereby leading to a similar lowering of κ.

Other Related Works. The work of [FKPR14] considers the prefix-fixing constrained PRF from the classical GGM construction [GGM86], and shows how to avoid an exponential (in n) loss in security when going from selective security to adaptive security. Their work also shows that any "simple" reduction, that proves full security of the bit-fixing constrained PRF of [BW13], from a non-interactive hardness assumption, must incur an exponential security loss. The work of [HKKW14] shows how to construct adaptively secure

---

[1] By symmetry, we can also start with a bit-fixing constrained PRF that fixes only one bit to 0.

constrained PRFs for circuits from indistinguishability obfuscation in the random oracle model. More recently, key-homomorphic constrained PRFs were constructed in [BV15,BFP+15]. Similar to us, Banerjee et al. [BFP+15] also observe that [BW13] is "key-homomorphic".

Security of Multilinear Maps. After the initial work of Garg et al. [GGH13a], Coron, Lepoint and Tibouchi proposed a multilinear maps construction over the integers [CLT13] also based on ideal lattices. But, Cheon, Han, Lee, Ryu and Stehlé [CHL+15] proposed an attack which completely broke the CLT scheme by recovering the secret parameters of the scheme in polynomial time. Coron et al. [CLT15] proposed another candidate construction. This was broken recently by Cheon et al. [CLR15] and Minaud et al. [MF15]. Hu and Jia [HJ15] also recently showed that the κ-MDDH assumption in [GGH13a] does not hold when encodings of zero are provided. Independent of these, Gentry, Gorbunov and Halevi [GGH15] proposed a multilinear maps construction based on *random* lattices but with the map defined with respect to a directed acyclic graph.

We do not rely on the security of any specific multilinear maps scheme. Since we do not give low-level encodings of zero in our construction, any scheme [GGH13a,CLT13,CLT15] which is secure under the κ-MDDH assumption can be used to instantiate our constructions.

1.2   Our Techniques

Our starting point is the constrained PRF construction of [BW13] for arbitrary circuit predicates. We first view this construction differently as follows. Let the PRF in [BW13] be denoted by $\mathsf{PRF}_{n+\ell}(u,x)$, where u is the key of the PRF, x, an n-bit string, is the input to the PRF, and $\mathsf{PRF}_{n+\ell}$ denotes that the PRF output is at the $(n+\ell)-$level of the multilinear map (where ℓ denotes the depth of the constraint f). Now, in order to give out a constrained key for f, we first pick a random value r_w for every wire w in the circuit. Let j denote the depth of this wire in the circuit. Now, for a given x such that $f(x) = 1$, the idea is to give a key that will enable the user to compute $\mathsf{PRF}_{n+j}(r_w,x)$ for all wires w in the circuit that evaluate to 1 on x. Doing this inductively will allow the compution of $\mathsf{PRF}_{n+\ell}(u,x)$. Let w be an output to some gate in the circuit and let $A(w), B(w)$ be the input wires corresponding to this gate. If this gate is an AND (respectively OR) gate, we give a key, that will allow a user to compute $\mathsf{PRF}_{n+j}(r_w,x)$ from the values $\mathsf{PRF}_{n+j-1}(r_{A(w)},x)$ AND (respectively OR) $\mathsf{PRF}_{n+j-1}(r_{B(w)},x)$.

Free AND Construction. Our first observation is that for AND gates, one must be able to compute the PRF value corresponding to w wire iff one has the PRF values corresponding to *both* $A(w)$ and $B(w)$. Now, suppose the PRF under consideration is "additively homomorphic" in some sense. Then, we observe that given $\mathsf{PRF}_{n+j-1}(r_{A(w)},x)$ and $\mathsf{PRF}_{n+j-1}(r_{B(w)},x)$, one can compute $\mathsf{PRF}_{n+j-1}(r_w,x)$, without the need for additional keys and without jumping a level in the multilinear map as long as we set $r_{A(w)}$ and $r_{B(w)}$ to be random additive shares of r_w. Now, this ensures that AND gates are "free" in the circuit. The OR gates are handled exactly as in the case of [BW13]. This leads to a construction that only makes use of a $(n + \ell_{OR} - 1)$−linear map.

While this is the main change made to the construction, the proof of security now requires attention. At a very high level, [BW13] could embed a part of the "hard problem" from the hardness assumption at every layer of the circuit as they give out keys for all gates in the circuits. In our case, we do not have that luxury. In particular, since we do not give any keys for AND gates, the structure of the hard problem may be distorted after multiple evaluations of AND gates. In order to overcome this, we must carefully give out the keys at OR levels to "reset" the problem to be of our preferred form. This enables us to then prove security.

Free OR Construction. Now, suppose we turn our attention towards the OR gates alone. Note, that one must be able to compute the PRF value corresponding to wire w iff one has the PRF values corresponding to *either* $A(w)$ or $B(w)$. Now, suppose we set $r_w = r_{A(w)} = r_{B(w)}$, then this enables the computation of $\mathsf{PRF}_{n+j-1}(r_w, x)$ from either $\mathsf{PRF}_{n+j-1}(r_{A(w)}, x)$ or $\mathsf{PRF}_{n+j-1}(r_{B(w)}, x)$, without the need for additional keys and without jumping a level in the multilinear map. However, doing this naïvely would lead to a similar "backtracking attack" as the attack described by [GGH+13c] in the context of ABE. In more detail, note that if $A(w) = 0$ and $B(w) = 1$, one can indeed (rightly) compute $\mathsf{PRF}_{n+j-1}(r_w, x)$ from $\mathsf{PRF}_{n+j-1}(r_{B(w)}, x)$ as both $B(w)$ and w are 1. However, this also enables the (unauthorized) computation of $\mathsf{PRF}_{n+j-1}(r_{A(w)}, x)$, and if this wire had a fan-out greater than 1, this would lead to an attack on the security of the PRF. Here, we show that if the circuit had a specific structure, then such a construction can still be made to work. We show that several circuits can be converted to this form (with a polynomial blowup) that results in a reduction in the number of multilinear levels needed. We remark that for the construction (and proof) to succeed, one must carefully select the random key values on the circuit for the constrained key, starting *backwards*, from the output wire in the circuit.

$\mathbf{NC}^1$ *Construction.* While we obtain our construction of constrained PRF for $\mathbf{NC}^1$ circuits by combining the above two techniques, we note that the proof of security is tricky and requires the simulator to carefully set the random keys in the simulation. In particular, let x^* be the challenge input to the PRF. Now, suppose, the simulator must give out a constrained key for a circuit f such that $f(x^*) = 0$. The simulator must choose all the random keys of the PRFs on each wire in such a way that for all wires that evaluate to 1 on x^*, the key is either chosen randomly by the simulator or can be computed from values that are chosen randomly by the simulator. We show that this can be indeed done by the simulator, thus resulting in the proof of security.

We then show how to generalize this construction to obtain a constrained PRF for $\mathbf{NC}^1$ circuits from any constrained PRF for bit-fixing predicates that fixes only *one bit* and has certain additively homomorphic properties. We believe this construction to be of independent interest as till date, constrained PRFs for any non-trivial predicate, are known only based on multilinear maps.

Finally, we show how to extend our Free AND/OR techniques to the case of ABE. This gives an ABE based on $(\ell_{OR} + 1)$−linear and $(\ell_{AND} + 1)$−linear maps respectively, improving upon the $(\ell+1)$−linear map construction of [GGH+13c].

1.3 Organization

In Sect. 2, we define constrained PRFs and ABE as well as state the hardness assumption that we make. We also present circuit notation that is used in the rest of the paper. In Sect. 3, we describe our $(n + \ell_{OR} - 1)$−linear map construction of constrained PRF for arbitrary circuits. We outline our $(n + \ell_{AND} - 1)$−linear map construction in Sect. 4. We present our n−linear map construction of constrained PRF for $\mathbf{NC}^1$ circuits in Sect. 5 and the black-box construction of constrained PRF for $\mathbf{NC}^1$ circuits from bit-fixing constrained PRFs in Sect. 6. We show how to extend our results to the setting of ABE in the full version of this paper [CRV15].

2 Preliminaries

2.1 Definitions

Constrained Pseudorandom Functions. A pseudorandom function (PRF) $F : \mathcal{K} \times \mathcal{X} \to \mathcal{Y}$, is a deterministic polynomial (in security parameter λ) time algorithm, that on input a key $k \in \mathcal{K}$ and an input $x \in \mathcal{X}$, outputs $F(k, x) \in \mathcal{Y}$. F has a setup algorithm $\mathsf{Setup}(1^\lambda)$ that on input λ, outputs a key $k \in \mathcal{K}$.

Definition 1. *A PRF $F : \mathcal{K} \times \mathcal{X} \to \mathcal{Y}$ is said to be constrained with respect to a set system $\mathcal{S} \subseteq \mathcal{X}$ if there is an additional key space $\mathcal{K}_c$, and there exist algorithms (F.Constrain, F.Evaluate) such that*

- *F.Constrain(k, S) is a randomized polynomial time algorithm that takes as input a PRF key $k \in \mathcal{K}$ and the description of a set $S \in \mathcal{S}$. It outputs a constrained key $k_S \in \mathcal{K}_c$ which enables the evaluation of $F(k, x)$ for all $x \in S$ and no other x;*
- *F.Evaluate(k_S, x) is a deterministic polynomial time algorithm that takes as input a constrained key $k_S \in \mathcal{K}_c$ and an input $x \in \mathcal{X}$. If k_S is the output of F.Constrain(k, S) for some $k \in \mathcal{K}$, then F.Evaluate(k_S, x) outputs $F(k, x)$ if $x \in S$ and $\perp$ otherwise, where $\perp \notin \mathcal{Y}$. We will use the shorthand $F(k_S, x)$ for F.Evaluate(k_S, x).*

The security of constrained PRFs informally states that given several constrained keys, as well as the output of the PRF on several points of the adversary's choice, the PRF looks random at all points that the adversary could not have computed himself. Let $F : \mathcal{K} \times \mathcal{X} \to \mathcal{Y}$ be a constrained PRF with respect to a set system $\mathcal{S}$. Define two experiments Exp_0 and Exp_1. For $b \in \{0, 1\}$, Exp_b proceeds as follows:

1. First, a random key $k \in \mathcal{K}$ is chosen, and two sets $C, V \subseteq \mathcal{X}$ are initialized to $\emptyset$. C will keep track of points on which the adversary will be challenged and V will keep track of points on which the adversary can compute the PRF himself. The experiments will maintain the invariant that $C \cap V = \emptyset$.
2. The adversary is given access to the following oracles:
   - F.Constrain: Given a set $S \in \mathcal{S}$, if $S \cap C = \emptyset$, the oracle returns F.Constrain(k, S) and updates $V \leftarrow V \cup S$; otherwise, it returns $\bot$.
   - F.Evaluate: Given an input $x \in \mathcal{X}$, if $x \notin C$, the oracle returns $F(k, x)$ and updates $V \leftarrow V \cup x$; otherwise, it returns $\bot$.
   - Challenge: Given $x \in \mathcal{X}$ where $x \notin V$, if $b = 0$, the oracle returns $F(k, x)$; if $b = 1$, the oracle returns a random (consistent) $y \in \mathcal{Y}$. C is updated as $C \leftarrow C \cup x$.
3. The adversary finally outputs a bit $b' \in \{0, 1\}$.
4. For $b \in \{0, 1\}$, define W_b to be the event that $b' = 1$ in experiment Exp_b. The adversary's advantage $\mathsf{Adv}_{\mathcal{A}, F, \mathcal{S}}(\lambda)$ is defined to be $|\Pr[W_0] - \Pr[W_1]|$.

Definition 2. *A constrained PRF $F : \mathcal{K} \times \mathcal{X} \to \mathcal{Y}$, is said to be secure, if for all PPT adversaries $\mathcal{A}$, we have that $\mathsf{Adv}_{\mathcal{A}, F, \mathcal{S}}(\lambda)$, is negligible in λ.*

Remark. When constructing constrained pseudorandom functions, it will be more convenient to work with the definition where the adversary is allowed to issue only a single challenge query. A standard hybrid argument shows that this definition is equivalent to the one where an adversary is allowed to issue multiple challenge queries. A constrained PRF is selectively secure if the adversary commits to this single challenge query at the beginning of the experiment.

Attribute-Based Encryption. An attribute-based encryption (ABE) scheme has the following algorithms:

- Setup$(1^\lambda, n, \ell)$: This algorithm takes as input the security parameter λ, the length n of input descriptors in the ciphertext, and a bound ℓ on the circuit depth. It outputs the public parameters PP and the master secret key MSK.
- Encrypt(PP, x, M): This algorithm takes as input the public parameters, $x \in \{0, 1\}^n$ (representing the assignment of boolean variables) and a message M. It outputs a ciphertext CT.
- KeyGen(MSK, f): This algorithm takes as input the master secret key and a circuit f. It outputs a secret key SK.
- Decrypt(SK, CT): This algorithm takes as input a secret key and ciphertext and outputs either M or $\bot$.

The correctness of the ABE requires that for all messages M, for all $x \in \{0, 1\}^n$, for all depth ℓ circuits f, with $f(x) = 1$, if Encrypt(PP, x, M) outputs CT, and KeyGen(MSK, f) outputs SK, where PP and MSK were obtained as the output of Setup$(1^\lambda, n, \ell)$, then Decrypt$(SK, CT) = M$. The security of an ABE scheme is defined through the following game between a challenger Chall and adversary Adv as described below:

- **Setup.** Chall runs Setup($1^\lambda, n, \ell$) and gives PP to Adv; it keeps SK to itself.
- **Phase 1.** Adv makes any polynomial number of queries for circuit descriptions f of its choice. Chall returns KeyGen(MSK, f).
- **Challenge.** Adv submits two equal length messages M_0 and M_1 as well as an $x^* \in \{0, 1\}$ such that for all f queried in Phase 1, $f(x^*) = 0$. Chall flips a bit b and returns $CT^* = $ Encrypt(PP, x^*, M_b) to Adv.
- **Phase 2.** Phase 1 is repeated with the restriction that $f(x^*) = 0$ for all queried f.
- **Guess.** Adv outputs a bit b'.

Definition 3. *The advantage of* Adv *in the above game is defined to be* $|\Pr[b' = b] - \frac{1}{2}|$. *An ABE for circuits is secure if for all PPT adversaries* Adv, *the advantage of* Adv *is negligible in the security parameter* λ. *An ABE scheme is said to be selectively secure, if* Adv *commits to* x^* *at the beginning of the security game.*

2.2 Assumptions

Leveled Multilinear Groups. We assume the existence of a group generator $\mathcal{G}$, which takes as input a security paramter 1^λ and a positive integer κ to indicate the number of levels. $\mathcal{G}(1^\lambda, \kappa)$ outputs a sequence of groups $\mathbb{G} = (\mathbb{G}_1, \ldots, \mathbb{G}_\kappa)$ each of large prime order $p > 2^\lambda$. In addition, we let g_i be a canonical generator of $\mathbb{G}_i$ that is known from the group's description. We let $g = g_1$. We assume the existence of a set of multilinear maps $\{e_{i,j} : \mathbb{G}_i \times \mathbb{G}_j \to \mathbb{G}_{i+j} | i, j \geq 1; i + j \leq \kappa\}$. The map $e_{i,j}$ satisfies the following relation: $e_{i,j}(g_i^a, g_j^b) = g_{i+j}^{ab}, \forall a, b \in \mathbb{Z}_p$. When the context is obvious, we will drop the subscripts i, j. For example, we may simply write $e(g_i^a, g_j^b) = g_{i+j}^{ab}$. We define the κ-Multilinear Decisional Diffie-Hellman (κ-MDDH) [GGH13a] assumption as follows:

Assumption 21. (κ-*Multilinear Decisional Diffie-Hellman: κ-MDDH) The κ-Multilinear Decisional Diffie-Hellman (κ-MDDH) problem is as follows: A challenger runs* $\mathcal{G}(1^\lambda, \kappa)$ *to generate groups and generators of order p. Then it picks random* $c_1, \ldots, c_{\kappa+1} \in \mathbb{Z}_p$. *The assumption states that given* $g = g_1, g^{c_1}, \ldots, g^{c_{\kappa+1}}$, *it is hard to distinguish the element* $T = g_\kappa^{\Pi_{j \in [\kappa+1]} c_j}$ *from a random group element in $\mathbb{G}_\kappa$ with better than negligible advantage in λ.*

2.3 Circuit Notation

We will consider layered circuits, where a gate at[2] depth j will receive both of its inputs from wires at depth $j-1$. We also assume that all NOT gates are restricted to the input level. Similar to [BW13], we restrict ourselves to monotonic circuits where gates are either AND or OR gates of two inputs.[3]

Formally, our circuits will be a five tuple $f = (n, q, A, B, \texttt{GateType})$. We let n be the number of inputs and q be the number of gates. We define inputs $= [n]$,

---

[2] When the term depth is used, it is synonymous to the notion of tot-depth described ahead.

[3] These restrictions are mostly useful for exposition and do not impact functionality.

Wires $= [n + q]$ and Gates $= [n + q] \backslash [n]$. The wire $n + q$ is designated as the output wire, outputwire. A : Gates $\rightarrow$ Wires$\backslash\{$outputwire$\}$ is a function where $A(w)$ identifies w's first incoming wire and B : Gates $\rightarrow$ Wires$\backslash\{$outputwire$\}$ is a function where $B(w)$ identifies w's second incoming wire. Finally, GateType : Gates $\rightarrow \{$AND, OR$\}$ is a function that identifies a gate as either an AND gate or an OR gate. We let $w > B(w) > A(w)$. Also, define three functions: tot-depth(w), AND-depth(w), and OR-depth(w) that are all 1, when $w \in$ inputs, and in general are equal to the number of gates (respectively AND and OR gates) on the shortest path to an input wire plus one. We let $f(x)$ be the evaluation of f on the input $x \in \{0, 1\}^n$, and $f_w(x)$ be the value of the wire w on the input x.

3   A Free-AND Circuit-Predicate Construction

We show how to construct a constrained PRF for arbitrary polynomial size circuit predicates, without giving any keys for AND gates, based on $\kappa = (n + \ell_{\mathsf{OR}} - 1)$−linear maps, where ℓ_{OR} denotes the OR-depth of the circuit. The starting point of our construction is the constrained PRF construction of [BW13] which is based on the ABE for circuits [GGH+13c]. [BW13] works with layered circuits. For ease of exposition, we assume a layered circuit where all gates in a particular layer are of the same type (either AND or OR). Circuits have a single output OR gate. Also a layer of gates is not followed by another layer of the same type. We stress that these are only for the purposes of exposition and can be removed as outlined later on in the section.

3.1   Construction

F.Setup$(1^\lambda, n, \ell_{\mathsf{OR}})$: The setup algorithm takes as input the security parameter λ, the bit length, n, of PRF inputs and ℓ_{OR}, the maximum OR-depth[4] of the circuit. The algorithm runs $\mathcal{G}(1^\lambda, \kappa = n + \ell_{\mathsf{OR}} - 1)$ and outputs a sequence of groups $\mathbb{G} = (\mathbb{G}_1, \ldots, \mathbb{G}_\kappa)$ of prime order p with canonical generators $g_1, \ldots, g_\kappa$, where $g = g_1$. It chooses random exponents $u \in \mathbb{Z}_p$ and $(d_{1,0}, d_{1,1}), \ldots, (d_{n,0}, d_{n,1}) \in \mathbb{Z}_p^2$ and computes $D_{m,\beta} = g^{d_{m,\beta}}$ for $m \in [n]$ and $\beta \in \{0, 1\}$. It then sets the key of the PRF as:

$$k = (\mathbb{G}, p, g_1, \ldots, g_\kappa, u, d_{1,0}, d_{1,1}, \ldots, d_{n,0}, d_{n,1}, D_{1,0}, D_{1,1}, \ldots, D_{n,0}, D_{n,1})$$

The PRF is $F(k, x) = g_\kappa^{u \prod_{m \in [n]} d_{m,x_m}}$, where x_m is the mth bit of $x \in \{0, 1\}^n$.

F.Constrain$(k, f = (n, q, A, B, \mathtt{GateType}))$: The constrain algorithm takes as input the key k and a circuit description f. The circuit has $n + q$ wires with n input wires, q gates and the wire $n + q$ designated as the output wire.

To generate a constrained key k_f, the key generation algorithm chooses random $r_1, \ldots, r_n \in \mathbb{Z}_p$, where we think of the random value r_w as being associated

---

[4] We can define OR-depth of a circuit which is in our specified form as the number of layers comprising of OR gates, plus 1.

with the wire w. For each $w \in [n+q-1]\backslash[n]$, if $\texttt{GateType}(w) = \text{AND}$, it sets $r_w = r_{A(w)} + r_{B(w)}$ (where $+$ denotes addition in the group $\mathbb{Z}_p$); otherwise, it chooses $r_w \in \mathbb{Z}_p$ at random. Finally, it sets $r_{n+q} = u$.

The first part of the constrained key is given out as simply all $D_{i,\beta}$ for $i \in [n]$ and $\beta \in \{0,1\}$. Next, the algorithm generates key components. The structure of the key components depends on whether w is an input wire or an output of an OR gate. For AND gates, we do not need to give out any keys. The key components in each case are described below.

- *Input wire.* By convention, if $w \in [n]$, then it corresponds to the w-th input. The key component is: $K_w = g^{r_w d_{w,1}}$.
- *OR gate.* Let $j = \texttt{OR-depth}(w)$. The algorithm chooses random $a_w, b_w \in \mathbb{Z}_p$. Then, the algorithm creates key components:

$$K_{w,1} = g^{a_w}, K_{w,2} = g^{b_w}, K_{w,3} = g_{j-1}^{r_w - a_w \cdot r_{A(w)}}, K_{w,4} = g_{j-1}^{r_w - b_w \cdot r_{B(w)}}$$

The constrained key k_f consists of all these key components along with $\{D_{i,\beta}\}$ for $i \in [n]$ and $\beta \in \{0,1\}$.

$F.\mathsf{Evaluate}(k_f, x)$: The evaluate algorithm takes as input a constrained key k_f for the circuit f and an input $x \in \{0,1\}^n$. The algorithm first checks that $f(x) = 1$, and if not, it aborts. Consider the wire w at OR-depth j. If $f_w(x) = 1$, then, the algorithm computes $E_w = g_{n+j-1}^{r_w \prod_{m \in [n]} d_{m,x_m}}$. If $f_w(x) = 0$, then nothing is computed for that wire. The algorithm proceeds iteratively starting with computing E_1 and proceeds, in order, to compute E_{n+q}. Computing these values in order ensures that the computation on a lower-depth wire that evaluates to 1 will be defined, before the compution on a higher-depth wire. Since $r_{n+q} = u$, $E_{n+q} = g_{n+\ell_{\mathsf{OR}}-1}^{u \prod_{m \in [n]} d_{m,x_m}}$. We show how to compute E_w for all w where $f_w(x) = 1$, case-wise, according to whether the wire is an input, an OR gate or an AND gate. Define $D = D(x) = g_n^{\prod_{m \in [n]} d_{m,x_m}}$, which is computable through pairings.

- *Input wire.* Suppose $f_w(x) = 1$. Through pairing operations, the algorithm computes $g_{n-1}^{\prod_{m \in [n]\backslash\{w\}} d_{m,x_m}}$. It then computes:

$$E_w = e\left(K_w, g_{n-1}^{\prod_{m \in [n]\backslash\{w\}} d_{m,x_m}}\right) = g_n^{r_w \prod_{m \in [n]} d_{m,x_m}}$$

- *OR gate.* Let $j = \texttt{OR-depth}(w)$. The computation is performed if $f_w(x) = 1$. Note that in this case, at least one of $f_{A(w)}(x)$ and $f_{B(w)}(x)$ must be 1. If $f_{A(w)}(x) = 1$, the algorithm computes:

$$\begin{aligned}
E_w &= e(E_{A(w)}, K_{w,1}) \cdot e(K_{w,3}, D) \\
&= e\left(g_{n+j-2}^{r_{A(w)} \prod_{m \in [n]} d_{m,x_m}}, g^{a_w}\right) \cdot e\left(g_{j-1}^{r_w - a_w \cdot r_{A(w)}}, g_n^{\prod_{m \in [n]} d_{m,x_m}}\right) \\
&= g_{n+j-1}^{r_w \prod_{m \in [n]} d_{m,x_m}}
\end{aligned}$$

Otherwise, we have $f_{B(w)}(x) = 1$ and the algorithm computes E_w from $E_{B(w)}, K_{w,2}, K_{w,4}$ in a similar manner.

– *AND gate*. Let $j = \texttt{OR-depth}(w)$. The computation is performed if $f_w(x) = 1$. Note that in this case, $f_{A(w)}(x) = f_{B(w)}(x) = 1$. The algorithm computes:

$$E_w = E_{A(w)} \cdot E_{B(w)} = g_{n+j-1}^{r_{A(w)} \prod_{m \in [n]} d_{m,x_m}} \cdot g_{n+j-1}^{r_{B(w)} \prod_{m \in [n]} d_{m,x_m}} = g_{n+j-1}^{r_w \prod_{m \in [n]} d_{m,x_m}}$$

The procedures above are evaluated in order for all w for which $f_w(x) = 1$. Thus, the algorithm computes $E_{n+q} = g_{n+\ell_{\mathsf{OR}}-1}^{u \prod_{m \in [n]} d_{m,x_m}} = F(k,x)$.

3.2 Proof of Pseudorandomness

The correctness of the constrained PRF is verifiable in a straightforward manner. The security proof is in the selective security model (where the adversary commits to the challenge input x^* at the beginning of the game). To get full security, the proof will use the standard complexity leveraging technique of guessing the challenge x^*; this guess will cause a loss of a $1/2^n$-factor in the reduction.

Theorem 1. *If there exists a PPT adversary $\mathcal{A}$ that breaks the pseudorandomness of our circuit-predicate construction for n-bit inputs with advantage $\epsilon(\lambda)$, then there exists a PPT algorithm $\mathcal{B}$ that breaks the $\kappa = (n+\ell_{\mathsf{OR}}-1)-Multilinear Decisional Diffie-Hellman assumption with advantage $\epsilon(\lambda)/2^n$.*

Proof. The algorithm $\mathcal{B}$ first receives a $\kappa = (n + \ell_{\mathsf{OR}} - 1)-$MDDH challenge consisting of the group sequence description $\mathbb{G}$ and $g = g_1, g^{c_1}, \dots, g^{c_{\kappa+1}}$ along with T, where T is either $g_\kappa^{\prod_{m \in [\kappa+1]} c_m}$ or a random group element in $\mathbb{G}_\kappa$.

Setup: It chooses an $x^* \in \{0,1\}^n$ uniformly at random. Next, it chooses random $z_1, \dots, z_n \in \mathbb{Z}_p$ and sets $D_{m,\beta} = g^{c_m}$ when $x_m^* = \beta$ and g^{z_m} otherwise, for $m \in [n]$ and $\beta \in \{0,1\}$. This corresponds to setting $d_{m,\beta} = c_m$ when $x_m^* = \beta$ and z_m otherwise. It then implicitly sets $u = c_{n+1} \cdot c_{n+2} \cdot \dots \cdot c_{n+\ell_{\mathsf{OR}}}$. The setup is executed as in the construction.

Constrain: Suppose a query is made for a secret key for a circuit $f = (n, q, A, B, \texttt{GateType})$. If $f(x^*) = 1$, then $\mathcal{B}$ aborts. Otherwise, $\mathcal{B}$ generates key components for every wire w, case-wise, according to whether w is an input wire or an OR gate as described below.

Input Wire. By convention, if $w \in [n]$, then it corresponds to the w-th input. If $x_w^* = 1$, then $\mathcal{B}$ chooses $\eta_w = r_w$ at random. The key component is:

$$K_w = (D_{w,1})^{r_w} = g^{r_w d_{w,1}}$$

If $x_w^* = 0$, then $\mathcal{B}$ implicitly sets $r_w = c_{n+1} + \eta_w$, where $\eta_w \in \mathbb{Z}_p$ is a randomly chosen element. The key component is:

$$K_w = (g^{c_{n+1}} \cdot g^{\eta_w})^{z_w} = g^{r_w d_{w,1}}$$

OR Gate. Suppose that $w \in$ Gates and that $\texttt{GateType}(w) = \text{OR}$. In addition, let $j = \texttt{OR-depth}(w)$. In order to show that $\mathcal{B}$ can simulate all the key components, we shall additionally show the following property:

Property 1. For any gate $w \in$ Gates, $\mathcal{B}$ will be able to compute $g_j^{r_w}$, where $j = \texttt{OR-depth}(w)$.

We will prove the above property through induction on the OR-depth j; doing this will enable us to prove that $\mathcal{B}$ can compute all the key components required to give out the constrained key. The base case of the input wires ($j = 1$) follows as we know that for an input wire w, $\mathcal{B}$ can compute g^{r_w}, where r_w is of the form η_w or $c_{n+1} + \eta_w$. We now proceed to show the computation of the key-components. In each case, we show that Property 1 is satisfied.

CASE 1: If $f_w(x^*) = 1$, then $\mathcal{B}$ chooses $\psi_w = a_w$, $\phi_w = b_w$ and $\eta_w = r_w$ at random. Then, $\mathcal{B}$ creates key components:

$$K_{w,1} = g^{a_w}, K_{w,2} = g^{b_w}, K_{w,3} = g_{j-1}^{r_w - a_w \cdot r_{A(w)}}, K_{w,4} = g_{j-1}^{r_w - b_w \cdot r_{B(w)}}$$

By virtue of Property 1, since $\texttt{OR-depth}(A(w)) = \texttt{OR-depth}(B(w)) = j - 1$, by the induction hypothesis, we know that $\mathcal{B}$ can compute $g_{j-1}^{r_{A(w)}}$ and $g_{j-1}^{r_{B(w)}}$. Hence, $\mathcal{B}$ can compute the above key-components, as the remaining exponents were all chosen at random by $\mathcal{B}$. Further, since r_w was chosen at random, note that $g_j^{r_w}$ can be be computed for this wire, and hence Property 1 holds for this wire as well (at OR-depth j).

CASE 2: If $f_w(x^*) = 0$, then $\mathcal{B}$ implicitly sets $r_w = c_{n+1} \cdot \ldots \cdot c_{n+j} + \eta_w$, where $\eta_w \in \mathbb{Z}_p$ is a randomly chosen element. Since η_w was chosen at random, note that $g_j^{r_w}$ can be be computed for this wire (since $g_j^{c_{n+1} \cdot \ldots \cdot c_{n+j}}$ can be computed using j pairings of g^{c_m}, $n+1 \leq m \leq n+j$), and hence Property 1 holds for this wire as well. For computing the key-components, the choices of a_w and b_w are done more carefully.

1. Suppose the level before the current level consists of the inputs. $\mathcal{B}$ would know the values of $\eta_{A(w)}$ and $\eta_{B(w)}$, since for input wires, these values are always chosen at random. In this case, $\mathcal{B}$ implicitly sets $a_w = c_{n+j} + \psi_w$ and $b_w = c_{n+j} + \phi_w$, where $\psi_w, \phi_w \in \mathbb{Z}_p$ are randomly chosen elements. Then, $\mathcal{B}$ creates key components:

$$K_{w,1} = g^{c_{n+j} + \psi_w} = g^{a_w}, K_{w,2} = g^{c_{n+j} + \phi_w} = g^{b_w},$$

$$K_{w,3} = g_{j-1}^{\eta_w - c_{n+j} \cdot \eta_{A(w)} - \psi_w(c_{n+1} \cdot \ldots \cdot c_{n+j-1} + \eta_{A(w)})} = g_{j-1}^{r_w - a_w \cdot r_{A(w)}},$$

$$K_{w,4} = g_{j-1}^{\eta_w - c_{n+j} \cdot \eta_{B(w)} - \phi_w(c_{n+1} \cdot \ldots \cdot c_{n+j-1} + \eta_{B(w)})} = g_{j-1}^{r_w - b_w \cdot r_{B(w)}}$$

$\mathcal{B}$ is able to create the last two key components due to a cancellation. Since $f_{A(w)}(x^*) = f_{B(w)}(x^*) = 0$, $\mathcal{B}$ would have set $r_{A(w)} = c_{n+1} \cdot \ldots \cdot c_{n+j-1} + \eta_{A(w)}$ and $r_{B(w)} = c_{n+1} \cdot \ldots \cdot c_{n+j-1} + \eta_{B(w)}$. Further, $g_{j-1}^{c_{n+1} \cdot \ldots \cdot c_{n+j-1}}$ can be computed using $j - 1$ pairings of g^{c_m}, $n + 1 \leq m \leq n + j - 1$.

2. Suppose the level before the current level consists of AND gates. Since $f_{A(w)}(x^*) = 0$, we have two cases: either one of $f_{A(A(w))}(x^*)$ and $f_{B(A(w))}(x^*)$ is zero, or both of them are zero. $\mathcal{B}$ sets $a_w = c_{n+j} + \psi_w$ in the former case, and $a_w = \frac{1}{2}c_{n+j} + \psi_w$ in the latter case, where $\psi_w \in \mathbb{Z}_p$ is a randomly chosen element. Similarly, since $f_{B(w)}(x^*) = 0$, we have two cases: either one of $f_{A(B(w))}(x^*)$ and $f_{B(B(w))}(x^*)$ must be zero, or both of them must be zero. $\mathcal{B}$ sets $b_w = c_{n+j} + \phi_w$ in the former case, and $b_w = \frac{1}{2}c_{n+j} + \phi_w$ in the latter case, where $\phi_w \in \mathbb{Z}_p$ is a randomly chosen element. Then, $\mathcal{B}$ creates key components:

$$K_{w,1} = g^{a_w}, K_{w,2} = g^{b_w}, K_{w,3} = g_{j-1}^{r_w - a_w \cdot r_{A(w)}}, K_{w,4} = g_{j-1}^{r_w - b_w \cdot r_{B(w)}}$$

We now show that these components can indeed be computed in every case. Note that the first two components can be computed in every case. Consider $K_{w,3}$ (a similar argument holds for $K_{w,4}$).

(a) Consider the first case, where one of $f_{A(A(w))}(x^*)$ and $f_{B(A(w))}(x^*)$ is zero. In particular, without loss of generality, assume that $f_{A(A(w))}(x^*) = 0$ and $f_{B(A(w))}(x^*) = 1$. Hence, $\mathcal{B}$ must have set $r_{A(A(w))} = c_{n+1} \cdots \cdot c_{n+j-1} + \eta_{A(A(w))}$ and $r_{B(A(w))} = \eta_{B(A(w))}$. Since $A(w)$ is an AND gate, we would have $r_{A(w)} = r_{A(A(w))} + r_{B(A(w))} = c_{n+1} \cdots \cdot c_{n+j-1} + \eta_{A(A(w))} + \eta_{B(A(w))}$. Hence, we have:

$$K_{w,3} = g_{j-1}^{\eta_w - c_{n+j}(\eta_{A(A(w))} + \eta_{B(A(w))}) - \psi_w(c_{n+1} \cdots \cdot c_{n+j-1} + \eta_{A(A(w))} + \eta_{B(A(w))})}$$
$$= g_{j-1}^{r_w - a_w \cdot r_{A(w)}}$$

which can be computed as follows. We know the values of $\eta_{A(A(w))}$ and $\eta_{B(A(w))}$. Further, $g_{j-1}^{c_{n+1} \cdots \cdot c_{n+j-1}}$ can be computed using $j - 1$ pairings of g^{c_m}, $n + 1 \leq m \leq n + j - 1$. Hence the key component can be computed.

(b) Consider the second case, where $f_{A(A(w))}(x^*) = f_{B(A(w))}(x^*) = 0$. Hence, $\mathcal{B}$ must have set $r_{A(A(w))} = c_{n+1} \cdots \cdot c_{n+j-1} + \eta_{A(A(w))}$ and $r_{B(A(w))} = c_{n+1} \cdots \cdot c_{n+j-1} + \eta_{B(A(w))}$. Since $A(w)$ is an AND gate, we would have $r_{A(w)} = r_{A(A(w))} + r_{B(A(w))} = 2c_{n+1} \cdots \cdot c_{n+j-1} + \eta_{A(A(w))} + \eta_{B(A(w))}$. Hence, we have:

$$K_{w,3} = g_{j-1}^{\eta_w - \frac{1}{2}c_{n+j}(\eta_{A(A(w))} + \eta_{B(A(w))}) - \psi_w(2c_{n+1} \cdots \cdot c_{n+j-1} + \eta_{A(A(w))} + \eta_{B(A(w))})}$$
$$= g_{j-1}^{r_w - a_w \cdot r_{A(w)}}$$

which can be computed as outlined in the former case.

Thus, the four key components can be given out in every case.

AND Gate. We now discuss the case of the AND gate. Suppose that $w \in \mathsf{Gates}$ and that $\mathtt{GateType}(w) = \mathrm{AND}$. In addition, let $j = \mathtt{OR\text{-}depth}(w)$. $\mathcal{B}$ implicitly sets $r_w = r_{A(w)} + r_{B(w)}$. Note that we need not choose any a_w or b_w. In fact, r_w is being chosen because the key components being given out for the OR gates involve $r_{A(w)}$, etc., which may potentially be from AND gates. Clearly, Property 1 holds here as well, i.e., $g_j^{r_w} = g_j^{r_{A(w)}} \cdot g_j^{r_{B(w)}}$ can be computed for this wire, since $g_j^{r_{A(w)}}$ and $g_j^{r_{B(w)}}$ can be computed by virtue of Property 1.

Finally, we set, for the output wire $w = n + q$, $\eta_w = 0$, so that $r_w = u$ in $\mathcal{B}$'s internal view. It is easy to see that a_w and b_w have the same distribution in the real game and the game executed by $\mathcal{B}$. In the real game, they are chosen at random and in the game executed by $\mathcal{B}$, they are either chosen at random or are values offset by some random values ψ_w and ϕ_w, respectively. For $w \in [n+q-1]$, r_w also has the same distribution in the real game and the game executed by $\mathcal{B}$. This is true, since in the real game, they are chosen so that randomness on the input wires of an AND gate add up to the randomness on its output wire, and they are chosen at random for an OR gate, while in the game executed by $\mathcal{B}$, they are chosen in the exact same way, where being "chosen at random" is either truly satisfied or are fixed values are offset by random η_w values. Now, we look at r_{n+q}. In the real game, it is a fixed value u, and in the game executed by $\mathcal{B}$, by setting $\eta_{n+q} = 0$, $r_{n+q} = c_{n+1} \cdot c_{n+2} \cdot \ldots \cdot c_{n+\ell_{OR}} = u$ internally. Hence, they too have the same distribution. Hence all the parameters in the real game and game executed by $\mathcal{B}$ have the identical distribution.

Evaluate: Suppose a query is made for a secret key for an input $x \in \{0,1\}^n$. If $x = x^*$, then $\mathcal{B}$ aborts. Otherwise, $\mathcal{B}$ identifies an arbitrary t such that $x_t \neq x_t^*$. Through ℓ_{OR} pairings of g^{c_m}, $n + 1 \leq m \leq n + \ell_{OR}$, it computes $H = g_{\ell_{OR}}^u = g_{\ell_{OR}}^{c_{n+1} \cdot \ldots \cdot c_{n+\ell_{OR}}}$. Then, through pairing of $D_{m,x_m} \forall m \in [n]\backslash\{t\}$, it computes $g_{n-1}^{\Pi_{m\in[n]\backslash\{t\}} d_{m,x_m}}$ and raises it to $d_{t,x_t} = z_t$ to get $H' = g_{n-1}^{\Pi_{m\in[n]} d_{m,x_m}}$. Finally, it computes $H'' = e(H, H') = g_{n+\ell_{OR}-1}^{u \Pi_{m\in[n]} d_{m,x_m}} = F(k,x)$ and outputs it. Eventually, $\mathcal{A}$ will issue a challenge input $\tilde{x}$. If $\tilde{x} = x^*$, $\mathcal{B}$ will return the value T and output the same bit as $\mathcal{A}$ does as its guess. If $\tilde{x} \neq x^*$, $\mathcal{B}$ outputs a random bit as its guess.

This completes the description of the adversary $\mathcal{B}$. We first note that in the case where T is part of a MDDH tuple, the real game and game executed by $\mathcal{B}$ have the identical distribution. Secondly, in both cases (i.e., whether or not T is part of the MDDH tuple), as long as $\mathcal{B}$ does not abort, once again, the real game and game executed by $\mathcal{B}$ have the identical distribution, except for the output of $\mathcal{B}$ on the challenge query x^*. We now analyze the probability that $\mathcal{B}$'s guess was correct. Let δ' denote $\mathcal{B}$'s output and let δ denote whether T is an MDDH tuple or not, $\delta, \delta' \in \{0,1\}$. Now

$$\Pr[\delta' = \delta] = \Pr[\delta' = \delta|\mathsf{abort}] \Pr[\mathsf{abort}] + \Pr[\delta' = \delta|\overline{\mathsf{abort}}] \Pr[\overline{\mathsf{abort}}]$$

$$= \frac{1}{2}(1 - 2^{-n}) + \Pr[\delta' = \delta|\overline{\mathsf{abort}}] \cdot (2^{-n})$$

$$= \frac{1}{2}(1 - 2^{-n}) + \left(\frac{1}{2} + \epsilon\right) \cdot (2^{-n}) = \frac{1}{2} + \epsilon \cdot (2^{-n})$$

The set of equations shows that the advantage of $\mathcal{B}$ is $\epsilon(\lambda)/2^n$. This completes the proof of the theorem, which establishes the pseudorandomness property of the construction. Hence, the constrained PRF construction for the circuit-predicate case is secure under the κ-MDDH assumption.

Removing the Restrictions. The restriction that $\mathtt{GateType}(n + q) = \mathtt{OR}$ enables us to set randomness as we do in the scheme above. But this restriction can be easily removed by setting the randomness corresponding to the last level of OR gates (or the input wires in case there is no OR gate in the circuit) appropriately so that r_{n+q} ends up being u.

The restriction that a layer of gates cannot follow another layer of the same type of gates can also be overcome. The case of several consecutive layers of OR gates poses no threat since we move up one level in the multilinear maps for layers of OR gates and hence the current proof method works as is. The case of several consecutive layers of AND gates can be handled by even more careful choices of the randomness a_w and b_w. When we had only one layer of AND gate (before a layer of OR gates), for an OR gate at $\mathtt{OR\text{-}depth}$ j, we set a_w to be either $1 \cdot c_{n+j} + \psi_w$ or $\frac{1}{2} \cdot c_{n+j} + \psi_w$ depending on whether $r_{A(w)} = 1 \cdot c_{n+1} \cdots \cdot c_{n+j-1} + \eta_{A(A(w))} + \eta_{B(A(w))}$ or $r_{A(w)} = 2 \cdot c_{n+1} \cdots \cdot c_{n+j-1} + \eta_{A(A(w))} + \eta_{B(A(w))}$. Similarly, we set b_w in accordance with $r_{B(w)}$. Now, when there are more than one layers of AND gates consecutively, for an OR gate at $\mathtt{OR\text{-}depth}$ j just after these AND gates, we set a_w (resp. $b(w)$) to be $\frac{1}{k} c_{n+j} + \psi_w$ where k is the coefficient of $c_{n+1} \cdots \cdot c_{n+j-1}$ in $r_{A(w)}$ (resp. $r_{B(w)}$). We present an illustration of this technique in the full version [CRV15].

Regarding the first assumption, any layered circuit can be trivially converted into a "homogeneous" layered circuit by "splitting" each layer in the layered circuit into two layers: one with only AND gates and the other with only OR gates. This doubles the depth of the circuit. But if we are a bit more careful and do the splitting such that the odd layers are split into an AND-layer followed by an OR-layer and the even layers are split into an OR-layer followed by an AND-layer, the resulting circuit will have layers of the form (AND-OR)-(OR-AND)-(AND-OR)-$\cdots$. Now, we can merge the consecutive OR layers into a single OR layer (because our scheme supports gates with arbitrary fan-in) with just a polynomial increase in the number of wires. So, we can convert a layered circuit of depth d into a layered circuit with each layer consisting of only AND or OR gates with depth $d + 1$ but with the OR-depth of the circuit being $d/2$ now. So even in the worst case we get improvements in parameters using our scheme.

4 A Free-OR Circuit-Predicate Construction

In this section, we show how to construct a constrained random function for polynomial size circuit predicates of a specific form, without giving any keys for the OR gates. Once again, we base our construction on multilinear maps and on the κ-MDDH assumption; however κ in our construction will only depend on n (the size of the input to the PRF) and now, the AND-depth of the circuit (informally, this is the maximum number of AND gates from input wires to the output wire along any path). Once again, the starting point of our construction is the constrained PRF construction of Boneh and Waters [BW13] which is based on the attribute-based encryption construction for circuits [GGH+13c]. We restrict the class of boolean circuits to be of a specific form. We assume layered circuits and that all gates in a particular layer are of the same type (either AND or OR). We assume that a layer of gates is not followed by another layer of the same type of gates. We also assume that all AND gates have a fanout of 1^5.

We introduce here a "gadget" which we call a "FANOUT-gate". This is done in order to deal with OR gates in the circuit that have a fanout greater than 1. To this end, we assume that a FANOUT-gate is placed just after the OR gate under consideration. We view such OR gates also to have a fanout of 1 and without loss of generality assume that the FANOUT-gate alone has a fanout greater than 1. However, we do not treat the FANOUT-gate while calculating the total depth of the circuit, etc. It is merely a construct which allows us to deal only with OR gates having fanout 1.

4.1   Construction

The setup and the PRF construction is identical to the construction in Sect. 3. We now outline the constrain and evaluate algorithms.

$F.\text{Constrain}(k, f = (n, q, A, B, \text{GateType}))$: The constrain algorithm takes as input the key k and a circuit description f. The circuit has $n + q$ wires with n input wires, q gates and the wire $n + q$ designated as the output wire. Assume that all gates have fanout 1 and that FANOUT-gates have been inserted at places where the gates have a fanout greater than 1.

To generate a constrained key k_f, the key generation algorithm sets $r_{n+q} = u$, where we think of the random value r_w as being associated with the wire w. Hence, in notation, if a gate w has fanout greater than 1, then, notation-wise, r_w would have multiple values: one associated with each of the fanout wires of the FANOUT-gate and one associated with the wire leading out of the gate w itself. We introduce notation for the same below.

Consider a FANOUT-gate placed after wire w, as shown in Fig. 1. We denote by r_w^{L} the randomness on the wire going as input to the FANOUT-gate (the actual output wire of the gate under consideration) and by $r_w^{\text{R},i}$ the randomness on the ith fanout wire of the FANOUT-gate (there would be as many of these as the fanout of the gate w), where $i \in [\Delta]$ and Δ is the fanout of the wire w.

We now describe how the randomness for each wire is set. For each $w \in [n + q] \setminus [n]$, if $\text{GateType}(w) = \text{OR}$, it sets $r_{A(w)} = r_{B(w)} = r_w$, otherwise, it

---

[5] This can always be ensured for circuits that have alternating AND and OR layers. Suppose there is an AND gate with fanout $\Delta > 1$. We simply replace it with Δ AND gates having the same inputs and now we have Δ wires with the required output as before. Note that this process would have forced us to make the fanout of gates driving the AND gate to be Δ times as large, but since a gate driving an AND gate would only be an OR gate by our imposed circuit structure, this blows up the size of the circuit by only a polynomial factor.

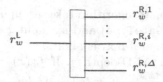

Fig. 1. FANOUT-gate

chooses $r_{A(w)}$ and $r_{B(w)}$ at random. The case of FANOUT-gates is handled as follows. Note that the above description already takes care of setting randomness on all the fanout wires of the FANOUT-gate. The randomness for the input wire to the FANOUT-gate (the output wire of the gate with fanout greater than 1) is chosen at random. Note that this completely describes how randomness on all wires in the circuit are chosen.

The first part of the constrained key is given out as simply all $D_{i,\beta}$ for $i \in [n]$ and $\beta \in \{0,1\}$. Next, the algorithm generates key components. The structure of the key components depends on whether w is an input wire or an output of an AND gate. For OR gates, we do not need to give out any keys, hence the name Free-OR. But, we also need to give out special key components for the FANOUT-gates. The key components in each case are described below.

- *Input wire*
  By convention, if $w \in [n]$, then it corresponds to the w-th input. The key component is:
  $$K_w = g^{r_w d_{w,1}}$$

- *AND gate*
  Suppose that $w \in$ Gates and that $\texttt{GateType}(w) = \text{AND}$. In addition, let $j = \texttt{AND-depth}(w)$. The algorithm chooses random $a_w, b_w \in \mathbb{Z}_p$. Then, the algorithm creates key components:
  $$K_{w,1} = g^{a_w}, K_{w,2} = g^{b_w}, K_{w,3} = g_{j-1}^{r_w - a_w \cdot r_{A(w)} - b_w \cdot r_{B(w)}}$$

- *FANOUT-gate*
  Suppose that $w \in$ Gates, $\texttt{GateType}(w) = \text{OR}$ and that the fanout of w is greater than 1. In addition, let $j = \texttt{AND-depth}(w)$. In this case, a FANOUT-gate would have been placed after w. Let r_w^L denote the randomness on the wire going as input to the FANOUT-gate (the actual output wire of the gate under consideration) and let $r_w^{\mathsf{R},i}$ denote the randomness on the ith fanout wire of the FANOUT-gate (there would be as many of these as the fanout of the gate w). The keys given out are:
  $$K_{w,w',i} = g_{j-1}^{\left(r_w^{\mathsf{R},i} - r_w^\mathsf{L}\right)}$$

for all $i \in [\Delta]$, where Δ is the fanout of the gate w.

The constrained key k_f consists of all these key components along with $\{D_{i,\beta}\}$ for $i \in [n]$ and $\beta \in \{0,1\}$.

F.Evaluate(k_f, x): The evaluate algorithm takes as input a constrained key k_f for the circuit $f = (n, q, A, B, \texttt{GateType})$ and an input $x \in \{0,1\}^n$. The algorithm first checks that $f(x) = 1$, and if not, it aborts.

Consider the wire w at AND-depth j. If $f_w(x) = 1$, then, the algorithm computes $E_w = g_{n+j-1}^{r_w \prod_{m \in [n]} d_{m,x_m}}$. If $f_w(x) = 0$, then nothing needs to be computed for that wire. The algorithm proceeds iteratively starting with computing E_1 and proceeds, in order, to compute E_{n+q}. Computing these values in order ensures that the computation on a lower-depth wire that evaluates to 1 will be defined before the computation for a higher-depth wire. Since $r_{n+q} = u$,
$$E_{n+q} = g_{n+\ell_{\mathsf{AND}}-1}^{u \prod_{m \in [n]} d_{m,x_m}}.$$

We show how to compute E_w for all w where $f_w(x) = 1$, case-wise, according to whether the wire is an input, an OR gate, an AND gate or a fanout wire of a FANOUT-gate. Define $D = D(x) = g_n^{\prod_{m \in [n]} d_{m,x_m}}$, which is computable through n pairing operations.

- *Input wire*
  By convention, if $w \in [n]$, then it corresponds to the w-th input. Suppose $f_w(x) = 1$. Through pairing operations, the algorithm computes $g_{n-1}^{\prod_{m \in [n]\setminus\{w\}} d_{m,x_m}}$. It then computes:

$$E_w = e\left(K_w, g_{n-1}^{\prod_{m \in [n]\setminus\{w\}} d_{m,x_m}}\right) = g_n^{r_w \prod_{m \in [n]} d_{m,x_m}}$$

- *OR gate*
  Consider a wire $w \in$ Gates with $\texttt{GateType}(w) = \text{OR}$. The computation is performed if $f_w(x) = 1$. Note that in this case, at least one of $f_{A(w)}(x)$ and $f_{B(w)}(x)$ must be 1. Hence, we must have been able to evaluate at least one of $E_{A(w)}$ and $E_{B(w)}$. Since, for an OR gate, $r_{A(w)} = r_{B(w)} = r_w$, we have $E_w = E_{A(w)} = E_{B(w)}$, which can now be computed.

- *AND gate*
  Consider a wire $w \in$ Gates with $\texttt{GateType}(w) = \text{AND}$. In addition, let $j = \texttt{AND-depth}(w)$. The computation is performed if $f_w(x) = 1$. Note that in this case, both $f_{A(w)}(x)$ and $f_{B(w)}(x)$ must be 1. The algorithm computes:

$$
\begin{aligned}
E_w &= e(E_{A(w)}, K_{w,1}) \cdot e(E_{B(w)}, K_{w,2}) \cdot e(K_{w,3}, D) \\
&= e\left(g_{n+j-2}^{r_{A(w)} \prod_{m \in [n]} d_{m,x_m}}, g^{a_w}\right) \cdot e\left(g_{n+j-2}^{r_{B(w)} \prod_{m \in [n]} d_{m,x_m}}, g^{b_w}\right) \cdot \\
&\quad\ e\left(g_{j-1}^{r_{A(w)} - a_w \cdot r_{A(w)} - b_w \cdot r_{B(w)}}, g_n^{u \prod_{m \in [n]} d_{m,x_m}}\right) \\
&= g_{n+j-1}^{r_w \prod_{m \in [n]} d_{m,x_m}}
\end{aligned}
$$

- *FANOUT-gate*
  Let r_w^{L} denote the randomness on the wire going as input to the FANOUT-gate (the actual output wire of the gate under consideration) and let $r_w^{\mathsf{R},i}$ denote the randomness on the ith fanout wire of the FANOUT-gate (there would be as many of these as the fanout of the gate w). The computation is

performed if $f_w(x) = 1$. In coherence with the previous notation, we define the quantities E_w^{L} and $E_w^{\mathsf{R},i}$. Note that the E_w^{L} would have been computed. It then computes:

$$E_w^{\mathsf{R},i} = e\left(K_{w,w',i}, D\right) \cdot E_w^{\mathsf{L}} = g_{n+j-1}^{r_w^{\mathsf{R},i} \prod_{m \in [n]} d_{m,x_m}}$$

The procedures above are evaluated in order for all w for which $f_w(x) = 1$. Thus, the algorithm computes $E_{n+q} = g_{n+\ell-1}^{u \prod_{m \in [n]} d_{m,x_m}} = F(k,x)$.

5   Combining the Free-AND and Free-OR Techniques

In this section, we show that for the case of $\mathbf{NC}^1$, we can indeed combine the Free-AND and Free-OR techniques to obtain a construction that has Free-ANDs and Free-ORs. While the main reason that the technique works is that for $\mathbf{NC}^1$ circuits we can consider only boolean formulas, proving that our construction is secure is non-trivial (and different from the case of ABE).

5.1   An $\mathbf{NC}^1$-predicate Construction

We construct a constrained PRF for arbitrary $\mathbf{NC}^1$ circuit predicates, without giving any keys for AND as well as OR gates. Again, we base our construction on the κ-MDDH assumption; however κ in our construction will only depend on n (the size of the input to the PRF) and **not** on the circuit in any way. We will be dealing with circuits of the form described in Sect. 2.3.

5.2   Construction

$F.\mathsf{Setup}(1^\lambda, 1^n)$: The setup algorithm that defines the master secret key and the PRF is identical to the setup algorithm from Sect. 3 with $\kappa = n$ instead of $n + \ell_{\mathsf{OR}} - 1$.

$F.\mathsf{Constrain}(k, f = (n, q, A, B, \mathsf{GateType}))$: The algorithm sets $r_{n+q} = u$. For each $w \in [n+q]\setminus[n]$, if $\mathsf{GateType}(w) = \mathsf{OR}$, it sets $r_{A(w)} = r_{B(w)} = r_w$, otherwise, it chooses $r_{A(w)}$ at random and sets $r_{B(w)} = r_w - r_{A(w)}$. Since the fanout of all gates is 1, for any wire $w \in [n+q]\setminus[n]$, r_w would have been uniquely set. However, since the same inputs may be re-used in multiple gates, for any wire $w \in [n]$, r_w may have multiple values (as many as the fanout of the input wire), i.e., different randomness values for each use of the input wire (to different gates). Note that this procedure sets randomness on all wires in the circuit. The first part of the constrained key (k_f) is given out as simply all $D_{i,\beta}$ for $i \in [n]$ and $\beta \in \{0,1\}$. The remaining key components are: $K_{w,i} = g^{r_{w,i} d_{w,1}}, \forall i \in [\Delta]$, where Δ is the fanout of the input wire w.

$F.\mathsf{Evaluate}(k_f, x)$: The evaluate algorithm takes as input a constrained key k_f and an input $x \in \{0,1\}^n$. The algorithm first checks that $f(x) = 1$, and if not, it aborts. Consider the wire w. If $f_w(x) = 1$, then, we show how to compute[6] $E_w = g_n^{r_w \prod_{m \in [n]} d_{m,x_m}}$, case-wise, according to whether the wire is an input, an OR gate or an AND gate.

- *Input wire.* Through pairing operations, compute $g_{n-1}^{\prod_{m \in [n] \setminus \{w\}} d_{m,x_m}}$. Then compute: $E_{w,i} = e\left(K_{w,i}, g_{n-1}^{\prod_{m \in [n] \setminus \{w\}} d_{m,x_m}}\right) = g_n^{r_{w,i} \prod_{m \in [n]} d_{m,x_m}} \forall i \in [\Delta]$, where Δ is the fanout of the input wire w.
- *OR gate.* In this case, at least one of $f_{A(w)}(x)$ and $f_{B(w)}(x)$ must be 1. Hence, we can evaluate at least one of $E_{A(w)}$ and $E_{B(w)}$. Since, for an OR gate, $r_{A(w)} = r_{B(w)} = r_w$, $E_w = E_{A(w)} = E_{B(w)}$, can now be computed.
- *AND gate.* In this case, $f_{A(w)}(x) = f_{B(w)}(x) = 1$. The algorithm computes:

$$E_w = E_{A(w)} \cdot E_{B(w)} = g_n^{r_{A(w)} \prod_{m \in [n]} d_{m,x_m}} \cdot g_n^{r_{B(w)} \prod_{m \in [n]} d_{m,x_m}} = g_n^{r_w \prod_{m \in [n]} d_{m,x_m}}$$

The procedures above are evaluated, in order, for all w for which $f_w(x) = 1$. Thus, the algorithm computes $E_{n+q} = g_n^{u \prod_{m \in [n]} d_{m,x_m}} = F(k, x)$.

5.3 Proof of Pseudorandomness

The correctness of the constrained PRF is verifiable in a straightforward manner. To show pseudorandomness, given an algorithm $\mathcal{A}$ that breaks security of the constrained PRF, we will construct algorithm $\mathcal{B}$ that breaks security of the $\kappa = n-$MDDH assumption. $\mathcal{B}$ receives a $\kappa-$MDDH challenge consisting of the group sequence description $\mathbb{G}$ and $g = g_1, g^{c_1}, \ldots, g^{c_{\kappa+1}}$ along with T, where T is either $g_\kappa^{\prod_{m \in [\kappa+1]} c_m}$ or a random group element in $\mathbb{G}_\kappa$. The security proof is in the selective security model (where the adversary commits to the challenge input x^* at the beginning of the game). To get full security, the proof will use the standard complexity leveraging technique of guessing the challenge x^*; this guess will cause a loss of a $1/2^n$-factor in the reduction. We formally show:

Theorem 2. *If there exists a PPT adversary $\mathcal{A}$ that breaks the pseudorandomness property of our $\mathbf{NC}^1$-predicate construction for n-bit inputs with advantage $\epsilon(\lambda)$, then there exists a PPT algorithm $\mathcal{B}$ that breaks the $\kappa = n-$Multilinear Decisional Diffie-Hellman assumption with advantage $\epsilon(\lambda)/2^n$.*

Proof. The algorithm $\mathcal{B}$ first receives a $\kappa = n-$MDDH challenge consisting of the group sequence description $\mathbb{G}$ and $g = g_1, g^{c_1}, \ldots, g^{c_{\kappa+1}}$ along with T, where T is either $g_\kappa^{\prod_{m \in [\kappa+1]} c_m}$ or a random group element in $\mathbb{G}_\kappa$.

---

[6] For input wires $w \in [n]$, we have $E_{w,i} = g_n^{r_{w,i} \prod_{m \in [n]} d_{m,x_m}}$ for all $i \in [\Delta]$, where Δ is the fanout of the input wire w. This feature has been present in our Free-OR construction as well. We pay attention to it specifically in this construction because of the absence of fanout for any wire other than the input wires.

Setup. It chooses an $x^* \in \{0,1\}^n$ uniformly at random. Next, it chooses random $z_1, \ldots, z_n \in \mathbb{Z}_p$ and sets $D_{m,\beta} = g^{c_m}$ if $x_m^* = \beta$ and g^{z_m} otherwise, for $m \in [n]$ and $\beta \in \{0,1\}$. It then implicitly sets $u = c_{n+1}$. The setup is executed as in the construction.

Constrain. Suppose a query is made for a secret key for a circuit $f = (n, q, A, B, \texttt{GateType})$. If $f(x^*) = 1$, then $\mathcal{B}$ aborts.

Otherwise, $\mathcal{B}$ sets the randomness on each wire in the circuit in the following way. It sets, for the output wire $w = n + q$, $r_w = u = c_{n+1}$. For each $w \in [n + q]\backslash[n]$, if $\texttt{GateType}(w) = \text{OR}$, it sets $r_{A(w)} = r_{B(w)} = r_w$. Suppose $\texttt{GateType}(w) = \text{AND}$. If $f_w(x^*) = 1$, then $f_{A(w)}(x^*) = f_{B(w)}(x^*) = 1$ and $\mathcal{B}$ chooses $r_{A(w)}$ at random and sets $r_{B(w)} = r_w - r_{A(w)}$. Suppose $f_w(x^*) = 0$. Then we know that at least one of $f_{A(w)}(x^*)$ and $f_{B(w)}(x^*)$ must be zero. If $f_{A(w)}(x^*) = 0$, it chooses $r_{B(w)}$ at random and sets $r_{A(w)} = r_w - r_{B(w)}$, while if $f_{A(w)}(x^*) = 1$ and hence $f_{B(w)}(x^*) = 0$, it chooses $r_{A(w)}$ at random and sets $r_{B(w)} = r_w - r_{A(w)}$. As we shall see later, such a choice of randomness is critical for the security proof. Since the fanout of all gates is 1, for any wire $w \in [n+q]\backslash[n]$, r_w would have been uniquely set. However, since the same inputs may be re-used in multiple gates, for any wire $w \in [n]$, r_w may have multiple values (as many as the fanout of the input wire), i.e., different randomness values for each use of the input wire (to different gates), which we denote by $r_{w,i}$ for all $i \in [\Delta]$, where Δ is the fanout of the input wire w. Note that this procedure sets randomness on all wires in the circuit.

To show that $\mathcal{B}$ can indeed compute all the key components, our proof will follow a similar structure to the Free-OR case (Sect. 4). We shall prove that for all wires in the circuit, $\mathcal{B}$ can compute g^{r_w}. To prove this, we shall prove the above statement, both when the wire w is such that $f_w(x^*) = 1$ (Lemma 2), and when the wire w is such that $f_w(x^*) = 0$ (Lemma 3). To prove Lemma 2, we shall first prove the following fact (Lemma 1): consider all wires in the circuit that evaluate to 1 on x^* and consider those wires among these that have maximum total depth; then, these wires must all be input wires to AND gates.

Lemma 1. *Define:*

- $S_1 = \{w : w \in [n + q] \wedge f_w(x^*) = 1\}$
- $S_1^{\textit{max-tot-depth}} = \{w : w \in S_1 \wedge \textit{tot-depth}(w) \geq \textit{tot-depth}(w') \; \forall w' \in S_1\}$

Then w is an input wire to an AND gate $\forall w \in S_1^{\textit{max-tot-depth}}$.

Proof. This fact is very easy to easy. Clearly, $w \neq n+q$, since $f_{n+q}(x^*) = 0$ while $f_w(x^*) = 1$. Hence there exist layers of gates after the one containing w. Suppose w is an input wire to an OR gate. Since $f_w(x^*) = 1$, for some OR gate w' in the next layer of gates, $f_{w'}(x^*) = 1$. Hence, $\exists w' \in S_1$ such that $\textit{tot-depth}(w) < \textit{tot-depth}(w')$ which contradicts the fact that $w \in S_1^{\textit{max-tot-depth}}$.

Lemma 2. *For any wire $w \in [n + q]$, if $f_w(x^*) = 1$, then r_w is known.*

Proof. We prove this by observing the randomness we have set on each wire, from the output wire to the input wires. From Lemma 1, we know that the first such wire we would see would be an input to an AND gate. For an input wire $A(w)$, of an AND gate, satisfying $f_{A(w)}(x^*) = 1$, first consider the case when $f_w(x^*) = 1$[7]. In this case, $\mathcal{B}$ explicitly chooses all random values associated with this gate and hence $\mathcal{B}$ chose $r_{A(w)}$. When $f_w(x^*) = 0$, note that $\mathcal{B}$ carefully chose the randomness on the input wires which may potentially evaluate to 1 on x^* at random (and set the value on the other input wire $B(w)$ based on this). Hence, if $f_{A(w)}(x^*) = 1$, $r_{A(w)}$ is known to $\mathcal{B}$. This forms the base case for the induction. Now, consider any other wire $A(w)$ such that $f_{A(w)} = 1$. Now, if $A(w)$ were an input to an AND gate, then by the same argument as above, $r_{A(w)}$ is known to $\mathcal{B}$. Suppose, $A(w)$ were an input to an OR gate w and $f_{A(w)}(x^*) = 1$, then $f_w(x^*) = 1$. By the induction hypothesis, r_w is known. We know that since w is an OR gate, $r_{A(w)} = r_w$ and hence $r_{A(w)}$ is known. This completes the proof. $\qquad\blacksquare$

Lemma 3. *For any wire $w \in [n + q]$, if $f_w(x^*) = 0$, then g^{r_w} is known.*

Proof. We can prove this by observing the randomness we have set on each wire, from the output wire to the input wires. The statement is true for the output wire $w = n + q$, since $g^{c_{n+1}}$ is known. This forms the base case. We can now argue inductively.

- Case 1: If w is an input to an OR gate w', then $r_w = r_{w'}$. If $f_w(x^*) = 1$, then by Lemma 2, $r_{w'}$ is known and hence g^{r_w} is known. If $f_{w'}(x^*) = 0$, then by the induction hypothesis, $g^{r_{w'}}$ is known and hence g^{r_w} is known.
- Case 2: If w is an input to an AND gate w', then $f_{w'}(x^*) = 0$. Now, by the induction hypothesis, $g^{r_{w'}}$ is known. If $w = A(w')$, then $r_{B(w')}$ was chosen at random and is known, and hence $g^{r_w} = g^{r_{w'} - r_{B(w')}}$ is known. Suppose $w = B(w')$. If $f_{A(w')}(x^*) = 0$, r_w was chosen at random and is known, and hence g^{r_w} is known. If $f_{A(w')}(x^*) = 1$, then $r_{A(w')}$ was chosen at random and is known, and hence $g^{r_w} = g^{r_{w'} - r_{A(w')}}$ is known.

Finally, $\mathcal{B}$ generates key components for input wires $w \in [n]$. By convention, if $w \in [n]$, then it corresponds to the w-th input. If $x^*_w = 1$, then $r_{w,i}$ is known, from Lemma 2, for all $i \in [\Delta]$, where Δ is the fanout of the input wire w. The key components are: $K_{w,i} = (D_{w,1})^{r_{w,i}} = g^{r_{w,i}d_{w,1}}$, for all $i \in [\Delta]$. If $x^*_w = 0$, then $g^{r_{w,i}}$ is known, from Lemma 3, for all $i \in [\Delta]$. The key components are: $K_{w,i} = (g^{r_{w,i}})^{z_w} = g^{r_{w,i}d_{w,1}}$, for all $i \in [\Delta]$.

Evaluate. Suppose a query is made for a secret key for an input $x \in \{0,1\}^n$. If $x = x^*$, then $\mathcal{B}$ aborts. Otherwise, $\mathcal{B}$ identifies an arbitrary t such that $x_t \neq x^*_t$. Through pairing of $D_{m,x_m} \forall m \in [n]\backslash\{t\}$, it computes $g_{n-1}^{\prod_{m \in [n]\backslash\{t\}} d_{m,x_m}}$ and raises it to $d_{t,x_t} = z_t$ to get $H = g_{n-1}^{\prod_{m \in [n]} d_{m,x_m}}$. Finally, it computes $H' = e(U, H) =$

---

[7] It is true that the first such wire when we go from output to input level would be an AND gate with $f_w(x^*) = 0$. However, the discussion on the case of $f_w(x^*) = 1$ is more a general one for all AND gates in the circuit.

$g_n^{u \prod_{m \in [n]} d_{m,x_m}} = F(k, x)$ and outputs it. Eventually, $\mathcal{A}$ will issue a challenge input $\tilde{x}$. If $\tilde{x} = x^*$, $\mathcal{B}$ will return the value T and output the same bit as $\mathcal{A}$ does as its guess. If $\tilde{x} \neq x^*$, $\mathcal{B}$ outputs a random bit as its guess.

This completes the description of the adversary $\mathcal{B}$. We first note that in the case where T is part of a MDDH tuple, the real game and game executed by $\mathcal{B}$ have the identical distribution. Secondly, in both cases (i.e., whether or not T is part of the MDDH tuple), as long as $\mathcal{B}$ does not abort, once again, the real game and game executed by $\mathcal{B}$ have the identical distribution, except for the output of $\mathcal{B}$ on the challenge query x^*. Similar to the analysis in Sect. 3, the probability that $\mathcal{B}$'s guess was correct can be shown to be $\epsilon(\lambda)/2^n$.

6 From Bit-Fixing PRFs to $\mathbf{NC}^1$ PRFs

In this section, we show that from any constrained PRF scheme supporting bit-fixing predicates that has certain additive homomorphic properties (let this be $\mathsf{F_{bf}}$), we can construct a constrained PRF scheme supporting $\mathbf{NC}^1$ circuit predicates ($\mathsf{F_{NC1}}$) in a black-box manner. We will be dealing with circuits of the form described in Sect. 2.3. It is sufficient if the PRF is able to fix a single bit to just one of the possibilities (i.e., either fixing the bits only to 0 or only to 1). The homomorphic properties that we require from the bit-fixing scheme are:

1. The PRF must have an additive key-homomorphism property. In other words, there exists a public algorithm $\mathsf{F_{bf}.KeyEval}$, such that, for all $k_1, k_2 \in \mathcal{K}$, $\mathsf{F_{bf}.KeyEval}$ outputs $\mathsf{F_{bf}}(k_1 + k_2, x)$ on inputs $\mathsf{F_{bf}}(k_1, x)$ and $\mathsf{F_{bf}}(k_2, x)$.
2. Let $\mathsf{F_{bf}.Constrain}(k, i)$ be the constrain algorithm that takes in a key and the position of the bit to be fixed to 1.[8] An additive key-homomorphism property should also exist among the constrained keys, that is, there exists a public algorithm, $\mathsf{F_{bf}.AddKeys}$, such that[9], for all $k_1, k_2 \in \mathcal{K}$ and index i,

$$\mathsf{F_{bf}.AddKeys}(\mathsf{F_{bf}.Constrain}(k_1, i), \mathsf{F_{bf}.Constrain}(k_2, i)) = \mathsf{F_{bf}.Constrain}(k_1 + k_2, i)$$

6.1 Construction

We follow the same template as in our $\mathbf{NC}^1$-predicate construction in Sect. 5.1. We observe that the component $K_{w,i}$ at the input level can be replaced with a constrained key from any bit-fixing scheme which satisfies the properties mentioned above. $\mathsf{F_{bf}}, \mathsf{F_{NC1}}$ denote the bit-fixing and $\mathbf{NC}^1$ schemes respectively.

$\mathsf{F_{NC1}.Setup}(1^\lambda, 1^n)$: The setup algorithm runs $\mathsf{F_{bf}.Setup}(1^\lambda, 1^n)$ to get the PRF $\mathsf{F_{bf}}$ and key k. It sets the key as k. The keyed pseudo-random function is defined as $\mathsf{F_{bf}}(k, x)$.

---

[8] By symmetry, the construction also works if the constrain algorithm fixes a bit to 0.
[9] We note here that $\mathsf{F_{bf}.Constrain}(k, i)$ could, in general, be a randomized algorithm and in this case, we require the distributions on the left and the right of the equality to be computationally indistinguishable. For ease of exposition, we assume that $\mathsf{F_{bf}.Constrain}(k, i)$ is deterministic and state our results accordingly.

F_{NC1}.Constrain$(k, f = (n, q, A, B, \texttt{GateType}))$: The constrain algorithm sets up randomness on the wires of the circuit using the procedure in the construction in Sect. 5.1 and computes key components for the input wires as $K_w = F_{bf}$.Constrain$(r_w, w)^{10}$. The constrained key k_f consists of all these key components.

F_{NC1}.Evaluate(k_f, x): The algorithm first checks that $f(x) = 1$, and if not, it aborts. As in the construction in Sect. 5.1, for every wire w, if $f_w(x) = 1$, then, the algorithm computes $F_{bf}(r_w, x)$. The algorithm proceeds iteratively and computes $F_{bf}(r_{n+q}, x) = F_{bf}(k, x)$. $F_{bf}(r_w, x)$ can be computed, case-wise, according to whether the wire is an input, an OR gate or an AND gate.

- *Input wire*
  If $f_w(x) = 1$, it computes $F_{bf}(r_w, x) = F_{bf}$.Eval(K_w, x).
- *OR gate*
  If $f_w(x) = 1$, at least one of $f_{A(w)}(x)$ and $f_{B(w)}(x)$ must be 1. Hence, we must have been able to evaluate at least one of $F_{bf}(r_{A(w)}, x)$ and $F_{bf}(r_{B(w)}, x)$. Since, $r_{A(w)} = r_{B(w)} = r_w$, $F_{bf}(r_w, x) = F_{bf}(r_{A(w)}, x) = F_{bf}(r_{B(w)}, x)$, which can be computed.
- *AND gate*
  If $f_w(x) = 1$, $f_{A(w)}(x) = f_{B(w)}(x) = 1$. Hence, we must have been able to evaluate both $F_{bf}(r_{A(w)}, x)$ and $F_{bf}(r_{B(w)}, x)$. The algorithm computes $F_{bf}(r_w, x) = F_{bf}$.KeyEval$(F_{bf}(r_{A(w)}, x), F_{bf}(r_{B(w)}x))$, since, $r_{A(w)} + r_{B(w)} = r_w$.

The procedures above are evaluated, in order, for all w for which $f_w(x) = 1$. Thus, the algorithm computes $F_{bf}(r_{n+q}, x) = F_{bf}(k, x)$.

6.2   Proof of Pseudorandomness

The correctness of the scheme is straightforward from the key-homomorphism property of the bit-fixing PRF scheme. We now prove the security.

Theorem 3. *If there exists a PPT adversary $\mathcal{A}$ that breaks the selective security of our construction for n-bit inputs supporting $\mathbf{NC}^1$-predicates with an advantage $\epsilon(\lambda)$, then there exists a PPT algorithm $\mathcal{B}$ that breaks the selective security of the underlying bit-fixing predicate construction with the same advantage $\epsilon(\lambda)$.*

Proof. Let $\overset{\bullet}{\mathcal{A}}$ be the adversary which breaks the selective security of our $\mathbf{NC}^1$ construction. We will construct an adversary $\mathcal{B}$ which will use $\mathcal{A}$ to break the selective security of the bit-fixing construction F_{bf}. Thus, $\mathcal{B}$ plays a dual role: one as an adversary in the security game breaking the bit-fixing construction and also as a challenger in the security game breaking the $\mathbf{NC}^1$ construction.

- First $\mathcal{A}$ provides its challenge x^* to $\mathcal{B}$ which in turn forwards it to its challenger. $\mathcal{B}$ receives the public parameters of the bit-fixing scheme from its challenger along with either $F_{bf}(k, x^*)$ or a random value which it forwards

---

[10] As in Sect. 5.1, the fanout of the input wires can be easily incorporated.

to $\mathcal{A}$. $\mathcal{B}$ is going to answer queries as though the PRF evaluated by the $\mathbf{NC}^1$ construction is the same as that evaluated by the bit-fixing construction F_{bf} used by the challenger. When $\mathcal{A}$ asks a query f to $\mathbf{NC}^1$.Constrain oracle with $f(x^*) = 0$, $\mathcal{B}$ follows a procedure similar to the one in Sect. 5.1.

- $\mathcal{B}$ *carefully* sets the randomness on all wires in the circuit as in the proof in Sect. 5.1. By virtue of this careful setting, the same properties hold: for any wire $w \in [n + q]$, if $f_w(x^*) = 1$, then r_w is known, and if $f_w(x^*) = 0$, then r_w would either be known or of the form $k + \sum r$, where each r is known. Note that $r_{n+q} = k$ which is the key of PRF used by $\mathcal{B}$ as well as $\mathcal{B}$'s challenger.

- To give out keys for the input wires, $\mathcal{B}$ does the following. For those wires w with $f_w(x^*) = 1$, r_w is known and hence $\mathcal{B}$ obtains $K_w = \mathsf{F}_{\mathsf{bf}}.\mathsf{Constrain}(r_w, w)$ by running $\mathsf{F}_{\mathsf{bf}}.\mathsf{Constrain}(r_w, w)$ by itself. For wires w with $f_w(x^*) = 0$, if r_w is known, then $\mathcal{B}$ obtains $K_w = \mathsf{F}_{\mathsf{bf}}.\mathsf{Constrain}(r_w, w)$ by running $\mathsf{F}_{\mathsf{bf}}.\mathsf{Constrain}(r_w, w)$ by itself. Otherwise, r_w is of the form $k + \sum r$, where each r is known. For each r, $\mathcal{B}$ obtains $K'_{r,w} = \mathsf{F}_{\mathsf{bf}}.\mathsf{Constrain}(r, w)$ by running $\mathsf{F}_{\mathsf{bf}}.\mathsf{Constrain}(r, w)$ by itself. Through repeated use of $\mathsf{F}_{\mathsf{bf}}.\mathsf{AddKeys}$, and by virtue of the homomorphism property of the constrained keys, $\mathcal{B}$ obtains $K'_{\sum r, w} = \mathsf{F}_{\mathsf{bf}}.\mathsf{Constrain}\left(\sum r, w\right)$. $\mathcal{B}$ then queries its challenger for the constrained key fixing the wth bit, i.e., it obtains $K'_{k,w} = \mathsf{F}_{\mathsf{bf}}.\mathsf{Constrain}(k, w)$ by querying its challenger. Finally, through the use of $\mathsf{F}_{\mathsf{bf}}.\mathsf{AddKeys}\left(K'_{k,w}, K'_{\sum r,w}\right)$, $\mathcal{B}$ obtains $K_w = \mathsf{F}_{\mathsf{bf}}.\mathsf{Constrain}\left(r_w, w\right)$.

- When answering $\mathcal{A}$'s queries to $\mathbf{NC}^1$.Constrain, it is important to note that $\mathcal{B}$ does not query for any predicate that allows it to evaluate $F(k, x^*)$ by itself. We achieve this because all queries by $\mathcal{B}$ to the challenger, $\mathsf{F}_{\mathsf{bf}}.\mathsf{Constrain}(k, w)$, fix the wth bit to 1, while if the query were made, $f_w(x^*) = 0$, i.e., the wth bit of x^* is 0.

- When $\mathcal{A}$ outputs a bit b', $\mathcal{B}$ outputs the same.

In the above game, if $\mathcal{A}$ breaks the selective security of the $\mathbf{NC}^1$ construction with an advantage of $\epsilon(\lambda)$ then $\mathcal{B}$ breaks the underlying bit-fixing construction with the same advantage.

References

[BFP+15] Banerjee, A., Fuchsbauer, G., Peikert, C., Pietrzak, K., Stevens, S.: Key-homomorphic constrained pseudorandom functions. In: Dodis, Y., Nielsen, J.B. (eds.) TCC 2015, Part II. LNCS, vol. 9015, pp. 31–60. Springer, Heidelberg (2015)

[BGI14] Boyle, E., Goldwasser, S., Ivan, I.: Functional signatures and pseudorandom functions. In: Public Key Cryptography, pp. 501–519 (2014)

[BV15] Brakerski, Z., Vaikuntanathan, V.: Constrained key-homomorphic PRFs from standard lattice assumptions. Or: how to secretly embed a circuit in your PRF. In: Dodis, Y., Nielsen, J.B. (eds.) TCC 2015, Part II. LNCS, vol. 9015, pp. 1–30. Springer, Heidelberg (2015)

[BW13]   Boneh, D., Waters, B.: Constrained pseudorandom functions and their applications. In: Sako, K., Sarkar, P. (eds.) ASIACRYPT 2013, Part II. LNCS, vol. 8270, pp. 280–300. Springer, Heidelberg (2013)

[CHL+15]   Cheon, J.H., Han, K., Lee, C., Ryu, H., Stehlé, D.: Cryptanalysis of the multilinear map over the integers. In: Oswald, E., Fischlin, M. (eds.) EUROCRYPT 2015, Part I. LNCS, vol. 9056, pp. 3–12. Springer, Heidelberg (2015)

[CLR15]   Cheon, J.H., Lee, C., Ryu, H.: Cryptanalysis of the new CLT multilinear maps. Cryptology ePrint Archive, Report 2015/934 (2015)

[CLT13]   Coron, J.-S., Lepoint, T., Tibouchi, M.: Practical multilinear maps over the integers. In: Canetti, R., Garay, J.A. (eds.) CRYPTO 2013, Part I. LNCS, vol. 8042, pp. 476–493. Springer, Heidelberg (2013)

[CLT15]   Coron, J.-S., Lepoint, T., Tibouchi, M.: New multilinear maps over the integers. In: Gennaro, R., Robshaw, M. (eds.) CRYPTO 2015, Part I. LNCS, vol. 9215, pp. 267–286. Springer, Heidelberg (2015)

[CRV14]   Chandran, N., Raghuraman, S., Vinayagamurthy, D.: Constrained pseudorandom functions: verifiable and delegatable. IACR Cryptology ePrint Archive, 2014:522 (2014)

[CRV15]   Chandran, N., Raghuraman, S., Vinayagamurthy, D.: Reducing depth in constrained PRFs: from bit-fixing to NC^1. IACR Cryptology ePrint Archive, 2015:829 (2015)

[FKPR14]   Fuchsbauer, G., Konstantinov, M., Pietrzak, K., Rao, V.: Adaptive security of constrained PRFs. In: Sarkar, P., Iwata, T. (eds.) ASIACRYPT 2014, Part II. LNCS, vol. 8874, pp. 82–101. Springer, Heidelberg (2014)

[Fuc14]   Fuchsbauer, G.: Constrained verifiable random functions. In: Abdalla, M., De Prisco, R. (eds.) SCN 2014. LNCS, vol. 8642, pp. 95–114. Springer, Heidelberg (2014)

[GGH13a]   Garg, S., Gentry, C., Halevi, S.: Candidate multilinear maps from ideal lattices. In: Johansson, T., Nguyen, P.Q. (eds.) EUROCRYPT 2013. LNCS, vol. 7881, pp. 1–17. Springer, Heidelberg (2013)

[GGH+13b] Garg, S., Gentry, C., Halevi, S., Raykova, M., Sahai, A., Waters, B.: Candidate indistinguishability obfuscation and functional encryption for all circuits. In: 54th Annual IEEE Symposium on Foundations of Computer Science, FOCS 2013, 26–29 October, 2013, Berkeley, CA, USA, pp. 40–49 (2013)

[GGH+13c] Garg, S., Gentry, C., Halevi, S., Sahai, A., Waters, B.: Attribute-based encryption for circuits from multilinear maps. In: Canetti, R., Garay, J.A. (eds.) CRYPTO 2013, Part II. LNCS, vol. 8043, pp. 479–499. Springer, Heidelberg (2013)

[GGH15]   Gentry, C., Gorbunov, S., Halevi, S.: Graph-induced multilinear maps from lattices. In: Dodis, Y., Nielsen, J.B. (eds.) TCC 2015, Part II. LNCS, vol. 9015, pp. 498–527. Springer, Heidelberg (2015)

[GGM86]   Goldreich, O., Goldwasser, S., Micali, S.: How to construct random functions. J. ACM **33**(4), 792–807 (1986)

[GPSW06]   Goyal, V., Pandey, O., Sahai, A., Waters, B.: Attribute-based encryption for fine-grained access control of encrypted data. In: ACM Conference on Computer and Communications Security, pp. 89–98 (2006)

[GVW13]   Gorbunov, S., Vaikuntanathan, V., Wee, H.: Attribute-based encryption for circuits. In: STOC, pp. 545–554 (2013)

[HJ15]   Hu, Y., Jia, H.: Cryptanalysis of GGH map. IACR Cryptology ePrint Archive, 2015:301 (2015)

[HKKW14] Hofheinz, D., Kamath, A., Koppula, V., Waters, B.: Adaptively secure constrained pseudorandom functions. IACR Cryptology ePrint Archive, 2014:720 (2014)

[KPTZ13] Kiayias, A., Papadopoulos, S., Triandopoulos, N., Zacharias, T.: Delegatable pseudorandom functions and applications. In: ACM SIGSAC Conference on Computer and Communications Security, CCS 2013, Berlin, Germany, 4–8 November, 2013, pp. 669–684 (2013)

[MF15] Minaud, B., Fouque, P.-A.: Cryptanalysis of the new multilinear map over the integers. Cryptology ePrint Archive, Report 2015/941 (2015)

[SW05] Sahai, A., Waters, B.: Fuzzy identity-based encryption. In: Cramer, R. (ed.) EUROCRYPT 2005. LNCS, vol. 3494, pp. 457–473. Springer, Heidelberg (2005)

Non-Malleable Functions and Their Applications

Yu Chen[1,2]($\boxtimes$), Baodong Qin[3], Jiang Zhang[4], Yi Deng[1,4],
and Sherman S.M. Chow[2]

[1] State Key Laboratory of Information Security, Institute of Information
Engineering, Chinese Academy of Sciences, Beijing 100093, China
[2] Department of Information Engineering, The Chinese University of Hong Kong,
Shatin, New Territories, Hong Kong
yuchen.prc@gmail.com
[3] School of Computer Science and Technology,
Southwest University of Science and Technology, Mianyang 621010, China
[4] State Key Laboratory of Cryptology, P.O. Box 5159, Beijing 100878, China

Abstract. We formally study "non-malleable functions" (NMFs), a general cryptographic primitive which simplifies and relaxes "non-malleable one-way/hash functions" (NMOWHFs) introduced by Boldyreva et al. (ASIACRYPT 2009) and refined by Baecher et al. (CT-RSA 2010). NMFs focus on deterministic functions, rather than probabilistic one-way/hash functions considered in the literature of NMOWHFs.

We mainly follow Baecher et al. to formalize a game-based definition. Roughly, a function f is non-malleable if, given an image $y^* \leftarrow f(x^*)$ for a randomly chosen x^*, it is hard to output a mauled image y with a ϕ from some transformation class s.t. $y = f(\phi(x^*))$. A distinctive strengthening of our non-malleable notion is that $\phi(x^*) = x^*$ is always allowed. We also consider adaptive non-malleability which stipulates non-malleability maintains even when an inversion oracle is available.

We investigate the relations between non-malleability and one-wayness in depth. In the non-adaptive setting, we show that for any achievable transformation class, non-malleability implies one-wayness for poly-to-one functions but not vise versa. In the adaptive setting, we show that for most algebra-induced transformation class, adaptive non-malleability (ANM) is equivalent to adaptive one-wayness (AOW) for injective functions. These two results establish interesting theoretical connections between non-malleability and one-wayness for functions, which extend to trapdoor functions as well, and thus resolve some open problems left by Kiltz et al. (EUROCRYPT 2010). Notably, the implication AOW $\Rightarrow$ ANM not only yields constructions of NMFs from adaptive trapdoor functions, which partially solves an open problem posed by Boldyreva et al. (ASIACRYPT 2009), but also provides key insight into addressing non-trivial copy attacks in the area of related-key attacks (RKA).

Finally, we show that NMFs lead to a simple black-box construction of continuous non-malleable key derivation functions recently proposed by Qin et al. (PKC 2015), which have proven to be very useful in achieving RKA-security for numerous cryptographic primitives.

© International Association for Cryptologic Research 2016
C.-M. Cheng et al. (Eds.): PKC 2016, Part II, LNCS 9615, pp. 386–416, 2016.
DOI: 10.1007/978-3-662-49387-8_15

Keywords: Non-malleable functions · One-way functions · Algebra-induced transformations · Related-key attacks · Copy attacks · Key derivation

1 Introduction

Non-malleability is an important notion for cryptographic primitives which ensures some level of independence of outputs with respect to related inputs. This notion, first treated formally in the seminal work of Dolev, Dwork and Naor [25], has been studied extensively for many randomized primitives, such as commitments [22, 23, 29, 44], encryptions [12], zero-knowledge proofs [39, 42, 49], obfuscations [20], and codes [26–28]. However, little attention has been paid on deterministic primitives. Particularly, the study dedicated to non-malleability for deterministic functions, which is arguably the most basic primitive, is still open. With the goal to fill this gap, we initiate the study of non-malleability for deterministic functions in this work.

1.1 Related Work

Non-Malleable One-Way and Hash Functions. Boldyreva et al. [16] initiated the foundational study of non-malleable one-way and hash functions (NMOWHFs).[1] They gave a simulation-based definition of non-malleability, basically saying that, for any adversary mauling a function value y^* into a related value y, there exists a simulator which does just well even without seeing y^*. They provided a construction of NMOWHFs from perfectly one-way hash functions (POWHF) and simulation-sound non-interactive zero-knowledge proof of knowledge (NIZKPoK). However, they regarded this construction as a feasibility result due to its inefficiency. They also discussed applications of NMOWHFs to partially instantiating random oracles in the Bellare-Rogaway encryption scheme [11] and OAEP [17], as well as enhancing the security of cryptographic puzzles.

Being aware of several deficiencies in the simulation-based definition of non-malleability [16],[2] Baecher et al. [3] reverted the core idea behind non-malleability and proposed a game-based definition which is more handy to work with. Their definition avoids simulator completely and rather asks for the following: given a function value $y^* \leftarrow f(x^*)$ of an unknown preimage x^*, no probabilistic polynomial time (PPT) adversary is able to output a mauled image y together with a transformation ϕ from a prefixed transformation class Φ such that $y = f(\phi(x^*))$. To demonstrate the usefulness of their game-based definition, they proved that the strengthened Merkle-Damgård transformation satisfies their non-malleability notion w.r.t. bit flips, and their non-malleability notion suffices for improving security of the Bellare-Rogaway encryption scheme.

---

[1] Historically, Boldyreva et al. [16] aggregated both one-way functions and hash functions under the term hash functions for simplicity.

[2] See [3] for a detailed discussion on simulation-based non-malleable notion.

We identify the following gaps in the NMOWHFs literature [3, 16].

- Both [16] and [3] considered non-malleability for a very general syntax of functions, comprising both classical one-way functions and collision resistant hash functions. In their cases, the underlying functions could be probabilistic and are assumed to be one-way.[3] Despite such treatment is of utmost generality, it is somewhat bulky and even inapplicable for some natural applications, e.g., when the functions are probabilistic, two independent parties computing with the same input will not necessarily get the same output [16]. Moreover, to some extent, it blurs the relations between non-malleability and one-wayness.
- The game-based non-malleable notion [3] is not strong enough in the sense that the adversary is restricted to output $\phi \in \Phi$ such that $\phi(x^*) \neq x^*$. Note that Φ is introduced to capture all admissible transformations chosen by the adversary, this restriction translates to the limit that Φ does not contain ϕ that has fixed points, which is undesirable because many widely used transformations (e.g., affine functions and polynomials) are excluded.
- Boldyreva et al.'s construction of NMOWHF is in the standard model, but the uses of POWHF and NIZKPoK render it probabilistic, and inefficient for practical applications [16] (e.g., cryptographic puzzles for network protocols). The strengthened Merkle-Damgård transformation does constitute an efficient NMOWHF construction [3], but its non-malleability inherently relies on modeling the compression function as a random oracle [3]. An efficient, deterministic solution in the standard model was left open [16].
- Though NMOWHFs are powerful, their cryptographic applications are only known for partially instantiating random oracles for some public-key encryption schemes and enhancing the design of cryptographic puzzles. Further applications of NMOWHFs in other areas were expected [16].

(Adaptive) One-Way Functions. As a fundamental primitive, one-way functions [24] and their variants [19,43] have been studied extensively. Roughly, one-way functions are a family of deterministic functions where each particular function is easy to compute, but most are hard to invert on average.

Kiltz et al. [38] introduced a strengthening of trapdoor one-way functions called adaptive one-way trapdoor functions (ATDFs), which remain one-way even when the adversary is given access to an inversion oracle. They gave a black-box construction of chosen-ciphertext secure public-key encryption (CCA-secure PKE) from ATDFs, and showed how to construct ATDFs from either lossy TDFs [45] or correlated-product TDFs [48]. Their work suggested a number of open problems; in particular, considering non-malleability for TDFs, exploring its relation to existing notions for TDFs and implications for PKE, and realizing them from standard assumptions.

1.2   Motivation

Based on the above discussion, we find that the state of the art of NMOWHFs is not entirely satisfactory. In particular, the study of non-malleability dedicated to deterministic functions and its relation to one-wayness are still open.

---

[3] The basic design principle for cryptographic hash functions is one-wayness.

In this work, we continue the study of non-malleable primitive, but restrict our attention to *deterministic* functions, rather than *probabilistic one-way/hash* functions considered in prior works. Apart from being a natural question which deserves study in its own right, a direct treatment of deterministic functions (without imposing any other cryptographic property) provides three main benefits. First, it shares the same underlying object of "classical" one-way functions and hence allows us to explore the relations between non-malleability and one-wayness. Second, this may further lead to efficient constructions of deterministic NMFs in the standard model, by leveraging a vast body of works on one-way functions. Third, deterministic primitives are more versatile, making deterministic NMFs more attractive being used a building block for higher-level cryptographic protocols.

In summary, we are motivated to consider the following intriguing questions:

What is the strong yet handy non-malleable notion for deterministic functions? What are the relations between non-malleability and one-wayness? Can we construct efficient deterministic NMFs in the standard model? Are there new appealing applications of deterministic NMFs?

1.3 Our Contributions

We give positive answers to the above questions, which we summarize below.

Non-Malleable Functions. In Sect. 3, we introduce a new cryptographic primitive called deterministic NMFs,[4] which simplifies and relaxes NMOWHFs in that the underlying functions are deterministic and not required to have any cryptographic property. Informally, NMFs stipulate no PPT adversary is able to modify a function value into a meaningfully related one. We mainly follow the game-based approach [3] to define non-malleability for deterministic functions w.r.t. related-preimage deriving transformation[5] (RPDT) class Φ, that is, given $y^* \leftarrow f(x^*)$ for a randomly chosen x^*, no PPT adversary is able to output a transformation $\phi \in \Phi$ and a function value y such that $y = f(\phi(x^*))$.

In our definition, adversary's power is neatly expressed through Φ and there is no other restriction. In particular, $\phi(x^*) = x^*$ is always allowed even when $y = y^*$, whereas existing definition of NMOWHFs [3, Section 3.1] demands $\phi(x^*) \neq x^*$. As we will see in Sects. 7 and 8, this strengthening surfaces as an important property when applying to the area of RKA security. We also introduce adaptive NMFs, which remain non-malleable even the adversary has access to an inversion oracle. This stronger notion is desirable when NMFs are used in more adversarial environment, as we will show in Sect. 8.4.

Novel Properties of RPDTs. Our non-malleability notion is stronger if Φ is larger. To capture broad yet achievable RPDT class, in Sect. 4 we introduce two novel properties for RPDT class that we call *bounded root space* (BRS) and

---

[4] We will omit "deterministic" and simply say NMFs when the context is clear.
[5] We use the term transformation to highlight that ϕ has the same domain and range. RPDT was refereed to as admissible transformation in [3].

sampleable root space (SRS). Let id and ϕ_c represent identity transformation and any constant transformation respectively. The two properties demand that for each $\phi \in \Phi$, the root spaces of composite transformations $\phi - \phi_c$ and $\phi - $ id are polynomially bounded and allow efficient uniform sampling.

BRS and SRS are general enough in that they are met by most algebra-induced transformations considered in the literature, including linear functions, affine functions, and low degree polynomials (with id and ϕ_c being punctured). We let Φ_{brs}^{srs} denote the general RPDT class satisfying the BRS & SRS properties.

Relations Among Non-Malleability and One-Wayness. In Sects. 5 and 6, we investigate the relations among non-malleability and one-wayness in depth. Figure 1 shows a (rough) pictorial summary.

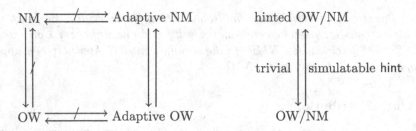

Fig. 1. Let unhatched arrows represent implications, and hatched arrows represent separations. The left figure is a rough overview of relations among (adaptive) Φ-non-malleability and (adaptive) one-wayness for deterministic functions. See Sect. 5 for concrete requirements on Φ and the underlying functions. The right figure depicts the relation between standard one-wayness/non-malleability and hinted one-wayness/non-malleability. See Sect. 6 for details.

In the non-adaptive setting, we show that w.r.t. any achievable RPDT class Φ, non-malleability (NM) implies one-wayness (OW) for poly-to-one functions (cf. Definition 1), but not vise versa. This rigorously confirms the intuition that in common cases NM is strictly stronger than OW. In the adaptive setting, we show that w.r.t. Φ_{brs}^{srs}, adaptive non-malleability (ANM) is equivalent to adaptive one-wayness (AOW) for injective functions. While the implication ANM $\Rightarrow$ AOW is obvious, the converse is much more technically involved. In Sect. 5.3, we prove the implication AOW $\Rightarrow$ ANM via a novel algebraic technique, leveraging the injectivity of the underlying functions and the BRS & SRS properties of Φ_{brs}^{srs}. The rough idea is that: if an adversary breaks non-malleability (outputting a mauled image along with a transformation), the reduction can obtain a solvable equation about the preimage and thus contradicts the assumed one-wayness.

All these results indicate that the preimage size is a fundamental parameter of NMFs. We also note that all the above results apply equally well to trapdoor functions. Most importantly, the equivalence AOW $\Leftrightarrow$ ANM answers the aforementioned open problems left by Kiltz et al. [38].

Both OW and NM can be considered with auxiliary information of preimage x^*, which is modeled by a hint function $\text{hint}(x^*)$. We refer to the standard (default) notions without hint as *hint-free notions*, and refer to the ones with hint as *hinted notions*. Compared to hint-free notions, hinted ones are generally more useful for cryptographic applications, as we will demonstrate in Sect. 8. While hinted notions trivially implies hint-free ones, the converse becomes more subtle. In Sect. 6, we will show that w.r.t. statistically/computationally simulatable $\text{hint}(x^*)$, hinted notions are implied by hint-free ones.

Benefits of AOW $\Rightarrow$ ANM. Given the fact that ATDFs are efficiently realizable from a variety of hardness assumptions, the implication AOW $\Rightarrow$ ANM immediately gives rise to efficient deterministic NMFs w.r.t. $\Phi_{\text{hrs}}^{\text{srs}}$ in the standard model. This partially[6] resolves an open question raised in [16]. In the full version [21] of this work, by using the technique underlying AOW $\Rightarrow$ ANM, we prove that the Merkle-Damgård transformation is actually $\Phi_{\text{brs}}^{\text{srs}}$-non-malleable. This greatly improves prior result [3], and thus provides an efficient candidate of NMFs w.r.t. a large RPDT class, though in the random oracle model.

Apart from yielding efficient constructions of NMFs, we find that the implication AOW $\Rightarrow$ ANM is also useful elsewhere. In Sect. 7, we discuss how the high-level idea underlying AOW $\Rightarrow$ ANM provides a key insight in the RKA area, that is, resilience against non-trivial copy attacks w.r.t. most algebra-induced related-key deriving class is in fact a built-in security.

Applications of NMFs. Boldyreva et al. [16] showed how to design cryptographic puzzles using NMOWHFs. We note that poly-to-one NMFs can replace NMOWHFs in their design, making it more applicable for securing practical network protocols.

In Sect. 8, we revisit continuous non-malleable key derivation functions (KDFs) recently proposed by Qin et al. [47], which have proven to be useful in achieving RKA-security for numerous cryptographic primitives. The existing construction of continuous non-malleable KDFs is somewhat complicated, which employs one-time lossy filter, one-time signature, and pairwise-independent functions as ingredients. We propose an exquisitely simple and elegant construction of continuous non-malleable KDFs based solely on poly-to-one NMFs. Comparatively, our construction not only has potential advantages in efficiency, but also admits a direct and modular proof.

1.4   Additional Related Work

Non-Malleable Codes. Dziembowski, Pietrzak and Wichs [26] introduced the notion of "non-malleable codes" (NMCs) which relaxes the notion of error-correction and error-detection codes. Roughly, NMCs require that given a code $c^* \leftarrow \text{NMC}(m^*)$ for a source-message m^*, the decoded message m of the tampered codeword $c = \phi(c^*)$ is either equal or completely unrelated to m^*. We note

---

[6] We say "partially" since the posed question in [16] is to construct efficient deterministic NMFs in the context of their simulation-based definition.

that NMFs are somehow dual to NMCs. The duality comes from the fact that NMFs stipulate given $y^* \leftarrow \mathsf{NMF}(x^*)$, $\mathsf{NMF}(\phi(x^*))$ is still hard to compute. Very informally, we can think of in NMCs the tampering takes place on code (which could be interpreted as image of message), whereas in NMFs the "tampering" takes place on preimage.

Correlated-Input Hash Functions. Goyal, O'Neill and Rao [35] undertook the study of correlated-input hash functions (CIHs), which maintain security when the adversary sees hash values $h(c_i(r))$ of related inputs $c_i(r)$ sharing the same random coins, where c_i is a sequence of circuits chosen by the adversary. In particular, unpredictable CIHs require that no PPT adversary is able to predicate $h(c_{n+1}(r))$ after seeing $h(c_i(r))$ for $i \in [n]$. NMFs can be roughly viewed as a weakening of unpredictable CIHs by restricting $n = 1$ and $c_1 = \mathsf{id}$. Yet, our motivation, definitional framework, as well as techniques are quite different from their work. Until now, instantiation of unpredictable CIHs is only known w.r.t. specific circuit class (tie to scheme algebra), and based on specific number-theoretic assumption.

2   Preliminaries

Basic Notations. For a distribution or random variable X, we write $x \leftarrow X$ to denote the operation of sampling a random x according to X. For a set X, we use $x \xleftarrow{\text{R}} X$ to denote the operation of sampling x uniformly at random from X, and use $|X|$ to denote its size. We denote $\lambda \in \mathbb{N}$ as the security parameter. Unless described otherwise, all quantities are implicit functions of λ (we reserve $n(\lambda)$ and $m(\lambda)$ to denote the input length and output length of a function respectively), and all cryptographic algorithms (including the adversary) take λ as an input.

We use standard asymptotic notation O, o, Ω, and ω to denote the growth of functions. We write $\mathsf{poly}(\lambda)$ to denote an unspecified function $f(\lambda) = O(\lambda^c)$ for some constant c. We write $\mathsf{negl}(\lambda)$ to denote some unspecified function $f(\lambda)$ such that $f(\lambda) = o(\lambda^{-c})$ for every constant c. We say that a probability is overwhelming if it is $1 - \mathsf{negl}(\lambda)$, and a probability is noticeable if it is $\Omega(1/\mathsf{poly}(\lambda))$.

A probabilistic polynomial time (PPT) algorithm is a randomized algorithm that runs in time $\mathsf{poly}(\lambda)$. If $\mathcal{A}$ is a randomized algorithm, we write $z \leftarrow \mathcal{A}(x_1, \ldots, x_n; r)$ to indicate that $\mathcal{A}$ outputs z on inputs $(x_1, \ldots, x_n)$ and random coins r. We will omit r and write $z \leftarrow \mathcal{A}(x_1, \ldots, x_n)$.

Implications and Separations. Consider security notions A and B for a cryptographic primitive Π, we say that

- $A \Rightarrow B$: if all constructions of Π meeting security notion A also meet security notion B.
- $A \nRightarrow B$: if there exists a construction of Π which meets security notion A but does not meet security notion B.

Following [7], we call a result of the first type an *implication*, and a result of the second type a *separation*. If $A \Rightarrow B$, we say A is stronger than B. If we further have $B \not\Rightarrow A$, we say that A is strictly stronger than B. If we further have $B \Rightarrow A$, we say that A is equivalent to B.

3 One-Way and Non-Malleable Functions

We first recall the general syntax of a family of efficiently computable deterministic functions.

Definition 1 (Efficiently Computable Deterministic Functions). *A family of efficiently computable functions $\mathcal{F}$ consists of three polynomial time algorithms* (Gen, Samp, Eval) *such that:*

- *Sample a function:* Gen(λ) *outputs a function index $i \in I_\lambda$. Each value of i output by* Gen(λ) *defines a deterministic function $f_i : D_\lambda \to R_\lambda$.*
- *Sample a preimage:* Samp(λ) *samples a random preimage $x \in D_\lambda$ according to some distribution $\mathcal{C}_\lambda$ over D_λ.[7] Typically $\mathcal{C}_\lambda$ is a uniform distribution over D_λ, and we simply write $x \xleftarrow{\text{R}} D_\lambda$ in this case.*
- *Evaluate a function: on input $(i, x) \in I_\lambda \times D_\lambda$,* Eval$(i, x)$ *outputs $f_i(x)$.*

In the rest of this work, we simply say $\mathcal{F}$ is a family of functions when the context is clear. For an element $y \in R_\lambda$ we denote its preimage set under f_i by $f_i^{-1}(y) = \{x \in D_\lambda : f_i(x) = y\}$. We say $\mathcal{F}$ is injective if each $f_i \in \mathcal{F}$ is injective. Following [8], we measure the amount of "non-injectivity" by looking at the maximum preimage size. Specifically, we say that $\mathcal{F}$ has polynomially bounded preimage size if $|f_i^{-1}(y)| \leq \mathsf{poly}(\lambda)$ for all $f_i \in \mathcal{F}$, all $y \in R_\lambda$ and all $\lambda \in \mathbb{N}$. For brevity, we simply say $\mathcal{F}$ is poly-to-one.

We say $\mathcal{F}$ is a family of trapdoor functions if Gen(λ) *additionally outputs a trapdoor td_i, and there is a PPT algorithm* TdInv(td_i, y) *that computes a preimage $x \in f_i^{-1}(y)$. If a value y is not in the image $f_i(D_i)$, i.e., $f_i^{-1}(y)$ is empty, then the behavior of* TdInv(td_i, y) *is unspecified.*

Remark 1. When things are clear from the context, we will slightly abuse the notation for simplicity and write: I for I_λ, D for D_λ, R for R_λ, $\mathcal{C}$ for $\mathcal{C}_\lambda$, td for td_i, $f \leftarrow \mathcal{F}.\mathsf{Gen}(\lambda)$ for $(i \leftarrow \mathcal{F}.\mathsf{Gen}(\lambda), f := f_i)$. The above definition considers the domains and ranges that depend only on λ. It is easy to generalize the definition so that the domains and ranges also depend on the function index i.

Next, we recall the notion of one-wayness and formally define the notion of non-malleability for deterministic functions. We also define the corresponding adaptive notions, in which the adversary is given access to an inversion oracle $\mathcal{O}_{\mathsf{inv}}(\cdot)$. For trapdoor functions, $\mathcal{O}_{\mathsf{inv}}(y) := \mathsf{TdInv}(td, y)$. For functions without trapdoor, $\mathcal{O}_{\mathsf{inv}}(y)$ returns a preimage $x \in f^{-1}(y)$ if $y \in f(D)$, while its behavior is unspecified otherwise. We emphasize that in the security experiments of adaptive notions the challenger is not necessarily to be efficient and could be unbounded for simulating $\mathcal{O}_{\mathsf{inv}}(\cdot)$.

---

[7] Virtually all "interesting" security notions are achievable only for well-spread distributions $\mathcal{C}_\lambda$ (i.e., with super-logarithmic min-entropy). Therefore, we will stick to this requirement in our work.

Definition 2 (One-Wayness and Adaptive One-Wayness). $\mathcal{F}$ *is one-way if for any PPT adversary $\mathcal{A}$ its advantage $\mathsf{Adv}^{\mathrm{ow}}_{\mathcal{A},\mathcal{F}}(\lambda)$ defined in the security experiment below is negligible in λ:*

$$\mathsf{Adv}^{\mathrm{ow}}_{\mathcal{A},\mathcal{F}}(\lambda) = \Pr\left[x \in f^{-1}(y^*) : \begin{array}{l} f \leftarrow \mathcal{F}.\mathsf{Gen}(\lambda); \\ x^* \leftarrow \mathcal{F}.\mathsf{Samp}(\lambda); y^* \leftarrow f(x^*); \\ x \leftarrow \mathcal{A}(f, y^*); \end{array}\right].$$

$\mathcal{F}$ *is adaptively one-way if one-wayness maintains even when $\mathcal{A}$ is allowed to query $\mathcal{O}_{\mathsf{inv}}(\cdot)$ on any point other than y^*.*

Definition 3 (Hardcore Functions). *Let $\mathcal{H}$ be a family of functions that map D_λ to $\{0,1\}^{m(\lambda)}$. $\mathcal{H}$ is a hardcore of $\mathcal{F}$ if for any PPT adversary $\mathcal{A}$ its advantage $\mathsf{Adv}^{\mathrm{rand}}_{\mathcal{A},\mathcal{H}}(\lambda)$ defined in the security experiment below is negligible in λ:*

$$\mathsf{Adv}^{\mathrm{rand}}_{\mathcal{A},\mathcal{H}}(\lambda) = \Pr\left[b = b' : \begin{array}{l} f \leftarrow \mathcal{F}.\mathsf{Gen}(\lambda); h \leftarrow \mathcal{H}.\mathsf{Gen}(\lambda, f); \\ x^* \leftarrow \mathcal{F}.\mathsf{Samp}(\lambda); y^* \leftarrow f(x^*); \\ r_0^* \leftarrow h(x^*); r_1^* \stackrel{\mathrm{R}}{\leftarrow} \{0,1\}^m; \\ b \stackrel{\mathrm{R}}{\leftarrow} \{0,1\}; \\ b' \leftarrow \mathcal{A}(f, h, y^*, r_b^*); \end{array}\right] - \frac{1}{2}.$$

The well-known Goldreich-Levin theorem [34] says that if $\mathcal{F}$ is one-way, then it has a hardcore $\mathcal{H}$. More precisely, Goldreich and Levin [34] showed that the inner product of preimage x with a random string r (the latter could be viewed as part of the description of h) is a hardcore predicate (which is a special hardcore function with one-bit outputs) for any OWFs.

Definition 4 (Non-Malleability and Adaptive Non-Malleability). *Let Φ be a RPDT class defined over the domain D. $\mathcal{F}$ is Φ-non-malleable if for any PPT adversary $\mathcal{A}$ its advantage $\mathsf{Adv}^{\mathrm{nm}}_{\mathcal{A},\mathcal{F}}$ defined in the security experiment below is negligible in λ:*

$$\mathsf{Adv}^{\mathrm{nm}}_{\mathcal{A},\mathcal{F}}(\lambda) = \Pr\left[\phi \in \Phi \wedge y = f(\phi(x^*)) : \begin{array}{l} f \leftarrow \mathcal{F}.\mathsf{Gen}(\lambda); \\ x^* \leftarrow \mathcal{F}.\mathsf{Samp}(\lambda); y^* \leftarrow f(x^*); \\ (\phi, y) \leftarrow \mathcal{A}(f, y^*); \end{array}\right].$$

$\mathcal{F}$ *is adaptively Φ-non-malleable if Φ-non-malleability maintains even when $\mathcal{A}$ is allowed to query $\mathcal{O}_{\mathsf{inv}}(\cdot)$ on any point other than y^*.*

We give several technical remarks about the above notions.

Impossible Classes. Obviously, our non-malleable notion is impossible to realize w.r.t. RPDT class that contains "regular" transformations, namely, identity transformation id and constant transformations ϕ_c. If Φ contains id, an adversary can simply win by outputting (id, y^*). If Φ contains ϕ_c, an adversary can win by outputting $(\phi_c, f(c))$. It is easy to see that inclusion of the transformations *near to* the regular ones[8] will also make Φ-non-malleability unachievable. In this regard, we call the regular transformations and the transformations near to the regular ones as "dangerous" transformations. So, a primary task is to distill the characterizations on Φ for excluding "dangerous" transformations yet maintaining its generality to the largest extent.

Parameterized Adaptivity. Let q be the maximum number of inversion queries that an PPT adversary is allowed to make in the experiments of adaptive one-wayness/non-malleability. Typically q is assumed to be polynomially bounded and omitted from the definitions. Nevertheless, explicitly parameterizing adaptive notions with q yields more refined notions, i.e., q-adaptive one-wayness/non-malleability. Clearly, adaptive notions degenerate to non-adaptive ones when $q = 0$. We will adopt the refined adaptive notions in Sect. 5.3 to give a dedicated relation between adaptive one-wayness and adaptive non-malleability.

Hinted Notions. In the non-malleability notions of one-way/hash functions considered in [3,16], in addition to the challenge y^*, the adversary is also given some hint of x^* to capture the auxiliary information that might has been collected from previous actions that involve x^*. The hint of x^* is modeled by $\mathsf{hint}(x^*)$, where hint is a probabilistic function from D_λ to $\{0,1\}^{m(\lambda)}$. Analogously, in the security experiments of both one-wayness and non-malleability for deterministic functions, we can also make the adversaries more powerful by giving them $\mathsf{hint}(x^*)$.[9] We say that the resulting notions are hinted, and the original notions are hint-free. Hinted notions are very useful in cryptographic applications in which the adversaries may obtain some auxiliary information about x^* other than merely its image y^*, as we demonstrate in Sect. 8.

Next, we first seek for an achievable yet large RPDT class in Sect. 4, then explore the connections among non-malleability and one-wayness in Sect. 5, working with hint-free notions for simplicity. We postpone the study of the relations between hint-free notions and hinted ones to Sect. 6, since we need some result in Sect. 5 as prerequisite.

4   Related-Preimage Deriving Transformation Class

Following [3], our notion of non-malleability for a family of deterministic functions is defined w.r.t. a RPDT class Φ, in which $\phi : D \to D$ maps a preimage to a related preimage. We require transformations in Φ should be efficiently recognizable and computable. Hereafter, we use id to denote the identity transformation $f(x) = x$ and use cf to denote the set of all constant transformations

---

[8] Roughly, we say f is near to g if they outputs agree on most inputs.

[9] Clearly, to make the hinted notions achievable, hint must meets some necessary condition. For instance of hinted non-malleability, hint should be at least uninvertible (finding the exact preimage is infeasible). We prefer to keep the definition as general as possible, so we do not explicitly impose concrete restriction to hint in definition.

$\{\phi_c(x) = c\}_{x \in D}$. When D under addition forms a group, we use 0 to denote the identity. For $\phi_1, \phi_2 \in \Phi$, we define $\phi := \phi_1 - \phi_2$ as $\phi(x) = \phi_1(x) - \phi_2(x)$.

As remarked before, we cannot hope to achieve non-malleability for any RPDT class Φ. We are thus motivated to distill some characterizations on Φ that make non-malleability achievable while keeping Φ still general enough. Towards this goal, we introduce two novel properties for RPDT classes as below.

Definition 5 (Bounded Root Space). *Let $r(\lambda)$ be a quantity of λ. A transformation ϕ has $r(\lambda)$-bounded root space if $|\phi^{-1}(0)| \leq r(\lambda)$. A RPDT class Φ has $r(\lambda)$-bounded root space if for each $\phi \in \Phi$ and each $\phi_c \in$ cf, the composite transformations $\phi' = \phi - $ id and $\phi' = \phi - \phi_c$ both have $r(\lambda)$-bounded root space.*

Definition 6 (Sampleable Root Space). *A transformation ϕ has sampleable root space if there exists a PPT algorithm SampRS that takes ϕ as input and outputs an element from $\phi^{-1}(0)$ uniformly at random.[10] A RPDT class Φ has sampleable root space if for each $\phi \in \Phi$ and each $\phi_c \in$ cf, the composite transformations $\phi' = \phi - $ id and $\phi'' = \phi - \phi_c$ both have sampleable root spaces.*

In this work, we restrict our attention to root spaces whose size is polynomially bounded,[11] i.e., $r(\lambda) \leq \mathsf{poly}(\lambda)$. Hereafter, we let $\Phi_{\mathrm{brs}}^{\mathrm{srs}}$ denote the RPDT class satisfying the bounded root space (BRS) & sampleable root space (SRS) properties. The BRS property immediately rules out the regular transformations from Φ and stipulates that each $\phi \in \Phi$ is far away from regular ones, i.e., having at most polynomially many intersection points with them. As we will see shortly, with the confining of the BRS property, an adversary's correct solution (ϕ, y) such that $f(\phi(x^*)) = y$ provides enough information about x^* and thus reduces the min-entropy of x^* to $O(\log(\lambda))$. The SRS property further guarantees that a polynomial-time reduction can extract the right x^* with noticeable probability.

Remark 2. Recent works [36,47] introduced two general properties called high output entropy (HOE) and input-output collision resistance (IOCR) for transformation class Φ. The former states that for each $\phi \in \Phi$, the min-entropy of $\phi(x)$ is sufficiently high when $x \xleftarrow{\mathrm{R}} D$, i.e., $\mathsf{H}_\infty(\phi(x)) = \omega(\log \lambda)$. The latter states that for each $\phi \in \Phi$, $\Pr[\phi(x) = x] = \mathsf{negl}(\lambda)$ when $x \xleftarrow{\mathrm{R}} D$. We observe here that BRS implies HOE & IOCR. To see this, notice that: (1) for each $c \in D$ the equation $\phi(x) - c = 0$ having at most polynomial number of roots implies that $\max_{c \in D} \Pr[\phi(x) = c] \leq \mathsf{poly}(\lambda)/|D| = \mathsf{negl}(\lambda)$ when $x \xleftarrow{\mathrm{R}} D$; (2) the equation $\phi(x) - x = 0$ having at most polynomial number of roots implies that $\Pr[\phi(x) = x] \leq \mathsf{poly}(\lambda)/|D| = \mathsf{negl}(\lambda)$ when $x \xleftarrow{\mathrm{R}} D$. We can alternatively think of the BRS property captures the characterization that all $\phi \in \Phi$ are far from regular transformations in an algebraic view.

The notion of root sampleable RPDTs (RPDT class that meets the SRS property) is reminiscent of the notion of preimage sampleable functions introduced in [32]. The former one is weaker than the latter one in that it only insists two

---

[10] If $\phi^{-1}(0)$ is empty, this algorithm simply outputs a distinguished symbol $\perp$.

[11] We will continue to use BRS to denote poly-bounded root space for simplicity.

special forms of transformations are preimage sampleable at zero point obeying uniform distribution. We note that it suffices to relax uniform distribution to some appropriate distribution.

We conclude this section by showing that the BRS & SRS properties are met by most algebra-induced transformation classes (excluding id and cf) considered in the literature, which we recall as below.

Group-Induced Transformations. When D under $\odot$ forms a group $\mathbb{G}$, let $\Phi^{\mathrm{lin}} = \{\phi_a\}_{a \in \mathbb{G}}$ with $\phi_a(x) = a \odot x$ be the class of linear transformations, which generalize several important classes, for example, "bit flips" (exclusive or, XOR) $\phi_a(x) = a \oplus x$ and modular additions $\phi_a(x) = a + x \mod 2^n$ when $D = \{0,1\}^n$.

Ring-Induced Transformations. When D under addition $+$ and multiplication $\cdot$ forms a ring $\mathbb{R}$, let $\Phi^{\mathrm{aff}} = \{\phi_{a,b}\}_{a,b \in \mathbb{R}}$ with $\phi_{a,b}(x) = ax + b$ be the class of affine transformations.

Field-Induced Transformations. When D under addition $+$ and multiplication $\cdot$ forms a field $\mathbb{F}$, let p be the characteristic of $\mathbb{F}$ and $d \geq 0$ be any fixed integer. Let $\Phi^{\mathrm{poly}(d)} = \{\phi_q\}_{q \in \mathbb{F}_d(x)}$ with $\phi_q(x) = q(x)$ be the class of polynomial functions, where $\mathbb{F}_d(x)$ denotes single variable polynomials over $\mathbb{F}$ with degree bounded by d. When d and p are small (i.e., $d = \mathrm{poly}(\lambda)$ and $p = \mathrm{poly}(\lambda)$), one can find all roots for any $q \in \mathbb{F}_d(x)$ in polynomial time $O(d^3 p)$ using Berlekamp's algorithm [14]. When d is small but p is large, one can find all roots for any $q \in \mathbb{F}_d(x)$ in expected polynomial time $O(d^{2+\varepsilon} + d^{1+\varepsilon} \log p)$ using Gathen and Shoup's algorithm [31].

It is easy to verify that $\Phi^{\mathrm{lin}} \backslash \mathrm{id}$, $\Phi^{\mathrm{aff}} \backslash (\mathrm{id} \cup \mathrm{cf})$, and $\Phi^{\mathrm{poly}(d)} \backslash (\mathrm{id} \cup \mathrm{cf})$ for $d = \mathrm{poly}(\lambda)$ all satisfy the BRS and SRS properties.

5   Relations Among Non-Malleability and One-Wayness

In this section, we explore the relations among (adaptive) non-malleability and (adaptive) one-wayness for deterministic functions. For simplicity, we work with hint-free notions. All the results obtained extend naturally among hinted notions.

5.1   Non-Malleability $\Rightarrow$ One-Wayness

Lemma 1. *For any achievable RPDT class Φ, Φ-Non-Malleability $\Rightarrow$ One-Wayness when $\mathcal{F}$ is poly-to-one.*

Proof. Suppose there is an adversary $\mathcal{A}$ that breaks the one-wayness of $\mathcal{F}$ with non-negligible probability, then we can build an algorithm $\mathcal{B}$ that breaks non-malleability of $\mathcal{F}$ also with non-negligible probability. $\mathcal{B}$ works by simulating $\mathcal{A}$'s challenger in the one-wayness experiment as follows:

Setup: Given $f \leftarrow \mathcal{F}.\mathsf{Gen}(\lambda)$ and a challenge $y^* \leftarrow f(x^*)$ for $x^* \leftarrow \mathcal{F}.\mathsf{Samp}(\lambda)$, $\mathcal{B}$ forwards (f, y^*) to $\mathcal{A}$.

Attack: When $\mathcal{A}$ outputs its solution x against one-wayness, $\mathcal{B}$ simply picks a random $\phi \in \Phi$, then outputs $(\phi, f(\phi(x))$ as its solution.

Since $\mathcal{F}$ is poly-to-one, conditioned on $\mathcal{A}$ succeeds $(x \in f^{-1}(y^*))$, we have $\Pr[x = x^*|y^*] \geq 1/\mathrm{poly}(\lambda)$, where the probability is over the choice of $x^* \leftarrow \mathcal{F}.\mathsf{Samp}(\lambda)$. This is because there are at most $\mathrm{poly}(\lambda)$ values x such that $f(x) = y^*$, and they are all equally likely in $\mathcal{A}$'s view. Therefore, if $\mathcal{A}$ breaks the one-wayness of $\mathcal{F}$ with non-negligible probability, then $\mathcal{B}$ breaks the non-malleability of $\mathcal{F}$ also with non-negligible probability. This lemma follows. $\square$

The above reduction loses a factor of $1/\mathrm{poly}(\lambda)$. When $\mathcal{F}$ is injective, the reduction becomes tight.

5.2 One-Wayness $\not\Rightarrow$ Non-Malleability

Lemma 2. *One-Wayness $\not\Rightarrow$ $\Phi_{\mathrm{brs}}^{\mathrm{srs}}$-Non-Malleability.*

Proof. Let $\mathcal{F}$ be a family of one-way functions. To prove this lemma, we show how to modify $\mathcal{F}$ into $\mathcal{F}'$ so that $\mathcal{F}'$ is still one-way but malleable w.r.t. $\Phi_{\mathrm{brs}}^{\mathrm{srs}}$. Suppose $\mathcal{F}.\mathsf{Gen}(\lambda)$ outputs a function $f : \{0,1\}^n \to \{0,1\}^m$, we construct $\mathcal{F}'.\mathsf{Gen}(\lambda)$ as follows: run $f \leftarrow \mathcal{F}.\mathsf{Gen}(\lambda)$, output a function $f' : \{0,1\}^{n+1} \to \{0,1\}^{m+1}$ where $f'(x||\beta) := f(x)||\beta$ and β denotes the last bit of its input. We then proceed to prove the following two claims.

Claim 1. $\mathcal{F}'$ *is one-way.*

Proof. It is easy to see that $\mathcal{F}'$ inherits the one-wayness from $\mathcal{F}$. We omit the proof here since it is straightforward. $\square$

Claim 2. $\mathcal{F}'$ *is* $(\Phi^{\mathrm{xor}} \backslash \mathsf{id})$-*malleable.*

Proof. Given f' and a challenge $y'^* = f'(x'^*)$ where $x'^* = x^*||\beta^*$ is randomly chosen from $\{0,1\}^{n+1}$, we build an adversary $\mathcal{A}'$ against the non-malleability of $\mathcal{F}'$ as follows: parse y'^* as $y^*||\beta^*$, set $a = 0^n||1$, then output ϕ_a together with $y' = y^*||(\beta^* \oplus 1)$. It is easy to see that $\phi_a \in \Phi^{\mathrm{xor}} \backslash \mathsf{id}$ and $y' = f'(x^*||(\beta^* \oplus 1)) = f'(\phi_a(x'^*))$. This proves Claim 2. $\square$

As shown in Sect. 4, Φ^{xor} is a special case of group-induced class, and thus $\Phi^{\mathrm{xor}} \backslash \mathsf{id} \subseteq \Phi_{\mathrm{brs}}^{\mathrm{srs}}$. The lemma immediately follows from the above two claims. $\square$

While this is just a contrived counterexample for one particular attempt, there exist more natural counterexamples. For instance, a Φ-homomorphic one-way function[12] f is also Φ-malleable since $f(x^*) = y^*$ implies $f(\phi(x^*)) = \phi(y^*)$. All these counterexamples indicate that functions with nice algebraic structure are unlikely to be non-malleable.

---

[12] Φ-homomorphism means that for any $\phi \in \Phi$ and any $x \in D$, $f(\phi(x)) = \phi(f(x))$.

5.3 Adaptive Non-Malleability $\Leftrightarrow$ Adaptive One-Wayness

Lemma 3. *For any achievable RPDT class Φ, q-Adaptive Φ-Non-Malleability $\Rightarrow$ q-Adaptive One-Wayness when $\mathcal{F}$ is poly-to-one.*

Proof. The proof can be easily adapted from that of Lemma 1. We omit it here for since it is straightforward. $\square$

Lemma 4. *$(q+1)$-Adaptive One-Wayness $\Rightarrow$ q-Adaptive $\Phi_{\mathrm{brs}}^{\mathrm{srs}}$-Non-Malleability when $\mathcal{F}$ is injective.*

We first outline the high-level idea of the proof. Since the task of finding the preimage x^* appears to be harder than that of mauling its image, the major technical difficulty is how to utilize the power of an adversary $\mathcal{A}$ against adaptive non-malleability to break adaptive one-wayness.

It is instructive to see that a challenge instance of one-wayness has already provided an equation about x^*, i.e., $f(x^*) = y^*$. When $\mathcal{A}$ outputs its solution (ϕ, y) against non-malleability, the reduction immediately obtains another equation about x^*, that is, $f(\phi(x^*)) = y$. However, these two equations are hard to solve on their own due to the involvement of f (which could be complex). Luckily, by utilizing either the injectivity of f or the inversion oracle, the reduction is able to obtain a new solvable equation about x^* without the presence of f: (1) for the case of $y = y^*$, the reduction gets $\phi(x^*) = x^*$ due to the injectivity of f; (2) for the case of $y \neq y^*$, the reduction first queries the inversion oracle at point y, then gets $\phi(x^*) = \mathcal{O}_{\mathrm{inv}}(y)$. In both cases, the reduction successfully confines x^* in a poly-bounded root space (due to the BRS property), then correctly extracts it with noticeable probability (due to the SRS property). This justifies the usefulness of BRS & SRS properties. See the formal proof as follows.

Proof. Suppose there is an adversary $\mathcal{A}$ against the adaptive non-malleability of $\mathcal{F}$, we can build an adversary $\mathcal{B}$ against the adaptive one-wayness of $\mathcal{F}$. $\mathcal{B}$ simulates $\mathcal{A}$'s challenger in the adaptive non-malleability experiment as follows:

Setup: Given $f \leftarrow \mathcal{F}.\mathsf{Gen}(\lambda)$ and a challenge $y^* \leftarrow f(x^*)$ for $x^* \leftarrow \mathcal{F}.\mathsf{Samp}(\lambda)$, $\mathcal{B}$ forwards (f, y^*) to $\mathcal{A}$.

Attack: When $\mathcal{A}$ issues an query to the inversion oracle, $\mathcal{B}$ forwards it to its own challenger and sends back the reply. When $\mathcal{A}$ outputs its solution (ϕ, y) against adaptive non-malleability, $\mathcal{B}$ proceeds as follows:

1. Case $y = y^*$: $\mathcal{B}$ runs $\mathsf{SampRS}(\phi')$ to output a random solution of $\phi'(\alpha) = 0$ where $\phi'(\alpha) = \phi(\alpha) - \alpha$.
2. Case $y \neq y^*$: $\mathcal{B}$ queries the inversion oracle $\mathcal{O}_{\mathrm{inv}}(\cdot)$ at point y and gets the response x, then runs $\mathsf{SampRS}(\phi'')$ to output a random solution of $\phi''(\alpha) = 0$ where $\phi''(\alpha) = \phi(\alpha) - x$.

We justify the correctness of $\mathcal{B}$'s strategy as follows. For case 1, conditioned on $\mathcal{A}$ succeeds ($f(\phi(x^*)) = y^*$), due to the injectivity of $\mathcal{F}$, we have $\phi(x^*) = x^*$, i.e., x^* is a solution of $\phi'(\alpha) = 0$. For case 2, conditioned on $\mathcal{A}$ succeeds

$(f(\phi(x^*)) = y)$, due to the injectivity of $\mathcal{F}$, we have $\phi(x^*) = x$, i.e., x^* is a solution of $\phi''(\alpha) = 0$. Taking the two cases together, conditioned on $\mathcal{A}$ succeeds by making at most q inversion queries, then according to the BRS & SRS properties of $\Phi_{\mathrm{brs}}^{\mathrm{srs}}$, $\mathcal{B}$ will output the right x^* with probability $1/\mathsf{poly}(\lambda)$ by making at most $(q+1)$ inversion queries. We stress that the probability here is taken over the randomness of SampRS, but not $\mathcal{F}$.Samp. Thereby, if $\mathcal{A}$ breaks the q-adaptive non-malleability with non-negligible probability, $\mathcal{B}$ breaks the $(q+1)$-adaptive one-wayness also with non-negligible probability. This proves this lemma.   □

Combining Lemmas 3 and 4 together, we conclude that for injective functions, adaptive $\Phi_{\mathrm{brs}}^{\mathrm{srs}}$-non-malleability is equivalent to adaptive one-wayness.

Remark 3. Analogous to the RKA security notion, our non-malleability notion is of "unique" flavor, in which the adversary is only considered to be successful if its output is a related image of the preimage x^* exactly chosen by the challenger. Precis for this reason, the injectivity of $\mathcal{F}$ is crucial for the reduction from adaptive non-malleability to adaptive one-wayness. If $\mathcal{F}$ is non-injective, the reduction is not guaranteed to get the right equation about x^*. For example, in case $y = y^*$, if the adversary $\mathcal{A}$ always outputs $\phi \in \Phi$ such that $\phi(x) \neq x$ for any $x \in D$, the reduction will never get a right solvable equation about x^*.

5.4 Non-Malleability $\nRightarrow$ Adaptive Non-Malleability

At first glance, one might think non-malleability does imply adaptive non-malleability based on the intuition that the inversion oracle does not help. Suppose $\mathcal{A}$ is an adversary against adaptive non-malleability. Given $y^* \leftarrow f(x^*)$ for randomly chosen x^* and an inversion oracle, $\mathcal{A}$ is asked to output (ϕ, y) such that $f(\phi(x^*)) = y$. Since $\mathcal{A}$ is not allowed to query the inversion oracle on y^*, it seems the only strategy is to firstly maul y^* to some related y, then query the inversion oracle on y, and use the answer x to help figuring out a transformation ϕ s.t. $\phi(x^*) = x$. As we showed in Lemma 1, if $\mathcal{F}$ is non-malleable and poly-to-one, it is also one-way and thus x^* is computationally hidden from $\mathcal{A}$. Thus, it seems impossible for $\mathcal{A}$ to determine ϕ without the knowledge of x^*.

However, the above intuition is deceptive in thinking that the inversion algorithm always behave benignly, namely, returning the preimages of its inputs. Actually, contrived inversion algorithm may reveal critical information (e.g. trapdoor) when its inputs fall outside the image of f, and thus make f not adaptively non-malleable. This is similar in spirit to the separation NM-CPA $\nRightarrow$ IND-CCA1 [7, Sect. 3.2] in the public-key encryption setting.

Lemma 5. *For any achievable RPDT class Φ, Φ-Non-Malleability $\nRightarrow$ Adaptive Φ-Non-Malleability when $\mathcal{F}$ is poly-to-one.*

Due to page limit, we defer the proof of this lemma to the full version [21].

In the above, we work with hint-free (standard) non-malleability notion and one-wayness notion for simplicity. It is easy to see that all these relations apply equally well to the hinted non-malleability notion and the hinted one-wayness notion, with respect to the same hint function.

Construction of NMFs. Baecher et al. [3, Construction4.1] showed that the strengthened Merkle-Damgård (MD) transformation is non-malleable w.r.t. $\Phi^{\text{xor}} \backslash \text{id}$), assuming the compression function is a random oracle. We improve over their result by showing that the strengthened MD transformation is essentially non-malleable w.r.t. $\Phi^{\text{srs}}_{\text{brs}}$. This result gives us an efficient candidate of NMFs w.r.t. large RPDT class, though in the random oracle model. Due to page limit, we defer the details of this part to the full version [21].

As to the construction of NMFs in the standard model, Lemma 4 shows that any injective ATDFs are indeed $\Phi^{\text{srs}}_{\text{brs}}$-non-malleable, while [38] demonstrates that injective ATDFs can be constructed from either a number of cryptographic primitives such as correlated-product TDFs [48], lossy TDFs [45] and CCA-secure deterministic encryption [4] (which in turn can be efficiently constructed from a variety of standard assumptions) or from some specific assumption, e.g. "instance-independent" RSA assumption. This indicates that deterministic NMFs are widely realizable in the standard model, and thus partially resolves an open question raised in [16].

Finally, we observe that for the purpose of constructing NMFs, 1-ATDFs (which only allows the adversary to query the inversion oracle once) are sufficient. Nevertheless, if 1-ATDFs are strictly weaker than q-ATDFs for $q > 1$ and if it allows more efficient instantiations, are still unknown to us. Besides, we are only able to construct NMFs w.r.t. $\Phi^{\text{srs}}_{\text{brs}}$ in this work. Though $\Phi^{\text{srs}}_{\text{brs}}$ is very general (comprising most algebra-induced transformations), it is still of great interest to know if it is possible to go beyond the algebraic barrier.

6 Relation Between Hint-Free and Hinted Notions

In this section, we investigate the relations between hint-free notions and hinted notions. While hinted notions obviously imply hint-free ones, if the reverse implication holds crucially depends on the hint functions. It is intriguing to know for what kind of hint functions, hint-free notions do imply hinted notions.

Let $\mathcal{F}$ be a family of deterministic functions, $f \leftarrow \mathcal{F}.\text{Gen}(\lambda)$, $x^* \leftarrow \mathcal{F}.\text{Samp}(\lambda)$ and $y^* \leftarrow f(x^*)$. Roughly, we say $\text{hint}(x^*)$ is $p(\lambda)$-*statistically simulatable* if there exists a PPT algorithm $\mathcal{R}$ such that $(y^*, \mathcal{R}(y^*)) \approx_s (y^*, \text{hint}(x^*))$ holds with probability $p(\lambda)$; we say $\text{hint}(x^*)$ is $p(\lambda)$-*computationally simulatable* if there exists a PPT algorithm $\mathcal{R}$ such that $(y^*, \mathcal{R}(y^*)) \approx_c (y^*, \text{hint}(x^*))$ holds with probability $p(\lambda)$ based on the hint-free hardness assumption. The probability is over the choice of $x^* \leftarrow \mathcal{F}.\text{Samp}(\lambda)$ and the random coins of $\mathcal{R}$. It is easy to see that when $\text{hint}(x^*)$ is either statistically simulatable or computationally simulatable for some noticeable probability $p(\lambda)$, a reduction algorithm is able to create a game with probability $p(\lambda)$ such that it is indistinguishable to the real hinted game, and thus reduces hinted notions to hint-free ones. We exemplify these two cases in Lemmas 7 and 8, respectively.

Next, we formally study the relation between one-wayness and hinted one-wayness, then show the analogous result also holds between non-malleability and hinted non-malleability for poly-to-one functions.

Lemma 6. *For a family of functions $\mathcal{F}$, hinted one-wayness w.r.t. any achievable hint function implies one-wayness.*

Proof. This direction is straightforward and hence the proof is omitted.   □

We then turn to the inverse direction. We first show that regardless of the construction of $\mathsf{hint}(\cdot)$, as long as its output length is short, i.e., bounded by $\log(\mathsf{poly}(\lambda))$, then $\mathsf{hint}(x^*)$ is $1/\mathsf{poly}(\lambda)$-perfectly simulatable (a special case of statistically simulatable) and thus one-wayness implies hinted one-wayness.

Lemma 7 (Statistically Simulatable Case). *For a family of functions $\mathcal{F}$, one-wayness implies hinted one-wayness w.r.t. any hint function with output length bounded by $\log(\mathsf{poly}(\lambda))$.*

Proof. Let $\mathcal{A}$ be an adversary against hinted one-wayness of $\mathcal{F}$ with advantage $\mathsf{Adv}_{\mathcal{A},\mathcal{F}}^{\mathsf{how}}(\lambda)$. We build an adversary $\mathcal{B}$ against one-wayness by using $\mathcal{A}$'s power. Given (f, y^*) where $f \leftarrow \mathcal{F}.\mathsf{Gen}(\lambda)$, $y^* \leftarrow f(x^*)$ for $x^* \leftarrow \mathcal{F}.\mathsf{Samp}(\lambda)$, $\mathcal{B}$ simply makes a random guess of $\mathsf{hint}(x^*)$, then sends $(f, y^*, \mathsf{hint}(x^*))$ to $\mathcal{A}$. Finally, $\mathcal{B}$ forwards $\mathcal{A}$'s solution as its solution. Since the output length is bounded by $\log(\mathsf{poly}(\lambda))$, $\mathcal{B}$ guesses the right hint value and thus simulates perfectly with probability $1/\mathsf{poly}(\lambda)$. Thereby, we conclude that $\mathsf{Adv}_{\mathcal{B},\mathcal{F}}^{\mathsf{ow}}(\lambda) \geq \mathsf{Adv}_{\mathcal{A},\mathcal{F}}^{\mathsf{how}}(\lambda)/\mathsf{poly}(\lambda)$. The lemma immediately follows.   □

We then show that, for some specific hint functions with output length could possibly beyond $\log(\mathsf{poly}(\lambda))$, $\mathsf{hint}(x^*)$ is computationally simulatable assuming the one-wayness of $\mathcal{F}$, and thus hint-free one-wayness also implies hinted one-wayness in this case.

Lemma 8 (Computationally Simulatable Case). *For a family of functions $\mathcal{F}$, one-wayness implies hinted one-wayness w.r.t. the following specific hint function:*

$$\mathsf{hint}(x; b) = \begin{cases} h(x) & \text{if } b = 0 \\ r \xleftarrow{\text{R}} \{0,1\}^{m(\lambda)} & \text{if } b = 1 \end{cases} \tag{1}$$

Here, $h : D \to \{0,1\}^{m(\lambda)}$ denotes a hardcore function for $f \in \mathcal{F}$. It is well-defined when $\mathcal{F}$ is one-way.

Proof. The high-level idea of the proof is to show that, assuming the one-wayness of $\mathcal{F}$, $\mathsf{hint}(x^*; b)$ for $x^* \xleftarrow{\text{R}} X$ and $b \xleftarrow{\text{R}} \{0,1\}$ is 1-computationally simulatable. We prove this theorem via a sequence of games. Let $\mathcal{A}$ be an adversary against the hinted one-wayness of $\mathcal{F}$ w.r.t. the hint function defined as above. Let S_i be the event that $\mathcal{A}$ wins in Game i.

Game 0 (The real experiment): $\mathcal{CH}$ interacts with $\mathcal{A}$ in the real hinted one-wayness experiment w.r.t. the hinted function defined as above. According to the definition, we have:

$$\text{Adv}_{\mathcal{A},\mathcal{F}}^{\text{how}}(\lambda) = \Pr[S_0]. \tag{2}$$

Game 1 (Modify the hint function): The same as Game 0 except that the hint function $\text{hint}(x^*; b)$ is modified to $\widetilde{\text{hint}}(x^*; b)$, which ignores its input (x^*, b) and always returns a random value $r \xleftarrow{\text{R}} \{0,1\}^{m(\lambda)}$. Observe that in this case the hint value carries no information of x^*.

We now state and prove two claims that establish the lemma.

Claim 3. *Game 0 and Game 1 are computationally indistinguishable, assuming the hint-free one-wayness of $\mathcal{F}$.*

Proof. Since one-wayness of $\mathcal{F}$ implies pseudorandomness of its hardcore $\mathcal{H}$ (c.f. Definition 3), it suffices to show that Game 0 and Game 1 are computationally indistinguishable based on the pseudorandomness of $\mathcal{H}$. We show how to turn a distinguisher $\mathcal{A}$ into an algorithm $\mathcal{B}$ against the pseudorandomness of $\mathcal{H}$.

Given (f, h, y^*, r_β^*) where $f \leftarrow \mathcal{F}.\text{Gen}(\lambda)$, h is a hardcore function for f, $y^* \leftarrow f(x^*)$ for $x^* \leftarrow \mathcal{F}.\text{Samp}(\lambda)$, and r_β^* is $h(x^*)$ if $\beta = 0$ or a random string from $\{0,1\}^{m(\lambda)}$ if $\beta = 1$, $\mathcal{B}$ is asked to determine the value of β. $\mathcal{B}$ picks a random bit b and computes the hint value as follows:

$$\text{hint}'(x^*; b) = \begin{cases} r_\beta^* & \text{if } b = 0 \\ r \xleftarrow{\text{R}} \{0,1\}^{m(\lambda)} & \text{if } b = 1 \end{cases}$$

$\mathcal{B}$ then sends $(f, y^*, \text{hint}'(x^*))$ to $\mathcal{A}$. Finally, $\mathcal{A}$ outputs a bit b' ($b' = 0$ indicates Game 0 and $b' = 1$ indicates Game 1), and $\mathcal{B}$ forwards b' to its own challenger. It is easy to verify that if $\beta = 0$ then $\text{hint}(x^*; b) = \text{hint}'(x^*; b)$ and thus $\mathcal{B}$ perfectly simulates Game 0; if $\beta = 1$ then $\widetilde{\text{hint}}(x^*; b) = \text{hint}'(x^*; b)$ and thus $\mathcal{B}$ perfectly simulates Game 1. Therefore, $\mathcal{B}$ breaks the pseudorandomness of $\mathcal{H}$ with at least the same advantage as $\mathcal{A}$ distinguishes Game 0 and Game 1. By assuming the one-wayness of $\mathcal{F}$, Game 0 and Game 1 are computationally indistinguishable. This proves the Claim 3. □

Claim 4. *No PPT adversary has non-negligible advantage in Game 2 assuming the one-wayness of $\mathcal{F}$.*

Proof. Suppose $\mathcal{A}$ is a PPT adversary that has non-negligible advantage in Game 2. We show how to use $\mathcal{A}$'s power to break the one-wayness of $\mathcal{F}$. Given the one-wayness challenge (f, y^*) where $y^* \leftarrow f(x^*)$ for randomly chosen x^*, $\mathcal{B}$ simply assigns $\widetilde{\text{hint}}(x^*; b)$ to be a random string from $\{0,1\}^{m(\lambda)}$, then sends $(f, y^*, \widetilde{\text{hint}}(x^*; b))$ to $\mathcal{A}$ as the challenge. Finally, $\mathcal{A}$ outputs its solution, and $\mathcal{B}$ forwards it to its own challenger. Clearly, $\mathcal{B}$ perfectly simulates Game 1. Therefore, $\mathcal{B}$ breaks the one-wayness of $\mathcal{F}$ with at least the same advantage as $\mathcal{A}$ succeeds in Game 1. By assuming the one-wayness of $\mathcal{F}$, $\mathcal{A}$'s advantage must be negligible in λ. This proves the Claim 4. □

From Claims 3 and 4, we have $\Pr[S_1] - \Pr[S_0] = \mathsf{negl}(\lambda)$ and $\Pr[S_1] = \mathsf{negl}(\lambda)$. Putting all the above together, we have $\mathsf{Adv}_{\mathcal{A},\mathcal{F}}^{\mathsf{how}}(\lambda) = \mathsf{negl}(\lambda)$ assuming the one-wayness of $\mathcal{F}$. In other words, one-wayness implies hinted one-wayness w.r.t. such specific hint function defined as above. The lemma follows. $\square$

The above results apply naturally to the adaptive setting.

Remark 4. It is easy to see that the above results also hold between hinted non-malleability and hint-free non-malleability for poly-to-one $\mathcal{F}$. Particularly, to see hinted NM w.r.t. the hint function defined in Eq. (1) is implied by hint-free NM, just note that such hint function is 1-computationally simulatable assuming the one-wayness of $\mathcal{F}$ (as we have shown in Lemma 8), which in turn implied by the non-malleability of $\mathcal{F}$ when $\mathcal{F}$ is poly-to-one (Lemma 1).

7 Built-In Resilience Against Non-trivial Copy Attacks

Here, we extend the idea underlying the implication $\mathrm{AOW} \Rightarrow \mathrm{ANM}$ further still to address non-trivial copy attacks in the RKA area. We begin by briefly introducing the background of RKA security and defining what it means for "copy attacks" (including trivial ones and non-trivial ones).

7.1 RKA-security Model and Copy Attacks

Traditional security models assume that the internal states (e.g., secret keys and random coins) of cryptographic hardware device are completely protected from the adversary. However, practical fault injection techniques [15,18] demonstrate that the adversaries are able to launch related-key attacks (RKAs), namely, to induce modifications to the keys stored in cryptographic hardware device and subsequently observe the outcome under the modified keys. Bellare and Kohno [9] initiated a theoretical study of RKA security. Their results mainly focused on pseudorandom function/permutation, and their constructions were subsequently improved by [1,5]. So far, the study of RKA security has expands to other primitives, such as private-key encryption [2], public-key encryption [51], signature [10], and identity-based encryption [10].

In the RKA-security model, modifications to the secret keys are modeled by related-key deriving transformation (RKDT) class Φ, and cryptographic hardware device is modeled by algorithm $\mathsf{Func}(sk, x)$, where $\mathsf{Func}(sk, \cdot)$ denotes some keyed-operations (e.g., signing, decryption) and x denotes its input (e.g., message, ciphertext). A primitive is said to be RKA-secure if it remains secure when the adversary can access to a RKA oracle $\mathcal{O}_{\mathsf{rka}}(\phi, x) := \mathsf{Func}(\phi(sk), x)$.

Let x^* be the challenge in the security experiment. The RKA queries $\langle \phi, x^* \rangle$ where $\phi(sk) = sk$ essentially capture a category of attacks known as "copy attacks". Among copy attacks, we refer to the ones with $\phi = \mathsf{id}$ as *trivial copy attacks* and the rest as *non-trivial copy attacks*. While trivial copy attacks must be excluded to ensure the meaningfulness of the RKA-security notion, non-trivial copy attacks should be allowed since they are possible in practice (e.g., via fault injection attacks [15,18]). However, attaining resilience against non-trivial copy attacks turns out to be difficult.

7.2   Known Techniques in Tackling Non-trivial Copy Attacks

Almost all the known constructions of RKA-secure primitives achieve RKA security by exploiting so called Φ-key-malleability as a vital property. Loosely speaking, this property provides a PPT algorithm T such that $\mathsf{Func}(\phi(sk), x) = \mathsf{Func}(sk, \mathsf{T}(\phi, x))$. Let $\mathcal{O}(x) := \mathsf{Func}(sk, x)$ be the original oracle of the starting primitive. With such property, the reduction is able to reduce the RKA security to the original security of the starting primitive by simulating the RKA oracle via the original oracle, that is, answering $\mathcal{O}_{\mathsf{rka}}(\phi, x)$ with $\mathcal{O}(\mathsf{T}(\phi, x))$. However, a subtlety in the above strategy is that the original oracle $\mathcal{O}(\cdot)$ will deny query $\langle x^* \rangle$. As a consequence, the reduction is unable to handle non-trivial copy attacks, i.e., answering RKA queries $\langle \phi, x^* \rangle$ where $\psi \neq \mathsf{id}$ but $\phi(sk) = sk$.

Prior works paid a lot of effort to address this problem. To date, there are three methods dealing with non-trivial copy attacks in the literature. The first method is assuming Φ is claw-free and contains id. Recall that claw-freeness requires that for all distinct $\phi, \phi' \in \Phi$ and all $x \in D$, $\phi(x) \neq \phi'(x)$. With this assumption, such a ϕ is not in Φ and non-trivial copy attacks are automatically ruled out. This is exactly the technical reason of why numerous constructions of Φ-RKA-secure-primitives [5,9,33,41] are restricted to claw-free Φ. However, as already pin-pointed by [1,6], this assumption is undesirable because many natural and practical RKDT classes are not claw-free. The second method is directly modifying the RKA security experiment to disallow RKA queries $\langle \phi, x^* \rangle$ where $\phi \neq \mathsf{id}$ but $\phi(sk) = sk$. Such method evades non-trivial copy attacks only in the conceptual sense by adopting a potentially weaker RKA notion. It also brings a new technical challenge, that is, checking if $\phi(sk) = sk$ without knowing sk. To overcome this hurdle, existing works either require the starting primitives to meet extra properties like Φ-fingerprinting [37,40,51] in the context of public-key encryption or resort to ad-hoc transform like identity-renaming [10] in the context of identity-based encryption.[13] The third method in the context of pseudorandom functions is to rely on Φ-key-collision-security [1], which requires that for a random key k it is impossible to find two distinct $\phi_1, \phi_2 \in \Phi$ such that $\phi_1(k) = \phi_2(k)$. However, such property is only known to hold w.r.t. specific Φ under concrete number-theoretic assumptions.

7.3   Our Insight in Addressing Non-trivial Copy Attacks

As discussed above, non-trivial copy attacks have not been well addressed at a general level. Being aware of the similarity between our non-malleability notion and the RKA security notion, we are curious to know if our strengthening of allowing $\phi(x^*) = x^*$ can shed light on this problem. Recall that in the proof of Lemma 4 for the case of $y = y^*$, we essentially proved that by assuming

---

[13] Briefly, Φ-fingerprinting for requires that $\phi(sk) \neq sk$ always invalidates the challenge ciphertext c^*. Notice that queries $\langle \phi, c^* \rangle$ such that $\phi(sk) = sk$ are already forbidden by the definition, the reduction can thus safely reject all RKA queries of the form $\langle \phi, c^* \rangle$ without even looking at ϕ, since either case $\phi(sk) = sk$ or case $\phi(sk) \neq sk$ yields the same output $\bot$ with respect to c^*.

the one-wayness of f, no PPT adversary is able to find a $\phi \in \Phi_{\mathrm{brs}}^{\mathrm{srs}}$ such that $\phi(x^*) = x^*$ with non-negligible probability. The high-level idea is that as long as the adversary is able to find such a $\phi \in \Phi_{\mathrm{brs}}^{\mathrm{srs}}$, then a reduction can obtain an efficiently solvable equation about x^*. Somewhat surprisingly, this idea immediately indicates that w.r.t. RKDT class $\Phi = \Phi_{\mathrm{brs}}^{\mathrm{srs}} \cup \mathsf{id} \cup \mathsf{cf}$, resilience against non-trivial copy attacks is in fact a built-in immunity guaranteed by the security of starting primitives.

We sketch the argument more formally as follows. Let $\mathcal{A}$ be a RKA adversary and denote by E the event that non-trivial attack happens, i.e., $\mathcal{A}$ makes at least one RKA query $\langle \phi, x^* \rangle$ such that $\phi \in \Phi_{\mathrm{brs}}^{\mathrm{srs}}$ and $\phi(sk) = sk$. Let $l(\lambda)$ be the maximum number of RKA queries $\mathcal{A}$ makes. Our aim is to prove $\Pr[E] = \mathsf{negl}(\lambda)$ by only assuming the original security of the starting primitives. Conditioned on E happens, a reduction $\mathcal{R}$ can pick out a non-trivial copy attack query say $\langle \phi, x^* \rangle$ and hence obtains a right equation $\phi(sk) = sk$ about sk, with probability at least $1/l(\lambda)$. Conditioned on getting the right equation, $\mathcal{R}$ can further compute the correct sk with probability $1/\mathsf{poly}(\lambda)$ due to the BRS & SRS properties of $\Phi_{\mathrm{brs}}^{\mathrm{srs}}$. Overall, $\mathcal{R}$ is able to recover sk with probability $\Pr[E]/l(\lambda)\mathsf{poly}(\lambda)$. Since $\mathcal{A}$ is a PPT adversary, $l(\lambda)$ is poly-bounded. Therefore, if $\Pr[E]$ is non-negligible, then $\mathcal{R}$ can recover sk with non-negligible probability. This contradicts the security of the starting primitives, and therefore we must have $\Pr[E] = \mathsf{negl}(\lambda)$.

Somewhat surprisingly, our result indicates that w.r.t. RKDT class $\Phi \subseteq \Phi_{\mathrm{brs}}^{\mathrm{srs}} \cup \mathsf{id} \cup \mathsf{cf}$, resilience against non-trivial copy attacks is essentially a built-in security guaranteed by the starting primitives. Previous RKA-secure schemes w.r.t. algebra-induced RKDTs could benefit from this, that is, "weak" RKA security (disallowing non-trivial copy attacks) can be enhanced automatically without resorting to claw-free assumption or additional properties/transformations.

8   Application to RKA-secure Authenticated KDFs

8.1   Continuous Non-Malleable KDFs, Revisited

Qin et al. [47] extended non-malleable key derivation functions (KDFs) [28] to continuous non-malleable KDFs, and showed how to use it to compile numerous cryptographic primitives into RKA-secure ones. In what follows, we briefly recall the syntax, security notion, as well as construction of continuously non-malleable KDFs presented in [47].

Syntax. KDFs consist of three polynomial time algorithms: (1) Setup(λ), on input λ, outputs system-wide public parameters pp, which define the key space S, the public key space Π, and the derived key space $\{0,1\}^m$. (2) Sample(pp), on input pp, samples a random key $s \xleftarrow{\mathrm{R}} S$ and computes public key $\pi \in \Pi$. (3) Derive(s, π), on input (s, π), outputs a derived key $r \in \{0,1\}^m$ or $\perp$ indicating that π is not a valid proof of s.

Security. The continuous non-malleability of KDFs is defined w.r.t. a transformation class Φ, which states that no PPT adversary can distinguish a real derived key $r \leftarrow$ Derive(s^*, π^*) from a random one, even if it can continuously query a key derivation oracle $\mathcal{O}^{\Phi}_{\text{derive}}(\cdot, \cdot)$, which on input $\phi \in \Phi$ and $\pi \in \Pi$, returns a special symbol same* if $\underline{(\phi(s^*), \pi) = (s^*, \pi^*)}$, or Derive$(\phi(s^*), \pi)$ otherwise.

Construction. Let LF $=$ (Gen, Eval, LTag) be a collection of one-time lossy filters [46] with domain S, range Y, and tag space $T = \{0,1\}^* \times T_c$. Let OTS $=$ (Gen, Sign, Vefy) be a strongly one-time signature. Let $\mathcal{H}$ be a family of pairwise independent functions from S to $\{0,1\}^m$. The construction is as below.

- KDF.Setup(λ): run $(ek, td) \leftarrow$ LF.Gen(λ), pick $h \xleftarrow{\text{R}} \mathcal{H}$, output $pp = (ek, h)$. Precisely, pp also includes the public parameters of LF and OTS.
- KDF.Sample(pp): run $(vk, sk) \leftarrow$ OTS.Gen(λ), pick $t_c \xleftarrow{\text{R}} T_c$, $s \xleftarrow{\text{R}} S$; compute $y \leftarrow$ LF.Eval$(ek, (vk, t_c), s)$ and $\sigma \leftarrow$ OTS.Sign$(sk, t_c \| y)$, then set $t = (vk, t_c, y, \sigma)$, and finally output (s, t).
- KDF.Derive(s, t): parse $t = (vk, t_c, y, \sigma)$, if LF.Eval$(ek, (vk, t_c), s) = y$ and OTS.Vefy$(vk, t_c \| y, \sigma) = 1$ hold simultaneously, output $h(s)$, else output $\bot$.

Qin et al.'s construction requires one-time lossy filter, one-time signature, and pairwise-independent functions as ingredients. Though ingenious, their construction is somewhat complicated and expensive. Its public parameters consist of those of three ingredients as well as an evaluation key; to compute a tag for a random key, its sampling procedure has to generate a fresh one-time signature key pair, pick a random tag, evaluate a function and also compute a signature; to derive a random key, its key derivation procedure has to verify a signature and a function value before deriving. Compared to standard KDFs, these do add noticeable storage and computation overhead, which could be critical in resource-constrained scenarios, e.g., embedded systems and low-end smart card.

More Accurate Naming. In standard KDFs, there is no the concept of "public key", and the key derivation algorithm never fails. In contrast, in the KDFs introduced by Qin et al. [47], each key s is accompanied with an auxiliary "public key" π, and the key derivation algorithm reports failure by outputting $\bot$ if π does not match s. Thus, it is preferable to use the name authenticated KDFs to highlight this functional difference. In addition, π is interpreted as a proof of knowledge of s in [47] . However, in the context of KDFs, the key s is not necessarily belong to any $\mathcal{NP}$ language. In this regard, it is more appropriate to simply view π as a tag of s, which we will denote by t.

We then reconsider its security notion. The continuous non-malleable notion considered in [47] is potentially weak in that key derivation queries of the form $\langle \phi, \pi^* \rangle$ with $\phi(s^*) = s^*$ are implicitly rejected by returning same*. As a consequence, this notion cannot guarantee the resilience against non-trivial copy attacks for its enabling RKA-secure schemes. Besides, non-malleability is conventionally used to capture the inability to maul the value of a cryptographic primitive in a controlled way, whereas RKA security ensures that a cryptographic primitive remains secure even an adversary may adaptively learn functions of a sequence of related keys. In light of this distinction, their "continuous non-malleability" is actually a form of related-key security and we use the term

"RKA-secure authenticated KDFs" instead of continuous non-malleable KDFs in the rest of this work.

8.2   RKA-secure Authenticated KDFs

Based on the above discussions, we are motivated to enhance the security notion and propose a simple yet efficient construction for RKA-secure authenticated KDFs (AKDFs) w.r.t. general RKDT class. For completeness, we first present authenticated KDFs with the refined terminology and enhanced security notions.

Definition 7 (Authenticated KDFs). *Authenticated KDFs are given by three polynomial time algorithms as follows:*

- Setup(λ): *on input λ, output system parameters pp, which define the derivation key space S, the tag space T, and the derived key space $\{0,1\}^m$.*
- Sample(pp): *on input pp, pick a random key $s \xleftarrow{\text{R}} S$ computes it associated tag $t \in T$, output (s,t).*
- Derive(s,t): *on input a key $s \in S$ and a tag $t \in T$, output a derived key $r \in \{0,1\}^m$ or a rejecting symbol $\perp$ indicating that t is not a valid tag of s.*

Definition 8 (RKA-Security). *AKDFs are said to be Φ-RKA-secure w.r.t. RKDT class Φ if for any PPT adversary $\mathcal{A}$ its advantage $\text{Adv}^{\text{rka}}_{\mathcal{A},AKDF}$ defined in the following experiment is negligible in λ.*

$$\text{Adv}^{\text{rka}}_{\mathcal{A},AKDF}(\lambda) = \Pr \left[b' = b : \begin{array}{l} pp \leftarrow \text{Setup}(\lambda); \\ (s^*,t^*) \leftarrow \text{Sample}(pp); \\ r_0^* \leftarrow \text{Derive}(s^*,t^*), r_1^* \xleftarrow{\text{R}} \{0,1\}^m; \\ b \xleftarrow{\text{R}} \{0,1\}; \\ b' \leftarrow \mathcal{A}^{\mathcal{O}^{\Phi}_{\text{derive}}(\cdot,\cdot)}(pp,t^*,r_b^*); \end{array} \right] - \frac{1}{2}.$$

Here $\mathcal{O}^{\Phi}_{\text{derive}}(\phi,\pi)$ on input $\phi \in \Phi$ and $t \in T$, returns a special symbol $\textsf{same}^*$ only if $\underline{\phi = \text{id and } t = t^*}$, and returns $\text{Derive}(\phi(s^*),t)$ otherwise.

Our RKA security notion is strong in the sense that only trivial query (underlined as above) is not allowed. By Qin et al.'s result [47], one can use RKA-secure AKDFs to transform a cryptographic primitive to a RKA-secure one in a modular way, as long as the key generation algorithm of the primitive takes uniform random coins to generate (public/secret) keys. Notably, this transform naturally transfers our strong RKA security of AKDFs to the resulting RKA-secure primitives.

8.3   RKA-secure AKDFs from Non-Malleable Functions

Before presenting our construction, we first sketch the high-level idea, which we think may be useful in other places. The main technical hurdle in constructing RKA-secure AKDFs is to answer related key derivation queries without knowing the secret key s^*. As we recalled in Sect. 7, a common approach addressing this hurdle is exploiting key-malleable like property to simulate RKA oracle based on the standard oracle of the starting primitive. However, this approach does not fit for our purpose. On one hand, efficient construction of the starting primitive namely AKDFs is yet unknown to us. On the other hand, key-malleable like property (if exists) is usually tied to some specific algebraic structure and thus cannot yield RKA-security w.r.t. general RKDT class. Here we take a complementary approach, that is, acquiring RKA security from non-malleability. Instead of trying to answer RKA queries, we aim to reject all RKA queries. We do so by stipulating that even after seeing a valid tag t^* of s^*, no PPT adversary is able to generate a legal related key derivation query (ϕ, π) (here legal means t is a valid tag of $\phi(s^*)$). In this way, the reduction can handle all related key derivation queries without knowing s^*, by simply returning $\perp$.

With this strategy, an incredibly simple construction of RKA-secure AKDFs comes out by twisting NMFs. Let $\mathcal{F}$ be a family of poly-to-one NMFs. The Setup algorithm randomly picks f from $\mathcal{F}$. Let h be a hardcore function of f. To generate a tag for a random key, one simply computes $t \leftarrow f(s)$. Intuitively, t serves as a deterministic non-malleable tag of s. To get a derived key from (s, t), one first checks if $f(s) = t$ and then outputs $r \leftarrow h(s)$ if so. On a high (and not entirely precise) level, due to the non-malleability of the underlying NMFs, all related-key derivation queries can be safely rejected, and thus the pseudorandomness of the derived key can be reduced to the one-wayness of f. A subtlety here is that, in addition to t^*, the adversary can obtain some auxiliary information about s^*, namely, the real or random derived key. In this regard, hinted non-malleability is required for $\mathcal{F}$. We present our generic construction and formal security proof in details as below.

Our Construction. Let $\mathcal{F} = (\mathsf{Gen}, \mathsf{Samp}, \mathsf{Eval})$ be a family of Φ-non-malleable poly-to-one functions and $\mathcal{H}$ be its hardcore that maps D to $\{0, 1\}^m$. We show how to build Φ'-RKA-secure AKDFs from it, where $\Phi' = \Phi \cup \mathsf{id} \cup \mathsf{cf}$.[14]

- AKDF.Setup(λ): run $f \leftarrow \mathcal{F}.\mathsf{Gen}(\lambda)$, $h \leftarrow \mathcal{H}.\mathsf{Gen}(\lambda, f)$, output $pp = (f, h)$.
- AKDF.Sample(pp): sample $s \leftarrow \mathcal{F}.\mathsf{Samp}(\lambda)$, compute $t \leftarrow f(s)$, output (s, t).
- AKDF.Derive(s, t): if $t \neq f(s)$, output $\perp$; otherwise output $r \leftarrow h(s)$.

The RKA security of the above construction follows from the theorem below.

Theorem 1. *The above construction of AKDFs is Φ'-RKA-secure if $\mathcal{F}$ is Φ-non-malleable and poly-to-one, where $\Phi' = \Phi \cup \mathsf{id} \cup \mathsf{cf}$.*

Proof. We prove this theorem via a sequence of games. Let S_i be the event that $\mathcal{A}$ wins in Game i.

Game 0 (The real experiment): $\mathcal{CH}$ interacts with $\mathcal{A}$ as follows:

---

[14] As we discussed in Sect. 3, non-malleability is impossible to achieve if Φ contains id or constant transformations. Thus, we assume $\Phi \cap (\mathsf{id} \cup \mathsf{cf}) = \emptyset$.

1. $\mathcal{CH}$ picks $f \leftarrow \mathcal{F}.\mathsf{Gen}(\lambda)$, $h \leftarrow \mathcal{H}.\mathsf{Gen}(\lambda, f)$, sets $pp = (f, h)$; picks $s^* \leftarrow \mathcal{F}.\mathsf{Samp}(\lambda)$, computes $t^* \leftarrow f(s^*)$, $r_0^* \leftarrow h(s^*)$, $r_1^* \xleftarrow{\text{R}} \{0,1\}^m$. Finally, $\mathcal{CH}$ picks $b \xleftarrow{\text{R}} \{0,1\}$, sends (pp, t^*, r_b^*) to $\mathcal{A}$ as the challenge.
2. Upon receiving a RKA key derivation query $\langle \phi, t \rangle$ from $\mathcal{A}$, if $\langle \phi, t \rangle = \langle \mathsf{id}, t^* \rangle$, $\mathcal{CH}$ returns same^*; else $\mathcal{CH}$ returns $h(\phi(s^*))$ if $\phi(s^*) = t$ or $\bot$ otherwise.
3. $\mathcal{A}$ outputs a guess b' for b and wins if $b' = b$.

According to the definition of $\mathcal{A}$, we have:

$$\mathsf{Adv}^{\text{rka}}_{\mathcal{A},\text{AKDF}}(\lambda) = |\Pr[S_0] - 1/2|. \tag{3}$$

Game 1 (Handling trivial queries without s^*): The same as Game 0 except that in step 2 $\mathcal{CH}$ handles trivial queries $\langle \phi, t \rangle$ without s^*. Here the term "trivial" means $\phi \in \mathsf{id} \cup \mathsf{cf}$. We break trivial queries into three cases:

- $\phi = \mathsf{id}$ and $t = t^*$: return same^* indicating that the query is illegal.
- $\phi = \mathsf{id}$ and $t \neq t^*$: return $\bot$ indicating that the query is invalid. This is because f is a deterministic function and hence each s has an unique tag.
- $\phi \in \mathsf{cf}$ and all t: suppose ϕ is a constant transform that maps all its inputs to a constant c, return $h(c)$ if $f(c) = t$ and $\bot$ otherwise.

These modifications are purely conceptual and hence

$$\Pr[S_1] = \Pr[S_0]. \tag{4}$$

Game 2 (Handling all queries without s^*): The same as Game 1 except $\mathcal{CH}$ directly returns $\bot$ for all non-trivial queries $\langle \phi, t \rangle$. Here the term "non-trivial" means $\phi \in \Phi$. Let E be the event that $\mathcal{A}$ issues a non-trivial query $\langle \phi, t \rangle$ such that $t = f(\phi(s^*))$. According to the definitions of Game 1 and Game 2, if this event happens, $\mathcal{CH}$ returns $\bot$ in Game 2, but not in Game 1. It is easy to see that unless event E occurs, Game 1 and Game 2 are identical from the view of the adversary. By the difference lemma, it follows that:

$$|\Pr[S_2] - \Pr[S_1]| \leq \Pr[E]. \tag{5}$$

We now state and prove two claims that establish the main theorem.

Lemma 9. $\Pr[E]$ *is negligible in* λ *assuming the* Φ*-non-malleability of* $\mathcal{F}$.

What we need to show is that, after seeing t^* and the auxiliary information r_b^* about s^*, no PPT adversary is able to output a valid non-trivial RKA query $\langle \phi, t \rangle$ such that $\phi(s^*) = t$. Therefore, hint-free non-malleability is inadequate and hinted non-malleability is needed. Notice that here the auxiliary information r_b^* is exactly $\mathsf{hint}(s^*; b)$, where hint is the special hint function defined in Eq. (1). As we have shown Sect. 6, hinted non-malleability w.r.t. this hint function is implied by hint-free non-malleability.

Proof. Suppose $\mathcal{B}$ is an adversary against hinted Φ-non-malleability of $\mathcal{F}$ w.r.t. the hint function defined in Equation (1). Given $(f, y^*, \mathsf{hint}(x^*; b))$, where $f \leftarrow \mathcal{F}.\mathsf{Gen}(\lambda)$, $y^* \leftarrow f(x^*)$ for $x^* \leftarrow \mathcal{F}.\mathsf{Samp}(\lambda)$, and $b \xleftarrow{\text{R}} \{0, 1\}$. $\mathcal{B}$ simulates $\mathcal{A}$'s challenger in Game 2 as below: set $pp = (f, h)$,[15] $t^* = y^*$, $r_b^* \leftarrow \mathsf{hint}(x^*; b)$, then send (pp, t^*, r_b^*) to $\mathcal{A}$. Here s^* is implicitly set to be x^*, which is unknown to $\mathcal{B}$. This is not a problem since according to the definition of Game 2, $\mathcal{B}$ is able to handle all RKA queries correctly without s^*. Let L be the list of all non-trivial queries issued by $\mathcal{A}$. Since $\mathcal{A}$ is a PPT adversary, we have $|L| \leq \mathsf{poly}(\lambda)$. At the end of the simulation, $\mathcal{B}$ picks a random tuple (ϕ, t) from the L list as its answer against hinted Φ-non-malleability. Conditioned on E happens, $\mathcal{B}$ succeeds with probability at least $1/\mathsf{poly}(\lambda)$. Therefore, if $\Pr[E]$ is non-negligible, $\mathcal{B}$'s advantage is at least $\Pr[E]/\mathsf{poly}(\lambda)$, which is also non-negligible. This breaks the hinted Φ-non-malleability of $\mathcal{F}$, which in turn contradicts the assumed hint-free Φ-non-malleability of $\mathcal{F}$ in this case. The lemma immediately follows. □

Lemma 10. $|\Pr[S_2] - 1/2| = \mathsf{negl}(\lambda)$ *assuming the Φ-non-malleability of $\mathcal{F}$.*

Proof. Since $\mathcal{F}$ is poly-to-one, according to Lemma 1 Φ-non-malleability implies one-wayness, and further implies pseudorandomness of its hardcore $\mathcal{H}$. Thereby, it suffices to prove $|\Pr[S_2] - 1/2| = \mathsf{negl}(\lambda)$ assuming the pseudorandomness of $\mathcal{H}$. Suppose $\mathcal{B}$ is an adversary against pseudorandomness of hardcore $\mathcal{H}$ associated with $\mathcal{F}$. Given (f, h, y^*, r_b^*), where $y^* \leftarrow f(x^*)$ for $x^* \xleftarrow{\text{R}} D$ and r_b^* is either $h(x^*)$ when $b = 0$ or a random string from $\{0, 1\}^m$ when $b = 1$, $\mathcal{B}$ simulates $\mathcal{A}$'s challenger in Game 2 as follows: set $pp = (f, h)$, $t^* = y^*$, send (pp, t^*, r_b^*) to $\mathcal{A}$. According to the definition of Game 2, $\mathcal{B}$ can handle all the queries without the knowledge of $s^* = x^*$. At the end of the game, $\mathcal{B}$ simply forwards $\mathcal{A}$'s output as its guess. It is easy to see that if $\mathcal{A}$ succeeds, so does $\mathcal{B}$. Therefore, we have $\mathsf{Adv}_{\mathcal{B}, \mathcal{H}}^{\mathrm{rand}}(\lambda) \geq |\Pr[S_2] - 1/2|$. By the hypothesis that $\mathcal{H}$ is pseudorandom, we have $|\Pr[S_2] - 1/2| = \mathsf{negl}(\lambda)$. This proves the lemma. □

Putting it all together, the theorem immediately follows. □

By instantiating our generic construction with poly-to-one NMFs w.r.t. $\Phi_{\mathrm{brs}}^{\mathrm{srs}}$ (which in turn can be constructed from ATDFs), we obtain RKA-secure AKDFs w.r.t. $\Phi_{\mathrm{brs}}^{\mathrm{srs}} \cup \mathsf{id} \cup \mathsf{cf}$.

Comparison to Qin et al.'s Construction. While both our construction and Qin et al.'s construction are generic, it is still instructive to make a rough comparison. For efficiency, our construction is built solely from deterministic NMFs, so its public parameters consist of merely the descriptions of a NMF f and a hardcore function h; and its tag generation and authentication procedures are both deterministic. In contrast, Qin et al.'s construction is built from three different cryptographic primitives, and thus its public parameters size is large and its tag generation procedure is randomized. In this regard, our construction has potential advantages over Qin et al.'s construction in terms of small footprint

---

[15] The description of h is implicit in hint.

of cryptographic code, compact public parameters size, short tag size, as well as quick tag generation and authentication. For security, our construction is RKA-secure in the strong sense w.r.t. a general RKDT class with a direct and modular proof, whereas Qin et al.'s construction is RKA-secure w.r.t. specific RKDT class [30] with a bit involved proof.

8.4 Optimizations

Relaxation on NMFs. We observe that in the above construction, NMFs can be relaxed to non-malleable verifiable relations (NMVRs). In NMVRs, instead of requiring f to be efficiently computable, we only require that the distribution $(x, f(x))$ for a random x is efficiently sampleable and the correctness of sampling is publicly verifiable.[16] It is easy to see that NMVRs are implied by adaptive trapdoor relations (ATDRs) [50] with publicly verifiability. As shown in [52], publicly verifiable ATDRs can be constructed from all-but-one verifiable lossy trapdoor relations, which permit efficient realizations from a variety of standard assumptions. Combining this result with our observation above, we are able to give more efficient constructions of RKA-secure AKDFs.

Stronger RKA Security. In the above RKA security notion for AKDFs, the adversary is only given access to a RKA oracle. In practice, it may also collect some tags and learn the corresponding derivation keys. To defend against such powerful adversaries, it is necessary to make the RKA security stronger by giving the adversary access to a reveal oracle $\mathcal{O}_{\mathsf{reveal}}$ that on input a tag t outputs a corresponding key s.[17] AKDFs satisfying such strong RKA notion can be constructed from adaptive NMFs, which in turn can be constructed from ATDFs. This not only justifies the utility of the adaptive non-malleability notion, but also supports the view of Kiltz et al. [38] that "ATDFs may be useful in the general context of black-box constructions of cryptographic primitives secure against adaptive attacks."

Increasing the Length of Derivation Key. We can always instantiate h via the Goldreich-Levin hardcore predicate [34]. Nevertheless, such general instantiation yields only one-bit derived key. We may also obtain a hardcore function with linearly-many hardcore bits either by iteration when $\mathcal{F}$ is a family of one-way permutations or relying on stronger decisional assumptions. A recent work [13] provides us an appealing hardcore function with poly-many hardcore bits from any one-way functions, assuming the existence of differing-inputs/indistinguishability obfuscation. In applications of RKA-secure AKDFs where the length of the derived key is of great importance, one can further stretch it by applying a normal pseudorandom generator.

---

[16] Here the publicly verifiable property means verification can be done without knowing the secret random coins used in sampling.

[17] Query on the challenge tag t^* is not allowed to avoid trivial attack.

9   Conclusion

We formally study non-malleable functions with simplified syntax and strong game-based security definition. We establish connections between (adaptive) non-malleability and (adaptive) one-wayness, by exploiting our newly abstracted algebraic properties of transformation class. Notably, the implication AOW $\Rightarrow$ ANM not only gives efficient construction of NMFs from adaptive trapdoor functions, but also provides insight in addressing non-trivial copy attacks in the RKA area. Using NMFs, we give a simple and efficient construction of RKA-secure authenticated KDFs.

Acknowledgments. We particularly thank Zongyang Zhang for bringing up the work [3] to our attention. We are grateful to Qiong Huang, Marc Fischlin, Jinyong Chang and Fei Tang for helpful discussions and advice. We also thank the anonymous reviewers of PKC 2016 for their useful comments.

Yu Chen is supported by the National Natural Science Foundation of China (Grant No. 61303257), the IIE's Cryptography Research Project (Grant No. Y4Z0061B02), and the Strategic Priority Research Program of CAS (Grant No. XDA06010701).

Baodong Qin is supported by the National Natural Science Foundation of China (Grant No. 61502400, 61373153 and 61572318).

Jiang Zhang is supported by the National Basic Research Program of China (Grant No. 2013CB338003).

Yi Deng is supported by the National Natural Science Foundation of China (Grant No. 61379141), the IIE's Cryptography Research Project (Grant No. Y4Z0061802), and the State Key Laboratory of Cryptology's Open Project (Grant No. MMKFKT201511).

Sherman S.M. Chow is supported by the Early Career Scheme and the Early Career Award of the Research Grants Council, Hong Kong SAR (CUHK 439713).

References

1. Abdalla, M., Benhamouda, F., Passelègue, A., Paterson, K.G.: Related-key security for pseudorandom functions beyond the linear barrier. In: Garay, J.A., Gennaro, R. (eds.) CRYPTO 2014, Part I. LNCS, vol. 8616, pp. 77–94. Springer, Heidelberg (2014)
2. Applebaum, B., Harnik, D., Ishai, Y.: Semantic security under related-key attacksand applications. In: ICS, pp. 45–60 (2010)
3. Baecher, P., Fischlin, M., Schröder, D.: Expedient non-malleability notions for hash functions. In: Kiayias, A. (ed.) CT-RSA 2011. LNCS, vol. 6558, pp. 268–283. Springer, Heidelberg (2011)
4. Bellare, M., Boldyreva, A., O'Neill, A.: Deterministic and efficiently searchable encryption. In: Menezes, A. (ed.) CRYPTO 2007. LNCS, vol. 4622, pp. 535–552. Springer, Heidelberg (2007)
5. Bellare, M., Cash, D.: Pseudorandom functions and permutations provably secure against related-key attacks. In: Rabin, T. (ed.) CRYPTO 2010. LNCS, vol. 6223, pp. 666–684. Springer, Heidelberg (2010)
6. Bellare, M., Cash, D., Miller, R.: Cryptography secure against related-key attacks and tampering. In: Lee, D.H., Wang, X. (eds.) ASIACRYPT 2011. LNCS, vol. 7073, pp. 486–503. Springer, Heidelberg (2011)

7. Bellare, M., Desai, A., Pointcheval, D., Rogaway, P.: Relations among notions of security for public-key encryption schemes. In: Krawczyk, H. (ed.) CRYPTO 1998. LNCS, vol. 1462, pp. 26–45. Springer, Heidelberg (1998)

8. Bellare, M., Halevi, S., Sahai, A., Vadhan, S.P.: Many-to-one trapdoor functions and their relation to public-key cryptosystems. In: Krawczyk, H. (ed.) CRYPTO 1998. LNCS, vol. 1462, p. 283. Springer, Heidelberg (1998)

9. Bellare, M., Kohno, T.: A theoretical treatment of related-key attacks: RKA-PRPs, RKA-PRFs, and applications. In: Biham, E. (ed.) EUROCRYPT 2003. LNCS, vol. 2656, pp. 491–506. Springer, Heidelberg (2003)

10. Bellare, M., Paterson, K.G., Thomson, S.: RKA security beyond the linear barrier: ibe, encryption and signatures. In: Wang, X., Sako, K. (eds.) ASIACRYPT 2012. LNCS, vol. 7658, pp. 331–348. Springer, Heidelberg (2012)

11. Bellare, M., Rogaway, P.: Random oracles are practical: a paradigm for designing efficient protocols. In: ACM CCS, pp. 62–73 (1993)

12. Bellare, M., Sahai, A.: Non-malleable encryption: equivalence between two notions, and an indistinguishability-based characterization. In: Wiener, M. (ed.) CRYPTO 1999. LNCS, vol. 1666, pp. 519–536. Springer, Heidelberg (1999)

13. Bellare, M., Stepanovs, I., Tessaro, S.: Poly-many hardcore bits for any one-way function and a framework for differing-inputs obfuscation. In: Sarkar, P., Iwata, T. (eds.) ASIACRYPT 2014, Part II. LNCS, vol. 8874, pp. 102–121. Springer, Heidelberg (2014)

14. Berlekamp, E.R.: Factoring polynomials over large finite fields. Math. Comput. **24**, 713–735 (1970)

15. Biham, E., Shamir, A.: Differential fault analysis of secret key cryptosystems. In: Kaliski Jr., B.S. (ed.) CRYPTO 1997. LNCS, vol. 1294, pp. 513–525. Springer, Heidelberg (1997)

16. Boldyreva, A., Cash, D., Fischlin, M., Warinschi, B.: Foundations of non-malleable hash and one-way functions. In: Matsui, M. (ed.) ASIACRYPT 2009. LNCS, vol. 5912, pp. 524–541. Springer, Heidelberg (2009)

17. Boldyreva, A., Fischlin, M.: On the security of OAEP. In: Lai, X., Chen, K. (eds.) ASIACRYPT 2006. LNCS, vol. 4284, pp. 210–225. Springer, Heidelberg (2006)

18. Boneh, D., DeMillo, R.A., Lipton, R.J.: On the importance of checking cryptographic protocols for faults. In: Fumy, W. (ed.) EUROCRYPT 1997. LNCS, vol. 1233, pp. 37–51. Springer, Heidelberg (1997)

19. Canetti, R., Dakdouk, R.R.: Extractable perfectly one-way functions. In: Aceto, L., Damgård, I., Goldberg, L.A., Halldórsson, M.M., Ingólfsdóttir, A., Walukiewicz, I. (eds.) ICALP 2008, Part II. LNCS, vol. 5126, pp. 449–460. Springer, Heidelberg (2008)

20. Canetti, R., Varia, M.: Non-malleable obfuscation. In: Reingold, O. (ed.) TCC 2009. LNCS, vol. 5444, pp. 73–90. Springer, Heidelberg (2009)

21. Chen, Y., Qin, B., Zhang, J., Deng, Y., Chow, S.S.: Non-malleable functions and their applications. Cryptology ePrint Archive, Report 2015/1253 (2015)

22. Di Crescenzo, G., Ishai, Y., Ostrovsky, R.: Non-interactive and non-malleable commitment. In: STOC, pp. 141–150 (1998)

23. Di Crescenzo, G., Katz, J., Ostrovsky, R., Smith, A.: Efficient and non-interactive non-malleable commitment. In: Pfitzmann, B. (ed.) EUROCRYPT 2001. LNCS, vol. 2045, pp. 40–59. Springer, Heidelberg (2001)

24. Diffie, W., Hellman, M.E.: New directions in cryptograpgy. IEEE Trans. Inf. Theor. **22**(6), 644–654 (1976)

25. Dolev, D., Dwork, C., Naor, M.: Nonmalleable cryptography. SIAM J. Comput. **30**(2), 391–437 (2000)

26. Dziembowski, S., Pietrzak, K., Wichs, D.: Non-malleable codes. In: ICS, pp. 434–452 (2010)
27. Faust, S., Mukherjee, P., Nielsen, J.B., Venturi, D.: Continuous non-malleable codes. In: Lindell, Y. (ed.) TCC 2014. LNCS, vol. 8349, pp. 465–488. Springer, Heidelberg (2014)
28. Faust, S., Mukherjee, P., Venturi, D., Wichs, D.: Efficient non-malleable codes and key-derivation for poly-size tampering circuits. In: Nguyen, P.Q., Oswald, E. (eds.) EUROCRYPT 2014. LNCS, vol. 8441, pp. 111–128. Springer, Heidelberg (2014)
29. Fischlin, M., Fischlin, R.: Efficient non-malleable commitment schemes. In: Bellare, M. (ed.) CRYPTO 2000. LNCS, vol. 1880, pp. 413–431. Springer, Heidelberg (2000)
30. Fujisaki, E., Xagawa, K.: Note on the rka security of continuously non-malleable key-derivation function from pkc 2015. Cryptology ePrint Archive, Report 2015/1088 (2015)
31. von zur Gathen, J., Shoup, V.: Computing frobenius maps and factoring polynomials. In: STOC, pp. 97–105 (1992)
32. Gentry, C., Peikert, C., Vaikuntanathan, V.: Trapdoors for hard lattices and new cryptographic constructions. In: STOC, pp. 197–206 (2008)
33. Goldenberg, D., Liskov, M.: On related-secret pseudorandomness. In: Micciancio, D. (ed.) TCC 2010. LNCS, vol. 5978, pp. 255–272. Springer, Heidelberg (2010)
34. Goldreich, O., Levin, L.A.: A hard-core predicate for all one-way functions. In: STOC, pp. 25–32 (1989)
35. Goyal, V., O'Neill, A., Rao, V.: Correlated-input secure hash functions. In: Ishai, Y. (ed.) TCC 2011. LNCS, vol. 6597, pp. 182–200. Springer, Heidelberg (2011)
36. Jafargholi, Z., Wichs, D.: Tamper detection and continuous non-malleable codes. In: Dodis, Y., Nielsen, J.B. (eds.) TCC 2015, Part I. LNCS, vol. 9014, pp. 451–480. Springer, Heidelberg (2015)
37. Jia, D., Lu, X., Li, B., Mei, Q.: RKA secure PKE based on the DDH and HR assumptions. In: Susilo, W., Reyhanitabar, R. (eds.) ProvSec 2013. LNCS, vol. 8209, pp. 271–287. Springer, Heidelberg (2013)
38. Kiltz, E., Mohassel, P., O'Neill, A.: Adaptive trapdoor functions and chosen-ciphertext security. In: Gilbert, H. (ed.) EUROCRYPT 2010. LNCS, vol. 6110, pp. 673–692. Springer, Heidelberg (2010)
39. Lin, H., Pass, R., Tseng, W.-L.D., Venkitasubramaniam, M.: Concurrent non-malleable zero knowledge proofs. In: Rabin, T. (ed.) CRYPTO 2010. LNCS, vol. 6223, pp. 429–446. Springer, Heidelberg (2010)
40. Lu, X., Li, B., Jia, D.: Related-key security for hybrid encryption. In: Chow, S.S.M., Camenisch, J., Hui, L.C.K., Yiu, S.M. (eds.) ISC 2014. LNCS, vol. 8783, pp. 19–32. Springer, Heidelberg (2014)
41. Lucks, S.: Ciphers secure against related-key attacks. In: Roy, B., Meier, W. (eds.) FSE 2004. LNCS, vol. 3017, pp. 359–370. Springer, Heidelberg (2004)
42. Ostrovsky, R., Persiano, G., Visconti, I.: Constant-round concurrent non-malleable zero knowledge in the bare public-key model. In: Aceto, L., Damgård, I., Goldberg, L.A., Halldórsson, M.M., Ingólfsdóttir, A., Walukiewicz, I. (eds.) ICALP 2008, Part II. LNCS, vol. 5126, pp. 548–559. Springer, Heidelberg (2008)
43. Pandey, O., Pass, R., Vaikuntanathan, V.: Adaptive one-way functions and applications. In: Wagner, D. (ed.) CRYPTO 2008. LNCS, vol. 5157, pp. 57–74. Springer, Heidelberg (2008)
44. Pass, R., Rosen, A.: Concurrent non-malleable commitments. In: FOCS, pp. 563–572 (2005)
45. Peikert, C., Waters, B.: Lossy trapdoor functions and their applications. In: STOC, pp. 187–196 (2008)

46. Qin, B., Liu, S.: Leakage-resilient chosen-ciphertext secure public-key encryption from hash proof system and one-time lossy filter. In: Sako, K., Sarkar, P. (eds.) ASIACRYPT 2013, Part II. LNCS, vol. 8270, pp. 381–400. Springer, Heidelberg (2013)
47. Qin, B., Liu, S., Yuen, T.H., Deng, R.H., Chen, K.: Continuous non-malleable key derivation and its application to related-key security. In: Katz, J. (ed.) PKC 2015. LNCS, vol. 9020, pp. 557–578. Springer, Heidelberg (2015)
48. Rosen, A., Segev, G.: Chosen-ciphertext security via correlated products. SIAM J. Comput. **39**(7), 3058–3088 (2010)
49. Sahai, A.: Non-malleable non-interactive zero knowledge and adaptive chosen-ciphertext security. In: FOCS, pp. 543–553 (1999)
50. Wee, H.: Efficient chosen-ciphertext security via extractable hash proofs. In: Rabin, T. (ed.) CRYPTO 2010. LNCS, vol. 6223, pp. 314–332. Springer, Heidelberg (2010)
51. Wee, H.: Public key encryption against related key attacks. In: Fischlin, M., Buchmann, J., Manulis, M. (eds.) PKC 2012. LNCS, vol. 7293, pp. 262–279. Springer, Heidelberg (2012)
52. Xue, H., Lu, X., Li, B., Liu, Y.: Lossy trapdoor relation and its applications to lossy encryption and adaptive trapdoor relation. In: Chow, S.S.M., Liu, J.K., Hui, L.C.K., Yiu, S.M. (eds.) ProvSec 2014. LNCS, vol. 8782, pp. 162–177. Springer, Heidelberg (2014)

On Public Key Encryption from Noisy Codewords

Eli Ben-Sasson[1]($\boxtimes$), Iddo Ben-Tov[1], Ivan Damgård[2], Yuval Ishai[1,3], and Noga Ron-Zewi[4,5]

[1] Department of Computer Science, Technion, Haifa, Israel
{eli,idddo,yuvali}@cs.technion.ac.il
[2] Department of Computer Science, Aarhus University, Aarhus, Denmark
ivan@cs.au.dk
[3] UCLA, Los Angeles, CA, USA
[4] School of Mathematics, Institute for Advanced Study, Princeton, NJ, USA
nogazewi@ias.edu
[5] DIMACS, Rutgers University, Piscataway, NJ, USA

Abstract. Several well-known public key encryption schemes, including those of Alekhnovich (FOCS 2003), Regev (STOC 2005), and Gentry, Peikert and Vaikuntanathan (STOC 2008), rely on the conjectured intractability of inverting noisy linear encodings. These schemes are limited in that they either require the underlying field to grow with the security parameter, or alternatively they can work over the binary field but have a low noise entropy that gives rise to sub-exponential attacks.

Motivated by the goal of efficient public key cryptography, we study the possibility of obtaining improved security over the binary field by using different noise distributions. Inspired by an abstract encryption scheme of Micciancio (PKC 2010), we study an abstract encryption scheme that unifies all the three schemes mentioned above and allows for arbitrary choices of the underlying field and noise distributions.

Our main result establishes an unexpected connection between the power of such encryption schemes and additive combinatorics. Concretely, we show that under the "approximate duality conjecture" from additive combinatorics (Ben-Sasson and Zewi, STOC 2011), every instance of the abstract encryption scheme over the binary field can be attacked in time $2^{O(\sqrt{n})}$, where n is the maximum of the ciphertext size and the public key size (and where the latter excludes public randomness used for specifying the code). On the flip side, counter examples to the above conjecture (if false) may lead to candidate public key encryption schemes with improved security guarantees.

We also show, using a simple argument that relies on agnostic learning of parities (Kalai, Mansour and Verbin, STOC 2008), that any such encryption scheme can be *unconditionally* attacked in time $2^{O(n/\log n)}$, where n is the ciphertext size. Combining this attack with the security proof of Regev's cryptosystem, we immediately obtain an algorithm that solves the *learning parity with noise (LPN)* problem in time $2^{O(n/\log\log n)}$ using only $n^{1+\epsilon}$ samples, reproducing the result of Lyubashevsky (Random 2005) in a conceptually different way.

A full version of this extended abstract can be found in [6].

© International Association for Cryptologic Research 2016
C.-M. Cheng et al. (Eds.): PKC 2016, Part II, LNCS 9615, pp. 417–446, 2016.
DOI: 10.1007/978-3-662-49387-8_16

Finally, we study the possibility of instantiating the abstract encryption scheme over constant-size rings to yield encryption schemes with no decryption error. We show that over the binary field decryption errors are inherent. On the positive side, building on the construction of matching vector families (Grolmusz, Combinatorica 2000; Efremenko, STOC 2009; Dvir, Gopalan and Yekhanin, FOCS 2010), we suggest plausible candidates for secure instances of the framework over constant-size rings that can offer perfectly correct decryption.

Keywords: Public key encryption · Noisy codewords · Learning parity with noise · Additive combinatorics

1   Introduction

Public key encryption is one of the most intriguing concepts of modern cryptography. Decades after the introduction of the first public key encryption schemes [13,17,31,38,42], there are still only a handful of candidate constructions. While public key encryption schemes such as RSA are widely deployed in practice, their concrete efficiency, including the size of keys and ciphertexts, leaves much to be desired. In particular, there is still a considerable efficiency gap between the best known public key encryption schemes and their private key counterparts.

Motivated by the goal of finding new public key encryption schemes with attractive efficiency features, we study an abstract encryption scheme which captures a class of known schemes that rely on the hardness of inverting a *noisy linear encoding*. This class includes the public key encryption scheme of Alekhnovich [3], whose security is based on the conjectured intractability of the "learning parity with noise" (LPN) problem, and the schemes of Regev [40] and of Gentry, Peikert and Vaikuntanathan (GPV) [18], whose security is based on the conjectured intractability of the "learning with errors" (LWE) problem.

In all of the above schemes, there is a publicly known linear code which is typically chosen at random, and the public keys and ciphertexts are generated by picking a secret uniform random codeword and adding a secret random noise vector, or alternatively by computing the syndrome of such a noisy codeword. Among other differences, the schemes differ in the choice of the underlying field and the distribution from which the noise is picked. In the schemes proposed by Regev and GPV, the field size grows polynomially with the security parameter and the noise distribution is a discrete Guassian. The scheme of Alekhnovich has the advantage of working over the *binary* field, but its noise distribution is restricted to noise patterns whose Hamming weight is smaller than the square root of the ciphertext size and public key size[1].

---

[1] We view the code specification as a global public parameter and do not count it towards the public key size. This is justified by the possibility of picking the code pseudorandomly or using special classes of codes that can be succinctly described (cf. [12,30]).

The choice of binary field made by Alekhnovich [3] is attractive because of the potential for better concrete efficiency, especially on light-weight devices [12,23, 37]. However, the choice of noise distribution made in [3] has a negative impact on efficiency since the low-weight noise makes a brute-force guessing attack possible. In particular, if we require the scheme to resist 2^t time attacks then this requires the public keys as well as the ciphertexts to be of size at least $\Omega(t^2)$, even when encrypting a single bit. In contrast, the known attacks on the schemes of Regev and GPV, using lattice algorithms, only require the public keys and ciphertexts to be of size $\Theta(t \log t)$. The main question we study is whether it is possible to obtain a similar or better level of succinctness by using linear codes over the binary field, thus obtaining a cryptosystem that enjoys the best of both worlds.

1.1 Overview of Contribution

Towards a systematic study of the above question, we study an abstract encryption scheme which unifies the schemes of Regev, GPV, and Alekhnovich, and allows for arbitrary choices of the underlying field and noise distributions. This scheme is inspired by an abstract encryption scheme of Micciancio described in the online talk [33], which unifies the encryption schemes of Regev and GPV.

Our first result unconditionally rules out the possibility of instantiating the abstract encryption scheme over the binary field to yield an *optimally succinct* cryptosystem, in the sense that the ciphertexts and public keys are only $O(t)$ bits long[2]. This result is obtained using a simple argument that relies on a previous result of Kalai et al. on agnostic learning of parities [24]. Combining this attack with the security proof of Regev's cryptosystem [40] immediately yields an algorithm that solves the learning parity with noise (LPN) problem in time $2^{O(n/\log\log n)}$ using only $n^{1+\epsilon}$ samples, providing a conceptually different proof for the main result of Lyubashevsky [29].

Our main result establishes an unexpected connection between the power of such encryption schemes and additive combinatorics. We show that under a conjecture from additive combinatorics it is also impossible to obtain near-optimal succinctness over the binary field in the case in which the decryption error of a single encryption is a sufficiently small constant. More concretely, every instance of the abstract encryption scheme over the binary field can be attacked in time $2^{O(\sqrt{n})}$, where n is the maximum of the ciphertext size and the public key size. This suggests that the parameters of Alekhnovich's original construction cannot be significantly improved by choosing different noise distributions.

---

[2] Recall that we do not include global public parameters, such as the specification of a random linear code, in the public key size. Currently, the only plausible candidates for public key encryption schemes that are optimally succinct in the above sense are based on special families of elliptic curves. Unlike typical code-based constructions, these schemes are inherently susceptible to quantum attacks. The work of Sahai and Waters [43] shows that public key encryption with optimally succinct ciphertexts can be based on indistinguishability obfuscation and an exponentially strong one-way function. However, obfuscation-based constructions have large public keys and their known instances are currently quite far from being practical.

The high level idea behind this result is as follows. The unified encryption scheme is parameterized by three independent noise distributions: a distribution μ_{sk}, applied during the key generation, and distributions μ_0 and μ_1 that are used for encrypting the messages 0 and 1 respectively. To enable correct decryption with high probability, it must be the case that the distributions $\langle \mu_{sk}, \mu_0 \rangle$ and $\langle \mu_{sk}, \mu_1 \rangle$ are statistically far (where $\langle \cdot, \cdot \rangle$ denotes the inner product of independent random samples). On the other hand, the security of the scheme implies that noisy linear encoding with respect to these noise distributions must be one-way, and in particular these distributions should *not* satisfy certain combinatorial properties that enable an adversary to guess the noise and solve the resulting system of linear equations. Our conditional negative results are obtained by applying the *approximate duality conjecture* from [8] to establish limits on the existence of distributions which satisfy the above. On the flip side, counter examples to the approximate duality conjecture (if false) would give distributions μ_{sk}, μ_0, μ_1 that can potentially serve as a basis for cryptosystems (over the binary field) that resist exponential time attacks.

As a secondary contribution of this work, we study the possibility of instantiating the unified scheme over constant-size rings to yield encryption schemes with no decryption error. We show that over the binary field, a small decryption error probability is inherent. On the positive side, building on the construction of matching vector families from [14], which builds in turn on the constructions of [16,21], we suggest plausible candidates for secure instances of the framework over constant-size rings that can offer perfectly correct decryption.

Before providing a more detailed account of our results, we provide some background on the problem of noisy linear decoding and public key encryption schemes based on its conjectured hardness.

1.2   Learning Parity with Noise

The *learning parity with noise* (LPN) problem is the problem of solving random linear equations over $\mathbb{F}_2$ which are corrupted by some noise. More specifically, in this problem there is an unknown vector $s \in \mathbb{F}_2^n$, and one is given independent random samples of the form (a_i, b_i), where a_i is a uniform random vector in $\mathbb{F}_2^n$, $b_i = \langle a_i, s \rangle + e_i$, and each noise bit $e_i \in \{0, 1\}$ is 1 with probability $\eta < \frac{1}{2}$ and 0 otherwise independently of a_i (all operations are performed over $\mathbb{F}_2$). The goal is to recover the unknown vector s from these samples. If the *noise rate* η equals 0 then this can simply be done using Gaussian elimination. When $\eta > 0$ the problem is conjectured to be intractable. Indeed, solving LPN given m samples can be viewed as the problem of decoding a noisy codeword in a random linear code of block length m and dimension n, a longstanding open problem in coding theory.

It is known that the hardness of solving the above *search* version of LPN with a uniform random unknown vector s implies the hardness of the *decision* version of LPN, namely distinguishing between samples of the form (a_i, b_i) as above and uniformly random and independent vectors in $\mathbb{F}_2^{n+1}$ [5,10]. From a coding theory perspective, this means that if it is hard to decode noisy random codewords in a random linear code, then the joint distribution (G, b) is pseudorandom, where G is a random generator matrix of a random linear code and b is a noisy random codeword in the code.

A naive approach for solving LPN is to search among all vectors in $\mathbb{F}_2^n$ to find a vector s' the largest number of equations. This algorithm takes $2^{O(n)}$ time and one can show, using the Chernoff bound, that $O(n)$ independent random samples suffice to ensure that s' will be the correct solution with high probability. In [11], Blum et al. showed that, quite surprisingly, one can solve the LPN problem in time $2^{O(n/\log n)}$. However, a drawback of this algorithm is that it requires $2^{O(n/\log n)}$ independent random samples. In [29] (see also [25]) it was shown that the number of samples could be reduced to $n^{1+\epsilon}$ at the price of increasing the running time to $2^{O(n/\log \log n)}$. More specifically, they showed that using only $n^{1+\epsilon}$ initial independent random samples one can generate additional "almost fresh" random samples by XORing sufficiently large random subsets of the initial samples. These new samples can be used in turn as an input to the algorithm of [11].

1.3 Alekhnovich's Public Key Encryption Scheme

In 2003, Alekhnovich [3] proposed a public key encryption scheme whose security was based on the intractability of the LPN problem. Roughly speaking, this scheme can be used to encrypt a bit $\sigma \in \{0, 1\}$ as follows. Let n be a security parameter, $m = 2n$, and $k = n^{1/2-\epsilon}$ for some small constant $\epsilon > 0$. The key generation proceeds by choosing a random noise vector $e \in \mathbb{F}_2^m$ in which each entry is set to 1 with independent probability $\eta = k/m$, a uniform random $m \times n$ matrix G over the binary field, and a uniform random $w \in \text{Image}(G)$ (that is, w is uniform in the column span of G). The private key is the noise vector e and the public key is the $m \times (n+1)$ matrix $\tilde{G} = (G \mid b)$ obtained from G by appending the noisy codeword $b = w + e$ to the right of the matrix G. (As discussed above, we do not count G towards the size of the public key.)

The encryption of $\sigma = 0$ is a random vector $c \in \mathbb{F}_2^m$ of the form $c = \tilde{w} + \tilde{e}$, where $\tilde{w}$ is a uniform random vector in $\ker(\tilde{G}^T)$ and $\tilde{e} \in \mathbb{F}_2^m$ is a random noise vector distributed identically to (but independently of) the private key e. The encryption of $\sigma = 1$ is a uniform random vector in $\mathbb{F}_2^m$. In order to decrypt a ciphertext $c \in \mathbb{F}_2^m$, one simply outputs the inner product $\langle c, e \rangle$. It can be easily seen that this inner product is a nearly uniform random bit when c is an encryption of 1, and is equal to the inner product $\langle e, \tilde{e} \rangle$ when c is an encryption of 0. By the birthday paradox, the inner product $\langle e, \tilde{e} \rangle$ is 0 with probability $1 - o(1)$ and consequently, by repeating the encryption process polylog(n) times, one can distinguish between encryptions of 0 and 1 with negligible error probability.

The security of the above scheme can be based on the intractability of the LPN problem with noise rate η. Indeed, since the matrix $\tilde{G}$ is indistinguishable from a uniform random matrix, the code from which $\tilde{w}$ is picked is indistinguishable from a random linear code, implying that the noisy codeword c is also pseudorandom. However, by the choice of the noise rate η, the Hamming weight of the private key e is bounded by $n^{1/2-\epsilon/2}$ with overwhelming probability. By trying all different possibilities for such a private key, the scheme can be attacked in time $2^{O(\sqrt{n})}$.

It is instructive to consider the abstract requirements from the noise distributions e and $\tilde{e}$ that are necessary for the correctness and security of the above scheme. To enable correct decryption with high probability, the inner product of e and $\tilde{e}$ (where the two noise vectors are independently sampled) should be statistically far from uniform, i.e., significantly biased towards either 0 or 1. On the other hand, a sufficient condition for security is that the LPN decision problem be intractable with respect to both of the noise distributions e and $\tilde{e}$. The main question that motivates this work is whether there can be other choices of noise distributions that satisfy the above correctness requirement and may provide substantially better security than the original choice of Alekhnovich.

1.4   Learning with Errors

The *learning with errors* (LWE) problem, introduced by Regev for the construction of his public key encryption scheme [40], is a generalization of the LPN problem to arbitrary rings $\mathbb{Z}_q$ (where q is a prime power). More specifically, in this problem one is given independent random samples of the form (a_i, b_i) where now a_i is a uniform random vector in $\mathbb{Z}_q^n$, $b_i = \langle a_i, s \rangle + e_i$ for a fixed unknown vector $s \in \mathbb{Z}_q^n$ and e_i is distributed according to some fixed distribution χ on $\mathbb{Z}_q$ independently of a_i (all operations are performed over $\mathbb{Z}_q$). Concretely, the distribution χ is usually chosen to be some small *discrete Gaussian*. The goal is again to recover the unknown vector s.

As was the case with LPN, assuming that the distribution χ is sufficiently far from uniform, one can solve LWE naively in time $q^{O(n)}$ using $O(n \log q)$ samples, and the algorithm of Blum et al. [11] can be adapted to solve this problem in time $q^{O(n/\log n)}$ using $q^{O(n/\log n)}$ samples. However, what is remarkable about LWE is that its hardness can be based on the *worst-case hardness* of well-studied lattice problems. This makes all cryptographic constructions based on the hardness of LWE secure under assumptions on the worst-case hardness of these lattice problems. See the survey [41] for more details.

1.5   Public Key Encryption Based on Learning with Errors

As mentioned above, Regev introduced the LWE problem as a basis for the construction of his public key encryption scheme [40] which can be used to encrypt a bit $\sigma \in \{0, 1\}$ as follows. Let n be a security parameter, $m = (1 + \epsilon)n \log q$ and $q = \text{poly}(n)$. The key generation proceeds by choosing a random noise vector $e \in \mathbb{F}_q^m$ in which each coordinate is distributed independently according to a small discrete Gaussian, a uniform random $m \times n$ matrix G over $\mathbb{F}_q$, and a uniform random $w \in \text{Image}(G)$. The private key is the noise vector e and the public key is the $m \times (n+1)$ matrix $\tilde{G} = (G \mid b)$ obtained from G by appending the noisy codeword $b = w + e$ to the right of the matrix G.

The encryption of a bit $\sigma \in \{0,1\}$ is a random vector $c \in \mathbb{F}_q^{n+1}$ of the form $c = \tilde{G}^T \cdot \tilde{e} + v_\sigma$ where $\tilde{e}$ is a uniform random vector in $\{0,1\}^m$ and $v_\sigma \in \mathbb{F}_q^{n+1}$ is the vector all of whose coordinates equal 0 except for the $(n+1)$-th coordinate which equals $\sigma \cdot \lfloor \frac{q}{2} \rfloor$. In order to decrypt a ciphertext $c \in \mathbb{F}_q^{n+1}$ one computes $\sigma' =: c_{n+1} - \langle x, P_n(c) \rangle$, where $P_n : \mathbb{F}_q^{n+1} \to \mathbb{F}_q^n$ denotes the projection on the first n coordinates and x is such that $w = Gx$, and outputs 0 if σ' is closer to 0 than to $\lfloor \frac{q}{2} \rfloor$ and 1 otherwise. Finally, it can be verified that $\sigma' = \sigma \cdot \lfloor \frac{q}{2} \rfloor + \langle e, \tilde{e} \rangle$. Consequently, if one chooses the Guassian distribution of the coordinates of e to be small enough then $\langle e, \tilde{e} \rangle$, which is the sum of at most m such independent Gaussians, would be smaller than $\lfloor \frac{q}{4} \rfloor$ in absolute value with high probability and therefore would enable one to distinguish between encryptions of 0 and 1 with small error probability. In fact, the error here can be completely eliminated by truncating the tail of the Gaussian noise distribution.

The main advantage of Regev's encryption scheme is that while Alekhnovich's encryption scheme can be attacked in time $2^{O(\sqrt{n})}$ by enumerating over all possible private keys, the best known attacks on Regev's encryption scheme, using lattice algorithms, run in time $2^{O(n)}$. This advantage of Regev's scheme stems from the possibility to exploit the large modulus q for picking noise distributions e and $\tilde{e}$ whose inner product is statistically far from uniform and yet the noisy decoding problem corresponding to these distributions can be conjectured to have nearly exponential hardness. Note, however, that since q is polynomial in n, the ciphertext is of size $\Omega(n \log n)$ and therefore falls slightly short of being optimally succinct.

Another related public key encryption scheme, based on the hardness of LWE, is the public key encryption scheme proposed by Gentry, Peikert and Vaiknutanathan (GPV) [18] which is described by the authors as a "dual of Regev's scheme in which the key generation and the encryption algorithms are swapped". A useful property of the encryption scheme of [18] is that it allows an *identity-based encryption* in which arbitrary strings are allowed to serve as public keys.

1.6   Related Work

Originating from the seminal work of Ajtai [1], there has been a large body of research on basing lattice-based cryptosystems on the minimal possible assumptions and improving the efficiency of such provably secure constructions. In particular, the work of Micciancio and Mol [34] considers the possibility of replacing the standard Gaussian noise by other noise distributions, which may admit a more efficient sampling algorithm, while maintaining provable security under standard assumptions. In contrast, the goal of the present work is to explore the space of constructions that *might* be secure, in the sense that they resist known attacks, regardless of the underlying intractability assumption or the way security is argued. Moreover, unlike the work on lattice-based cryptography, our main focus is on constructions that use linear codes over the *binary* field.

As noted above, the unified encryption scheme we study is inspired by the abstract encryption scheme described in Micciancio's online talk [33] which generalizes the encryption schemes of Regev and GPV. In particular, as in [33], this unified scheme relies on duality between noisy codeword encoding and syndrome encoding. This duality has also been noticed and used in other settings in the context of lattice-based public key encryption, for example in [34,44][3].

Finally, one should note that the unified scheme we study does not capture all of the code-based and lattice-based public key encryption schemes from the literature. For instance, it does *not* capture the code-based McEliece cryptosystem and its variants [31,36], as well as lattice- and LWE-based cryptosystems such as [2,4,19,22,30,32,35,39]. However, these alternative constructions do not seem well suited to the goal of obtaining near-optimal succinctness over binary fields. The former code-based schemes require the public key size to grow quadratically with the security parameter, whereas the latter lattice-based schemes do not admit a "native" implementation over binary fields.

2   Our Results in More Detail

To study the public key encryption schemes of Alekhnovich [3], Regev [40] and Gentry, Peikert and Vaikuntanathan (GPV) [18] in a unified way, we start by defining an abstract encryption scheme that captures these encryption schemes. More specifically, for each of the schemes [3,18,40] we define an abstract version that we call $\Pi_{\text{Alek}}, \Pi_{\text{Reg}}, \Pi_{\text{GPV}}$, respectively, in which the field size as well as the noise distributions used in the key generation and encryption processes are allowed to be arbitrary.

Following Miciancio [33], we observe that for an identical choice of parameters all the abstract schemes are equivalent to each other in terms of security: Given a pair of schemes $E, E' \in \{\Pi_{\text{Alek}}, \Pi_{\text{Reg}}, \Pi_{\text{GPV}}\}$, there exists an efficiently computable randomized mapping which for every bit $\sigma \in \{0,1\}$ maps the joint distribution of the public key pk and the encryption of σ using pk in E to the joint distribution of the public key pk$'$ and the encryption of σ using pk$'$ in E'[4].

At a high level, all the abstract schemes work as follows (see Table 1 in the full version [6] for more details). Each of the schemes is parametrized by integers $n < m$, a field $\mathbb{F}_q$ (whose size may depend on n), a distribution μ_{sk} over $\mathbb{F}_q^m$ and a pair of distributions μ_0, μ_1 over $\mathbb{F}_q^{m+1}$. In all three schemes the private key is a random noise vector $e \sim \mu_{\text{sk}}$. The public key consists of two parts: A random linear code $C : \mathbb{F}_q^n \to \mathbb{F}_q^m$, specified by either a uniform random

---

[3] A different unified view of the schemes of Regev and Alekhnovich was previously given by Lindner and Peikert [26] who suggested to add an additional noise vector in the encryption process of Regev's scheme. This allowed them to argue about the security of Regev's scheme using Alekhnovich-style security proof and consequently reduce key sizes in Regev's scheme.

[4] Note that we do not claim that the original encryption schemes of Alekhnovich, Regev and GPV are equivalent to each other in terms of security but rather that for each pair of schemes $E, E' \in \{\text{Alekhnovich, Regev, GPV}\}$ one can change the field size and noise distributions in E (but not the syntactics of E!) to obtain an encryption scheme that is equivalent to E' in terms of security.

generator matrix $G^T \in \mathbb{F}_q^{n \times m}$ (in Π_{Alek} and Π_{Reg}) or a uniform random parity-check matrix $H^T \in \mathbb{F}_q^{(m-n) \times m}$ (in Π_{GPV}), together with either a noisy codeword $b = w + e$ where w is a random codeword in C (in Π_{Alek} and Π_{Reg}) or its syndrome $u = H^T \cdot e$ (in Π_{GPV}).

The encryption process is similar: Let $\tilde{C} : \mathbb{F}_q^{m-n} \to \mathbb{F}_q^{m+1}$ be the code specified by the parity-check matrix

$$\tilde{G}^T = \begin{pmatrix} G & b \\ 0_n^T & -1 \end{pmatrix}^T,$$

where $\tilde{C}$ is the $(m+1) \times (n+1)$ matrix obtained by appending the column b to the right of the matrix G and adding below a row whose first n entries equal zero and whose last entry equals -1. Let

$$\tilde{H} = \begin{pmatrix} H \\ u^T \end{pmatrix}$$

be the $(m+1) \times (m-n)$ matrix obtained by adding the row u^T below the matrix H, and note that $\tilde{H}^T$ is a generator matrix for the code $\tilde{C}$. In order to encrypt a bit $\sigma \in \{0,1\}$ one chooses a random noise vector $\tilde{e} \sim \mu_\sigma$. The encryption of σ is either a noisy codeword $b = \tilde{w} + \tilde{e}$ where $\tilde{w}$ is a uniform random codeword in $\tilde{C}$ (in Π_{Alek} and Π_{GPV}) or its syndrome $\tilde{G}^T \cdot \tilde{e}$ (in Π_{Reg}).

Finally, in all the three schemes using the private key e one can obtain the inner product $\langle e \circ (-1), \tilde{e} \rangle$, where $e \circ (-1)$ denotes the vector obtained from e by adding -1 below the vector e. To enable decryption one has to choose noise distributions μ_{sk}, μ_0 and μ_1 such that it is possible to distinguish between the distributions $\langle \mu_{\text{sk}} \circ (-1), \mu_0 \rangle$ and $\langle \mu_{\text{sk}} \circ (-1), \mu_1 \rangle$ efficiently.

2.1 Unconditional Negative Result

Our first result shows a simple unconditional attack running in time $2^{O(n/\log n)}$ on any instance of the abstract encryption scheme over the binary field. The attack uses a simple argument based on the algorithm for agnostic learning of parities of Kalai et al. [24], a powerful algorithm that learns parities with noise from *arbitrary* distributions. More specifically, this algorithm is given independent random samples of the form (a_i, b_i), where $b_i = \langle a_i, s \rangle + e_i$ for a fixed unknown vector $s \in \mathbb{F}_2^n$ and (a_i, e_i) are distributed according to an arbitrary distribution over $\mathbb{F}_2^n \times \mathbb{F}_2$ (In particular, the e_i's may depend on the a_i's). Assuming that the noise bit e_i is non-zero with probability at most η (or alternatively, $b_i \neq \langle a_i, s \rangle$ with probability at most η), the algorithm returns a circuit $h : \mathbb{F}_2^n \to \mathbb{F}_2$ that errs with probability at most η on future examples, that is $\Pr_{(a_i, b_i)}[h(a_i) \neq b_i] \leq \eta$. The running time and number of samples used by this algorithm is $2^{O(n/\log n)}$ which matches the performance of the original LPN algorithm of [11]. Note that though quite powerful, this algorithm is not a proper learner since it returns an arbitrary circuit which is not necessarily a parity function. For simplicity, assume for now that the algorithm returns the original vector s.

By the equivalence of the abstract encryption schemes Π_{Alek}, Π_{Reg} and Π_{GPV} it suffices to show an attack on the encryption scheme Π_{Reg}. The property of this scheme that we shall use for the attack is that the decryption of a ciphertext $c \in \mathbb{F}_2^{n+1}$ is $c_{n+1} - \langle s, P_n(c) \rangle$ where $P_n : \mathbb{F}_2^{n+1} \to \mathbb{F}_2^n$ denotes the projection on the first n bits and $s \in \mathbb{F}_2^n$ is such that $w = Gs$. Using the public key we generate $2^{O(n/\log n)}$ samples of the form $(P_n(c'), c'_{n+1} - \xi)$ where $\xi \in \{0, 1\}$ is a uniform random bit and c' is a random encryption of ξ and feed them to the algorithm for agnostic learning of parities described above. Assuming that the decryption algorithm has low error probability we have that $c'_{n+1} - \langle s, P_n(c') \rangle = \xi$ with probability at least $1 - \eta$, or alternatively, $\langle s, P_n(c') \rangle \neq c'_{n+1} - \xi$ with probability at most η. Hence the algorithm of [24] will recover the vector s and consequently we can recover the private key $e = b - Gs$.

The attack described above has also some *positive* consequences to learning, where it can be used for learning parities corrupted by arbitrary noise distributions in sub-exponential time using a relatively small number of samples. More specifically, we observe that Regev's security proof [40], which shows that his original encryption scheme is secure assuming the hardness of LWE, can be generalized to show the security of the abstract encryption scheme under similar assumptions. In more detail, one can show that any instance of the abstract encryption scheme over an arbitrary field $\mathbb{F}_q$, using an arbitrary noise distribution μ_{sk} and noise distributions μ_0, μ_1 of sufficiently high min-entropy, is secure assuming the hardness of learning linear functions over $\mathbb{F}_q$ corrupted by noise coming from the distribution μ_{sk}. We further observe that this security guarantee holds even assuming the hardness of learning such functions using a relatively small number of samples.

Stated positively, the above says that any attack on an instance of the abstract encryption scheme as above can be turned into an algorithm that learns linear functions over $\mathbb{F}_q$ corrupted by noise coming from the distribution μ_{sk} using a relatively small number of samples. In particular, the attack described above can be turned into such an algorithm. We further observe that an instance of this latter algorithm solves the LPN problem in time $2^{O(n/\log \log n)}$ using $n^{1+\epsilon}$ samples, reproducing the result of [29] (see also [25]) in a conceptually different way.

2.2   Conditional Negative Results

Our main result is a (non-uniform) attack running in time $2^{O(\sqrt{m})}$ on any instance of the abstract encryption scheme over the binary field in the case in which the decryption error of a single encryption is a sufficiently small constant, assuming the 'approximate duality conjecture' of [8]. For the attacks we first formulate combinatorial properties of the distributions μ_{sk}, μ_0 and μ_1 that imply an attack on the abstract encryption scheme and then show that these combinatorial properties are satisfied assuming the approximate duality conjecture or its variant. We elaborate on these two parts below.

Attacks based on combinatorial properties of $\mu_{\text{sk}}, \mu_0, \mu_1$. The main combinatorial property we shall use for the attacks is *sparsity*. More precisely, we say that a distribution μ over $\mathbb{F}_2^m$ for $m \geq n$ is (n, k, ρ)-*sparse* if there exist k subsets $A_1, \ldots, A_k \subseteq \mathbb{F}_2^m$ (not necessarily distinct) and k full rank linear transformations $L_1, \ldots, L_k : \mathbb{F}_2^m \to \mathbb{F}_2^n$ (not necessarily distinct) such that $\text{Pr}_\mu \left(\bigcup_{i=1}^k A_i \right) \geq \rho$ and $L_i(A_i)$ is constant for every $i \in [k]$. In other words, this means that there exist k affine subspaces $V_1, \ldots, V_k \subseteq \mathbb{F}_2^m$, of co-dimension n each, such that with probability at least ρ a random vector sampled from μ falls into the union of these subspaces.

We show that if an instance of the abstract encryption scheme over the binary field satisfies that the distribution μ_{sk} is (n, k, ρ)-sparse or one of the distributions μ_0 or μ_1 is $(m + 1 - n + \log k + \log(1/\rho), k, \rho)$-sparse, and the decryption error of a single encryption is relatively small compared to ρ, then one can attack this instance in time $O(k)$. To illustrate the idea behind our attacks assume that we are attacking Π_{Alek} and that the distribution μ_{sk} is (n, k, ρ)-sparse. In this case one can search for a 'good' private key e' by enumerating over all $i \in [k]$ and solving a corresponding system of linear equations to find a vector $e' \in \bigcup_{i=1}^k V_i$ and a vector $x' \in \mathbb{F}_2^n$ such that $b = Gx' + e'$. We can further test whether e' is a 'good' private key by generating random encryptions of 0 and 1 using the public key and computing the success probability of e' in decrypting these encryptions. Since the distribution μ_{sk} is (n, k, ρ)-sparse, with probability at least ρ we will succeed in finding a 'good' private key e' which can be used in turn in order to decrypt the ciphertext.

The case in which one of the distributions μ_0 or μ_1 is $(m + 1 - n + \log k + \log(1/\rho), k, \rho)$-sparse is a bit more tricky. In this case it will be convenient to attack the scheme Π_{GPV} and by symmetry it suffices to show such an attack in the case in which μ_0 is $(m + 1 - n + \log k + \log(1/\rho), k, \rho)$-sparse. As in the μ_{sk} case, we can still search in time $O(k)$ for $e' \in \bigcup_{i=1}^k V_i$ and a vector $x' \in \mathbb{F}_2^{m-n}$ such that $c = \tilde{H} \cdot x' + e'$. Our main observation is that since $\bigcup_{i=1}^k V_i$ is not too large, with high probability over the choice of the matrix $\tilde{H}$, there is no $e' \neq \tilde{e}$ such that $e' \in \bigcup_{i=1}^k V_i$ and $c = \tilde{H}x' + e'$ for some $x' \in \mathbb{F}_2^{m-n}$. This implies in turn that by enumerating over all $i \in [k]$ and solving a corresponding system of linear equations, with high probability one can verify whether $\tilde{e} \in \bigcup_{i=1}^k V_i$ and if this is the case one can also find $\tilde{e}$. It thus suffices to be able to distinguish between $\tilde{e} \sim \mu_0$ and $\tilde{e} \sim \mu_1$, conditioned on the event that $\tilde{e} \in \bigcup_{i=1}^k V_i$. Assuming that the decryption error is sufficiently small compared to ρ, this can be done by computing the inner product $\langle e^{(sk)} \circ (-1), \tilde{e} \rangle$ with a random $e^{(sk)} \sim \mu_{\text{sk}}$.

Attacks based on the approximate duality conjecture. For a pair of subsets $A, B \subseteq \mathbb{F}_2^m$ their *duality measure* is given by

$$D(A, B) = \mathbb{E}_{a \in A, b \in B} \left[(-1)^{\langle a, b \rangle} \right]. \tag{1}$$

Note that $D(A, B) = 1$ implies that $\langle a, b \rangle$ is constant. The question is what can be said about the structure of A, B when $D(A, B)$ is sufficiently large but strictly smaller than 1. The approximate duality conjecture of [8] (cf., also Conjecture 1.7.2 in [27]) postulates that in this case there exist large subsets $A' \subseteq A$, $B' \subseteq B$, of density at least $2^{-O(\sqrt{m})}$ inside A, B respectively, with $D(A', B') = 1$.

We note that the bound of $2^{-O(\sqrt{m})}$ in the approximate duality conjecture is tight, and to see this take $A = B = \binom{m}{\sqrt{m}}$ to be the set of vectors that have $\sqrt{m}$ ones. The birthday paradox shows that $D(A, B)$ is a fixed positive constant, independent of m (in fact, taking vectors of weight $\alpha\sqrt{m}$ for α approaching 0 makes $D(A, B)$ approach 1). But it can be verified that for any pair $A' \subset A$ and $B' \subset B$ satisfying $D(A', B') = 1$, the size of one of the sets A' or B' is a $2^{-\sqrt{m}}$ fraction of $|A|$. Such a pair is obtained by taking A' (B' respectively) to contain all vectors supported on the first (last, respectively) $m/2$ coordinates.

In [7] it was shown that assuming the well-known polynomial Freiman-Ruzsa conjecture from additive combinatorics (cf., [20]), the approximate duality conjecture holds when replacing the lower bound $2^{-O(\sqrt{m})}$ on the ratios $|A'|/|A|$ and $|B'|/|B|$ with the weaker bound of $2^{-O(m/\log m)}$. Furthermore, in [28] a version of the approximate duality conjecture over the reals was shown to hold (unconditionally) with the stronger bound of $2^{-O(\sqrt{m})}$. The approximate duality conjecture has found so far various applications in complexity theory: To the construction of two-source extractors [8], to relating rank to communication complexity [7] and to lower bounds on matching vector codes [9].

We show that the approximate duality conjecture implies that in any instance of the abstract encryption scheme over the binary field one of the distributions μ_{sk}, μ_0 or μ_1 is sparse which by the above implies an attack on this instance. To see this suppose that Π is an instance of the abstract encryption scheme over the binary field in which $\mu_{sk} \circ (-1), \mu_0, \mu_1$ are distributed uniformly over subsets $A, B_0, B_1 \subseteq \mathbb{F}_2^{m+1}$ respectively. Then by correctness of the decryption algorithm we have that either $D(A, B_0) \geq 1 - \epsilon$ or $D(A, B_1) \leq -(1 - \epsilon)$ for some constant $\epsilon < 1$. Without loss of generality assume that $D(A, B_0) \geq 1 - \epsilon$ and note that in this case the approximate duality conjecture implies that there exist subsets $A' \subseteq A$, $B' \subseteq B_0$, of density at least $2^{-c\sqrt{m}}$ inside A, B_0 respectively, with $D(A', B') = 1$. The latter implies in turn that $\dim(\text{span}(A')) + \dim(\text{span}(B')) \leq m + 2$. Consequently, we have that either $\dim(\text{span}(A')) \leq m + 2 - n + 2c\sqrt{m}$ in which case A' is contained in the union of $2^{2c\sqrt{m}+1}$ affine subspaces of co-dimension n and so $\mu_{sk} \circ (-1)$ is $(n, 2^{2c\sqrt{m}+1}, 2^{-c\sqrt{m}})$-sparse or that $\dim(\text{span}(B')) \leq n - 2c\sqrt{m}$ in which case μ_0 is $(m - n + 2c\sqrt{m}, 1, 2^{-c\sqrt{m}})$-sparse. This implies in turn an attack running in time $2^{O(\sqrt{m})}$ in the case in which the decryption error is $2^{-\Omega(\sqrt{m})}$. Note that the attack is non-uniform since the attacker needs to know the subsets A' and B'.

In order to show such an attack in the case in which μ_{sk}, μ_0, μ_1 are general distributions, not necessarily uniform over a subset, we prove that the standard formulation of the approximate duality conjecture implies a generalized version of it that holds also when the expectation in (1) is taken over arbitrary distributions. In order to handle larger decryption errors we apply the approximate duality conjecture iteratively to obtain $t = 2^{O(\sqrt{m})}$ pairs of subsets $A_1, B_1, \ldots, A_t, B_t$ such that $D(A_i, B_i) = 1$ for all $1 \leq i \leq t$ and such that the probability of being contained in the union of $\Omega(t)$ such subsets is $\Omega(1 - \epsilon)$. This implies that either $\mu_{sk} \circ (-1)$ is $(n, 2^{3c\sqrt{m}+1}, \Omega(1-\epsilon))$-sparse or μ_0 is $(m-n+2c\sqrt{m}, 2^{c\sqrt{m}}, \Omega(1-\epsilon))$-sparse which implies in turn an attack that runs in time $2^{O(\sqrt{m})}$ in the case in which the decryption error is a sufficiently small constant.

Finally, we note that if the approximate duality conjecture is false, then a counter example to this conjecture would be a pair of sets $A, B \subseteq \mathbb{F}_2^m$ such that $D(A, B)$ is high but no large pair of subsets A', B' of A, B respectively are dual. In this case, if we let Π be a (possibly non-uniform) instance of the unified scheme in which μ_{sk}, μ_0, μ_1 are distributed uniformly over the sets $A, B \circ 0, B \circ 1$ respectively, then the fact that $D(A, B)$ is high implies that the advantage of the decryption algorithm in Π is high. On the other hand, the lack of linear structure in the above distributions makes them secure against our brute-force linear algebra attacks which could potentially make Π secure against sub-exponential time attacks.

2.3 Perfectly Correct Decryption

Our last collection of results is concerned with the possibility of achieving perfectly correct decryption in the abstract encryption scheme over constant-size rings. As mentioned above, when the field size is polynomial in n, one can truncate the tail of the Gaussian noise distribution used in Regev's original encryption scheme [40] to achieve a perfectly correct decryption. We investigate whether one can achieve perfect decryption also over constant-size rings.

Our first result in this regard is negative, showing that over the binary field any instance of the abstract encryption scheme with perfectly correct decryption can be attacked in time poly(m). On the positive side, we propose to use the construction of matching vector families from [14], which builds on the constructions of [16,21], to obtain candidates for instances of the abstract encryption scheme over constant-size rings that achieve perfectly correct decryption but resist poly(m)-time attacks.

It should be noted that Dwork et al. [15] provide a general method for eliminating decryption errors in public key encryption schemes. However, applying their method has a high toll on efficiency and it only guarantees perfectly correct decryption with high probability over the randomness of the key generation.

2.4 Open Problems

We end this section by highlighting several open problems for future research.

The approximate duality conjecture and its implications to public key encryption. This work presents a new connection between additive combinatorics and public key encryption by showing non-trivial attacks on any binary instance of an abstract public key encryption scheme that captures the schemes of Alekhnovich [3], Regev [40] and Gentry, Peikert and Vaikuntanathan [18], assuming the approximate duality conjecture from additive combinatorics. On the positive side, if the approximate duality conjecture is false then counter examples to this conjecture may lead to candidate binary instances of the abstract encryption scheme with improved security guarantees. This motivates further study of the connection between public key encryption from noisy codewords and additive combinatorics in general and the approximate duality conjecture in particular.

Extending to non-binary fields. Our unconditional results could be possibly extended to show an attack in time $q^{O(n/\log n)}$ on any instance of the generalized encryption schemes over an arbitrary finite field $\mathbb{F}_q$, given an algorithm for agnostic learning of linear functions over $\mathbb{F}_q$. However, we are not aware of such an algorithm over non-binary fields and it seems that the results of [24] do not immediately apply in this setting. Our conditional results, on the other hand, do generalize to show an attack in time $q^{O(\sqrt{n})}$ on any instance of the generalized encryption schemes over an arbitrary constant-size field $\mathbb{F}_q$ assuming a variant of the approximate duality conjecture over such fields (see e.g. Conjecture 1.7.2 in [27]).

Perfectly correct decryption. We have shown that, over the binary field, our general framework *cannot* be instantiated to yield an encryption scheme with perfect decryption. We proposed a plausible approach for obtaining perfect decryption over constant-size rings by using matching vectors. The security of this construction, as well as the possibility of obtaining perfect security over constant-size *fields*, remain to be further studied.

2.5 Paper Organization

Some of the material is omitted due to space limitations but can be found in the full version of this paper [6]. In Sect. 3 we fix some notation and terminology, and in Sect. 4 we formally define the abstract encryption scheme we study. In Sect. 5 we present our unconditional attack, running in time $2^{O(n/\log n)}$, on the abstract encryption scheme over the binary field and consequences of this attack to learning. In Sect. 6 we present combinatorial properties of the distributions μ_{sk}, μ_0 and μ_1 that imply an attack on the abstract encryption scheme over the binary field. In Sect. 7 we show that these latter properties are satisfied assuming the approximate duality conjecture which implies an attack on the abstract encryption scheme over the binary field running in time $2^{O(\sqrt{m})}$.

3 Preliminaries

We start with fixing some notation. For a prime power q let $\mathbb{F}_q$ denote the finite field with q elements. All operations below are performed over $\mathbb{F}_q$ and all vectors are assumed to be column vectors unless otherwise stated. For integers $m \geq n$ let $\mathcal{M}^*_{m \times n}(q)$ denote the set of all $m \times n$ full rank matrices over $\mathbb{F}_q$. For an integer m let $P_m : \mathbb{F}_q^{m+1} \to \mathbb{F}_q^m$ denote the projection on the first m coordinates. Let $0_m, 1_m$ denote the all-zeros and all-ones vectors of length m, respectively. For a pair of vectors u, v let $u \circ v$ denote their concatenation.

Let μ be a distribution over $\mathbb{F}_q^m$. For an element $a \in \mathbb{F}_q^m$ let $\Pr_\mu(a) = \Pr_{e \sim \mu}[e = a]$. The *support* $\text{supp}(\mu)$ of μ is the set containing all elements $a \in \mathbb{F}_q^m$ for which $\Pr_\mu(a) > 0$. For a subset $A \subseteq \mathbb{F}_q^m$ we let $\Pr_\mu(A) = \Pr_{e \sim \mu}[e \in A]$ and we denote by $\mu|A$ the distribution μ conditioned on the event that $e \in A$. For a pair of distributions μ, μ' over $\mathbb{F}_q^m$ we denote by $\langle \mu, \mu' \rangle$ the distribution of $\langle e, e' \rangle$ where $e \sim \mu$ and $e' \sim \mu'$ independently. Finally, we write that $a \in_R A$ if a is chosen uniformly at random from the set A.

3.1   Public Key Encryption

A *public key encryption scheme* Π consists of three randomized polynomial time algorithms: the *key generation algorithm* Gen, the *encryption algorithm* Enc and the *decryption algorithm* Dec, which satisfy:

1. The key generation algorithm Gen takes as input the *security parameter* 1^n and outputs a pair of keys (sk, pk) where sk is the *private key* and pk is the *public key*. We write this as $(\text{sk}, \text{pk}) \leftarrow \text{Gen}(1^n)$.
2. The encryption algorithm Enc takes as input a public key pk and a *message bit* $\sigma \in \{0, 1\}$ and outputs a *ciphertext* c. We write this as $c \leftarrow \text{Enc}_{\text{pk}}(\sigma)$.
3. The decryption algorithm Dec takes as input a private key sk and a ciphertext c and outputs a bit $\sigma' \in \{0, 1\}$. We assume without loss of generality that Dec is deterministic and write this as $\sigma' := \text{Dec}_{\text{sk}}(c)$.

The *advantage of the decryption algorithm* is given by

$$\text{Adv}^{\text{Dec}}(n) = \Pr[\text{Dec}_{\text{sk}}(\text{Enc}_{\text{pk}}(1)) = 1] - \Pr[\text{Dec}_{\text{sk}}(\text{Enc}_{\text{pk}}(0)) = 1], \quad (2)$$

where the probabilities in (2) are taken over the internal coin tosses of the algorithms Gen and Enc. We say that the decryption algorithm is *perfectly correct* if $\text{Adv}^{\text{Dec}}(n) = 1$.

A typical choice of parameters in public key encryption schemes is that $\text{Adv}^{\text{Dec}}(n) = 1 - \eta(n)$ for $\eta(n)$ which is a negligible function in n. However, in the case where $\text{Adv}^{\text{Dec}}(n)$ is a fixed constant one can achieve $(1 - \eta(n))$-advantage in the decryption process by repeating the key generation and encryption processes $\text{polylog}(n)$ times. In this work we are interested in negative results and our unconditional results hold even when $\text{Adv}^{\text{Dec}}(n)$ is negligible in n. Our conditional results, on the other hand, hold only if a single encryption (without repetitions) achieves advantage $\text{Adv}^{\text{Dec}}(n) = 1 - \epsilon$ where $\epsilon > 0$ is a sufficiently small constant.

A *(uniform) attack* $\mathcal{A}$ on a public key encryption scheme Π is a randomized algorithm that takes as input a public key pk and a ciphertext c and outputs a bit $\sigma' \in \{0, 1\}$ and we write this as $\sigma' \leftarrow \mathcal{A}(\text{pk}, c)$. The *advantage of the attack* $\mathcal{A}$ is given by

$$\text{Adv}^{\mathcal{A}}(n) = \Pr[\mathcal{A}(\text{pk}, \text{Enc}_{\text{pk}}(1)) = 1] - \Pr[\mathcal{A}(\text{pk}, \text{Enc}_{\text{pk}}(0)) = 1], \quad (3)$$

where the probabilities in (3) are taken over the internal coin tosses of the algorithms Gen and Enc as well as the attack $\mathcal{A}$. A *non-uniform attack* $\mathcal{A}$ is defined similarly to the above except that it is modeled as a non-uniform Boolean circuit and we say that it has running time $t(n)$ if the associated circuit family has size $t(n)$.

4   Unified Encryption Scheme

In what follows we present the formal definition of the abstract encryption scheme Π_{Alek}, Π_{Reg} and Π_{GPV} and show their equivalence.

General Parameters: Integers $m > n$, field $\mathbb{F}_q$ (q may depend on n), efficiently samplable distribution μ_{sk} over $\mathbb{F}_q^m$, a pair of efficiently samplable distributions μ_0, μ_1 over $\mathbb{F}_q^{m+1}$, efficiently computable *decryption function* $g : \mathbb{F}_q \to \{0, 1\}$.

Π_{Alek} **scheme:**

- **Private key:** Choose a random vector $e \in \mathbb{F}_q^m$ according to the distribution μ_{sk}. The private key is e.
- **Public key:** Choose a uniform random matrix $G \in \mathcal{M}_{m \times n}^*(q)$ and a uniform random vector $w \in \text{Image}(G)$ and let $b = w + e$. The public key is $\tilde{G} = \begin{pmatrix} G & b \\ 0_n^T & -1 \end{pmatrix}$.
- **Encryption:** In order to encrypt a bit $\sigma \in \{0, 1\}$ choose a random vector $\tilde{e} \in \mathbb{F}_q^{m+1}$ according to the distribution μ_σ and a uniform random vector $\tilde{w} \in \ker(\tilde{G}^T)$. The encryption of σ is $\tilde{w} + \tilde{e}$.
- **Decryption:** The decryption of a vector $c \in \mathbb{F}_q^{m+1}$ is $g(\langle e \circ (-1), c \rangle)$.

Π_{Reg} **scheme:**

- **Private key:** Choose a random vector $e \in \mathbb{F}_q^m$ according to the distribution μ_{sk}. The private key is e.
- **Public key:** Choose a uniform random matrix $G \in \mathcal{M}_{m \times n}^*(q)$ and a uniform random $w \in \text{Image}(G)$ and let $b = w + e$. The public key is $\tilde{G} = \begin{pmatrix} G & b \\ 0_n^T & -1 \end{pmatrix}$.
- **Encryption:** In order to encrypt a bit $\sigma \in \{0, 1\}$ choose a random vector $\tilde{e} \in \mathbb{F}_q^{m+1}$ according to the distribution μ_σ. The encryption of σ is $\tilde{G}^T \cdot \tilde{e}$.
- **Decryption:** The decryption of a vector $c \in \mathbb{F}_q^{n+1}$ is $g(-\langle x \circ (-1), c \rangle)$ where $x \in \mathbb{F}_q^n$ is such that $b = Gx + e$.

Π_{GPV} **scheme:**

- **Private key:** Choose a random vector $e \in \mathbb{F}_q^m$ according to the distribution μ_{sk}. The private key is e.
- **Public key:** Choose a uniform random matrix $H \in \mathcal{M}_{m \times (m-n)}^*(q)$ and let $u = H^T \cdot e$. The public key is $\tilde{H} = \begin{pmatrix} H \\ u^T \end{pmatrix}$.
- **Encryption:** In order to encrypt a bit $\sigma \in \{0, 1\}$ choose a random vector $\tilde{e} \in \mathbb{F}_q^{m+1}$ according to the distribution μ_σ and a uniform random vector $\tilde{w} \in \text{Image}(\tilde{H})$. The encryption of σ is $\tilde{w} + \tilde{e}$.
- **Decryption:** The decryption of a vector $c \in \mathbb{F}_q^{m+1}$ is $g(\langle e \circ (-1), c \rangle)$.

A straightforward computation gives the following.

Claim 1 (Advantage of Decryption). For every $\Pi \in \{\Pi_{\text{Alek}}, \Pi_{\text{Reg}}, \Pi_{\text{GPV}}\}$,

$$\text{Adv}^{\text{Dec}}(n) = \Pr[g(\langle \mu_{\text{sk}} \circ (-1), \mu_1 \rangle) = 1] - \Pr[g(\langle \mu_{\text{sk}} \circ (-1), \mu_0 \rangle) = 1].$$

The following claim shows that for an identical setting of parameters all the abstract encryption schemes defined above are equivalent in terms of security. For an encryption scheme Π and a bit $\sigma \in \{0,1\}$ let $(\text{pk}^{\Pi}, \text{Enc}_{\text{pk}}^{\Pi}(\sigma))$ denote the joint distribution of the public key and the encryption of the bit σ using this public key in Π.

Claim 2 (Equivalence of Abstract Encryption Schemes). For every pair of encryption schemes $\Pi, \Pi' \in \{\Pi_{\text{Alek}}, \Pi_{\text{Reg}}, \Pi_{\text{GPV}}\}$ there exists a randomized mapping $\varphi_{\Pi \to \Pi'}$, computable in time $\text{poly}(m, q)$, such that for every bit $\sigma \in \{0,1\}$ the distributions $\varphi_{\Pi \to \Pi'}(\text{pk}^{\Pi}, \text{Enc}_{\text{pk}}^{\Pi}(\sigma))$ and $(\text{pk}^{\Pi'}, \text{Enc}_{\text{pk}}^{\Pi'}(\sigma))$ are identical.

5   Unconditional Attack

In this section we show an unconditional simple attack running in time $2^{O(n/\log n)}$ on any instance of the abstract encryption scheme over the binary field. The attack is based on the following algorithm for agnostic learning of parities (The theorem below is given as Theorem 2 in [24] for the special case in which $a = \log n/1000$, $b = n/a$, $\epsilon = 2^{-n^{0.99}}$ and the success probability is 0.99. The general parameters can be deduced from the proof of this theorem.)

Theorem 1 (Agnostic Learning of Parities, [24]). *For any integers a, b such that $ab \geq n$ and for any $\epsilon > 0$ there exists a randomized algorithm running in time $\text{poly}(\epsilon^{-2^a}, 2^b)$ which satisfies the following guarantees for every distribution D over $(x, y) \in \mathbb{F}_2^n \times \mathbb{F}_2$. With probability at least $1 - \exp(-n)$, given $\text{poly}(\epsilon^{-2^a}, 2^b)$ independent random samples from D, the algorithm outputs a circuit computing $h : \mathbb{F}_2^n \to \mathbb{F}_2$ such that*

$$\Pr_{(x,y) \sim D}[h(x) \neq y] \leq \min_{s \in \mathbb{F}_2^n} \Pr_{(x,y) \sim D}[\langle x, s \rangle \neq y] + \epsilon.$$

Our main result in this section is the following.

Theorem 2. *Let $\Pi \in \{\Pi_{\text{Alek}}, \Pi_{\text{Reg}}, \Pi_{\text{GPV}}\}$ be with $q = 2$ and $\text{Adv}^{\text{Dec}}(n) \geq \epsilon$. Then for any integers a, b such that $ab \geq n$ and for any $\gamma > 0$ there exists a (uniform) attack $\mathcal{A}_{\text{agnost}}$ Π running in time $\text{poly}(\gamma^{-2^a}, 2^b, m)$ with $\text{Adv}^{\mathcal{A}_{\text{agnost}}}(n) \geq \epsilon - \gamma - \exp(-n)$.*

By setting $a = \log n/1000$, $b = n/a$ and $\gamma = 2^{-n^{0.99}}$ in the above theorem we obtain the following corollary.

Corollary 1. *Let $\Pi \in \{\Pi_{\text{Alek}}, \Pi_{\text{Reg}}, \Pi_{\text{GPV}}\}$ be with $q = 2$ and $\text{Adv}^{\text{Dec}}(n) \geq \epsilon$. Then there exists a (uniform) attack $\mathcal{A}_{\text{agnost}}$ on Π running in time $\text{poly}(2^{n/\log n}, m)$ with $\text{Adv}^{\mathcal{A}_{\text{agnost}}}(n) \geq \epsilon - 2^{-n^{0.99}} - \exp(-n)$,*

Proof (Proof of Theorem 2). By Claim 2 it suffices to prove the theorem for $\Pi = \Pi_{\text{Reg}}$ and without loss of generality we may assume that the decryption function g is the identity function over $\mathbb{F}_2$. Let D be the distribution over $(x, y) \in \mathbb{F}_2^n \times \mathbb{F}_2$ where $x = G^T \cdot P_m(e')$ and $y = \langle b \circ (-1), e' \rangle - \xi$ for $\xi \in_R \{0, 1\}$ and $e' \sim \mu_\xi$. Note that D can be generated efficiently using the public key $\tilde{G}$. The attack $\mathcal{A}_{\text{agnost}}$ runs the algorithm guaranteed by Theorem 1 with the parameters a, b and $\gamma/2$ on the distribution D and outputs $c_{n+1} - h(P_n(c))$. By Theorem 1 we clearly have that the attack runs in time $\text{poly}(\gamma^{-2^a}, 2^b, m)$. It remains to analyze the advantage of the attack in guessing the message bit σ.

For a vector $y \in \mathbb{F}_2^m$ let

$$\epsilon(y) := \Pr[\langle y \circ (-1), \mu_1 \rangle = 1] - \Pr[\langle y \circ (-1), \mu_0 \rangle = 1],$$

and note that by Claim 1 we have that $\text{Adv}^{\text{Dec}}(n) = \mathbb{E}[\epsilon(\mu_{\text{sk}})]$. Let $s \in \mathbb{F}_2^n$ be such that $w = Gs$. Then we have that

$$
\begin{aligned}
&\Pr_{(x,y) \sim D}[\langle x, s \rangle \neq y] \\
&= \frac{1}{2} \cdot \Pr\big[\langle G^T \cdot P_m(\mu_1), s \rangle = \langle b \circ (-1), \mu_1 \rangle\big] \\
&\quad + \frac{1}{2} \cdot \Pr\big[\langle G^T \cdot P_m(\mu_0), s \rangle = 1 + \langle b \circ (-1), \mu_0 \rangle\big] \\
&= \frac{1}{2} \cdot \Pr\big[\langle P_m(\mu_1), Gs \rangle = \langle b \circ (-1), \mu_1 \rangle\big] + \frac{1}{2} \cdot \Pr\big[\langle P_m(\mu_0), Gs \rangle = 1 + \langle b \circ (-1), \mu_0 \rangle\big] \\
&= \frac{1}{2} \cdot \Pr[\langle \mu_1, (b - w) \circ (-1) \rangle = 0] + \frac{1}{2} \cdot \Pr[\langle \mu_0, (b - w) \circ (-1) \rangle = 1] \\
&= \frac{1}{2} \cdot \Pr[\langle \mu_1, e \circ (-1) \rangle = 0] + \frac{1}{2} \cdot \Pr[\langle \mu_0, e \circ (-1) \rangle = 1] \\
&= \frac{1}{2} - \frac{1}{2} \cdot \Big(\Pr[\langle \mu_1, e \circ (-1) \rangle = 1] - \Pr[\langle \mu_0, e \circ (-1) \rangle = 1]\Big) \\
&= \frac{1 - \epsilon(e)}{2}.
\end{aligned}
$$

Consequently, with probability at least $1 - \exp(-n)$, the circuit h satisfies

$$\Pr_{(x,y) \sim D}[h(x) \neq y] \leq \frac{1 - \epsilon(e)}{2} + \frac{\gamma}{2} = \frac{1 - (\epsilon(e) - \gamma)}{2}.$$

Suppose that c is an encryption of a bit $\sigma \in \{0, 1\}$. Conditioned on the above, we have that

$$
\begin{aligned}
&\Pr[c_{n+1} - h(P_n(c)) = 1 \mid \sigma = 1] - \Pr[c_{n+1} - h(P_n(c)) = 1 \mid \sigma = 0] \\
&= \Pr\big[\langle b \circ (-1), \mu_1 \rangle - h(G^T \cdot P_m(\mu_1)) = 1\big] \\
&\quad - \Pr\big[\langle b \circ (-1), \mu_0 \rangle - h(G^T \cdot P_m(\mu_0)) = 1\big] \\
&= 1 - \Pr\big[h(G^T \cdot P_m(\mu_1)) \neq 1 + \langle b \circ (-1), \mu_1 \rangle\big] \\
&\quad - \Pr\big[h(G^T \cdot P_m(\mu_0)) \neq \langle b \circ (-1), \mu_0 \rangle\big] \\
&= 1 - 2\Pr_{(x,y) \sim D}[h(x) \neq y] \\
&\geq \epsilon(e) - \gamma.
\end{aligned}
$$

Averaging over all $e \sim \mu_{sk}$ we obtain that the advantage of the attack is at least

$$\mathbb{E}[\epsilon(\mu_{sk})] - \gamma - \exp(-n) = \text{Adv}^{\text{Dec}}(n) - \gamma - \exp(-n) \geq \epsilon - \gamma - \exp(-n).$$

6 Attacks Based on Combinatorial Properties of μ_{sk}, μ_0, μ_1

In Sects. 6.1 and 6.2 we present combinatorial properties of the distribution μ_{sk} and the pair of distributions μ_0, μ_1, respectively, that imply an attack on the abstract encryption scheme over the binary field. In Sect. 7 we shall show that assuming the approximate duality conjecture at least one of the distributions μ_{sk}, μ_0 or μ_1 satisfies these combinatorial properties. This will imply in turn an attack on the abstract encryption scheme over the binary field assuming the approximate duality conjecture.

The main combinatorial property we shall utilize for the attacks is *sparsity*, defined as follows.

Definition 1 ((n, k, ρ)-Sparse Distribution). Suppose that μ is a distribution over $\mathbb{F}_2^m$ for $m \geq n$. We say that μ is (n, k, ρ)-*sparse* if there exist k subsets $A_1, \ldots, A_k \subseteq \mathbb{F}_2^m$ and k full rank linear transformations $L_1, \ldots, L_k : \mathbb{F}_2^m \to \mathbb{F}_2^n$ such that $\text{Pr}_\mu \left(\bigcup_{i=1}^k A_i \right) \geq \rho$ and $L_i(A_i)$ is constant for every $i \in [k]$.

Note that $A_1, \ldots, A_k$ and $L_1, \ldots, L_k$ in the definition above are not required to be distinct. At a high level, assuming that one of the noise distributions μ_{sk}, μ_0 or μ_1 is sparse one can 'guess' the noise vector used in the key generation process (in the case in which μ_{sk} is sparse) or in the encryption process (in the case in which μ_0 or μ_1 are sparse) by enumerating over all $i \in [k]$ and solving a corresponding system of linear equations.

6.1 Attack Based on Combinatorial Properties of μ_{sk}

Lemma 1 (Attack Based on Combinatorial Properties of μ_{sk}). *Let $\Pi \in \{\Pi_{\text{Alek}}, \Pi_{\text{Reg}}, \Pi_{\text{GPV}}\}$ be with $q = 2$ and $\text{Adv}^{\text{Dec}}(n) \geq 1 - \epsilon$ and suppose that the distribution μ_{sk} is (n, k, ρ)-sparse. Then there exists a non-uniform attack $\mathcal{A}_{sk}$ on Π running in time $(k/\epsilon) \cdot \text{poly}(m)$ with $\text{Adv}^{\mathcal{A}_{sk}}(n) \geq (\rho - 4\sqrt{\epsilon})/10$.*

Proof. By Claim 2 it suffices to prove the lemma for $\Pi = \Pi_{\text{Alek}}$ and without loss of generality we may assume that g is the identity function over $\mathbb{F}_2$. Since μ_{sk} is (n, k, ρ)-sparse there exist k subsets $A_1, \ldots, A_k \subseteq \mathbb{F}_2^m$ and k full rank linear transformations $L_1, \ldots, L_k : \mathbb{F}_2^m \to \mathbb{F}_2^n$ such that $\text{Pr}_{\mu_{sk}} \left(\bigcup_{i=1}^k A_i \right) \geq \rho$ and $L_i(A_i)$ is constant for every $i \in [k]$.

Our main observation is that if e' satisfies that $b = w' + e'$ for some $w' \in \text{Image}(G)$ and in addition

$$\text{Pr}[\langle e' \circ (-1), \mu_1 \rangle = 1] - \text{Pr}[\langle e' \circ (-1), \mu_0 \rangle = 1] \geq 1 - \epsilon' \qquad (4)$$

then decrypting the ciphertext using e' as the private key achieves advantage $1 - \epsilon'$. We search for e' that satisfies the above by enumerating over all $i \in [k]$ and solving a corresponding system of linear equations and we test whether e' satisfies (4) via sampling.

Fix $y \in \mathbb{F}_2^m$. By the Hoeffding bound for sampling if we draw $\ell = m/(\sqrt{\epsilon}/2)^2$ independent random samples $e_1^{(0)}, \ldots, e_\ell^{(0)} \sim \mu_0$ and ℓ independent random samples $e_1^{(1)}, \ldots, e_\ell^{(1)} \sim \mu_1$ then

$$\left| \left(\Pr[\langle y \circ (-1), \mu_1 \rangle = 1] - \Pr[\langle y \circ (-1), \mu_0 \rangle = 1] \right) \right. \tag{5}$$

$$\left. - \left(\Pr_{j \in [\ell]}[\langle y \circ (-1), e_j^{(1)} \rangle = 1] - \Pr_{j \in [\ell]}[\langle y \circ (-1), e_j^{(0)} \rangle = 1] \right) \right| \leq \sqrt{\epsilon}$$

with probability at least $1 - 4 \cdot 2^{-2m}$. By union bound this implies in turn that (5) holds for every $y \in \mathbb{F}_2^m$ with probability at least $1 - 4 \cdot 2^{-m}$. In particular, there exist ℓ vectors $e_1^{(0)}, \ldots, e_\ell^{(0)} \in \mathrm{supp}(\mu_0)$ and ℓ vectors $e_1^{(1)}, \ldots, e_\ell^{(1)} \in \mathrm{supp}(\mu_1)$ for which (5) holds for every $y \in \mathbb{F}_2^m$.

$\mathcal{A}_{\mathrm{sk}}$

- For every $i = 1, 2, \ldots, k$:
    - Solve the system of linear equations

    $$L_i b = L_i G x' + L_i(A_i)$$

    in the indeterminate x'.
    - If there is no solution continue to the next i.
    - Else let x' be an arbitrary solution and let $e' := b - Gx'$.
    - If e' satisfies that

    $$\Pr_{j \in [\ell]}[\langle e' \circ (-1), e_j^{(1)} \rangle = 1] - \Pr_{j \in [\ell]}[\langle e' \circ (-1), e_j^{(0)} \rangle = 1] \geq 1 - 2\sqrt{\epsilon}, \tag{6}$$

    output $\langle e' \circ (-1), c \rangle$, else continue to the next i.
- Else if no e' satisfies (6), output a random bit.

Inspection reveals that the attack above can be implemented using a non-uniform circuit of size $(k/\epsilon) \cdot \mathrm{poly}(m)$. Next we analyze the advantage of the attack in guessing the message bit σ. We will show that with probability at least $(\rho - \sqrt{\epsilon})/10$ the attack finds e' which satisfies (6) and that in this case the advantage of guessing the correct message bit is at least $1 - 3\sqrt{\epsilon}$. This will imply in turn that $\mathrm{Adv}^{\mathcal{A}_{\mathrm{sk}}}(n) \geq (\rho - 4\sqrt{\epsilon})/10$.

We start by showing a lower bound on the probability that the attack finds e' which satisfies (6). Since $\mathrm{Adv}^{\mathrm{Dec}}(n) \geq 1 - \epsilon$ by Claim 1, together with a standard probabilistic argument, we have that e satisfies

$$\Pr[\langle e \circ (-1), \mu_1 \rangle = 1] - \Pr[\langle e \circ (-1), \mu_0 \rangle = 1] \geq 1 - \sqrt{\epsilon}$$

with probability at least $1 - \sqrt{\epsilon}$. By (5) this implies in turn that e satisfies (6) with probability at least $1 - \sqrt{\epsilon}$. Furthermore, since μ_{sk} is (n, k, ρ)-sparse with probability at least ρ we have that $e \in \bigcup_{i=1}^{k} A_i$. So with probability at least $\rho - \sqrt{\epsilon}$ we have that e satisfies (6) and in addition $e \in A_i$ for some $i \in [k]$. Finally, the matrix $L_i G$ is non-singular with probability at least $1/10$ (say), independently of the above.

Conditioned on all the above, in the i-th iteration we have that

$$e' = b - Gx' = b - G \cdot (L_i G)^{-1}(L_i b - L_i(A_i)) = b - G \cdot (L_i G)^{-1} \cdot (L_i b - L_i e) = e.$$

Consequently we have that the attack finds e' which satisfies (6) with probability at least $(\rho - \sqrt{\epsilon})/10$.

Next we show that if the attack finds e' which satisfies (6) then the advantage of guessing the correct message bit using e' is high. Since $e' = b - Gx'$ we have that

$$\begin{aligned}
\langle e' \circ (-1), c \rangle &= \langle (b - Gx') \circ (-1), \tilde{w} \rangle + \langle (b - Gx') \circ (-1), \tilde{e} \rangle \\
&= \langle b \circ (-1), \tilde{w} \rangle - \langle x', G^T \cdot P_m(\tilde{w}) \rangle + \langle (b - Gx') \circ (-1), \tilde{e} \rangle \\
&= 0 - 0 + \langle e' \circ (-1), \tilde{e} \rangle \\
&= \langle e' \circ (-1), \tilde{e} \rangle.
\end{aligned}$$

Furthermore, since e' satisfies (6), by (5) we have that

$$\Pr[\langle e' \circ (-1), \mu_1 \rangle = 1] - \Pr[\langle e' \circ (-1), \mu_0 \rangle = 1] \geq 1 - 3\sqrt{\epsilon},$$

so the advantage of the attack in this case is $1 - 3\sqrt{\epsilon}$.

6.2   Attack Based on Combinatorial Properties of μ_0, μ_1

Lemma 2 (Attack Based on Combinatorial Properties of μ_0, μ_1). *Let $\Pi \in \{\Pi_{\mathrm{Alek}}, \Pi_{\mathrm{Reg}}, \Pi_{\mathrm{GPV}}\}$ be with $q = 2$ and $\mathrm{Adv}^{\mathrm{Dec}}(n) \geq 1 - \epsilon$ and suppose that there exists $\xi \in \{0, 1\}$ such that the distribution μ_ξ is $(m + 1 - n + r, k, \rho)$-sparse. Then there exists a non-uniform attack $\mathcal{A}_\xi$ on Π running in time $k \cdot \mathrm{poly}(m)$ with $\mathrm{Adv}^{\mathcal{A}_\xi}(n) \geq \rho/2 - \epsilon - 2k2^{-r}$.*

Proof. By Claim 2 it suffices to prove the lemma for $\Pi = \Pi_{\mathrm{GPV}}$ and by symmetry we may further assume that $\xi = 0$. Without loss of generality we may assume that g is the identity function over $\mathbb{F}_2$. Since μ_0 is $(m + 1 - n + r, k, \rho)$-sparse there exist k subsets $A_1, \ldots, A_k \subseteq \mathbb{F}_2^{m+1}$ and k full rank linear transformations $L_1, \ldots, L_k : \mathbb{F}_2^{m+1} \to \mathbb{F}_2^{m+1-n+r}$ such that $\Pr_{\mu_0}\left(\bigcup_{i=1}^k A_i\right) \geq \rho$ and $L_i(A_i)$ is constant for every $i \in [k]$. For every $i \in [k]$ let $V_i = \{v \in \mathbb{F}_2^{m+1} \mid L_i(v) = L_i(A_i)\}$ and let $S = \bigcup_{i=1}^k V_i$. Since $\mathrm{Adv}^{\mathrm{Dec}}(n) \geq 1 - \epsilon$, by averaging there exists $e^{(\mathrm{sk})} \in \mathrm{supp}(\mu_{sk})$ such that

$$\Pr[\langle e^{(\mathrm{sk})} \circ (-1), \mu_1 \rangle = 1] - \Pr[\langle e^{(\mathrm{sk})} \circ (-1), \mu_0 \rangle = 1] \geq 1 - \epsilon.$$

Our main observation is that since S is not too large, with high probability over the choice of the matrix $\tilde{H}$, there is no $e' \in S \setminus \{\tilde{e}\}$ such that $c = \tilde{H}x' + e'$ for some $x' \in \mathbb{F}_2^{m-n}$. This implies in turn that by enumerating over all $i \in [k]$ and solving a corresponding system of linear equations, with high probability one can verify whether $\tilde{e} \in S$ and if this is the case one can also find $\tilde{e}$. It thus suffices to be able to distinguish between $\tilde{e} \sim \mu_0$ and $\tilde{e} \sim \mu_1$, conditioned on the event that $\tilde{e} \in S$. Assuming that ϵ is sufficiently small compared to ρ, this can be done by computing the inner product $\langle e^{(sk)} \circ (-1), \tilde{e} \rangle$.

$\mathcal{A}_0$

- For every $i = 1, 2, \ldots, k$:
    - Solve the system of linear equations

$$L_i c = L_i \tilde{H} x' + L_i(A_i) \qquad (7)$$

    in the indeterminate x'.
    - If there is no solution continue to the next i.
    - Else let x' be an arbitrary solution and let $e' := c - \tilde{H}x'$.
    - If e' satisfies that $\langle e^{(\text{sk})} \circ (-1), e' \rangle = 0$ output 0, else continue
    to the next i.
- Else if no e' satisfies the above, output a random bit.

Inspection reveals that the attack above can be implemented using a non-uniform circuit of size $k \cdot \text{poly}(m)$. Next we analyze the advantage of the attack in guessing the message bit σ.

We say that $\tilde{H}$ is S-*good* for $\tilde{e}$ if there is no $z \in S \setminus \{\tilde{e}\}$ such that $z - \tilde{e} \in \text{Image}(\tilde{H})$. We will show that for every $\tilde{e}$ the probability that $\tilde{H}$ is S-good for $\tilde{e}$ is at least $1 - k \cdot 2^{-r}$. Consequently, for every $\tilde{e}$ there exists a collection $\mathcal{H}_{\tilde{e}}$ of S-good matrices for $\tilde{e}$ such that $\Pr[\tilde{H} \in \mathcal{H}_{\tilde{e}}] = 1 - k \cdot 2^{-r}$. We will then show that conditioned on the event that $\tilde{H} \in \mathcal{H}_{\tilde{e}}$ the attack outputs 0 with probability at least $(1 + \rho - \epsilon)/2$ when c is an encryption of 0 and it outputs 1 with probability at least $(1 - \epsilon)/2$ when c is an encryption of 1. This will imply in turn that the advantage of the attack is at least $(1 - k2^{-r})(\rho/2 - \epsilon) - k2^{-r} \geq \rho/2 - \epsilon - 2k2^{-r}$.

We start by showing that for every $\tilde{e}$ the probability that $\tilde{H}$ is S-good for $\tilde{e}$ is at least $1 - k \cdot 2^{-r}$. For this note that for every $i \in [k]$ the subspace V_i has co-dimension $m + 1 - n + r$ and hence $|V_i| = 2^{n-r}$ and consequently $|S| \leq k2^{n-r}$. Thus by union bound it suffices to show that for every $z \in S \setminus \{\tilde{e}\}$ it holds that $z - \tilde{e} \in \text{Image}(\tilde{H})$ with probability at most 2^{-n}. To see this fix $z \in S \setminus \{\tilde{e}\}$ and suppose that $z - \tilde{e} \in \text{Image}(\tilde{H})$. Since $\tilde{H} = \begin{pmatrix} H \\ u^T \end{pmatrix}$ this implies in turn that $P_m(z - \tilde{e}) \in \text{Image}(H)$. Furthermore, since $z - \tilde{e} \neq 0$ and H is full rank we also have that $P_m(z - \tilde{e}) \neq 0$. So we obtained that $P_m(z - \tilde{e})$ is a non-zero point contained in $\text{Image}(H)$, a uniform random $(m - n)$-dimensional space, which happens with probability at most 2^{-n}.

Next we show a lower bound on the probability that the attack outputs 0 when c is an encryption of 0, conditioned on the event that $\tilde{H} \in \mathcal{H}_{\tilde{e}}$. Since the event $\tilde{H} \in \mathcal{H}_{\tilde{e}}$ is independent of the choice of $\tilde{e}$, by union bound we have that the events $\tilde{e} \in \bigcup_{i=1}^{k} A_i$ and $\langle e^{(\mathrm{sk})} \circ (-1), \tilde{e} \rangle = 0$ hold simultaneously with probability at least $\rho - \epsilon$. We will show that if these two events hold then the attack outputs 0. This will imply in turn that in the case in which c is an encryption of 0, conditioned on the event that $\tilde{H} \in \mathcal{H}_{\tilde{e}}$, the attack outputs 0 with probability at least $\rho - \epsilon$ and it outputs a random bit otherwise. So it outputs 0 in this case with probability at least $(1 + \rho - \epsilon)/2$.

Suppose that $\tilde{e} \in \bigcup_{i=1}^{k} A_i$ and $\langle e^{(\mathrm{sk})} \circ (-1), \tilde{e} \rangle = 0$. Then in this case we have that

$$L_i c = L_i \tilde{w} + L_i \tilde{e} = L_i \tilde{H} \tilde{x} + L_i(A_i),$$

where $i \subset [k]$ is such that $\tilde{e} \in A_i$ and $\tilde{x}$ is such that $\tilde{w} = \tilde{H} \tilde{x}$. Consequently, the attack will find a solution for (7). Furthermore, we claim that if the attack finds a solution x' to (7) for some $j \in [k]$ then $e' = c - \tilde{H} x' = \tilde{e}$. To see this note that $L_j e' = L_j c - L_j \tilde{H} x' = L_j(A_j)$ and therefore $e' \in S$. Furthermore, we have that $e' - \tilde{e} = (c - \tilde{H} x') - (c - \tilde{H} \tilde{x}) = \tilde{H}(\tilde{x} - \tilde{x}')$ and so $e' - \tilde{e} \in \mathrm{Image}(\tilde{H})$. But due to our assumption that $\tilde{H}$ is S-good for $\tilde{e}$ this implies in turn that $\tilde{e} = e'$. So we have that $\tilde{e} = e'$ and due to our assumption that $\langle e^{(\mathrm{sk})} \circ (-1), \tilde{e} \rangle = 0$ this implies in turn that the attack will output 0.

Finally, we show a lower bound on the probability that the attack outputs 1 when c is an encryption of 1, conditioned on the event that $\tilde{H} \in \mathcal{H}_{\tilde{e}}$. Since the event $\tilde{H} \in \mathcal{H}_{\tilde{e}}$ is independent of the choice of $\tilde{e}$, we have that $\langle e^{(\mathrm{sk})} \circ (-1), \tilde{e} \rangle = 1$ with probability at least $1 - \epsilon$. Suppose that this latter event holds. If there is no solution for (7) for every $j \in [k]$ the attack outputs a random bit. Otherwise if the attack finds a solution x' for (7) for some $j \in [k]$ then similarly to the above the assumption that $\tilde{H} \in \mathcal{H}_{\tilde{e}}$ implies that $e' = c - \tilde{H} x' = \tilde{e}$. Due to our assumption that $\langle e^{(\mathrm{sk})} \circ (-1), \tilde{e} \rangle = 1$ this implies in turn that the attack will output a random bit. Concluding, we obtained that in the case in which c is an encryption of 1, conditioned on the event that $\tilde{H} \in \mathcal{H}_{\tilde{e}}$, the attack outputs 1 with probability at least $(1 - \epsilon)/2$.

7 Attacks Based on the Approximate Duality Conjecture

Recall the definition of the duality measure given in (1). All results presented in this section assume that the following conjecture holds.

Conjecture 1 (Approximate duality conjecture [8]). For every constant $\epsilon > 0$ there exists a constant c which depends only on ϵ such that the following holds. If $A, B \subseteq \mathbb{F}_2^m$ have $D(A, B) \geq \epsilon$ then there exist subsets $A' \subseteq A$ and $B' \subseteq B$ such that $|A'| \geq 2^{-c\sqrt{m}}|A|$, $|B'| \geq 2^{-c\sqrt{m}}|B|$ and $D(A', B') = 1$.

Our main result in this section is the following.

Theorem 3. *Assuming the approximate duality conjecture (Conjecture 1) there exist constants $\epsilon, \gamma > 0$ such that the following holds. Let $\Pi \in \{\Pi_{\mathrm{Alek}}, \Pi_{\mathrm{Reg}}, \Pi_{\mathrm{GPV}}\}$ be with $q = 2$ and $\mathrm{Adv}^{\mathrm{Dec}}(n) \geq 1 - \epsilon$. Then there exists a non-uniform attack $\mathcal{A}$ on Π running in time $2^{O(\sqrt{m})}$ with $\mathrm{Adv}^{\mathcal{A}}(n) \geq \gamma$.*

For the proof of the above theorem we first prove two consequences of Conjecture 1. The first consequence is a generalized form of this conjecture that applies to arbitrary distributions, not necessarily uniform over subsets A, B. For a pair of distributions μ_1, μ_2 over $\mathbb{F}_2^m$ we define their duality measure as

$$D(\mu_1, \mu_2) = \mathbb{E}\left[(-1)^{\langle \mu_1, \mu_2 \rangle}\right].$$

Note that in the special case where μ_1, μ_2 are uniform distributions over subsets $A, B \subseteq \mathbb{F}_2^m$ respectively then $D(\mu_1, \mu_2) = D(A, B)$.

Lemma 3. *Assuming Conjecture 1, for every constant $\epsilon > 0$ there exists a constant c which depends only on ϵ such that the following holds. If a pair of distributions μ_1, μ_2 over $\mathbb{F}_2^m$ have $D(\mu_1, \mu_2) \geq \epsilon$ then there exist subsets $A', B' \subseteq \mathbb{F}_2^m$ such that $\Pr_{\mu_1}(A') \geq 2^{-c\sqrt{m}}$, $\Pr_{\mu_2}(B') \geq 2^{-c\sqrt{m}}$ and $D(A', B') = 1$.*

The proof of the above lemma is given in Sect. 7.1. Note that the probability of being contained in the sets A' and B' in the above lemma is $2^{-c\sqrt{m}}$ and so using this lemma one can only obtain an attack on the abstract encryption scheme in the case in which the decryption error of a single encryption is $2^{-\Omega(\sqrt{m})}$. However, we are interested in an attack that works in the case in which the decryption error of a single encryption is a sufficiently small constant. For this we apply Lemma 3 iteratively to obtain $t \approx 2^{c\sqrt{m}}$ pairs of subsets A_i, B_i such that $D(A_i, B_i) = 1$ for all $1 \leq i \leq t$ and such that the probability of being contained in the union of $\Omega(t)$ of these subsets is $\Omega(\epsilon)$.

Lemma 4. *Assuming Conjecture 1, for every constant $\epsilon > 0$ there exists a constant c which depends only on ϵ such that the following holds for every integer $t \leq 2^{c\sqrt{m}}\epsilon/4$. If a pair of distributions μ_1, μ_2 over $\mathbb{F}_2^m$ have $D(\mu_1, \mu_2) \geq \epsilon$, then there exist subsets $A_1, \ldots, A_t \subseteq \mathbb{F}_2^m$ and $B_1, \ldots, B_t \subseteq \mathbb{F}_2^m$ such that $D(A_i, B_i) = 1$ for all $i \in [t]$, and in addition for every $I \subseteq [t]$ it holds that $\Pr_{\mu_1}(\bigcup_{i \in I} A_i) \geq |I| \cdot 2^{-c\sqrt{m}}/4$ and $\Pr_{\mu_2}(\bigcup_{i \in I} B_i) \geq |I| \cdot 2^{-c\sqrt{m}}/4$.*

Note that the sets $A_1, \ldots, A_t$ and $B_1, \ldots, B_t$ in the above lemma may have non-empty intersections and in particular are not required to be distinct. The proof of the above lemma is omitted due to space limitations.

In what follows we present the proof of our main Theorem 3 based on Lemma 4.

Proof (Proof of Theorem 3). We will show that assuming Conjecture 1 we have that the conditions of either Lemmas 1 or 2 hold. Let c be the constant guaranteed by Lemma 4 for the constant $1 - 2\epsilon$. We shall show that the conclusion of the theorem holds for

$$\gamma = \min\left\{(1 - 4\sqrt{\epsilon})/10, ((1 - 2\epsilon)/32 - 4\sqrt{\epsilon})/10, (1 - 2\epsilon)/64 - \epsilon - 2 \cdot 2^{-c\sqrt{m}}\right\}.$$

If $n \leq 2c\sqrt{m}$ we clearly have that the distribution μ_{sk} is $(n, 2^{2c\sqrt{m}}, 1)$-sparse and consequently Lemma 1 implies an attack in time $2^{O(\sqrt{m})}$ with advantage $(1 - 4\sqrt{\epsilon})/10$. Hence from now on we shall assume that $n > 2c\sqrt{m}$.

Let $\xi \in \{0,1\}$ be such that the decryption function g satisfies $g(0) = \xi$. Our main observation is that the assumption that $\mathrm{Adv}^{\mathrm{Dec}}(n) \geq 1 - \epsilon$ implies that $\Pr[\langle \mu_{\mathrm{sk}} \circ (-1), \mu_\xi \rangle = 0] \geq 1-\epsilon$ and consequently $D(\mu_{\mathrm{sk}} \circ (-1), \mu_\xi) \geq 1-2\epsilon$. Thus we may apply Lemma 4 to the distributions $\mu_{\mathrm{sk}} \circ (-1)$ and μ_ξ and conclude the existence of $t = 2^{c\sqrt{m}}(1-2\epsilon)/4$ subsets $A_1, \dots, A_t \subseteq \mathbb{F}_2^{m+1}$ and $B_1, \dots, B_t \subseteq \mathbb{F}_2^{m+1}$ such that $D(A_i, B_i) = 1$ for all $i \in [t]$, and in addition for every $I \subseteq [t]$ it holds that $\Pr_{\mu_{\mathrm{sk}} \circ (-1)}(\bigcup_{i \in I} A_i) \geq |I| \cdot 2^{-c\sqrt{m}}/4$ and $\Pr_{\mu_\xi}(\bigcup_{i \in I} B_i) \geq |I| \cdot 2^{-c\sqrt{m}}/4$.

Fix $i \in [t]$. The fact that $D(A_i, B_i) = 1$ implies in turn that $\dim(\mathrm{span}\,(A_i)) + \dim(\mathrm{span}\,(B_i)) \leq m + 2$ and in particular we have that either $\dim(\mathrm{span}\,(A_i)) \leq m + 2 - n + 2c\sqrt{m}$ or $\dim(\mathrm{span}\,(B_i)) \leq n - 2c\sqrt{m}$. Let $I \subseteq [t]$ be the set of all indices i for which $\dim(\mathrm{span}\,(A_i)) \leq m + 2 - n + 2c\sqrt{m}$. We shall show that if $|I| \geq t/2$ the conditions of Lemma 1 hold while if $|I| < t/2$ the conditions of Lemma 2 hold.

We start with the case in which $|I| \geq t/2$. Fix $i \in I$ and let $v_1, \dots, v_{m+1}$ be a basis for $\mathbb{F}_2^{m+1}$ such that the subspace spanned by $v_1, \dots, v_{m+2-n+2c\sqrt{m}}$ contains $\mathrm{span}\,(A_i)$. Let $L_i : \mathbb{F}_2^{m+1} \to \mathbb{F}_2^n$ be the linear transformation which satisfies $L_i(\sum_{j=1}^{m+1} \alpha_j v_j) = (\alpha_{m-n+2}, \dots, \alpha_{m+1})$ for every $\alpha_1, \dots, \alpha_{m+1} \in \mathbb{F}_2$. Then $L_i(A_i)$ is supported only on the first $2c\sqrt{m} + 1$ bits and consequently $|L_i(A_i)| \leq 2^{2c\sqrt{m}+1}$. Furthermore, we have that $|I| \leq t = 2^{c\sqrt{m}}(1 - 2\epsilon)/4$ and $\Pr_{\mu_{\mathrm{sk}} \circ (-1)}(\bigcup_{i \in I} A_i) \geq (t/2) \cdot 2^{-c\sqrt{m}}/4 = (1 - 2\epsilon)/32$. This implies in turn that the distribution $\mu_{\mathrm{sk}} \circ (-1)$, and consequently also μ_{sk}, are $(n, 2^{3c\sqrt{m}+1}(1 - 2\epsilon)/4, (1 - 2\epsilon)/32)$-sparse. Lemma 1 implies in turn that the encryption scheme can be attacked in time $2^{O(\sqrt{m})}$ with advantage $((1 - 2\epsilon)/32 - 4\sqrt{\epsilon})/10$.

Next we deal with the case in which $|I| < t/2$. Similarly to the previous case for every $i \notin I$ there exists a full rank linear transformation $L_i : \mathbb{F}_2^{m+1} \to \mathbb{F}_2^{m+1-n+2c\sqrt{m}}$ such that $L_i(B_i) \equiv 0$ and $\Pr_{\mu_\xi}(\bigcup_{i \notin I} B_i) \geq (1 - 2\epsilon)/32$. This implies in turn that μ_ξ is $(m + 1 - n + 2c\sqrt{m}, 2^{c\sqrt{m}}(1 - 2\epsilon)/4, (1 - 2\epsilon)/32)$-sparse. So by Lemma 2 we have that the encryption scheme can be attacked in time $2^{O(\sqrt{m})}$ with advantage $(1 - 2\epsilon)/64 - \epsilon - 2 \cdot 2^{-c\sqrt{m}}$.

7.1 From Uniform to General Distributions – Proof of Lemma 3

We start with the following lemma which says that every distribution can be approximated by a distribution which is a convex combination of not too many uniform distributions.

Lemma 5. *Let μ be a distribution with support S, $|S| = N$, and let $t = \log(2N/\epsilon)/\log(1 + \epsilon/2)$. Then there exist a partition of S into at most $t + 2$ subsets $S_0, \dots, S_{t+1}$ and a distribution χ which is a convex combination of uniform distributions on $S_0, \dots, S_t$ such that μ is ϵ-close to χ.*

Proof. Choose an arbitrary element $\beta \in S$. Let

$$S_0 = \left\{ \alpha \in S \setminus \{\beta\} \,\middle|\, \Pr_\mu(\alpha) \leq \frac{\epsilon}{2N} \right\},$$

for all $1 \leq i \leq t$ let

$$S_i = \left\{ \alpha \in S \setminus \{\beta\} \,\middle|\, \frac{\epsilon}{2N} \cdot (1 + \epsilon/2)^{i-1} < \mathrm{Pr}_\mu(\alpha) \leq \frac{\epsilon}{2N} \cdot (1 + \epsilon/2)^i \right\}$$

and let $S_{t+1} = \{\beta\}$.

Let χ be the distribution which satisfies

$$\mathrm{Pr}_\chi(\alpha) = \begin{cases} 0, & \alpha \in S_0 \\ \frac{\epsilon}{2N} \cdot (1 + \epsilon/2)^{i-1}, & \alpha \in S_i \text{ for } 1 \leq i \leq t \\ 1 - \sum_{\gamma \in S \setminus \{\beta\}} \mathrm{Pr}_\chi(\gamma), & \alpha = \beta. \end{cases}$$

We clearly have that $S_0, \ldots, S_{t+1}$ is a partition of S and that χ is a convex combination of uniform distributions on $S_0, \ldots, S_{t+1}$.

It remains to show that μ is ϵ-close to the distribution χ. For this we compute

$$|\mu - \chi| = \frac{1}{2} \sum_{\alpha \in S} |\mathrm{Pr}_\mu(\alpha) - \mathrm{Pr}_\chi(\alpha)| = \sum_{\alpha \in S \setminus \{\beta\}} (\mathrm{Pr}_\mu(\alpha) - \mathrm{Pr}_\chi(\alpha))$$

$$\leq \sum_{\alpha \in S_0} \frac{\epsilon}{2N} + \sum_{i=1}^t \sum_{\alpha \in S_i} \frac{\epsilon}{2} \mathrm{Pr}_\mu(\alpha) \leq \frac{\epsilon}{2N} \cdot N + \frac{\epsilon}{2} \sum_{\alpha \in S} \mathrm{Pr}_\mu(\alpha) = \epsilon.$$

We shall also use the definition of the *spectrum* given below.

Definition 2 (Spectrum). For a distribution μ over $\mathbb{F}_2^m$ and $\epsilon \in [0, 1]$ let the ϵ-*spectrum* of μ be the set

$$\mathrm{Spec}_\epsilon(\mu) = \left\{ x \in \mathbb{F}_2^m \,\middle|\, \mathbb{E}\left[(-1)^{\langle x, \mu \rangle}\right] \geq \epsilon \right\}. \tag{8}$$

Note that if $\mathrm{supp}(\mu_1) \subseteq \mathrm{Spec}_\epsilon(\mu_2)$ then $D(\mu_1, \mu_2) \geq \epsilon$. Conversely, a standard probabilistic argument shows that if $D(\mu_1, \mu_2) \geq \epsilon$ then $\mathrm{Pr}_{\mu_1}(\mathrm{Spec}_{\epsilon/2}(\mu_2)) \geq \epsilon/2$.

Proof (Proof of Lemma 3). Let c' be the constant guaranteed by Conjecture 1 for the constant $\epsilon/4$.

Let $\mu_1' = \mu_1 | \mathrm{Spec}_{\epsilon/2}(\mu_2)$ and note that the fact that $D(\mu_1, \mu_2) \geq \epsilon$ implies that $\mathrm{Pr}_{\mu_1}(\mathrm{Spec}_{\epsilon/2}(\mu_2)) \geq \epsilon/2$. By Lemma 5 there exists a partition of $\mathrm{supp}(\mu_1')$ into $t + 2$ subsets $A_0, \ldots, A_{t+1} \subseteq \mathbb{F}_2^m$ for $t = \log(2 \cdot 2^m / \delta) / \log(1 + \delta/2)$ such that μ_1' is δ-close to a distribution χ_1 which is a convex combination of uniform distributions on $A_0, \ldots, A_{t+1}$. Since $\mathrm{supp}(\mu_1') \subseteq \mathrm{Spec}_{\epsilon/2}(\mu_2)$ we have that $A_i \subseteq \mathrm{Spec}_{\epsilon/2}(\mu_2)$ for all $0 \leq i \leq t + 1$ and so $D(A_i, \mu_2) \geq \epsilon/2$ for all $0 \leq i \leq t + 1$.

Fix $0 \leq i \leq t + 1$. Similarly to the above, let $\mu_2^{(i)} = \mu_2 | \mathrm{Spec}_{\epsilon/4}(A_i)$ and note that the fact that $D(A_i, \mu_2) \geq \epsilon/2$ implies that $\mathrm{Pr}_{\mu_2}(\mathrm{Spec}_{\epsilon/4}(A_i)) \geq \epsilon/4$. By Lemma 5 there exists a partition of $\mathrm{supp}(\mu_2^{(i)})$ into $t + 2$ subsets $B_0^{(i)}, \ldots, B_{t+1}^{(i)} \subseteq \mathbb{F}_2^m$ for $t = \log(2 \cdot 2^m / \delta) / \log(1 + \delta/2)$ such that $\mu_2^{(i)}$ is δ-close to a distribution $\chi_2^{(i)}$ which is a convex combination of uniform distributions on $B_0^{(i)}, \ldots, B_{t+1}^{(i)}$.

Since $\mathrm{supp}(\mu_2^{(i)}) \subseteq \mathrm{Spec}_{\epsilon/4}(A_i)$ we have that $B_j^{(i)} \subseteq \mathrm{Spec}_{\epsilon/4}(A_i)$ for all $0 \leq j \leq t+1$ and so $D(A_i, B_j^{(i)}) \geq \epsilon/4$ for all $0 \leq j \leq t+1$.

Summarizing, so far we found a collection of subsets $\{A_i\}_{0 \leq i \leq t+1}$ and a collection $\{B_j^{(i)}\}_{0 \leq i,j \leq t+1}$ such that:

- $\mu_1' = \mu_1 | \mathrm{Spec}_{\epsilon/2}(\mu_2)$ is close to a convex combination of uniform distributions on $A_0, \ldots, A_{t+1}$.
- $\mu_2^{(i)} = \mu_2 | \mathrm{Spec}_{\epsilon/4}(A_i)$ is close to a convex combination of uniform distributions on $B_0^{(i)}, \ldots, B_{t+1}^{(i)}$ for all $0 \leq i \leq t+1$.
- $D(A_i, B_j^{(i)}) \geq \epsilon/4$ for all $0 \leq i, j \leq t+1$.

For every $0 \leq i, j \leq t+1$ we can apply Conjecture 1 to the sets $A_i, B_j^{(i)}$ and conclude the existence of subsets $\tilde{A}_j^{(i)} \subseteq A_i$, $\tilde{B}_j^{(i)} \subseteq B_j^{(i)}$ such that $D(\tilde{A}_j^{(i)}, \tilde{B}_j^{(i)}) = 1$ and $|\tilde{A}_j^{(i)}| \geq 2^{-c'\sqrt{m}}|A_i|$, $|\tilde{B}_j^{(i)}| \geq 2^{-c'\sqrt{m}}|B_j^{(i)}|$. So in order to prove the lemma it suffices to show the existence of a constant c and indices $0 \leq k, \ell \leq t+1$ for which $\mathrm{Pr}_{\mu_1}(\tilde{A}_\ell^{(k)}) \geq 2^{-c\sqrt{m}}$ and $\mathrm{Pr}_{\mu_2}(\tilde{B}_\ell^{(k)}) \geq 2^{-c\sqrt{m}}$.

By the pigeonhole principle, for every $0 \leq i \leq t+1$ there exists an index $0 \leq j_i \leq t+1$ such that

$$\mathrm{Pr}_{\mu_2}\left(\tilde{B}_{j_i}^{(i)}\right) \geq \frac{\mathrm{Pr}_{\mu_2}\left(\bigcup_{j=0}^{t+1} \tilde{B}_j^{(i)}\right)}{t+2}.$$

Similarly, there exists $0 \leq k \leq t+1$ such that

$$\mathrm{Pr}_{\mu_1}\left(\tilde{A}_{j_k}^{(k)}\right) \geq \frac{\mathrm{Pr}_{\mu_1}\left(\bigcup_{i=0}^{t+1} \tilde{A}_{j_i}^{(i)}\right)}{t+2}.$$

Let $A' = \tilde{A}_{j_k}^{(k)}$ and $B' = \tilde{B}_{j_k}^{(k)}$. Then we have that $D(A', B') = 1$ and in order to bound the probabilities $\mathrm{Pr}_{\mu_1}(A')$ and $\mathrm{Pr}_{\mu_2}(B')$ from below it suffices to bound the probabilities $\mathrm{Pr}_{\mu_2}\left(\bigcup_{j=0}^{t+1} \tilde{B}_j^{(k)}\right)$ and $\mathrm{Pr}_{\mu_1}\left(\bigcup_{i=0}^{t+1} \tilde{A}_{j_i}^{(i)}\right)$ from below. For this we compute

$$\mathrm{Pr}_{\mu_2}\left(\bigcup_{j=0}^{t+1} \tilde{B}_j^{(k)}\right) \geq \frac{\epsilon}{4} \cdot \mathrm{Pr}_{\mu_2^{(k)}}\left(\bigcup_{j=0}^{t+1} \tilde{B}_j^{(k)}\right) \quad \text{(Since } \mathrm{Pr}_{\mu_2}(\mathrm{Spec}_{\epsilon/4}(A_k)) \geq \epsilon/4\text{)}$$

$$\geq \frac{\epsilon}{4} \cdot \left(\mathrm{Pr}_{\chi_2^{(k)}}\left(\bigcup_{j=0}^{t+1} \tilde{B}_j^{(k)}\right) - \delta\right) \quad \text{(Since } \mu_2^{(k)} \text{ and } \chi_2^{(k)} \text{ are } \delta\text{-close)}$$

$$\geq \frac{\epsilon}{4} \cdot \left(2^{-c'\sqrt{m}} - \delta\right),$$

where the last inequality follows since $\chi_2^{(k)}$ is a convex combination of uniform distributions on $B_0^{(k)}, \ldots, B_{t+1}^{(k)}$ and $|\tilde{B}_j^{(k)}| \geq 2^{-c'\sqrt{m}}|B_j^{(k)}|$ for all $0 \leq j \leq t+1$.

Similarly, we have that

$$\Pr_{\mu_1}\left(\bigcup_{i=0}^{t+1}\tilde{A}_{j_i}^{(i)}\right)\geq\frac{\epsilon}{2}\cdot\Pr_{\mu_1'}\left(\bigcup_{i=0}^{t+1}\tilde{A}_{j_i}^{(i)}\right)\geq\frac{\epsilon}{2}\cdot\left(\Pr_{\chi_1'}\left(\bigcup_{i=0}^{t+1}\tilde{A}_{j_i}^{(i)}\right)-\delta\right)\geq\frac{\epsilon}{2}\cdot\left(2^{-c'\sqrt{m}}-\delta\right).$$

Concluding, we have found subsets A', B' such that $D(A', B') = 1$ and such that both $\Pr_{\mu_1}(A')$ and $\Pr_{\mu_2}(B')$ are bounded from below by $\frac{\epsilon}{4(t+2)}\cdot\left(2^{-c'\sqrt{m}}-\delta\right)$. The proof is completed by letting $\delta = 2^{-c'\sqrt{m}}/2$ and $t = \frac{\log(2\cdot 2^m/\delta)}{\log(1+\delta/2)}$ and noting that with this setting of parameters there exists a constant c which depends only on ϵ such that $\frac{\epsilon}{4(t+2)}\cdot\left(2^{-c'\sqrt{m}}-\delta\right)\geq 2^{-c\sqrt{m}}$ for a sufficiently large m.

Acknowledgements. We thank Parikshit Gopalan, Elad Haramaty, Swastik Kopparty, Shachar Lovett, Oded Regev, Amir Shpilka, Shubhangi Saraf and Ben Lee Volk for useful discussions, and the anonymous reviewers for helpful comments and pointers.

The research of the first two authors was supported by ERC grant no. 240258 (PaC) and ISF grant 1501/14. The research of the third author was supported by the CFEM center funded by the Danish Council for Strategic Research, the FP7 EU-project PRACTICE, the MPCPRO project funded by ERC and the CTIC center funded by the Danish National Research Foundation. The research of the fourth author was supported by ERC grant no. 259426 CaC, ISF grant 1709/14, and BSF grant 2012378. His research is also supported from a DARPA/ARL SAFEWARE award, NSF Frontier Award 1413955, NSF grants 1228984, 1136174, 1118096, and 1065276. This material is based upon work supported by the Defense Advanced Research Projects Agency through the ARL under Contract W911NF-15-C-0205. The views expressed are those of the author and do not reflect the official policy or position of the Department of Defense, the National Science Foundation, or the U.S. Government. The research of fifth author was partially supported by NSF grants CCF-1412958 and CCF-1445755 and the Rothschild fellowship.

References

1. Ajtai, M.: Generating hard instances of lattice problems (extended abstract). In: Proceedings of the Twenty-Eighth Annual ACM Symposium on the Theory of Computing (STOC), pp. 99–108. ACM Press (1996)
2. Ajtai, M., Dwork, C.: A public-key cryptosystem with worst-case/average-case equivalence. In: Proceedings of the Twenty-Ninth Annual ACM Symposium on the Theory of Computing (STOC), pp. 284–293. ACM Press (1997)
3. Alekhnovich, M.: More on average case vs approximation complexity. Comput. Complex. **20**(4), 755–786 (2011). Preliminary version in Proceedings of the 44th Annual IEEE Symposium on Foundations of Computer Science (FOCS 2003)
4. Applebaum, B., Cash, D., Peikert, C., Sahai, A.: Fast cryptographic primitives and circular-secure encryption based on hard learning problems. In: Halevi, S. (ed.) CRYPTO 2009. LNCS, vol. 5677, pp. 595–618. Springer, Heidelberg (2009)
5. Applebaum, B., Ishai, Y., Kushilevitz, E.: Cryptography with constant input locality. J. Cryptology **22**(4), 429–469 (2009)

6. Ben-Sasson, E., Ben-Tov, I., Damgård, I., Ishai, Y., Ron-Zewi, N.: On public key encryption from noisy codewords. IACR Cryptology ePrint Archive, 2015:572 (2015)

7. Ben-Sasson, E., Lovett, S., Ron-Zewi, N.: An additive combinatorics approach relating rank to communication complexity. J. ACM (2013) (to appear)

8. Ben-Sasson, E., Zewi, N.: From affine to two-source extractors via approximate duality. In: Proceedings of the 43rd Annual ACM Symposium on Theory of Computing (STOC), pp. 177–186. ACM Press (2011)

9. Bhowmick, A., Dvir, Z., Lovett, S.: New bounds for matching vector families. In: Proceedings of the 47th ACM Symposium on Theory of Computing (STOC), pp. 823–832. ACM Press (2013)

10. Blum, A., Furst, M.L., Kearns, M., Lipton, R.J.: Cryptographic primitives based on hard learning problems. In: Stinson, D.R. (ed.) CRYPTO 1993. LNCS, vol. 773, pp. 278–291. Springer, Heidelberg (1994)

11. Blum, A., Kalai, A., Wasserman, H.: Noise-tolerant learning, the parity problem, the statistical query model. J. ACM $50(4)$, 506–519 (2003)

12. Damgård, I., Park, S.: Is public-key encryption based on LPN practical? IACR Cryptology ePrint Archive, 2011:699 (2012)

13. Diffie, W., Hellman, M.E.: New directions in cryptography. IEEE Trans. Inf. Theory $22(6)$, 644–654 (1976)

14. Dvir, Z., Gopalan, P., Yekhanin, S.: Matching vector codes. SIAM J. Comput. $40(4)$, 1154–1178 (2011). Preliminary version in Proceedings of the IEEE 51st Annual Symposium on Foundations of Computer Science (FOCS 2011)

15. Dwork, C., Naor, M., Reingold, O.: Immunizing encryption schemes from decryption errors. In: Cachin, C., Camenisch, J.L. (eds.) EUROCRYPT 2004. LNCS, vol. 3027, pp. 342–360. Springer, Heidelberg (2004)

16. Efremenko, K.: 3-query locally decodable codes of subexponential length. SIAM J. Comput. $41(6)$, 1694–1703 (2012). Preliminary version in Proceedings of the 41st Annual ACM Symposium on Theory of Computing (STOC 2009)

17. ElGamal, T.: A public key cryptosystem and a signature scheme based on discrete logarithms. IEEE Trans. Inf. Theory $31(4)$, 469–472 (1985)

18. Gentry, C., Peikert, C., Vaikuntanathan, V.: Trapdoors for hard lattices and new cryptographic constructions. In: Proceedings of the 40th Annual ACM Symposium on Theory of Computing (STOC). ACM Press (2008)

19. Goldreich, O., Goldwasser, S., Halevi, S.: Public-key cryptosystems from lattice reduction problems. In: Kaliski Jr., B.S. (ed.) CRYPTO 1997. LNCS, vol. 1294, pp. 112–131. Springer, Heidelberg (1997)

20. Green, B.: Finite field models in additive combinatorics. In London Mathematical Society Lecture Note Series, vol. 324. Cambridge University Press, Cambridge (2005)

21. Grolmusz, V.: Superpolynomial size set-systems with restricted intersections mod 6 and explicit ramsey graphs. Combinatorica **20**, 71–86 (2000)

22. Hoffstein, J., Pipher, J., Silverman, J.H.: NTRU: a ring-based public key cryptosystem. In: Buhler, J.P. (ed.) ANTS 1998. LNCS, vol. 1423, pp. 267–288. Springer, Heidelberg (1998)

23. Hopper, N.J., Blum, M.: Secure human identification protocols. In: Boyd, C. (ed.) ASIACRYPT 2001. LNCS, vol. 2248, pp. 52–66. Springer, Heidelberg (2001)

24. Kalai, A.T., Mansour, Y., Verbin, E.: On agnostic boosting and parity learning. In: Proceedings of the 40th Annual ACM Symposium on Theory of Computing (STOC), pp. 629–638. ACM Press (2008)

25. Kopparty, S., Saraf, S.: Local list-decoding and testing of random linear codes from high error. SIAM J. Comput. **42**(3), 1302–1326 (2013)
26. Lindner, R., Peikert, C.: Better key sizes (and attacks) for LWE-based encryption. In: Kiayias, A. (ed.) CT-RSA 2011. LNCS, vol. 6558, pp. 319–339. Springer, Heidelberg (2011)
27. Lovett, S.: Additive combinatorics and its applications in theoretical computer science (2013)
28. Lovett, S.: Communication is bounded by root of rank. In: Proceedings of the 46th ACM Symposium on Theory of Computing (STOC). ACM Press (2014)
29. Lyubashevsky, V.: The parity problem in the presence of noise, decoding random linear codes, and the subset sum problem. In: Chekuri, C., Jansen, K., Rolim, J.D.P., Trevisan, L. (eds.) APPROX 2005 and RANDOM 2005. LNCS, vol. 3624, pp. 378–389. Springer, Heidelberg (2005)
30. Lyubashevsky, V., Peikert, C., Regev, O.: On ideal lattices and learning with errors over rings. J. ACM **60**(6), 43 (2013)
31. McEliece, R.J.: A public-key cryptosystem based on algebraic coding theory. JPL DSN Progress Report (1978)
32. Micciancio, D.: Improving lattice based cryptosystems using the hermite normal form. In: Silverman, J.H. (ed.) CaLC 2001. LNCS, vol. 2146, pp. 126–145. Springer, Heidelberg (2001)
33. Micciancio, D.: Duality in lattice-based cryptography. In Public Key Cryptography (invited talk) (2010)
34. Micciancio, D., Mol, P.: Pseudorandom Knapsacks and the sample complexity of LWE search-to-decision reductions. In: Rogaway, P. (ed.) CRYPTO 2011. LNCS, vol. 6841, pp. 465–484. Springer, Heidelberg (2011)
35. Micciancio, D., Regev, O.: Lattice-based cryptography. In: Bernstein, D.J., Buchmann, J., Dahmen, E. (eds.) Post-Quantum Cryptography, pp. 147–192. Springer, Heidelberg (2009)
36. Niederreiter, H.: Knapsack-type cryptosystems and algebraic coding theory. Prob. Control Inf. Theory (Problemy Upravlenija i Teorii Informacii) **15**, 159–166 (1986)
37. Pietrzak, K.: Cryptography from learning parity with noise. In: Bieliková, M., Friedrich, G., Gottlob, G., Katzenbeisser, S., Turán, G. (eds.) SOFSEM 2012. LNCS, vol. 7147, pp. 99–114. Springer, Heidelberg (2012)
38. Rabin, M.: Digitalized signatures and public-key functions as intractable as factorization. MIT LCS TR-212 (1979)
39. Regev, O.: New lattice-based cryptographic constructions. J. ACM **51**(6), 899–942 (2004)
40. Regev, O.: On lattices, learning with errors, random linear codes, and cryptography. J. ACM **56**(6), 34:1–34:40 (2009). Preliminary version in Proceedings of the 37th Annual ACM Symposium on Theory of Computing (STOC 2005)
41. Regev, O.: The learning with errors problem (invited survey). In: IEEE Conference on Computational Complexity, pp. 191–204 (2010)
42. Rivest, R.L., Shamir, A., Adleman, L.M.: A method for obtaining digital signatures and public-key cryptosystems (reprint). Commun. ACM **26**(1), 96–99 (1983)
43. Sahai, A., Waters, B.: How to use indistinguishability obfuscation: deniable encryption, and more. In: Proceedings of the 46th Annual ACM Symposium on the Theory of Computing (STOC), pp. 475–484. ACM Press (2014)
44. Stehlé, D., Steinfeld, R., Tanaka, K., Xagawa, K.: Efficient public key encryption based on ideal lattices. In: Matsui, M. (ed.) ASIACRYPT 2009. LNCS, vol. 5912, pp. 617–635. Springer, Heidelberg (2009)

Indistinguishability Obfuscation
with Non-trivial Efficiency

Huijia Lin[1]([⊠]), Rafael Pass[2], Karn Seth[2], and Sidharth Telang[2]

[1] University of California at Santa Barbara, Santa Barbara, USA
rachel.lin@cs.ucsb.edu
[2] Cornell University, Ithaca, USA
{rafael,karn,sidtelang}@cs.cornell.edu

Abstract. It is well known that *inefficient* indistinguishability obfuscators (iO) with running time $\mathrm{poly}(|C|, \lambda) \cdot 2^n$, where C is the circuit to be obfuscated, λ is the security parameter, and n is the input length of C, exists *unconditionally*: simply output the function table of C (i.e., the output of C on all possible inputs). Such inefficient obfuscators, however, are not useful for applications.

We here consider **iO** with a slightly "non-trivial" notion of efficiency: the running-time of the obfuscator may still be "trivial" (namely, $\mathrm{poly}(|C|, \lambda) \cdot 2^n$), but we now require that the obfuscated code is just slightly smaller than the truth table of C (namely $\mathrm{poly}(|C|, \lambda) \cdot 2^{n(1-\epsilon)}$, where $\epsilon > 0$); we refer to this notion as *iO with exponential efficiency*, or simply *exponentially-efficient iO (Xio)*. We show that, perhaps surprisingly, under the subexponential LWE assumption, subexponentially-secure **XiO** for polynomial-size circuits implies (polynomial-time computable) **iO** for all polynomial-size circuits.

1 Introduction

The goal of *program obfuscation* is to "scramble" a computer program, hiding its implementation details (making it hard to "reverse-engineer"), while preserving the functionality (i.e., input/output behavior) of the program. In recent years, the notion of *indistinguishability obfuscation (iO)* [BGI+01,GGH+13b] has emerged as the central notion of obfuscation. Roughly speaking, this notion requires that obfuscations $\mathbf{iO}(C_1)$, $\mathbf{iO}(C_2)$ of any two *functionally equivalent* circuits C_1 and C_2 (i.e., whose outputs agree on all inputs) from some class $\mathcal{C}$ (of circuits of some bounded size) are computationally indistinguishable.

H. Lin—Work supported in part by NSF grants CNS-1528178 and CNS-1514526.
R. Pass—Work supported in part by a Microsoft Faculty Fellowship, Google Faculty Award, NSF Award CNS-1217821, NSF Award CCF-1214844, AFOSR Award FA9550-15-1-0262 and DARPA and AFRL under contract FA8750-11-2-0211. The views and conclusions contained in this document are those of the authors and should not be interpreted as representing the official policies, either expressed or implied, of the Defense Advanced Research Projects Agency or the US Government.

© International Association for Cryptologic Research 2016
C.-M. Cheng et al. (Eds.): PKC 2016, Part II, LNCS 9615, pp. 447–462, 2016.
DOI: 10.1007/978-3-662-49387-8_17

On the one hand, this notion of obfuscation is strong enough for a plethora of amazing applications (see e.g., [SW14, BCP14, BZ14, GGHR14, BGL+15, CHJV14, KLW14]); on the other hand, it may plausibly exist [GGH+13b, BGK+13, PST14, GLSW14], whereas stronger notion of obfuscations have run into strong impossibility results, even in idealized models (see e.g., [BGI+01, GK05, CKP15, PS15, MMN15, LPST15])

However, despite all these amazing progress, to date, all candidate constructions of **iO** rely on candidate constructions of *multi-linear maps* [GGH13a, CLT13, GGH15, CLT15], all of which have non-trivial attacks [CHL+15, MF15], and it is not clear to what extent the security of the obfuscators that rely on them are affected.

Can Inefficient *iO* *be Useful?* Let us emphasize that for all known application of **iO**, it is important that the obfuscator is *efficient*—namely, polynomial-time. Indeed, as already observed by [BGI+01], it is "trivial" to provide an *inefficient* **iO** with running time $\text{poly}(|C|, \lambda) \cdot 2^n$, where C is the circuit to be obfuscated, λ is the security parameter, and n is the input length of C, exists *unconditionally*: simply output the function table of C (i.e., the output of C on all possible inputs). Recall that, in contrast, for "standard" (efficient) **iO**, the running time and size of the obfuscator is required to be $\text{poly}(|C|, \lambda)$—namely, *polylogarithmic* in the size of the truth table of C).

In this paper, we consider **iO** with just a slightly "non-trivial" notion of efficiency: the running-time of the obfuscator may still be "trivial" (namely, $\text{poly}(|C|, \lambda) \cdot 2^n$), but we now require that the obfuscated code is just slightly smaller than the truth table of C (namely $\text{poly}(|C|, \lambda) \cdot 2^{n(1-\epsilon)}$, where $\epsilon > 0$); we refer to this notion as *iO with exponential efficiency*, or simply *exponentially-efficient iO (Xio)*. The main question investigated in this paper is the following:

Can iO with just slightly non-trivial efficiency be useful for applications?

Main Theorem. Perhaps surprisingly, we show that in the regime of subexponential security, under the LWE assumption, **XiO** for P/poly implies (standard) **iO** for P/poly.

Theorem 1. *Assume subexponential security of the LWE assumption, and the existence of subexponentially secure **XiO** for $P^{\log}$/poly. Then there exists subexponentially secure iO for P/poly.*

Let us remark that in the proof of Theorem 1, we only employ the **XiO** on circuits that take inputs of length $O(\log \lambda)$ (it would be surprising if we didn't since we aim is to achieve an obfuscator with polynomial efficiency). As a consequence, the proof of Theorem 1 also shows that (under the subexponential LWE assumption), subexponentially secure **XiO** for circuits with such "short" inputs (i.e., inputs of length $O(\log \lambda)$)—we refer to this class of circuits as $P^{\log}$/poly—implies **iO** for all polynomial-size circuits (with "long" inputs).[1] We remark that in [BGL+15], the authors (implicitly) considered a notion of "short-input" iO (as opposed to **XiO**) and demonstrate that for *some* (but far from all) applications of iO, this weaker notion actually suffices. Our results show that in the regime of subexponential security, "short-input" iO (and in fact, even **XiO**) implies standard iO (and thus suffices for all applications of iO).

Techniques. Our starting point are the recent beautiful works by Ananth and Jain [AJ15] and Bitansky and Vaikuntanathan [BV15] which show that the existence of subexponentially-secure *functional encryption with sublinearly compact ciphertexts (a.k.a. sublinear compact FE)* for P/poly implies iO for P/poly. Roughly speaking, a (single-key) functional encryption scheme is a public-key encryption scheme for which it is possible to release a (single) functional secret-key sk_C (for circuit C of some a-priori bounded size S) such that knowledge of sk_C enables efficiently computing $C(m)$ given any encryption of the message m, (but nothing more); sublinear compactness means that the encryption time is sublinear in the upper bound S on the circuit-size.[2] We recently demonstrated in [LPST15] that assuming subexponential LWE, it in fact suffices to start off with an FE satisfying an even weaker notion of compactness—which we refer to as *weak sublinear compactness*—which simply requires that the *size* of the ciphertext (but not the encryption time) is sublinear in the circuit-size.

Our main technical contribution will be showing that **XiO** for $\mathsf{P}^{\log}$/poly implies weakly sublinear compact FE for P/poly, which by the above-mentioned result implies our main theorem.

Theorem 2. *Assume the LWE assumption (resp. subexponential security of the LWE assumption) holds, and the existence of* **XiO** *for* $\mathsf{P}^{\log}$/poly *(resp. subexponentially-secure* **XiO** *for* $\mathsf{P}^{\log}$/poly*). Then there exists weakly sublinear compact FE for* P/poly *(resp. subexponentially-secure weakly sublinear compact FE for* P/poly*).*

Note that Theorem 2 is interesting in its own right as it applies also in the regime of polynomial security.[3]

---

[1] "Short-input" iO is more appealing than standard iO (for P/poly) in the sense that it can be efficiently checked whether an attack on a candidate scheme succeeds [Nao03] (an attacker needs to come up with two circuits C_1, C_2 that are functionally equivalent for which it can distinguish obfuscations; checking whether two circuits are functionally equivalent may be hard in general, but becomes efficient if the circuits are restricted to inputs of length $O(\log \lambda)$ by simply enumerating all inputs).

[2] More precisely, in a functional encryption scheme (Setup, KeyGen, Enc, Dec), Setup samples a public-key, secret-key pair (pk, msk), KeyGen(msk, C) generates the functional secret key sk_C; Enc(pk, m) outputs an encryption c of m, and Dec(sk_C, c) outputs $C(m)$ if c is an encryption of m.

[3] Furthermore, as we remark later on, weakly sublinear compact FE trivially implies a variant of **XiO** and this variant of **XiO** is also sufficient for our theorems. As such, by our results, **XiO** may be viewed as a new way to characterize the complexity of weakly sublinear compact FE.

The proof of Theorem 2 proceeds as follows. Following a proof template from [AJ15] (we discuss this result in more detail below), we start off with the result of Goldwasser et al. [GKP+13] which shows that under the LWE assumption, there exists a functional encryption scheme for *boolean* functions (i.e., functions with 1-bit outputs) in NC^1 that has *logarithmic* compactness. Combined with the bootstrapping result of [ABSV14], this can be used to construct a functional encryption scheme for *boolean* functions in P/poly that still has logarithmic compactness. We next show how to use **XiO** for $P^{\log}$/poly to extend any such compact FE scheme for boolean functions to one that handles arbitrary polynomial-sized circuits (with potentially long outputs). ([AJ15] provided a similar transformation assuming, so-called, *compact randomized encoding (for Turing machines)* instead of **XiO**.)

We now turn to describe our transformation from "single-bit compact FE" to "multi-bit weakly sublinear compact FE". As an initial approach, instead of simply encrypting a message m, encrypt the sequence $(m; 1)$, $(m; 2)$, $\dots (m; \ell)$, where ℓ is the maximum output length of the class of functions we want to be able to evaluate. Then, instead of simply releasing a functional secret key for a circuit C, release a secret key for the function $C'(m; i) = C_i(m)$, where $C_i(m)$ denotes the ith output bit of $C(m)$. This approach clearly enables evaluating circuits with multi-bit outputs; but the encryption scheme is no longer (even weakly) compact! The length of the ciphertext grows *linearly* with the number of output bits. To retain compactness (or at least weakly sublinear compactness), we have the encryption algorithm release an obfuscation of a program Π that generates all the ℓ encryptions—more precisely, given an index i, it applies a PRF (with a hard-coded seed) to the index i to generate randomness r_i and then outputs an encryption of $(m; i)$. As long as obfuscation size is "just-slightly-compressing", the functional encryption will have weak sublinear compactness; furthermore, the program we obfuscate only needs to take inputs of length $O(\log \lambda)$. Thus, it suffices to assume the obfuscator satisfies **XiO** for $P^{\log}$/poly.

To prove security of the construction, we use the "one-input-at-a-time" technique from [BCP14, GLW14, PST14, GLSW14, CLTV15], and the punctured program technique of Sahai and Waters [SW14]; the crucial point that enables us to keep the obfuscation small is that the output of the program Π on different inputs uses independent randomness (since they are independent encryptions) and thus in the hybrid arguments it suffices to puncture the PRF on a single point.

Let us end this section by briefly comparing our transformation to the above-mentioned transformation by Ananth and Jain [AJ15]; [AJ15] shows how to use, so-called, "compact randomized encoding" to transform single-bit compact FE for NC^1 into multi-bit compact FE for NC^1. As we explain in more detail in Remark 3, compact randomized encoding can be viewed as a special case of **XiO** for the class of *Turing machines* (as opposed to circuits) with short input. Turing machine obfuscation is a significantly more challenging task than circuit obfuscation. We provide a brief description of their transformation in Appendix A and explain why the transformation fails when using **XiO** (for circuits).

2   Preliminaries

Let $\mathcal{N}$ denote the set of positive integers, and $[n]$ denote the set $\{1, 2, \ldots, n\}$. We denote by PPT probabilistic polynomial time Turing machines, and by nuPPT non-uniform probabilistic polynomial time Turing machines. The term negligible is used for denoting functions that are (asymptotically) smaller than one over any polynomial. More precisely, a function $\nu(\cdot)$ from non-negative integers to reals is called negligible if for every constant $c > 0$ and all sufficiently large n, it holds that $\nu(n) < n^{-c}$. For any algorithm A and input x we denote by $\mathsf{outlen}_A(x)$, the output length of A when run with input x.

Definition 1. *We denote by* $\mathsf{P}^{\log}/\mathsf{poly}$ *the class of circuits* $\{\mathcal{C}_\lambda\}$ *where* $\mathcal{C}_\lambda$ *are* $\mathrm{poly}(\lambda)$-*size circuits that have input length* $c \log \lambda$ *for some constant* c.

2.1   Puncturable PRF

Puncturable PRFs defined by Sahai and Waters [SW14], are PRFs for which a key can be given out that allows evaluation of the PRF on all inputs, except for a designated polynomial-size set of inputs.

Definition 2 (Puncturable PRF [SW14]). *A puncturable pseudo-random function* F *is given by a triple of efficient algorithms* $(\mathsf{F.Key}, \mathsf{F.Punc}, \mathsf{F.Eval})$, *and a pair of computable functions* $n(\cdot)$ *and* $m(\cdot)$, *satisfying the following conditions:*

– **Functionality preserved under puncturing**: *For every polynomial size set* $S \subseteq \{0,1\}^{n(\lambda)}$ *and for every* $x \in \{0,1\}^{n(\lambda)} \setminus S$, *we have that:*

$$\Pr[K \leftarrow \mathsf{F.Key}(1^\lambda), K_S = \mathsf{F.Punc}(K, S) \; : \; \mathsf{F.Eval}(K, x) = \mathsf{F.Eval}(K_S, x)] = 1$$

– **Pseudorandom at punctured points**: *For every polynomial size set* $S \subseteq \{0,1\}^{n(\lambda)}$ *and for every nuPPT adversary* A *we have that:*

$$|\Pr[A(K_S, \mathsf{F.Eval}(K, S)) = 1] - \Pr[A(K_S, U_{m(\lambda) \cdot |S|}) = 1]| = \mathrm{negl}(\lambda)$$

where $K \leftarrow \mathsf{F.Key}(1^\lambda)$ *and* $K_S = \mathsf{F.Punc}(K, S)$ *and* $\mathsf{F.Eval}(K, S)$ *denotes the concatenation of* $\mathsf{F.Eval}(K, x_1), \ldots \mathsf{F.Eval}(K, x_k)$ *where* $S = \{x_1, \ldots, x_k\}$ *is the enumeration of the elements of* S *in lexicographic order,* U_ℓ *denotes the uniform distribution over* ℓ *bits.*

The GGM tree-based construction of PRFs [GGM86] from one-way functions are easily seen to yield puncturable PRFs, as recently observed by [BW13, BGI14, KPTZ13]. Furthermore, it is easy to see that if the PRG underlying the GGM construction is sub-exponentially hard (and this can in turn be built from sub-exponentially hard OWFs), then the resulting puncturable PRF is sub-exponentially pseudorandom.

2.2 Functional Encryption

We recall the definition of public-key functional encryption (FE) with selective indistinguishability based security [BSW12, O'N10]. We note that in this work, we only need the security of the functional encryption scheme to hold with respect to statically chosen challenge messages and functions. We further consider FE schemes that only produce a single functional secret key for each public key.

Definition 3 (Functional Encryption [O'N10, BSW12]). *A public key functional encryption scheme for a class of circuits $\{\mathcal{C}_\lambda\}$ is a tuple of PPT algorithms* (FE.Setup, FE.KeyGen, FE.Enc, FE.Dec) *that behave as follows:*

- $(msk, pk) \leftarrow$ FE.Setup(1^λ)*:* FE.Setup *takes as input the security parameter λ and outputs the master secret key msk and public key pk.*
- $sk_C \leftarrow$ FE.KeyGen(msk, C)*:* FE.KeyGen *takes as input the master secret key and a circuit $C \in \mathcal{C}_\lambda$ and outputs the functional secret key sk_C.*
- $c \leftarrow$ FE.Enc(pk, m)*:* FE.Enc *takes as input the public key and message $m \in \{0,1\}^*$ and outputs the ciphertext c.*
- $y \leftarrow$ FE.Dec(sk_C, c)*:* FE.Dec *takes as input the functional secret key and ciphertext and outputs $y \in \{0,1\}^*$.*

We require the following conditions to hold:

- **Correctness***: For every $\lambda \in \mathbb{N}$, $C \in \mathcal{C}_\lambda$ with input length n and message $m \in \{0,1\}^n$, we have that*

$$\Pr \left[\begin{array}{c} (pk, msk) \leftarrow \mathsf{FE.Setup}(1^\lambda) \\ sk_C \leftarrow \mathsf{FE.KeyGen}(msk, C) : C(m) = \mathsf{FE.Dec}(sk_C, c) \\ c \leftarrow \mathsf{FE.Enc}(pk, m) \end{array} \right] = 1$$

- **Selective Security***: For every nuPPT A there exists a negligible function μ such that for every $\lambda \in \mathbb{N}$, every circuit $C \in \mathcal{C}_\lambda$ with input length n and pair of messages $m_0, m_1 \in \{0,1\}^n$ such that $C(m_0) = C(m_1)$ we have that $|\Pr[A(\mathcal{D}_0) = 1] - \Pr[A(\mathcal{D}_1) = 1]| \leq \mu(\lambda)$ where*

$$\mathcal{D}_b = Pr \left[\begin{array}{c} (pk, msk) \leftarrow \mathsf{FE.Setup}(1^\lambda) \\ sk_C \leftarrow \mathsf{FE.KeyGen}(msk, C) : (pk, sk_C, c_b) \\ c_b \leftarrow \mathsf{FE.Enc}(pk, m_b) \end{array} \right]$$

We say the scheme has sub-exponential security *if there exists a constant ϵ such that for every λ, every 2^{λ^ϵ}-size adversary A, $|\Pr[A(\mathcal{D}_0) = 1] - \Pr[A(\mathcal{D}_1) = 1]| \leq 1/2^{\lambda^\epsilon}$ where $\mathcal{D}_b$ is defined above.*

We recall the definition of compactness and succinctness for functional encryption schemes, as defined in [BV15, AJ15].

Definition 4 (Compact Functional Encryption [BV15, AJ15]). *We say a functional encryption scheme for a class of circuits* $\{\mathcal{C}_\lambda\}$ *is* compact *if for every* $\lambda \in \mathbb{N}$, $pk \leftarrow$ FE.Setup(1^λ) *and* $m \in \{0,1\}^*$ *we have that*

$$\mathsf{Time}(\mathsf{FE.Enc}(pk, m)) = \mathrm{poly}(\lambda, |m|, \log s)$$

where $s = \max_{C \in \mathcal{C}_\lambda} |C|$. *We say the scheme has* sub-linear compactness *if the running time of* FE.Enc *is bounded as*

$$\mathsf{Time}(\mathsf{FE.Enc}(pk, m)) = \mathrm{poly}(\lambda, |m|) \cdot s^{1-\epsilon}$$

where $\epsilon > 0$.

Definition 5 (Succinct Functional Encryption). *A* compact functional encryption scheme for a class of circuits that output only a single bit *is called a* succinct *functional encryption scheme.*

Theorem 3 ([GKP+13]). *Assuming (sub-exponentially secure) LWE, there exists a (sub-exponentially secure) succinct functional encryption scheme for* NC^1.

We note that [GKP+13] do not explicitly consider sub-exponentially secure succinct functional encryption, but their construction satisfies it (assuming sub-exponentially secure LWE). Additionally, we have the following bootstrapping theorem:

Theorem 4 ([GHRW14, ABSV14, AJ15]). *Assuming the existence of symmetric-key encryption with decryption in* NC^1 *(resp. sub-exponentially secure) and succinct functional encryption for* NC^1 *(resp. sub-exponentially secure), there exists succinct functional encryption for* P/poly *(resp. sub-exponentially secure).*

Following [LPST15], we here also consider a weaker compactness notion, where only the ciphertext *size* (but not the encryption time) is sublinear in the output length of the function being evaluated.

Definition 6 (Weakly Sublinear Compact Functional Encryption [LPST15]). *We say a functional encryption scheme for a class of circuits* $\{\mathcal{C}_\lambda\}$ *is* weakly sublinear compact *if there exists* $\epsilon > 0$ *such that for every* $\lambda \in \mathbb{N}$, $pk \leftarrow$ FE.Setup(1^λ) *and* $m \in \{0,1\}^*$ *we have that*

$$\mathsf{Time}_{\mathsf{FE.Enc}}(pk, m) = \mathrm{poly}(\lambda, |m|, s)$$

$$\mathsf{outlen}_{\mathsf{FE.Enc}}(pk, m) = s^{1-\epsilon} \cdot \mathrm{poly}(\lambda, |m|)$$

where $s = \max_{C \in \mathcal{C}_\lambda} |C|$.

454   H. Lin et al.

2.3   Indistinguishability Obfuscation

We recall the notion of indistinguishability obfuscation (**iO**).

Definition 7 (Indistinguishability Obfuscator [BGI+01,GGH+13b]**).** *A PPT machine* iO *is an* indistinguishability obfuscator *(also referred to as **iO**) for a circuit class* $\{C_\lambda\}_{\lambda \in \mathcal{N}}$ *if the following conditions are satisfied:*

– **Functionality:** *for all security parameters* $\lambda \in \mathbb{N}$, *for all* $C \in C_\lambda$, *for all inputs* x, *we have that*

$$\Pr[C' \leftarrow iO(C) \; : \; C'(x) = C(x)] = 1 \;.$$

– **Indistinguishability:** *for any polysize distinguisher* $\mathcal{D}$, *there exists a negligible function* μ *such that the following holds: For all security parameters* $\lambda \in \mathbb{N}$, *for all pairs of circuits* $C_0, C_1 \in C_\lambda$ *of the same size, we have that if* $C_0(x) = C_1(x)$ *for all inputs* x, *then*

$$\left| \Pr\left[\mathcal{D}(iO(C_0)) = 1\right] - \Pr\left[\mathcal{D}(iO(C_1)) = 1\right] \right| \leq \mu(\lambda) \;.$$

We say the scheme has sub-exponential security *if there exists a constant* ϵ *such that for every* λ, *every* 2^{λ^ϵ}-*size adversary* $\mathcal{D}$, $|\Pr[\mathcal{D}(iO(C_0)) = 1] - \Pr[\mathcal{D}(iO(C_1)) = 1]| \leq 1/2^{\lambda^\epsilon}$.

The recent beautiful results of [AJ15], Bitansky and Vaikuntanathan [BV15] show that subexponentially secure sublinear compact functional encryption schemes implies **iO** for P/poly. In an earlier work [LPST15], we demonstrated that (if we additionally assume subexponential LWE), it suffices to start off with just a *weakly* sublinear compact functional encryption scheme (recall that in such a scheme only the length of the ciphertext needs to be sublinear, but encryption time may be polynomial).

Theorem 5 ([LPST15]**).** *Assume the existence of sub-exponentially secure LWE. If there exists a weakly sublinear compact functional encryption scheme for* P/poly *with sub-exponential security, then there exists a sub-exponentially secure indistinguishability obfuscator for* P/poly.

3   Exponentially-Efficient iO (XiO)

In this section, we define our new notion of exponentially-efficient indistinguishability obfuscation (**XiO**), which allows the obfuscator to have running time as long as a brute-force canonicalizer that outputs the entire truth table of the function, but requires the obfuscated program to be slightly smaller in size than a brute-force canonicalization.

Definition 8 (Exponentially-Efficient Indistinguishability Obfuscation (XiO)). *A machine* XiO *is an* exponentially-efficient indistinguishability obfuscator *(also referred to as **XiO**) for a circuit class* $\{C_\lambda\}_{\lambda \in \mathbb{N}}$ *if it satisfies the same functionality and indistinguishability property of indistinguishability obfuscators as in Definition 7 and the following efficiency requirement.*

– **Non-trivial Efficiency**[4]. *There exists a constant $\epsilon > 0$ such that for any security parameter $\lambda \in \mathbb{N}$, circuit $C \in \mathcal{C}_\lambda$ with input length n and $C' \in$ $\mathsf{XiO}(1^\lambda, C)$, we have that*

$$\mathsf{Time}_{\mathsf{XiO}}(1^\lambda, C) = \mathrm{poly}(\lambda, |C|, 2^n)$$
$$\mathsf{outlen}_{\mathsf{XiO}}(1^\lambda, C) = \mathrm{poly}(\lambda, |C|) \cdot 2^{n(1-\epsilon)}$$

Remark 1 *(Circuits with logarithmic input length). Note that if we want the obfuscation to be efficient (i.e., polynomial-time in λ and the size of the circuit to be obfuscated), then the above definition is only meaningful when the class of circuits $\mathcal{C}_\lambda$ has input length $O(\log \lambda)$. Our results in this paper hold assuming XiO for $\mathsf{P}^{\log}/\mathsf{poly}$.*

Remark 2 *(XiO in the preprocessing model and comparison with Compact Functional Encryption). We can consider further a relaxation of the running-time requirement of the obfuscator. The obfuscator may first perform a long "pre-processing" step (without having seen the program to be obfuscated), taking time $\mathrm{poly}(\lambda, s, 2^n)$ (where s is the size bound on circuits to be obfuscated), and outputting a (potentially long) pre-processing public-key O_{pk}. The actual obfuscation then takes O_{pk}, and the circuit C as inputs, runs in time $\mathrm{poly}(\lambda, s, 2^n)$ and outputs an obfuscated program of size $\mathrm{poly}(\lambda, s) \cdot 2^{n(1-\epsilon)}$, and then the evaluation of the obfuscated program may finally also access the public-key O_{pk}. All our results also apply to this relaxed notion of XiO.*

Additionally, we note that weakly sublinear compact FE directly implies this notion as follows: pre-processing public key O_{pk} (generated in the pre-processing step) is the public key pk for the FE and the functional secret key sk_{FT} corresponding to a function table generator program that takes as input a circuit and outputs the function table of it; the obfuscation of a circuit C is an encryption of the circuit C (w.r.t., the FE public key pk), and evaluation of the obfuscated code uses the functional secret key sk_{FT} inside O_{pk} to compute the function table of C and selects the appropriate output. Sub-linear compactness of the functional encryption scheme implies the obfuscator has exponential efficiency.

Remark 3 *(Comparison with Compact Randomized Encoding for Turing machines). [AJ15] and [LPST15] study a notion of compact randomized encodings [IK02, AIK04]. Roughly speaking, a randomized encoding (RE) is a method for encoding a Turing Machine Π, an input x and a running-time bound T, into a randomized encoding $\widehat{\Pi(x)}$ from which $\Pi(x)$ can be efficiently decoded; furthermore the encodings does not leak anything more about Π and x than what*

---

[4] Our notion of "trivial" running-time is even more relaxed than the notion used in the introduction. We here allow the running-time be polynomial in 2^n, and opposed to just linear (as we described it in the introduction). This even more relaxed notion of efficiency is useful in order to more cleanly compare **XiO** with the notion of compact FE; see Remark 2.

can be (inefficiently) deduced from just the output $\Pi(x)$ (truncated at T steps).[5] A randomized encodings is compact (resp. sublinearly compact) if the encoding time is poly-logarithmic (resp sublinear) in T (and polynomial in the size of Π and x). We note that sublinear compact RE directly implies **XiO** as follows: to obfuscate a circuit C, compute an encoding $\widehat{FT_C}$ of the function table generator Turing machine FT_C that has the circuit C hardcoded (i.e., FT_C takes no inputs and simply computes the function table of C); evaluation of the obfuscation on an input i simply decodes the encoding $\widehat{FT_C}$ and picks out the ith output. Sublinear compactness of the RE implies that the obfuscator is exponentially-efficient. In fact, this obfuscator has a stronger efficiency guarantee than **XiO**: the running time of the obfuscator is $\mathrm{poly}(\lambda, |C|) \cdot 2^{n(1-\epsilon)}$ whereas **XiO** allows for a longer running time.

In fact, the above methods extend to show that (sublinearly) compact RE implies a notion of **XiO** for Turing machines. We note that Turing machine obfuscation is a significantly harder task than circuit obfuscation (indeed, all known construction of Turing machine obfuscators first go through circuit obfuscation). We also point out that whereas (subexponentially-secure) **iO** for circuits is known to imply **iO** for Turing machine [BGL+15, CHJV14, KLW14], these techniques do not apply in the regime of programs with short input (and thus do not seem amenable in the regime of inefficient **iO** either).

4 iO from XiO

In this section, we show how to achieve "standard" (polynomially-efficient) **iO** from **XiO**.

4.1 Weakly Sublinear Compact FE from Succinct FE and XiO

We first give our construction of weakly sublinear compact FE from succinct FE and **XiO** for circuits with input-size $O(\log(\lambda))$. At a high-level, our idea is to have the ciphertext for the FE scheme be **XiO** of a circuit that, on input i, generates a succinct FE encryption of (m, i). The secret key corresponding to C consists of a single key for the succinct FE scheme, that, given a ciphertext encrypting (m, i), computes the ith output bit of $C(m)$.

Let F be a puncturable pseudorandom function, XiO be an exponentially-efficient indistinguishability obfuscator for $\mathsf{P}^{\log}/\mathrm{poly}$ and sFE be a succinct functional encryption scheme (resp. with sub-exponential security) for an appropriate class of circuits $\{\mathcal{C}'_\lambda\}$ that includes C' defined below. We define a compact functional encryption scheme FE for a class of poly-size circuits $\{\mathcal{C}_\lambda\}$ as follows:

$(msk, pk) \leftarrow \mathsf{FE.Setup}(1^\lambda)$: FE.Setup is identical to sFE.Setup and has the same output.

---

[5] Or equivalently, for any two programs Π_1, Π_2 and inputs x_1, x_2 such that $\Pi_1(x_1) = \Pi_2(x_2)$, a randomized encoding of Π_1, x_1 is indistinguishable from an encoding of Π_2, x_2.

$c \leftarrow \mathsf{FE.Enc}(pk, m)$: $\mathsf{FE.Enc}$ samples a puncturable PRF key $K \leftarrow \mathsf{F.Key}(1^\lambda)$ and outputs $\Pi \leftarrow \mathsf{XiO}(1^\lambda, G[pk, K, m])$ where $G[pk, K, m]$ is a circuit with input length $n = \log s$ where $s = \max_{C \in \mathcal{C}_\lambda} \mathsf{outlen}(C)$, defined as follows:

$$G[pk, K, m](i) = \mathsf{sFE.Enc}(pk, (m, i); \mathsf{F.Eval}(K, i))$$

G is padded to be the same size as circuits G' and G'' that we will define later in the security proof. All circuits G, G', and G'' will ultimately have size bounded by $S = \mathrm{poly}(\lambda, |m|, \log s)$ where $s = \max_{C \in \mathcal{C}_\lambda} |C|$, and are padded to size S.

$sk_C \leftarrow \mathsf{FE.KeyGen}(msk, C)$: $\mathsf{FE.KeyGen}$ outputs $\mathsf{sFE.KeyGen}(msk, C')$ where C' on input (m, i) outputs the ith bit of $C(m)$, or outputs $\bot$ if i is greater than the output length of C.

$y \leftarrow \mathsf{FE.Dec}(sk_C, \Pi)$: $\mathsf{FE.Dec}$ runs $c_i \leftarrow \Pi(i)$ and $y_i \leftarrow \mathsf{sFE.Dec}(sk_C, c_i)$ for every i and outputs $y_1, \ldots y_{2^n}$.

Let $\{\mathcal{C}'_\lambda\}$ be a class of circuits that includes C' as defined above for every $C \in \mathcal{C}_\lambda$.

Theorem 6. *Assuming* F *is a puncturable pseudorandom function (resp. with subexponential security),* XiO *is an exponentially efficient indistinguishability obfuscator for* $\mathsf{P}^{\log}/\mathsf{poly}$ *(resp. with subexponential security) and* sFE *is a succinct functional encryption scheme for* $\{\mathcal{C}'_\lambda\}$ *(resp. with subexponential security), we have that* FE *as defined above is a functional encryption scheme for* $\{\mathcal{C}_\lambda\}$ *with weakly sub-linear compactness (resp. and with subexponential security).*

Proof. We first show weak sublinear compactness of FE. Consider any λ, $C \in \mathcal{C}_\lambda$, message m, $pk \in \mathsf{FE.Setup}(1^\lambda)$ and puncturable PRF key $K \in \mathsf{F.Key}(1^\lambda)$. $\mathsf{Time}(\mathsf{FE.Enc}(pk, m))$ is the time XiO takes to obfuscate the circuit $G[pk, K, m]$, which is of size $S = \mathrm{poly}(\lambda, |m|, \log s)$ where $s = \max_{C \in \mathcal{C}_\lambda} |C|$. Hence we have that

$$\mathsf{Time}_{\mathsf{XiO}}(1^\lambda, G[pk, K, m]) = \mathrm{poly}(\lambda, |m|, \log s, 2^n) \le \mathrm{poly}(\lambda, |m|, s)$$
$$\mathsf{outlen}_{\mathsf{XiO}}(1^\lambda, G[pk, K, m]) = \mathrm{poly}(\lambda, |m|, \log s) \cdot 2^{n(1-\epsilon)} \le \mathrm{poly}(\lambda, |m|) \cdot s^{1-\epsilon'}$$

where ϵ' is a constant with $0 < \epsilon' < \epsilon$.

Next we show the selective security of FE. We proceed by using the "one-input-at-a-time" technique from [BCP14, GLW14, PST14, GLSW14, CLTV15]. More precisely, we proceed by a hybrid argument where in each hybrid distribution, the circuit being obfuscated, on input i, produces ciphertexts of m_1 when i is less than a "threshold", and ciphertexts of m_0 otherwise. Indistinguishability of neighboring hybrids is shown using the "punctured programming" technique of [SW14], as was done in [CLTV15] for constructing iO for probabilistic functions. (This technique is also used extensively in other applications of iO, eg., [BGL+15], [CHJV14], [KLW14] and more.)

Assume for contradiction there exists a nuPPT A and polynomial p such that for sufficiently large λ, circuit $C \in \mathcal{C}_\lambda$ and messages m_0, m_1 such that

$C(m_0) = C(m_1)$, A distinguishes $\mathcal{D}_0$ and $\mathcal{D}_1$ with advantage $1/p(\lambda)$, where

$$\mathcal{D}_b = \left(\begin{array}{l} (msk, pk) \leftarrow \mathsf{FE.Setup}(1^\lambda) \\ K \leftarrow \mathsf{F.Key}(1^\lambda) \\ sk_C \leftarrow \mathsf{FE.KeyGen}(msk, C) \end{array} : pk, sk_C, \mathsf{XiO}(G[pk, K, m_b]) \right)$$

For $j \in [\ell]$, we define the jth hybrid distribution H_j as follows:

$$H_j = \left(\begin{array}{l} (msk, pk) \leftarrow \mathsf{FE.Setup}(1^\lambda) \\ K \leftarrow \mathsf{F.Key}(1^\lambda) \\ sk_C \leftarrow \mathsf{FE.KeyGen}(msk, C) \end{array} : pk, sk_C, \mathsf{XiO}(G'[pk, K, j, m_0, m_1]) \right)$$

where $G'[pk, K, j, m_0, m_1]$, where G' is defined as follows

$$G'[pk, K, j, m_0, m_1](i) = \begin{cases} \mathsf{sFE.Enc}(pk, (m_0, i); \mathsf{F}(K, i)) \text{ if } i > j \\ \mathsf{sFE.Enc}(pk, (m_1, i); \mathsf{F}(K, i)) \text{ if } i \leq j \end{cases}$$

We also require G' to be padded to be of the same size S as $G[pk, K, m]$.

We consider the hybrid sequence $\mathcal{D}_0, H_1, \ldots, H_\ell, \mathcal{D}_1$. By a hybrid argument, there exists a pair of neighboring hybrids in this sequence such that A distinguishes the pair with probability $\frac{1}{p(\lambda)\cdot(\ell+2)} = \frac{1}{\mathsf{poly}(\lambda)}$. We show a contradiction by proving that each pair of neighboring hybrids is computationally indistinguishable.

We first note that $\mathcal{D}_0$ is indistinguishable from H_0. This follows by observing that $G'[pk, K, 0, m_0, m_1]$ is functionally identical to $G[pk, K, m_0]$, and applying the security of XiO. The same argument also shows that H_ℓ is indistinguishable from $\mathcal{D}_1$.

Next, we show H_{j^*} and H_{j^*+1} are indistinguishable for each $j^* \in [\ell]$. Define hybrid distribution H_0' which is identical to H_{j^*} except that XiO obfuscates a different circuit $G''[pk, K_{j^*}, j^*, m_0, m_1, c]$ where $K_{j^*} \leftarrow \mathsf{F.Punc}(\lambda, j^*)$ and $c \leftarrow \mathsf{sFE.Enc}(pk, (m_0, j^*); R)$ using uniformly sampled randomness R. G'' on input i has the same behavior as G' except $i = j^*$, where it outputs the hardcoded ciphertext c. By the "punctured programming" technique of Sahai-Waters [SW14], which relies on the security of the obfuscator XiO and puncturable PRF F, it follows that for sufficiently large λ, A distinguishes between H_{j^*} and H_0' with negligible probability.

The puncturing programming technique itself works in two hybrid steps:

- First the circuit G' is replaced with circuit $G''[pk, K_{j^*}, j^*, m_0, m_1, c]$ where the hardwired ciphertext is $c = \mathsf{sFE.Enc}(pk, (m_0, j^*); \mathsf{F}(K, j^*))$, which is the same ciphertext G' previously computed. Since this doesn't change the functionality of the circuit, indistinguishability follows from the security of XiO.
- Second, the hardcoded ciphertext is modified to be generated from real randomness R, and indistinguishability follows from the security of the puncturable PRF.

Next, we define hybrid distribution H_1' which is identical to H_0' except that the hardcoded ciphertext c is generated as $\mathsf{sFE.Enc}(pk, (m_1, j^*); R)$ for uniformly sampled randomness R. Since $C(m_0)$ is identical to $C(m_1)$, from the security of sFE, A distinguishes H_0' and H_1' with negligible probability.

Finally, note that H_1' and H_{j*+1} differ in the same way H_0' and H_{j*} do, and are hence indistinguishable by a similar argument. Hence A distinguishes H_{j*} and H_{j*+1} with negligible probability and we have a contradiction. This completes the proof.

We note that the proof above is described in terms of computational indistinguishability, but in fact also can be applied to show that FE is subexponentially-secure, if both XiO and sFE are subexponentially secure.

4.2 Putting Pieces Together

Theorem 7. *Assuming sub-exponentially hard LWE, if there exists a subexponentially secure exponentially efficient indistinguishability obfuscator for* $P^{\log}/poly$ *then there exists an indistinguishability obfuscator for* P/poly *with subexponential security.*

Proof. By Theorems 3 and 4, assuming subexponentially secure LWE, there exists a succinct functional encryption scheme for P/poly that is subexponentially secure. Using this with a subexponentially secure exponentially efficient indistinguishability obfuscator for $P^{\log}/poly$, by Theorem 6, we get weakly sublinear compact function encryption for P/poly with sub-exponential selective security. Together with Theorem 5, this gives us **iO** for P/poly.

Remark 4 (XiO *for* NC^1 *suffices).* *We remark it in fact suffices to assume* XiO *for only* NC^1 *(instead of* P/poly*) if rely on the existence of puncturable PRFs in* NC^1. *Indeed, if encryption algorithm of the succinct FE scheme and the puncturable PRF are both in* NC^1, *then in our construction it suffices to obfuscate* NC^1 *circuits (we also need to verify that the "merged" circuit used in the hybrid argument is in NC1, which directly follows). By the result of [AIK04], assuming the existence of pseudorandom generators in* NC^1, *we can assume without loss of generality that the succinct FE encryption we rely on also has encryption in* NC^1 *(in fact even* NC^0, *but this will not be useful to us): the encryption algorithm for the new succinct FE scheme computes the "randomized encoding" of the original encryption function.*

Acknowledgments. We thank Vinod Vaikuntanathan for insightful discussions.

A   Comparison with [AJ15]

In this section we briefly describe the related result by [AJ15] and compare it with our result. [AJ15] show how to construct a compact functional encryption scheme from a succinct functional encryption scheme and "compact randomized encodings for Turing machines" (see Remark 3 for an informal description of randomized encodings). The rough idea is as follows: the compact functional secret key for a function f is a sequence of ℓ independent succinct functional secret keys where ℓ is the output length of f. The ith succinct functional secret key corresponds to the function that outputs the ith bit of f. The compact functional ciphertext for a message m is the randomized encoding of a machine Π that takes no input and when run, outputs $\{Enc(pk_i, m)\}_{i\in[\ell]}$ where pk_i is the public key corresponding to the ith instance of the succinct functional scheme (these instances are generated using a PRF, hence the description size of Π is independent of ℓ). The compactness of the functional encryption scheme follows from the compactness of the randomized encoding scheme.

Note that the above result necessarily requires the computation being encoded to be represented as a Turing machine, since the description size is required to be independent of the output length. As we explain in Remark 3, such a notion of randomized encodings for Turing machine does not seem useful for our purposes.

References

[ABSV14] Ananth, P., Brakerski, Z., Segev, G., Vaikuntanathan, V.: The trojan method in functional encryption: from selective to adaptive security. Technical report, generically. Cryptology ePrint Archive, Report 2014/917 (2014)

[AIK04] Applebaum, B., Ishai, Y., Kushilevitz, E.: Cryptography in nc^0. In: FOCS, pp. 166–175 (2004)

[AJ15] Ananth, P., Jain, A.: Indistinguishability obfuscation from compact functional encryption. IACR Cryptology ePrint Archive, 2015:173 (2015)

[BCP14] Boyle, E., Chung, K.-M., Pass, R.: On extractability obfuscation. In: Lindell, Y. (ed.) TCC 2014. LNCS, vol. 8349, pp. 52–73. Springer, Heidelberg (2014)

[BGI+01] Barak, B., Goldreich, O., Impagliazzo, R., Rudich, S., Sahai, A., Vadhan, S.P., Yang, K.: On the (im)possibility of obfuscating programs. In: Kilian, J. (ed.) CRYPTO 2001. LNCS, vol. 2139, pp. 1–18. Springer, Heidelberg (2001)

[BGI14] Boyle, E., Goldwasser, S., Ivan, I.: Functional signatures and pseudorandom functions. In: Krawczyk, H. (ed.) PKC 2014. LNCS, vol. 8383, pp. 501–519. Springer, Heidelberg (2014)

[BGK+13] Barak, B., Garg, S., Kalai, Y.T., Paneth, O., Sahai, A.: Protecting obfuscation against algebraic attacks. In: Nguyen, P.Q., Oswald, E. (eds.) EUROCRYPT 2014. LNCS, vol. 8441, pp. 221–238. Springer, Heidelberg (2014)

[BGL+15] Bitansky, N., Garg, S., Lin, H., Pass, R., Telang, S.: Succinct randomized encodings and their applications. IACR Cryptology ePrint Archive, 2015:356 (2015)

[BSW12] Boneh, D., Sahai, A., Waters, B.: Functional encryption: a new vision for public-key cryptography. Commun. ACM 55(11), 56–64 (2012)

[BV15] Bitansky, N., Vaikuntanathan, V.: Indistinguishability obfuscation from functional encryption. IACR Cryptology ePrint Archive, 2015:163 (2015)

[BW13] Boneh, D., Waters, B.: Constrained pseudorandom functions and their applications. In: Sako, K., Sarkar, P. (eds.) ASIACRYPT 2013, Part II. LNCS, vol. 8270, pp. 280–300. Springer, Heidelberg (2013)

[BZ14]   Boneh, D., Zhandry, M.: Multiparty key exchange, efficient traitor tracing, and more from indistinguishability obfuscation. In: Garay, J.A., Gennaro, R. (eds.) CRYPTO 2014, Part I. LNCS, vol. 8616, pp. 480–499. Springer, Heidelberg (2014)

[CHJV14]   Canetti, R., Holmgren, J., Jain, A., Vaikuntanathan, V.: Indistinguishability obfuscation of iterated circuits and RAM programs. IACR Cryptology ePrint Archive, 2014:769 (2014)

[CHL+15]   Cheon, J.H., Han, K., Lee, C., Ryu, H., Stehlé, D.: Cryptanalysis of the multilinear map over the integers. In: Oswald, E., Fischlin, M. (eds.) EUROCRYPT 2015, Part I. LNCS, pp. 3–12. Springer, Heidelberg (2015)

[CKP15]   Canetti, R., Kalai, Y.T., Paneth, O.: On obfuscation with random oracles. In: Dodis, Y., Nielsen, J.B. (eds.) TCC 2015, Part II. LNCS, vol. 9015, pp. 456–467. Springer, Heidelberg (2015)

[CLT13]   Coron, J.-S., Lepoint, T., Tibouchi, M.: Practical multilinear maps over the integers. In: Canetti, R., Garay, J.A. (eds.) CRYPTO 2013, Part I. LNCS, vol. 8042, pp. 476–493. Springer, Heidelberg (2013)

[CLT15]   Coron, J.-S., Lepoint, T., Tibouchi, M.: New multilinear maps over the integers. In: Gennaro, R., Robshaw, M. (eds.) CRYPTO 2015, Part I. LNCS, pp. 267–286. Springer, Heidelberg (2015)

[CLTV15]   Canetti, R., Lin, H., Tessaro, S., Vaikuntanathan, V.: Obfuscation of probabilistic circuits and applications. In: Dodis, Y., Nielsen, J.B. (eds.) TCC 2015, Part II. LNCS, vol. 9015, pp. 468–497. Springer, Heidelberg (2015)

[GGH13a]   Garg, S., Gentry, C., Halevi, S.: Candidate multilinear maps from ideal lattices. In: Johansson, T., Nguyen, P.Q. (eds.) EUROCRYPT 2013. LNCS, vol. 7881, pp. 1–17. Springer, Heidelberg (2013)

[GGH+13b] Garg, S., Gentry, C., Halevi, S., Raykova, M., Sahai, A., Waters, B.: Candidate indistinguishability obfuscation and functional encryption for all circuits. In: Proceedings of FOCS 2013 (2013)

[GGH15]   Gentry, C., Gorbunov, S., Halevi, S.: Graph-induced multilinear maps from lattices. In: Dodis, Y., Nielsen, J.B. (eds.) TCC 2015, Part II. LNCS, vol. 9015, pp. 498–527. Springer, Heidelberg (2015)

[GGHR14]   Garg, S., Gentry, C., Halevi, S., Raykova, M.: Two-round secure MPC from indistinguishability obfuscation. In: Lindell, Y. (ed.) TCC 2014. LNCS, vol. 8349, pp. 74–94. Springer, Heidelberg (2014)

[GGM86]   Goldreich, O., Goldwasser, S., Micali, S.: How to construct random functions. J. ACM **33**(4), 792–807 (1986)

[GHRW14]   Gentry, H., Raykova, W.: Outsourcing private ram computation. In: Proceedings of the FOCS 2014 (2014)

[GK05]   Goldwasser, S., Kalai, Y.T.: On the impossibility of obfuscation with auxiliary input. In: 46th Annual IEEE Symposium on Foundations of Computer Science (FOCS 2005), 23–25 October 2005, Pittsburgh, PA, USA, Proceedings, pp. 553–562 (2005)

[GKP+13]   Goldwasser, S., Kalai, Y.T., Popa, R.A., Vaikuntanathan, V., Zeldovich, N.: Reusable garbled circuits and succinct functional encryption. In: Symposium on Theory of Computing Conference, STOC 2013, Palo Alto, CA, USA, 1–4 June 2013 pp. 555–564 (2013)

[GLSW14]   Gentry, C., Lewko, A., Sahai, A., Waters, B.: Indistinguishability obfuscation from the multilinear subgroup elimination assumption. Cryptology ePrint Archive, Report 2014/309 (2014)

[GLW14] Gentry, C., Lewko, A., Waters, B.: Witness encryption from instance inde-
          pendent assumptions. In: Garay, J.A., Gennaro, R. (eds.) CRYPTO 2014,
          Part I. LNCS, vol. 8616, pp. 426–443. Springer, Heidelberg (2014)

  [IK02] Ishai, Y., Kushilevitz, E.: Perfect constant-round secure computation via
          perfect randomizing polynomials. In: Widmayer, P., Triguero, F., Morales,
          R., Hennessy, M., Eidenbenz, S., Conejo, R. (eds.) ICALP 2002. LNCS,
          vol. 2380, pp. 244–256. Springer, Heidelberg (2002)

[KLW14] Koppula, V., Lewko, A.B., Waters, B.: Indistinguishability obfuscation for
          turing machines with unbounded memory. Technical report, Cryptology
          ePrint Archive, Report 2014/925 (2014). http://eprint.iacr.org

[KPTZ13] Kiayias, A., Papadopoulos, S., Triandopoulos, N., Zacharias, T.: Dele-
          gatable pseudorandom functions and applications. In CCS, pp. 669–684
          (2013)

[LPST15] Lin, H., Pass, R., Seth, K., Telang, S.: Output-compressing randomized
          encodings and applications (2015)

  [MF15] Minaud, B., Fouque, P.-A.: Cryptanalysis of the new multilinear map over
          the integers. Cryptology ePrint Archive, Report 2015/941 (2015). http://
          eprint.iacr.org/

[MMN15] Mahmoody, M., Mohammed, A., Nematihaji, S.: More on impossibility
          of virtual black-box obfuscation in idealized models. IACR Cryptology
          ePrint Archive, 2015:632 (2015)

 [Nao03] Naor, M.: On cryptographic assumptions and challenges. In: Boneh, D.
          (ed.) CRYPTO 2003. LNCS, vol. 2729, pp. 96–109. Springer, Heidelberg
          (2003)

 [O'N10] O'Neill, A.: Definitional issues in functional encryption. Cryptology ePrint
          Archive, Report 2010/556 (2010). http://eprint.iacr.org/

 [PS15] Pass, R., Shelat, A.: Impossibility of VBB obfuscation with ideal constant-
          degree graded encodings. IACR Cryptology ePrint Archive, 2015:383
          (2015)

[PST14] Pass, R., Seth, K., Telang, S.: Indistinguishability obfuscation from
          semantically-secure multilinear encodings. In: Garay, J.A., Gennaro, R.
          (eds.) CRYPTO 2014, Part I. LNCS, vol. 8616, pp. 500–517. Springer,
          Heidelberg (2014)

 [SW14] Sahai, A., Waters, B.: How to use indistinguishability obfuscation: deni-
          able encryption, and more. In: Proceedings of STOC 2014 (2014)

Author Index

Printed in the United States
by Bookmasters

Printed in the United States
By Bookmasters